International Migration Outlook 2012

OECD
BETTER POLICIES FOR BETTER LIVES

This work is published on the responsibility of the Secretary-General of the OECD. The opinions expressed and arguments employed herein do not necessarily reflect the official views of the Organisation or of the governments of its member countries.

This document and any map included herein are without prejudice to the status of or sovereignty over any territory, to the delimitation of international frontiers and boundaries and to the name of any territory, city or area.

Please cite this publication as:
OECD (2012), *International Migration Outlook 2012*, OECD Publishing.
http://dx.doi.org/10.1787/migr_outlook-2012-en

ISBN 978-92-64-17720-8 (print)
ISBN 978-92-64-17723-9 (PDF)

Series:
ISSN 1995-3968 (print)
ISSN 1999-124X (online)

The statistical data for Israel are supplied by and under the responsibility of the relevant Israeli authorities. The use of such data by the OECD is without prejudice to the status of the Golan Heights, East Jerusalem and Israeli settlements in the West Bank under the terms of international law.

Photo credits: Cover © David Rooney.

Corrigenda to OECD publications may be found on line at: *www.oecd.org/publishing/corrigenda*.
© OECD 2012

You can copy, download or print OECD content for your own use, and you can include excerpts from OECD publications, databases and multimedia products in your own documents, presentations, blogs, websites and teaching materials, provided that suitable acknowledgement of OECD as source and copyright owner is given. All requests for public or commercial use and translation rights should be submitted to *rights@oecd.org*. Requests for permission to photocopy portions of this material for public or commercial use shall be addressed directly to the Copyright Clearance Center (CCC) at *info@copyright.com* or the Centre français d'exploitation du droit de copie (CFC) at *contact@cfcopies.com*.

Foreword

This publication constitutes the thirty-sixth report of the OECD's Continuous Reporting System on Migration. The report is divided into four parts plus a statistical annex.

Part I contains three main sections. The first of these provides a broad overview of recent trends in international migration flows. In 2010 permanent migration to the OECD reached 4.1 million and temporary migration 1.9 million, an annual decline of 3 and 6% respectively. The strongest drop in permanent-type migration was recorded for labour migration, as well as, in Europe, free movement migration. Other categories of migration, namely family and humanitarian migration, less responsive to economic conditions, saw smaller changes compared with 2009. Preliminary figures for 2011 show that immigration started to increase again in most European OECD countries, as well as in Australia and New Zealand.

The second section of Part I takes a close look at the impact of the economic crisis on the employment situation of immigrants. Overall, in OECD countries, the foreign-born unemployment rate increased by four percentage points between 2008 and 2011, compared with 2.5 points for the native-born. The report also outlines some forthcoming challenges, including addressing long-term unemployment of immigrants, and the integration of young migrants in the labour market, which appears to be one of the most vulnerable groups.

The final section of Part I highlights major changes in migration policy. It specifically looks at the impact of the recent economic crisis on the management of labour migration and presents recent policy changes on family and humanitarian migration as well as on border controls, which generally illustrate a tightening of migration legislation.

Parts II and III are devoted to special topics. The first one analyses the contribution of migration to labour force changes by education level and occupation in the past decade. The second special chapter emphasises the growing importance of Asian migration to OECD countries and identifies upcoming challenges to existing labour migration systems in Asia.

Part IV presents succinct country-specific notes and statistics on developments in international migration movements and policies in OECD countries in recent years. Finally the statistical annex includes a broad selection of recent and historical statistics on immigrant flows, foreign and foreign-born populations, naturalisations and migrant workers.

This year's edition of the OECD International Migration Outlook is the joint work of staff of the Directorate for Employment, Labour and Social Affairs. Part I and Part II are a collective work of the staff of the International Migration Division with contributions from John Salt and Martina Lubyova (Part I.C). Part III was prepared by Jonathan Chaloff and Part IV by Maria Vincenza Desiderio. Jean-Christophe Dumont edited the report. Research assistance and statistical work were carried out by Véronique Gindrey and Philippe Hervé. Editorial assistance was provided by Sylviane Yvron.

Table of contents

Editorial 17
Executive summary 21

Part I

TRENDS IN INTERNATIONAL MIGRATION

A. Trends in international migration flows and in the immigrant population 28
    1. Introduction: The context for migration in 2010/11 28
    2. Permanent migration 28
    3. Temporary migration and asylum seeking 35
    4. A first glance at migration trends in 2011 42
    5. Regional and gender composition of migration flows: Evolution since 2000 ... 47
    6. The migrant population 50
    7. Conclusion 54
Notes 55
References 56

Annex I.A1. Changes in inflows of migrants by country of origin,
            selected OECD countries, 2000-09 and 2010 57

B. Employment 60
    1. Introduction 60
    2. The labour market situation of migrants has changed during the crisis 61
    3. The impact of the crisis has not been uniform 69
    4. The crisis is putting additional pressure on already disadvantaged
       migrant youth 73
    5. Conclusion 79
Notes 80
References 80

Annex I.B1. Employment, unemployment and participations rates by gender
            and place of birth in selected OECD countries, 2008-11 81
Annex I.B2. Foreign-born unemployment in selected OECD countries
            by unemployment duration, Q1 2008-Q4 2011 91
Annex I.B3. NEET, short-term and long-term unemployment rates for foreign-
            and native-born in selected OECD countries, 2011 93
Annex I.B4. Foreign-born employment by sector of activity 94

TABLE OF CONTENTS

  C. Migration policy developments 97
    1. Introduction.. 97
    2. Framework legislation, changes in governments leading to policy shifts 97
    3. Labour migration.. 100
    4. Family and humanitarian policies 109
    5. Irregular migration and regularisation 112
    6. EU legislation and other forms of intergovernmental and international
      co-operation... 113
    7. Integration and citizenship policies.. 116
    8. Conclusion 120
 Notes.. 121
 References 121

Part II
RENEWING THE SKILLS OF AGEING WORKFORCES: THE ROLE OF MIGRATION

1. Introduction.. 124
2. Main findings 125
3. General methodological approach... 126
4. The role of immigrants in the labour market....................................... 126
5. The demography of changes in the educational attainment of the labour force .. 127
6. The composition of changes in the educational attainment of the labour force ... 130
7. The demography of occupational change.. 134
8. Demographic components of occupational change 137
9. Conclusion... 147

Notes.. 148
References 149
Annex II.A1. Methodology for estimating the components of demographic change ... 150
Annex II.A2. 152

Part III
THE CHANGING ROLE OF ASIA IN INTERNATIONAL MIGRATION

1. Introduction.. 158
2. Main findings 158
3. The importance of Asian migration to the OECD and within the region.......... 160
4. Can OECD countries continue to compete with Asia for highly skilled migrants? .. 170
5. Key challenges for managing low-skilled and family migration.................. 181
6. Key priorities for origin countries in Asia....................................... 194
7. Conclusion... 201

Notes.. 202
References 203
Annex III.A1. Supplementary tables... 206

Part IV

COUNTRY NOTES: RECENT CHANGES IN MIGRATION MOVEMENTS AND POLICIES

Australia	210	Lithuania	248
Austria	212	Luxembourg	250
Belgium	214	Mexico	252
Bulgaria	216	Netherlands	254
Canada	218	New Zealand	256
Chile	220	Norway	258
Czech Republic	222	Poland	260
Denmark	224	Portugal	262
Estonia	226	Romania	264
Finland	228	Russian Federation	266
France	230	Slovak Republic	268
Germany	232	Slovenia	270
Greece	234	Spain	272
Hungary	236	Sweden	274
Ireland	238	Switzerland	276
Israel	240	Turkey	278
Italy	242	United Kingdom	280
Japan	244	United States	282
Korea	246		

STATISTICAL ANNEX

Introduction	288
General comments	288
Inflows and outflows of foreign population	290
Inflows of asylum seekers	315
Stocks of foreign and foreign-born populations	335
Acquisitions of nationality	374
List of correspondents of the Continuous Reporting System on Migration	393
List of OECD Secretariat members involved in the preparation of this publication	395

TABLE OF CONTENTS

Figures and tables

Part I

TRENDS IN INTERNATIONAL MIGRATION

Figures

A. Trends in international migration flows and in the immigrant population	28
I.1. Permanent migration inflows into selected OECD and non-OECD countries, 2007 and 2010	30
I.2. Permanent movements as an estimated percentage of entries into the working-age population, 2010	31
I.3. Estimated entries into the working-age population of youth and new immigrants relative to exits, by 2015, assuming current migration levels	32
I.4. Permanent inflows into selected OECD and non-OECD countries, by category of entry, 2010	33
I.5. Changes in annual permanent migration between 2007 and 2010, by category	34
I.6. Main fields of study of international students, 2009	39
I.7. Recent trends in migration from Greece, Ireland, Portugal and Spain into Germany	44
I.8. Detections at the external borders of the European Union, by quarter	45
I.9. Change in the scale and composition by origin of migration flows between 2000 and 2010	48
I.10. Share of women in migration flows, 2000-10	49
I.11. Evolution of the share of foreign and foreign-born populations among the total population in OECD countries, 2000-10	51
I.12. Population growth between 2000 and 2010 and its components	52
I.13. Number of acquisitions of citizenship between 2000 and 2010, by region	52
I.14. Number of acquisitions of citizenship between 2000 and 2010, per thousand host-country citizens of 2000	53
I.15. Percentage of high-educated among the foreign-born population, 2000 and 2010	54
I.A1.1. Changes in inflows of migrants by country of origin, selected OECD countries, 2000-09 and 2010	57
B. Employment	60
I.16. Changes in monthly harmonised unemployment rates in OECD countries, December 2007 to January 2012	60
I.17. Quarterly employment by place of birth in selected OECD countries, Q1 2007 to Q4 2011	62
I.18. Changes in unemployment and employment rates by place of birth, 2008-11	63
I.19. Contribution of various factors to changes in foreign- and native-born employment in European OECD countries and in the United States	64
I.20. Changes in long-term unemployed foreign-born workers in selected OECD countries, 2008-11	69
I.21. Changes in participation and employment rates by gender and country of birth, 2008-11	71

I.22. Changes in unemployment rates by place of birth and by education level in selected OECD countries, 2008-11 72
I.23. Changes in employment rates by place of birth and age in selected OECD countries, 2008-11 74
I.24. Unemployment rates by place of birth for youth and adults in selected OECD countries, 2011 75
I.25. Changes in NEET rates and long-term and short-term unemployment for youth by place of birth, in selected OECD countries, 2008-11 75
I.26. Changes in temporary employment by place of birth and age in selected OECD countries, 2008-11 77
I.27. Share of part-time employment (2011) and its evolution (2008-11), by place of birth for youth (15-24) in selected OECD countries 78
I.28. Changes in migrant youth (15-24) employment by education level in selected OECD countries, 2008-11 78
I.B2.1. Evolution of foreign-born unemployment in selected OECD countries by unemployment duration, Q1 2008-Q4 2011 91
I.B3.1. NEET, short-term and long-term unemployment rates among youth (15-24), 2011 93

Tables

A. Trends in international migration flows and in the immigrant population 28
I.1. Inflows of permanent immigrants into selected OECD and non-OECD countries, 2000-10 29
I.2. Temporary worker migration in OECD countries, 2005-10 35
I.3. International tertiary-level students in OECD countries and the Russian Federation, 2004-09 37
I.4. Main origin countries of international students in OECD countries, 2009 38
I.5. Asylum seekers in OECD countries and the Russian Federation, 2000-10 40
I.6. Top 25 countries of origin of asylum seekers in OECD countries in 2009 and 2010, and top 2000-10 total 41
I.7. Preliminary trends in immigration for 2011 42
I.8. Top 25 countries of immigration into OECD countries, 2000-10 47
I.9. Countries with strong gender imbalances in migration flows to the OECD, 2010 50

B. Employment 60
I.10. Ten industries with the largest changes in foreign- and native-born employment, in selected OECD countries, 2008-11 66
I.11. Employment, unemployment and participation rates by region of origin in selected OECD countries, 2011 70
I.B1.1. Quarterly employment rates by gender and place of birth in selected OECD countries, 2008-11 82
I.B1.2. Quarterly unemployment rates by gender and place of birth in selected OECD countries, 2008-11 85
I.B1.3. Quarterly participation rates by gender and place of birth in selected OECD countries, 2008-11 88
I.B4.1. Ten industries with the largest changes in foreign- and native-born employment, in selected OECD countries, 2010-11 94
I.B4.2. Employment of foreign-born persons by sector, 2011 96

Part II
RENEWING THE SKILLS OF AGEING WORKFORCES: THE ROLE OF MIGRATION

Figures

- II.1. Changes in the educational attainment of the labour force, 2000-10, by source 131
- II.2a. Composition of the change in the tertiary-educated labour force, by demographic group, 2000-10 132
- II.2b. Composition of the change in the labour force with upper secondary attainment, by demographic group, 2000-10 132
- II.2c. Composition of the change in the labour force with less than upper secondary education, by demographic group, 2000-10 133
- II.3. Total change in the distribution of employment by occupation, 2000-10 137
- II.4. Demographic components of net occupational change by occupational growth quintile, 2000-10 139
- II.5a. Contribution of different demographic groups to occupational growth, average over European countries, 2000-10 142
- II.5b. Contribution of various demographic groups to occupational growth, United States, 2000-10 143
- II.6. Differences in the distribution of occupational skills of workers entering or changing jobs (2000-10) by skill level, new immigrants compared to young resident workers 145
- II.7a. Skill level composition of occupational entries or exits, 2000-10, by demographic group 146
- II.7b. Demographic composition of occupational entries or exits, 2000-10, by skill level 146

Tables

- II.1. Contributions to growth in the labour force by demographic group, 2000-10 ... 128
- II.2. Educational attainment of the labour force, new entrants, new immigrants and retirees, 2000-10 129
- II.3. Growing and declining occupations, 2000-10 135
- II.4. Occupational entry and exit and occupational growth and decline, 2000-10 140
- II.5. Entries of new immigrants into growing and declining occupations, 2010 ... 141
- II.6. Employment growth, by occupational skill level, 2000-10 144
- II.A2.1. Decomposition of growth in the labour force by educational attainment and source, 2000-10 152
- II.A2.2. Decomposition of occupational change (2000-10) by growth quintile and source 154

Part III

THE CHANGING ROLE OF ASIA IN INTERNATIONAL MIGRATION

Figures

- III.1. Emigration rates to OECD countries, by place of birth and gender, total and tertiary educated, 2005/2006 164
- III.2. Total fertility rate, by Asian region, 1970-2010 165
- III.3. Age structure of the population in Asian and OECD economies, 2010 165
- III.4. Educational structure of the population aged 15 and over in Asian economies, 2010 166
- III.5. Share of Asian recipients of selected permanent and temporary skilled worker visas/permits in selected OECD countries, 2009-11 170
- III.6. International students from Asia (including Japan and Korea) in OECD countries, 2009 173
- III.7. International tertiary education students from Asia (incl. Japan and Korea) in OECD countries, 2009, as a percentage of international students and of all students 173
- III.8. Global middle class consumption, in 2005 USD PPP, 2010-20 176
- III.9. Inflows and outflows of Chinese students, 1996-2011 181
- III.10. Outflow of overseas workers relative to the size of the active population, Asian countries 182
- III.11. Proportion of marriages involving a foreign bride and a foreign spouse in Japan, Korea, Chinese Taipei and Singapore, 1998-2010 190

Tables

- III.1. Migrant stock of persons born in Asia (including Japan and Korea) living in OECD countries, 2005/06 160
- III.2. Inflows from Asia to OECD countries, by country of origin, 2000-10 161
- III.3. Migrants from Asia in OECD countries by place of birth, gender, education level, and recent migration, 2005/06 162
- III.4. Foreign workers, total and as percentage of total employment in different Asian economies, 2010 or most recent year, by selected sectors 168
- III.5. Foreign workers from selected Asian countries, by destination, 2010-11 169
- III.6. Share of native-born, foreign-born Asians and other foreign-born in life science and health professional occupations 172
- III.7. Engineering and science graduates for selected countries, 2009 175
- III.8. Outflows of overseas workers, 2005-10, by origin country 182
- III.9. Estimated stocks of undocumented workers in selected Asian economies 184
- III.10. Sex ratio at birth (SRB) or for 0-4 age cohort, selected Asian economies, 1990-2010 191
- III.11. Estimated remittance flows, by origin and receiving country and region, 2010 .. 195
- III.A1.1. Migrants from Asia in OECD countries by place of birth, gender, education level, and recent migration, 2005/06 206
- III.A1.2. Migration flows from Asian countries by destination, 2010 or most recent year 208

Part IV
COUNTRY NOTES: RECENT CHANGES IN MIGRATION MOVEMENTS AND POLICIES

Recent trends in migrants' flows and stocks

Australia 211	Lithuania 249
Austria 213	Luxembourg 251
Belgium 215	Mexico 253
Bulgaria 217	Netherlands 255
Canada 219	New Zealand 257
Chile 221	Norway 259
Czech Republic 223	Poland 261
Denmark 225	Portugal 263
Estonia 227	Romania 265
Finland 229	Russian Federation 267
France 231	Slovak Republic 269
Germany 233	Slovenia 271
Greece 235	Spain 273
Hungary 237	Sweden 275
Ireland 239	Switzerland 277
Israel 241	Turkey 279
Italy 243	United Kingdom 281
Japan 245	United States 283
Korea 247	

STATISTICAL ANNEX

Inflows and outflows of foreign population 290
    A.1. Inflows of foreign population into selected OECD countries
         and the Russian Federation 292
    B.1. Inflows of foreign population by nationality. 293

B.1. Australia (permanent).	293	B.1. Luxembourg	301
B.1. Austria.	293	B.1. Mexico	302
B.1. Belgium	294	B.1. Netherlands	302
B.1. Canada (permanent)	294	B.1. New Zealand.	303
B.1. Chile.	295	B.1. Norway	303
B.1. Czech Republic.	295	B.1. Poland	304
B.1. Denmark	296	B.1. Portugal	304
B.1. Estonia.	296	B.1. Russian Federation	305
B.1. Finland.	297	B.1. Slovak Republic	305
B.1. France	297	B.1. Slovenia.	306
B.1. Germany	298	B.1. Spain	306
B.1. Hungary.	298	B.1. Sweden	307
B.1. Iceland.	299	B.1. Switzerland.	307
B.1. Israel	299	B.1. Turkey	308
B.1. Italy	300	B.1. United Kingdom	308
B.1. Japan	300	B.1. United States (permanent) . .	309
B.1. Korea	301		

    A.2. Outflows of foreign population from selected OECD countries 310
Metadata related to Tables A.1, A.2 and B.1. Migration flows 311

Inflows of asylum seekers 315
    A.3. Inflows of asylum seekers into OECD countries and the Russian Federation . . 316
    B.3. Inflows of asylum seekers by nationality. 317

B.3. Australia	317	B.3. Korea	326
B.3. Austria.	317	B.3. Luxembourg	326
B.3. Belgium	318	B.3. Mexico	327
B.3. Canada.	318	B.3. Netherlands	327
B.3. Chile.	319	B.3. New Zealand.	328
B.3. Czech Republic.	319	B.3. Norway	328
B.3. Denmark	320	B.3. Poland	329
B.3. Estonia.	320	B.3. Portugal	329
B.3. Finland.	321	B.3. Russian Federation	330
B.3. France	321	B.3. Slovak Republic	330
B.3. Germany	322	B.3. Slovenia.	331
B.3. Greece	322	B.3. Spain	331
B.3. Hungary.	323	B.3. Sweden	332
B.3. Iceland.	323	B.3. Switzerland.	332
B.3. Ireland	324	B.3. Turkey	333
B.3. Israel	324	B.3. United Kingdom	333
B.3. Italy	325	B.3. United States	334
B.3. Japan	325		

Metadata related to Tables A.3 and B.3. Inflows of asylum seekers 334

Stocks of foreign and foreign-born populations ... 335

A.4. Stocks of foreign-born population in OECD countries and the Russian Federation ... 336

B.4. Stock of foreign-born population by country of birth ... 338

B.4. Australia ... 338	B.4. Luxembourg ... 346	
B.4. Austria ... 338	B.4. Mexico ... 346	
B.4. Belgium ... 339	B.4. Netherlands ... 347	
B.4. Canada ... 339	B.4. New Zealand ... 347	
B.4. Chile ... 340	B.4. Norway ... 348	
B.4. Czech Republic ... 340	B.4. Poland ... 348	
B.4. Denmark ... 341	B.4. Portugal ... 349	
B.4. Finland ... 341	B.4. Russian Federation ... 349	
B.4. France ... 342	B.4. Slovak Republic ... 350	
B.4. Germany ... 342	B.4. Slovenia ... 350	
B.4. Greece ... 343	B.4. Spain ... 351	
B.4. Hungary ... 343	B.4. Sweden ... 351	
B.4. Iceland ... 344	B.4. Switzerland ... 352	
B.4. Ireland ... 344	B.4. Turkey ... 352	
B.4. Israel ... 345	B.4. United Kingdom ... 353	
B.4. Italy ... 345	B.4. United States ... 353	

Metadata related to Tables A.4 and B.4. Stocks of foreign-born population ... 354

A.5. Stocks of foreign population by nationality in OECD countries and the Russian Federation ... 356

B.5. Stock of foreign population by nationality ... 358

B.5. Austria ... 358	B.5. Luxembourg ... 365
B.5. Belgium ... 358	B.5. Mexico ... 365
B.5. Czech Republic ... 359	B.5. Netherlands ... 366
B.5. Denmark ... 359	B.5. Norway ... 366
B.5. Finland ... 360	B.5. Poland ... 367
B.5. France ... 360	B.5. Portugal ... 367
B.5. Germany ... 361	B.5. Russian Federation ... 368
B.5. Greece ... 361	B.5. Slovak Republic ... 368
B.5. Hungary ... 362	B.5. Slovenia ... 369
B.5. Iceland ... 362	B.5. Spain ... 369
B.5. Ireland ... 363	B.5. Sweden ... 370
B.5. Italy ... 363	B.5. Switzerland ... 370
B.5. Japan ... 364	B.5. Turkey ... 371
B.5. Korea ... 364	B.5. United Kingdom ... 371

Metadata related to Tables A.5 and B.5. Stocks of foreign population ... 372

Acquisitions of nationality 374
    A.6. Acquisitions of nationality in OECD countries and the Russian Federation . . 375
    B.6. Acquisitions of nationality by country of former nationality 376

B.6. Australia	376		B.6. Korea	384
B.6. Austria	377		B.6. Luxembourg	384
B.6. Belgium	377		B.6. Mexico	385
B.6. Canada	378		B.6. Netherlands	385
B.6. Chile	378		B.6. New Zealand	386
B.6. Czech Republic	379		B.6. Norway	386
B.6. Denmark	379		B.6. Poland	387
B.6. Finland	380		B.6. Portugal	387
B.6. France	380		B.6. Russian Federation	388
B.6. Germany	381		B.6. Slovak Republic	388
B.6. Greece	381		B.6. Spain	389
B.6. Hungary	382		B.6. Sweden	389
B.6. Iceland	382		B.6. Switzerland	390
B.6. Ireland	383		B.6. Turkey	390
B.6. Italy	383		B.6. United Kingdom	391
B.6. Japan	384		B.6. United States	391

    Metadata related to Tables A.6 and B.6. Acquisitions of nationality 392

This book has...

StatLinks
A service that delivers Excel® files from the printed page!

Look for the *StatLinks* at the bottom right-hand corner of the tables or graphs in this book. To download the matching Excel® spreadsheet, just type the link into your Internet browser, starting with the *http://dx.doi.org* prefix.
If you're reading the PDF e-book edition, and your PC is connected to the Internet, simply click on the link. You'll find *StatLinks* appearing in more OECD books.

Editorial

Immigrant labour wanted? Recent lessons

The great recession which began in late 2008 brought an abrupt halt to the upward trend in international migration inflows to OECD countries. Three years later, with a sluggish recovery underway in the OECD area and many countries still grappling with high unemployment, the first tentative signs of a recovery in migration flows appeared. Now is a good moment to look back and draw the lessons learned about labour migration from the crisis and from other recent experiences in this area.

The first lesson, and it is a key one, is that it is job opportunities and demand by employers which drive labour migration. Migration policy can of course set limits which employers have to respect, such as minimum wages and working conditions or education levels or even occupations for which recruitment of immigrant workers is allowed, but the bottom line is … no work, no labour migrants.

Of course, labour migration did not come to a complete halt in the recession. Indeed in 2010 inflows of labour migrants to OECD countries totalled around 780 000 compared with 880 000 in 2007. The reasons are that not all countries were hit hard by the recession, that some recruitments were already in the pipeline and that even in a downturn there are still vacant jobs for which employers cannot find enough takers in the domestic labour market. Unemployed construction workers cannot take up jobs in engineering or health care.

The most telling evidence on the importance of job opportunities for labour migration was the large drop (by more than one-third) in free-circulation flows from the new accession countries of the European Union. Employers cut down on hiring and EU workers were quick to pick up the message – fewer of them left home for work in other countries of the European Union.

At the same time, temporary labour migration fell almost everywhere during the recession, including Australia, Canada, Japan and the United States. The quotas for skilled H-1B visas in the United States, for example, were often all filled on the first day the visas were made available in the pre-crisis era. In 2009 and 2010, however, it took at least nine months to exhaust the supply. In 2011 it still took eight months.

The United Kingdom last year imposed what it thought were strict caps on skilled migration, but employers were hiring so little that these were not even reached.

Unauthorised movements of migrants looking for work went down as well during the recession. Such movements are not cost-free and with no guarantee of finding a job, they no longer look so attractive to potential migrants and their families. Part of the large drop in unauthorised movements to the United States from Mexico and Central America (border patrol apprehensions decreased from 875 000 in 2007 to 350 000 in 2011) is due to the impact of the recession.

In short, economic conditions in destination countries are a major determinant of the scale of labour migration.

A *second lesson* is that employers do not automatically switch to hiring immigrant workers when the opportunity to do so is made easier. Finding and recruiting workers from other countries is generally more expensive and candidates who apply may not speak the language of the host country well or be familiar with the work culture. If in addition employers also have to pay wages in line with collective agreements or national minimum wages to workers recruited from abroad, it is likely that requests for such workers will be made only if the need is strong enough. With the introduction in late 2008 of the liberal Swedish labour migration regime, for example, requests by employers for workers from abroad have increased, but they have not exploded. While some aspects of the Swedish case are specific to that country and it is early yet to pass a final judgement, it does provide an interesting case-study of a demand-driven labour migration system with few restrictions which has not given rise to large and uncontrolled inflows.

A *third lesson*, this one based on the impact of the crisis, is that governments must be careful about employer permit requests for specific jobs which tend to be cut during downturns (*e.g.* construction, as seen in Ireland and Spain) and which build a strong feed-back loop into the system (*e.g.* more migrants needed to build housing for more migrants).

A *fourth lesson* is that supply-driven migration systems, in which immigrants are selected for admission on the basis of their perceived aptitude for integration and which generally favour highly educated candidates, are not working quite as well as they used to. Some immigrants accepted for admission under these systems have had a hard time finding adequate work after arrival and may have had to take jobs for which they are overqualified implying a productivity loss to the host country and dissatisfaction for the immigrants. Both Australia and Canada have introduced stronger links to labour market needs in their selection systems in order to minimize these concerns.

A *fifth lesson* is that in demand-driven labour migration systems, it is employers who determine which migrants are recruited from abroad, because they are the ones who select among candidates applying for particular jobs, subject to the constraints imposed by receiving country governments. Employers' hiring choices will be guided by their own experience with immigrant workers, by whatever knowledge they may possess about the qualifications and work experience of applicants and by preconceptions which they may have about expected productivity levels of potential migrants. Recent years have seen a rise in skilled labour migration from Asia, which suggests that the Asian continent may be a more and more important source of labour migrants for OECD countries in the short-to-medium term. In the long run, however, it is not so obvious that, as Asia develops, OECD countries will be able to rely on a steady stream of skilled workers from that region.

While the experience of the past has been useful in establishing a few signposts for the future, it has not eliminated the need for safeguards against abuse in the regulation of labour migration, for example with respect to substandard wages and working conditions or questionable recruitment practices. These are among the areas where best and cost-effective safeguards have not necessarily been identified.

The current slowdown in labour migration movements represents a good opportunity for governments to reflect on these lessons and adapt their policies accordingly, before the economic recovery picks up and migration accelerates.

John P. Martin

Director for Employment, Labour and Social Affairs

Executive summary

The slowdown in migration into OECD countries caused by the global economic crisis seems to have come to an end. Migration into OECD countries fell in 2010 for the third year in a row, but started to rise again in most countries in 2011. Temporary labour migration continued to fall, albeit more slowly, while the number of people coming to OECD countries to study continued to grow.

With the recovery still fragile, and public opinion sensitive to migration issues against a backdrop of continuing high unemployment, many governments have introduced more restrictive migration policies. Jobless young migrants are a particular cause for concern, requiring targeted policy action from governments.

For the future, population ageing in the OECD area is likely to have a significant effect on migration trends, but perhaps in unexpected ways.

At the same time, it is not clear how much longer high-skilled migration from Asia will continue to rise as demand for high-skilled labour increases in fast-growing economies in the region.

This edition of the *International Migration Outlook* looks at trends in migration and migration policy, as well as employment trends among migrants. Special chapters focus on how changes in educational attainment and occupations affect migration, and on the changing role of Asia in international migration.

Migration flows to OECD countries

Overall permanent migration inflows into 23 OECD countries plus the Russian Federation declined in 2010, for the third year in a row. However, the decline was modest overall (–3% compared with 2009) and the number of migrants – over 4.1 million – was higher than in any year prior to 2005 for which standardised statistics are available. Preliminary figures show that immigration started to increase again in 2011 in most European OECD countries except Italy, as well as in Australia and New Zealand.

Still limited evidence of increasing emigration from Southern Europe, Ireland

In the OECD, 2011 was marked by a worsening of economic conditions in some Eurozone countries, in particular Greece, Ireland, Italy, Portugal and Spain, generating some speculation about an increase in emigration. The evidence available to date suggests that emigration from these countries has indeed increased, but only modestly. Outflows of nationals have also been rather small, with the exception of Ireland, where language barriers to emigration may be less of a problem.

Free movement and labour migration is falling...

In 2010, free movement migration, strongly on the decline since 2007, accounted for 20% of all permanent migration flows. Because of the drop in employer demand, labour migration also decreased and represented only 21% of the total. Overall, family migration was the main category of entry in 2010, accounting for 36% of the flows (45% if accompanying family of workers are included). Humanitarian migration accounted for only 6% of migration in the EU and 13% in the United States.

... but temporary labour migration remains significant

Temporary worker migration tends to react quickly and strongly to changes in economic conditions. In fact, it experienced a sharp drop in 2008 and 2009 but only a modest 4% decline was observed in 2010. The size of temporary worker migration flows now stands at about 1.9 million, significantly more than the 1.4 million estimated for permanent migration for employment.

International student numbers continue to grow...

In contrast to both permanent migration and temporary labour migration, the number of international students continued to grow in 2009, increasing by 6% to reach more than 2.6 million in the OECD countries and the Russian Federation. Australia replaced France as the third main destination after the United States and the United Kingdom. International students account on average for more than 6% of all students in OECD countries. China and India between them account for a full 25% of international students, who are an important source of future labour migration.

... while asylum seeker figures remain stable

Arrivals of asylum seekers in OECD countries were at a slightly lower level in 2010 than in 2009, and well below the high numbers observed at the turn of the millennium. The economic crisis thus did not lead to large increases in asylum-seeking. France remained the country which received the most asylum seekers in 2010, followed by the United States and Germany. The main country of origin in 2010 was Serbia, followed by Afghanistan and China. In 2011, this trend was reversed as asylum applications increased by more than 20%, notably because of the "Arab Spring" and increasing requests from Afghanistan.

China accounts for almost 10% of migrant flows

In 2010, China was again the main country of origin of migration flows to the OECD, nearly one in ten migrants being a Chinese citizen. Romania, India and Poland follow – each contributing about 5% of the total.

Migrants hit hardest by crisis job losses

The economic downturn hit immigrants hard, and almost immediately, in most OECD countries. The evidence suggests that overall the impact of the economic crisis on unemployment has been more pronounced for migrants than for the native-born. Overall, in the OECD, the foreign-born unemployment rate increased by four percentage points between 2008 and 2011, compared with 2.5 points for the native-born. Even more worrysome is the increase in long-term unemployment among immigrants. In most countries, migrants are responsible for between 14% and 30% of the increase in total long-term unemployment, a figure which is, in most cases, well above their share in total employment.

The crisis affected different migrant groups in different ways. In most countries, migrant women have been less affected than foreign-born men – in several countries an increasing number of migrant women have taken jobs to compensate for income losses suffered by migrant men. In terms of skill levels, low-skilled foreign-born workers have been hit harder than the medium- and high-skilled. This is not only related to differences in employement distribution by sector, but also to the type of jobs they occupy (often temporary) and their lower seniority, which imply a lower firing cost to employers.

Young migrants are particularly vulnerable…

The increase between 2008 and 2011 in the share of young people not in education, employment, or training (NEET), an indicator which captures the "joblessness" of young people, has been especially marked among migrants. This is true most notably in Greece, Spain, Sweden, Ireland and Italy. In addition, in the majority of countries, the incidence of temporary employment has increased more for young foreign-born workers than for their native-born counterparts or foreign-born adults (aged 25-54). Similarly, in a number of countries, the share of part-time employment in total employment has increased more for migrant youth than for native-born young people.

… requiring adequate and immediate policy responses

Both during the crisis and in the recovery, adopting specific policies to help young people to find and keep a job is even more important for low-skilled foreign-born youth who suffer a combination of disadvantages (low skill levels, weak language skills, limited access to networks), who are at a higher risk of future unemployment and who are more likely to experience reduced total lifetime earnings (the so-called "scarring" effect).

Governments are reviewing migration policies…

Several countries shifted towards more restrictive immigration policies in 2010-11 in response to changing economic conditions and to increasing public sensitivity on migration issues. New governments tightened controls over the immigration process and restricted the possibilities of long-term immigration for migrants with poor employment prospects. More generally, many governments reviewed their skills shortage lists and temporary work programmes and subjected employers to more scrutiny. Points systems for admission have become more demand-driven, with supply-driven channels restrictive.

... including integration policies

Integration continues to be a top priority for immigration policy of OECD countries. Countries have adopted a wide range of integration-related initiatives – ranging from establishing comprehensive national strategies to fine-tuning and refining existing action plans and integration programs. The focus also oscillates between established and newly-arrived migrants. A common trend among these policies is to prioritise labour market integration and reinforce the educational aspects of integration, including language training.

Impact of population ageing on migration

Population ageing and the role of migration in meeting this challenge is not just a question of how many new workers there are to replace those who retire. By looking at the contribution of migration to labour force changes – instead of at changes in working age population – in terms of education level and occupation, it becomes clear that the labour market is changing too rapidly for demographic imbalances alone to be a reliable indicator of future occupational needs.

The educational attainment of new entrants into the labour force was much higher than that of retiring workers over the period 2000-10. New immigrants had educational levels that were between those of new entrants and retirees, with proportionally more highly educated workers among new immigrants than among retirees. New entrants are, however, playing a more significant role in maintaining the size of the labour force than in its upskilling in most countries.

There is also the question of the type of occupation that will be available in the future, and the skills that will be needed, compared with the jobs and skill sets of the past. New immigrants represented 15% of entries into strongly growing occupations in Europe over the decade and 22% in the United States. They are thus playing a significant role in the most dynamic portions of the economy, even under conditions when most migration has not been demand-driven. But a higher number of immigrants were entering the most strongly declining occupations – 24% in Europe and 28% in the United States. In some countries, the figure is significantly higher for low-skilled jobs, which risks creating a segmented labour market.

Growing importance of Asian migration to OECD countries...

Migrants from Asia accounted for 17% of all migrants over age 15 in OECD countries in the mid-2000s, and 30% of migration inflows in 2010 were from the region. Furthermore, Asia, notably India and China, provides a large part of skilled migration to OECD countries. In the short term it is most likely that Asia will remain a key source region for highly skilled workers. In the longer-term, however, as Asia develops, it will produce more skilled workers, but also foster the conditions for them to remain, and to attract skilled workers from other parts of the world.

... and future challenges for labour migration systems in Asia

Management of less-skilled migration in Asia is difficult because of a large surplus of labour and limited opportunities, leading to frequent rent-taking and rising migration costs for the less educated to a significant portion of expected overseas earnings. Some schemes, such as Korea's Employment Permit Scheme (EPS), have been successful in dealing with these challenges. In the meantime, countries of origin look to the Philippines as a model of how to integrate surplus labour into the global labour market – in different sectors, towards different destinations, and at different skill levels – while protecting their rights. As the growth in demand for low skilled migration remains limited in Gulf Co-operation Council (GCC) and OECD destination countries as well as within Asia, there might be little scope to significantly increase the supply of this type of migrant.

In the future Asian countries will also face a number of challenges, notably to manage increasing family and marriage migration but also to develop more comprehensive integration strategies as settlement – or at least longer duration of stay – is becoming more frequent for both high- and less skilled migrants.

PART I

Trends in international migration

Part I begins with a broad overview of recent trends in international migration flows, including preliminary 2011 data. It then turns to the impact of the economic crisis on immigrants' employment situation. Finaly, it examines recent major changes in migration policies, including how the crisis has affected the management of migration flows and how migration legislation has tightened, as illustrated by changes in family and humanitarian migration policy and in border controls.

A. Trends in international migration flows and in the immigrant population

1. Introduction: The context for migration in 2010/11

Following the strong decline in 2009, macroeconomic conditions improved in most OECD countries in 2010/11. However, the recovery generally remained fragile, in particular in Southern Europe, where the debt crisis dampened economic prospects. With the earthquake and tsunami in 2011, Japan also re-entered into recession. Unemployment hit a high of 8.3% in 2010 and declined only marginally in 2011, to 8.1%. It thus remained well above the pre-crisis level of 5.7% in 2007.

In this context, the demand for new labour migration remained limited. Major geopolitical events have also affected migration trends, particularly in European OECD countries, namely the so-called "Arab Spring" and the entry into force of full labour mobility with the countries that joined the European Union (EU) in 2004.

Against this background, this section analyses the main trends in international migration. The section starts with an overview of the trends in permanent migration in 2010 (sub-section 2). This is followed by a description of trends in temporary migration and asylum seeking (sub-section 3). Sub-section 4 gives a glance at preliminary migration trends in 2011. Sub-section 5 provides an overview on the regional and gender composition of migration flows. Sub-section 6 looks at the immigrant population and highlights the contribution of migrants to the growth of population in OECD countries over the past decade. The section ends with a summary of recent key developments (sub-section 7).

2. Permanent migration

Overall across the 23 OECD countries plus the Russian Federation for which standardised statistics are available, permanent migration inflows continued to decline, for the third year in a row. However, the decline has been modest overall (–3% compared with 2009) and levels – more than 4.1 million – were still higher than in any year prior to 2007 for which standardised statistics are available (Table I.1). Indeed, among the 21 countries for which data are available since 2005, only six showed a decline over that period. Furthermore, virtually all of the decline in absolute numbers in 2010 was attributable to the United States, which saw an 8% decline.

In relative terms, the decline in immigration continued to be significant in several other countries, in particular Ireland, which was hard hit by the crisis and where permanent inflows declined by a full 55% to drop below a fifth of their pre-crisis levels. Declines also continued to be significant in the Czech Republic and Japan, as well as in Southern Europe (Portugal, Italy and Spain). The Russian Federation also saw a decline of 12%, following a peak in 2009.

Table I.1. **Inflows of permanent immigrants into selected OECD and non-OECD countries, 2000-10**

	Standardised statistics (number of persons)							Variation (%)	
	2000	2005	2006	2007	2008	2009	2010	2010/09	2010/07
United States	841 000	1 122 400	1 266 300	1 052 400	1 107 100	1 130 200	1 041 900	-8	-1
United Kingdom	..	369 600	355 200	355 900	338 500	375 900	414 300	10	16
Italy	..	193 500	171 300	537 200	489 100	369 000	331 700	-10	-38
Spain	..	..	..	691 900	409 600	334 000	300 000	-10	-57
Canada	227 500	262 200	251 600	236 800	247 200	252 200	280 700	11	19
Russian Federation	..	..	..	252 000	268 500	299 000	263 900	-12	5
Germany	264 100	196 600	165 200	232 800	228 300	201 400	222 400	10	-4
Australia	..	167 300	179 800	191 900	205 900	221 000	209 000	-5	9
France	..	190 000	195 300	184 500	192 200	178 700	193 100	8	5
Korea	58 600	153 600	189 500	178 400	192 400	137 900	156 900	14	-12
Switzerland	..	78 800	86 300	122 200	139 100	114 800	115 000	0	-6
Netherlands	66 200	69 400	73 000	80 600	90 600	89 500	95 600	7	19
Sweden	47 600	53 800	78 500	74 400	71 000	71 300	64 400	-10	-13
Norway	..	25 800	28 300	43 700	48 900	48 500	55 900	15	28
Japan	107 900	98 700	104 100	108 500	97 700	65 500	55 700	-15	-49
Portugal	15 300	11 500	25 100	42 900	65 900	59 900	49 500	-17	15
New Zealand	..	59 200	54 600	51 700	51 200	47 500	47 700	0	-8
Austria	..	56 800	30 800	47 100	49 500	45 700	45 900	0	-3
Denmark	..	21 600	23 900	30 300	45 600	38 400	41 300	7	36
Belgium	..	35 000	35 600	40 300	43 900	37 700	35 900	-5	-11
Czech Republic	7 800	55 900	63 000	98 800	71 800	39 000	30 500	-22	-69
Mexico	6 400	9 200	6 900	6 800	15 100	23 900	26 400	11	287
Finland	9 100	12 700	13 900	17 500	19 900	18 100	18 200	1	4
Ireland	..	66 000	88 900	89 600	67 600	38 900	17 400	-55	-81
Total number of persons									
All countries				4 768 300	4 556 600	4 237 900	4 113 300		
Excluding settlement countries				3 235 500	2 945 200	2 587 000	2 534 000		
EU included above				2 523 800	2 183 500	1 897 500	1 860 200		
EU excl. free movements				1 369 800	1 296 400	1 203 800	1 173 300		
Annual per cent change									
All countries					-4	-7	-3		
Excluding settlement countries					-9	-12	-2		
EU included above					-13	-13	-2		
EU excl. free movements					-5	-7	-3		

	National statistics (unstandardised)							Variation (%)	
	2000	2005	2006	2007	2008	2009	2010	2010/09	2010/07
Turkey	..	..	..	..	..	..	29 910	..	..
Chile	..	38 150	48 520	79 380	68 380	57 060	63 910	12	-19
Poland	15 900	38 510	34 210	40 640	41 830	41 280	41 060	-1	1
Greece	..	..	..	..	..	33 540	22 980	-31	..
Slovenia	5 300	13 290	18 250	27 500	28 060	27 390	12 710	-54	-54
Hungary	20 200	25 580	23 570	22 610	35 550	25 580	23 880	-7	6
Luxembourg	10 800	13 760	13 730	15 770	16 800	14 640	15 810	8	0
Israel	60 200	21 180	19 270	18 130	13 700	14 570	16 630	14	-8
Slovak Republic	4 600	7 670	11 310	14 850	16 470	14 440	12 660	-12	-15
Iceland	2 500	4 680	7 070	9 320	7 470	3 390	2 990	-12	-68
Estonia	..	980	1 490	1 950	1 930	2 230	1 200	-46	-39
Total		163 800	177 420	230 150	230 190	200 580	190 850		
Per cent change			8	30	0	-13	-5		

Notes: Includes only foreign nationals; the inflows include status changes, namely persons in the country on a temporary status who obtained the right to stay on a longer-term basis.
Series for some countries have been significantly revised.
Information on data for Israel: http://dx.doi.org/10.1787/888932315602.
Source: OECD International Migration Database.

StatLink http://dx.doi.org/10.1787/888932616695

With the exception of those countries particularly hard hit by the crisis, it appears that overall the cyclical decline in migration came to an end in 2010.[1] There were double-digit increases in a number of rather large immigration countries with strong growth, such as Canada, which had a record-high level of immigration, Germany and Korea. The biggest increase was in Norway, where immigration reached a new record high. The United Kingdom also saw an increase, which was nevertheless due to status changes of people already in the country while immigration from outside the country declined.[2]

National statistics for the countries for which no standardised data are available suggest somewhat stronger declines for these, with the exception of Chile, Israel[3] and Luxembourg where economic conditions are more favourable. Since flows to the countries without standardised data tend to be small in numbers, their inclusion nevertheless does not alter the overall picture.

This edition of the *International Migration Outlook* presents, for the first time, standardised migration figures for the EU area as a whole. Since free movement essentially concerns intra-EU movements,[4] the EU figures in this publication exclude free movement, where possible. About 1.2 million permanent-type migrants joined the EU area in 2010, virtually the same number as in 2009, compared with slightly more than 1 million for the United States and 540 000 for Australia, Canada and New Zealand altogether.

The contribution of migration to population dynamics

In 2010, as in every year since 2007, the year when it fully opened its labour market for migration from the EU15, Switzerland has been the country that received the largest number of permanent migrants in per-capita terms (Figure I.1). Three quarters of new arrivals are from EU countries, mainly from Switzerland's neighbours, attracted by good labour market conditions and high wage levels. The situation in this respect is similar in Norway, where new migrant inflows – mainly from the enlarged EU – also accounted for

Figure I.1. **Permanent migration inflows into selected OECD and non-OECD countries, 2007 and 2010**
Percentage of the total population

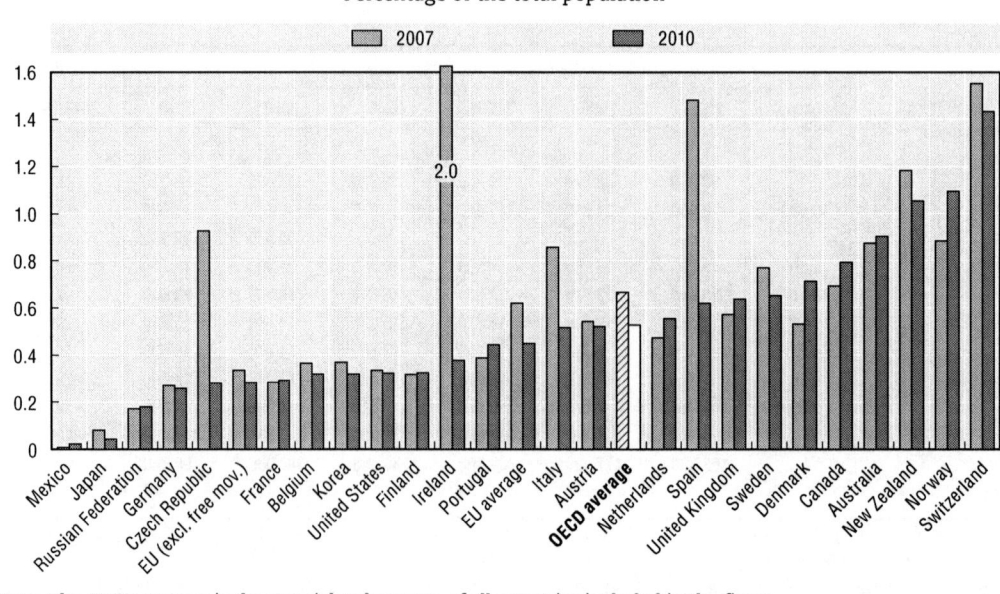

Note: The OECD average is the unweighted average of all countries included in the figure.
Source: OECD International Migration Database.
StatLink ⟶ http://dx.doi.org/10.1787/888932614985

more than 1% of the population. The next three countries in per-capita terms are New Zealand, Australia and Canada. All three of these have been settled by migration and take significant numbers of labour migrants through their migration programmes which operate with targeted migration levels. Targets are not necessarily set to react to immediate labour market needs, in contrast to the respective temporary migration programmes in these countries (see below). These three settlement countries thus decided to broadly maintain their migration intake during the crisis, which was also less pronounced in these countries than elsewhere in the OECD.

Migration levels in per-capita terms are lowest in Mexico, Japan and the Russian Federation. Permanent flows are also low in a number of European countries such as Germany and France, both of which have per capita inflows that are only about half of the OECD average and a third of those observed in Australia, Canada and New Zealand. The EU area as a whole has permanent migration that is, in per capita terms, at about the same level as the United States.

Comparing 2010 data with pre-crisis levels, the salient observation is that the crisis has been associated with strong declines in inflows in Ireland, Spain and, to a lesser degree, Italy.[5] All three of these had migration flows prior to the crisis that were well above the OECD average, in response to labour market needs. In most other countries, changes were modest either way.

In spite of the crisis, the relative scale of migration movements remains at significant levels, particularly when considering new permanent immigrants as a percentage of all new entries into the working-age population (Figure I.2).[6] With the exception of Mexico and Japan, in all OECD countries for which standardised data are available, new immigrants

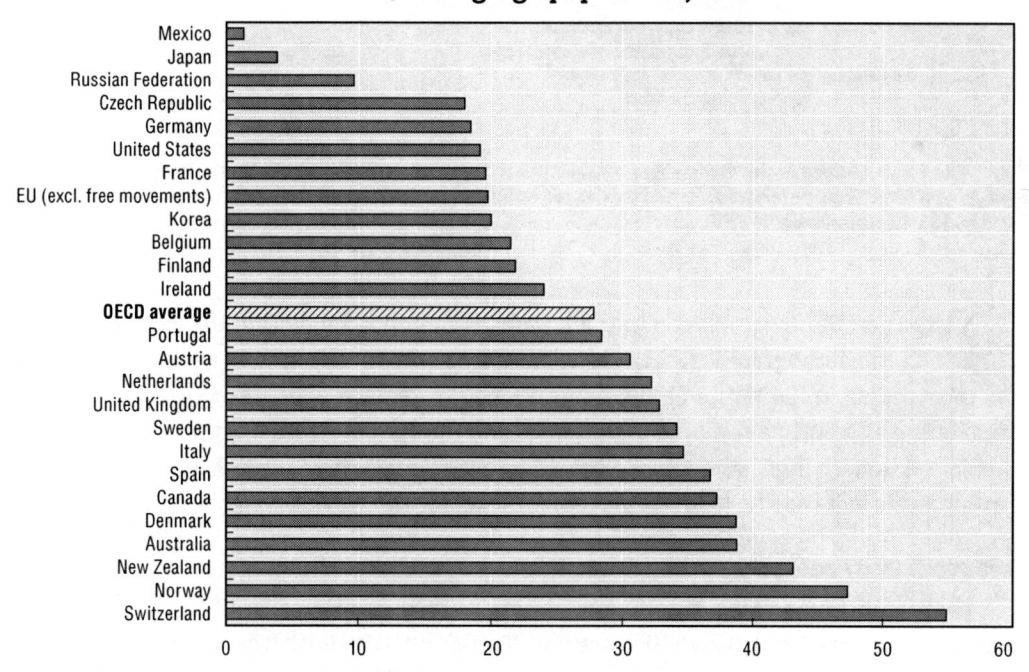

Figure I.2. **Permanent movements as an estimated percentage of entries into the working-age population, 2010**

Note: The OECD average is the unweighted average of all countries included in the figure.
Source: OECD International Migration Database.

StatLink http://dx.doi.org/10.1787/888932615004

make up for more than 10% of new entries – on average almost 30%.[7] In Switzerland, Norway and New Zealand, new immigrants even comprise about half of all new entries into the working-age population.

Without migration by 2015 there will be more old people leaving the working-age population than young people entering it in 13 of the 23 OECD countries for which standardised migration data are available (Figure I.3). However, assuming current migration trends, new migration will suffice to keep the working-age population at its previous level, except in the Czech Republic and Japan.

Figure I.3. **Estimated entries into the working-age population of youth and new immigrants relative to exits, by 2015, assuming current migration levels**

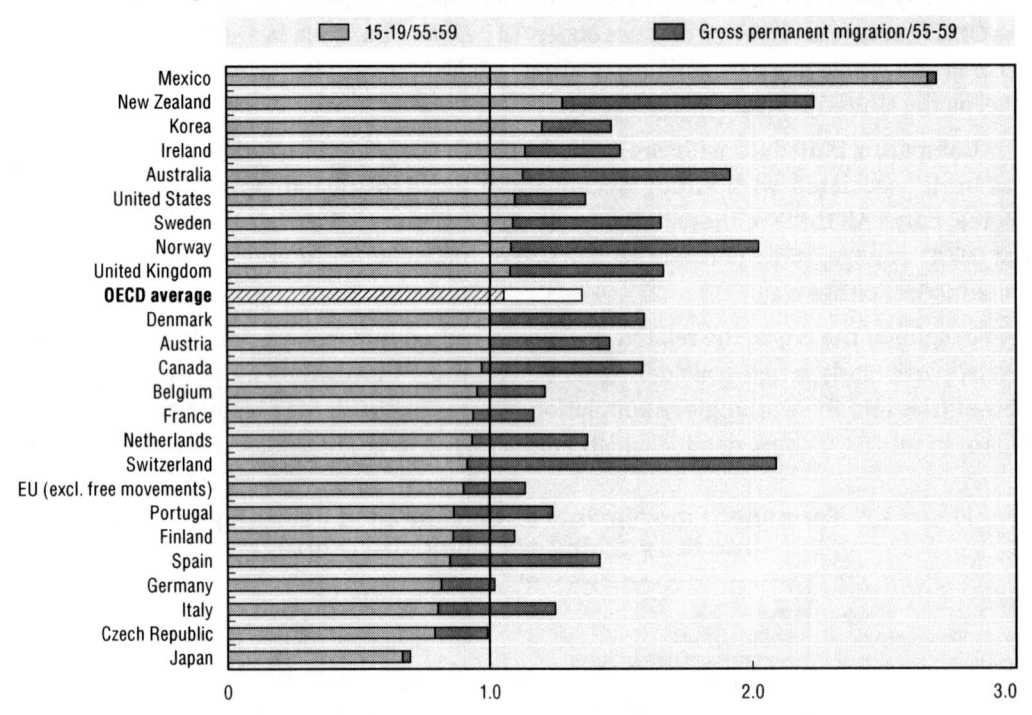

Notes: The OECD average is the unweighted average of all countries included in the figure. The ratio of 1 is the replacement level. The age-related exits and entries are estimated on the basis of the average size of the cohort aged 55-59 and 15-19, respectively, in 2010.
Source: OECD International Migration Database.   StatLink http://dx.doi.org/10.1787/888932615023

A large part of new migration in the EU area is free mobility within the European Union (EU), which – in demographic terms – is a zero-sum game for the area as a whole. Excluding free movements, migration will just about suffice to replace age-related exits in the EU.[8] Considering also emigration of both nationals and foreigners – which is not included in the calculation underlying Figure I.3 – for the EU as a whole, starting around 2015, migration at current levels will thus be below replacement level for the working-age population.

Composition by category

There continues to be significant variety across countries in the composition of international migration flows (Figure I.4). The countries with the largest inflows in per-capita terms, Switzerland and Norway, draw the bulk of their migrant intake from the enlarged European Union. Free movement migrants respond to labour demand and are attracted by high salary levels in these two countries.[9] Both free movement within the

Figure I.4. **Permanent inflows into selected OECD and non-OECD countries, by category of entry, 2010**
Percentage of the total population

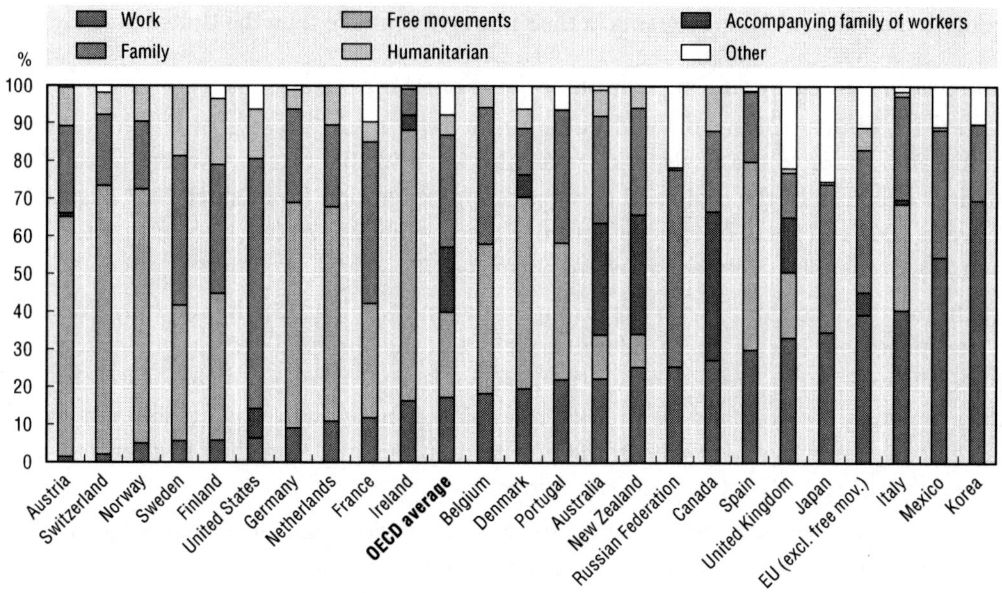

Legend: Work, Family, Free movements, Humanitarian, Accompanying family of workers, Other

Countries (left to right): Austria, Switzerland, Norway, Sweden, Finland, United States, Germany, Netherlands, France, Ireland, OECD average, Belgium, Denmark, Portugal, Australia, New Zealand, Russian Federation, Canada, Spain, United Kingdom, Japan, EU (excl. free mov.), Italy, Mexico, Korea

Note: The OECD average is the unweighted average of all countries included in the figure.
Source: OECD International Migration Database. StatLink http://dx.doi.org/10.1787/888932615042

enlarged European Union, Norway and Switzerland and labour migration remained roughly at their 2009 levels, accounting each for slightly more than 20% of permanent migration in the OECD. Not considering free movement, labour migration accounts for almost 40% of immigration flows into the EU, compared with only 6% in the United States.

In terms of the composition of migration for employment, there seems to be some "trade-off" between labour migration (that is, from outside of free mobility areas) and free movement. Countries which have large proportions of their migrant intakes through free movement, such as Switzerland, Norway and Austria, but also Germany and the Netherlands, tend to have little labour migration. The reverse is the case for Korea which does not currently have the option to satisfy possible labour needs through free movement migration. Mexico and Japan also have large shares of labour migrants, but in the context of low overall immigration levels.

There are a few exceptions to this pattern regarding the composition of migration for employment, namely Spain, Italy and the United States. For both Italy and Spain, the significant free mobility movements seem to consist, to a large part, of family migration to already resident migrants who have benefited from free mobility migration for employment prior to the crisis. In the United States, there is little permanent ("green card") labour migration, because its system, which is based on numerical limits, favours family migration.

Indeed, the United States has the largest share of family migrants in the OECD – about three out of four new permanent immigrants are in this category. Overall in OECD countries, in spite of some decline, family migration continued to be the main category for permanent migration in 2010, accounting for 36% of the flows. If the family members who are accompanying the labour migrant are included, this figure rises to 45%. Accompanying family of workers notably make up a large part of family migration in Australia, Canada and New Zealand.

I. TRENDS IN INTERNATIONAL MIGRATION

Humanitarian and other forms of migration account for the remainder of migration flows. Humanitarian migration to the EU makes up only 5% of all migration into the area, compared with 13% in the United States. Indeed, only Sweden (19%) and Finland (17%) have a larger proportion of humanitarian migrants in their immigrant intake than the United States.

Changes in the scale and composition of flows with the crisis

Free mobility migration had been among the main drivers of the increase in immigration prior to the crisis, and it has also been in this category where most of the changes occurred in the scale and composition of migration flows since 2007 (Figure I.5). Between 2007 and 2010, free movement declined by about 470 000, accounting for more than 75% of the total decline in movements in the OECD.

In the three countries with the strongest decline – Ireland, Spain and Italy – declines in free movement have accounted for at least 60% of the observed decrease in immigration flows. Likewise, for the countries which experienced the strongest increases in migration flows – namely Norway and Denmark – the bulk of the growth was attributable to free movement. Free movement within the enlarged European Union thus has reacted quite strongly to the changing economic conditions.

Some adjustment also came through the labour migration channel, notably in Spain, where labour migration from outside of the EU declined strongly in light of a slack labour market, by more than 90 000. Spain thereby accounted for virtually the entire global decline in labour migration in the OECD area over this period. Indeed, with the exception of Spain, declines in labour migration in some countries were compensated by increases in other countries, for example in Denmark and Canada, where labour migration increased in response to growing labour demand. The Russian Federation also saw a significant rise in labour migration.[10]

Humanitarian and family migration are less responsive to economic conditions. Indeed, family migration (including accompanying family) even experienced a slight increase over the crisis. In contrast, humanitarian migration – which accounts only for a small part of the overall inflows – tended to decline somewhat in most countries.

Figure I.5. **Changes in annual permanent migration between 2007 and 2010, by category**
Percentage of the total population

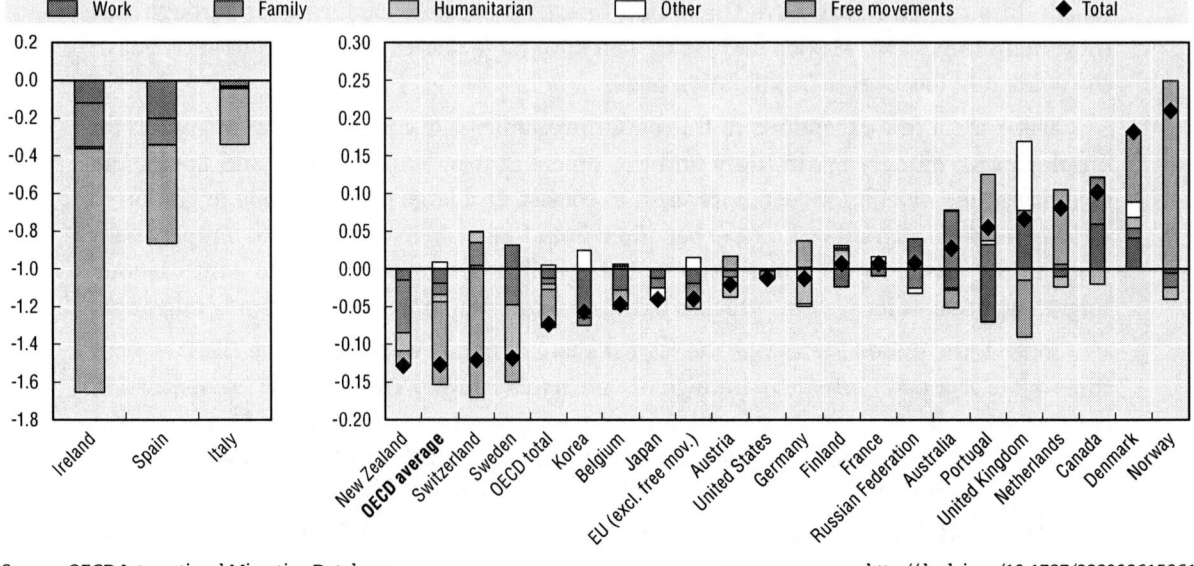

Source: OECD International Migration Database.

StatLink ᔆ http://dx.doi.org/10.1787/888932615061

I. TRENDS IN INTERNATIONAL MIGRATION

3. Temporary migration and asylum seeking

Worker migration

Together with free movement migration, temporary worker migration is the component of migration flows which reacts most strongly to economic conditions and thus experienced a sharp drop in 2009. In 2010, there had been little change overall, with a further but modest decline by 4%. The number of temporary worker migration flows now stands at about 1.9 million, significantly more than the estimated 1.4 million permanent migration for employment (including both labour migrants and work-related free movement).[11] The number of 1.9 million is a lower boundary, since the coverage of temporary worker migration is incomplete, both with respect to countries and categories. Nonetheless, Table I.2 below provides a reasonably complete overview of developments regarding temporary worker migration across the OECD, on the basis of data that are consistent over time.

Table I.2. **Temporary worker migration in OECD countries, 2005-10**

	2005	2006	2007	2008	2009	2010	2010/2009 change (%)
Trainees	115	129	164	146	114	83	−27
Working holiday makers	312	335	397	430	403	398	−1
Intra-company transfers	91	104	118	117	92	108	17
Seasonal workers	603	609	614	610	553	520	−6
Other temporary workers	1 093	1 165	1 138	1 085	794	765	−4
All categories	**2 187**	**2 313**	**2 393**	**2 350**	**1 956**	**1 875**	**−4**
Annual change (%)	7	6	3	−2	−17	−4	

	2005	2006	2007	2008	2009	2010	2010/2009 change (%)
United States	454	482	562	595	453	468	3
Germany	400	362	347	331	336	341	1
Australia	183	221	258	307	326	277	−15
Canada	117	133	157	183	169	173	2
Japan	202	164	165	161	134	103	−23
Switzerland	102	113	106	92	87	92	7
United Kingdom	275	266	226	194	114	88	−23
New Zealand	78	87	100	100	87	85	−3
Korea	29	39	53	47	39	39	2
Norway	25	36	43	38	37	33	−11
Mexico	46	40	28	23	31	29	−7
Italy	85	98	66	42	35	28	−20
Finland	19	22	24	25	23	21	−7
Netherlands	56	83	77	25	18	18	−1
Sweden	6	6	12	18	19	18	−8
France	24	26	26	19	13	14	11
Austria	18	15	14	15	14	13	−7
Belgium	5	16	30	35	6	13	121
Spain	42	85	82	92	6	12	90
Denmark	5	5	7	7	6	5	−9
Portugal	8	7	5	3	3	3	0
All countries	**2 187**	**2 313**	**2 393**	**2 350**	**1 956**	**1 875**	**−4**

Source: OECD International Migration Database.

StatLink ⟹ http://dx.doi.org/10.1787/888932616714

Temporary worker migration is a heterogeneous category in terms of the migrants it covers and the occupations in which they work. Seasonal workers, mainly low-skilled workers in agriculture, continue to be the single most important group of temporary worker migrants in the OECD. As in previous years, more than half of all seasonal workers in 2010 went to Germany, mainly from the new EU member countries, in particular Poland.

The next largest group are the so-called "working holiday makers", about 400 000 in 2010. Working holiday maker programmes – also designated "youth mobility" or summer work programmes – allow young people to work in a variety of jobs, generally for up to one year. Australia receives almost half of migrants in this category. Its admissions of such migrants declined in 2010, whereas the other settlement countries (i.e. the United States, Canada and New Zealand) increased their intakes of people on working holidays in 2010.

Trainees are a prominent category in Japan, which receives about two thirds of all trainees in the OECD. In response to the 2008 economic downturn, Japan had strongly reduced its trainee intake in 2009 and further in 2010. As a result, trainees were the group that experienced the relatively strongest decline in recent years.

For working holiday makers and trainees, the work carried out is, in principle, incidental. The main purpose of the migration may be tourism and cultural exchange (working holiday makers) or training (trainees). At the same time, working holiday makers and trainees have been sometimes been used to satisfy lesser skilled labour needs where low-skilled labour migration is not allowed. From a host-country perspective, these programmes are relatively "low-risk" forms of migration – with high compliance with stay requirements and employment in sectors where labour is needed.

Intra-corporate transfers are movements within the same company. Some are for permanent-type assignments, and not necessarily considered as or included in the figures for temporary work migration. In addition, and more importantly, registered intra-corporate transfers as shown in Table I.2 do generally not include intra-corporate transfers within the European Union. Those registered as intra-corporate transfers (outside of such free mobility) were the only group among temporary workers which was growing in 2010, driven by increases in the United States (which accounts for about 70% of all intra-corporate movements), Canada and Germany.

The remaining category of "other" temporary workers is a heterogeneous one, including au pairs, researchers and short-term workers. This latter group is prominent in the Russian Federation, which is not included in the table above and where such short-term workers account for the vast majority of overall migration. The Russian Federation recorded almost 800 000 short-term workers in 2010, a decline by more than 20% over 2009 and less than two thirds of the 2008 figure.

International students

Next to labour migration, international students are the other main category of temporary migration movements. In contrast to both permanent migration and temporary labour migration, the number of international students continued to grow in 2009, by 6%, and reached more than 2.6 million in the OECD countries and the Russian Federation. Australia replaced France as the third main destination after the United States and the United Kingdom. The numbers of international students also continued to grow strongly in Korea, Spain, New Zealand and a number of smaller destinations. The Netherlands, in contrast, registered a significant decline.

International students account on average for more than 6% of all students in OECD countries. Relative to the overall student population, their presence is strongest in Australia, where more than one out of five students is an international one. In the United Kingdom, Austria, New Zealand and Switzerland, about 15% of all students are international students.

Table I.3. **International tertiary-level students in OECD countries and the Russian Federation, 2004-09**

	Definition of international student (see notes)	2009	Average growth 2004-09	Year-over-year growth 2008-09	International students		
					% from OECD countries 2004	% from OECD countries 2009	Per 100 tertiary students
United States	N	660 600	3	6	35.0	33.7	3.5
United Kingdom	N	369 000	4	8	43.1	38.0	15.3
Australia	N	257 600	9.1	11.7	17.1	11.8	21.5
France	F	249 100	..	2	21.0	..	..
Germany	N	180 100	-2	1	43.9	35.1	..
Russian Federation	F	129 700	..	-5	..	..	1.4
Japan	N	119 600	2	4	23.2	..	3.1
Canada	N	93 500	-3	1	23.2	23.8	6.5
Italy	F	65 900	10	9	36.2	..	..
Korea	F	50 000	36	24	14.8	..	..
Spain	N	48 500	26	32	..	33.0	2.7
Austria	N	46 500	12	5	67.3	..	15.1
New Zealand	N	38 400	-2	21	12.0	29.6	14.6
Switzerland	N	34 800	7	10	67.9	69.0	14.9
Belgium	N	34 000	12	14	59.0	30.1	9.2
Czech Republic	F	30 600	15	10	58.5	..	..
Sweden	N	27 000	9	19	55.0	25.2	6.4
Greece	F	26 200	..	..	2.3	..	m
Netherlands	N	23 700	..	-21	59.0	77.0	3.8
Turkey	F	21 900	7	8	12.3	..	..
Poland	F	17 000	16	13	26.2	..	0.8
Hungary	N	14 500	4	8	38.1	52.7	3.7
Ireland	N	12 900	0	1	55.9	62.2	7.1
Denmark	N	12 600	..	..	41.5	66.0	5.4
Finland	N	11 000	1	14	32.0	..	3.7
Portugal	N	9 100	-11	13	19.1	20.0	2.4
Slovak Republic	N	6 300	32	21	39.3	80.3	2.7
Norway	N	5 100	8	15	39.8	..	2.3
Chile	N	2 200	..	..	..	7.6	0.3
Slovenia	N	2 000	..	49	..	12.0	1.8
Estonia	N	1 100	..	5	..	67.9	1.6
Iceland	N	800	10	9	66.5	77.5	4.6
Average of above countries				11	37.4	42.6	6.4
Total of above countries		2 601 300		6			

Notes: N = non-resident students, F = foreign students. The data cover international students enrolled in full-degree programmes.
Source: OECD Education Database.

StatLink http://dx.doi.org/10.1787/888932616733

On average, about 43% of all international students are from OECD countries, although the proportion varies strongly. In Australia and Chile, less than one out of eight international students comes from the OECD area, in contrast to more than three out of four in the Netherlands, the Slovak Republic and Iceland.

The main nationalities involved in international student migration are China and India, which together accounted for more than a quarter of the international student population in 2009 (Table I.4). The numbers were also large for Korea and Germany, where about 120 000 and 90 000, or 4% and 2% of the 20-24 year old population, respectively, were abroad as international students.[12]

Table I.4. **Main origin countries of international students in OECD countries, 2009**

Nationality	2009		
	Number of students in OECD countries	Per cent of total	Per 100 persons 20-24 in origin country
China	453 000	18.1	0.4
India	181 700	7.3	0.2
Korea	119 500	4.8	3.8
Germany	91 000	3.6	1.8
France	62 000	2.5	1.5
Malaysia	46 700	1.9	1.9
United States	45 900	1.8	0.2
Canada	44 500	1.8	1.9
Japan	44 000	1.8	0.7
Morocco	40 700	1.6	1.3
Viet Nam	37 700	1.5	0.4
Italy	35 300	1.4	1.1
Russian Federation	32 700	1.3	0.3
Hong Kong, China	32 500	1.3	7.3
Poland	31 700	1.3	1.0
Turkey	31 000	1.2	0.5
Slovak Republic	28 400	1.1	6.5
Greece	26 100	1.0	4.0
Pakistan	25 900	1.0	0.1
Mexico	25 300	1.0	0.3
Nigeria	25 200	1.0	0.2
Romania	24 600	1.0	1.4
Indonesia	24 500	1.0	0.1
Saudi Arabia	24 000	1.0	1.0
Brazil	23 800	1.0	0.1
Total above countries	1 557 800	62.3	0.4
Other countries/Unspecified origin	941 800	37.7	0.5
Total	2 499 600	100.0	0.4

Source: OECD Education Database.

StatLink http://dx.doi.org/10.1787/888932616752

International students are well represented in all major fields of study and the differences in terms of specialisation compared with the total student population are generally not large – at least not at the aggregated level (Figure I.6). Compared with the total student population, they are more often found in the social sciences and business, as well as in the sciences and in engineering. In contrast, they are underrepresented in the humanities, where full mastery of the host-country language is particularly important. International students are also underrepresented among the students in the health and welfare areas.

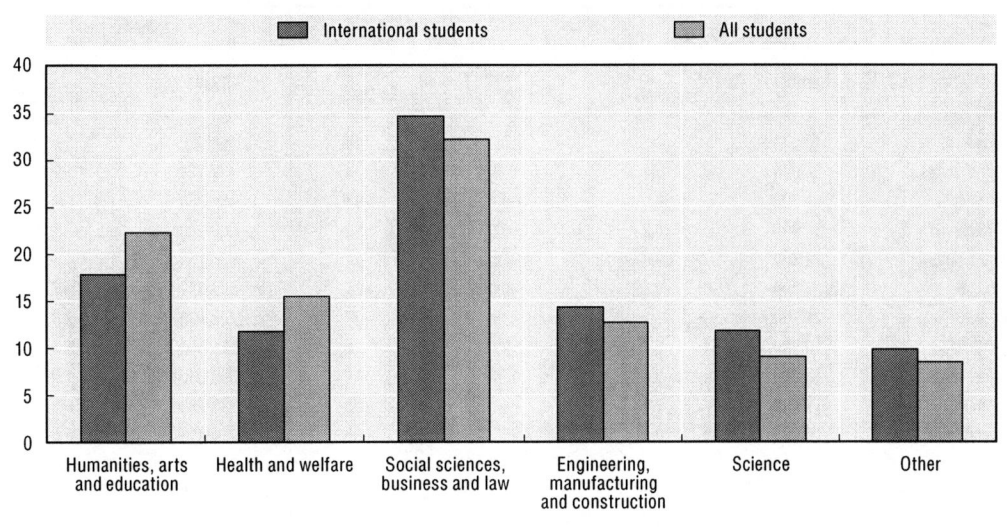

Figure I.6. **Main fields of study of international students, 2009**

Source: OECD Education Database.

StatLink http://dx.doi.org/10.1787/888932615080

Asylum seekers

Arrivals of asylum seekers in OECD countries were at a slightly lower level in 2010 than in 2009, and well below the high numbers seen at the turn of the millennium (Table I.5). The economic crisis thus did not lead to large increases in asylum seeking. France remained the most important recipient country in 2010 with 48 000 requests, followed by the United States (43 000), Germany (41 000, a 50% increase over 2009) and Sweden (32 000). Sweden was also the main destination in per capita terms, followed by Norway and Belgium.

In contrast to previous years, which saw a strong increase in asylum seeking at the periphery of the European Union such as Greece, Italy and Poland, the number of requests in all three of these countries declined significantly in 2010. Still, compared with the situation at the beginning of the millennium, the countries which had the strongest growth tend to be the ones which had little asylum seeking. Overall, however, the main recipient countries have remained the same since 2000, although the ranking within this group has changed. Whereas asylum seeking declined by more than half in the United Kingdom, the Netherlands and Belgium, it almost doubled in Sweden.

Asylum seekers are not migrants *per se*, but candidates for the status of humanitarian migrant. Only a minority of asylum requests lead to some form of protection, that is, relatively few eventually obtain migrant status. In many countries, less than one out of five asylum seekers are formally recognised as refugees under the Geneva Convention, although more are allowed to stay under a subsidiary or temporary protection status. These latter forms concern particularly those who have come from war zones, to which a return is problematical under existing conditions.

Almost three quarters of all asylum seekers in 2010 have gone to European OECD countries. However, recognition rates tend to be much higher in Canada and the United States, the main destinations outside of Europe. In addition, these countries take also significant numbers of humanitarian migrants through humanitarian resettlement programmes.[13] As a result, the share of humanitarian migrants among permanent migration intakes is in both of these countries higher than overall in European OECD countries.

Table I.5. **Asylum seekers in OECD countries and the Russian Federation, 2000-10**

	2010				2000-10	
	Number	Per '000 population	Change since 2000 (%)	Change since 2009 (%)	Total	Per '000 population in 2000
France	48 070	0.7	21	14	491 930	8.0
United States	42 970	0.1	5	14	487 820	1.7
Germany	41 330	0.5	-47	49	484 330	5.7
Sweden	31 820	3.2	95	32	285 940	30.7
United Kingdom	22 650	0.3	-72	-26	526 750	8.6
Canada	22 540	0.6	-34	-34	338 310	10.7
Belgium	21 760	1.9	-49	27	208 190	19.8
Switzerland	13 520	1.7	-23	-16	176 540	23.7
Netherlands	13 330	0.8	-70	-11	193 880	11.8
Austria	11 010	1.3	-40	-30	232 170	28.0
Greece	10 270	0.9	233	-36	119 410	10.5
Norway	10 060	2.0	-7	-42	125 980	26.9
Italy	10 050	0.2	-35	-43	156 310	2.6
Turkey	9 230	0.1	62	18	68 540	1.1
Australia	8 250	0.4	-37	33	68 710	3.5
Poland	6 530	0.2	42	-38	72 070	1.8
Denmark	4 970	0.9	-62	30	54 340	9.8
Finland	4 020	0.7	27	-32	36 690	6.9
Russian Federation	3 890	0.0	165	-32	26 180	0.2
Ireland	3 410	0.7	-69	27	68 140	17.5
Spain	2 740	0.1	-65	-9	63 660	1.5
Hungary	2 100	0.2	-73	-55	44 810	4.3
Israel	1 450	0.2	-76	79	25 520	4.2
Japan	1 200	0.0	456	-14	7 930	0.1
Mexico	1 040	0.0	275	53	5 210	0.1
Czech Republic	980	0.1	-89	-28	65 320	6.2
Luxembourg	740	1.4	18	55	8 920	19.9
Slovak Republic	540	0.1	-65	-34	52 490	9.5
Korea	430	0.0	900	33	2 870	0.1
New Zealand	340	0.1	-78	1	7 370	1.9
Chile	260	0.0	277	..	3 320	0.2
Slovenia	250	0.1	-97	37	16 940	8.3
Portugal	160	0.0	-28	15	1 830	0.2
Iceland	50	0.2	108	43	680	2.4
Estonia	30	0.0	900	-17	160	0.1
OECD	**351 970**	**0.2**	**-35**	**-4**	**4 529 100**	**3.4**

Information on data for Israel: http://dx.doi.org/10.1787/888932315602.
Source: UNHCR.

StatLink ⟶ http://dx.doi.org/10.1787/888932616771

Looking at the accumulated flows between 2000 and 2010, four G8 countries – the United Kingdom, the United States, Germany and France – all recorded about half a million requests each. Together they hosted almost half of all asylum flows. In per-capita terms, however, the flows were largest into four smaller European countries – Sweden, Austria, Norway and Switzerland. In each of these countries, between 20 and 30 asylum seekers per one thousand populations were recorded from 2000 to 2010.

The main country of origin of asylum seeking to the OECD and the Russian Federation in 2010 was Serbia (Table I.6). The strong increase by about 50% compared with 2009 appears to be linked with the introduction of visa-free travel to the Schengen area since December 2009.

Most asylum seekers from Serbia are either Roma or from the Albanian minority (Swiss Federal Office for Migration, 2012), and the overwhelming majority of requests are rejected.

Asylum seeking from Afghanistan and China, the two next important countries, remained at roughly the same level as in 2009. In contrast, the number of asylum seekers from Iraq and Somalia, which were next to Afghanistan the second and third main origin countries in 2009, decreased significantly. It nevertheless remained at high levels, as conditions in these countries remained difficult.

Overall, the main origin countries of asylum seeking have been remarkably stable. The top nine most important origin countries in 2010 were also among the ten main origin countries over the period 2000-10. The principal origin country was Iraq, followed by Serbia (including Montenegro) and Afghanistan. The only country which left the list is Turkey, which was among the main origin countries at the beginning of the decade – when annually about 30 000 persons from Turkey sought asylum in other OECD countries. Turkish nationals accounted for fewer than 6 000 asylum seekers in 2010.

Preliminary figures for 2011 show an increase of more than 20% for the OECD area. A particularly strong increase has been observed in Italy, which saw its number triple. This is mainly due to a large growth in asylum seeking from some African and Arab countries following the "Arab Spring" (see below).

Table I.6. **Top 25 countries of origin of asylum seekers in OECD countries in 2009 and 2010, and top 2000-10 total**

		2009	% of total			2010	% of total			2000-10	% of total
1	Afghanistan	28 300	7.7	1	Serbia	29 100	8.3	1	Iraq	347 300	7.7
2	Iraq	24 300	6.6	2	Afghanistan	24 800	7.0	2	Serbia	277 400	6.1
3	Somalia	21 300	5.8	3	China	21 000	6.0	3	Afghanistan	244 800	5.4
4	Russian Federation	20 200	5.5	4	Iraq	18 700	5.3	4	Russian Federation	235 000	5.2
5	China	19 500	5.3	5	Russian Federation	18 600	5.3	5	China	224 200	5.0
6	Serbia	19 000	5.2	6	Somalia	16 800	4.8	6	Turkey	182 200	4.0
7	Georgia	14 800	4.0	7	Iran	13 800	3.9	7	Iran	160 200	3.5
8	Nigeria	13 500	3.7	8	Pakistan	10 700	3.0	8	Somalia	157 600	3.5
9	Mexico	11 700	3.2	9	Nigeria	8 300	2.4	9	Pakistan	124 600	2.8
10	Iran	11 300	3.1	10	Georgia	8 000	2.3	10	Nigeria	120 200	2.7
11	Pakistan	11 200	3.0	11	Sri Lanka	7 900	2.2	11	Sri Lanka	98 200	2.2
12	Eritrea	10 100	2.7	12	Eritrea	6 900	2.0	12	India	97 700	2.2
13	Sri Lanka	9 800	2.7	13	Former Yug. Rep. of Macedonia	6 700	1.9	13	Dem. Rep. of the Congo	89 700	2.0
14	Zimbabwe	8 700	2.4	14	Bangladesh	6 100	1.7	14	Mexico	86 900	1.9
15	Turkey	7 000	1.9	15	Turkey	6 000	1.7	15	Colombia	82 700	1.8
16	Armenia	6 200	1.7	16	Dem. Rep. of the Congo	5 800	1.6	16	Georgia	80 900	1.8
17	Bangladesh	6 100	1.7	17	Mexico	5 200	1.5	17	Haiti	77 000	1.7
18	Dem. Rep. of the Congo	5 200	1.4	18	Guinea	5 200	1.5	18	Eritrea	73 000	1.6
19	Guinea	5 000	1.4	19	Armenia	5 200	1.5	19	Algeria	67 600	1.5
20	Syria	4 900	1.3	20	India	4 600	1.3	20	Armenia	65 700	1.5
21	Haiti	4 800	1.3	21	Syria	4 500	1.3	21	Bangladesh	63 200	1.4
22	India	4 200	1.1	22	Haiti	4 300	1.2	22	Bosnia and Herzegovina	53 500	1.2
23	Algeria	3 800	1.0	23	Algeria	3 600	1.0	23	Zimbabwe	50 300	1.1
24	Colombia	3 700	1.0	24	El Salvador	3 500	1.0	24	Ukraine	46 100	1.0
25	Ethiopia	3 500	1.0	25	Ethiopia	3 100	0.9	25	Guinea	45 400	1.0
Top 25 countries		**278 100**	**75.6**			**248 400**	**70.6**			**3 151 400**	**69.6**
Total		**367 900**	**100.0**			**352 000**	**100.0**			**4 528 600**	**100.0**

Source: UNHCR.

StatLink http://dx.doi.org/10.1787/888932616790

4. A first glance at migration trends in 2011

Preliminary trends in immigration

A key challenge in identifying trends in international migration is the availability of recent data, since most annual migration statistics are only available with a time-lag of a year. The reasons for this vary from country to country and are often linked with the administrative nature of the underlying data. This edition presents, for the first time, preliminary migration data for part of the year preceding the annual OECD *International Migration Outlook* – that is, 2011 data for this 2012 edition. These preliminary data do not necessarily come from the same sources as the migration data regularly included in this publication. They are often estimates and thus tend to be subject to revisions, but they do provide an indication of the more recent evolution of migration trends if compared with the same data for the same period in the previous year. Table I.7 below summarises the available data on recent trends.

On the basis of these preliminary figures, it seems that immigration increased again in 2011 in most European OECD countries, with the exception of Italy, Spain and Sweden, and in Australia, New Zealand and the United States. In most cases, however, the increases are not large, with the exception of Ireland, Germany, Luxembourg, Chile and Austria. Immigration to Ireland thus seems to recover again, albeit at a much more modest level than prior to the crisis. The relatively strong increases in Austria and Germany have been mainly driven by the full implementation of free movement with the countries that joined the European Union in 2004. Most increases in the other European OECD countries are also associated with free movement.

Table I.7. **Preliminary trends in immigration for 2011**

	2010	2011	% change	Period covered
Australia	206 700	210 700	2	July-June
Austria	72 600	83 400	15	Jan.-Sept.
Canada	223 100	188 900	-15	Jan.-Sept.
Chile	63 900	76 300	19	Jan.-Dec.
Denmark	53 400	53 900	1	Jan.-Dec.
Finland	18 200	20 600	13	Jan.-Dec.
Germany	314 000	381 000	21	Jan.-June
Ireland	17 500	25 200	44	May-Apr.
Italy	340 100	289 400	-15	Jan.-Sept.
Luxembourg	15 800	19 100	21	Jan.-Dec.
Netherlands	144 700	150 900	4	Jan.-Nov.
New Zealand	57 600	61 000	6	Jan.-Dec.
Norway	73 900	79 500	8	Jan.-Dec.
Spain	430 400	415 500	-3	Jan.-Dec.
Sweden	98 800	96 500	-2	Jan.-Dec.
Switzerland	134 200	142 500	6	Jan.-Dec.
United Kingdom	487 000	505 000	4	July-June
United States	1 042 600	1 062 000	2	Jan.-Dec.

Source: OECD International Migration Database, national sources.

StatLink http://dx.doi.org/10.1787/888932616809

Key economic and political events and their likely impact on migration

Emigration and the crisis in European OECD countries

2011 has been marked by the worsening of the economic conditions in some countries of the Eurozone, in particular Greece, Ireland, Italy, Portugal and Spain. From a migration perspective, these countries share two characteristics. First, they all have been, for most of the post-war era, countries of significant emigration. Second, they have all transformed into countries of immigration over the past fifteen years, hosting significant numbers of labour migrants.

Data on emigration based on origin countries often tends to underestimate actual outflows, since people do not necessarily de-register when they emigrate, or do so only after having left the country already for some time. Some countries try to account for this, at least in part. *Spain* provides detailed estimates on emigration, based on adjusted data from municipal registers and other sources. These data show that in 2011, for the first time since the series are available, there has been a net emigration (including both nationals and foreigners) of more than 50 000 people, compared with a net immigration of more than 60 000 in 2010. The decline was mainly attributable to an increase in emigration by more than 100 000. Most of the increase concerned foreign nationals. A recent report (González Enríquez, 2012), based, however, on 2010 data, looked into the issue of emigration from Spain and found that only 7% of the emigrants registered in 2010 were Spanish citizens born in Spain. The vast majority of emigration thus concerned return migrants, some of whom had taken Spanish nationality in recent years.

Ireland also provides estimates on emigration on the basis of various sources, the main one being the labour force survey. According to these, Ireland – which was among the countries first hit by the crisis – had net emigration already in 2009, and in each of the following two years, Ireland lost about 0.8% of its population.[14] The initial phase of the crisis (2007-09) was marked by a sharp drop in immigration (from 110 000 to 57 000), in particular from the new EU member countries (EU12) for whom Ireland was previously a prime destination country (a decline from 53 000 in 2007 to 13 500 in 2009). Later, in 2009, outflows of foreign nationals increased (by about 15 000), again mainly from the EU12. As the crisis persisted, emigration of Irish nationals began to rise strongly in 2010 (to 28 000, compared with 18 000 in 2009) and experienced a further strong growth in the year ending April 2011 when it reached more than 40 000. That year notably saw a strong rise in the emigration of women.

Similar figures are not available for Greece, Italy and Portugal. However, as far as emigration of nationals is concerned, the bulk of the flows can be captured by looking at the immigration statistics of the main destination countries. *Portugal*, in particular, has established an emigration observatory which provides data based on destination country sources. The quality of these varies widely, and they often date back a while. According to these, Angola – a Portuguese-speaking, resource-rich country that was, until the beginning of the downturn, among the fastest-growing economies of the world – had experienced a strong increase of Portuguese immigrants in 2009; more recent data are not available for this country. In 2010/2011, there have generally been little changes in Portuguese migration to European OECD countries for which data are available, and also to Brazil. In most European OECD countries, there have also been few increases in immigration from *Italy* and *Greece*.

I. TRENDS IN INTERNATIONAL MIGRATION

The only notable exception is Germany which, in light of growing labour shortages in some occupations, has tried to recruit actively from some of the above-mentioned countries. The 2010 figures already show a slight increase for all of these countries which accelerated in the first eight months of 2011 (Figure I.7). The increases in 2011 compared with the same period in the previous year varied from a rather modest 20% for Portugal and Italy to about 50% for Spain and more than 80% in the case of Greece; adding further to an almost 50% increase recorded for 2010. However, the numbers involved remained modest, with the exception of Greek migration, for which Germany has traditionally been the main destination country, hosting more than a third of all Greek expatriates. Nevertheless, the numbers involved in 2011 are only marginally higher than those observed prior to Greece joining the Eurozone. Indeed, the migration inflows from all four Southern European countries and Ireland taken together were only about a quarter of the inflows that were recorded in Germany from Poland alone.

Figure I.7. **Recent trends in migration from Greece, Ireland, Portugal and Spain into Germany**

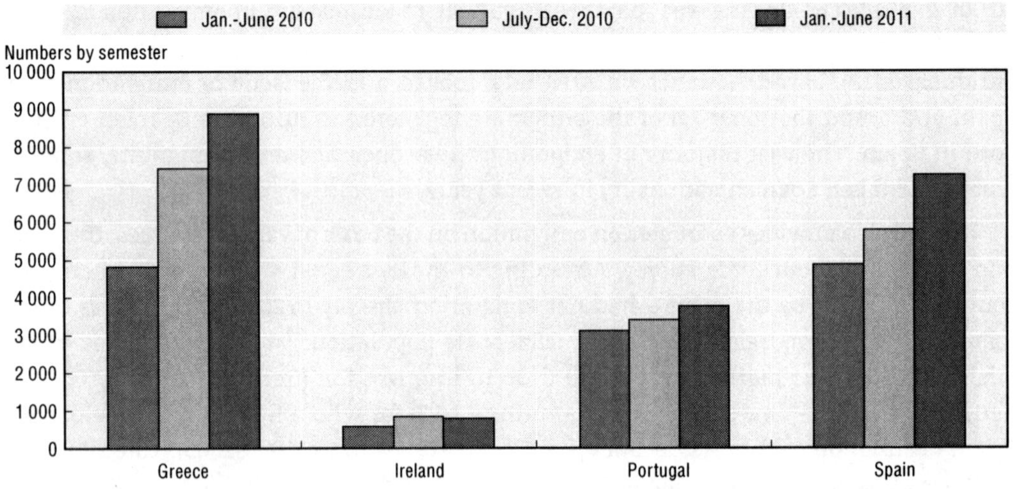

Source: DESTATIS (Statistisches Bundesamt).   StatLink http://dx.doi.org/10.1787/888932615099

In the OECD settlement countries, which have managed migration programmes with a strong selection for permanent migration – often linked with considerable delays between application and admission – increases in immigration from the above-mentioned countries, if any, have also been limited. An exception is Irish emigration to Australia, the second most important destination of recent Irish emigration after the United Kingdom. In Australia, the inflows in permanent migration of Irish increased almost twofold between the migration programme years ending 2008 and 2011. The increase was even stronger in the case of temporary business visas, where the reaction period is shorter and where selection is less pronounced. The number of business visa granted to Irish nationals more than doubled over the same period – in spite of an overall crisis-related reduction in this category.

In summary, the tentative evidence available to date thus suggests that emigration from the most affected countries has increased, but at a modest level overall. In addition, the evidence from Spain suggests that some of this increase concerned previous immigrants who had naturalised in the meantime. Crisis-related increases in the outflows of nationals have been rather small, with the exception of Ireland where language barriers to emigration may be less of a problem.

Migration and the "Arab Spring"

One key geopolitical event in 2011 has undoubtedly been the revolutions in the Arab countries. Starting with Tunisia in late 2010, revolutionary movements eventually spread through most Arab countries, and led thus far to new governments in Tunisia, Egypt and Libya. These three countries are all Mediterranean neighbours to the Southern European OECD countries. Due to this geographic proximity, and the strategic role played by some of the Arab countries concerned in terms of control of migration routes from African countries, there has been some concern about the likely impact on migration flows, in particular to Southern Europe. Yet, in the recent past, none of the countries involved has been a major origin country of migration flows, with the exception of France, for which Tunisia was one of the three main countries of origin (outside free movement) in 2009 and 2010.

It is too early to fully assess the impact of the "Arab Spring" on migration flows, but a number of observations can already be made. Since migration through legal channels takes time, depends on the decisions of host country authorities and is often not a possibility, most of the observed movements to date relate to detections of irregular border crossings and to asylum requests.

Thus far, it is mainly Tunisians – *Tunisia* being the country where the revolutionary movements started – for which most of the movements have been observed (see Figure I.8). For *Libya*, most of the flows to OECD countries concerned non-Libyans. With respect to *Egypt*, no major changes have been recorded.

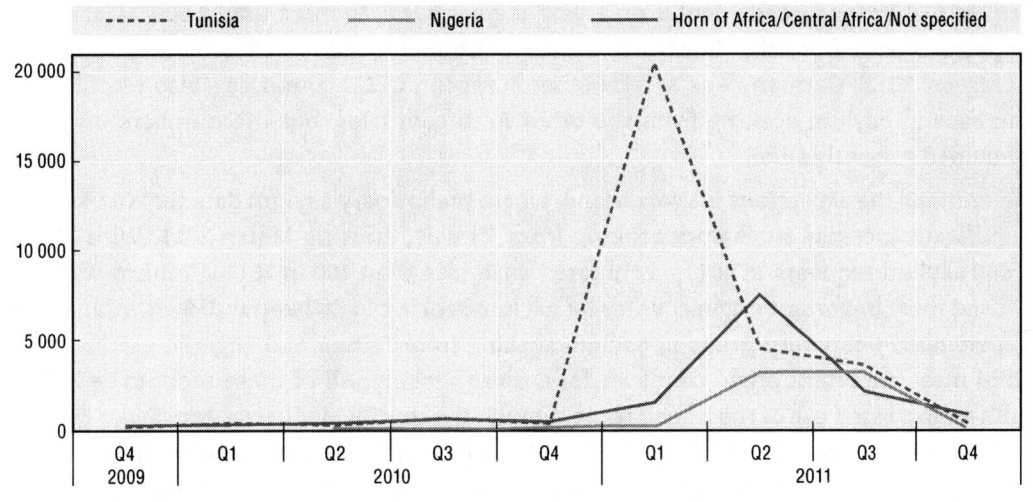

Figure I.8. **Detections at the external borders of the European Union, by quarter**

Note: Central Africa/Horn of Africa is the presumed origin; Nationalities have not been reported.
Source: FRONTEX.
StatLink http://dx.doi.org/10.1787/888932615118

Italy is the OECD country that is closest to both Libya and Tunisia. The Italian Island of Lampedusa is situated only about 100 km from the Tunisian coast. Due to this geographic proximity, Italy has been the main entry gate of the flows from Tunisia and Libya. According to data from the European border control agency FRONTEX, the number of detections of illegal border crossings in Italy reached 56 000 in 2011. The peak in flows from Tunisia was reached in March 2011, when 191 boats carrying more than 14 000 Tunisians arrived in Lampedusa. In April, a repatriation agreement was signed between Italy and Tunisia, which led to a strong reduction in the flows of Tunisians. In parallel, however, the situation in Libya led to increased flows, largely consisting of migrants from sub-Saharan Africa and the Horn of Africa who had been living in Libya and were expelled by the Gaddafi regime when the conflict broke out. Between April and August, over 25 000 persons arrived. However, the situation eased significantly from August 2011 onwards, when the National Transitional Council gained control of Libya. Between September and December 2012 only two more boats arrived in Italy (FRONTEX, 2012).

In France, according to national sources, about 10 000 illegally staying Tunisians were apprehended in 2011, four times as many as in 2010. However, increases in apprehensions do not necessarily provide an indication of the magnitude of the increase in flows, since they may be due to increased control efforts.

The "Arab Spring" had an effect not only on detections of irregular border crossing, but also on asylum requests – either at the border or, for those who are not detected at the border, inland. Again, most of the increase related to the "Arab Spring" concerned nationals from countries not directly involved in the events and who either fled or were expelled from Libya or took advantage of the open central Mediterranean route via Libya and the Mediterranean to Italy and Malta. Italy, for example, saw a strong increase in the number of asylum requests from Nigeria. The share of Tunisians who passed through the asylum channel seems to have been more limited, partly because the prospects of receiving asylum are dim, and partly because some legal channels were ultimately open to them. Italy notably issued about 11 800 temporary permits to Tunisians.

The situation in *Syria* has led, later in the year 2011 and in early 2012, to significant increases in asylum seeking in several countries, namely in Germany, which saw asylum requests of Syrians nearly double on a year-to-year basis, to more than 2 600. Most of the applicants were from the Kurdish community (German Federal Office for Migration and Refugees, 2012). Germany – as several other European OECD countries – also recorded an increase in asylum seeking from the other Arab countries, but the numbers involved remained generally small.

Among the exceptions is Switzerland, where preliminary asylum data for 2011 show a significant increase in asylum seeking from Tunisia, starting March 2011. With about 2 600 asylum requests in 2011 – compared with less than 400 in 2010 – Tunisia was the second most important origin country for asylum seeking to Switzerland. Switzerland also experienced temporary peaks in asylum seeking from Eritrea and Nigeria, the first and third most important origin countries for asylum seeking. All of these seem to be linked with an increased use of the transit route through the central Mediterranean (Swiss Federal Office for Migration, 2012) and indeed, the situation in terms of the timing of the increases notably for Tunisians and Nigerians has been quite similar to that observed in Italy. The number of asylum seekers from Syria also almost doubled in Switzerland, although it remained at a modest level (about 800 in 2011).

In the non-European OECD countries, the impact of the "Arab Spring" has been even more limited. For example, since January 2011, Canada recorded on average about 40 privately sponsored refugees per month from Syria – compared to virtually none before. A similar, albeit temporary, increase in this category was also observed for *Egypt*. Much more significant in the case of Egypt, however, was the increase in visitor applications to Canada. In the first six months of 2011 alone, 3 500 such applications were recorded from Egypt, compared with 900 for the whole of 2010. An even stronger increase was observed for *Iran* (which is not an Arab country), from about 100 in 2010 to 10 500 in the first six months of 2011.

5. Regional and gender composition of migration flows: Evolution since 2000

The discussion of permanent and temporary migration in previous sub-sections was generally based on standardised definitions which aim at making the scale and composition of migration movements comparable across countries. These data are not yet available by gender and geographical origin, except for a few countries. The latter information is, however, generally available from population and foreigner registers. What is considered a "migrant" in order to enter into these registers varies a lot between countries (see Lemaître, Liebig, Thoreau and Fron, 2008). Adding up register-based data, as below, is therefore not without caveats. The figures nevertheless provide an indication of the magnitude and composition of flows regarding gender and origin.[15]

In 2010, China was again the main country of origin of migration flows to the OECD, accounting for nearly one in ten migrants, followed by Romania, India and Poland – each of which accounted for about 5% of the flows (Table I.8). Among the main origin countries, it

Table I.8. **Top 25 countries of immigration into OECD countries, 2000-10**

	2000	2005	2009	2010	2010			
					% of all immigration	% change since 2009	% change since 2000	Emigration rate per '000 population
	Thousands							
China	282	438	460	508	9.6	11	80	0.4
Romania	88	212	276	289	5.5	5	229	13.0
India	113	212	227	252	4.8	11	123	0.2
Poland	104	264	220	223	4.2	1	114	5.6
Philippines	165	191	163	167	3.2	2	1	1.8
Mexico	181	174	180	156	3.0	–13	–13	1.4
United States	99	113	133	139	2.6	5	39	0.4
Morocco	99	150	137	124	2.3	–10	25	3.8
United Kingdom	95	157	129	118	2.2	–9	24	1.8
Germany	71	98	126	117	2.2	–7	64	1.4
Pakistan	54	74	77	100	1.9	31	86	0.6
France	70	68	93	91	1.7	–2	29	1.4
Viet Nam	52	78	77	88	1.7	14	69	1.0
Ukraine	57	105	79	81	1.5	2	42	1.7
Bulgaria	27	43	66	78	1.5	18	190	10.0
Italy	61	53	73	78	1.5	6	27	1.2
Korea	58	66	79	76	1.4	–3	30	1.6
Peru	22	66	78	71	1.3	–9	215	2.4
Dominican Republic	26	44	66	69	1.3	4	168	6.8
Russian Federation	84	86	66	68	1.3	2	–19	0.5
Brazil	72	107	63	63	1.2	0	–12	0.3
Colombia	67	64	72	63	1.2	–12	–6	1.4
Turkey	83	75	63	62	1.2	–1	–25	0.9
Thailand	32	47	47	51	1.0	7	57	0.7
Bangladesh	23	38	51	49	0.9	–2	118	0.3
Total of above countries	2 085	3 023	3 101	3 179	62.6	3	52	0.7
Total other countries	1 750	2 063	2 108	2 098	37.4	0	20	0.9
Total of above countries	100	145	149	152				
Total other countries	100	118	120	120				
Africa	329	496	546	515	9.8	–6	57	0.5
Americas	809	979	970	925	17.5	–5	14	1.0
Asia	1 169	1 562	1 677	1 823	34.5	9	56	0.4
Europe	1 189	1 609	1 686	1 759	33.3	4	48	2.3
Oceania	89	80	81	76	1.4	–6	–15	2.0

Source: OECD International Migration Database.

StatLink http://dx.doi.org/10.1787/888932616828

is Romania which saw the largest increase in migration to the OECD compared with the situation in 2000. Romania is also the country with the largest migration in per-capita terms – in 2010, more than 1.3% of its population migrated to OECD countries. The only other country for which such large outflows were recorded is Bulgaria, which also lost about 1% of its population. In both cases, the large flows are mainly due to migration to other EU countries, following Bulgaria's and Romania's accession to the EU in 2007.

Migrants from Africa account for less than one out of ten new migrants to OECD countries, and overall migration from Africa has declined by 6% in 2010. A strong decrease has also been registered for migration from the Americas (–5%), whereas migration from Asia and, to a lesser extent, from Europe, increased.

Compared with the beginning of the millennium, in terms of regional origin, migration has increased from all regions except Oceania, albeit to a different extent (Figure I.9). The increase in migration flows was mainly driven by increases from Asia and Europe, which account for 43% and 38% of the increase in flows in 2010 compared with 2000. Over this period, Asia has also overtaken Europe as the main origin region for new migration flows (see also Part III of this publication).

Figure I.9. **Change in the scale and composition by origin of migration flows between 2000 and 2010**

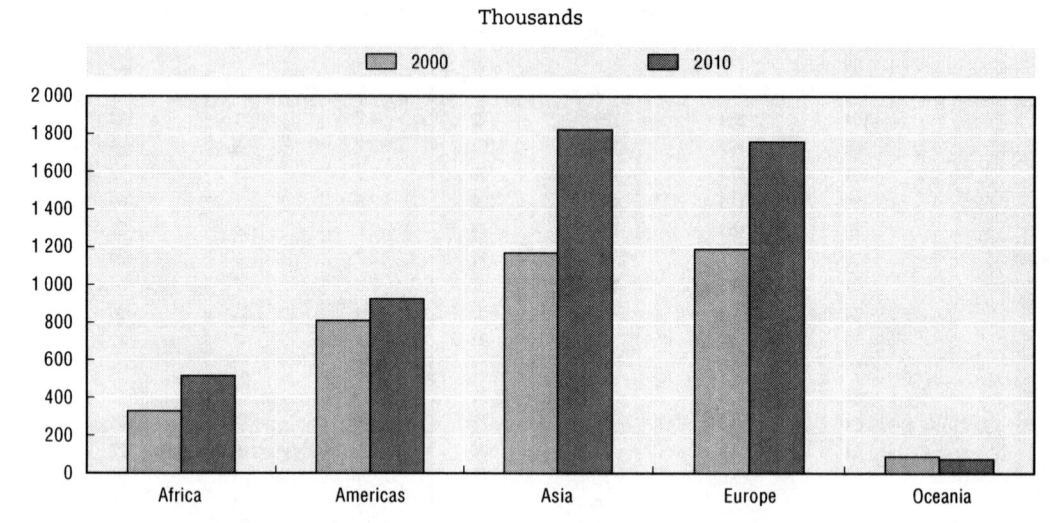

Thousands

Source: OECD International Migration Database. StatLink http://dx.doi.org/10.1787/888932615137

The large increases in migrants from Romania, Poland, Germany and Lithuania are all associated with expansion of free mobility in European OECD countries.[16] This is clearly visible when looking at the top ten origin countries in 2010 by country of destination (see the figures in the Annex). Romanians were the main nationality of new migrants in Hungary, Italy, Portugal and Spain. Linguistic proximity seems to explain the orientation of Romanian emigration to the latter three countries. In addition, Romanians were also the second most important origin group for Austria, Denmark and Germany. Poles were the top origin group for migration to Denmark, Germany, Iceland, the Netherlands and Norway. Chinese migration, in turn, was still predominantly to non-European OECD countries. Chinese were the main nationality of foreign migration to Japan and Korea – accounting for about 40% and 50% of all inflows, respectively – the second most important origin group for Australia and the United States, and the third main group for Canada.

I. TRENDS IN INTERNATIONAL MIGRATION

The gender composition of migration flows

Women account for the majority of the immigrant population in all but six OECD countries (see OECD, forthcoming), and these latter have small immigrant populations. Yet, women are underrepresented in migration flows in most countries (Figure I.10). This is not a recent phenomenon and suggests that women tend to be less inclined to return to their origin countries. This, in turn, appears to be due to the fact that they are overrepresented among family migrants, for whom return to the origin country is less likely than for labour migrants. In addition, women also have a higher life expectancy.

Figure I.10. **Share of women in migration flows, 2000-10**

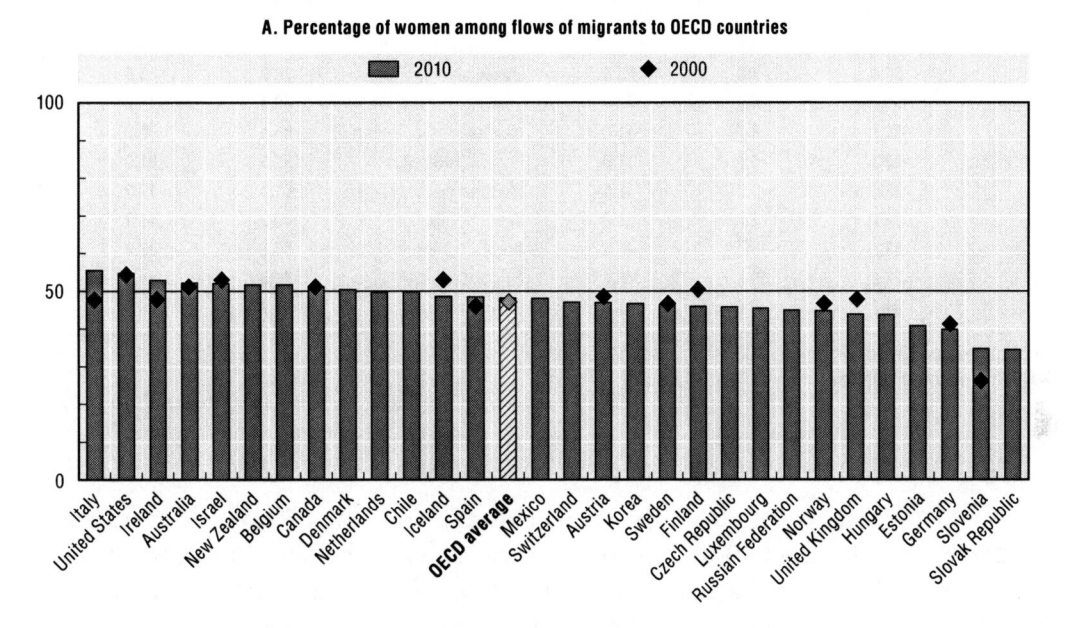

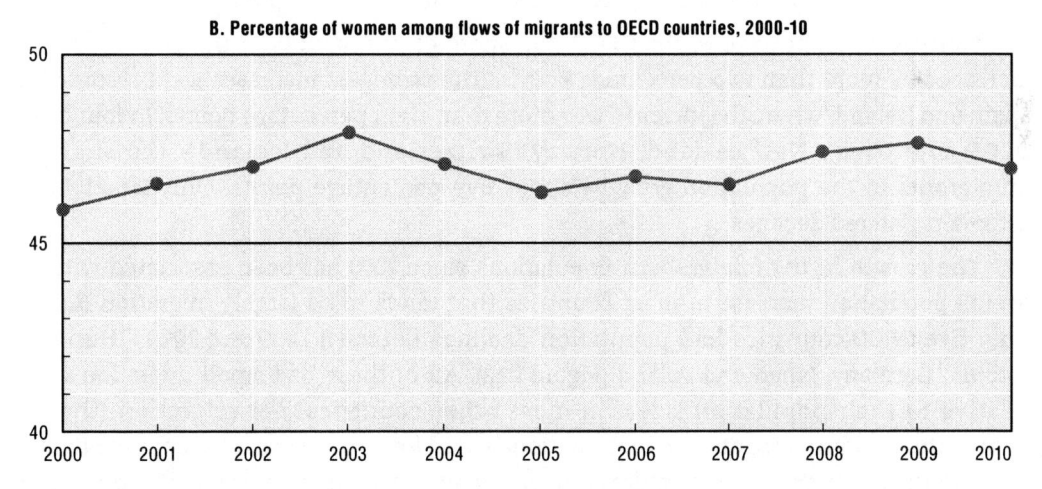

A. Percentage of women among flows of migrants to OECD countries

B. Percentage of women among flows of migrants to OECD countries, 2000-10

Notes: Figure on the Panel A: Belgium: data refer to 2009 instead of 2010; United States: data refer to 2002 instead of 2000. The figure on the Panel B includes the data from the 14 countries for which data are available since 2000. Information on data for Israel: http://dx.doi.org/10.1787/888932315602.

Source: OECD International Migration Database.

StatLink ⟶ http://dx.doi.org/10.1787/888932615156

Although the share of women varies across destination countries, gender imbalances are much greater with respect to the origin countries. Women account for a large part of migration from many Latin American countries, as well as from Thailand and Ukraine. In contrast, migrants from Central Asian countries and from North Africa tend to be predominantly men (Table I.9).

Table I.9. **Countries with strong gender imbalances in migration flows to the OECD, 2010**

Top 10 countries with the highest percentage of emigrant men[1]				Top 10 countries with the largest percentage of emigrant women[1]			
Country of origin	% Women in flows to OECD countries	Number of women ('000)	Total flows ('000)	Country of origin	% Women in flows to OECD countries	Number of women ('000)	Total flows ('000)
Uzbekistan	29.6	3.1	10.6	Paraguay	73.9	9.4	12.5
Bangladesh	30.4	7.0	23.0	Honduras	70.2	5.5	7.8
Afghanistan	31.6	6.3	19.8	Thailand	69.4	15.9	19.5
Senegal	31.7	3.7	11.6	Ukraine	66.4	34.2	44.6
Bosnia and Herzegovina	32.3	5.7	17.6	Russian Federation	63.5	31.6	14.2
Croatia	32.5	5.0	15.5	Moldova	61.9	13.5	33.7
Nepal	32.7	2.7	8.3	Japan	60.2	11.9	21.0
Pakistan	33.7	15.7	46.5	Brazil	60.2	23.9	33.7
Hungary	33.9	15.7	46.2	Peru	58.5	14.8	79.5
Egypt	34.7	6.4	18.4	Philippines	57.2	48.5	24.5

1. Among countries sending more than 5 000 migrants to OECD countries.
Source: OECD International Migration Database.

StatLink ⟶ http://dx.doi.org/10.1787/888932616847

6. The migrant population

In 2010, immigrants accounted on average for 13% of the populations in OECD countries (Figure I.11) and in 20 countries, at least one out of ten persons is an immigrant. The largest shares are in Luxembourg, Switzerland, Australia and Israel,[17] where immigrants comprised a quarter or more of the resident population.

Since 2000, on average in the OECD, the share of immigrants in the population has increased by more than two percentage points. The strongest increases were recorded in Spain and Ireland, where the increase was more than eight percentage points. In four other OECD countries – New Zealand, Norway, Switzerland and Iceland – the share of immigrants in the population grew by about five percentage points. Only Israel[18] and Estonia registered declines.

The growth in the foreign-born populations since 2000 has been associated with an overall population increase in most countries that tends to be largely migration-driven. Only five OECD countries had population declines between 2000 and 2010 – Hungary, Estonia, Germany, Japan and Poland (Figure I.12). All of these had small migration flows relative to their population sizes. In most other countries, net migration (that is, immigration minus emigration, of both nationals and foreigners) accounted for the bulk of the population increase. Particularly strong was the migration-induced population increase in Spain, where net migration added about 12% to the population.[19] Population increases through migration of more than 5% were also recorded for Luxembourg, Australia, Ireland, Canada, Switzerland and Norway.

Figure I.11. **Evolution of the share of foreign and foreign-born populations among the total population in OECD countries, 2000-10**
Percentage points

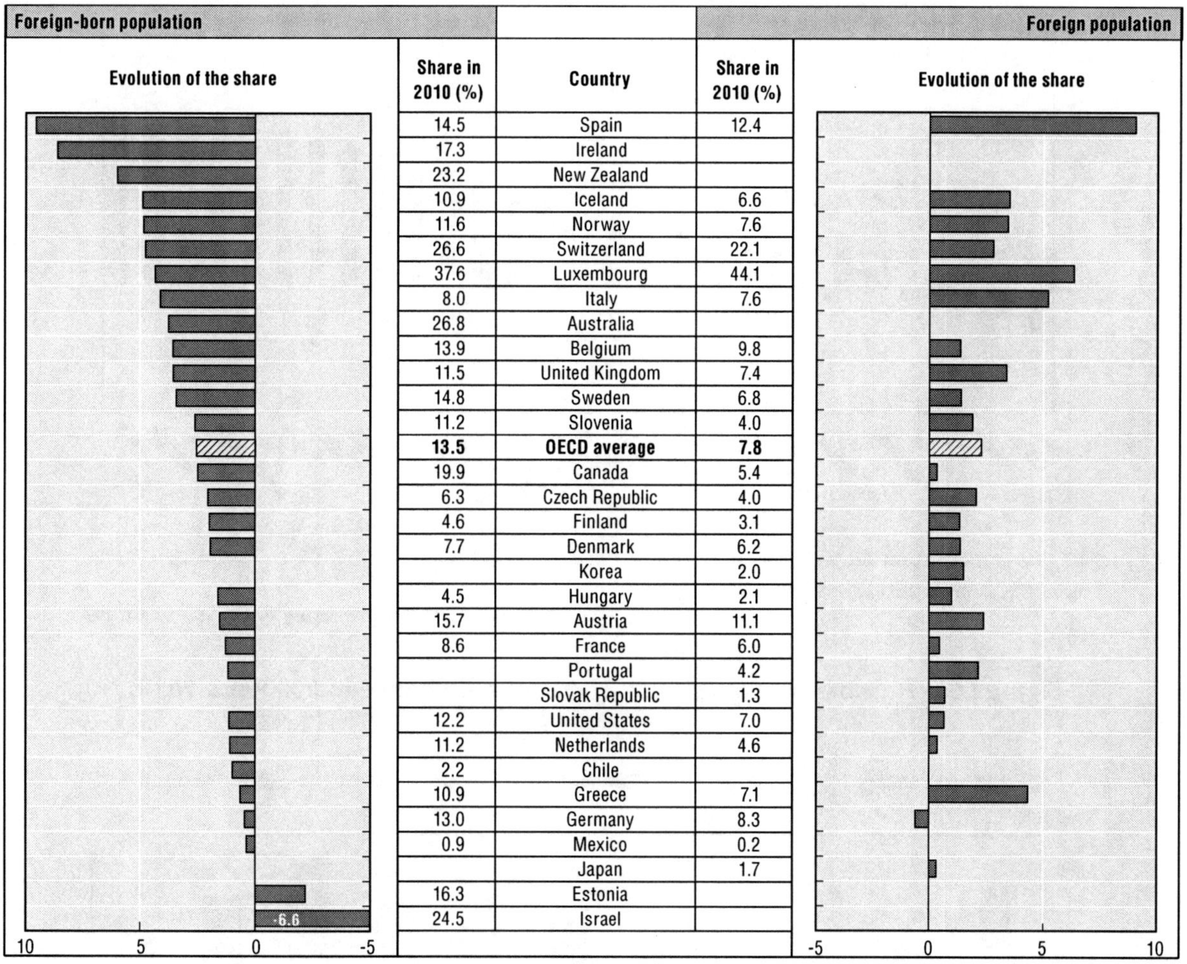

Foreign-born population — Evolution of the share	Share in 2010 (%)	Country	Share in 2010 (%)	Foreign population — Evolution of the share
	14.5	Spain	12.4	
	17.3	Ireland		
	23.2	New Zealand		
	10.9	Iceland	6.6	
	11.6	Norway	7.6	
	26.6	Switzerland	22.1	
	37.6	Luxembourg	44.1	
	8.0	Italy	7.6	
	26.8	Australia		
	13.9	Belgium	9.8	
	11.5	United Kingdom	7.4	
	14.8	Sweden	6.8	
	11.2	Slovenia	4.0	
	13.5	OECD average	7.8	
	19.9	Canada	5.4	
	6.3	Czech Republic	4.0	
	4.6	Finland	3.1	
	7.7	Denmark	6.2	
		Korea	2.0	
	4.5	Hungary	2.1	
	15.7	Austria	11.1	
	8.6	France	6.0	
		Portugal	4.2	
		Slovak Republic	1.3	
	12.2	United States	7.0	
	11.2	Netherlands	4.6	
	2.2	Chile		
	10.9	Greece	7.1	
	13.0	Germany	8.3	
	0.9	Mexico	0.2	
		Japan	1.7	
	16.3	Estonia		
	24.5	Israel		

Information on data for Israel: http://dx.doi.org/10.1787/888932315602.
Source: OECD International Migration Database.

StatLink http://dx.doi.org/10.1787/888932615175

Trends in naturalisation

In 2010, more than 1.7 million foreigners took up the citizenship of an OECD country. Whereas the number of naturalisations in Australia, Canada and New Zealand continued their decline which has been ongoing since their 2006 peak – partly following more stringent access rules – the number of naturalisations in the EU in 2009 passed, for the first time, the mark of 700 000 and hit in 2010 a new record of 756 000. The increase in 2010 is driven by the United Kingdom and Spain, following large numbers of migrants in the preceding decade who have become eligible for naturalisation in the meantime.[20]

Since 2000, more than 19 million people have been naturalised in the OECD. Naturalisations followed a somewhat cyclical pattern, with peaks in 2000 and 2006-08 (Figure I.13), ranging between about 1.4 and 2.1 million. Most of the changes concerned the United States, which accounted for about half of all naturalisations in the OECD area.

I. TRENDS IN INTERNATIONAL MIGRATION

Figure I.12. **Population growth between 2000 and 2010 and its components**
Percentages

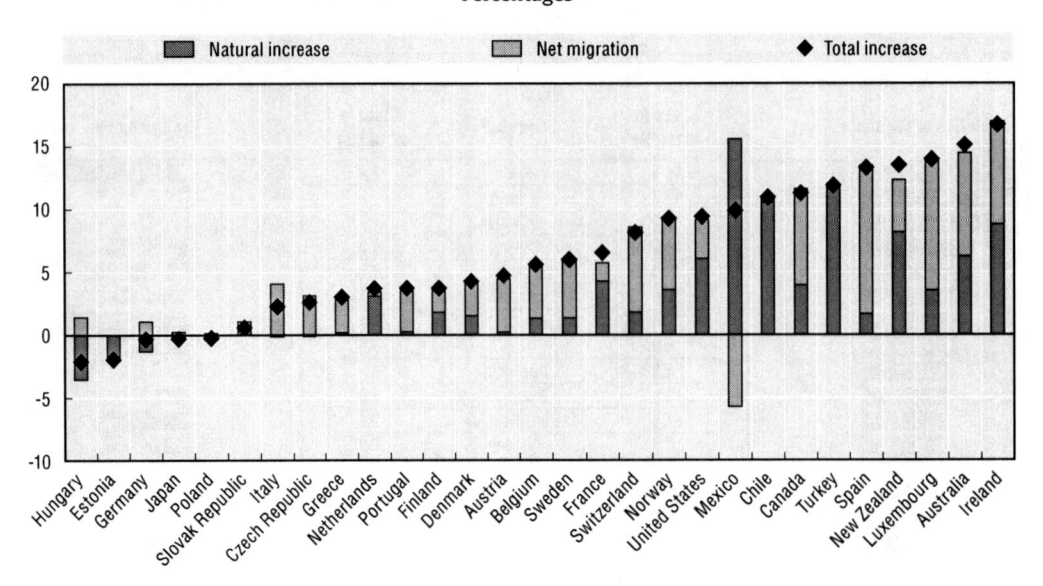

Note: 2010 or most recent available year.
Sources: OECD Population and Vital Statistics Database.

StatLink http://dx.doi.org/10.1787/888932615194

Figure I.13. **Number of acquisitions of citizenship between 2000 and 2010, by region**

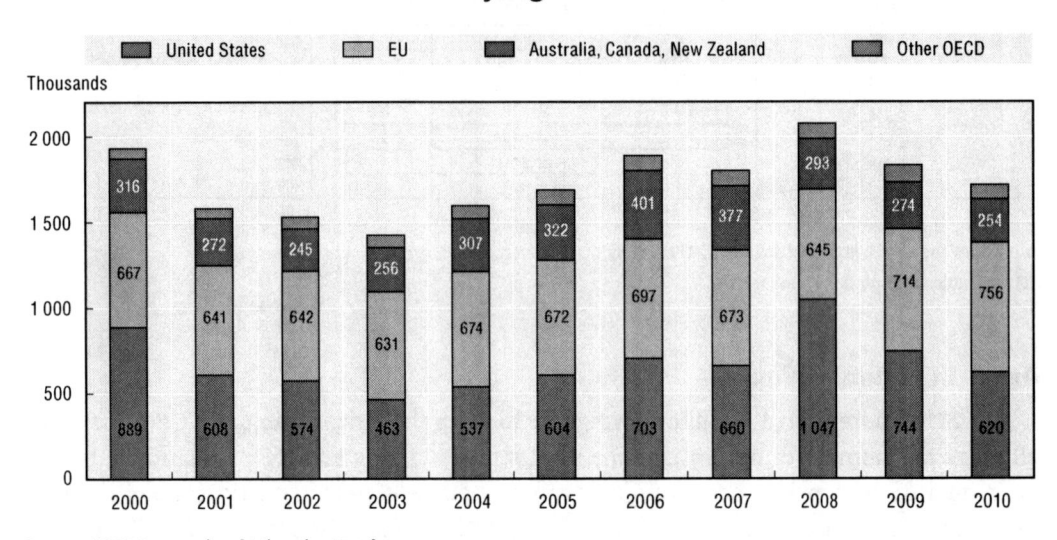

Source: OECD International Migration Database.

StatLink http://dx.doi.org/10.1787/888932615213

Figure I.14 shows the degree to which naturalisation has contributed to increases in the population. The increase has been largest in New Zealand, Canada, Switzerland, Australia and Belgium. In all of these countries, naturalisations added about 5% or more to the national population. This group of countries is a rather heterogeneous one. Not surprisingly figure the OECD countries which have been settled by migration and which have significant intakes of migrants through their migration programmes (Australia,

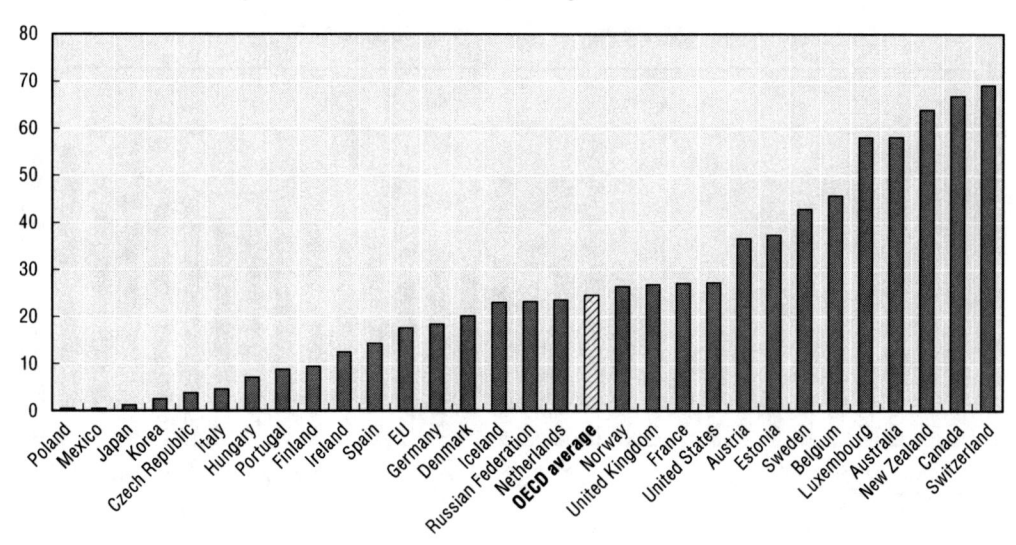

Figure I.14. **Number of acquisitions of citizenship between 2000 and 2010, per thousand host-country citizens of 2000**

Note: Estimates for Australia and New Zealand.
Source: OECD International Migration Database.

StatLink http://dx.doi.org/10.1787/888932615232

Canada and New Zealand). In these countries, it is natural for immigrants to naturalise soon after arrival; access to citizenship is liberal and its take-up actively encouraged. Belgium had relatively small migrant intakes in recent years, but strongly facilitated access to citizenship in 2000, introducing one of the most liberal regimes in the OECD. Switzerland, in turn, has the most restrictive access to nationality in the OECD. However, it has one of the largest and most longstanding immigrant populations in the OECD. In addition, the share of its population with foreign nationality in 2000 was the largest in the OECD – next to Luxembourg, where 40% of the population in 2000 were foreigners (see Figure I.12 above). In both Luxembourg and Switzerland, the population potentially eligible for naturalisation over the period was thus much larger than in all other OECD countries.

At the other end of the scale in terms of increases of population with host-country nationality are countries for which migrant populations are small (Poland, Mexico, Japan, Korea) or recent (Italy, Portugal, Ireland, Spain).

Trends in the qualification structure of migrants

The percentage of high-educated among the immigrant population has been growing over the past decade in most OECD countries (Figure I.15). The only exceptions are Spain, Greece, Italy and Mexico. In all of these latter countries, a large part of migration over the past decade consisted of labour migrants for low-skilled employment. The share of high-educated is now highest in Canada, where over 50% of the immigrant population have tertiary education, followed by the United Kingdom and Ireland. On average over the OECD, about 30% of immigrants now have a tertiary education, compared with less than 25% in 2000.

Figure I.15. **Percentage of high-educated among the foreign-born population, 2000 and 2010**

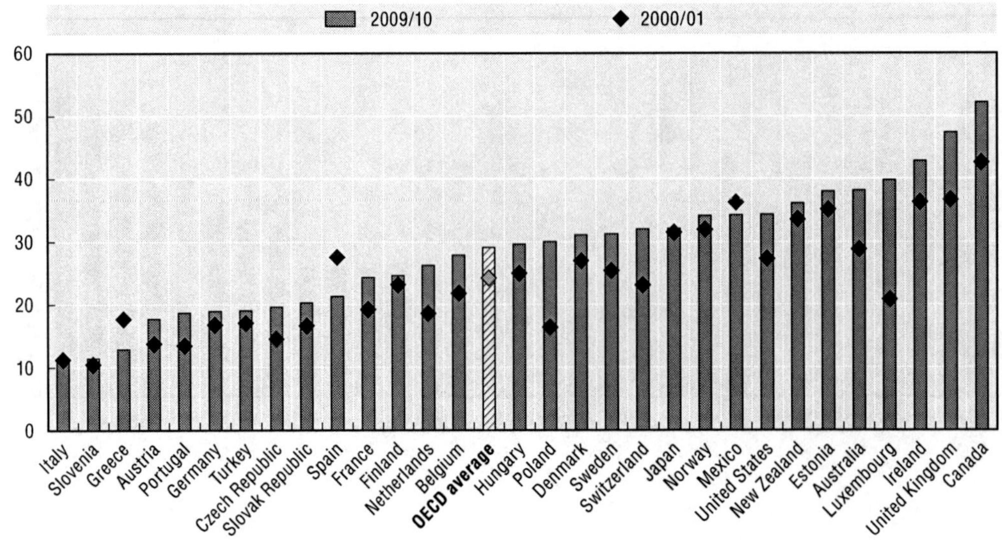

Sources: DIOC, Labour Force Surveys.

StatLink http://dx.doi.org/10.1787/888932615251

The growing share of highly-educated among the immigrant population mirrors a global increase in education levels of roughly the same level that is observed among the total resident population in OECD countries. In some countries, notably in Canada, Australia and the United Kingdom which all saw significant intakes of skilled labour migrants through their migration programmes, the increase also reflects shifts in migration policy with a stronger focus on skilled labour migration. This is also the case in Switzerland, Luxembourg and Ireland, where a large part of migration over the past decade consisted of highly-educated migrants from the European Union.

7. Conclusion

The past decade has seen an increasing trend in migration movements, driven by a growing importance of labour and free movement migration, both of which are more affected by economic conditions than family and humanitarian migration.

Prior to the crisis, immigration had been at record-high levels in many countries, and some of the countries subsequently hardest hit by the downturn were among the main drivers behind the preceding growth in migration. Indeed, the past decade saw countries which were previously mainly countries of emigration emerging as significant destinations for immigrants, such as notably Greece, Ireland, Italy, Portugal and Spain.

The crisis has slowed migration, but in the OECD area as a whole, the crisis-related decline appears to have come to an end in 2010. Indeed, it seems that the underlying factors which had been driving the growth in migration for employment prior to the crisis – namely demographic trends, the enlargement of free mobility zones, the globalisation of education and labour markets and the emergence of a growing middle class in developing countries which has the skills and resources to respond to labour demand in OECD countries – start to be acting again more strongly as there are some signs of improvements in economic conditions in many destination countries. To which degree this will materialise over the short term is, however, unclear, as the global economic situation remains fragile. In any case, even during the severe crisis, the decline in labour migration has generally been modest.

In the European OECD countries, a large part of the increase in migration flows over the past decade has been due to the expansion of free mobility. Indeed, free mobility, notably from the countries that joined the EU in 2004 and 2007, has often been more significant than previously projected. Free movement declined strongly with the crisis, but it seems that it is now on the rise again in many countries.

Globally, however, migration from Asia is increasingly dominating the trends (see Part III in this publication), in particular China and India which together now account for 14% of new migrants to the OECD area. This trend is likely to continue, as a look at international students indicates. China and India notably account for a full 25% of international students, who are an important resource for future labour migration.

Notes

1. Preliminary figures for 2011 seem to confirm this trend (sub-section 4 below).
2. The bulk of the increase was due to large numbers of grants on a discretionary basis. These have been granted with the aim of clearing the previous backlog of outstanding unresolved cases, especially in the domain of asylum.
3. The statistical data for Israel are supplied by and under the responsibility of the relevant Israeli authorities. The use of such data by the OECD is without prejudice to the status of the Golan Heights, East Jerusalem and Israeli settlements in the West Bank under the terms of international law.
4. Norway and Switzerland also participate in the free movement area, but are not included in this figure as they are not part of the EU. The figures are based on the EU countries for which standardised migration data are available; those which are not included generally have small immigration flows.
5. The strong decline in the Czech Republic is to some degree due to a break in the series.
6. The other component of entries are entries from domestic sources and concern school leavers, proxied in Figure I.2 by the average size of a single-age cohort between the ages of 20 and 24.
7. In practice, there are a number of factors that tend to reduce this proportion. Not all arriving immigrants are in the working-age population. Some are retired and some are children, although the latter will eventually enter the population of working age. Likewise, some immigrants will not remain in the destination country, but return to their countries of origin or migrate elsewhere. In addition, some native-born persons also emigrate, although in most countries not nearly to the same extent as immigrants. Finally, in terms of contributions to the labour force, one should remember that the participation rate of many arriving immigrants, and in particular of family and humanitarian migrants, is generally low immediately after arrival, although over time it tends to converge to the participation rate of native-born.
8. Most of the EU countries that are not included in this calculation (which is based on the countries for which standardised information is available) are at best in a similar demographic situation as the Czech Republic.
9. The terms "free movement" and "free mobility" are used synonymously in this section.
10. The reported increase in the United Kingdom largely relates to a treatment of backlogs and status changes of persons already in the country.
11. This figure assumes that three quarters of free movement migration is for employment; based on the participation rate of recent free mobility migrants which is on average at this level.
12. Note that the figures on international students only include full degree programmes; short-term exchange programmes (*e.g.* students benefiting from the European student mobility programme ERASMUS) are excluded. The number of students who were in 2009 at an educational institution abroad thus tends to be significantly higher.
13. Australia also has a large humanitarian resettlement programme, but the number of humanitarian migrants passing through the asylum channel is low. Several European OECD countries also take resettled refugees.

14. The figures for Ireland refer to the respective year ending April.
15. The data below generally refer to the nationality of the migrants, which is not necessarily the same as their country of origin, although this will generally be the case. For the sake of convenience, the country names are used for describing the flows in terms of nationality.
16. In the case of Germany, almost 40% of the increase was related with the introduction of free mobility with Switzerland.
17. See Note 3.
18. See Note 3.
19. However, as noted above, reported net migration tends to be higher than actual net migration flows, since many people leaving the countries do not necessarily de-register.
20. The particularly strong increase in the United Kingdom was related to administrative changes and backlogs.

References

FRONTEX (2012), *FRAN*, Quarterly Issue 3, July-September 2011. European Agency for the Management of Operational Co-operation at the External Borders of the Member States of the European Union.

German Federal Office for Migration and Refugees (2012), *Umsturz und Unruhen in der arabischen Welt*, Nuremberg.

González Enríquez, C. (2012), "La emigración desde España, una migración de retorno", Research Note, Real Instituto Elcano.

Lemaitre, G., T. Liebig, C. Thoreau and P. Fron (2008), "Standardised statistics on immigrant inflows results, sources and methods", OECD Publishing, Paris.

OECD (2011a), *International Migration Outlook*, OECD Publishing, Paris.

OECD (2011b), *Naturalisation: A Passport for the Better Integration of Immigrants?*, OECD Publishing, Paris.

OECD (forthcoming), *Settling in: OECD Indicators on Immigrant Integration – 2012*, OECD Publishing, Paris.

Swiss Federal Office for Migration (2012), *Asylstatistik 2011*, Berne.

ANNEX I.A1

Figure I.A1.1. **Changes in inflows of migrants by country of origin, selected OECD countries, 2000-09 and 2010**

2010 top ten countries of origin as a percentage of total inflows

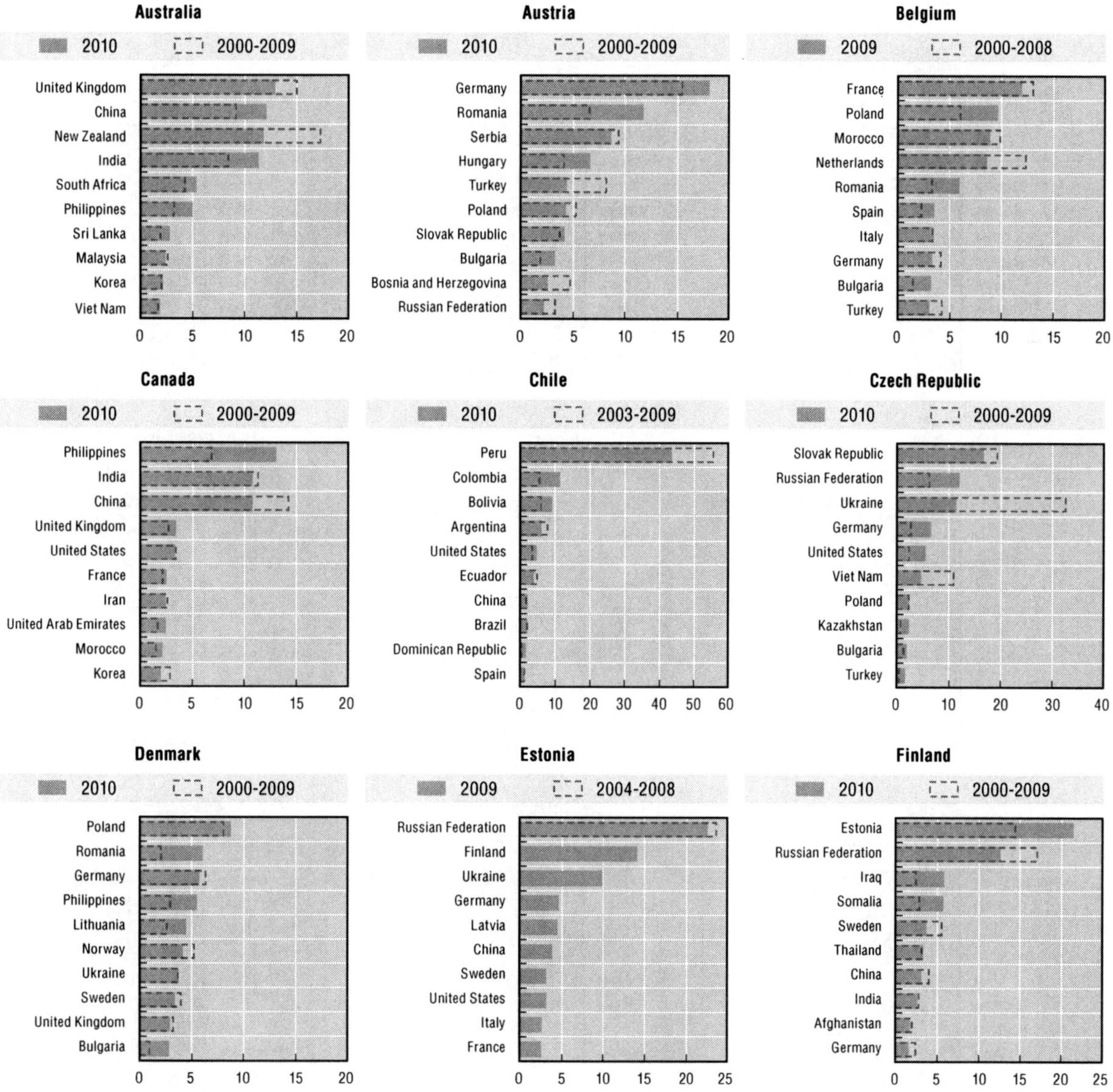

I. TRENDS IN INTERNATIONAL MIGRATION

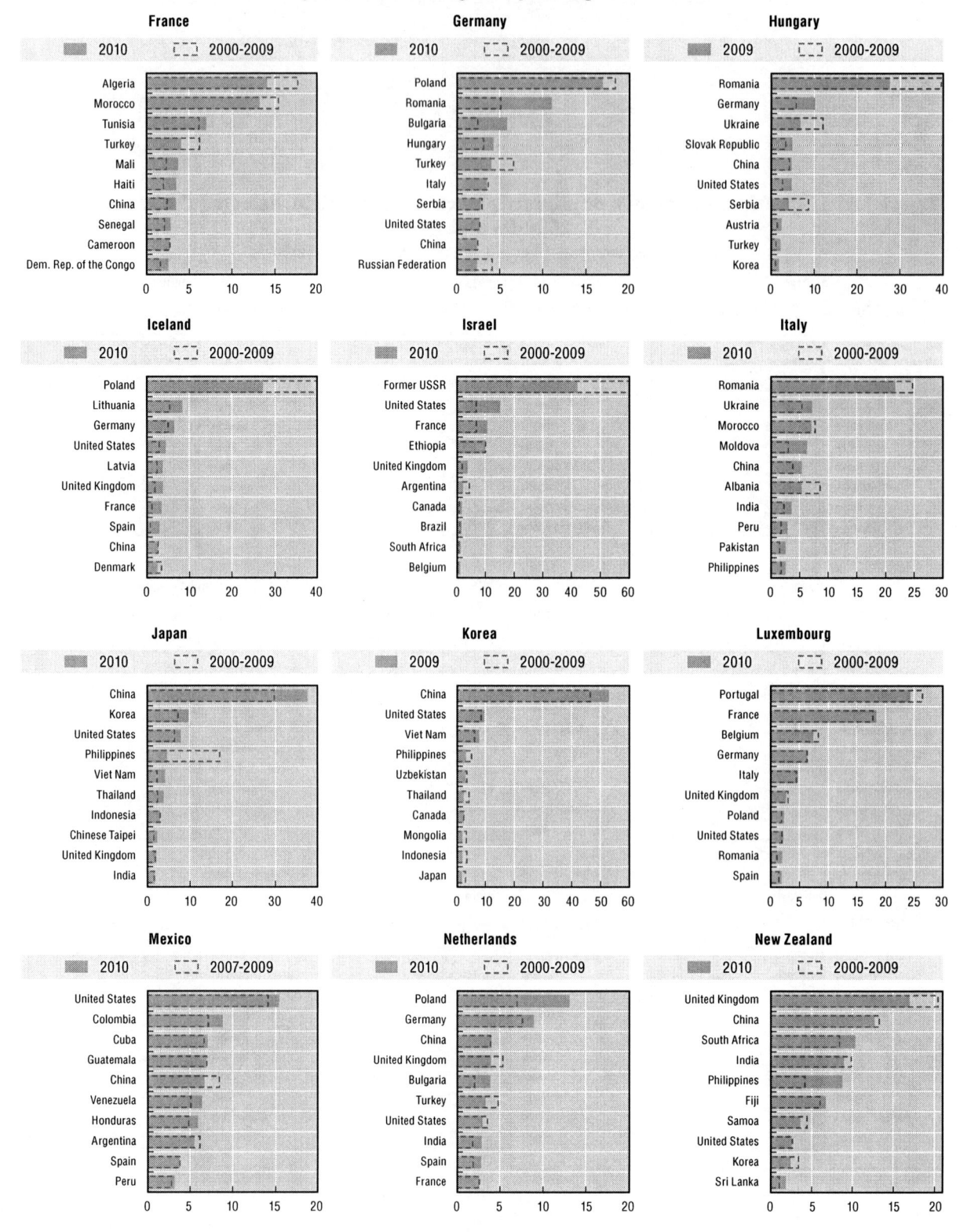

Figure I.A1.1. **Changes in inflows of migrants by country of origin, selected OECD countries, 2000-09 and 2010** (cont.)

2010 top ten countries of origin as a percentage of total inflows

I. TRENDS IN INTERNATIONAL MIGRATION

Figure I.A1.1. **Changes in inflows of migrants by country of origin, selected OECD countries, 2000-09 and 2010** (cont.)

2010 top ten countries of origin as a percentage of total inflows

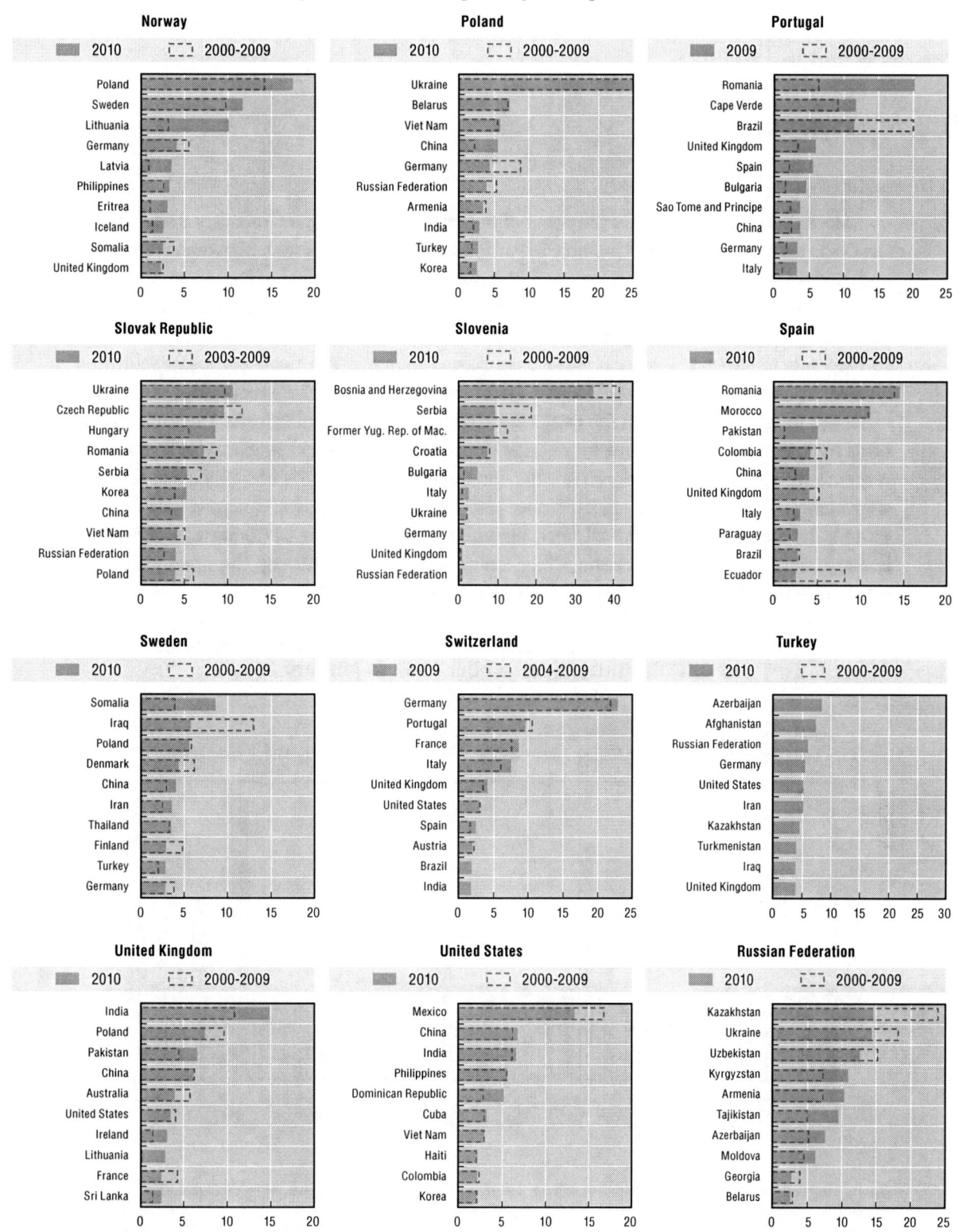

Information on data for Israel: http://dx.doi.org/10.1787/888932315602.
Source: OECD International Migration Database.

StatLink http://dx.doi.org/10.1787/888932615270

B. Employment

1. Introduction

More than three years after the onset of the crisis, with a sluggish recovery underway in the OECD area, many countries, notably in Europe, are still grappling with high unemployment and increasing long-term unemployment. The magnitude of the effect of the recession on the labour market has however been varying among OECD countries. Overall, in the OECD area, unemployment increased by 54.5% between December 2007 and January 2012, which corresponds to about 13.7 million more unemployed persons. The three European countries greatest hit by the crisis in Europe, Ireland, Spain and Greece, have also experienced the largest increases in unemployment in the OECD together with Iceland and Estonia. Unemployment rates in Spain and Greece have more than doubled in this period reaching 23% and 20% respectively, while those in Iceland, Estonia and Ireland at 6.7%, 11.7% and 14.8% respectively, were close to three times those in December 2007 (Figure I.16). Portugal, Hungary, Italy, France, Poland, the Slovak Republic had all unemployment rates above the OECD average of 8.4% in January 2012. In contrast, in Austria, Chile, Israel,[1] Germany and Turkey, the unemployment rate had returned to its pre-crisis level (or below that) in January 2012.

Figure I.16. **Changes in monthly harmonised unemployment rates in OECD countries, December 2007 to January 2012**

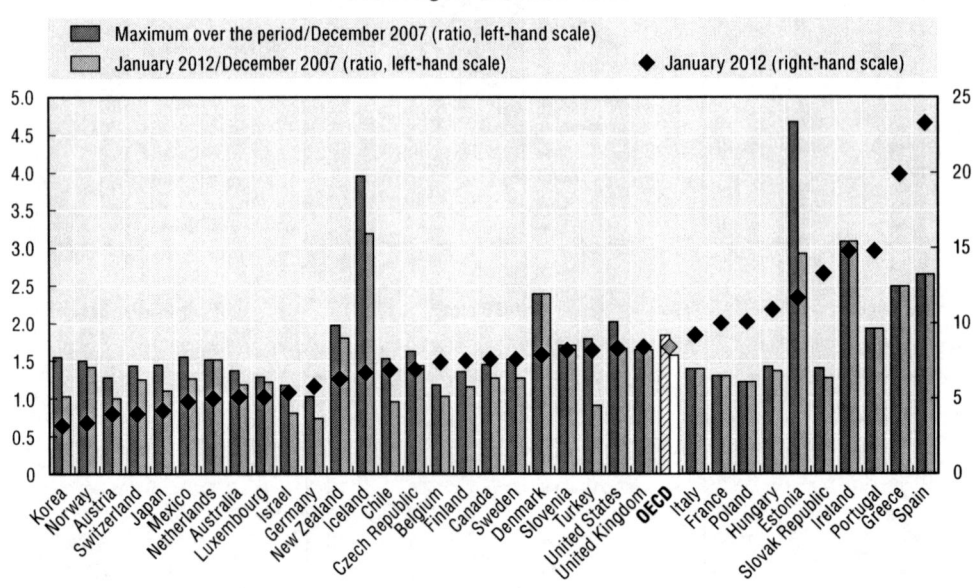

Percentage of the labour force

Notes: Instead of January 2012, rates for Chile, Estonia, Iceland, Israel, Japan, New Zealand, Turkey and the United Kingdom are for December 2011; rates for Greece and Norway are for November 2011 and the rate for Switzerland is for September 2011. They are compared with the corresponding month four years earlier. Information on data for Israel: http://dx.doi.org/10.1787/888932315602.

Source: OECD, *Main Economic Indicators.* StatLink ⟶ http://dx.doi.org/10.1787/888932615289

Since the onset of the crisis, OECD countries have adopted policies and temporary measures aiming to minimise the adverse labour market effects of the crisis and provide support to the increasing numbers of unemployed. Short-time work schemes, job subsidies and labour cost cuts are among the measures adopted to cushion the adverse effects on the labour market. At the same time, countries introduced policies to protect job losers and their households against the income losses through changes in the unemployment benefit (UB) systems as well as social assistance programmes (see Chapter 1 in OECD, 2011b). Temporary policies have been adopted in most countries aiming to provide replacement or supplementary income to job losers and more importantly those experiencing long spells of joblessness. This includes measures to increase the generosity of unemployment benefits either by raising the benefit level or extending its duration. At the same time, countries have modified the eligibility requirements for UB by for example weakening the link between past labour market experience and access to unemployment insurance. Such measures were adopted to increase coverage among the unemployed with weak attachment to the labour market (or greater representation in informal jobs) and hence limited prior formal labour market experience, such as youth, the low-skilled and certain groups of migrants who have been seriously hit by the economic crisis.

This section examines the labour market situation of foreign-born persons in comparison with their native counterparts over the past five years in OECD countries. By presenting evidence on labour market outcomes and distribution across sectors, the next sub-section shows that in many OECD countries migrants have been more negatively affected than natives. Sub-section 3 argues that not all migrant groups have been badly affected by the crisis and identifies those groups of foreign-born persons who are fairing better relative to other foreigners but also natives. Sub-section 4 focuses on migrant youth, the group experiencing not only the greatest increase in unemployment in the majority of OECD countries, but also substantial increases in inactivity, temporary and part-time work.

2. The labour market situation of migrants has changed during the crisis

Immigrants have been heavily hit by the crisis...

As pointed out in the previous editions of the *International Migration Outlook* (OECD, 2009 and 2010a), immigrants have been hard hit, and almost immediately, by the economic downturn in most OECD countries. This fact is mainly explained by the greater presence of immigrants in sectors[2] (*e.g.* construction, manufacturing and wholesale, retail trade and financial sectors – see OECD, 2010b) that have been mostly affected by the crisis in comparison with natives and also by the over-representation of the foreign-born in precarious and often informal jobs with no or limited protection. However, the situation has not been uniform across the OECD and great differences exist both across OECD countries and between migrant groups.

Figure I.17 presents data on employment over the past five years for selected European countries, the United States, Canada and Australia. Employment trends by place of birth in OECD European countries (except Germany, Switzerland and Turkey[3]) show important differences between the foreign-born and the natives. Foreign-born employment in Europe increased by 6.3% between the first quarter of 2008 and the third quarter of 2011, while that of native-born decreased by 2.6% over the same period. In contrast, in the United States, both groups have seen their employment levels decline between the last

Figure I.17. **Quarterly employment by place of birth in selected OECD countries, Q1 2007 to Q4 2011**

Index 100 in Q1 2007 (Q1 2008 in Canada)

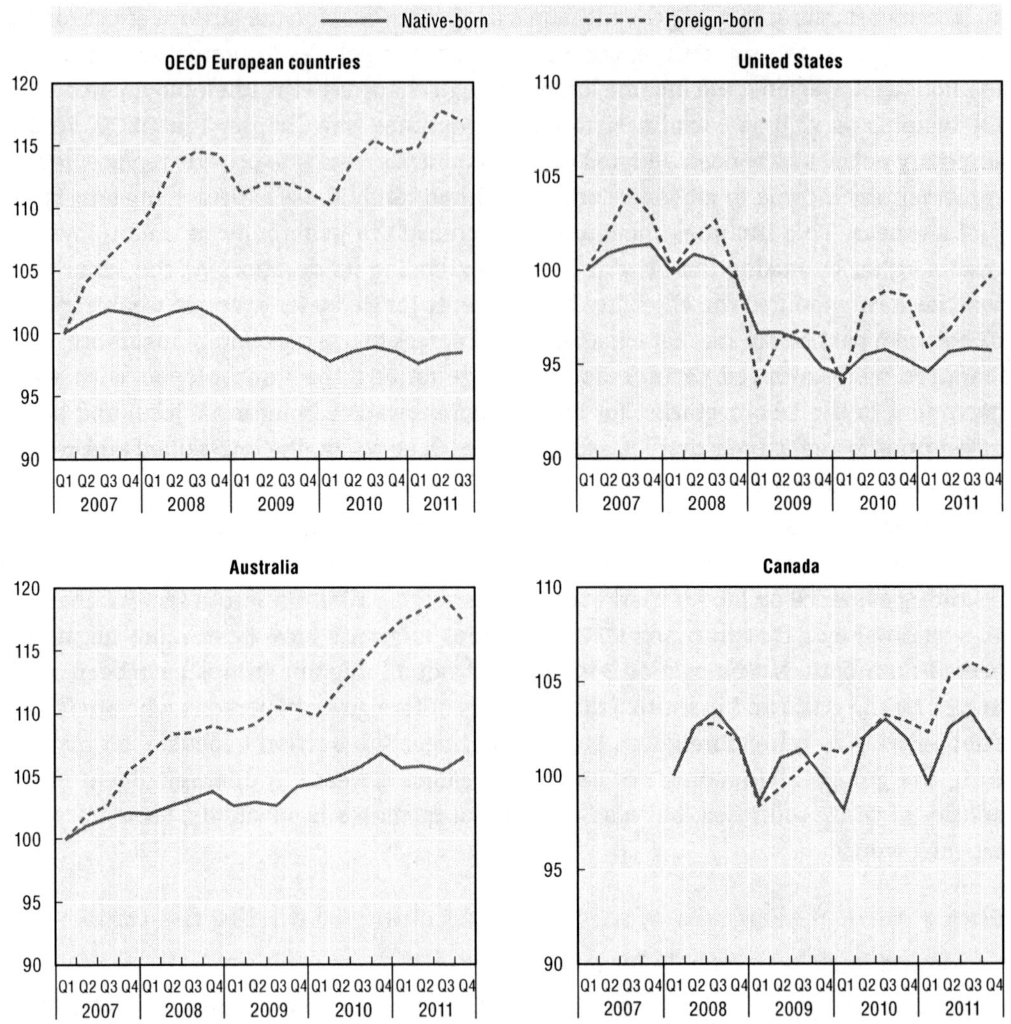

——— Native-born   ----- Foreign-born

[OECD European countries, United States, Australia, Canada charts]

Notes: The population refers to working-age population (15-64). Germany and Turkey were excluded because of a break in the series in 2008 and 2009 respectively, and Switzerland because quarterly data are only available since 2010.
Sources: European Labour Force Surveys (Eurostat); Australia, Canada: Labour Force Surveys; United States: Monthly Current Population Surveys.   StatLink ⏵ http://dx.doi.org/10.1787/888932615308

quarter of 2007 and the end of 2011, and the drop has been more important for the native-born (5.6% versus 3% for the foreign-born). Data for the last quarter of 2011 for the United States reveal that the employment level of migrants is close to its level at the beginning of the crisis while that of the native-born remains about 4% lower than in the first quarter of 2008.

The impact of the crisis on the labour market has been small in Canada in comparison with Europe and the United States. Employment of the foreign-born had already returned to its pre-crisis level in the third quarter of 2010 and an additional 84 000 migrant jobs were created between the end of 2010 and 2011. In Australia, there has been constant employment growth over the past five years for both natives and foreign-born and at a more rapid pace for the latter.

Figure I.18 presents the changes in unemployment and employment rates for migrants and natives for a set of OECD countries between 2008 and 2011 (also between 2007 and 2011 for the United States, where the crisis started earlier). The evidence suggests that the impact of the economic crisis on unemployment has been more pronounced for migrants than for the native-born in most OECD countries (countries located on the right of the identity line). In Spain, Greece and Estonia migrant unemployment increased by 15, 13 and 12 percentage points respectively between 2008 and 2011 whereas that of the native-born increased by 10, 9 and 8 percentage points. In contrast, in some countries such as Switzerland, the Czech Republic and Luxembourg, native unemployment rose more in comparison with that of immigrants.

The right panel in Figure I.18 suggests that, contrary to unemployment, migrant employment has shown more resilience to adverse economic conditions. In some central European countries (Austria, the Czech Republic and Germany) and Luxembourg employment increased for migrants and this to a greater extent than for the native-born (for more details see Annex I.B1). At the same time, with the exception of Germany, unemployment increased over the same period. Similarly, in the United Kingdom and the United States, the drop in employment was more important for the native-born than for migrants while the opposite was true for unemployment. One of the factors responsible for this trend is the increase in labour force participation for some groups of migrants, notably women throughout the crisis (see also OECD, 2011c and next section).

Changes in aggregate employment reflect the dynamics of unemployment on the one hand, and changes in the size of the working-age population and labour force participation on the other. All these dynamics can differ between immigrants and natives. For instance, although changes in the growth of the native working-age population can only be minimal from one year to the other and are related to population ageing, those of the migrant

Figure I.18. **Changes in unemployment and employment rates by place of birth, 2008-11**

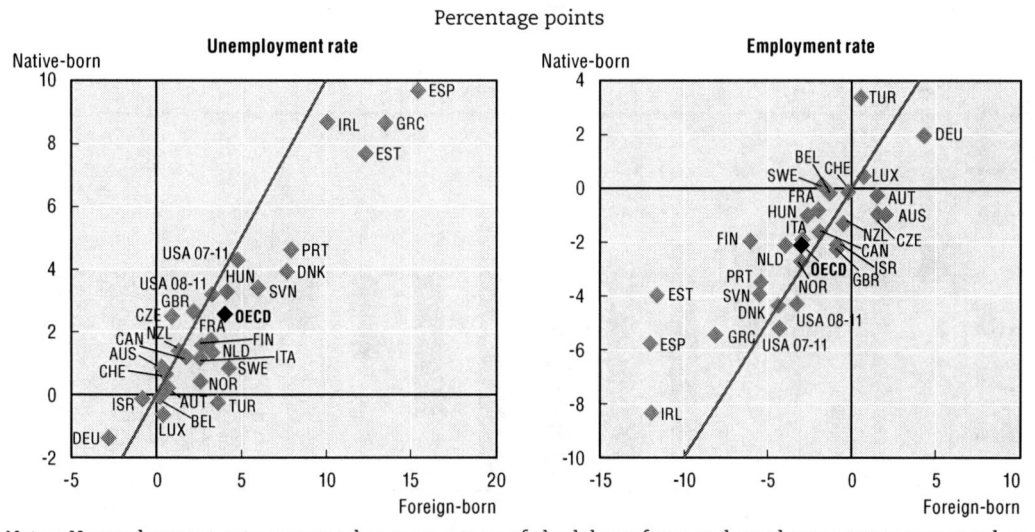

Percentage points

Notes: Unemployment rate measured as percentage of the labour force and employment rate measured as percentage of the population of working-age (15-64). Data for EU countries refer to changes between Q1-3 2008 and Q1-3 2011. Data for the United States refer to changes between 2007 and 2011 (US 07-11) and between 2008 and 2011 (US 08-11). Data for Australia, Canada and New Zealand refer to changes between 2008 and 2011.

Sources: European Labour Force Surveys (Eurostat); Australia, Canada, New Zealand: Labour Force Surveys; United States: Current Population Surveys.

StatLink ⟶ http://dx.doi.org/10.1787/888932615327

population can be more important. The economic crisis has affected new entries into OECD countries and the return rates of existing migrants, but also the way migration policy is shaped in the destination countries as a response to the drop in labour demand. As a result, it is important to identify and analyse the different factors contributing to aggregate employment change, separately for the foreign- and the native-born.

Figure I.19 presents a shift-share analysis on these factors contributing to changes in employment in selected European countries (Figure I.19a) and the United States (Figure I.19b). The evidence presented confirms the expectation of considerable differences between immigrants and natives in Europe and the United States. In Europe, unemployment increased substantially at the very beginning of the crisis (already in the

Figure I.19. **Contribution of various factors to changes in foreign- and native-born employment in European OECD countries and in the United States**

A. European OECD countries (excluding Germany, Switzerland and Turkey),
Q1 2007-Q3 2010 compared to Q1 2008-Q3 2011
Thousands

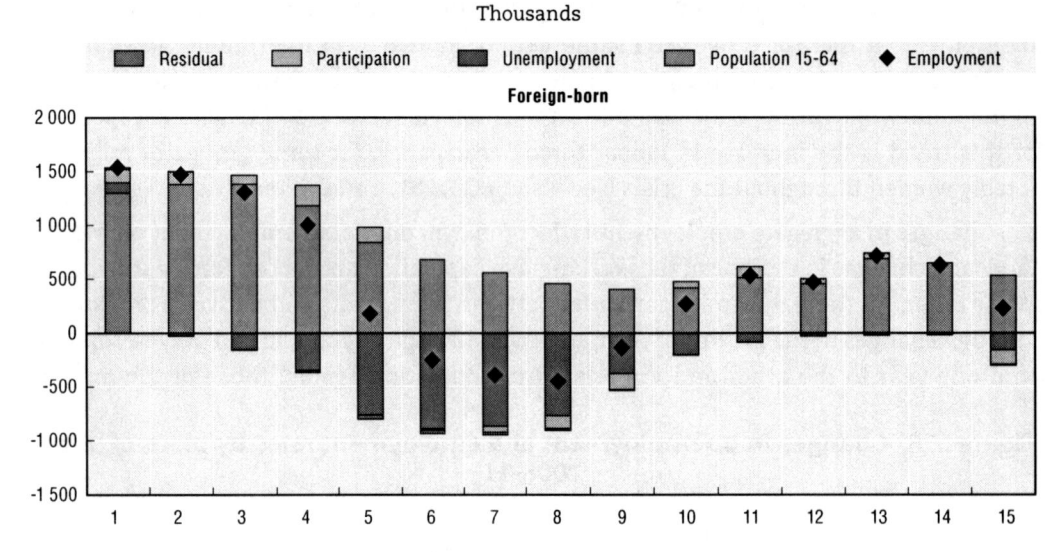

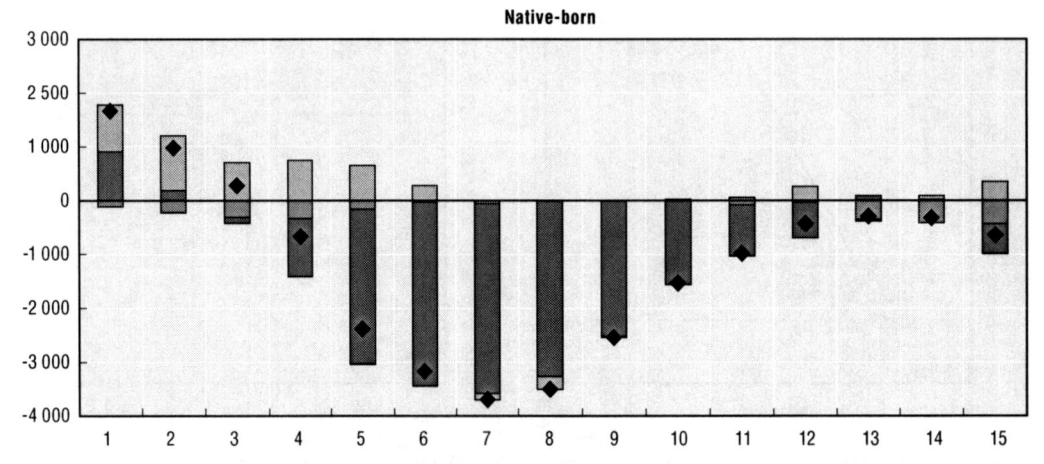

Notes: The population refers to working-age population (15-64). Comparisons are made for the same quarters and not for successive quarters. For example, period 1 compares employment in Q1 2007 to employment in Q1 2008. Period 2 is a comparison between employment in Q2 2007 and Q2 2008. Germany and Turkey were excluded because of a break in the series in 2008 and 2009 respectively, and Switzerland because quarterly data are only available since 2010.

Sources: European Labour Force Surveys (Eurostat).

I. TRENDS IN INTERNATIONAL MIGRATION

Figure I.19. **Contribution of various factors to changes in foreign- and native-born employment in European OECD countries and in the United States** *(cont.)*

B. United States, Q1 2006-Q4 2010 compared to Q1 2007-Q4 2011
Thousands

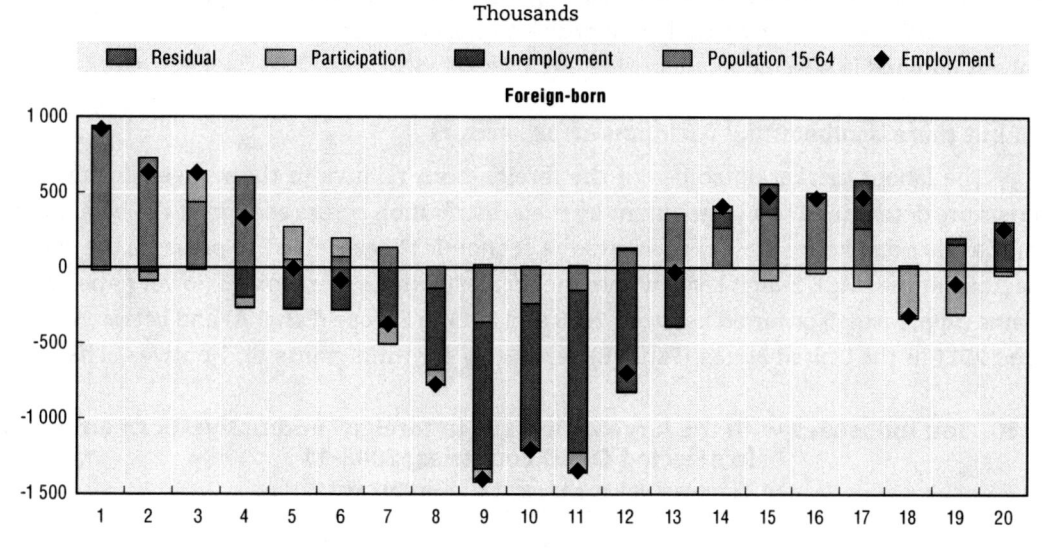

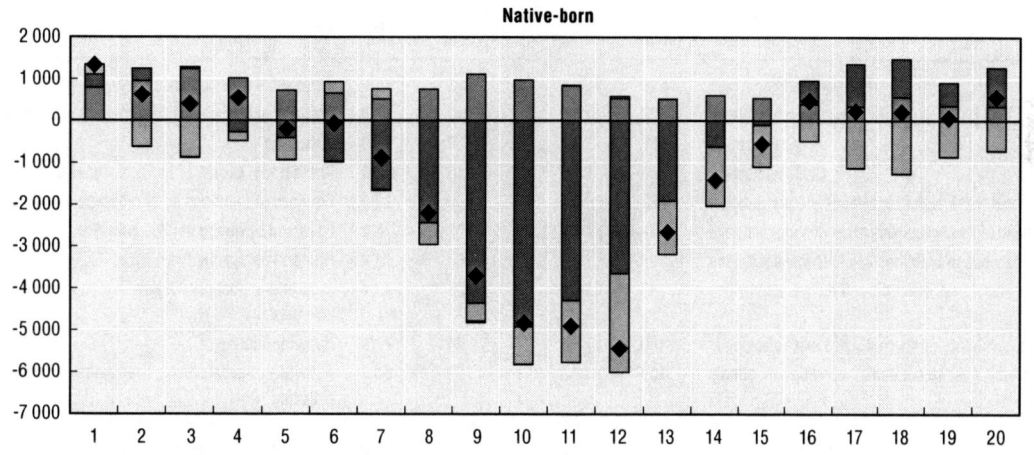

Legend: Residual | Participation | Unemployment | Population 15-64 | ◆ Employment

Notes: The population refers to working-age population (15-64). Comparisons are made for the same quarters and not for successive quarters. For example, period 1 compares employment in Q1 2006 to employment in Q1 2007. Period 2 is a comparison between employment in Q2 2006 and Q2 2007.

Sources: Monthly Current Population Surveys, 2006-11.

StatLink ᕙ http://dx.doi.org/10.1787/888932615346

third quarter of 2008) while employment responded with some delay and started going down only in the second quarter of 2009. The reason behind this time lag is the belated slowdown in the growth of the foreign-born working-age population, which started in the first quarters of 2009 and was also a consequence of the crisis. With the economic recovery in some European countries and the policies adopted to tackle the labour market effects of the crisis, employment picked up again from the second trimester of 2010 and was accompanied by an increase in net migration. In contrast, the decline in employment among the native-born followed closely in pace the increase in unemployment. Employment growth has indeed remained negative through 2011 among natives and this has been somewhat exacerbated by the negative and continuous growth in the working-age population.

I. TRENDS IN INTERNATIONAL MIGRATION

The situation is rather different in the United States in comparison with Europe. The employment drop among natives has been more marked in the first as is also the decline in the foreign-born population during the crisis. Indeed, migration flows to the United States have been fairly responsive to the economic conditions and the drop in labour demand in specific sectors.

... but there is substantial variation across sectors

The labour market outcomes of the foreign-born relative to the natives during the crisis are determined to a large extent by their distribution across sectors at the beginning of the crisis and hence their exposure to the economic shock. Table I.10 presents the list of sectors (at the NACE 2-digit level) where the greatest employment losses (lower panel) and gains (upper panel) occurred between 2008 and 2011 in Europe (Panel A) and between 2007 and 2011 in the United States (Panel B) separately for immigrants and natives. The two

Table I.10. **Ten industries with the largest changes in foreign- and native-born employment, in selected OECD countries, 2008-11**

A. European Union, changes between 2008 and 2011

	Native-born		Foreign-born		
	Change (000)	%	Change (000)	%	
Human health activities	511	4.7	216	46.9	Residential care activities
Residential care activities	427	12.6	193	17.8	Activities of households as employers of domestic personnel
Education	422	3.1	128	12.0	Education
Civil engineering	296	25.6	115	6.5	Retail trade, except of motor vehicles and motorcycles
Social work activities without accommodation	273	6.7	109	12.9	Services to buildings and landscape activities
Activities of head offices; management consultancy activities	204	21.4	102	6.2	Food and beverage service activities
Services to buildings and landscape activities	193	8.0	90	7.4	Human health activities
Other professional, scientific and technical activities	186	24.2	85	23.4	Crop and animal production, hunting and related service activities
Computer programming, consultancy and related activities	186	8.8	76	17.9	Accommodation
Electricity, gas, steam and air conditioning supply	159	12.8	60	58.2	Activities of head offices; management consultancy activities
Other personal service activities	−215	−8.2	−20	−11.0	Office administrative, office support and other business support activities
Manufacture of furniture	−237	−20.0	−22	−14.1	Manufacture of electrical equipment
Manufacture of wearing apparel	−266	−25.7	−26	−16.4	Manufacture of other non-metallic mineral products
Manufacture of machinery and equipment n.e.c.	−278	−9.9	−28	−27.5	Manufacture of textiles
Crop and animal production, hunting and related service activities	−405	−6.2	−29	−23.7	Manufacture of wearing apparel
Wholesale trade, except of motor vehicles and motorcycles	−413	−6.3	−42	−18.2	Legal and accounting activities
Manufacture of fabricated metal products, except machinery and equipment	−455	−12.8	−45	−35.1	Manufacture of furniture
Construction of buildings	−517	−12.2	−68	−13.3	Manufacture of fabricated metal products, except machinery and equipment
Retail trade, except of motor vehicles and motorcycles	−526	−3.3	−119	−9.1	Specialised construction activities
Specialised construction activities	−1 592	−17.2	−271	−26.4	Construction of buildings

Notes: The population refers to working-age population (15-64). European members of the OECD, excluding Turkey and Switzerland where data are not available on the whole period; NACE Rev. 2.
Sources: European Labour Force Surveys, Q1-Q3 2008 and Q1-Q3 2011.

Table I.10. **Ten industries with the largest changes in foreign- and native-born employment, in selected OECD countries, 2008-11** (cont.)

B. United States, changes between 2007 and 2011

	Native-born		Foreign-born		
	Change (000)	%	Change (000)	%	
Health care services, except hospitals	449	6.3	82	20.5	Social assistance
Hospitals	290	5.9	78	19.9	Agriculture
Food services and drinking places	220	3.6	71	5.8	Educational services
Professional and technical services	95	1.3	69	5.5	Health care services, except hospitals
Mining	64	9.7	61	4.2	Administrative and support services
Arts, entertainment, and recreation	54	2.3	59	13.5	Food manufacturing
Miscellaneous and not specified manufacturing	40	4.2	39	2.9	Professional and technical services
Internet publishing and broadcasting	30	151.2	32	6.2	Public administration
Agriculture	29	2.4	28	39.2	Utilities
Management of companies and enterprises	27	20.2	18	8.8	Insurance
Primary metals and fabricated metal products	-225	-14.3	-39	-23.6	Machinery manufacturing
Transportation equipment manufacturing	-226	-11.9	-43	-29.1	Paper and printing
Plastics and rubber products	-234	-38.9	-45	-12.9	Private households
Paper and printing	-244	-25.0	-50	-35.6	Furniture and fixtures manufacturing
Real estate	-281	-13.6	-56	-8.4	Wholesale trade
Finance	-430	-11.0	-73	-18.6	Real estate
Wholesale trade	-555	-15.7	-92	-4.0	Retail trade
Retail trade	-559	-4.1	-95	-32.8	Textile, apparel, and leather manufacturing
Transportation and warehousing	-566	-11.0	-138	-19.8	Finance
Construction	-1 988	-23.0	-852	-28.9	Construction

Notes: The population refers to working-age population (15-64). Industries are derived from the 2002 Census Classification.
Sources: Current Population Surveys.

StatLink ⟶ http://dx.doi.org/10.1787/888932616866

sectors with the greatest job losses for migrants in Europe were manufacturing and construction, which together accounted for more than a quarter of total foreign-born employment in 2008. In the "construction of buildings" sectors, about 271 000 migrant jobs were lost, and more than 1.5 million jobs for natives. Migrants lost about 220 000 jobs in six manufacturing sectors and important losses were also recorded for immigrants in "office administration, office support and other business support activities" (20 000 jobs) as well as "legal and accounting activities" (42 000 jobs), two sectors that typically employ medium- and high-skilled workers.

In the United States, as in Europe, the construction sector has been the most heavily hit by the crisis. Close to three million jobs were lost in total in "construction", of which one third were migrant jobs. Sectors that typically employ high-skilled workers have also recorded substantial losses. Immigrants have lost 138 000 jobs in "finance", representing one quarter of the total losses in the sector.

The greatest increases in migrant employment in Europe were recorded in the services sector. Specifically, a total of 643 000 jobs were created in "residential care activities" of which more than 50% were taken by foreign-born workers. An additional 193 000 jobs were filled by immigrants in "activities of households as employers of domestic personnel" and migrants have also benefited from 109 000 jobs created in "services to building and landscape activities" (193 000 new jobs for natives). Moreover, important employment gains have occurred in certain medium- and high-skilled sectors. Migrant employment in education has increased by

12% (128 000 extra jobs for the foreign-born and 422 000 for natives) while 60 000 additional jobs were created for migrants in "activities of head offices; management consultancy activities". With the exception of the last sector, women benefited from more than 70% of the new jobs created in these sectors (94% in "activities of households as employers of domestic personnel" and 84% in "services to buildings and landscape activities").

In the United States, job creation among the foreign-born has been the greatest in "social assistance" (82 000 jobs) and "agriculture" (78 000 jobs). In the latter, more than 70% of the total jobs created were taken by foreign-workers. Similarly to Europe, migrant employment has also expanded in medium- and high-skilled sectors. In "professional and technical services", "public administration" and "educational services" 142 000 migrant jobs were created between 2007 and 2011.

It is interesting to compare the above changes with those that occurred during the last year when the economies of many OECD countries starting to show some first signs of recovery. Table I.B4.1 in annex presents the ten sectors with the greatest employment gains (upper panel) and losses (lower panel) between 2010 and 2011 in Europe (Panel A) and the United States (Panel B).[4] In Europe, "specialised construction activities" has changed lists and is now found among the sectors with the greatest increase in migrant employment. Likewise, in the United States, some manufacturing sectors (*e.g.* "computer and electronic product manufacturing") in which foreign-born employment had been seriously hit by the recession, have now started to recover the migrant employment has marked substantial increases.

Long-term unemployment continues to increase

As a result of the economic crisis and the slow recovery, the duration of unemployment increased in many OECD countries both for native and migrant workers. In 2011, more than half of the foreign-born unemployed were looking for a job for at least 12 months in Ireland, Germany and some Central European countries (Figure I.20). However differences exist among OECD countries. While in the majority of countries, this percentage ranged between 30 and 50%, in Austria, Australia, Finland, Turkey, New Zealand and Sweden less than 30% of their unemployed migrants were in long-term unemployment. The contribution of foreign-labour to the increase in the increase in total long-term unemployment has been substantial. In all OECD countries for which data are available except the Slovak Republic and Hungary, immigrants are responsible for between 14 and 30% of the increase in total long-term unemployment (Figure I.20), a figure which is well above their share in total employment. In two countries, Sweden and Switzerland, the contribution of the foreign-born to the total increase in long-term unemployment was as high as 56%.

Figure I.B2.1 (in annex) shows a clear progression of unemployment duration for the foreign-born in many OECD countries over the period 2008-11. The increase in unemployment duration continued throughout 2011 and has been particularly marked among those who have been unemployed for more than two years in France, Italy, Spain, the United Kingdom and the United States. Similar increases have occurred in the numbers of the "18 months plus" category in Ireland, the Netherlands and Greece.

Figure I.20. **Changes in long-term unemployed foreign-born workers in selected OECD countries, 2008-11**

Percentages

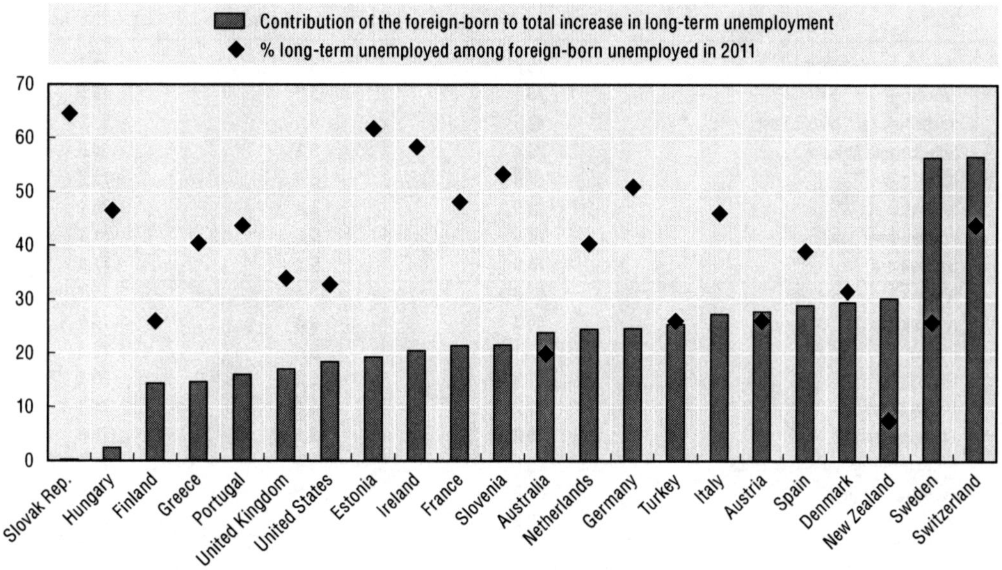

■ Contribution of the foreign-born to total increase in long-term unemployment
♦ % long-term unemployed among foreign-born unemployed in 2011

Notes: The population refers to working-age population (15-64). Data for EU countries refer to changes between Q1-Q3 2008 and Q1-Q3 2011 (for each period, the number considered is the sum of the values for the three quarters). Data for the United States refer to changes between 2007 and 2011.

Sources: European Labour Force Surveys (Eurostat); Australia, New Zealand: Labour Force Surveys; United States: Current Population Surveys.

StatLink ⟶ http://dx.doi.org/10.1787/888932615365

3. The impact of the crisis has not been uniform

Differences in the labour market outcomes of migrants across the OECD are related to their characteristics (in terms of age and education) and their distribution across sectors (as was shown above), occupations as well as countries of residence. Overall, there exist striking differences in the labour market situation of the foreign-born across countries. Table I.11 presents the main labour market indicators for migrants by county of residence (Australia, Canada, Europe, and the United States) and by region of origin. Foreign-born record on average higher employment and participation rates than the natives in the United States whereas in Europe they lag significantly behind their native counterparts (at least with respect to employment rates). In addition, in Europe, they face unemployment rates that are close to twice the unemployment of natives.

The region of origin matters...

These aggregate figures mask important differences among the foreign born according to their region of origin. Immigrants from North Africa in Europe and Australia (North Africa and Middle East in the second) record the lowest employment rates (48%) and the weakest attachment to the labour markets (65% in Europe and 53% in Australia), in comparison with all other migrant groups both in Europe and the United States. Migrants from those countries and from Latin America and the Caribbean in Europe experience record unemployment rates of 25 and 22% respectively. This is not surprising given the over-representation of these groups of migrants in sectors (construction) and countries (Spain, Italy, Greece) greatly affected by the economic crisis. Migrants from Mexico and Central and Latin America are also faring worse than the other migrant groups in the United States, a situation which is related to lower levels of education and language skills as well as discriminatory practices of employers.

Table I.11. **Employment, unemployment and participation rates by region of origin in selected OECD countries, 2011**

Percentages

		Employment rates	Unemployment rates	Participation rates
Australia	Oceania and Antartica	76.8	6.2	81.8
	Europe	73.6	3.7	76.5
	North Africa and Middle East	48.0	9.5	53.0
	Sub-Saharan Africa	76.4	5.3	80.6
	Asia	67.5	5.9	71.7
	Americas	73.9	5.3	78.1
	Foreign-born (total)	**70.5**	**5.2**	**74.4**
	Native-born	**73.9**	**5.2**	**77.9**
Canada	Africa	65.6	13.4	75.7
	Asia and Middle East	66.3	9.3	73.1
	Europe	73.1	6.6	78.3
	Oceania	77.2	3.3	79.8
	United States	72.2	5.4	76.3
	South America	70.3	10.9	78.9
	Other North and Central America	69.6	9.4	76.8
	Foreign-born (total)	**68.9**	**8.9**	**75.6**
	Native-born	**72.8**	**7.2**	**78.5**
European OECD countries	EU27 + EFTA	68.1	11.1	76.6
	Other European countries	59.4	14.3	69.3
	North Africa	48.3	25.2	64.6
	Other African countries and Middle East	58.0	19.6	72.1
	North America	67.4	7.1	72.6
	Other American countries and Caribbean	62.0	22.2	79.6
	Asia	62.4	9.8	69.2
	Others	78.7	3.2	81.2
	Foreign-born (total)	**61.6**	**15.5**	**72.9**
	Native-born	**65.4**	**8.8**	**71.7**
United States	Mexico	65.2	10.2	72.6
	Other Central American countries	69.9	10.7	78.3
	South America and Caribbean	68.6	10.7	76.8
	Canada	70.3	5.7	74.5
	Europe	71.1	7.4	76.8
	Africa	66.9	11.4	75.5
	Asia	67.4	7.0	72.5
	Other regions	63.0	10.1	70.1
	Foreign-born (total)	**67.5**	**9.1**	**74.3**
	Native-born	**65.1**	**9.2**	**71.7**

Notes: The population refers to working-age population (15-64). OECD European countries do not include Turkey because no data by region of birth are available for this country. The regions of origin could not be more comparative across countries of residence because of the way aggregate data provided to the Secretariat were coded.
Sources: European Labour Force Surveys (Eurostat), Q1-Q3 2011; Australia, Canada: Labour Force Surveys; United States: Current Population Surveys. StatLink http://dx.doi.org/10.1787/888932616885

The labour market situation of migrants in Australia and Canada is somewhat between that in Europe and the United States, but possibly closely to the latter, in that they fare similar to the natives in terms of unemployment rates and only slightly worse in terms of labour force participation and employment rates. The foreign-born in Australia, have on average better labour market outcomes than immigrants in Europe and the United States, but in some cases are still behind the native-born. Immigrants from the Middle East and North Africa record the lowest participation and highest unemployment rates in the country. In Canada, migrants from Europe, Oceania and the United States (who tend to be more qualified on average) have on average better labour market outcomes than the native-born.

... as do gender and level of education

The labour market effects of the crisis differ significantly across migrant groups with different education levels (Figure I.22) and between men and women (Figure I.21). In most countries, migrant women have been less affected by the economic crisis than foreign-born men. In more than half of the OECD countries, participation rates of foreign-born women increased between 2008 and 2011. In Austria, Canada, Denmark, France, Germany, Greece, Israel,[5] Portugal, the United Kingdom and the United States, the increase in participation in percentage points has been greater for migrant women than for migrant men but also

Figure I.21. **Changes in participation and employment rates by gender and country of birth, 2008-11**

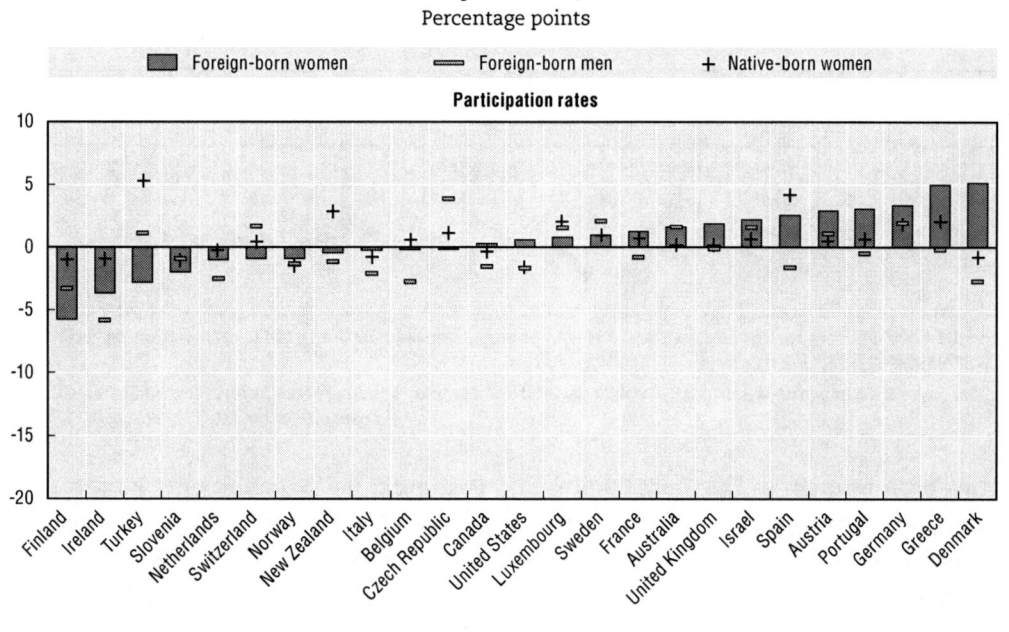

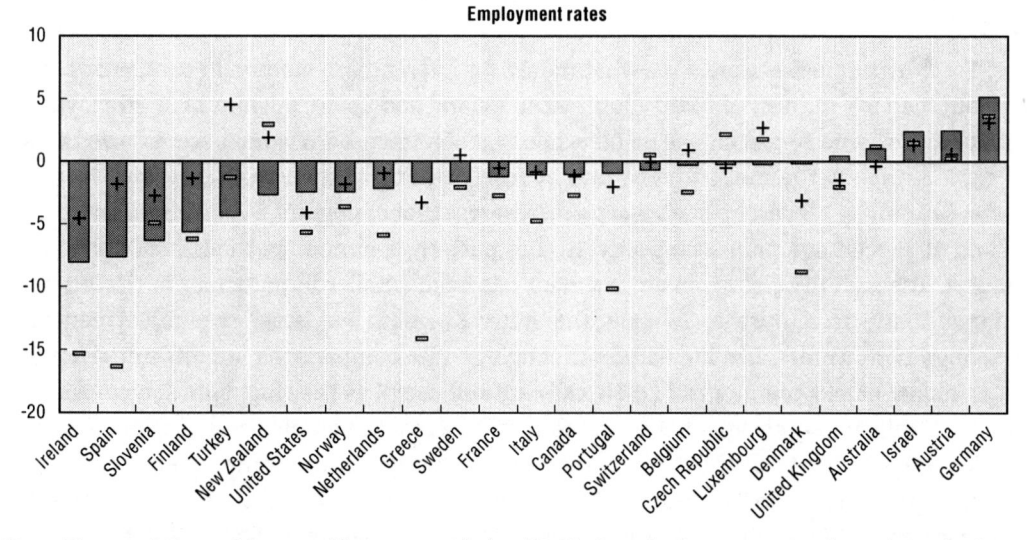

Percentage points

Notes: The population refers to working-age population (15-64). Data for European countries and Israel refer to changes between Q1-Q3 2008 and Q1-Q3 2011. Data for the United States refer to changes between 2007 and 2011. Information on data for Israel: http://dx.doi.org/10.1787/888932315602.

Sources: European Labour Force Surveys (Eurostat); Australia, Canada, Israel, New Zealand: Labour Force Surveys; United States: Current Population Surveys. StatLink ⟶ http://dx.doi.org/10.1787/888932615384

Figure I.22. **Changes in unemployment rates by place of birth and by education level in selected OECD countries, 2008-11**
Percentage points

Native-born ------ Foreign-born

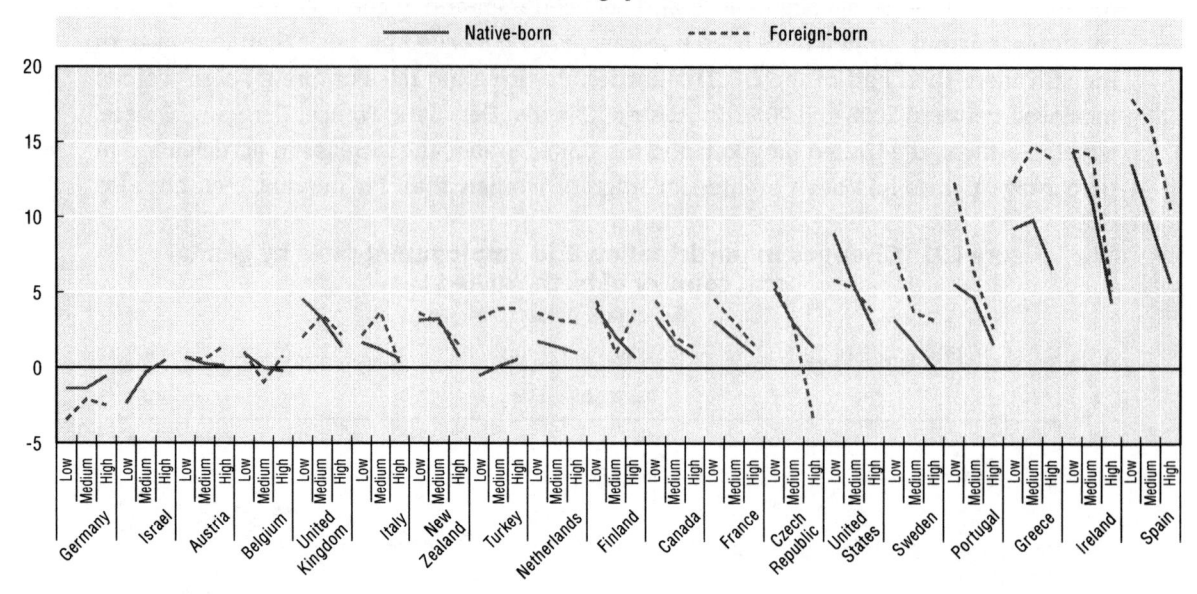

Notes: The population refers to working-age population (15-64). Data for European countries and Israel refer to changes between Q1-Q3 2008 and Q1-Q3 2011. Data for the United States refer to changes between 2007 and 2011. Information on data for Israel: http://dx.doi.org/10.1787/888932315602.

Sources: European Labour Force Surveys (Eurostat), Canada, Israel, New Zealand: Labour Force Surveys; United States: Current Population Surveys.
StatLink ⟶ http://dx.doi.org/10.1787/888932615403

native-born women. In the United States and Denmark, participation only increased for foreign-born women, whereas it went down for the other two groups. There is some evidence suggesting an "added worker effect" in Greece, Spain, Portugal, France and Denmark, where participation rates of foreign-born men went down whereas those of foreign-born women increased and in some cases quite substantially (by five percentage points in Denmark and Greece).

Employment losses were somewhat muted for foreign-born women in comparison with migrant men in a number of OECD countries. In Ireland and Spain, migrant male employment dropped by close to 16 percentage points while that of foreign-born women went down by half of that. Similarly, the employment rate of foreign-born women in Greece and Portugal decreased only by 1.6 and 1 percentage point, whereas that of migrant men drooped sharply by 14 and 10 percentage points respectively. The pattern is similar in the United States and Canada, although the change in employment has been smaller in particular in the latter. In contrast, in Australia, Austria, Germany, the United Kingdom and Israel[6] the employment rate of foreign-born women has increased. Although gender comparisons are difficult given the much higher employment rates of men, they are still useful as they highlight some resilience of female migrant employment. The distribution of female migrants across sectors is one of the key determinants of this trend. Only 10% of foreign-born women were working in manufacturing in 2008 in European OECD countries (11% in the United States) and another 4% in construction (13% in the "construction of buildings" in the United States), the two sectors heavily hit by the crisis and where many foreign-born men worked.

On average, low-skilled foreign-born workers have been more adversely affected than the medium- and high-skilled in many countries. This is not only related to their different distribution across sectors, but also to the type of jobs they occupy (often temporary) and their lower seniority, which imply a lower firing cost to employers. In more than three quarters of the OECD countries with available data, the unemployment gap between low-skilled and high-skilled migrants has increased between 2008 and 2011 (Figure I.22). The situation of the low-skilled has got worse both in absolute terms and relative to high-skilled foreign-born in Portugal, Spain, Ireland, and the Czech Republic. In countries such as the United Kingdom, Italy and Greece, the increase in unemployment has been more important among the medium-skilled foreign-born than others, less or more educated migrants.

The differences between migrants and natives are especially sharp in the three countries experiencing important increases in unemployment among the foreign-born, that is Greece, Spain, Portugal (for the low skilled), but also in Turkey and Sweden (for the low- and high-skilled). Substantial differences also exist for the medium-skilled in Italy and Ireland, possibly because of the over-representation of migrants in semi-skilled sectors and occupations mainly affected by the economic downturn.

4. The crisis is putting additional pressure on already disadvantaged migrant youth

The recent crisis had devastating effects for young persons (15-24 years), further exacerbating their existing disadvantages in terms of access to secure and well-paid jobs (see also OECD, 2010b for a thorough analysis of this issue). Youth unemployment has been more responsive to the business cycle than adult unemployment in many OECD countries (Scarpetta et al., 2010). In the OECD, the total number of unemployed youth increased by more than two million persons between December 2007 and January 2012. The limited work experience of youth, their disproportionate presence among temporary job holders and their concentration in sectors which are heavily volatile (such as construction and manufacturing) are some of the factors explaining why youth have been particularly hurt by the recent economic crisis in the OECD. In many countries, even young persons with permanent labour contracts may have been disproportionally hurt in comparison with older workers because of the application of the "last in, first out" rule. Youth have on average less job tenure and hence less firm specific human capital and as a result firms are less inclined to invest in them. In addition, because, in most countries, severance pay is a function of past work experience, firing young workers is less costly than firing older ones.

Significant employment losses for foreign-born youth in many OECD countries...

Foreign-born youth have experienced sizeable declines in their employment rates in many OECD countries. Foreign-born youth employment has declined by 28 percentage points in Ireland and 16 percentage points in Spain between 2008 and 2011 (Figure I.23). This drop is substantially higher than that for prime-age and older workers in the majority of countries (except Slovenia, Portugal, Belgium and Finland) but also higher than for their native-born youth. In countries such as Turkey and Ireland, there are up to 14 and 11 percentage points differences in the drop in employment between migrant and native youth. The only country in which all youth, irrespectively of their origin, have seen their employment rates decrease by 14-16 percentage points is Spain, the country with the highest increase in unemployment for all groups as a consequence of the recession.

In most countries older foreign-born workers have been fairly protected relative to younger ones (except in Finland). This is partly due to the limited availability of early-retirement schemes during the crisis associated with the restrictions imposed by the

I. TRENDS IN INTERNATIONAL MIGRATION

Figure I.23. **Changes in employment rates by place of birth and age in selected OECD countries, 2008-11**

Percentage points

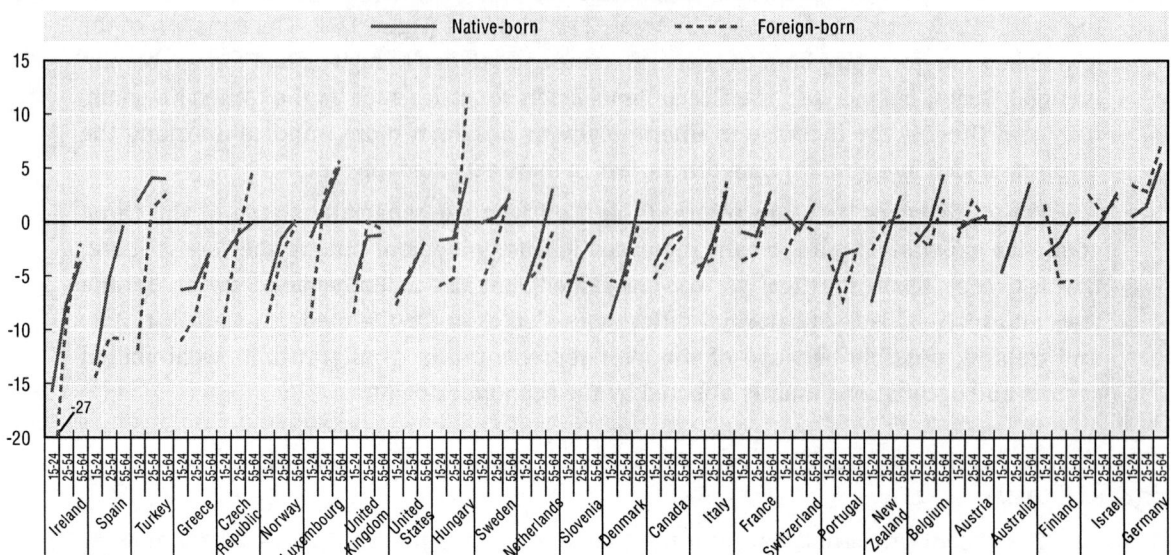

Notes: The population refers to working-age population (15-64). Data for European countries and Israel refer to changes between Q1-Q3 2008 and Q1-Q3 2011. Data for the United States refer to changes between 2007 and 2011. Information on data for Israel: http://dx.doi.org/10.1787/888932315602.

Sources: European Labour Force Surveys (Eurostat), Australia, Israel, New Zealand Labour: Force Surveys, United States: Current Population Surveys.

StatLink ⟶ http://dx.doi.org/10.1787/888932615422

OECD member countries on such potential exists towards e.g. sickness and disability benefits. In addition, it is likely that older workers chose to work longer in countries experiencing large reductions in pension incomes as part of their fiscal consolidation measures. In Spain, prime-age and older workers among the foreign-born have been particularly badly hit in comparison with the natives of the same age. These differences are even more pronounced than those between foreign-born and native-born youth.

Although the ratio of migrant to native youth unemployment rate in 2011 (Q1-Q3) was close to one for the OECD on average, there are large differences across countries (Figure I.24). In the Netherlands, Austria, Slovenia, Luxembourg, Switzerland and Sweden, foreign-born youth are two times more likely than native youth to be unemployed. In contrast, the differences are in favour of foreign-born youth in the Czech Republic, Italy, Greece, Ireland, Israel and the United States. Comparisons are striking when conducted between migrant youth and migrant adults. In all OECD countries, among the migrant population, the probability of unemployment for youth is close to or more than two times that for adults. This ratio is close to four in Luxembourg and New Zealand and between 2.5 and 3 in Austria, Australia, France, Italy, Slovenia, Sweden, Turkey and the United Kingdom.

... and increasing numbers of young persons out of the labour market

The unemployment rate for youth is only partially measuring labour market outcomes for this age-group. Getting a job or searching for one is only one of the possible outcomes for young persons who have just left school. Some youth may choose not to enter the labour force, or engage in irregular employment or in domestic unpaid work, etc. The numbers of youth in these situations can be large especially in some OECD countries and it is important to be able to measure them and compare them across countries. Figure I.25 follows the analysis in OECD

I. TRENDS IN INTERNATIONAL MIGRATION

Figure I.24. **Unemployment rates by place of birth for youth and adults in selected OECD countries, 2011**
Percentage of the labour force

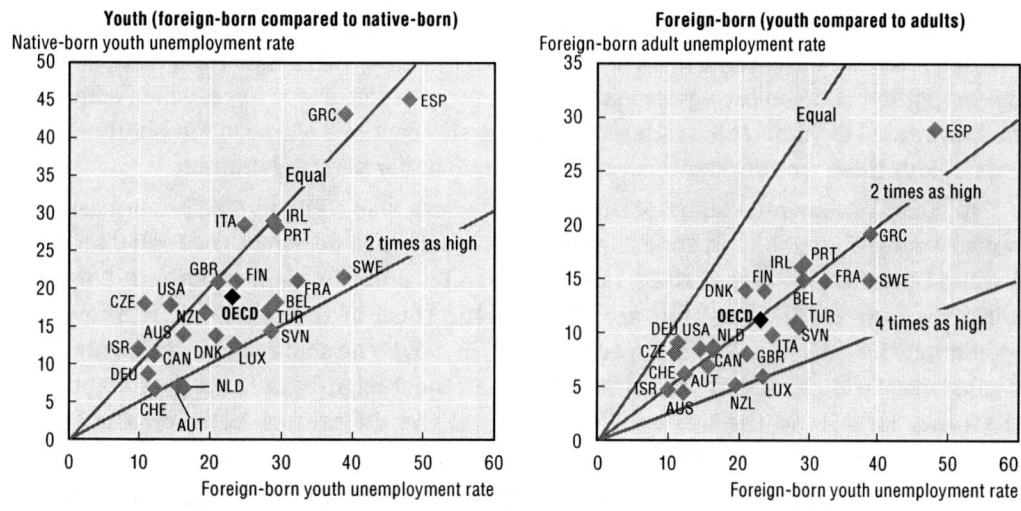

Notes: The population refers to adults 25-54 and youth 15-24. Data for European countries and Israel refer to Q1-Q3 2011. Data for the United States refer to 2011.
Information on data for Israel: http://dx.doi.org/10.1787/888932315602.
Sources: European Labour Force Surveys (Eurostat); Australia, Canada, Israel, New Zealand: Labour Force Surveys; United States: Current Population Surveys. StatLink http://dx.doi.org/10.1787/888932615441

Figure I.25. **Changes in NEET rates and long-term and short-term unemployment for youth by place of birth, in selected OECD countries, 2008-11**
Percentage points

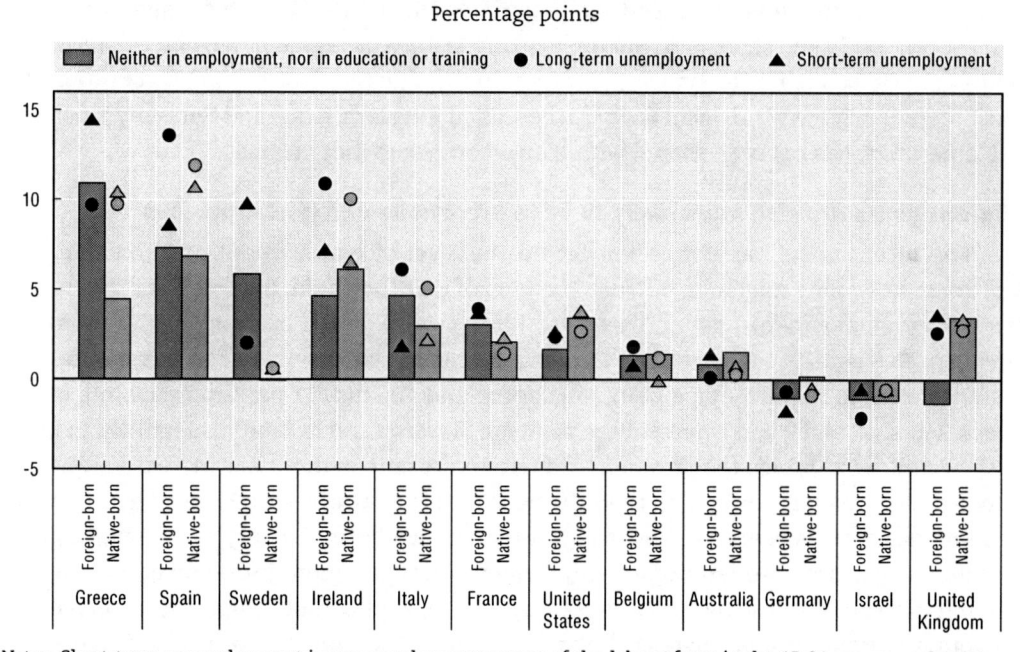

Notes: Short-term unemployment is measured as percentage of the labour force in the 15-24 age-group. Long-term unemployment is expressed as a share of total unemployment. NEET is expressed as a share of the total population. Data for European countries and Israel refer to changes between Q1-Q3 2008 and Q1-Q3 2011 (for each period, the number considered is the sum of the values for the three quarters). Data for the United States refer to changes between 2007 and 2011 The results for NEET in Europe and Israel are overestimated because they are based on three quarters, including summertime, when under declaration of school enrolment of students is commonly observed.
Information on data for Israel: http://dx.doi.org/10.1787/888932315602.
Sources: European Labour Force Surveys (Eurostat); Australia, Israel: Labour Force Surveys; United States: Current Population Surveys. StatLink http://dx.doi.org/10.1787/888932615460

(2010b) and presents data on the numbers of youth not in education, employment or training (NEET), which is an indicator seeking to capture the "joblessness" of young people, many of whom are not captured by conventional measures of unemployment. A youth is considered as NEET if he or she has left the school system and is not employed (nor in continuing education). The NEET has two advantages relative to the youth unemployment rate. First, it is calculated as a proportion of the entire age category, and not only of the labour force, which eliminates the bias related to youth still in school. Second, it also captures all individuals without jobs, and not only those who are identified as unemployed under the ILO definition.

In 2011, a substantial share of foreign-born youth was NEET in OECD countries with available data (Figure I.B3.1 in annex). Australia, Germany, Ireland, Israel, the United Kingdom and the United States record NEET rates between 6% and 21% while Southern European countries have NEET rates that are close to one third of the total size of the youth population (38% in Spain, 32% in Greece and 30% in Italy). The share of youth who are NEET is substantially lower among the native-born than the foreign-born (with the exception of Australia, Israel and the United Kingdom) and the difference between the two is particularly high in Greece and in Spain.

The increase in the share of youth in NEET between 2008 and 2011 has been especially marked among migrant youth in Greece, followed by Spain, Sweden, Ireland and Italy (Figure I.25). The increase has been more marked among the foreign-born than the native-born in all those countries except Australia, Ireland, the United Kingdom and the United States. In particular in Greece, the share of youth in NEET has increased by 15 percentage points for foreign-born and by 11 percentage points for natives. The situation for migrant youth is particularly worrisome in Spain as long-term unemployment for foreign-born youth has increased by 14 percentage points (12 percentage points for native-born youth) and short-term unemployment has also increased by 8.6 percentage points (11 percentage points for the natives). Contrary to the situation in most OECD countries, the NEET rates of migrant youth went down in the United Kingdom, Israel and Germany, a positive outcome which has not been shared with native-born youth (not in Israel).

Migrant youth are also more likely to be in precarious and part-time jobs

The recent crisis has not only affected the level of employment and likelihood of joblessness of young migrants, but also the type of jobs they hold. Indeed, the incidence of temporary employment has increased for foreign-born youth in many OECD countries between 2008 and 2011 (Figure I.26). In some countries the rise has been substantial, for instance close to 15 percentage points in Greece and Finland, 11 percentage points in the Czech Republic, and 9 and 7 percentage points in Slovenia and Ireland respectively. In most of the countries in which the prevalence of temporary employment has increased, this has affected more foreign-born youth than the native-born. In Greece and Finland for instance, this rate has decreased or remained stable for the native-born and only in Ireland, Belgium and Italy the increase in temporary employment has been more pronounced among the native-born youth. In the majority of countries, the likelihood of temporary employment for young foreign-born has increased by more than that for foreign-born adults (25-54).

For some youth, temporary contracts may be a first – and possibly the only one – valuable labour market experience, the passport to a more stable permanent job. However, this is not the rule and many young persons find themselves trapped in a series of temporary jobs followed by short – or longer unemployment spells. This is more likely to be the case for foreign-born youth who start on average with substantial disadvantages relative to native youth in terms of human capital including language skills and access to social networks.

Figure I.26. **Changes in temporary employment by place of birth and age in selected OECD countries, 2008-11**
Percentage points

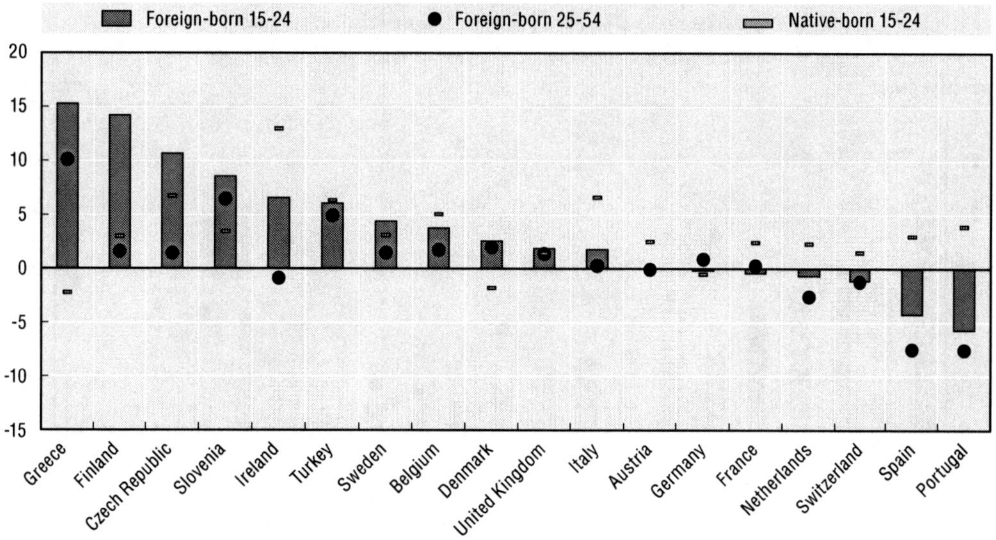

Legend: Foreign-born 15-24 (bars); Foreign-born 25-54 (dots); Native-born 15-24 (bars)

Countries (left to right): Greece, Finland, Czech Republic, Slovenia, Ireland, Turkey, Sweden, Belgium, Denmark, United Kingdom, Italy, Austria, Germany, France, Netherlands, Switzerland, Spain, Portugal.

Note: Data refer to changes between Q1-Q3 2008 and Q1-Q3 2011.
Sources: European Labour Force Surveys (Eurostat), Q1-Q3 2008 and Q1-Q3 2011.
StatLink http://dx.doi.org/10.1787/888932615479

In all OECD countries in Figure I.27, the share of part-time in total employment increased substantially between 2008 and 2011 both for natives and migrants (except for Germany for the first, Belgium for the latter and Israel for both). This can be closely linked to the use of short-time work schemes by many countries which allowed companies to retain their employees and hence mitigate the effects of the crisis on employment. In the countries with the greatest increase in the incidence of part-time employment (Ireland, the Netherlands, the United Kingdom, Portugal and Greece), foreign-born youth have been more affected than the natives. In some countries the rise has been substantial, for example 20 in Ireland, and about 13 percentage points in the Netherlands, the United Kingdom and Portugal, where part-time employment accounts for 34%, 48%, 29% and 22% of total migrant youth employment respectively.

Migrant youth of all education levels have experienced important employment losses over the crisis

Although, in the majority of OECD countries, the labour market performance of foreign-born youth of all skill levels has been heavily affected by the crisis, differences exist across countries.[7] In all OECD countries with available data except Belgium, Germany, Israel and the United Kingdom, the employment rates of low-skilled foreign-born youth dropped between 2008 and 2011 (Figure I.28). The greatest losses were experienced in Ireland, Spain, Estonia, Iceland and the United States, while in France and New Zealand the employment drop was substantially smaller (4 and 6 percentage points respectively). In contrast, in the United Kingdom, Germany, Belgium and Israel the employment rates of low-skilled foreign-born youth increased over the crisis.

The medium- and high-skilled foreign-born youth have not been spared the adverse consequences of the crisis. In fact, in Ireland, Spain, France and Luxembourg, better educated foreign-born youth (medium- and high-skilled) suffered greater employment

I. TRENDS IN INTERNATIONAL MIGRATION

Figure I.27. **Share of part-time employment (2011) and its evolution (2008-11), by place of birth for youth (15-24) in selected OECD countries**

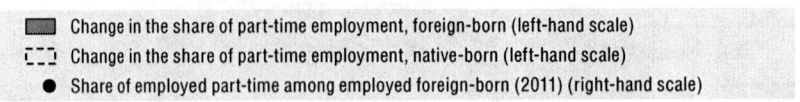

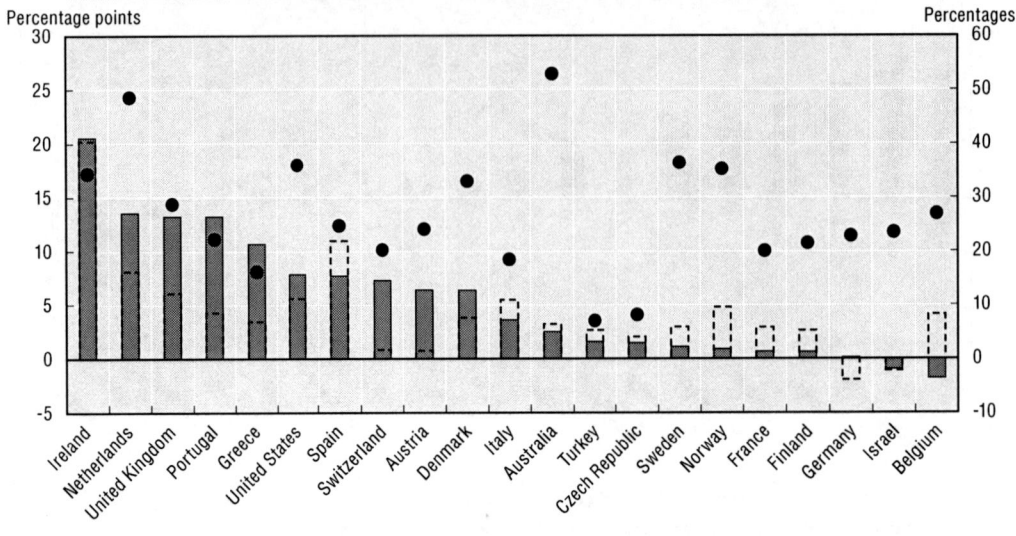

Notes: Changes in the share of part-time employment in total employment in Europe and in Israel refer to changes between Q1-Q3 2008 and Q1-Q3 2011. Information on data for Israel: http://dx.doi.org/10.1787/888932315602.

Sources: European Labour Force Surveys (Eurostat), Q1-Q3 2008 and Q1-Q3 2011; Australia, Israel: Labour Force Surveys; United States: Current Population Surveys. *StatLink* http://dx.doi.org/10.1787/888932615498

Figure I.28. **Changes in migrant youth (15-24) employment by education level in selected OECD countries, 2008-11**

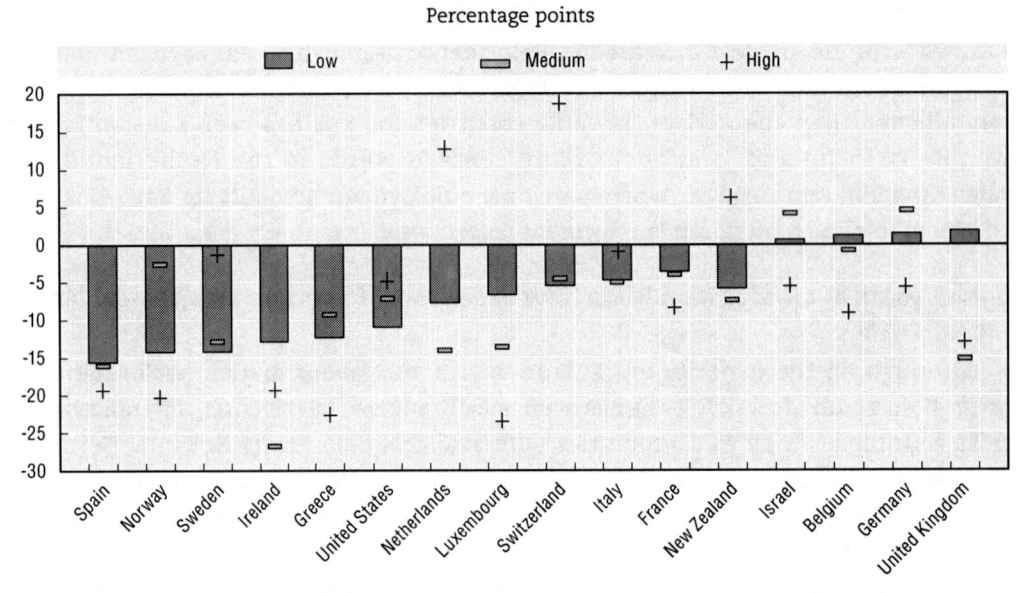

Percentage points

Notes: Data for European countries and Israel refer to changes between Q1-Q3 2008 and Q1-Q3 2011 (for each period, the number considered is the sum of the values for the three quarters). Data for the United States refer to changes between 2007 and 2011. Information on data for Israel: http://dx.doi.org/10.1787/888932315602.

Sources: European Labour Force Surveys (Eurostat); Israel, New-Zealand: Labour Force Surveys; United States: Current Population Surveys. *StatLink* http://dx.doi.org/10.1787/888932615517

losses than the low-skilled. Especially high-skilled young migrants in Luxembourg, Greece, Norway, Spain and Ireland have seen their employment rates decline by 19-23 percentage points between 2008 and 2011. This situation is not different from that of native-born skilled youth in these countries (except Luxembourg).

These trends have contributed in some countries to the narrowing of the existing employment gap between low-skilled and better educated young migrants. This is not a surprising finding given the availability of low-skilled foreign-born youth to work in jobs that better educated persons would not accept. Moreover, in some cases this trend can be explained by a delayed entry into the labour market for skilled migrants (see also Table I.11) or a return to the educational system for those with no other way of staying legally in the country. Overall, it is possible that the employment gap will increase again when economies will pick-up because skilled young migrants will be in a better position to benefit from the recovery whereas the effects of the crisis may be more long-lasting for their low-skilled counterparts.

5. Conclusion

OECD countries have reacted quickly to address the labour market adverse effects of the crisis by implementing various measures to help the unemployed and the most disadvantaged groups, including youth. To minimise the labour market losses for young persons, they have provided them with additional opportunities for education and training, but also valuable work experience i.e. through apprenticeship schemes. Providing quality job-search training is particularly important for foreign-born young jobseekers (and even more so for the low-skilled among them) who lack access to social networks and resources allowing them to search effectively for a job. However, meeting quality and quantity objectives in times of budget cuts may be complicated, as it may also be reaching out to the most disadvantaged migrant youth.

Although the economies in certain OECD countries have started to recover, the need for such measures targeting the youth is likely to continue. According to preliminary evidence (OECD, 2012) the employment situation for youth and low-skilled workers continued to deteriorate while that of other groups had stabilised or improved during the recovery. This is not surprising given the unusually large number of jobseekers with valuable skills and substantial labour-market experience who push young job-seekers at the back of the hiring queue. Adopting policies to support youth in finding and keeping a job is even more important for low-skilled foreign-born youth who accumulate various disadvantages (low skills levels, weak language skills, limited access to networks) who are at a higher risk of future unemployment and are more likely to experience reduced earnings in their lives (the so-called "scarring" effect). For this group of youth, additional measures may be needed.

Policies used by OECD countries range from specific measures targeting the children of immigrants (some of which are born abroad), those targeting young migrants (often not exclusively) to general active labour market policies which target all unemployed groups. Evidence suggests that measures to promote participation in early education for those arriving at a young age and language and integration courses for those arriving later, as well as measures to improve access to apprenticeships and training courses are necessary to improve the labour market outcomes of immigrants (OECD, 2010c). Furthermore, mentoring programmes have proved useful means for young migrants as they provide them with personalised information on the labour market and facilitate their access to business-related networks. OECD countries have made considerable efforts over recent years to improve the labour market integration of foreign-born youth. However, countries greatly hit by the jobs crisis, where greater efforts are needed, are also the least likely to implement them given their weak post-crisis economic performance and the substantial budget cuts they are implementing.

Notes

1. The statistical data for Israel are supplied by and under the responsibility of the relevant Israeli authorities. The use of such data by the OECD is without prejudice to the status of the Golan Heights, East Jerusalem and Israeli settlements in the West Bank under the terms of international law.
2. The distribution of migrant employment across sectors after the end of the crisis (in 2011) is presented in Table I.B4.2 in annex. Similarly to the situation prior to the crisis, the vast majority of foreign-born workers in the European countries of the OECD are employed in three main sectors: "other services" which excludes education, health and households, manufacturing and construction. The greatest increases in foreign-born employment over the past four years have occurred in construction in Ireland, Portugal, Spain, Greece and Denmark and this despite the fact that this sector has been severely hit by the recession in these countries.
3. Germany and Turkey were excluded because of a break in the series in 2008 and 2009 respectively, and Switzerland because quarterly data are only available since 2010.
4. Table I.B4.2 presents the distribution of migrant employment across sectors in 2011.
5. See Note 1.
6. See Note 1.
7. It has not been possible to analyse the evolution of unemployment over the crisis by country of birth, age and education level because of the small number of persons in some groups and countries.

References

OECD (2009), *International Migration Outlook*, OECD Publishing, Paris.

OECD (2010a), *International Migration Outlook*, OECD Publishing, Paris.

OECD (2010b), *Off to a Good Start? Jobs for Youth*, OECD Publishing, Paris.

OECD (2010c), *Equal Opportunities? The Labour Market Integration of the Children of Immigrants*, OECD Publishing, Paris.

OECD (2011a), *OECD Economic Outlook*, No. 90, OECD Publishing, Paris.

OECD (2011b), *OECD Employment Outlook*, OECD Publishing, Paris.

OECD (2011c), *International Migration Outlook*, OECD Publishing, Paris.

OECD (2012), "The role of policies for labour market resilience", EC Project Grant: VS2010/0617-SI576449, February 2012.

Scarpetta, S., A. Sonnet and T. Manfredi (2010), "Rising Youth Unemployment During The Crisis: How to Prevent Negative Long-term Consequences on a Generation?", *OECD Social, Employment and Migration Working Papers* No. 106, OECD Publishing.

ANNEX I.B1

Employment, unemployment and participations rates by gender and place of birth in selected OECD countries, 2008-11

I. TRENDS IN INTERNATIONAL MIGRATION

Table I.B1.1. **Quarterly employment rates by gender and place of birth in selected OECD countries, 2008-11**
Percentages

Men + women		AUS	AUT	BEL	CAN	CHE	CZE	DEU	DNK	ESP	EST	FIN	FRA	GBR	GRC	HUN	IRL	ISL	ISR	ITA	LUX	NLD	NOR	NZL	POL	PRT	SVK	SVN	SWE	TUR	USA
Native-born	2008 Q1	74.8	72.6	64.1	73.1	..	66.1	71.6	78.4	64.5	68.7	69.7	65.3	72.2	60.8	56.0	67.6	–	58.5	57.8	58.6	78.0	78.0	75.9	58.1	67.7	61.3	67.0	75.4	42.4	69.3
	2008 Q2	75.1	73.5	63.2	75.1	81.0	66.6	71.9	79.4	64.5	68.9	72.6	65.7	72.2	61.7	56.3	67.3	–	59.0	58.7	58.9	78.7	78.9	76.4	59.0	68.1	61.6	68.4	76.8	46.2	69.9
	2008 Q3	75.0	74.4	64.0	75.5	..	66.7	72.9	79.6	64.2	69.9	72.4	66.1	72.2	61.6	57.1	67.6	–	58.5	58.2	60.4	78.9	79.0	76.0	60.1	67.6	63.1	70.3	77.7	46.5	69.6
	2008 Q4	74.9	73.7	63.7	74.0	..	66.8	73.0	79.3	62.7	68.8	70.6	65.4	72.2	61.1	56.5	65.1	83.8	58.2	57.7	59.7	79.1	77.9	76.9	60.0	67.3	62.9	68.6	75.2	44.2	68.6
	2008	**75.0**	**73.6**	**63.8**	**74.4**	..	**66.6**	**72.4**	**79.2**	**64.0**	**69.1**	**71.3**	**65.6**	**72.1**	**61.3**	**56.5**	**66.9**	**83.8**	**58.5**	**58.1**	**59.4**	**78.7**	**78.5**	**76.3**	**59.3**	**67.7**	**62.2**	**68.6**	**76.3**	**44.8**	**69.4**
	2009 Q1	73.9	72.4	63.2	71.4	..	65.5	72.0	77.1	60.7	64.2	68.6	64.8	71.0	60.5	54.9	62.8	–	57.8	56.8	60.2	78.8	77.4	75.0	59.3	66.6	61.0	66.9	73.8	41.2	66.5
	2009 Q2	74.0	73.1	63.2	72.9	80.3	65.4	72.3	77.2	60.3	63.0	70.0	65.4	70.4	61.0	55.4	62.1	–	57.9	57.3	63.3	78.7	77.8	74.4	59.3	66.3	60.4	67.8	74.9	44.6	66.5
	2009 Q3	73.8	73.8	63.1	73.1	..	65.2	72.5	76.8	60.1	63.3	69.5	65.3	70.4	61.0	55.3	61.9	–	57.2	56.9	62.9	78.6	76.8	73.6	59.9	65.4	60.1	68.6	74.9	45.8	66.2
	2009 Q4	74.0	73.0	63.4	71.9	..	65.3	73.2	75.2	59.5	61.2	67.5	64.5	70.4	60.2	55.3	60.5	–	57.2	56.5	61.0	78.1	76.4	74.6	59.4	65.5	59.2	67.5	73.3	44.9	65.1
	2009	**73.9**	**73.1**	**63.2**	**72.3**	..	**65.4**	**72.5**	**76.6**	**60.1**	**62.9**	**68.9**	**65.0**	**70.5**	**60.7**	**55.2**	**61.8**	**78.4**	**57.5**	**56.9**	**61.9**	**78.6**	**77.1**	**74.4**	**59.4**	**66.0**	**60.2**	**67.7**	**74.2**	**44.1**	**66.1**
	2010 Q1	73.4	71.9	63.6	70.6	80.3	64.1	71.8	74.0	58.7	59.0	66.7	64.6	69.7	59.5	54.3	59.7	–	57.5	56.1	60.5	77.6	75.6	74.1	58.2	65.5	58.0	66.3	73.1	43.6	64.6
	2010 Q2	73.8	72.7	63.1	73.0	79.9	64.8	72.4	75.3	59.0	59.9	69.5	65.0	69.9	59.6	55.1	60.4	–	58.7	56.6	60.3	78.0	76.5	73.5	59.3	65.3	58.6	66.4	75.4	47.3	65.3
	2010 Q3	74.0	73.7	63.6	73.5	80.2	65.3	72.7	75.0	59.1	62.6	69.7	65.3	70.5	59.1	55.8	60.5	–	58.7	56.0	62.0	76.4	76.2	73.8	60.0	65.1	59.2	66.6	76.5	47.4	65.6
	2010 Q4	74.4	73.4	64.2	72.6	80.5	65.4	73.2	74.2	58.9	63.7	68.1	64.4	70.2	57.8	55.6	59.6	–	59.1	56.5	59.9	76.3	76.0	74.0	59.6	64.9	59.3	65.9	75.3	46.4	65.2
	2010	**73.9**	**72.9**	**63.6**	**72.4**	**80.3**	**64.9**	**72.5**	**74.7**	**58.9**	**61.3**	**68.5**	**64.7**	**70.1**	**59.0**	**55.2**	**60.1**	**78.5**	**58.5**	**56.3**	**60.7**	**76.2**	**76.1**	**73.8**	**59.3**	**65.2**	**58.8**	**66.3**	**75.1**	**46.2**	**65.2**
	2011 Q1	73.8	72.3	63.0	71.3	80.9	64.9	72.8	74.3	58.3	63.6	67.6	64.2	69.9	56.6	54.5	59.1	–	59.0	56.1	60.0	76.0	75.5	75.1	58.9	64.4	59.0	64.0	75.1	46.0	64.6
	2011 Q2	74.0	73.2	64.3	73.5	81.1	65.6	73.6	74.9	58.3	64.8	70.4	64.9	69.9	56.0	55.7	59.5	–	59.5	56.5	60.0	76.5	75.8	74.5	59.7	64.4	59.6	64.6	77.1	49.2	65.1
	2011 Q3	73.8	74.3	63.5	73.9	80.7	66.1	74.0	75.2	58.6	67.2	70.7	65.2	70.0	55.1	56.3	58.9	–	59.0	56.3	60.5	76.8	76.4	74.5	60.2	64.0	59.9	65.4	78.0	49.9	65.4
	2011 Q4	73.9	73.5	64.0	72.6	81.4	66.0	74.6	74.5	57.6	65.8	68.9	64.7	70.2	53.3	56.3	59.3	–	59.1	56.4	58.8	77.0	76.2	75.4	59.9	62.3	59.5	64.7	76.1	49.9	65.3
	2011	**73.9**	**73.3**	**63.7**	**72.8**	**90.9**	**65.7**	**73.8**	**74.7**	**58.4**	**65.3**	**69.4**	**64.8**	**70.0**	**55.2**	**55.7**	**59.2**	**78.7**	**59.2**	**56.3**	**59.5**	**76.0**	**76.0**	**75.0**	**59.7**	**63.8**	**59.5**	**64.7**	**76.6**	**48.4**	**65.1**
Foreign-born	2008 Q1	68.6	63.3	52.8	70.4	..	65.2	61.8	61.3	68.0	74.6	66.8	59.2	67.9	66.5	63.8	72.4	–	64.4	63.7	68.5	66.0	72.5	68.3	40.3	73.0	68.2	68.3	62.7	44.9	70.5
	2008 Q2	68.6	66.5	54.5	71.0	75.4	66.8	62.2	68.2	67.0	75.5	66.7	60.4	67.6	67.7	64.3	71.3	–	63.8	64.3	71.9	67.4	73.2	70.2	46.8	74.7	67.5	66.9	64.3	49.9	71.3
	2008 Q3	68.5	65.4	53.8	70.8	..	66.4	63.8	68.6	66.0	74.1	66.4	59.9	67.4	68.4	65.1	70.0	–	63.1	66.6	68.9	68.4	73.6	70.5	45.7	74.1	70.3	67.6	65.3	51.4	71.5
	2008 Q4	69.1	65.3	54.7	70.7	..	67.2	62.7	67.2	63.6	75.1	61.9	59.2	67.3	67.4	65.4	67.9	–	64.2	65.5	66.6	67.5	73.3	71.1	39.4	74.1	66.6	71.0	63.9	48.5	69.8
	2008	**68.7**	**65.1**	**54.0**	**70.7**	..	**66.4**	**62.6**	**66.3**	**66.1**	**74.8**	**65.4**	**59.7**	**67.6**	**67.5**	**64.7**	**70.4**	**81.4**	**63.8**	**65.1**	**69.0**	**67.5**	**73.2**	**70.0**	**43.5**	**74.0**	**68.1**	**68.4**	**64.0**	**48.8**	**70.8**
	2009 Q1	67.9	63.4	53.3	68.3	..	65.3	63.1	67.7	56.7	73.2	66.9	58.4	67.0	65.5	64.8	62.9	–	63.6	62.9	69.6	67.8	70.5	69.3	43.4	71.0	64.9	64.7	62.2	46.2	67.3
	2009 Q2	67.0	64.8	51.4	68.4	75.7	66.9	63.4	67.0	58.3	69.4	61.9	58.4	65.5	66.3	66.0	62.9	–	62.9	63.5	68.6	65.9	71.0	69.4	44.4	71.3	61.4	66.1	61.9	48.2	68.3
	2009 Q3	66.8	65.1	51.4	68.4	..	65.1	63.7	71.8	58.2	64.0	59.5	58.1	67.1	64.9	65.3	61.5	–	64.4	62.5	69.4	66.6	68.6	68.0	43.1	69.0	56.6	66.0	62.8	47.5	67.9
	2009 Q4	67.6	65.5	52.6	68.8	..	64.9	64.0	65.6	56.8	65.1	61.8	56.9	66.6	62.4	65.8	60.7	–	63.8	62.3	69.6	66.0	68.9	67.9	52.6	68.0	58.1	67.4	61.5	47.2	67.4
	2009	**67.3**	**64.7**	**52.2**	**68.5**	..	**65.8**	**63.5**	**68.1**	**58.0**	**67.8**	**63.8**	**57.8**	**66.6**	**66.0**	**65.5**	**62.0**	**77.2**	**63.7**	**62.8**	**69.3**	**66.6**	**70.2**	**68.6**	**45.7**	**69.8**	**60.6**	**66.1**	**62.1**	**47.2**	**67.7**
	2010 Q1	67.9	64.5	51.8	67.9	..	65.5	62.7	64.1	56.4	57.8	61.6	56.9	66.9	65.0	64.3	59.7	–	63.2	61.4	70.1	64.6	69.4	68.0	47.3	68.8	55.9	66.8	60.6	47.9	66.1
	2010 Q2	67.7	65.6	52.5	69.0	75.3	67.5	64.2	63.6	56.8	56.6	61.9	58.4	67.6	64.3	66.2	62.9	–	65.3	62.6	69.8	65.4	69.1	67.8	49.1	69.5	56.2	67.1	60.9	49.6	68.8
	2010 Q3	68.5	67.4	53.2	69.3	75.8	69.8	65.3	63.8	57.8	58.8	59.5	58.1	67.1	64.9	67.1	59.4	–	65.3	62.5	69.4	65.0	68.6	68.0	54.7	69.3	55.9	63.1	62.5	49.7	68.2
	2010 Q4	69.9	67.6	54.5	68.8	..	64.9	64.2	65.6	56.3	63.4	59.0	57.8	66.6	62.4	64.2	58.5	–	64.9	61.0	71.7	65.2	68.5	67.9	53.0	68.7	57.9	64.1	61.4	50.9	67.4
	2010	**68.5**	**66.3**	**53.0**	**68.8**	**74.6**	**68.1**	**64.1**	**63.4**	**56.8**	**59.2**	**60.5**	**57.7**	**66.2**	**64.0**	**65.5**	**59.5**	**74.8**	**64.7**	**61.9**	**70.7**	**64.4**	**68.9**	**68.3**	**50.7**	**69.1**	**56.5**	**65.3**	**61.3**	**49.5**	**67.6**
	2011 Q1	69.9	65.6	52.4	67.8	74.0	68.5	65.0	59.7	54.6	61.0	57.5	57.6	66.7	59.6	61.1	58.0	–	64.9	61.5	72.3	64.1	68.2	69.1	54.2	66.8	58.7	66.8	60.6	47.9	66.7
	2011 Q2	69.6	67.1	52.9	69.0	75.7	67.9	66.9	61.6	55.7	60.7	62.6	58.4	66.7	60.5	60.9	59.7	–	66.4	63.0	69.4	62.7	70.7	67.8	55.8	69.2	56.2	67.1	60.9	49.6	68.8
	2011 Q3	69.9	67.2	52.0	69.5	76.1	67.1	67.1	63.4	54.5	67.4	61.8	57.6	67.1	58.2	63.2	60.2	–	66.0	61.5	70.0	63.1	69.4	69.4	56.6	69.6	60.2	63.1	63.5	49.0	67.5
	2011 Q4	69.7	66.8	53.0	69.0	76.0	67.9	66.9	61.8	52.7	66.2	62.8	56.3	65.9	55.3	62.9	59.3	–	65.8	60.1	69.7	64.4	70.4	70.0	55.1	69.2	61.3	61.2	63.3	50.5	68.2
	2011	**69.8**	**66.7**	**52.6**	**68.8**	**75.5**	**67.8**	**66.5**	**61.7**	**54.4**	**63.9**	**61.1**	**57.4**	**66.5**	**58.4**	**62.1**	**59.3**	**76.3**	**65.8**	**61.5**	**70.3**	**63.6**	**70.2**	**69.5**	**55.3**	**68.7**	**59.7**	**61.9**	**62.6**	**49.7**	**67.5**

I. TRENDS IN INTERNATIONAL MIGRATION

Table I.B1.1. **Quarterly employment rates by gender and place of birth in selected OECD countries, 2008-11** (cont.)

Percentages

Men

		AUS	AUT	BEL	CAN	CHE	CZE	DEU	DNK	ESP	EST	FIN	FRA	GBR	GRC	HUN	IRL	ISL	ISR	ITA	LUX	NLD	NOR	NZL	POL	PRT	SVK	SVN	SWE	TUR	USA
Native-born	2008 Q1	80.7	78.2	69.5	75.2	..	74.9	76.0	81.6	74.8	73.1	71.2	69.3	77.3	73.7	62.3	75.2	–	62.4	68.8	66.3	83.6	80.2	81.6	65.0	73.6	68.9	71.0	77.2	64.1	73.3
	2008 Q2	80.8	79.3	68.7	77.6	86.1	75.2	76.4	83.0	74.4	72.3	74.8	69.9	77.3	74.4	63.0	74.6	–	63.1	70.0	68.5	84.3	81.4	81.8	66.0	73.7	69.2	72.6	78.4	68.0	74.3
	2008 Q3	80.8	80.2	69.5	79.0	..	75.7	77.1	83.5	73.9	72.8	74.7	70.2	77.4	74.2	63.7	74.7	–	62.8	69.5	69.8	84.3	81.6	80.9	67.3	73.3	70.8	74.5	79.3	68.6	73.9
	2008 Q4	80.6	79.0	69.1	76.3	..	75.8	77.2	82.4	71.3	72.3	72.2	69.6	76.8	73.6	62.4	71.4	87.5	61.7	68.7	68.3	84.4	80.2	82.2	67.1	73.1	70.8	72.1	76.8	65.6	72.1
	2008	**80.7**	**79.2**	**69.2**	**77.0**	..	**75.4**	**76.8**	**82.6**	**73.6**	**72.6**	**73.2**	**69.7**	**77.2**	**74.0**	**62.8**	**74.0**	–	**62.5**	**69.3**	**68.2**	**84.2**	**80.8**	**81.6**	**66.4**	**73.4**	**69.9**	**72.6**	**77.9**	**66.6**	**73.4**
	2009 Q1	79.0	76.5	68.4	72.3	..	74.2	76.0	79.5	68.7	65.0	69.2	68.8	75.5	72.6	60.5	67.4	–	60.6	67.6	67.3	83.8	79.0	80.1	65.7	71.7	68.6	69.8	75.1	61.6	69.3
	2009 Q2	78.7	77.7	67.8	74.5	84.5	73.9	76.1	79.4	67.9	62.8	70.6	69.2	74.6	73.1	61.3	66.3	–	60.9	68.1	71.1	83.9	79.8	80.1	66.1	71.2	68.0	71.4	76.0	64.8	69.5
	2009 Q3	78.6	78.6	67.9	75.8	..	73.7	76.6	79.1	67.5	65.4	70.6	69.1	74.6	73.1	61.0	66.0	–	60.4	67.9	70.0	83.6	78.7	78.1	66.9	70.2	67.4	71.9	76.3	66.7	69.8
	2009 Q4	78.9	78.2	68.5	73.4	..	73.6	76.9	77.3	66.6	60.8	67.9	68.2	74.6	72.0	60.8	64.2	–	59.8	67.3	68.4	82.8	77.8	79.6	65.9	70.0	66.1	71.1	74.8	65.5	68.0
	2009	**78.8**	**77.7**	**68.1**	**74.0**	..	**73.8**	**76.4**	**78.8**	**67.7**	**63.5**	**69.6**	**68.8**	**74.8**	**72.7**	**60.9**	**66.0**	**80.3**	**60.4**	**67.7**	**69.2**	**83.5**	**78.8**	**79.5**	**66.2**	**70.8**	**67.5**	**71.0**	**75.6**	**64.6**	**69.1**
	2010 Q1	78.6	76.0	68.3	71.4	85.2	72.2	75.8	75.3	65.5	56.7	67.2	68.1	73.6	71.1	59.0	63.2	–	60.6	66.8	67.6	82.0	77.2	79.2	64.3	70.0	64.3	69.8	74.4	63.7	67.0
	2010 Q2	79.0	78.0	68.3	74.8	85.1	73.3	76.5	76.6	65.9	58.7	70.4	68.5	74.3	70.9	60.2	64.1	–	62.0	67.0	67.6	82.4	78.1	78.5	65.5	69.6	65.2	68.9	76.9	67.8	68.5
	2010 Q3	79.3	78.8	68.6	76.4	85.1	74.1	77.0	77.5	66.0	65.1	71.4	68.9	75.2	70.3	61.0	64.4	–	62.0	66.4	70.5	81.4	78.2	79.4	66.6	69.7	65.5	70.3	78.2	68.3	69.2
	2010 Q4	79.9	78.7	68.7	74.5	85.6	73.9	77.4	77.2	65.1	66.0	69.1	68.3	74.7	68.6	60.7	63.0	–	61.5	66.7	67.7	81.1	77.8	79.2	66.2	69.5	65.7	69.3	76.6	67.2	68.2
	2010	**79.2**	**77.9**	**68.5**	**74.3**	**85.3**	**73.4**	**76.7**	**76.6**	**65.6**	**61.6**	**69.5**	**68.4**	**74.5**	**70.2**	**60.2**	**63.7**	**80.6**	**61.5**	**66.7**	**68.4**	**81.2**	**77.8**	**79.1**	**65.6**	**69.7**	**65.2**	**69.6**	**76.6**	**66.7**	**68.2**
	2011 Q1	79.2	76.8	67.5	72.6	85.6	73.4	76.7	76.5	64.6	65.7	68.8	68.1	74.2	67.0	59.5	62.6	–	61.6	66.3	67.5	80.6	76.8	81.0	65.1	68.6	65.5	67.2	76.4	66.7	67.2
	2011 Q2	79.1	78.4	69.1	75.5	85.5	74.0	77.5	77.0	64.8	66.6	72.0	68.7	74.2	66.6	61.0	62.9	–	62.8	66.6	65.6	80.9	77.3	80.7	66.4	68.4	66.4	67.3	78.5	69.9	68.4
	2011 Q3	78.5	79.4	67.4	77.1	86.0	74.4	78.0	77.7	64.8	69.7	72.1	69.0	74.4	65.4	61.8	62.8	–	63.0	66.7	66.0	81.4	78.0	81.0	67.3	68.5	66.7	68.5	79.3	71.3	69.2
	2011 Q4	78.9	78.8	68.7	74.7	86.0	74.2	78.7	77.0	63.3	67.7	70.1	68.2	74.5	63.0	61.8	63.0	–	62.0	66.2	64.4	81.5	78.0	81.0	66.7	66.1	66.4	67.5	77.5	..	68.8
	2011	**78.9**	**78.3**	**68.2**	**75.0**	**85.8**	**73.9**	**77.7**	**77.1**	**64.4**	**67.4**	**70.8**	**68.5**	**74.3**	**65.5**	**61.0**	**62.8**	**80.6**	**62.3**	**66.5**	**65.9**	**81.1**	**77.6**	**80.7**	**66.3**	**67.9**	**66.3**	**67.6**	**77.9**	**69.3**	**68.4**
Foreign-born	2008 Q1	77.6	71.0	63.1	77.1	..	77.4	70.8	70.0	76.6	84.8	71.3	67.7	78.2	84.3	73.8	80.5	–	70.0	80.2	76.9	75.1	76.2	78.4	46.9	80.2	74.5	74.6	67.9	61.5	81.3
	2008 Q2	77.0	77.2	65.3	77.9	83.6	79.6	71.5	76.6	74.6	83.3	73.1	68.9	77.8	85.7	71.9	79.5	–	69.1	79.5	78.6	76.4	78.0	78.9	54.0	81.2	74.0	72.8	70.1	70.0	82.7
	2008 Q3	76.5	75.9	62.1	78.4	..	77.3	72.9	77.5	72.3	78.6	73.1	69.4	77.1	86.1	72.6	78.3	–	68.5	82.8	76.2	77.6	77.1	78.2	54.8	81.0	77.0	73.0	71.8	69.0	83.5
	2008 Q4	76.8	75.4	67.0	77.9	..	75.9	71.5	76.0	68.9	74.4	67.4	68.5	77.7	84.0	73.1	76.1	85.3	69.8	80.8	71.8	76.8	75.4	79.2	47.2	79.6	75.9	75.8	69.9	65.7	80.5
	2008	**77.0**	**74.9**	**64.4**	**77.8**	..	**77.5**	**71.7**	**74.9**	**73.1**	**80.5**	**71.2**	**68.6**	**77.7**	**85.0**	**72.9**	**78.6**	–	**69.4**	**80.9**	**75.9**	**76.5**	**76.7**	**78.7**	**51.2**	**80.5**	**75.4**	**74.0**	**69.9**	**66.6**	**82.0**
	2009 Q1	75.5	70.0	62.1	73.8	..	73.9	71.5	73.3	62.6	75.6	68.6	66.2	76.9	80.3	75.6	69.5	–	69.2	77.8	76.4	76.1	72.6	77.2	46.2	76.1	75.7	67.9	66.8	59.8	76.7
	2009 Q2	74.7	72.4	61.3	73.6	84.1	74.2	71.1	70.0	61.8	74.9	67.9	65.4	74.6	80.9	75.7	68.8	–	69.0	77.9	79.0	74.5	75.2	76.8	52.9	75.7	71.6	71.4	66.3	63.3	78.8
	2009 Q3	74.8	74.1	61.7	74.0	..	74.8	72.3	76.8	60.7	63.3	68.5	65.9	75.2	81.3	71.2	66.7	–	69.2	77.5	78.8	74.8	74.0	74.8	53.8	73.5	67.7	71.3	67.5	62.4	77.8
	2009 Q4	75.6	73.4	60.4	74.1	..	75.4	71.9	74.0	59.4	61.0	65.7	64.6	73.7	79.3	73.0	65.8	–	67.8	76.0	78.2	73.7	74.0	75.3	66.2	73.7	73.7	72.7	66.1	62.6	76.6
	2009	**75.1**	**72.5**	**61.4**	**73.9**	..	**74.6**	**71.7**	**73.5**	**61.1**	**68.8**	**67.7**	**65.5**	**75.1**	**80.5**	**74.0**	**67.7**	**76.5**	**68.8**	**77.3**	**78.1**	**74.8**	**74.0**	**76.0**	**54.2**	**74.8**	**72.4**	**70.9**	**66.7**	**61.9**	**77.5**
	2010 Q1	76.7	70.7	58.7	72.6	82.7	73.9	71.5	72.1	58.5	55.3	66.3	64.9	72.9	77.6	69.4	64.8	–	67.0	74.5	78.3	71.3	73.0	75.9	60.1	73.5	75.7	71.2	65.9	61.5	75.2
	2010 Q2	76.2	73.3	61.6	75.6	84.5	78.9	72.7	66.0	60.0	57.6	68.6	67.0	74.6	80.9	67.9	66.3	–	69.0	76.4	79.0	74.5	73.4	75.1	60.8	75.0	74.3	70.5	66.8	64.3	78.8
	2010 Q3	76.7	75.0	62.1	75.7	84.0	81.3	74.2	65.3	61.5	59.7	68.5	67.3	76.1	77.4	69.0	65.1	–	70.5	78.1	79.7	74.8	72.3	75.5	55.4	74.8	74.9	69.9	68.3	62.6	78.7
	2010 Q4	78.2	75.1	63.4	75.4	83.0	80.5	73.3	67.6	60.1	70.4	65.1	66.4	76.1	75.3	70.3	63.8	–	69.4	75.3	80.1	73.2	72.3	76.6	60.1	73.7	73.8	69.4	68.0	62.6	76.8
	2010	**77.0**	**73.5**	**61.4**	**74.5**	**82.8**	**79.1**	**72.9**	**67.6**	**60.0**	**60.8**	**67.7**	**66.4**	**74.8**	**80.5**	**69.2**	**65.0**	**74.6**	**69.3**	**77.3**	**78.1**	**74.8**	**74.0**	**76.0**	**54.2**	**74.8**	**75.4**	**72.4**	**70.9**	**66.7**	**77.4**
	2011 Q1	78.7	72.4	60.9	73.7	82.4	80.7	74.0	63.2	58.2	68.0	64.3	65.6	75.6	77.6	67.0	62.3	–	68.9	74.4	80.5	70.5	73.0	75.9	59.6	69.4	71.6	74.8	65.9	61.5	75.2
	2011 Q2	77.8	76.1	60.4	75.6	84.5	80.5	75.8	66.4	58.6	64.6	68.1	66.2	75.8	71.8	67.9	64.3	–	71.6	77.7	77.3	69.8	74.5	77.4	58.7	71.0	75.2	74.3	66.8	64.3	78.8
	2011 Q3	78.2	76.4	61.9	76.0	85.4	79.7	75.8	67.7	57.7	73.4	66.6	66.1	75.7	70.2	75.2	65.7	–	71.6	76.3	79.4	71.1	75.1	77.0	63.6	71.5	76.0	74.9	69.3	67.1	78.4
	2011 Q4	77.8	75.0	62.1	75.2	84.6	80.0	76.6	67.0	56.3	72.1	68.2	66.4	75.1	66.0	72.1	64.7	–	71.1	73.8	78.6	71.9	73.6	77.9	69.9	71.0	70.6	73.8	68.5	65.4	78.6
	2011	**78.1**	**75.0**	**61.3**	**75.1**	**84.2**	**80.2**	**75.6**	**66.1**	**57.7**	**69.6**	**66.8**	**65.6**	**75.5**	**70.0**	**71.1**	**64.3**	**77.9**	**70.8**	**75.6**	**78.9**	**70.8**	**73.5**	**77.5**	**62.7**	**70.7**	**73.3**	**68.4**	**68.0**	**65.9**	**78.1**

Table I.B1.1. Quarterly employment rates by gender and place of birth in selected OECD countries, 2008-11 (cont.)
Percentages

Women

		AUS	AUT	BEL	CAN	CHE	CZE	DEU	DNK	ESP	EST	FIN	FRA	GBR	GRC	HUN	IRL	ISL	ISR	ITA	LUX	NLD	NOR	NZL	POL	PRT	SVK	SVN	SWE	TUR	USA
Native-born	2008 Q1	68.8	67.0	58.6	71.0	..	57.3	67.2	75.2	53.9	64.6	68.0	61.4	67.1	47.9	50.0	59.8	–	54.5	46.7	50.9	72.3	75.8	70.4	51.4	61.8	53.7	62.8	73.6	20.9	65.6
	2008 Q2	69.5	67.6	57.5	72.5	75.8	57.9	67.3	75.7	54.4	65.7	70.3	61.7	67.2	49.0	50.0	60.0	–	54.8	47.1	49.0	72.8	76.3	71.2	52.1	62.5	54.1	64.0	75.0	24.7	65.8
	2008 Q3	69.2	68.5	58.4	71.9	..	57.7	68.0	75.7	54.2	67.1	70.0	62.1	67.0	49.0	50.8	60.5	–	54.0	46.6	50.9	73.4	76.3	71.2	53.1	61.9	55.4	65.9	76.0	24.7	65.5
	2008 Q4	69.2	68.3	58.2	71.7	..	57.7	68.7	76.1	53.8	65.5	68.9	61.4	67.1	48.7	50.9	58.8	–	54.7	46.6	50.8	73.6	75.6	71.9	53.2	61.5	55.1	65.0	73.6	23.0	65.3
	2008	**69.2**	**67.9**	**58.2**	**71.8**	**..**	**57.6**	**67.8**	**75.7**	**54.1**	**65.7**	**69.3**	**61.7**	**67.1**	**48.6**	**50.4**	**59.8**	**79.8**	**54.5**	**46.8**	**50.4**	**73.0**	**76.0**	**71.2**	**52.4**	**62.0**	**54.6**	**64.4**	**74.5**	**23.3**	**65.5**
	2009 Q1	68.7	68.2	57.9	70.4	..	56.7	67.9	74.6	52.4	63.5	68.1	61.0	66.5	48.5	49.5	58.1	–	54.9	46.4	53.1	73.8	75.7	70.1	52.3	61.6	53.3	63.8	72.5	21.5	63.8
	2009 Q2	69.4	68.5	58.5	71.4	75.9	56.7	68.5	74.9	52.4	63.1	69.3	61.7	66.0	49.0	49.7	57.8	–	55.0	46.4	55.3	73.8	75.7	69.0	52.7	61.3	52.8	64.0	73.7	24.9	63.6
	2009 Q3	68.8	69.0	58.3	70.5	..	56.6	68.3	74.5	52.4	61.3	68.4	61.7	66.3	48.9	49.7	57.8	–	53.8	45.6	55.4	73.4	74.9	69.2	53.1	60.7	52.8	65.0	73.4	25.4	62.8
	2009 Q4	69.0	67.7	58.2	70.5	..	56.7	69.4	73.0	52.2	61.5	67.1	60.8	66.3	48.3	50.0	56.9	–	54.5	45.6	53.5	73.3	74.9	69.8	53.0	61.1	52.3	63.7	71.7	24.8	62.4
	2009	**69.0**	**68.4**	**58.2**	**70.7**	**..**	**56.7**	**68.5**	**74.3**	**52.3**	**62.4**	**68.2**	**61.3**	**66.3**	**48.7**	**49.7**	**57.6**	**76.4**	**54.5**	**45.9**	**54.4**	**73.5**	**75.3**	**69.5**	**52.8**	**61.2**	**52.8**	**64.1**	**72.8**	**24.2**	**63.2**
	2010 Q1	68.1	67.6	58.9	69.8	..	55.8	67.7	72.7	51.8	61.1	66.2	61.2	65.7	47.9	49.8	56.2	–	54.3	45.2	53.1	73.1	74.1	69.2	52.3	61.1	51.7	62.6	71.7	24.2	62.3
	2010 Q2	68.6	67.4	57.7	71.2	74.6	56.2	68.1	74.0	51.8	61.0	68.6	61.5	65.5	48.3	50.3	56.8	–	55.4	46.0	53.2	73.6	74.7	68.7	53.3	61.1	52.1	63.7	73.8	27.3	62.3
	2010 Q3	68.6	68.6	58.6	70.5	74.8	56.8	68.3	72.5	52.0	60.2	68.1	61.8	65.8	47.9	50.7	56.5	–	55.4	45.4	53.3	71.4	74.2	68.5	53.6	60.5	52.9	62.6	74.8	27.0	62.1
	2010 Q4	68.9	68.0	59.5	70.6	75.3	56.8	69.0	71.1	52.4	61.5	67.0	60.5	65.6	46.9	50.6	56.2	–	56.7	46.2	51.4	71.4	74.1	68.9	53.1	60.3	53.0	62.4	73.7	26.1	62.2
	2010	**68.5**	**67.9**	**58.7**	**70.5**	**75.1**	**56.3**	**68.3**	**72.6**	**52.0**	**61.0**	**67.5**	**61.1**	**65.7**	**47.8**	**50.4**	**56.4**	**76.4**	**55.5**	**45.7**	**52.8**	**71.1**	**74.3**	**68.8**	**53.1**	**60.8**	**52.4**	**62.8**	**73.5**	**26.1**	**62.2**
	2011 Q1	68.2	67.7	58.4	70.0	75.9	56.7	68.8	71.9	51.9	61.6	66.4	60.5	65.7	46.0	49.7	55.5	–	56.3	45.9	52.4	71.2	74.2	70.1	52.8	60.2	52.5	60.6	73.7	25.9	62.0
	2011 Q2	68.9	67.9	59.4	71.4	76.4	57.2	69.6	72.8	52.8	63.1	68.8	61.2	65.5	45.3	50.5	56.0	–	56.2	46.2	51.8	72.0	74.4	70.0	53.2	60.5	52.8	61.7	75.6	29.0	61.9
	2011 Q3	69.1	69.1	59.5	70.6	75.2	57.6	69.9	72.7	52.3	64.8	69.2	61.5	65.6	44.8	50.8	55.1	–	54.9	45.7	54.7	72.1	69.7	69.7	53.3	59.5	53.0	62.2	76.6	28.9	61.7
	2011 Q4	69.0	68.1	59.3	70.4	76.5	57.8	70.5	71.8	51.8	64.0	67.7	61.3	65.6	43.5	51.0	55.7	–	56.1	46.6	53.1	72.4	74.2	70.8	53.3	58.6	52.5	61.9	74.7	–	61.9
	2011	**68.8**	**68.2**	**59.1**	**70.6**	**76.0**	**57.3**	**69.7**	**72.3**	**52.2**	**63.4**	**68.0**	**61.1**	**65.7**	**44.9**	**50.5**	**55.6**	**76.9**	**55.9**	**46.1**	**53.0**	**71.9**	**74.3**	**70.1**	**53.1**	**59.7**	**52.7**	**61.6**	**75.1**	**27.9**	**61.9**
Foreign-born	2008 Q1	59.9	56.6	43.2	63.9	..	53.2	53.0	53.6	59.5	65.7	62.3	51.5	57.8	48.4	55.9	63.9	–	59.2	48.9	59.5	57.8	68.9	59.1	32.5	66.1	60.1	61.5	57.9	28.6	59.2
	2008 Q2	60.4	57.2	44.8	64.5	67.5	54.0	53.3	60.6	59.3	68.5	60.4	52.5	57.7	49.3	58.4	62.6	–	59.0	51.1	65.1	59.2	68.4	62.2	39.6	68.5	60.5	60.8	59.1	30.9	59.2
	2008 Q3	60.6	56.2	45.9	63.7	..	55.5	54.9	60.8	59.8	70.0	59.6	51.2	58.3	50.3	59.4	61.2	–	58.4	52.3	61.0	60.0	70.1	63.4	36.5	68.0	63.4	60.9	59.5	32.4	58.8
	2008 Q4	61.3	56.2	42.4	64.0	..	58.4	54.4	59.7	58.2	75.7	56.4	50.5	57.4	50.1	59.5	59.5	–	59.3	52.0	61.3	60.3	71.1	63.4	33.2	69.2	57.6	65.4	58.4	29.9	58.5
	2008	**60.6**	**56.6**	**44.1**	**64.0**	**..**	**55.4**	**53.9**	**58.6**	**59.2**	**70.0**	**59.6**	**51.4**	**57.8**	**49.5**	**58.3**	**61.8**	**77.4**	**59.0**	**51.1**	**61.8**	**59.3**	**69.7**	**62.0**	**35.8**	**68.0**	**60.3**	**62.1**	**58.7**	**30.5**	**58.9**
	2009 Q1	60.1	57.3	44.7	63.2	..	58.5	54.9	62.5	54.9	71.2	60.5	51.2	57.6	49.2	56.9	55.8	–	58.7	49.6	62.3	60.4	68.5	62.0	41.2	66.6	54.7	61.3	58.0	26.7	57.4
	2009 Q2	59.4	57.7	42.2	63.5	67.6	59.4	56.0	64.3	54.8	64.4	60.8	51.5	56.9	51.4	56.8	57.0	–	57.5	51.0	58.2	58.2	66.8	62.1	37.1	67.4	53.4	60.9	57.9	27.3	57.4
	2009 Q3	58.8	56.8	41.4	63.3	..	55.5	55.4	67.4	55.7	64.5	59.9	50.0	57.3	52.3	60.9	56.1	–	60.2	49.0	60.1	59.2	67.0	63.4	35.7	65.2	47.7	60.2	58.7	25.8	57.6
	2009 Q4	59.7	58.3	45.2	63.8	..	53.9	56.5	58.6	54.2	68.1	58.4	49.8	57.7	51.5	60.6	55.5	–	60.3	50.2	60.6	59.2	63.8	60.6	43.8	63.1	45.1	61.5	57.2	25.5	57.6
	2009	**59.5**	**57.5**	**43.4**	**63.4**	**..**	**56.8**	**55.7**	**63.2**	**54.9**	**67.0**	**59.8**	**50.6**	**57.4**	**51.1**	**59.2**	**56.1**	**75.0**	**59.2**	**50.2**	**60.3**	**59.3**	**66.5**	**61.5**	**39.4**	**65.6**	**50.6**	**61.0**	**58.0**	**26.4**	**57.4**
	2010 Q1	59.2	58.9	45.3	63.5	65.0	54.4	54.6	57.5	54.4	59.8	57.1	49.3	57.4	50.7	56.9	54.6	–	59.9	50.0	61.9	58.8	65.7	60.4	36.9	64.8	39.5	62.0	55.8	27.4	56.6
	2010 Q2	59.4	58.6	44.1	64.0	66.9	55.0	56.1	61.5	53.9	55.7	55.5	50.5	57.9	51.9	64.8	54.7	–	60.7	50.5	61.5	59.4	64.6	60.7	39.4	64.7	39.9	63.4	55.5	28.0	58.1
	2010 Q3	60.6	60.6	44.5	63.2	67.5	55.3	56.9	62.6	54.2	58.1	54.3	49.4	58.5	52.5	65.5	53.8	–	60.6	48.9	62.6	58.2	64.7	60.8	54.2	64.4	36.5	56.2	57.3	26.7	57.4
	2010 Q4	61.8	60.9	46.3	62.7	67.1	58.3	55.6	58.2	52.6	58.1	53.7	50.0	57.9	49.8	59.1	53.2	–	61.1	48.6	63.6	57.9	64.5	62.5	46.8	64.3	39.9	58.0	55.5	29.3	57.7
	2010	**60.3**	**59.8**	**45.0**	**63.3**	**66.6**	**56.2**	**55.7**	**60.0**	**53.8**	**58.0**	**55.1**	**49.7**	**58.0**	**51.2**	**62.4**	**54.1**	**75.0**	**60.5**	**49.5**	**62.4**	**57.8**	**64.8**	**61.1**	**43.7**	**64.5**	**38.9**	**59.8**	**56.0**	**27.8**	**57.4**
	2011 Q1	61.4	59.4	44.6	62.5	65.9	55.3	56.5	57.0	51.3	55.5	51.0	50.2	58.4	47.7	56.3	53.8	–	61.4	50.4	63.6	58.2	65.5	60.7	48.2	64.6	45.4	55.7	56.5	27.3	56.4
	2011 Q2	61.5	59.0	45.7	62.9	67.3	53.7	58.3	57.7	53.0	57.6	57.4	51.2	58.1	49.2	53.9	55.2	–	61.7	50.3	61.1	56.5	66.9	61.8	52.9	67.7	43.5	55.3	57.0	25.1	56.5
	2011 Q3	61.7	59.0	42.7	63.3	67.1	53.1	58.8	59.6	51.7	62.8	57.1	50.0	58.6	46.3	53.0	54.7	–	61.0	48.7	60.3	55.9	67.7	62.0	50.7	67.4	45.6	53.8	58.1	26.7	56.1
	2011 Q4	61.5	59.4	44.8	63.3	67.8	54.4	57.7	57.5	49.3	61.3	57.8	48.9	57.3	44.8	55.6	54.1	–	61.3	48.5	61.4	57.6	67.2	62.0	43.4	67.4	43.4	54.3	58.5	28.7	57.6
	2011	**61.6**	**59.2**	**44.4**	**63.0**	**67.0**	**54.1**	**57.8**	**58.0**	**51.3**	**59.4**	**55.8**	**50.1**	**58.1**	**47.0**	**54.7**	**54.5**	**74.9**	**61.4**	**49.4**	**61.4**	**57.0**	**66.8**	**61.6**	**48.5**	**66.8**	**46.9**	**54.3**	**57.5**	**27.0**	**56.7**

Notes: Data are not adjusted for seasonal variations. Comparisons should therefore be made for the same quarters of each year, and not for successive quarters within a given year. Information on data for Israel: http://dx.doi.org/10.1787/888932315602.
Sources: EU Labour Force Survey data (Eurostat); United States: Current Population Surveys; Australia, Canada, Israel, New Zealand: Labour Force surveys.

StatLink http://dx.doi.org/10.1787/888932616904

Table I.B1.2. Quarterly unemployment rates by gender and place of birth in selected OECD countries, 2008-11
Percentages

Men + Women

		AUS	AUT	BEL	CAN	CHE	CZE	DEU	DNK	ESP	EST	FIN	FRA	GBR	GRC	HUN	IRL	ISL	ISR	ITA	LUX	NLD	NOR	NZL	POL	PRT	SVK	SVN	SWE	TUR	USA
Native-born	2008 Q1	4.5	3.4	5.8	6.2	..	4.7	7.3	2.9	8.7	–	6.5	6.8	4.9	8.4	8.1	4.4	–	6.5	7.0	2.7	2.5	2.3	4.1	8.2	7.9	10.5	5.0	5.4	10.7	5.4
	2008 Q2	4.3	2.9	5.3	5.9	2.4	4.2	7.0	2.8	9.3	–	7.1	6.4	5.1	7.4	7.7	5.0	–	5.9	6.6	4.7	2.3	2.6	3.8	7.2	7.6	10.1	4.1	6.0	8.3	5.5
	2008 Q3	3.9	3.2	6.6	5.9	..	4.3	6.4	3.2	10.2	6.2	5.3	6.7	6.0	7.3	7.8	6.5	–	6.9	6.0	4.1	2.1	2.2	4.2	6.7	8.0	9.0	4.1	4.7	9.3	6.3
	2008 Q4	4.2	3.2	5.8	5.9	..	4.4	6.1	3.2	12.5	7.9	5.8	7.4	6.1	8.0	8.1	7.2	2.8	6.7	6.9	3.4	2.2	2.2	4.3	6.8	8.1	8.7	4.3	5.2	11.5	6.8
	2008	**4.2**	**3.2**	**5.9**	**6.0**	..	**4.4**	**6.7**	**3.0**	**10.2**	–	**6.2**	**6.8**	**5.5**	**7.8**	**7.9**	**5.8**	–	**6.5**	**6.6**	**3.7**	**2.3**	**2.3**	**4.1**	**7.2**	**7.9**	**9.6**	**4.4**	**5.3**	**9.9**	**6.0**
	2009 Q1	5.7	3.7	6.6	8.1	..	5.8	7.1	4.9	15.2	12.3	7.5	8.2	7.0	9.2	9.7	9.4	–	7.4	7.8	3.9	2.7	2.7	5.6	8.3	9.0	10.5	5.1	6.9	14.4	8.9
	2009 Q2	5.4	3.9	6.3	8.0	3.2	6.3	6.9	5.6	15.9	13.5	9.4	8.1	7.5	8.7	9.7	11.4	–	7.8	7.0	3.2	2.8	3.0	5.7	8.0	9.3	11.3	5.5	8.0	12.4	9.4
	2009 Q3	5.2	4.3	6.8	8.1	..	7.3	7.0	5.9	16.1	14.4	7.3	8.4	7.9	9.2	10.4	12.0	–	8.6	7.0	3.5	3.0	3.0	6.4	8.2	10.1	12.5	6.2	7.0	12.3	9.7
	2009 Q4	5.1	3.8	6.8	7.4	..	7.3	6.4	6.4	16.7	15.6	8.0	9.1	7.5	10.1	10.6	11.9	–	8.1	8.2	2.7	3.3	2.5	6.6	8.6	10.4	13.9	6.7	7.1	11.9	9.7
	2009	**5.3**	**3.9**	**6.6**	**7.9**	..	**6.7**	**6.9**	**5.7**	**16.0**	**14.0**	**8.0**	**8.5**	**7.5**	**9.3**	**10.1**	**11.2**	**7.0**	**8.0**	**7.5**	**3.3**	**2.9**	**2.8**	**6.0**	**8.3**	**9.7**	**12.1**	**5.9**	**7.2**	**12.8**	**9.4**
	2010 Q1	5.8	3.9	7.1	8.4	3.5	8.1	7.2	7.4	17.9	20.1	9.1	9.0	7.9	11.4	11.9	12.5	–	7.3	8.8	2.6	3.9	3.2	6.5	10.7	10.9	15.2	7.0	8.0	13.2	10.5
	2010 Q2	5.3	3.6	6.7	7.6	3.1	7.2	6.3	6.6	18.1	18.3	9.3	8.3	7.6	11.5	11.3	13.3	–	6.4	8.0	2.7	3.7	3.3	6.5	9.6	10.9	14.4	7.0	8.0	10.0	9.9
	2010 Q3	5.0	3.8	7.0	7.7	3.7	7.2	6.1	6.6	17.9	14.0	6.9	8.4	7.9	12.2	11.0	13.3	–	7.7	7.4	2.7	3.8	2.9	6.3	9.2	11.2	14.2	7.0	6.4	10.3	9.8
	2010 Q4	4.9	3.4	6.6	6.8	3.1	7.0	5.8	6.9	18.4	13.2	7.2	8.8	7.7	14.0	11.0	13.4	–	6.8	8.3	4.0	3.8	2.7	6.7	9.4	11.2	13.9	7.7	5.9	9.9	9.2
	2010	**5.3**	**3.7**	**6.9**	**7.6**	**3.3**	**7.4**	**6.3**	**6.9**	**18.1**	**16.4**	**8.1**	**8.7**	**7.8**	**12.3**	**11.3**	**13.1**	**7.2**	**7.1**	**8.1**	**3.0**	**4.0**	**3.0**	**6.5**	**9.7**	**11.0**	**14.4**	**7.2**	**7.1**	**10.8**	**9.9**
	2011 Q1	5.6	3.6	5.9	7.9	3.2	7.3	6.1	7.3	19.2	14.1	8.4	8.7	7.7	15.5	11.7	13.7	–	5.9	8.3	3.5	3.9	2.7	5.5	10.2	12.3	13.9	8.1	6.6	10.5	9.6
	2011 Q2	5.0	3.4	5.1	7.2	2.7	6.8	5.3	6.6	18.8	12.8	8.7	8.0	7.8	16.2	10.9	14.1	–	5.5	7.4	2.8	3.5	3.0	5.3	9.6	12.3	13.2	7.5	6.8	8.6	9.2
	2011 Q3	5.1	3.1	6.5	7.0	3.4	6.6	5.2	6.8	19.4	10.6	6.5	8.3	8.4	17.5	10.8	14.7	–	6.8	7.4	3.4	3.6	2.7	5.4	9.5	12.7	13.2	7.7	5.3	8.4	9.4
	2011 Q4	5.1	3.4	5.8	6.5	3.0	6.5	4.8	6.8	20.6	11.1	6.6	8.9	8.1	20.3	10.8	14.0	–	5.9	9.0	4.0	4.1	2.5	5.4	9.9	14.5	14.0	8.6	5.5	..	8.5
	2011	**5.2**	**3.4**	**5.8**	**7.2**	**3.1**	**6.8**	**5.4**	**6.9**	**19.5**	**12.1**	**7.6**	**8.5**	**8.0**	**17.4**	**11.1**	**14.1**	**6.7**	**6.0**	**8.0**	**3.4**	**3.8**	**2.7**	**5.4**	**9.8**	**13.0**	**13.6**	**8.0**	**6.0**	**9.2**	**9.2**
Foreign-born	2008 Q1	4.6	8.5	15.6	7.1	..	8.1	13.4	9.3	14.1	5.0	12.7	12.4	7.1	8.3	5.2	5.8	–	4.8	9.0	6.2	6.9	5.0	5.3	–	9.5	–	6.5	12.1	10.4	5.8
	2008 Q2	4.6	6.6	13.8	7.1	6.2	6.8	12.3	6.2	15.7	4.6	13.2	11.1	6.7	7.2	6.0	6.8	–	5.5	8.7	5.4	6.4	4.7	4.3	–	8.6	–	5.7	12.8	7.4	5.2
	2008 Q3	4.7	7.0	15.6	7.5	..	6.7	11.5	5.6	16.7	6.7	12.4	11.6	7.1	6.8	5.6	8.4	–	5.8	7.3	7.2	4.3	5.7	4.4	–	9.8	–	4.5	11.5	6.4	5.7
	2008 Q4	4.6	8.1	13.3	7.1	..	6.4	12.1	7.3	20.3	7.6	13.3	12.1	7.4	8.8	7.4	9.2	4.7	5.9	8.9	7.7	5.7	5.8	5.4	–	9.9	–	4.3	12.3	11.5	6.7
	2008	**4.6**	**7.5**	**14.6**	**7.2**	..	**7.0**	**12.3**	**7.1**	**16.7**	**6.0**	**12.9**	**11.8**	**7.1**	**7.8**	**6.1**	**7.5**	**4.7**	**5.5**	**8.5**	**6.6**	**5.8**	**5.3**	**4.8**	–	**9.5**	–	**5.3**	**12.2**	**8.8**	**5.9**
	2009 Q1	6.6	10.0	16.2	9.7	..	8.5	13.2	9.1	27.1	8.1	14.0	13.9	7.9	12.0	9.2	14.2	–	7.0	10.6	7.7	6.3	6.9	6.4	–	12.6	–	8.6	14.3	16.8	9.8
	2009 Q2	7.1	9.2	15.3	10.6	6.9	9.5	13.0	10.1	26.9	14.2	17.2	13.8	9.0	11.4	8.9	15.2	–	7.7	10.7	7.3	7.2	7.1	6.9	–	12.4	–	7.5	16.7	13.8	9.1
	2009 Q3	6.8	9.5	17.4	10.8	..	10.3	13.0	8.8	26.5	18.6	14.9	14.0	9.7	11.4	10.1	16.6	–	6.6	10.4	5.6	6.6	5.9	6.8	–	13.9	–	8.1	15.0	16.1	10.0
	2009 Q4	6.2	9.5	16.0	9.7	..	10.0	12.2	11.5	28.3	17.8	15.6	15.2	9.3	13.2	8.2	15.8	–	6.8	12.3	8.1	7.3	7.3	8.3	–	13.6	–	5.5	15.5	14.1	10.0
	2009	**6.7**	**9.5**	**16.2**	**10.2**	..	**9.6**	**12.8**	**9.9**	**27.2**	**14.8**	**15.4**	**14.3**	**8.9**	**12.0**	**9.1**	**15.4**	**11.8**	**7.0**	**11.0**	**7.1**	**6.8**	**6.8**	**7.1**	–	**13.1**	–	**7.4**	**15.4**	**15.1**	**9.7**
	2010 Q1	6.2	9.2	18.0	10.2	9.8	8.3	13.0	13.4	29.6	22.6	16.8	15.5	9.1	15.7	9.5	15.5	–	6.5	12.6	7.3	8.7	8.6	6.4	–	14.4	–	9.7	16.2	16.8	11.4
	2010 Q2	5.7	8.6	15.3	10.2	7.4	9.5	11.6	14.8	29.1	25.5	18.7	14.4	9.2	17.1	8.9	16.2	–	5.2	11.5	5.6	7.7	9.1	6.9	–	13.9	–	9.6	17.4	13.8	8.7
	2010 Q3	5.2	7.7	17.9	10.5	7.4	6.6	10.7	13.9	28.3	26.0	17.8	14.3	8.9	15.4	10.1	17.3	–	6.4	9.7	5.4	7.9	8.5	6.8	–	14.6	–	8.9	15.0	16.1	10.0
	2010 Q4	5.1	7.4	15.5	8.9	7.1	6.3	11.3	12.2	29.3	17.3	15.5	15.1	8.4	17.9	6.1	18.1	11.8	6.4	12.2	5.1	7.8	8.0	7.0	–	16.9	–	10.1	15.7	14.1	10.0
	2010	**5.6**	**8.2**	**17.1**	**10.0**	**7.9**	**7.2**	**11.6**	**13.6**	**29.1**	**22.8**	**17.2**	**14.8**	**8.9**	**16.2**	**9.1**	**16.8**	**13.4**	**6.1**	**11.5**	**5.8**	**8.5**	**8.5**	**7.1**	**11.6**	**15.0**	**11.8**	**9.6**	**16.3**	**15.1**	**9.8**
	2011 Q1	5.5	9.4	14.6	9.3	7.7	7.3	10.4	15.7	30.9	19.1	17.1	15.7	8.7	21.2	9.3	17.6	–	5.5	11.8	6.9	9.2	8.3	6.5	–	19.2	–	13.2	16.9	15.1	10.1
	2011 Q2	5.3	7.8	15.5	8.7	6.1	8.1	9.5	14.4	30.5	19.5	14.1	14.4	9.0	19.5	10.5	17.2	–	4.8	10.8	7.6	9.3	8.4	5.9	15.0	16.7	–	10.9	17.0	13.3	8.7
	2011 Q3	5.1	6.8	15.6	9.1	6.5	8.8	9.1	14.1	31.3	15.0	15.1	14.6	9.7	21.9	9.3	17.0	–	5.0	10.1	5.3	9.0	6.6	5.8	15.0	15.9	–	10.3	15.3	9.8	9.0
	2011 Q4	4.9	8.6	14.8	8.7	6.9	7.7	9.0	13.8	33.4	14.5	14.4	15.8	10.0	26.3	8.7	17.2	11.1	4.9	13.9	5.4	9.1	7.4	6.4	15.3	16.0	15.3	11.2	14.8	9.7	8.7
	2011	**5.2**	**8.2**	**15.1**	**8.9**	**6.8**	**8.0**	**9.5**	**14.5**	**31.5**	**16.9**	**15.2**	**15.1**	**9.4**	**22.2**	**9.5**	**17.3**	**11.1**	**5.0**	**11.7**	**6.3**	**9.2**	**7.7**	**6.2**	**12.1**	**16.9**	**15.3**	**11.5**	**16.0**	**11.1**	**9.1**

I. TRENDS IN INTERNATIONAL MIGRATION

Table I.B1.2. **Quarterly unemployment rates by gender and place of birth in selected OECD countries, 2008-11** (cont.)
Percentages

Men

		AUS	AUT	BEL	CAN	CHE	CZE	DEU	DNK	ESP	EST	FIN	FRA	GBR	GRC	HUN	IRL	ISL	ISR	ITA	LUX	NLD	NOR	NZL	POL	PRT	SVK	SVN	SWE	TUR	USA
Native-born	2008 Q1	4.2	3.3	5.3	7.2	..	3.7	7.4	2.7	7.0	3.9	6.3	6.4	5.4	5.7	7.8	5.3	–	5.9	5.8	2.3	2.4	2.5	3.9	7.7	6.8	9.2	4.7	5.1	10.7	5.9
	2008 Q2	4.1	2.6	4.9	6.6	2.1	3.5	6.9	2.3	7.9	4.7	6.9	5.8	5.6	4.8	7.5	6.2	–	5.3	5.4	3.9	2.1	2.7	4.0	6.6	6.6	9.1	3.4	5.8	8.3	5.7
	2008 Q3	3.6	2.9	5.7	5.9	..	3.3	6.0	2.6	9.0	7.1	4.8	6.2	6.6	4.8	7.5	7.5	–	6.0	5.0	2.4	2.0	2.3	4.6	5.8	6.8	7.7	4.0	4.5	8.9	6.5
	2008 Q4	4.2	2.8	5.1	6.7	..	3.4	6.1	3.3	11.3	8.3	5.7	6.8	6.9	5.3	8.1	9.1	3.1	6.2	6.1	1.3	2.0	2.2	4.4	6.1	7.1	7.7	4.0	5.1	11.4	7.5
	2008	**4.0**	**2.9**	**5.3**	**6.6**	..	**3.5**	**6.6**	**2.7**	**8.8**	**6.0**	**5.9**	**6.3**	**6.1**	**5.2**	**7.7**	**7.0**	**3.1**	**5.8**	**5.6**	**2.5**	**2.1**	**2.4**	**4.3**	**6.5**	**6.8**	**8.4**	**4.0**	**5.1**	**9.8**	**6.4**
	2009 Q1	5.8	3.8	6.3	10.1	..	5.0	7.5	5.7	14.3	15.1	8.3	8.0	8.0	6.5	10.1	12.3	–	7.0	6.7	4.3	2.7	3.0	5.5	7.8	8.3	9.7	5.2	7.1	14.6	10.6
	2009 Q2	5.8	3.8	6.3	9.6	3.0	5.5	7.2	6.2	15.0	17.9	10.3	7.8	8.9	6.0	10.0	14.7	–	7.9	6.2	2.6	2.7	3.1	5.4	7.6	8.9	10.5	5.4	8.2	12.5	10.8
	2009 Q3	5.5	4.2	6.2	8.6	..	6.4	7.3	6.5	15.3	16.7	7.5	7.8	9.1	6.3	10.6	15.1	–	8.2	6.2	2.7	2.9	3.1	6.5	7.7	9.2	11.9	6.4	7.3	12.0	10.4
	2009 Q4	5.4	3.9	6.7	8.8	..	6.5	6.7	7.1	15.9	19.6	8.7	9.0	8.7	7.3	10.8	15.3	–	8.2	7.2	2.7	3.3	2.9	6.7	8.3	9.8	13.5	6.6	7.5	12.0	11.0
	2009	**5.6**	**3.9**	**6.4**	**9.3**	..	**5.9**	**7.2**	**6.4**	**15.1**	**17.3**	**8.7**	**8.2**	**8.7**	**6.5**	**10.4**	**14.4**	**8.3**	**7.8**	**6.6**	**3.0**	**2.9**	**3.1**	**6.0**	**7.9**	**9.0**	**11.4**	**5.9**	**7.5**	**12.7**	**10.7**
	2010 Q1	6.0	4.2	6.7	10.3	3.1	7.6	7.8	9.1	17.3	25.9	10.4	9.1	9.3	8.5	12.7	16.2	–	7.5	7.9	2.8	3.9	3.7	6.1	10.6	10.2	15.1	7.2	8.5	13.2	12.4
	2010 Q2	5.4	3.7	6.6	8.8	3.2	6.3	6.7	7.9	17.2	22.7	10.0	8.2	8.6	8.7	11.9	16.7	–	6.5	7.4	4.7	3.7	4.0	6.4	9.4	10.2	14.2	7.4	8.4	9.7	11.0
	2010 Q3	4.9	3.9	6.8	7.7	2.9	6.1	6.4	6.7	17.1	14.7	7.2	8.1	8.6	9.2	11.1	16.5	–	7.3	6.7	1.9	3.8	3.1	5.6	8.7	10.0	14.0	7.2	6.6	9.8	10.3
	2010 Q4	4.8	3.3	6.5	7.5	2.9	6.0	6.0	7.2	17.7	14.3	7.8	8.4	8.6	11.1	11.2	16.9	–	6.6	7.5	2.7	3.6	3.1	6.5	9.0	10.3	13.9	7.9	6.1	9.4	10.1
	2010	**5.3**	**3.8**	**6.7**	**8.6**	**3.1**	**6.5**	**6.7**	**7.7**	**17.3**	**19.4**	**8.8**	**8.4**	**8.7**	**9.4**	**11.7**	**16.6**	**7.9**	**7.0**	**7.4**	**2.5**	**3.9**	**3.5**	**6.2**	**9.4**	**10.2**	**14.3**	**7.4**	**7.4**	**10.5**	**10.9**
	2011 Q1	5.4	3.6	5.9	9.2	3.0	6.5	6.6	7.9	18.5	15.7	9.1	8.3	8.6	12.7	12.2	17.1	–	6.3	7.7	1.6	3.9	3.0	4.9	10.1	12.0	14.0	8.3	6.5	10.2	10.9
	2011 Q2	5.0	3.3	4.8	8.0	2.7	5.9	5.7	7.2	18.3	13.7	9.3	7.6	8.5	13.2	10.9	17.6	–	5.6	6.9	2.8	3.6	2.6	4.8	9.1	12.1	13.5	8.0	6.8	8.2	9.8
	2011 Q3	5.3	3.1	6.3	7.0	3.0	5.6	5.3	6.7	18.6	10.4	6.9	7.8	9.2	14.5	10.7	17.7	–	5.9	6.6	3.6	3.6	2.6	5.0	8.4	12.2	13.1	8.1	5.5	7.5	9.5
	2011 Q4	5.1	3.0	5.7	7.2	2.7	5.6	4.9	6.8	20.0	12.5	7.5	8.7	8.8	17.2	10.7	17.4	–	5.4	8.4	3.8	4.0	2.8	5.3	9.0	14.6	13.8	8.4	5.6	..	9.0
	2011	**5.2**	**3.3**	**5.7**	**7.8**	**2.8**	**5.9**	**5.6**	**7.2**	**18.8**	**13.1**	**8.2**	**8.1**	**8.8**	**14.4**	**11.1**	**17.5**	**7.6**	**5.8**	**7.4**	**3.0**	**3.8**	**2.9**	**5.0**	**9.1**	**12.7**	**13.6**	**8.2**	**6.1**	**8.6**	**9.8**
Foreign-born	2008 Q1	4.1	8.8	15.9	6.8	..	5.7	13.7	7.8	12.5	–	13.1	12.5	6.7	5.0	4.3	6.3	–	5.0	6.1	2.6	6.2	4.7	4.4	–	6.9	–	6.3	11.7	9.8	5.9
	2008 Q2	4.1	6.1	13.7	7.1	..	4.0	12.0	4.5	14.8	–	14.4	11.0	6.8	4.3	7.7	7.1	–	6.2	6.0	4.7	5.9	5.6	3.7	–	7.5	–	5.0	11.9	6.0	4.8
	2008 Q3	4.4	6.5	16.8	7.0	..	3.4	11.2	5.4	17.2	–	9.5	10.6	6.8	4.3	5.6	8.9	–	5.8	5.0	8.0	3.8	6.1	3.9	–	7.7	–	3.6	10.6	7.2	5.3
	2008 Q4	4.1	7.9	11.2	6.7	..	5.0	12.2	7.9	20.8	–	12.5	11.4	7.0	6.3	7.4	10.6	–	6.0	6.6	10.4	5.5	7.4	4.8	–	8.9	–	4.1	11.9	11.5	6.9
	2008	**4.2**	**7.3**	**14.3**	**6.9**	..	**4.5**	**12.3**	**6.4**	**16.4**	–	**12.4**	**11.4**	**6.8**	**5.0**	**6.3**	**8.2**	**6.0**	**5.8**	**5.9**	**6.4**	**5.3**	**6.0**	**4.2**	–	**7.8**	–	**4.7**	**11.5**	**8.6**	**5.7**
	2009 Q1	6.3	11.6	15.9	10.4	..	7.8	13.6	8.8	29.1	–	12.1	13.7	7.8	10.3	7.4	16.2	–	7.3	8.9	6.0	6.3	9.9	6.6	–	11.6	–	10.1	14.7	16.5	10.4
	2009 Q2	7.3	10.6	15.4	11.3	6.2	9.6	14.3	10.2	29.5	13.1	19.9	14.1	8.9	9.8	8.0	18.2	–	8.0	8.9	6.2	7.5	7.3	6.9	–	12.6	–	8.9	18.0	13.8	9.3
	2009 Q3	6.6	10.1	17.0	11.1	..	8.2	13.2	9.9	29.3	23.0	15.7	13.5	10.0	9.8	10.6	19.2	–	6.8	9.4	4.9	7.1	7.8	7.2	–	14.9	–	6.3	16.2	16.0	10.2
	2009 Q4	5.9	10.5	17.0	10.0	..	8.2	13.3	11.2	31.4	26.5	16.1	15.4	8.9	11.5	8.6	19.3	14.8	7.9	10.4	6.4	8.0	8.8	8.0	–	13.8	–	5.1	16.0	12.7	10.6
	2009	**6.5**	**10.7**	**16.3**	**10.7**	..	**8.5**	**13.6**	**10.0**	**29.8**	**17.7**	**16.1**	**14.2**	**8.9**	**10.4**	**8.6**	**18.2**	**14.8**	**7.5**	**9.4**	**5.9**	**7.2**	**8.5**	**7.2**	–	**13.2**	–	**7.5**	**16.2**	**14.7**	**10.1**
	2010 Q1	5.7	10.6	18.6	10.7	7.4	7.1	14.3	14.9	32.5	26.5	17.3	14.7	9.4	14.2	9.1	19.1	–	7.7	11.2	6.5	9.4	9.5	7.1	–	12.9	–	10.6	16.3	14.6	12.1
	2010 Q2	5.2	9.2	17.1	10.5	9.8	5.4	12.1	17.8	31.4	26.2	19.7	14.1	9.4	15.2	8.2	18.5	–	5.9	10.0	5.7	8.1	10.3	8.5	–	10.9	–	9.7	16.8	14.2	8.8
	2010 Q3	5.0	8.4	16.9	10.0	6.3	4.6	11.4	15.0	29.8	26.8	19.8	13.5	8.7	14.9	6.8	20.0	–	7.2	8.0	3.8	7.1	9.7	6.5	–	12.0	–	7.5	15.3	9.5	9.0
	2010 Q4	4.5	7.1	15.0	8.7	6.4	5.0	11.7	12.4	30.7	15.5	16.7	13.0	8.9	16.6	6.4	21.0	–	6.7	11.0	4.7	8.3	9.6	6.7	–	14.9	–	9.7	15.1	11.1	10.0
	2010	**5.1**	**8.8**	**16.9**	**10.0**	**7.2**	**5.6**	**12.4**	**15.1**	**31.1**	**23.6**	**18.4**	**13.7**	**8.8**	**15.2**	**7.6**	**19.7**	**16.5**	**6.9**	**10.0**	**5.2**	**8.8**	**9.8**	**7.2**	**12.1**	**12.7**	**8.9**	**9.4**	**15.9**	**12.4**	**10.0**
	2011 Q1	4.7	10.2	16.0	9.1	7.3	4.4	10.9	16.3	31.9	16.0	17.2	14.4	8.6	19.7	10.5	20.9	–	6.2	10.4	4.8	9.8	9.2	5.6	–	12.9	–	13.0	16.9	14.6	10.4
	2011 Q2	4.6	7.9	15.0	8.2	5.9	6.5	9.8	12.9	31.8	19.0	15.7	13.9	9.0	19.4	9.7	20.0	–	5.1	8.2	5.9	8.1	9.3	5.7	–	10.9	–	8.8	16.8	14.2	8.4
	2011 Q3	4.5	6.0	15.0	8.3	5.3	7.4	9.3	13.1	33.1	13.6	16.4	13.7	9.3	21.3	8.5	19.2	–	5.8	8.4	3.5	9.4	6.8	5.2	–	12.0	–	8.2	15.0	9.0	8.2
	2011 Q4	4.6	7.9	14.9	8.0	6.2	6.2	9.0	13.2	34.6	14.3	14.7	14.7	9.5	25.9	7.1	19.2	–	5.1	11.9	4.7	9.5	7.8	5.8	–	14.9	–	9.7	15.4	9.2	8.4
	2011	**4.6**	**8.0**	**15.5**	**8.4**	**6.2**	**6.1**	**9.7**	**13.8**	**32.9**	**15.6**	**16.0**	**14.2**	**9.1**	**21.5**	**8.9**	**19.8**	**11.7**	**5.6**	**9.7**	**4.7**	**9.7**	**8.3**	**5.6**	**9.9**	**18.0**	**11.1**	**9.7**	**16.0**	**10.3**	**8.9**

I. TRENDS IN INTERNATIONAL MIGRATION

Table I.B1.2. **Quarterly unemployment rates by gender and place of birth in selected OECD countries, 2008-11** (cont.)

Percentages

Women

		AUS	AUT	BEL	CAN	CHE	CZE	DEU	DNK	ESP	EST	FIN	FRA	GBR	GRC	HUN	IRL	ISL	ISR	ITA	LUX	NLD	NOR	NZL	POL	PRT	SVK	SVN	SWE	TUR	USA
Native-born	2008 Q1	4.9	3.5	6.5	5.0	..	5.9	7.2	3.2	11.1	4.3	6.7	7.2	4.3	12.3	8.4	3.3	–	7.1	8.6	3.1	2.7	2.0	4.3	8.8	9.2	12.2	5.4	5.6	10.7	4.7
	2008 Q2	4.4	3.1	5.7	5.0	2.7	5.1	7.1	3.3	11.3	3.4	7.4	7.0	4.4	11.0	8.0	3.4	–	6.6	8.3	5.9	2.7	2.4	3.5	7.8	8.8	11.3	4.8	6.2	8.3	5.2
	2008 Q3	4.2	3.5	7.6	6.0	..	5.5	6.8	3.9	11.9	5.4	5.9	7.2	5.3	10.9	8.1	5.2	–	8.0	7.6	6.2	2.3	2.1	3.7	7.9	9.4	10.5	4.3	5.0	10.4	6.1
	2008 Q4	4.2	3.7	6.6	4.9	..	5.7	6.1	3.2	14.1	7.4	5.9	8.0	5.1	11.7	8.0	4.8	2.5	7.3	8.2	6.2	2.4	2.2	4.1	7.7	9.3	10.0	4.7	5.3	11.6	5.9
	2008	**4.4**	**3.5**	**6.6**	**5.3**	..	**5.6**	**6.8**	**3.4**	**12.1**	**5.2**	**6.5**	**7.4**	**4.8**	**11.5**	**8.1**	**4.2**	**2.5**	**7.3**	**8.2**	**5.4**	**2.5**	**2.2**	**3.9**	**8.0**	**9.1**	**11.0**	**4.8**	**5.5**	**10.2**	**5.5**
	2009 Q1	5.6	3.6	7.1	5.9	..	6.8	6.7	4.1	16.4	9.5	6.6	8.5	5.8	12.9	9.4	5.7	–	7.8	9.2	3.3	2.7	2.3	5.6	9.0	9.9	11.4	5.0	6.6	13.9	7.1
	2009 Q2	5.0	4.0	6.3	6.2	3.4	7.4	6.5	5.0	17.1	9.1	8.4	8.4	6.1	12.5	9.2	7.3	–	7.8	8.3	3.9	2.8	2.5	6.0	8.4	9.8	12.3	5.6	7.8	12.3	8.0
	2009 Q3	4.7	4.5	7.5	7.5	..	8.5	6.6	5.2	17.0	12.0	7.2	8.4	6.4	13.1	10.1	8.1	–	9.0	8.2	4.5	3.1	2.8	6.2	8.7	11.1	13.3	5.9	6.6	13.2	9.0
	2009 Q4	4.7	3.7	7.0	5.9	..	8.2	6.1	5.5	17.8	11.5	7.2	9.3	6.2	14.0	10.3	7.6	–	7.9	9.6	2.8	3.3	2.0	6.4	8.9	11.1	14.4	6.7	6.6	11.9	8.3
	2009	**5.0**	**3.9**	**7.0**	**6.4**	..	**7.7**	**6.5**	**5.0**	**17.1**	**10.5**	**7.4**	**8.8**	**6.1**	**13.2**	**9.8**	**7.2**	**5.5**	**8.1**	**8.8**	**3.6**	**3.0**	**2.4**	**6.1**	**8.7**	**10.5**	**12.9**	**5.8**	**6.9**	**12.8**	**8.1**
	2010 Q1	5.6	3.5	7.6	6.3	3.7	8.9	6.6	5.5	18.8	14.3	7.7	9.0	6.4	15.3	11.1	8.0	–	7.1	10.1	2.3	3.9	2.6	6.9	10.7	11.6	15.4	6.8	7.5	13.1	8.3
	2010 Q2	5.1	3.5	6.9	6.3	3.4	8.3	5.8	5.2	19.3	13.8	8.5	8.4	6.4	15.3	10.6	9.0	–	6.3	8.9	2.8	3.7	2.6	6.6	9.9	11.6	14.7	6.5	7.7	10.6	8.8
	2010 Q3	5.2	3.6	7.3	7.6	4.1	8.6	5.7	6.5	19.0	13.4	6.7	8.8	7.1	16.2	10.9	9.3	–	8.3	8.3	3.8	3.8	2.8	7.0	9.8	12.5	14.3	6.9	6.2	11.6	9.3
	2010 Q4	5.0	3.6	6.8	6.8	3.3	8.5	5.5	6.7	19.3	12.2	6.5	9.4	6.7	17.9	10.8	9.1	–	7.0	9.5	5.8	4.0	2.2	6.9	10.0	12.2	14.0	7.5	5.6	11.0	8.3
	2010	**5.2**	**3.6**	**7.1**	**6.6**	**3.6**	**8.5**	**5.9**	**6.0**	**19.1**	**13.4**	**7.4**	**8.9**	**6.6**	**16.2**	**10.8**	**8.9**	**6.4**	**7.2**	**9.2**	**3.6**	**4.0**	**2.5**	**6.8**	**10.1**	**12.0**	**14.6**	**6.9**	**6.8**	**11.6**	**8.7**
	2011 Q1	5.8	3.6	5.9	6.5	3.5	8.2	5.6	6.6	20.1	12.4	7.6	9.2	6.7	19.2	11.2	9.4	–	5.4	9.1	5.8	4.0	2.4	5.3	10.3	12.7	13.9	8.0	6.6	11.2	8.2
	2011 Q2	5.0	3.4	5.4	6.4	2.7	8.0	4.9	5.9	19.4	11.9	8.1	8.4	6.9	20.2	10.9	9.8	–	5.4	8.2	2.7	3.5	2.8	5.0	10.2	12.6	12.8	6.9	6.7	9.7	8.5
	2011 Q3	4.9	3.1	6.7	7.1	3.8	7.8	5.1	6.8	20.4	10.9	6.1	8.9	7.4	21.5	10.9	11.0	–	7.7	8.5	3.1	3.6	2.9	5.2	10.7	13.3	13.3	7.4	5.0	10.5	9.2
	2011 Q4	5.2	3.9	5.9	5.7	3.3	7.6	4.8	6.8	21.3	9.6	5.6	9.0	7.2	24.5	10.9	9.8	–	6.4	10.0	4.3	4.2	2.1	5.1	10.9	14.5	14.3	8.9	5.4	..	7.9
	2011	**5.2**	**3.5**	**6.0**	**6.4**	**3.3**	**7.9**	**5.1**	**6.5**	**20.3**	**11.2**	**6.9**	**8.9**	**7.0**	**21.4**	**11.0**	**10.0**	**5.8**	**6.2**	**8.9**	**4.0**	**3.8**	**2.5**	**5.1**	**10.5**	**13.3**	**13.6**	**7.8**	**5.9**	**10.5**	**8.5**
Foreign-born	2008 Q1	5.3	8.1	15.2	7.4	..	11.4	13.1	11.0	16.0	–	12.2	12.3	7.6	13.7	6.2	5.1	–	4.5	13.1	10.7	7.8	5.3	6.3	–	12.4	–	6.8	12.5	11.6	5.6
	2008 Q2	5.2	7.3	13.9	7.2	7.7	10.6	12.7	8.1	16.7	–	11.8	11.2	6.8	11.9	4.4	6.5	–	4.7	12.2	6.3	6.9	3.7	5.0	–	9.9	–	6.7	13.7	10.3	5.8
	2008 Q3	5.2	7.5	14.1	8.1	..	11.0	12.0	5.8	16.0	–	15.8	12.9	6.6	10.9	5.5	7.7	–	5.8	10.3	6.1	5.9	5.3	5.0	–	11.9	–	5.9	12.4	4.6	6.3
	2008 Q4	5.2	8.3	16.6	7.5	..	8.1	12.0	6.6	19.7	–	14.3	13.0	7.9	12.7	7.3	7.3	–	5.7	11.9	4.1	5.9	4.0	6.0	–	10.8	–	4.6	12.8	11.3	6.5
	2008	**5.2**	**7.8**	**14.9**	**7.6**	..	**10.2**	**12.4**	**7.8**	**17.2**	–	**13.5**	**12.4**	**7.5**	**12.3**	**5.9**	**6.6**	–	**5.2**	**11.8**	**6.8**	**6.4**	**4.6**	**5.6**	–	**11.2**	–	**6.0**	**12.9**	**9.4**	**6.0**
	2009 Q1	6.9	8.1	16.6	8.8	..	9.3	12.6	9.4	24.8	–	16.1	14.2	8.1	14.8	10.9	11.4	–	6.8	12.8	9.8	6.3	3.5	6.1	–	13.5	–	6.8	13.9	17.5	8.9
	2009 Q2	6.8	7.4	15.3	9.9	7.8	9.3	11.2	10.1	23.8	15.4	13.6	13.5	9.2	13.7	9.6	11.2	–	7.4	12.9	8.8	6.8	6.8	6.8	–	12.2	–	5.8	15.3	13.8	9.0
	2009 Q3	7.1	8.8	17.9	10.5	..	13.0	12.7	7.7	23.2	15.0	14.1	14.6	9.4	13.8	9.7	13.1	–	6.4	11.7	6.2	6.1	3.6	6.3	–	12.8	–	10.1	13.7	16.4	9.7
	2009 Q4	6.7	8.3	14.7	9.3	..	12.4	10.9	11.8	24.7	11.0	15.2	15.0	9.0	15.6	7.9	13.7	–	5.8	14.6	6.5	6.5	5.5	8.7	–	13.4	–	6.1	15.0	18.5	9.3
	2009	**6.9**	**8.2**	**16.1**	**9.6**	..	**11.0**	**11.8**	**9.7**	**24.1**	**12.3**	**14.7**	**14.3**	**8.9**	**14.5**	**9.6**	**11.7**	**8.6**	**6.6**	**13.0**	**6.4**	**6.4**	**4.9**	**7.0**	–	**13.0**	–	**7.2**	**14.5**	**16.6**	**9.2**
	2010 Q1	6.9	7.6	17.3	9.6	9.8	9.9	11.3	11.8	26.2	19.4	16.2	16.6	8.7	17.9	9.7	10.8	–	5.4	14.3	8.3	7.9	7.5	8.4	–	15.8	–	8.5	16.2	16.5	10.3
	2010 Q2	6.3	8.0	16.5	8.8	8.8	10.5	10.9	11.6	26.4	25.0	17.4	15.0	9.0	16.6	7.1	13.2	–	4.3	13.4	5.5	7.4	7.5	7.7	–	16.8	–	9.5	18.1	10.4	8.6
	2010 Q3	5.5	7.0	19.2	11.0	8.7	9.4	10.0	13.0	26.6	25.3	15.4	16.0	9.4	16.2	7.0	13.7	–	5.5	11.9	6.6	7.8	7.1	7.3	–	17.1	–	10.5	16.1	15.1	9.4
	2010 Q4	5.9	7.7	16.2	9.2	7.9	8.1	10.7	12.0	27.6	18.9	14.1	16.6	9.0	19.9	–	14.4	–	6.0	13.7	5.7	7.4	6.0	7.4	–	19.0	–	10.7	16.4	14.2	9.8
	2010	**6.1**	**7.6**	**17.3**	**9.9**	**8.8**	**9.5**	**10.7**	**12.1**	**26.7**	**22.2**	**15.8**	**16.0**	**9.0**	**17.7**	**7.4**	**13.0**	**10.4**	**5.3**	**13.3**	**6.5**	**8.2**	**7.0**	**7.7**	**11.1**	**17.2**	**16.7**	**9.8**	**16.7**	**14.1**	**9.5**
	2011 Q1	6.5	8.5	12.8	9.4	8.1	11.6	9.8	15.2	29.9	21.8	16.9	17.3	9.0	23.3	8.2	13.5	–	4.8	13.5	9.5	8.6	7.3	7.3	–	18.1	–	13.5	16.8	16.5	9.6
	2011 Q2	6.2	7.6	14.9	9.1	6.3	10.8	9.1	15.7	29.1	20.0	12.3	14.9	9.0	19.7	11.4	14.0	–	4.4	14.1	9.8	8.5	7.3	6.0	–	16.1	–	13.8	17.1	16.1	9.1
	2011 Q3	5.9	7.8	16.3	7.8	7.8	11.0	9.0	15.1	29.4	16.2	13.6	15.7	10.2	22.8	10.3	14.3	–	4.2	12.3	7.8	8.4	6.4	5.7	–	13.7	–	13.2	15.6	15.1	10.1
	2011 Q4	5.3	9.4	14.6	9.4	7.7	10.2	8.9	14.4	32.1	14.7	14.0	17.0	10.6	26.9	10.4	14.7	–	4.6	16.5	6.4	8.6	7.0	6.7	–	15.6	–	15.5	14.2	12.3	9.2
	2011	**6.0**	**8.3**	**14.6**	**9.5**	**7.5**	**10.9**	**9.2**	**15.1**	**30.1**	**18.1**	**14.2**	**16.3**	**9.7**	**23.2**	**10.1**	**14.1**	**10.4**	**4.5**	**14.1**	**8.4**	**8.5**	**7.0**	**6.4**	**14.5**	**15.9**	**20.8**	**14.0**	**15.9**	**13.6**	**9.5**

Notes: Data are not adjusted for seasonal variations. Comparisons should therefore be made for the same quarters of each year, and not for successive quarters within a given year. Information on data for Israel: http://dx.doi.org/10.1787/888932315602.
Sources: EU Labour Force Survey data (Eurostat); United States: Current Population Surveys; Australia, Canada, Israel, New Zealand: Labour Force Surveys.

StatLink ⟶ http://dx.doi.org/10.1787/888932616923

Table I.B1.3. Quarterly participation rates by gender and place of birth in selected OECD countries, 2008-11
Percentages

Men + Women

		AUS	AUT	BEL	CAN	CHE	CZE	DEU	DNK	ESP	EST	FIN	FRA	GBR	GRC	HUN	IRL	ISL	ISR	ITA	LUX	NLD	NOR	NZL	POL	PRT	SVK	SVN	SWE	TUR	USA
Native-born	2008 Q1	78.3	75.2	68.1	78.0	..	69.4	77.3	80.8	70.7	71.6	74.5	70.0	75.9	66.4	60.9	70.7	–	62.5	62.1	67.1	80.1	79.9	79.2	63.3	73.5	68.5	70.6	79.7	47.5	73.3
	2008 Q2	78.5	75.7	66.7	79.8	83.0	69.5	77.4	81.7	71.2	71.8	78.1	70.2	76.1	66.6	61.0	70.8	–	62.7	62.8	67.4	80.5	80.9	79.4	63.5	73.7	68.5	71.3	81.6	50.4	74.0
	2008 Q3	78.1	76.8	68.5	80.3	..	69.7	77.8	82.3	71.5	74.5	76.4	70.8	76.7	66.5	62.0	72.3	–	62.8	61.9	68.7	80.6	80.8	79.3	64.4	73.5	69.3	73.3	81.5	51.2	74.3
	2008 Q4	78.1	76.1	67.6	78.7	..	69.9	77.8	82.0	71.6	74.7	74.9	70.7	76.6	66.4	61.5	70.2	86.2	62.4	62.0	69.1	80.8	79.7	80.4	64.4	73.2	68.9	71.8	79.4	49.9	73.6
	2008	**78.3**	**76.0**	**67.7**	**79.2**	..	**69.6**	**77.6**	**81.7**	**71.2**	**73.1**	**76.0**	**70.4**	**76.3**	**66.5**	**61.3**	**71.0**	–	**62.6**	**62.2**	**68.1**	**80.5**	**80.3**	**79.6**	**63.9**	**73.5**	**68.8**	**71.7**	**80.6**	**49.7**	**73.8**
	2009 Q1	78.3	75.2	67.6	77.7	..	69.6	77.5	81.1	71.6	73.2	74.2	70.7	76.3	66.6	60.8	69.2	–	62.4	61.6	69.2	81.0	79.5	79.4	64.3	73.3	68.1	70.5	79.3	48.2	73.0
	2009 Q2	78.3	76.1	67.4	79.3	82.9	69.8	77.9	81.9	71.7	72.8	77.2	71.2	76.0	66.9	61.3	70.1	–	62.9	61.7	69.6	81.0	80.2	78.9	64.4	73.1	68.1	71.7	81.4	50.9	73.4
	2009 Q3	77.8	77.2	67.7	79.6	..	70.4	77.9	81.6	71.7	74.0	75.0	71.3	76.5	67.2	61.7	70.3	–	62.5	61.2	70.1	81.0	79.2	78.6	65.3	72.8	68.8	73.1	80.5	52.2	73.4
	2009 Q4	78.0	75.8	68.1	77.7	..	70.0	78.2	80.3	71.5	72.5	73.4	70.9	76.1	66.9	61.8	68.7	–	62.2	61.5	69.6	80.8	78.3	79.9	65.0	73.1	68.7	72.3	78.9	51.0	72.1
	2009	**78.1**	**76.1**	**67.7**	**78.6**	..	**70.0**	**77.9**	**81.2**	**71.6**	**73.1**	**74.9**	**71.0**	**76.2**	**66.9**	**61.4**	**69.6**	**84.3**	**62.5**	**61.5**	**69.6**	**80.9**	**79.3**	**79.2**	**64.7**	**73.1**	**68.4**	**71.9**	**80.0**	**50.6**	**73.0**
	2010 Q1	77.9	74.8	68.5	77.1	83.2	69.8	77.4	80.0	71.6	73.8	73.4	71.0	75.6	67.2	61.7	68.3	–	62.1	61.5	69.2	79.3	78.1	79.2	65.2	73.5	68.4	71.3	79.5	50.3	72.2
	2010 Q2	78.0	75.4	67.6	79.0	82.5	69.9	77.2	80.7	72.0	73.3	76.6	70.9	75.7	67.4	62.2	69.7	–	62.8	61.5	69.3	79.3	79.1	78.6	65.6	73.3	68.5	71.4	82.0	52.5	72.5
	2010 Q3	77.9	76.6	68.4	80.3	..	70.4	77.4	80.3	72.0	72.8	74.9	71.5	76.5	67.3	62.7	69.7	–	63.7	60.4	71.2	79.4	78.5	78.8	66.1	73.3	69.0	71.6	81.8	52.9	72.7
	2010 Q4	78.3	76.0	68.8	77.9	..	70.3	77.7	79.8	72.1	73.4	73.3	70.6	76.0	67.2	62.5	68.8	–	63.4	61.6	62.4	79.3	78.1	79.3	65.8	73.1	68.9	71.4	80.0	51.5	71.8
	2010	**78.0**	**75.7**	**68.3**	**78.4**	**83.0**	**70.1**	**77.4**	**80.2**	**71.9**	**73.3**	**74.6**	**70.8**	**76.0**	**67.3**	**62.3**	**69.1**	**84.6**	**63.0**	**61.2**	**62.6**	**79.3**	**78.5**	**79.0**	**65.7**	**73.3**	**68.7**	**71.4**	**80.8**	**51.8**	**72.3**
	2011 Q1	78.1	75.0	66.9	77.4	83.5	70.0	77.6	80.1	72.2	74.0	73.8	70.4	75.8	66.6	61.8	68.4	–	62.7	61.2	62.2	79.1	77.6	79.4	65.5	73.5	68.6	69.6	80.4	51.4	71.4
	2011 Q2	77.9	75.7	67.7	79.2	83.3	70.4	77.7	80.3	72.5	74.3	77.2	70.5	75.8	66.8	62.5	69.2	–	63.0	61.0	60.4	79.3	78.2	79.0	66.0	73.5	68.7	69.8	82.7	53.9	71.7
	2011 Q3	77.8	76.7	67.9	79.5	83.5	70.7	78.1	80.7	72.8	75.2	75.6	71.2	76.4	66.8	63.1	69.1	–	63.3	60.8	62.6	79.7	78.5	78.8	66.5	73.3	69.0	70.9	82.3	54.5	72.2
	2011 Q4	77.9	76.1	67.9	77.6	83.9	70.6	78.4	79.9	72.6	74.0	73.8	71.0	76.4	66.9	63.1	69.0	–	62.8	62.0	61.2	80.3	78.1	79.7	66.5	72.9	69.2	70.8	80.5	..	71.3
	2011	**77.9**	**75.9**	**67.6**	**78.5**	**83.5**	**70.4**	**77.9**	**80.2**	**72.5**	**74.4**	**75.1**	**70.8**	**76.1**	**66.8**	**62.6**	**68.9**	**84.4**	**62.9**	**61.3**	**61.6**	**79.6**	**78.1**	**79.2**	**66.1**	**73.3**	**68.8**	**70.3**	**81.5**	**53.3**	**71.7**
Foreign-born	2008 Q1	72.0	69.1	62.6	75.7	..	71.0	71.4	67.6	79.2	78.5	76.5	67.7	73.1	72.6	67.3	76.8	–	67.6	70.0	70.9	70.9	76.3	72.1	43.9	80.7	74.1	73.0	71.3	50.2	74.8
	2008 Q2	71.9	71.3	63.3	76.5	80.4	71.6	71.0	72.8	79.4	79.1	76.9	68.0	72.4	73.0	68.4	76.5	–	67.5	70.4	75.3	72.0	76.8	73.3	48.4	81.7	72.5	71.0	73.7	53.9	75.2
	2008 Q3	71.9	70.3	63.8	76.6	..	71.2	72.1	72.6	79.2	79.4	75.8	67.8	72.6	73.4	69.0	76.4	–	67.0	71.9	81.1	71.5	78.1	73.8	47.7	82.1	74.6	70.8	73.8	54.9	75.8
	2008 Q4	72.4	71.0	63.2	76.1	..	71.7	71.4	72.5	79.8	81.4	71.5	67.4	72.7	73.8	70.6	74.8	–	68.2	71.9	75.9	72.3	77.7	75.1	41.9	82.2	71.5	74.2	72.8	54.8	74.9
	2008	**72.1**	**70.4**	**63.2**	**76.2**	**80.4**	**71.4**	**71.5**	**71.3**	**79.4**	**79.6**	**75.1**	**67.7**	**72.7**	**73.2**	**68.9**	**76.2**	**85.5**	**67.5**	**71.1**	**75.9**	**71.7**	**77.3**	**73.6**	**45.8**	**81.7**	**73.1**	**72.2**	**72.9**	**53.5**	**75.2**
	2009 Q1	72.6	70.4	63.7	75.6	..	72.4	72.6	74.5	80.5	79.7	75.3	67.9	72.7	73.9	71.4	73.3	–	68.4	70.3	72.2	72.4	75.7	74.1	51.3	81.3	70.9	70.8	72.6	55.5	74.6
	2009 Q2	72.1	71.3	60.8	76.5	81.4	73.9	72.9	74.6	79.8	80.9	77.9	67.6	72.0	74.8	72.4	74.2	–	68.1	71.1	69.1	71.0	76.4	74.6	51.0	81.3	71.2	71.5	74.3	55.9	75.2
	2009 Q3	71.7	72.0	62.3	76.5	..	72.6	73.2	78.8	79.2	78.6	75.3	67.1	73.1	75.6	72.6	73.7	–	69.0	69.9	74.4	71.3	74.9	72.9	48.9	80.1	68.5	71.8	73.9	56.6	75.4
	2009 Q4	72.1	72.3	62.6	76.1	..	72.0	72.9	74.1	79.2	79.3	73.2	67.1	72.0	75.6	71.7	72.0	–	68.5	71.0	73.3	71.2	74.5	74.1	55.6	78.7	67.7	71.4	72.8	54.9	74.9
	2009	**72.1**	**71.5**	**62.3**	**76.3**	**81.0**	**72.7**	**72.9**	**75.5**	**79.7**	**79.6**	**75.4**	**67.4**	**72.4**	**75.0**	**72.0**	**73.3**	**87.4**	**68.5**	**70.6**	**74.7**	**71.5**	**75.3**	**73.9**	**51.6**	**80.4**	**69.7**	**71.3**	**73.4**	**55.7**	**75.0**
	2010 Q1	72.4	71.0	63.2	75.6	80.1	73.0	72.1	74.0	80.2	74.7	74.0	67.3	71.5	76.3	71.1	70.6	–	67.6	70.3	76.6	69.2	75.8	73.7	54.8	80.4	64.1	74.0	72.3	56.3	74.6
	2010 Q2	71.8	71.8	63.2	76.9	81.4	73.0	72.6	74.6	80.1	76.0	76.1	67.9	72.7	76.4	71.6	72.1	–	68.1	70.7	77.0	71.0	76.0	73.9	56.7	80.8	63.4	74.2	73.7	57.2	75.4
	2010 Q3	72.3	73.1	64.9	77.4	81.9	74.7	73.2	74.2	80.6	79.5	72.3	67.8	73.7	76.8	72.1	71.9	–	69.7	69.2	78.2	70.6	75.0	73.0	59.5	81.2	61.9	69.3	74.2	55.7	75.1
	2010 Q4	73.7	73.1	64.6	75.6	80.6	74.4	72.4	70.9	79.5	76.7	69.9	68.0	72.7	76.1	68.4	71.4	–	69.3	69.4	75.6	70.7	74.5	74.6	59.4	82.8	66.8	71.3	72.8	57.7	74.8
	2010	**72.6**	**72.3**	**64.0**	**76.4**	**81.0**	**73.3**	**72.6**	**73.4**	**80.1**	**76.7**	**73.0**	**67.7**	**72.7**	**76.4**	**70.8**	**71.5**	**86.4**	**68.9**	**69.9**	**75.0**	**70.4**	**75.3**	**73.8**	**57.4**	**81.3**	**64.0**	**72.2**	**73.3**	**56.8**	**75.0**
	2011 Q1	74.0	72.5	61.4	74.7	80.1	73.9	72.6	70.9	79.1	75.4	69.3	68.3	73.1	75.6	67.4	70.6	–	68.7	69.7	77.6	70.6	74.4	73.9	59.1	82.7	66.5	71.1	73.8	56.9	74.2
	2011 Q2	73.5	72.7	62.7	75.6	80.6	73.8	73.9	72.0	80.1	75.4	72.9	68.1	73.2	75.2	68.1	72.1	–	69.7	70.6	75.1	69.2	77.2	73.9	61.7	83.1	70.6	70.8	74.8	56.2	74.3
	2011 Q3	73.7	73.1	61.5	76.4	81.3	73.5	73.9	71.8	79.4	79.3	72.7	67.4	74.1	74.5	69.7	72.5	–	69.5	68.4	74.0	69.3	76.4	73.7	66.6	82.7	72.8	68.7	74.9	54.4	74.1
	2011 Q4	73.3	73.1	62.2	75.6	81.7	73.5	73.5	72.1	79.1	77.5	73.3	66.8	73.4	75.1	68.9	71.6	–	69.2	69.8	73.7	70.8	76.1	74.8	65.0	82.4	72.9	68.9	74.4	55.9	74.7
	2011	**73.6**	**72.6**	**61.9**	**75.6**	**80.9**	**73.7**	**73.5**	**72.1**	**79.4**	**76.9**	**72.0**	**67.7**	**73.4**	**75.1**	**68.6**	**71.7**	**85.8**	**69.3**	**69.6**	**75.1**	**70.0**	**76.0**	**74.1**	**62.9**	**82.7**	**70.5**	**69.9**	**74.5**	**55.9**	**74.3**

I. TRENDS IN INTERNATIONAL MIGRATION

Table I.B1.3. **Quarterly participation rates by gender and place of birth in selected OECD countries, 2008-11** (cont.)
Percentages

Men

		AUS	AUT	BEL	CAN	CHE	CZE	DEU	DNK	ESP	EST	FIN	FRA	GBR	GRC	HUN	IRL	ISL	ISR	ITA	LUX	NLD	NOR	NZL	POL	PRT	SVK	SVN	SWE	TUR	USA
Native-born	2008 Q1	84.2	80.9	73.4	81.1	..	77.7	81.9	83.9	80.4	76.0	76.0	73.9	81.8	78.2	67.5	79.5	–	66.3	73.1	67.9	85.6	82.3	84.9	70.4	79.0	75.9	74.5	81.3	71.9	77.9
	2008 Q2	84.2	81.4	72.3	83.1	88.0	77.9	82.0	85.0	80.8	75.8	80.3	74.1	81.9	78.1	68.1	79.5	–	66.6	74.0	71.3	86.1	83.6	85.2	70.7	78.9	76.1	75.2	83.2	74.2	78.8
	2008 Q3	83.9	82.5	73.7	83.9	..	78.2	82.5	85.7	81.1	78.3	78.5	74.8	82.8	78.0	68.9	80.7	–	66.8	73.2	71.5	86.0	83.5	84.8	71.4	78.6	76.7	77.6	83.0	75.3	79.1
	2008 Q4	84.1	81.3	72.9	81.8	..	78.4	82.1	85.2	80.4	78.9	76.6	74.6	82.5	77.7	67.9	78.5	–	65.7	73.1	69.2	86.1	82.1	86.0	71.4	78.7	76.6	75.1	81.0	74.1	78.0
	2008	**84.1**	**81.5**	**73.1**	**82.5**	**88.0**	**78.1**	**82.1**	**84.9**	**80.7**	**77.3**	**77.8**	**74.4**	**82.3**	**78.0**	**68.1**	**79.6**	**90.2**	**66.4**	**73.4**	**70.0**	**86.0**	**82.9**	**85.2**	**71.0**	**78.8**	**76.3**	**75.6**	**82.1**	**73.9**	**78.4**
	2009 Q1	83.9	79.6	72.9	80.5	..	78.0	82.1	84.3	80.1	76.5	75.5	74.6	82.1	77.6	67.3	76.9	–	65.2	72.5	70.3	86.1	81.5	84.7	71.3	78.2	76.0	73.6	80.8	72.1	77.5
	2009 Q2	83.5	80.8	72.3	82.4	87.1	78.2	81.9	84.7	80.0	76.5	78.7	74.9	81.8	77.7	68.1	77.8	–	66.1	72.6	73.0	86.2	82.6	84.6	71.5	78.2	76.0	75.5	82.8	74.0	77.9
	2009 Q3	83.2	82.1	72.4	82.9	..	78.7	82.5	84.6	79.7	78.5	76.3	75.0	82.1	78.0	68.3	77.7	–	65.8	72.4	72.0	86.0	81.2	83.6	72.5	77.3	76.6	76.9	82.3	75.8	77.9
	2009 Q4	83.5	81.3	73.4	80.4	..	78.7	82.3	83.2	79.2	75.6	74.4	74.8	81.6	77.6	68.2	75.8	–	65.1	72.5	70.3	85.6	80.1	85.4	71.9	77.6	76.4	76.1	80.9	74.4	76.4
	2009	**83.5**	**80.9**	**72.8**	**81.6**	**87.1**	**78.4**	**82.2**	**84.2**	**79.8**	**76.8**	**76.2**	**74.9**	**81.9**	**77.7**	**67.9**	**77.0**	**87.5**	**65.6**	**72.5**	**71.4**	**86.0**	**81.3**	**84.6**	**71.8**	**77.8**	**76.2**	**75.5**	**81.7**	**74.1**	**77.4**
	2010 Q1	83.6	79.4	73.2	79.6	..	78.1	82.1	82.9	79.1	76.5	75.0	74.8	81.1	77.7	67.6	75.5	–	65.5	72.5	69.5	84.5	80.1	84.4	71.9	77.9	75.7	75.2	81.3	73.4	76.5
	2010 Q2	83.5	81.0	73.1	82.0	87.6	78.3	82.1	83.2	79.7	75.9	78.2	74.5	81.3	77.6	68.3	77.0	–	66.3	72.3	69.5	84.5	81.4	83.8	72.2	77.5	76.0	74.5	84.0	75.1	77.0
	2010 Q3	83.4	82.0	73.6	82.8	..	78.9	82.2	83.0	79.5	76.3	76.9	74.9	82.2	77.4	68.7	77.1	–	66.9	71.2	71.9	84.7	80.7	84.1	72.9	77.5	76.2	75.7	83.7	75.7	77.1
	2010 Q4	83.9	81.4	73.5	80.6	..	78.6	82.3	83.1	79.1	76.9	74.9	74.4	81.7	75.8	68.4	75.8	–	65.8	72.0	69.7	84.2	80.3	84.1	72.7	77.5	76.3	75.2	81.9	74.2	75.8
	2010	**83.6**	**80.9**	**73.4**	**81.3**	**88.0**	**78.5**	**82.2**	**83.1**	**79.4**	**76.4**	**76.2**	**74.7**	**81.6**	**77.5**	**68.2**	**76.3**	**87.4**	**66.1**	**72.0**	**70.1**	**84.4**	**80.6**	**84.3**	**72.5**	**77.6**	**76.0**	**75.1**	**82.7**	**74.6**	**76.6**
	2011 Q1	83.7	79.7	71.7	80.0	..	78.0	82.1	83.1	79.2	77.9	75.7	74.2	81.1	76.8	67.7	75.6	–	65.7	71.9	68.6	83.9	79.1	85.1	72.3	78.0	76.2	73.3	81.8	74.3	75.4
	2011 Q2	83.3	81.1	72.6	82.1	87.8	78.6	82.1	83.0	79.3	77.1	79.4	74.3	81.2	76.7	68.5	76.4	–	66.5	71.6	67.5	83.9	79.7	84.7	73.0	77.8	76.8	73.2	84.3	76.1	75.8
	2011 Q3	82.9	82.0	71.9	82.9	..	78.8	82.3	83.3	79.6	77.8	77.4	74.8	81.9	76.5	69.3	76.3	–	66.9	71.5	68.5	84.4	80.4	84.5	73.4	78.0	76.8	74.5	84.0	77.1	76.5
	2011 Q4	83.2	81.2	72.8	80.5	..	78.5	82.7	82.7	72.1	77.4	75.8	74.6	81.7	76.0	69.2	76.3	–	65.5	72.2	66.9	84.9	80.3	85.5	73.2	77.3	77.0	73.6	82.1	..	75.6
	2011	**83.3**	**81.0**	**72.3**	**81.4**	**88.3**	**78.5**	**82.3**	**83.0**	**79.3**	**77.5**	**77.1**	**74.5**	**81.5**	**76.5**	**68.6**	**76.1**	**87.2**	**66.2**	**71.8**	**67.9**	**84.3**	**79.9**	**85.0**	**73.0**	**77.8**	**76.7**	**73.7**	**83.0**	**75.8**	**75.8**
Foreign-born	2008 Q1	80.9	77.8	75.0	82.8	..	82.1	81.8	75.9	87.5	86.5	82.1	77.5	83.8	88.7	77.1	85.9	–	73.8	85.4	79.0	80.1	80.0	82.0	50.3	86.1	79.6	79.6	77.0	68.1	86.4
	2008 Q2	80.3	82.2	75.7	83.9	88.0	82.9	81.1	80.2	87.6	86.6	85.3	77.5	83.3	89.6	77.9	85.6	–	73.7	84.6	82.5	81.1	82.6	81.9	54.4	87.7	77.9	76.6	79.6	74.4	86.9
	2008 Q3	79.9	81.2	74.7	84.2	..	80.1	81.8	81.9	87.3	84.3	80.8	77.5	82.7	89.9	77.0	86.0	–	72.7	87.2	82.9	80.6	82.1	81.3	55.2	87.7	80.3	75.7	80.4	74.4	88.2
	2008 Q4	80.1	81.9	75.4	83.5	..	79.9	81.3	82.5	87.1	82.7	77.0	77.3	83.6	89.7	78.9	85.1	–	74.3	86.5	80.1	81.3	81.3	83.2	49.6	87.4	80.2	79.1	79.3	74.2	86.5
	2008	**80.3**	**80.8**	**75.2**	**83.6**	**88.0**	**81.2**	**81.5**	**80.1**	**87.4**	**85.1**	**81.3**	**77.5**	**83.4**	**89.5**	**77.8**	**85.6**	**90.7**	**73.6**	**86.0**	**81.1**	**80.8**	**81.5**	**82.1**	**52.8**	**87.3**	**79.5**	**77.7**	**79.1**	**72.9**	**87.0**
	2009 Q1	80.6	79.2	73.8	82.4	..	80.2	81.9	80.4	88.2	82.5	78.1	76.6	83.4	89.6	81.6	83.0	–	74.6	85.4	81.3	81.2	80.5	82.6	59.5	86.1	80.8	75.5	78.3	71.6	85.6
	2009 Q2	80.6	81.0	72.4	83.0	89.6	82.1	82.3	78.0	87.6	86.1	84.7	76.1	81.8	89.7	82.3	84.0	–	74.9	85.5	84.2	80.5	81.2	82.5	60.9	86.7	80.8	78.4	80.8	73.5	86.8
	2009 Q3	80.1	82.5	74.3	83.2	..	81.4	82.5	85.2	85.9	82.2	81.2	76.1	83.6	90.2	79.6	82.5	–	74.2	85.6	82.9	80.6	80.3	80.6	58.1	86.4	83.3	76.1	80.5	74.2	86.6
	2009 Q4	80.3	82.0	72.8	82.3	..	82.1	82.3	83.3	86.5	83.1	78.3	76.4	80.9	89.6	79.9	81.5	–	73.5	84.8	83.5	80.1	81.2	81.9	67.4	85.5	85.3	76.6	78.7	71.7	85.7
	2009	**80.4**	**81.2**	**73.3**	**82.7**	**89.6**	**81.5**	**82.2**	**81.8**	**87.0**	**83.6**	**80.6**	**76.3**	**82.4**	**89.8**	**80.9**	**82.8**	**89.9**	**74.3**	**85.3**	**83.0**	**80.6**	**80.8**	**81.9**	**61.2**	**86.2**	**82.3**	**76.6**	**79.6**	**72.6**	**86.2**
	2010 Q1	81.4	79.1	72.1	81.3	..	80.2	83.1	84.7	86.7	75.2	80.2	76.1	80.5	90.4	76.4	80.1	–	72.6	83.9	83.7	76.6	80.6	81.7	68.4	84.4	82.8	79.7	78.7	72.0	85.5
	2010 Q2	80.4	80.7	74.3	83.0	89.6	82.1	82.8	80.3	87.4	78.1	85.4	77.1	81.8	89.7	73.9	81.3	–	74.8	84.9	82.1	79.3	81.2	82.5	67.8	84.2	82.7	78.0	80.3	74.9	86.5
	2010 Q3	80.8	81.8	74.8	84.2	..	81.8	83.7	76.9	87.7	81.6	81.1	77.3	83.4	90.9	74.1	81.4	–	75.9	84.9	82.9	78.8	80.3	80.6	62.5	85.0	83.3	75.6	80.6	73.1	86.5
	2010 Q4	81.9	80.8	74.6	82.5	..	82.1	83.0	77.2	86.8	83.3	78.1	76.9	82.5	90.2	75.2	80.7	–	74.4	84.7	84.0	79.7	80.0	82.1	70.1	86.6	81.6	76.9	80.1	74.5	85.3
	2010	**81.1**	**80.6**	**74.0**	**82.8**	**89.2**	**81.5**	**83.1**	**79.7**	**87.1**	**79.6**	**81.2**	**76.9**	**82.1**	**90.4**	**74.9**	**80.9**	**89.3**	**74.4**	**84.6**	**83.2**	**78.6**	**80.6**	**81.6**	**67.4**	**85.1**	**81.7**	**77.5**	**79.9**	**73.6**	**86.0**
	2011 Q1	82.6	80.6	72.4	81.1	..	84.4	83.0	75.5	85.5	81.0	77.7	76.6	82.7	89.4	74.8	78.8	–	73.5	83.0	84.6	78.2	78.0	82.1	65.1	86.9	79.1	76.7	80.3	73.9	85.6
	2011 Q2	81.5	82.6	71.9	82.4	89.8	86.1	84.0	76.2	85.9	79.7	80.7	76.9	83.2	89.1	77.2	80.3	–	75.5	84.7	82.1	77.7	82.1	82.0	64.1	85.9	81.8	76.6	81.4	74.6	85.7
	2011 Q3	81.9	81.2	72.8	82.9	..	86.1	83.6	77.9	86.1	84.9	79.7	76.5	83.4	89.2	82.2	81.3	–	76.0	83.3	82.2	78.5	80.6	81.3	72.0	87.3	86.5	75.4	81.5	71.9	85.5
	2011 Q4	81.6	81.5	73.0	81.8	..	85.3	84.2	77.2	86.1	84.2	80.0	75.5	83.0	89.1	77.6	80.2	–	74.9	83.7	82.4	79.5	79.8	82.7	78.7	85.0	83.1	74.3	80.9	73.3	85.8
	2011	**81.9**	**81.5**	**72.5**	**82.0**	**89.8**	**85.5**	**83.7**	**76.7**	**85.9**	**82.5**	**79.5**	**76.4**	**83.1**	**89.2**	**78.1**	**80.2**	**88.2**	**75.0**	**83.7**	**82.8**	**78.4**	**80.1**	**82.0**	**69.6**	**86.3**	**82.5**	**75.8**	**81.0**	**73.5**	**85.6**

I. TRENDS IN INTERNATIONAL MIGRATION

Table I.B1.3. **Quarterly participation rates by gender and place of birth in selected OECD countries, 2008-11** (cont.)
Percentages

Women

		AUS	AUT	BEL	CAN	CHE	CZE	DEU	DNK	ESP	EST	FIN	FRA	GBR	GRC	HUN	IRL	ISL	ISR	ITA	LUX	NLD	NOR	NZL	POL	PRT	SVK	SVN	SWE	TUR	USA
Native-born	2008 Q1	72.4	69.4	62.7	74.8	..	60.9	72.4	77.6	67.5	60.6	73.0	66.2	70.1	54.6	54.5	61.9	–	58.6	51.1	52.5	74.3	77.4	73.5	56.3	68.0	61.2	66.4	78.0	23.4	68.8
	2008 Q2	72.7	69.8	61.0	76.4	78.0	61.1	72.5	78.2	68.1	61.3	76.0	66.4	70.3	55.0	54.3	62.1	–	58.7	51.4	52.1	74.8	78.2	73.8	56.6	68.5	61.0	67.2	80.0	26.9	69.4
	2008 Q3	72.3	71.0	63.2	76.5	..	61.0	72.9	78.7	70.9	61.5	74.4	66.9	70.7	55.0	55.3	63.8	–	58.7	50.5	75.1	75.1	77.9	74.0	57.6	68.3	61.9	68.8	80.0	27.5	69.7
	2008 Q4	72.2	70.9	62.3	75.5	..	61.1	73.2	78.6	70.7	62.6	73.2	66.8	70.7	55.1	55.3	61.8	–	59.0	50.8	54.2	75.4	77.2	75.0	57.6	67.9	61.2	68.2	77.7	26.1	69.4
	2008	**72.4**	**70.3**	**62.3**	**75.8**	..	**61.0**	**72.8**	**78.3**	**69.3**	**61.5**	**74.1**	**66.6**	**70.4**	**54.9**	**54.9**	**62.4**	**81.9**	**58.8**	**51.0**	**53.3**	**74.9**	**77.7**	**74.1**	**57.0**	**68.2**	**61.3**	**67.7**	**78.9**	**26.0**	**69.3**
	2009 Q1	72.8	70.8	62.3	74.8	..	60.9	72.8	77.9	70.2	62.8	72.9	66.7	70.6	55.7	54.6	61.6	–	59.5	50.7	55.0	75.8	77.4	74.3	57.5	68.4	60.2	67.2	77.7	24.9	68.7
	2009 Q2	73.0	71.3	62.5	76.1	78.6	61.2	73.2	78.9	69.4	63.2	75.7	67.4	70.3	56.0	54.8	62.3	–	59.6	50.6	57.5	75.6	77.7	73.4	57.6	68.0	60.2	67.8	79.9	28.4	69.2
	2009 Q3	72.3	72.3	63.0	76.2	..	61.2	73.2	78.6	69.6	63.1	73.7	67.7	70.9	56.4	55.3	62.9	–	59.1	49.7	58.0	75.8	77.1	73.8	58.2	68.3	61.0	69.1	78.7	29.0	69.0
	2009 Q4	72.6	72.3	62.6	74.9	..	61.8	73.9	77.3	69.5	63.5	72.4	67.1	70.6	56.2	55.7	61.6	–	59.1	50.4	57.5	75.8	76.5	74.7	58.2	68.7	61.1	68.3	76.7	28.1	68.0
	2009	**72.6**	**71.1**	**62.6**	**75.5**	..	**61.4**	**73.3**	**78.2**	**69.7**	**63.2**	**73.7**	**67.2**	**70.6**	**56.1**	**55.1**	**62.1**	**80.9**	**59.3**	**50.4**	**56.4**	**75.8**	**77.2**	**74.0**	**57.9**	**68.3**	**60.6**	**68.1**	**78.2**	**27.7**	**68.7**
	2010 Q1	72.1	70.1	63.8	74.5	..	61.2	72.5	77.0	71.3	63.8	71.7	67.2	70.2	56.6	56.0	61.1	–	58.5	50.3	54.4	76.1	76.0	74.3	58.6	69.2	61.1	67.2	77.5	27.8	68.0
	2010 Q2	72.3	69.8	61.9	76.0	77.2	61.3	72.3	78.1	70.8	64.1	75.0	67.2	70.0	57.0	56.3	62.4	–	59.1	50.5	54.8	76.4	76.7	73.6	59.2	69.2	61.1	68.2	79.0	30.5	68.3
	2010 Q3	72.4	71.2	63.2	76.3	..	61.6	72.5	77.5	69.6	64.2	72.9	67.8	70.8	57.2	56.9	61.8	–	60.4	49.5	55.4	74.0	76.3	73.6	59.5	69.2	61.8	67.3	79.7	30.5	68.5
	2010 Q4	72.5	70.5	63.9	75.1	..	61.9	73.0	76.2	65.0	70.0	71.7	66.8	70.3	57.2	56.7	61.8	–	60.9	51.0	54.6	75.8	75.8	74.0	59.0	68.7	61.6	67.4	78.1	29.3	67.9
	2010	**72.3**	**70.4**	**63.2**	**75.5**	..	**61.5**	**72.6**	**77.2**	**64.3**	**70.4**	**72.8**	**67.1**	**70.3**	**57.0**	**56.5**	**61.9**	**81.6**	**59.7**	**50.3**	**54.8**	**74.1**	**76.2**	**73.9**	**59.0**	**69.1**	**61.4**	**67.5**	**78.8**	**29.5**	**68.1**
	2011 Q1	72.4	70.3	62.1	74.9	..	61.8	72.9	77.0	65.0	70.3	71.3	66.6	70.4	57.0	56.0	61.3	–	59.5	50.4	55.6	74.2	76.0	74.0	58.9	69.0	61.0	65.8	79.0	29.1	67.6
	2011 Q2	72.5	72.1	62.7	76.3	78.5	61.8	72.9	77.4	65.5	71.6	74.8	66.8	70.4	56.8	56.6	62.1	–	59.5	50.4	53.3	74.6	76.5	73.7	59.2	69.2	60.6	66.3	81.0	32.2	67.7
	2011 Q3	72.6	71.3	63.8	76.1	..	62.5	73.7	78.0	65.7	72.7	73.7	67.5	70.9	57.1	57.1	61.9	–	59.5	49.9	56.5	74.8	76.5	73.5	59.6	68.7	61.2	67.1	80.6	32.3	68.0
	2011 Q4	72.7	70.9	63.0	74.7	..	62.5	74.0	77.0	65.8	70.8	71.7	67.4	71.0	57.6	57.3	61.7	–	59.9	51.7	55.4	75.6	75.8	74.6	59.8	68.5	61.3	67.9	78.9	–	67.2
	2011	**72.6**	**70.7**	**62.9**	**75.5**	..	**62.2**	**73.3**	**77.3**	**65.5**	**71.3**	**73.0**	**67.1**	**70.7**	**57.1**	**56.7**	**61.8**	**81.5**	**59.6**	**50.6**	**55.2**	**74.8**	**76.2**	**73.9**	**59.4**	**68.8**	**61.0**	**66.8**	**79.9**	**31.2**	**67.6**
Foreign-born	2008 Q1	63.2	61.6	50.9	69.0	..	60.1	61.0	60.2	71.6	70.9	70.9	58.7	62.5	56.1	59.6	67.3	–	62.0	56.3	66.6	62.7	72.8	63.0	36.9	75.5	67.0	66.1	66.2	32.4	62.7
	2008 Q2	63.7	61.7	52.1	69.5	73.1	60.4	61.0	65.9	72.5	71.2	68.5	59.1	61.9	56.0	61.0	66.9	–	61.9	58.1	69.4	63.7	71.0	65.5	42.1	76.1	66.7	65.1	68.5	34.4	62.8
	2008 Q3	64.0	63.5	53.5	69.4	..	62.4	62.4	64.6	75.1	71.2	70.8	63.1	61.3	56.5	62.9	66.4	–	62.0	58.4	65.0	63.2	74.1	66.8	39.9	77.2	68.7	64.7	67.9	34.0	63.0
	2008 Q4	64.7	61.3	50.9	69.2	..	63.6	61.8	63.9	80.3	72.5	65.8	58.1	62.3	57.3	64.2	65.0	–	62.9	59.0	64.0	63.2	74.1	67.5	36.4	77.6	63.0	68.6	67.0	33.7	62.6
	2008	**63.9**	**61.4**	**51.8**	**69.3**	..	**61.7**	**61.6**	**63.6**	**74.8**	**71.5**	**69.0**	**58.7**	**62.5**	**56.5**	**62.0**	**66.2**	**80.0**	**62.2**	**58.0**	**66.3**	**63.4**	**73.0**	**65.7**	**39.1**	**76.6**	**66.2**	**66.1**	**67.4**	**33.6**	**62.7**
	2009 Q1	64.6	62.3	53.6	69.3	..	64.5	62.8	69.0	77.4	73.0	72.2	59.6	62.6	57.8	63.9	62.9	–	63.0	56.9	69.1	64.4	70.9	66.0	45.4	77.0	61.4	65.8	67.4	32.4	63.0
	2009 Q2	63.7	62.4	49.8	70.4	73.3	65.5	63.1	71.5	76.0	71.9	70.4	59.5	62.7	59.5	65.1	64.2	–	62.1	58.6	63.8	62.4	71.7	66.7	41.8	76.8	63.4	64.7	68.4	31.7	63.0
	2009 Q3	63.3	62.3	50.5	70.7	..	63.7	63.4	73.1	75.9	72.5	69.6	58.6	63.2	60.7	67.4	64.6	–	64.4	56.5	64.0	63.1	69.5	65.4	42.4	74.8	56.4	67.0	68.1	30.8	63.5
	2009 Q4	64.0	63.5	53.0	70.3	..	63.4	63.4	66.4	76.5	72.0	68.8	58.6	63.0	61.1	65.8	62.5	–	64.0	58.8	64.0	63.8	67.6	66.1	47.3	72.9	53.0	65.4	67.3	31.2	63.3
	2009	**63.9**	**62.6**	**51.7**	**70.2**	..	**63.8**	**63.2**	**70.0**	**76.4**	**72.4**	**70.2**	**59.1**	**63.0**	**59.8**	**65.5**	**63.5**	**85.0**	**63.3**	**57.7**	**66.1**	**63.3**	**69.9**	**66.1**	**44.2**	**75.4**	**58.9**	**65.7**	**67.8**	**31.6**	**63.3**
	2010 Q1	63.6	63.4	54.7	70.2	..	60.4	61.6	65.2	74.2	73.7	68.1	59.1	62.9	61.8	67.0	61.2	–	63.3	58.3	67.5	63.9	71.1	65.9	43.7	77.0	47.7	66.1	66.5	32.8	63.1
	2010 Q2	63.4	63.7	52.8	71.0	73.4	61.5	62.9	69.7	74.3	73.2	67.2	59.4	63.7	62.3	69.8	63.0	–	63.4	58.4	65.0	64.1	69.8	66.7	47.5	77.7	45.9	70.0	67.7	31.2	63.6
	2010 Q3	64.1	65.2	55.1	71.0	..	63.2	63.1	71.9	77.8	73.9	64.1	58.8	64.4	62.7	70.4	62.3	–	64.1	55.5	67.0	63.1	69.7	65.6	57.3	77.7	43.6	62.8	68.4	31.4	63.3
	2010 Q4	65.7	66.0	55.2	69.1	..	63.2	62.2	66.2	72.7	71.7	62.5	59.9	63.6	62.2	72.7	62.3	–	65.0	56.3	67.5	62.5	68.6	67.4	49.9	79.3	50.0	65.0	66.4	34.1	64.0
	2010	**64.2**	**64.7**	**54.5**	**70.3**	..	**62.1**	**62.4**	**68.2**	**73.4**	**74.5**	**65.4**	**59.2**	**63.7**	**62.2**	**67.4**	**62.2**	**83.7**	**63.9**	**57.1**	**66.8**	**63.0**	**69.7**	**66.2**	**49.1**	**77.9**	**46.8**	**66.3**	**67.4**	**32.4**	**63.5**
	2011 Q1	65.7	65.0	51.1	68.9	..	62.5	62.6	67.3	73.2	71.0	61.4	60.8	64.2	62.2	61.2	62.2	–	64.5	58.2	70.3	63.6	70.6	65.3	52.5	78.9	53.5	64.4	66.5	32.1	63.6
	2011 Q2	65.6	63.8	53.7	71.9	72.8	60.2	64.2	68.4	74.7	72.0	65.5	60.1	63.8	61.2	60.8	64.1	–	64.6	58.5	67.8	61.7	70.1	65.7	59.3	80.7	59.8	64.2	68.8	29.8	63.6
	2011 Q3	65.6	64.1	51.0	70.3	..	59.7	64.6	70.2	73.2	75.0	66.0	59.2	65.2	60.0	59.1	63.9	–	63.8	55.6	65.4	61.1	72.3	65.7	62.0	78.5	60.0	61.5	68.9	30.5	63.3
	2011 Q4	65.0	65.6	52.4	69.8	..	60.5	63.3	67.3	72.6	71.9	67.2	59.0	64.0	61.3	62.0	63.4	–	64.2	58.0	64.8	63.0	72.3	66.5	54.2	79.9	64.3	62.5	68.2	32.4	63.4
	2011	**65.5**	**64.6**	**52.1**	**69.6**	..	**60.7**	**63.7**	**68.3**	**73.4**	**72.5**	**65.1**	**59.8**	**64.3**	**61.2**	**60.8**	**63.4**	**83.6**	**64.3**	**57.6**	**67.0**	**62.4**	**71.9**	**65.8**	**56.8**	**79.5**	**59.2**	**63.1**	**68.4**	**31.2**	**62.6**

Notes: Data are not adjusted for seasonal variations. Comparisons should therefore be made for the same quarters of each year, and not for successive quarters within a given year. Information on data for Israel: http://dx.doi.org/10.1787/888932315602.
Sources: EU Labour Force Survey data (Eurostat); United States: Current Population Surveys; Australia, Canada, Israel, New Zealand: Labour Force Surveys.

StatLink ⟶ http://dx.doi.org/10.1787/888932616942

ANNEX I.B2

Foreign-born unemployment in selected OECD countries by unemployment duration, Q1 2008-Q4 2011

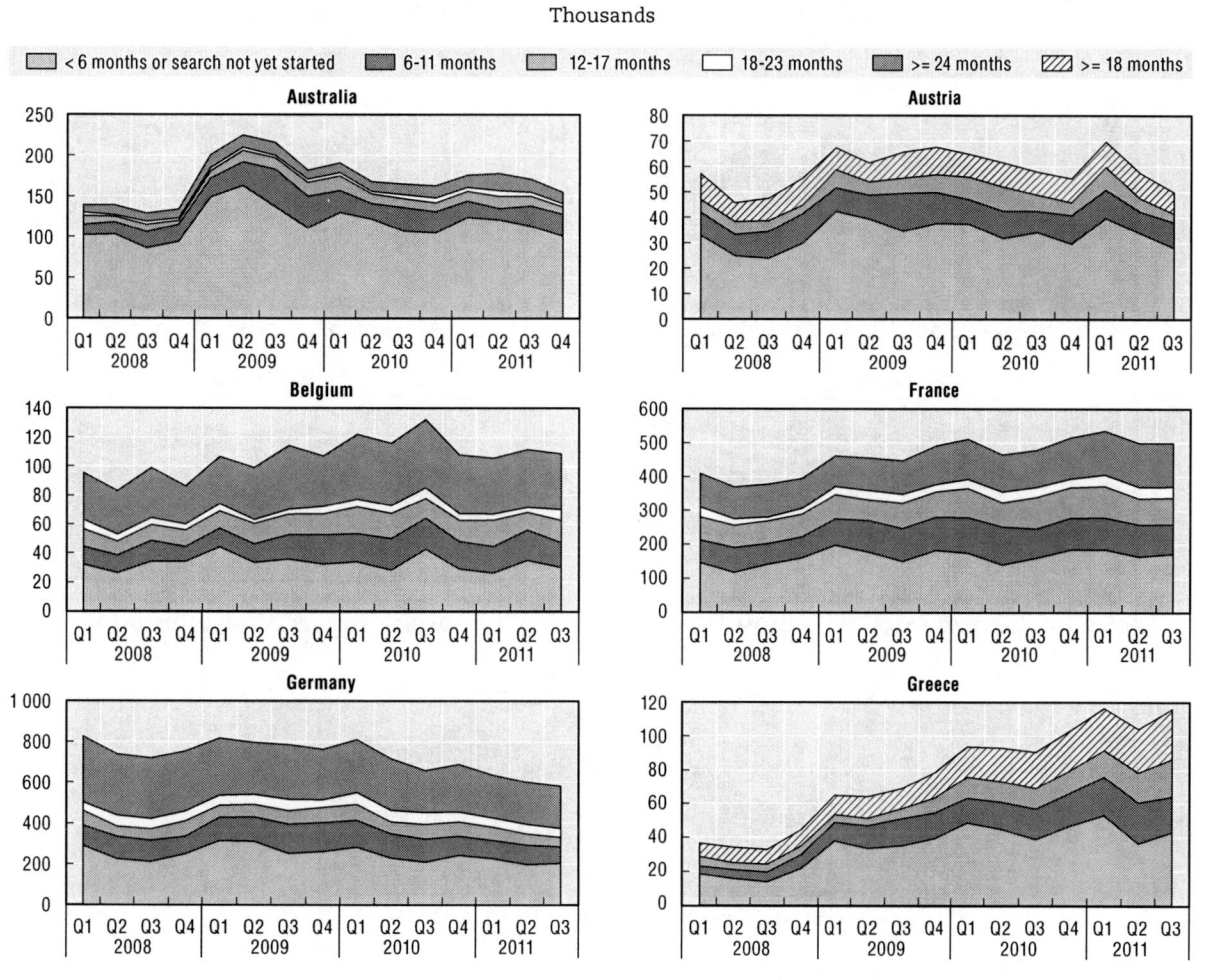

Figure I.B2.1. **Evolution of foreign-born unemployment in selected OECD countries by unemployment duration, Q1 2008-Q4 2011**
Thousands

Legend: < 6 months or search not yet started; 6-11 months; 12-17 months; 18-23 months; >= 24 months; >= 18 months

Australia · Austria · Belgium · France · Germany · Greece

I. TRENDS IN INTERNATIONAL MIGRATION

Figure I.B2.1. **Evolution of foreign-born unemployment in selected OECD countries by unemployment duration, Q1 2008-Q4 2011** (cont.)
Thousands

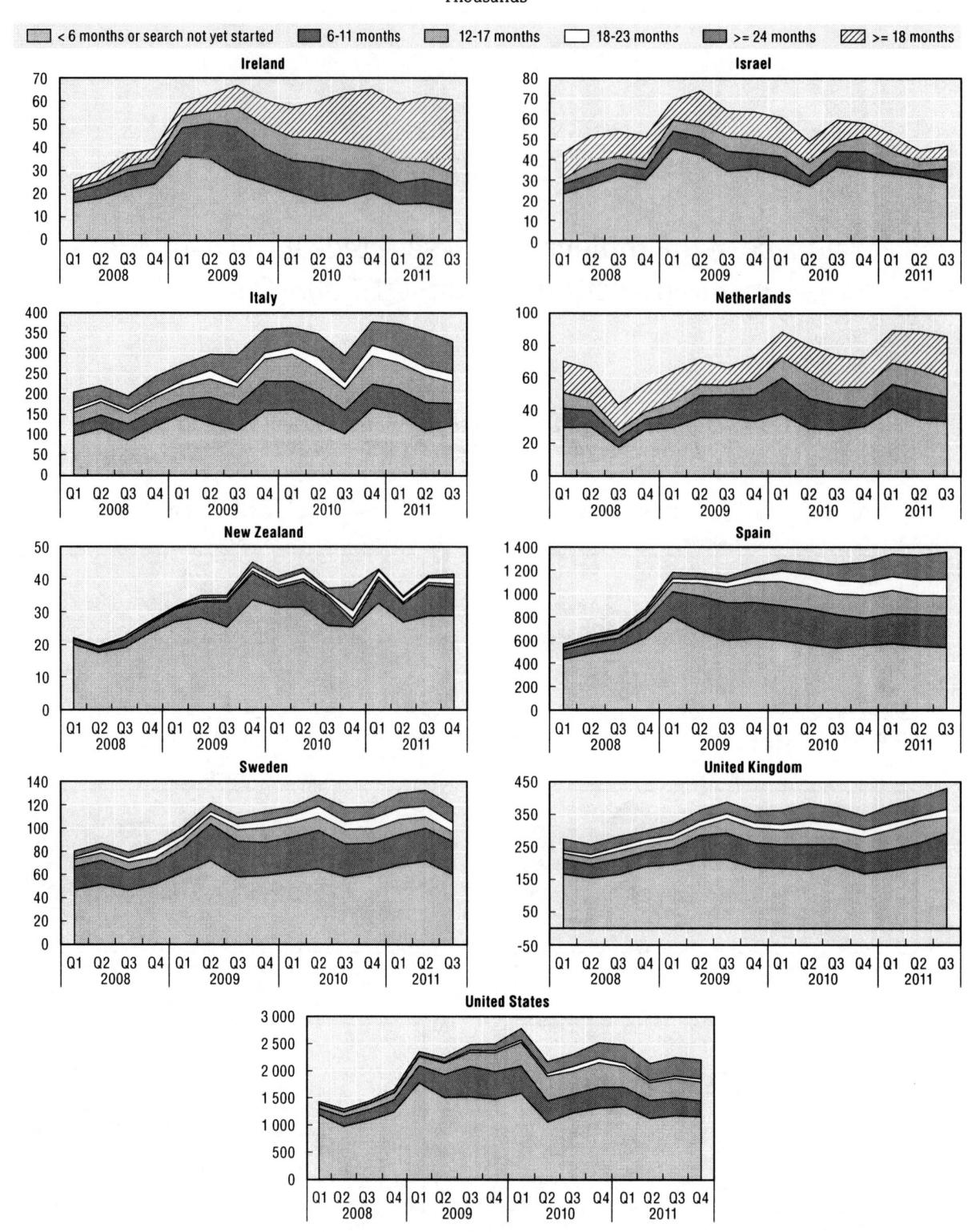

□ < 6 months or search not yet started   ■ 6-11 months   ▨ 12-17 months   □ 18-23 months   ■ >= 24 months   ▨ >= 18 months

Note: Information on data for Israel: http://dx.doi.org/10.1787/888932315602.

Sources: EU Labour Force Survey data (Eurostat); United States: Current Population Survey; Australia, Israel, New Zealand: Labour Force surveys.

StatLink http://dx.doi.org/10.1787/888932615536

ANNEX I.B3

NEET, short-term and long-term unemployment rates for foreign- and native-born in selected OECD countries, 2011

Figure I.B3.1. **NEET, short-term and long-term unemployment rates among youth (15-24), 2011**
Percentages

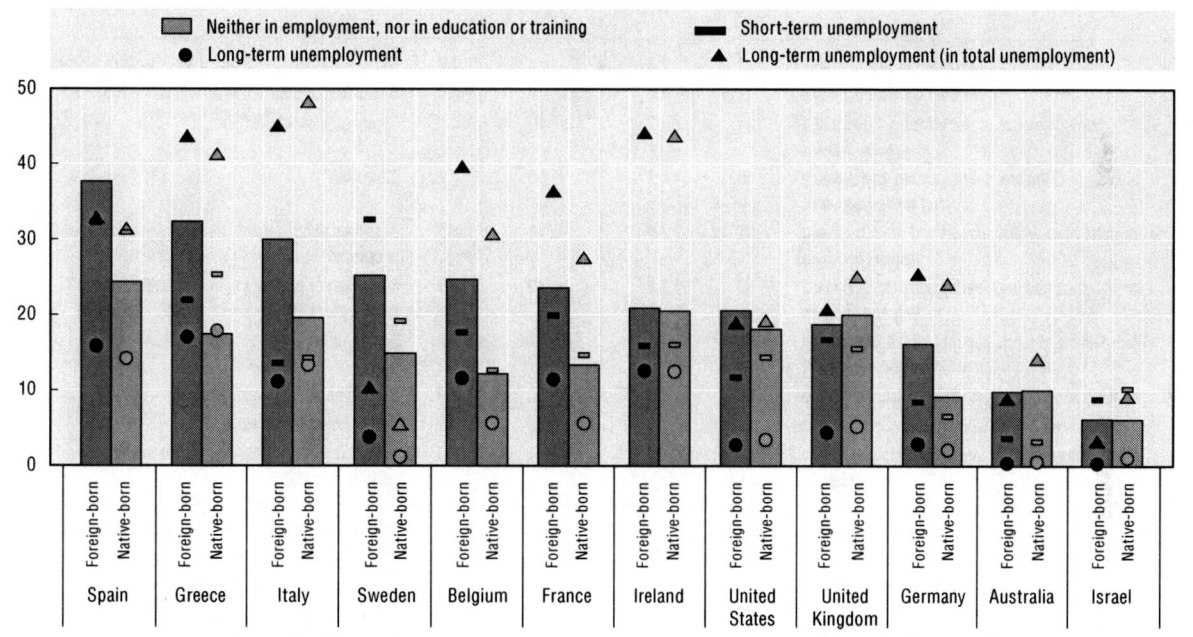

Notes: 2007 instead of 2008 for the United States. Short- and long-term unemployment are measured as percentage of the labour force in the 15-24 age-group. Long-term unemployment is expressed as a share of total unemployment. NEET is expressed as a share of the total population. Information on data for Israel: *http://dx.doi.org/10.1787/888932315602*.

Sources: European Labour Force Surveys (Eurostat), Q1-Q3 2008 and Q1-Q3 2011; Israel: Labour Force Survey, Q1-Q3 2008 and Q1-Q3 2011; United States: Current Population Surveys, 2007 and 2011. The results for NEET in Europe are overestimated because they are based on three quarters, including summertime, when under declaration of school enrolment of students is commonly observed.

StatLink ⟶ http://dx.doi.org/10.1787/888932615555

ANNEX I.B4

Foreign-born employment by sector of activity

Table I.B4.1. **Ten industries with the largest changes in foreign- and native-born employment, in selected OECD countries, 2010-11**

A. European Union, 2010-11

	Native-born		Foreign-born		
	Change (000)	%	Change (000)	%	
Human health activities	156	1.4	78	4.3	Retail trade, except of motor vehicles and motorcycles
Residential care activities	147	4.0	67	6.0	Specialised construction activities
Manufacture of motor vehicles, trailers and semi-trailers	134	5.7	66	10.8	Residential care activities
Computer programming, consultancy and related activities	95	4.3	53	4.7	Education
Office administrative, office support and other business support activities	91	7.8	43	3.5	Activities of households as employers of domestic personnel
Architectural and engineering activities; technical testing and analysis	66	2.8	43	12.5	Manufacture of motor vehicles, trailers and semi-trailers
Manufacture of fabricated metal products, except machinery and equipment	65	2.2	37	2.2	Food and beverage service activities
Warehousing and support activities for transportation	56	2.8	36	2.9	Human health activities
Social work activities without accommodation	55	1.3	35	19.5	Employment activities
Manufacture of computer, electronic and optical products	52	4.0	34	12.3	Financial service activities, except insurance and pension funding
Manufacture of furniture	−53	−5.3	−6	−7.3	Insurance, reinsurance and pension funding, except compulsory social security
Printing and reproduction of recorded media	−60	−6.5	−6	−0.9	Wholesale trade, except of motor vehicles and motorcycles
Manufacture of other transport equipment	−63	−7.1	−7	−7.7	Manufacture of furniture
Wholesale trade, except of motor vehicles and motorcycles	−73	−1.2	−7	−9.7	Manufacture of paper and paper products
Postal and courier activities	−79	−4.9	−8	−5.8	Creative, arts and entertainment activities
Wholesale and retail trade and repair of motor vehicles and motorcycles	−85	−2.5	−8	−10.0	Manufacture of basic pharmaceutical products and pharmaceutical preparations
Specialised construction activities	−91	−1.2	−8	−5.8	Manufacture of other non-metallic mineral products
Crop and animal production, hunting and related service activities	−137	−2.2	−9	−4.4	Manufacture of rubber and plastic products
Public administration and defence; compulsory social security	−141	−1.0	−19	−4.9	Other personal service activities
Construction of buildings	−274	−6.8	−70	−8.5	Construction of buildings

Notes: Working-age population (15-64). European members of the OECD, except Turkey and Switzerland where data are not available on the whole period; NACE Rev. 2.
Sources: European Labour Force Surveys, Q1-Q3 2008 and Q1-Q3 2011.

Table I.B4.1. **Ten industries with the largest changes in foreign- and native-born employment, in selected OECD countries, 2010-11** (cont.)

B. United States, 2010-11

	Native-born		Foreign-born		
	Change (000)	%	Change (000)	%	
Food services and drinking places	206	3.3	119	9.7	Professional and technical services
Professional and technical services	180	2.4	53	3.7	Administrative and support services
Management of companies and enterprises	98	151.6	41	19.5	Primary metals and fabricated metal products
Miscellaneous and not specified manufacturing	94	10.5	31	7.0	Agriculture
Primary metals and fabricated metal products	78	6.2	26	7.9	Computer and electronic product manufacturing
Mining	71	11.0	23	11.7	Chemical manufacturing
Transportation and warehousing	66	1.5	19	293.0	Management of companies and enterprises
Private households	63	19.5	10	16.6	Mining
Chemical manufacturing	58	6.0	10	11.2	Utilities
Transportation equipment manufacturing	55	3.4	10	1.8	Personal and laundry services
Motion picture and sound recording industries	−29	−7.5	−11	−1.2	Hospitals
Nonmetallic mineral product manufacturing	−34	−9.8	−16	−1.4	Transportation and warehousing
Retail trade	−35	−0.3	−16	−7.4	Textile, apparel, and leather manufacturing
Construction	−36	−0.5	−17	−3.5	Social assistance
Paper and printing	−38	−5.0	−18	−4.2	Repair and maintenance
Arts, entertainment, and recreation	−42	−1.7	−21	−16.6	Paper and printing
Membership associations and organisations	−71	−4.7	−26	−1.2	Construction
Personal and laundry services	−72	−4.4	−30	−5.7	Food manufacturing
Public administration	−124	−2.0	−30	−4.8	Wholesale trade
Educational services	−237	−2.1	−42	−3.0	Health care services, except hospitals

Notes: Working-age population (15-64). Industries are derived from the 2002 census Classification.
Sources: Current Population Surveys.

StatLink http://dx.doi.org/10.1787/888932616961

Table I.B4.2. **Employment of foreign-born persons by sector, 2011**
Percentage of total foreign-born employment

	Agriculture and fishing	Mining, Manufacturing and Energy	Construction	Wholesale and retail trade	Hotels and restaurants	Education	Health	Households	Admin. and ETO	Other services
Austria	0.9	17.8	11.8	14.6	12.1	4.3	9.5	–	2.6	25.8
Belgium	0.6	13.3	9.6	11.8	8.2	5.5	10.9	2.2	9.9	28.0
Czech Republic	1.2	31.1	10.1	15.1	5.6	5.2	4.6	–	3.1	23.9
Denmark	2.4	13.9	1.8	11.8	7.5	9.5	21.5	–	3.2	28.0
Finland	2.6	15.3	6.1	12.8	8.5	8.1	11.7	–	2.5	32.3
France	1.3	11.7	12.3	11.7	7.0	5.2	11.6	5.4	6.4	27.5
Germany	0.7	25.6	7.0	12.7	8.8	4.5	10.7	1.1	2.4	26.6
Greece	8.9	13.4	19.2	14.6	12.1	1.5	3.2	14.7	0.9	11.5
Hungary	–	23.9	7.9	16.1	5.7	9.8	9.4	–	4.5	20.0
Iceland	–	19.1	–	8.2	11.2	8.9	14.5	–	–	26.6
Ireland	2.2	17.1	4.2	16.3	11.7	4.9	14.4	1.0	2.2	26.0
Israel	1.2	19.7	4.9	13.3	4.1	9.2	13.5	3.7	3.4	25.7
Italy	4.0	20.6	13.6	10.1	8.8	1.9	4.8	17.0	1.4	17.7
Luxembourg	–	6.8	9.9	10.8	5.9	4.1	7.4	3.5	14.4	37.0
Netherlands	1.7	14.5	4.2	12.6	6.8	6.6	16.4	–	6.3	30.8
Norway	–	12.0	6.2	11.2	6.8	6.5	24.3	–	3.0	28.5
Portugal	–	14.1	9.9	13.3	10.5	9.1	7.2	5.1	7.1	22.2
Slovenia	–	31.0	17.7	7.9	8.2	5.0	5.9	0.0	2.8	20.0
Spain	5.7	9.3	10.5	13.6	16.1	2.2	5.0	14.9	2.0	20.6
Sweden	0.6	13.2	4.1	11.1	7.2	11.3	19.3	–	3.7	29.4
Switzerland	1.2	18.4	8.0	14.2	7.7	5.3	13.1	1.3	2.2	28.6
Turkey	12.2	20.5	11.1	15.9	4.7	6.6	3.0	2.0	5.9	18.1
United Kingdom	0.5	10.6	5.7	13.2	9.2	8.2	15.6	0.4	4.1	32.4
United States	2.2	12.9	9.3	13.9	10.5	5.8	12.1	1.4	2.4	29.5

Notes: A dash indicates that the estimate is not reliable enough for publication. ETO stands for extra-territorial organisations. Information on data for Israel: *http://dx.doi.org/10.1787/888932315602*.
Sources: European Labour Force Surveys (Eurostat), Q1-Q3 2011; United States: Current Population Survey 2011; Israel: Labour Force Survey.

StatLink http://dx.doi.org/10.1787/888932616980

C. Migration policy developments

1. Introduction

Behind the migration policy changes in OECD and other countries in recent years have been a number of factors. In some cases, policies have been changed to deal with the effects of the global economic crisis, often through more restrictive measures. In other cases, policy changes reflect a shift in paradigm, due to changes in governments or other shifts in the social and political situation in countries. While long-standing concerns about the impact of ageing populations and the need to attract skilled workers remain in the background, and even in crisis drive some reforms, this has been counteracted by a souring of public opinion regarding migration in some countries. Finally, many reforms are a response not to external factors but to efficiency issues, such as bottlenecks and backlogs in processing, or to refinements made based on operational experience, such as tweaks to admission criteria to prevent abuse.

Overall, in 2010-11, labour migration policy has generally become more selective, and family and humanitarian entry policy more restrictive. Measures designed to better integrate migrants in host societies have continued at a pace in line with previous years.

This section aims at providing overview of the main trends and changes of migration policies in OECD countries, as well as Bulgaria, Romania, Lithuania and the Russian Federation. The main trends in the framework legislation and policy shifts induced by political change are summarised in sub-section 2, followed by an overview of recent changes in labour migration policies (sub-section 3) and family and humanitarian policies (sub-section 4). Sub-section 5 deals with the developments in the fields of irregular migration and regularisation. The main implications for migration policies resulting from the EU legislation and other intergovernmental and international co-operation are discussed in sub-section 6. Sub-section 7 describes the recent trends in integration and naturalisation policies. The section then summarises the findings and identifies the principle common trends in the migration policy developments.

2. Framework legislation, changes in governments leading to policy shifts

In several OECD countries recent political changes led to migration policy shifts

Several OECD countries witnessed major political changes during 2010-11 as a result of elections or changes of political paradigm that triggered shifts in migration policies either in the direction of strengthening a rights-based approach and migrants' protection (for example in Mexico, Greece and Denmark), or in the direction of more restrictive migration policies (for example in the United Kingdom and the Netherlands).

Elections in the United Kingdom in 2010 led to a government committed to reducing total net migration to the country, with consequent impact on admission and stay policy for most categories of migrant, from labour migrants to students to family members.

A country where political change led to stricter migration policies was the Netherlands, where the newly elected government in 2010 announced its focus on restructuring, reducing and controlling immigration. A new "Modern Migration Policy Bill", passed in

February 2010, introduced changes to the admission system, although implementation has been delayed to 2012. In 2011, issuance of temporary work permits to non-EU/EFTA nationals was significantly restricted with the aim to secure work opportunities for Dutch citizens. In September 2011, new measures were announced that will limit possibilities for family reunification by restricting the eligibility to the "core" family, introducing a waiting period of one year, and increasing the length of period of stay required for further independent stay from three to five years. Asylum policy was also tightened. Finally, illegal stay was classified as a criminal offence punishable by a detention of up to four months or a fine (not applicable to minors).

In Denmark, elections in 2011 also led to the formation of a government pledged to ease several provisions of migration law, especially regarding family reunification and migrant integration.

Important changes were also implemented in Greece towards a more open approach to immigration and naturalisation. New acts adopted in 2010 significantly facilitated naturalisation of immigrants and their children, and introduced local political rights for migrants who have lived in Greece for at least five years. Links between integration and local policy were strengthened by the means of new Councils for Migrant Integration at the municipal level. The councils, advisory bodies to the mayors for the issues concerning the local migrant population, comprise members of the municipal council, social stakeholders and representatives of migrants.

Several countries introduced new migration policy strategies and frameworks

Another development in the field of migration policy was the adoption of new comprehensive migration policy frameworks in the form of national migration strategies in those countries that have not experienced a substantial immigration so far (Poland, Mexico, and Bulgaria). In these countries, emigration traditionally prevailed over immigration. Therefore, securing skilled labour force and competitiveness stands as a prominent priority that motivated the development of the national migration frameworks. Issues such as the reversal of negative migration balance, attraction of skilled labour force, return of own citizens from abroad, better integration of the existing migrants are among the key focuses of the new migration strategies. In Poland, the Inter-Ministerial Committee on Migration adopted in July 2011 a strategic document entitled "The Polish Migration Policy: Current state of play and further actions", which constitutes the first comprehensive strategic document on migration policy in Poland. The strategy stresses the need for the country to be more open for immigrants with needed skills and to facilitate their integration. The adoption of the strategy was preceded and accompanied by legislative changes aimed at increasing the country's attractiveness to migrants (see also the third Polish regularisation described in sub-section 7). Similarly, the Slovak Republic has been recently placing more and more importance on its migration policy in order to secure growth through mobilising qualified and skilled labour: in 2011 it adopted a comprehensive Migration Policy, stipulating a leading role for the EU political and legal framework in determining policy.

A major development occurred in 2011 in Mexico where the government has enacted the first Migration Act in the history of the country. A new Act on Refugees and Complementary Protection was also enacted. These changes materialised within a broader framework of constitutional reform of 2011 that represents a major shift towards strengthening human rights agenda in Mexico and is considered the most important reform in the field of Mexico's international human rights commitments in the last twenty years.[1] The National Human Rights Commission gained the right to carry out investigations and to officially request that local and federal laws that violate human rights be declared unconstitutional. The new Migration Law emphasises dignity and human rights approach towards migration, simplifies the number of categories of migrants, reduces the discretion of migration authorities and explicitly defines migration forms and procedures. Emphasis is also placed on family unification issues as well as health care and education rights of migrants, especially minors. The new Law on Refugees and Complementary Protection, enacted in January 2011, adopts the definition of refugee from the 1951 Geneva Convention and includes fundamental protection principles (no forced returns, non-discrimination, family unity, best interests of the child and confidentiality). The law also introduces a new legal concept of complementary protection for persons who do not legally qualify as refugees but may still require protection on other grounds. An important feature of the new act is the recognition of gender violence and discrimination as grounds for requesting refugee status.

Bulgaria adopted a new National Migration, Asylum and Integration Strategy for 2011-20 that aims to prevent illegal migration and improve management of labour migration. The new strategy is based on the recognition of opportunities that migration could provide for demographic and economic development. The Strategy also emphasises the integration of migrants.

Lithuania incorporated migration issues into its broader Global Lithuania Strategy, which includes initiatives to reinforce links with emigrants and diaspora outside the country.

New measures and changes occurred also within the existing migration policy frameworks

In several other OECD countries, where broader migration policy frameworks remained, unchanged, new measures were introduced to align these frameworks with national development goals. More significant changes in this regard occurred mainly in settlement countries (Australia, Canada, New Zealand), as well as in Ireland and Austria. The Australian government introduced in its 2011-12 budget three new migration initiatives to facilitate the process of structural adjustment in the economy. Following the recommendations made in 2010 by the National Resource Sector Employment Taskforce, the government will allow the developers of major new resource projects to source the necessary labour supply from abroad to prevent labour supply bottlenecks. Developers will enter into Enterprise Migration Agreements with the government, which will specify for each project the type, number and visa duration for temporary migrant workers. This sectoral initiative will be complemented by a regional one that aims to mitigate shortfall of skilled workers or overall shortfall of workers in some Australian regions. Regional Migration Agreements will be concluded among employers, unions and local and federal governments that will permit concessional arrangements to create incentives for skilled and semi-skilled migrant workers to be recruited into those regions.

In Canada, the process aimed at accelerating immigration procedures and reducing backlogs of applications, launched in 2008 under the Action Plan for Faster Immigration, continued through issuance of four sets of ministerial instructions until 2011. These provided, *inter alia*, for defining eligibility criteria for foreign workers, capping new applications to be considered under the priority occupation scheme, and inviting selected foreign PhD students to apply as foreign workers.

A new Immigration Act came into force in November 2010 in New Zealand, and the major policy developments in 2010-11 related to its implementation, introducing interim visas, establishing an Immigration and Protection Tribunal, and strengthening the sponsorship system. The new Act unifies entry and stay documents under a single "visa".

An amendment of the Residence Act came into effect in Austria in July 2011 introducing a new points-based system ("Red-White-Red Card", see next section) inspired by schemes in use, for example, in Canada or New Zealand. The change, along with the transposition of the EU Blue Card Directive, will have also have implications in broadening the scope for family reunifications in Austria.

3. Labour migration

Labour migration is seen in some countries as linked to demographic or population issues

Australia has introduced a policy initiative directly linking labour migration with broader population issues during the period of this review, with the release of its first Sustainable Population Strategy in 2011. Initiatives include a programme to support the marketing of regional settlements outside Australia's major cities as an alternative to living in a major capital city, and new Regional Migration Agreements aimed at enhancing the effectiveness of the migration programme by ensuring it responds to changing economic needs, in regions outside of the major cities. It allocated more migration places to the latter and introduced regional and enterprise migration agreements.

Measures to reinforce protection of the domestic labour market

A common objective among member countries in the last few years has been to acquire and maintain a favourable position in the international competition for skills and talents, with a trend towards greater selectivity in labour migration which favours the young and highly skilled. As the recession has unfolded, a number of trends have become manifest. While attention is still focused on endemic skill shortages, lack of demand from employers has reduced their need to import skills. At the same time, governments have sought to protect their domestic workforces in the face of rising unemployment and have become more restrictive towards foreign recruitment. They have also introduced measures to ease the situation for foreign workers who have lost their jobs, mainly by allowing them to stay on and search for work. The role of sponsors has also come under scrutiny.

These trends are still continuing. Four countries introduced major new policy initiatives designed to protect their labour markets and to monitor sponsors: the United Kingdom, Ireland, the Netherlands and Israel.[2] In the United Kingdom, a general election was held in May 2010, which resulted in the formation of a new government committed to reducing net migration, leading to imposition of restrictions on a series of categories of immigration. In July 2010 limits on economic migration from non-EEA countries were implemented by capping the visas issued for labour migrants under Tier 1 (highly skilled workers) and Tier 2 (skilled workers with a job offer) of the labour immigration scheme to the United Kingdom managed by the points-based system. The interim limits were aimed at keeping the numbers of issued visas 5% under the levels for the same period of the previous year. Further long-term limits were announced to take effect as of April 2011 and set at 1 000 visas annually for Tier 1 (not including investors and entrepreneurs who are not subject to a limit). The new government also announced its plan to condition the link between temporary and permanent migration. A number of further changes have been implemented to the immigration system following a review in 2011, tightening conditions on employment-related settlement, raising education thresholds for labour migrants, and launching new provisions for exceptionally talented migrants.

In 2010, in light of the economic crisis, the Irish government restated its policy to limit the issue of new employment permits to specific groups: those in highly skilled, highly paid positions; non-EEA nationals who were already legally resident in the country on valid employment permits; or those in occupations where there is an officially recognised scarcity of workers of a particular type or qualification. New arrangements saw a consolidated set of policies introduced, with a general scheme for current holders of work permits (including spousal/dependant permits) and work authorisations/visas for at least five consecutive years exempted from the requirement to hold a work permit on the next renewal of their immigration registration. In the case of persons working in Ireland on a work permit for less than five continuous years and who became redundant involuntarily, and those with five or more years of residence but not eligible for the aforementioned waiver, a six-month "grace period" is available under which they may seek alternative work without a labour market test being applied.

As a response to recession and to lower the unemployment rate of Dutch citizens, in 2011 the Dutch Cabinet further restricted the issuance of temporary work permits to migrants from outside the EU, so that only in exceptional cases would a permit be granted. In addition, a labour migrant from outside the EU must hold a work permit for five, instead of three, years, before being eligible for a permit with full labour market access. The new system streamlines the admission and residence procedure so that migrants no longer have to submit two separate applications for a provisional residence permit and a regular residence permit. Employers, in their role as sponsors, have been given more responsibility. They may submit residency applications on behalf of foreign nationals and applications for residence permits on their behalf while they are still abroad. However, the authorities now have greater powers to act against sponsors and foreign nationals who do not fulfil their legal obligations, such as better supervision of the payment of salaries to foreign bank accounts. Payment of salaries to bank accounts outside the Netherlands will be prevented where possible and employer-borne expenses, such as housing and travel costs, no longer count towards minimum salary requirements.

Economic conditions led to restrictions, from 2010 onwards, on the immigration of foreign workers in Israel, through reduced quotas available to employers. Agreements were signed with agriculture and construction employers for a gradual reduction in quotas up to 2016. In the construction sector, the quota will be eliminated. Despite complaints from the private sector, the government has tightened regulations on the employment of foreign care workers by restricting work permits to certain regions of the country or to certain sub-branches of the care-giving sector.

Ongoing cutbacks to shortage occupation lists

For much of the last decade, the policy tide flowed strongly in the direction of attempts to recruit the highly skilled across a wide range of occupations, as countries competed for international experts and talent. As the economic downturn persisted, countries reconsidered their positions. Recruitment of highly skilled workers slowed, quotas were lowered and selectivity increased.

While countries still seek highly skilled immigrants – for example, in 2010 the government of Luxembourg provided more favourable tax treatment of costs related to recruitment of highly skilled workers – the main trend recently has been for governments to become much more selective. The principal tools in this trend are shortage occupation lists. The permanent immigration countries and some European ones have used such lists as a basis for migrant selection for some time. In the last few years, the practice has been increasingly embraced, including by Portugal, Denmark, Ireland, the United Kingdom and Lithuania. With recession, reviews of shortage lists have been more frequent, in most cases reducing the number of occupations they contain.

It is clear that some chronic shortages do continue independent of the economic situation. Three countries, Germany, Ireland and New Zealand, have targeted certain occupations they require. As part of its plan to safeguard the supply of skilled workers, the German government introduced a "positive list", whereby the labour market test is suspended for those professions in which there is already an obvious shortage of skilled workers and for non-EU/EFTA citizens with a foreign degree. This applies initially to medical doctors and mechanical, automotive and electrical engineers. The list is reviewed by the Federal Employment Agency every six months. In addition, the salary limit for granting an immediate, indefinite residence permit to highly-qualified specialists and executive staff with exceptional professional experience is to be reduced from the previous EUR 66 000 per year to EUR 48 000.

As with Germany, during 2010 new arrangements in Ireland mean that entry has been eased for certain categories of doctors. They no longer require a work permit, nor would a labour market needs test be necessary.

In an effort to engage more with the knowledge economy, New Zealand has taken steps to attract visiting academic researchers. A new special visitor's visa was introduced in early 2011 to allow academics from 50 countries with which New Zealand has special visa waiver arrangements to travel to New Zealand to undertake academic work without first obtaining a visa offshore. The new visa allows established academics who are invited by a tertiary institution to stay for up to three months to undertake academic, research, or pedagogical work. In a separate development, New Zealand's new interim visa system, introduced in 2011, allows people to remain lawfully in the country between two visas and is valid for six months or until a decision is made on their application, whichever is the earliest. The conditions of interim visas (allowing work, study, or visitor rights) depend on the combination of the visa recently expired and the visa applied for. For instance, all applicants for student visas and student visa holders are granted study conditions, and workers applying for a visa to stay in the same job for the same employer are allowed to continue working.

Several countries have used shortage lists and labour market tests to tighten up on foreign recruitment. In August 2011, France reduced the number of occupations on its list of shortage occupations from thirty to fourteen. As part of its review of the immigration system, in February 2011 the United Kingdom government announced that Tier 2 visas would only be available for occupations at university graduate level. Successive reviews of the Shortage Occupation List by the Migration Advisory Committee during 2011 have reduced the number of occupations included. In a further attempt to reduce labour immigration, the intra-company transfer route to the United Kingdom was restricted: the job has to be in an occupation on the graduate occupation list; only those paid GBP 40 000 or more will be able to stay for more than a year up to a maximum of three years; and those paid between GBP 24 000 and GBP 40 000 will be allowed to come to the United Kingdom for no longer than 12 months, after which they must leave and will not be able to re-apply for 12 months. In 2011, Lithuania further shortened its Shortage Occupation List: from seven occupations in the first half of 2010 to four in 2011. However, the government took steps to attract the foreign labour required by accelerating admission and increasing flexibility in assessing employers' needs.

Spain changed the conditions for inclusion in its skill shortage list and adds mechanisms to take the domestic labour market situation into account in issuing temporary work permits and work permits for collective recruitment abroad. Self-employment permits are now limited by region and sector of activity. Financial requirements for employers of foreign labour, including households, have been made stricter. For skilled workers whose jobs are not on the shortage list, permits are only available after a resident labour market test has been carried out; the salary must be above average for the job; and ethical recruitment to prevent brain drain from sending countries is contemplated.

Administrative reasons lie, at least in part, behind Canada's decision in 2010 to reduce its intake under the priority occupation component of its Federal Skilled Worker programme. Because of a backlog, in 2010 Canada capped new applications to be considered under the priority occupation scheme to a total of 20 000 per year and a total of 1 000 per occupation. This was lowered to 10 000 and 500 per occupation in 2011. In addition, all permanent labour migrants now need to prove language proficiency through an independent test.

Points systems provide flexibility in the face of recession and change of government

Following the lead of Australia, Canada and New Zealand, some European member countries have adopted Points-Based Systems (PBS) for selecting immigrants (OECD, 2011). In most cases, the systems are related to shortage lists, with more points available for shortage occupations. Since 2008, the United Kingdom, Denmark, the Netherlands and Austria have adopted a PBS. Korea now also uses a PBS for accelerated permanent residence. Japan, as part of its strategy to promote economic growth, introduced a PBS in 2012 for selecting highly qualified immigrant workers. Elsewhere, countries are adjusting the parameters of their PBS to change the characteristics and numbers of immigrants accepted.

Australia's revised points test for General Skilled Migration applicants, with effect since July 2011, is designed to increase the overall skills base in the country. The new system recognises a broader range of skills and attributes than before, focusing on: better English levels; more extensive skilled employment; higher level qualifications obtained in Australia and overseas; and certain age ranges. Points are still awarded for study in Australia, including regional study, community languages, partner skills and the completion of an approved professional year. Points will no longer be awarded for specific occupations, although eligibility requires an occupation included in the Skilled Occupation List (SOL) and a skills assessment. The government will also introduce a new skilled migrant selection register, SkillSelect, in July 2012. Under the electronic two-stage process, prospective migrants first submit an expression of interest and may then be invited by the Immigration Department to make a skilled migration visa application.

Austria replaced its quota system for immigration of non-EU/EFTA citizens with a PBS during 2011. The new system differentiates four types of skilled persons: highly skilled; with scarce occupational skills; with other (medium to higher) skills; and university graduates. Points are given for educational qualifications and recognition of competences, occupational experience, language skills and age. Further points are attributed from graduation from an Austrian university. The permit is called Red-White-Red (RWR) Card. Highly skilled third country citizens must obtain at least 70 out of 100 possible points; for the other categories, 50 out of 75 points must be reached. Two types of cards may be issued, an RWR Card and an RWR Card plus. The former grants settlement and work with a specific employer (employer nomination), the latter allows settlement and free access to work anywhere in Austria. Family members of RWR Card holders receive an RWR Card plus, allowing them to work in Austria. Non-EU/EFTA citizens without a job offer in hand receive a job search visa, convertible into an RWR card if the required points are achieved.

The United Kingdom, where the PBS was introduced in 2008, imposed an annual limit on Tier 2 Certificates of Sponsorship from April 2011. Under the new system, employers have to apply for a certificate of sponsorship from the United Kingdom Border Agency for a specific post if they wish to bring someone to the United Kingdom, a change from the previous system which gave businesses an annual allocation. The annual limit of 20 700 certificates of sponsorship is divided into 12 monthly allocations, with unused monthly allocations rolled over to the following month. If the monthly allocation is oversubscribed, applications are ranked according to their score on the PBS. Once a certificate of sponsorship has been granted to an employer it must be assigned to the prospective employee within three months. Workers from outside the EU who want to come to the United Kingdom must have a graduate level job, speak at least an intermediate level of English, and meet specific salary and employment requirements.

Countries continue to scrutinise their temporary worker programmes

While most OECD countries continue to support policies designed to bring in the required skills, temporary work programmes and the agencies involved in them are increasingly under scrutiny. For example, in June 2010, Australia began the process of halving the number of types of temporary work visas by 2012, with a similar reduction in the total number of visa sub-classes by 2015. The Czech government announced in 2011 that private employment agencies would be allowed to supply clients only with those non-EU/EFTA nationals who have free access to the Czech labour market. It also gave greater responsibility to employers in case workers lose their job before the expiration of their work permit, and established a two-year residence requirement prior to change of status to self-employment.

In Canada, amendments to the broader Temporary Foreign Worker Programme were introduced in April 2011 to improve compliance by employers and better safeguard temporary workers. Among other provisions, employers who violate the terms of their job offers are now denied future access to the programme. The amount of time temporary foreign workers may stay is now limited, reinforcing the temporary nature of work under the programme and encouraging eligible workers and employers to use appropriate pathways to permanent residence.

The role of sponsoring employers was strengthened in New Zealand. The Immigration Act 2009 created a new framework for sponsorship, giving more protection to sponsored individuals and New Zealand taxpayers by ensuring sponsorship requirements and obligations are applied consistently across different categories. Key changes included extending mandatory sponsorship obligations to cover all aspects of maintenance, accommodation and repatriation (or deportation) for the sponsored person; making sponsorship a condition of a visa, rather than a requirement for an application; introducing a clear duration for sponsorship of temporary visa holders; introducing eligibility criteria for sponsors, while extending eligibility to organisations and government agencies; and facilitating the recovery of costs incurred by a sponsored person by organisations and agencies external to the Department of Labour.

Temporary care workers were the subject of new regulations in Israel in 2010. Despite complaints from the private sector about recruitment restrictions, Israel tightened its regulations on the employment of foreign care workers by issuing work permits tied to certain regions or sub-branches of the care giving sector. However, a foreign care worker's employment may be extended beyond 63 months, even if the worker has not been employed for at least one year.

From 2010, Korea established rules for foreign nationals previously employed under its temporary scheme who wish to re-enter under the same scheme. A Korean-language exam, as well as a good employment history, are required for workers to return to the same employer, and in 2011 a quota was established so that not all workers entering would be "repeats".

Most new developments, however, relate to seasonal employment in agriculture. The Australian Government is exploring with a number of Pacific countries the possibility of expanding the Pacific Seasonal Worker Pilot Scheme to make it more flexible and reflect better the needs of the horticulture sector. It is also implementing a small scale pilot involving tourism industry employers in Western Australia and workers from East Timor.

Alongside the gradual reduction in foreign worker quotas, Israel in 2010 piloted a programme to examine the possibility of employing seasonal workers in agriculture. In view of the results, the government decided in September 2011 to continue the programme and to allow workers who had been employed in Israel during the pilot to return to Israel for an additional half year during 2012.

In contrast to Australia and Israel, Italy adopted a more restrictive approach to seasonal migration, reducing its quota of seasonal workers from 80 000 in 2010 to 60 000 in 2011 and 35 000 in 2012, also reflecting the fact that the quota had not been fully utilised in past years.

Emigration countries still have an eye on attracting labour migrants

While Central and Eastern European countries are trying to attract more (highly skilled) foreign workers, they have been taking steps to persuade their own skilled emigrants to return. Continuing skill shortages are common and in several cases countries have sought to attract highly skilled migrants during 2010-11. However, there now seems to be a greater emphasis on measures to formalise existing work permit systems, to protect domestic workforces through more rigorous resident labour market tests and to prevent abuse by employers.

New measures in the Slovak Republic and Hungary have been designed to attract entrepreneurs and highly skilled migrants. In 2010 the Slovak Republic made it easier for high level employees, such as investors and posted workers, to start work immediately after legally entering the country without having to wait for a temporary stay permit. New legislation in Hungary exempted senior management from the mandatory labour market test, while immigrant entrepreneurs may obtain a residence permit for gainful employment if they have employed at least three persons for a period of at least six months or if their presence in the country is essential for the operation of the business.

Poland, too, has taken steps to facilitate foreigners' access to the Polish labour market by simplifying and shortening the procedure for issuing work permits. In August 2011 the government introduced a single permit covering both residence and work and extended the maximum time for which a permit for a fixed period may be issued from two to three years. Five different types of work permits were introduced, with simpler procedures and much lower fees. Also, in order to meet Polish labour market needs more effectively, the shortage occupation list granting a labour market test exemption was extended. Students and graduates of Polish full-time higher education studies or full-time doctorate studies in Polish universities may now work without a permit. In order to protect the domestic workforce and prevent social dumping, employers are now required to pay foreigners a salary no lower than that received by Polish citizens working in a similar position. Finally, citizens of Belarus, the Russian Federation, Ukraine, Moldova and Georgia may now work in Poland without a work permit for up to six months on the basis of an employer's declaration of intent to recruit a foreigner, with full contractual details, rather than the standard work permit procedure. The new system is being more closely monitored in order to prevent abuse.

The Russian Federation also liberalised its regulatory framework for migration. Since July 2010, foreigners from visa-free countries may access the labour market through purchase of a "patent" (license) to work in private households. A monthly payment of RUB 1 000 (about USD 34) is sufficient for the acceptance of legal status. The procedure for recruiting highly-qualified foreign specialists, especially those coming on intra-company transfers, has also been simplified. The main criterion for acceptance is an annual salary of at least RUB 2 million (about USD 68 000), but only half that figure for high-level professors and researchers. Eligible migrants may also bring along their families.

In contrast, policy in Romania has become more restrictive. Work permit regulations have been tightened to prevent undeclared work or illegal employment of foreign workers. A special visa for posted workers has also been introduced to protect the Romanian workforce by curbing improper use of the posted worker system by employers.

Investors are still wanted but countries are becoming more selective

Most new policies designed to attract permanent migrants relate to investors and entrepreneurs. This route of entry is widely promoted, although numbers are usually small. In the recent past, Germany, Netherlands, Norway, New Zealand and the United Kingdom were among the countries that introduced measures to attract them (see OECD, 2011 for a comprehensive review). In many cases, however, requirements for entry and settlement have now been increased.

The United Kingdom government switched its investor route to Tier 1 of its points based system in 2011. An applicant can achieve the required number of points if he/she is able to invest GBP 1 million in the United Kingdom, and is exempt from the quota.

In contrast to other countries, a review of New Zealand's migrant investment policy resulted in a relaxation of conditions, making it easier for investors to enter. The residence requirement during the three-year investment period was reduced. On the other hand, migrant investors who wish to receive an extension for transfer of funds must demonstrate reasonable efforts to transfer funds within the first year, before being granted a six-month extension, whereas a 12-month extension was previously possible. A business now needs either to employ at least five full-time employees, or make at least NZL 1 million in turnover per annum, instead of both criteria being required at the same time.

New regulations for immigrant investors in Canada introduced in December 2010 double the personal net worth requirement for investor applicants and increase the investment amount. These amendments were prompted by changing client profiles, international competitiveness and increased provincial and territorial participation in the programme, as well as to take account of inflation. Further, an administrative backlog led to a temporary moratorium on the acceptance of federal immigrant investor applications. In 2011, Romania tightened investor visa conditions by increasing the minimum investment threshold.

International students are still welcomed but with more caution

Over the last decade there has been a trend towards granting foreign students the possibility of subsequently allowing them to stay and take up employment. It is with regard to the last of these that recent policies in OECD countries with respect to international students have been most concerned. New developments have focused on this and two additional areas: recruitment of students and dealing with fraud.

Over the past years many OECD countries have introduced policies to attract international students to their universities. New legislation was adopted in Finland, Lithuania, the Slovak Republic, Spain and Sweden in 2010-12 with this objective in mind. Finland has allowed universities to collect fees in individual programmes from students coming from outside the European Economic Area. The Slovak Republic and Lithuania have facilitated access to temporary residence permits. Sweden introduced tuition fees for non-EU/EFTA students from 2011 onwards. To maintain its attractiveness, in 2011 it assigned a number of universities and colleges to arrange supplementary courses for non-EU/EFTA with a foreign university degree. Access to programmes was increased and courses designed for specific professions. In addition, scholarships for international students will increase.

In September 2010, the Irish government published a new five-year strategy designed to enhance the country's competitive position as a centre for international education, with the aim of increasing the number of international students in tertiary education by 50% by 2015. Immigration rules will reflect the course of study, with visas for degree programmes fast-tracked and short-term English language students viewed as "educational tourists" subject to fewer conditions for entry. The education and immigration authorities will co-ordinate for entry management.

In an attempt to reduce fraud, several countries have introduced measures designed to restrict student entry and to ensure compliance by sponsors and students. In some cases, such measures have been accompanied by more liberal conditions for those already in the country. Beginning in 2011, New Zealand has put greater emphasis on compliance, including attendance, course completion and ensuring that students genuinely have funds available. A visa was introduced in 2011 for visiting academics. The Student Policy was reviewed in parallel with the pathways to work and residence for international students, with changes implemented in April 2012 including limiting student work rights to tertiary education students, and additional points for residence under the Skilled Migrant category.

The Australian government is considering the recommendations of a strategic review of the student visa programme. Recommendations include: streamline visa processing for international students enrolled in Bachelor programmes or certain types of higher degree courses; grant access to a post-study work visa dependent upon the duration and level of an applicant's study; apply a "genuine temporary entrant" requirement for all student visa applicants; and review student-visa risk management. The implementation of the resulting changes is expected to be ongoing until 2013.

In July 2011, the United Kingdom introduced major changes to the student entry route, mainly aimed at closing fictitious colleges used as avenues for irregular migration. Work entitlements and rights to bring in dependants were restricted, educational institutions were required to provide courses with academic progress, and applications streamlined for students from "low risk" countries and trusted sponsors. Subsequently, the government stipulated that only "highly trusted" sponsors approved by one of the publicly-recognised inspection bodies may sponsor students. At the same time, visa fees for international students were sharply increased.

The integrity of international student programmes is a general concern, with a number of countries working with genuine educational institutions and local governments. For example, the Canadian government has begun discussions with provinces and territories to reduce fraud and improve services to legitimate students, while Korea has made universities responsible for monitoring compliance of international students.

There is mostly strong support for foreign graduates to stay on and work

Over the last few years there has been strong support from both employers and governments for policies aimed at encouraging international students to stay on and seek work in the countries of their graduation. Recently, many countries have changed their rules in this regard.

Since 2011, graduates from Austrian universities may be granted a visa to look for a job in Austria. If they find adequate employment, obtaining at least 45% of the social security contributions ceiling (in 2011, monthly gross earnings of EUR 1 900), they receive the RWR card. Family members also receive full labour market access.

Two settlement countries have amended their regulations to facilitate transition from study to work. Since 2011, New Zealand awards international students points for residence under the skilled migrant category. Meanwhile, faced with a backlog of applications for permanent migration, Canada invited up to 1 000 foreign nationals currently studying for a PhD or recently graduated to apply under the temporary foreign worker programme.

In 2011, France and the United Kingdom both adopted stricter rules and control. France allows those with higher educational qualifications to stay and gain work experience in their specialist field, as temporary workers. Criteria for correspondence between employment and field of study were published in 2011, which in some cases represented a restriction compared with previous practice. The United Kingdom government announced a change of its post-study route into the labour market starting in 2012, with future foreign graduates from United Kingdom universities needing sponsorship from an employer under the Tier 2 skilled migrant route. However, in 2012, the government also announced a new route for international graduate entrepreneurs: students who have engaged in innovative entrepreneurial activity during their studies may stay on afterwards to develop their business ideas.

Finally, several countries in Eastern Europe have taken steps in 2010-11 to ease the entry of international students into their labour markets after graduation. Poland introduced a temporary residence permit, valid one year, for international graduates of Polish tertiary education institutions to allow them to search for a job in Poland. Graduating students in the Slovak Republic may, after completing their studies, change status to conduct business activities without having to leave and re-enter the country. Romania now allows international graduates with a study visa to stay on after graduation and work, contingent on full-time employment in the same domain as the area of studies.

4. Family and humanitarian policies

Family migration policies are generally getting more restrictive but there are exceptions

Developments in family migration policies since 2010 continue the trends of the previous decade. Overall, family reunion has become more restrictive, although in a few cases the reverse is true. The main settlement countries have long taken the characteristics of accompanying family members of labour migrants into account when making decisions about applications under their permanent immigration programmes, providing additional points for family characteristics. Some European countries are introducing or increasing conditions for family reunification more generally, including prior levels of language knowledge, housing and finance availability, age and length of marriage.

The new Danish government, elected in late 2011, announced a simplified family reunion system. The points system is to be revoked, the age requirement is again set at 24, and the "dispensation rule" (the length of time one partner must have had Danish citizenship) is reduced from 28 to 26 years. The previous immigration test and application fees are to be abolished, and the amount of collateral finance required from the sponsor reduced.

With the entry into force in 2011 of the 2009 Immigration Act, conditions for family reunion have changed in Spain. Income thresholds are set for each family member to be sponsored, non-marital cohabitation is accepted as a route to family reunion providing there is proof of a relationship, and greater flexibility is granted in allowing reunion of family members aged under 65. Total family income is now counted for renewal of the primary permit-holder's residence permit. For highly skilled workers, family reunion may occur without a year of prior residence, although applicants must show that they have appropriate housing available.

In contrast, other countries have imposed stricter requirements for family reunion. In 2010, the new Dutch government raised the minimum age for partners from 21 to 24 years, and the minimum income requirement from 100 to 120% of the minimum wage. In 2010, Austria raised the age of the partner who wants to enter Austria on the basis of family reunion to 21.

In April 2010, Sweden introduced new maintenance requirements as a prerequisite for family migration. A person who intends to bring in a family member to Sweden must have accommodation of adequate size and standard, in addition to sufficient income, that can sustain both him/her self and the family member. However, a sponsor is exempted from these requirements if the family tie involves a child or if the sponsor is a citizen of Sweden, an EEA-country, or if the sponsor is granted a residence permit as a refugee or a holder of a permanent residence permit and has lived in Sweden for at least four years.

Several governments have introduced or are contemplating new measures to deter fraudulent marriages, namely Finland, the United Kingdom, the Netherlands, Canada and Ireland. Amendments to family reunion provisions in Finland in 2011 are aimed at sponsors and designed to ensure that the sponsor's own residence permit was not based on false information about his or her identity or family relations. A sponsor who has received international protection is required to have secure income to be able to be reunited with his/her family if the family has been formed after arriving in Finland.

The United Kingdom government announced proposals in 2011 to introduce measures to prevent abuse of the family reunion system through sham marriages and also to curb forced marriage. In the same year, the Dutch government trod a similar path by adopting measures to limit family reunification and formation to the "core family", i.e. partners who are married or have a registered partnership and their underage children. It also imposed a one year waiting period for those wishing to bring in a partner and increased the required term to qualify for "continued independent stay" from three to five years.

Canada and Ireland both took steps in 2011 to deter marriages of convenience. Canadian proposals would bar a sponsored spouse or partner from sponsoring a new spouse or partner for five years after becoming a permanent resident. Ireland has taken steps to deter marriages of conveniences for non-EEA spouses of EU nationals. New guidelines for registrars conducting marriage ceremonies have been introduced containing more stringent identification requirements, restrictions on the use of interpreters and the number of persons who may be admitted to a registrar's office.

Growing concerns about the integration of family members have led several countries to introduce "integration tests" as a prerequisite for gaining residence permits. The Netherlands, Denmark, France, Germany and Austria have already taken this route (see OECD, 2011). Recently, Italy, Poland and the United Kingdom also introduced language tests. From December 2010, certain foreign citizens applying for permit renewal or permanent residence permits in Italy must demonstrate their knowledge of the Italian language. Poland has imposed a requirement of a basic knowledge of the Polish language to be granted a permanent residence permit. In 2010, the new United Kingdom government introduced an English-language requirement for migrants seeking to enter or remain in the country as the spouse of a British citizen or permanent resident.

Asylum procedures continue to be streamlined

Asylum has not been at the sharp end of national migration policies in recent years. Many countries overhauled their policies in the early 2000s and more recent measures have focused on greater efficiency. For example, a revision of Switzerland's asylum legislation in 2011 is intended to simplify and streamline procedures while providing asylum seekers with greater legal protection.

In the new member countries of the EU, most of the main asylum policy developments in recent years have been associated with the requirement to incorporate the 1951 Geneva Convention as well as EU directives and regulations into their national systems. In 2011 Bulgaria adopted a National Plan for Temporary Support of Refugees and Asylum Seekers, to deal with any sudden inflows. At the same time, a programme for integration of refugees was adopted. New legislation that came into force in Hungary in late 2010 clarified the conditions under which asylum is granted and sped up processes of determination, with applicants arriving from a safe third country able to be rejected in an accelerated procedure.

In March 2011, a new streamlined refugee assessment process for irregular maritime arrivals commenced in Australia. The new process addresses issues of procedural fairness in two stages. A departmental officer conducts an initial Protection Obligations Evaluation. If the applicant is found not to be in need of protection at that stage, the case will be automatically referred to an independent assessor for an Independent Protection Assessment. In September 2011, new complementary protection legislation was passed to clarify processes for people seeking a protection visa who are deemed to be at risk of torture, inhumane treatment or likely death if returned to their home country. In October 2011, the Australian government announced that asylum claims of individuals arriving in Australia by irregular maritime means will be processed in Australia.

A new law in Greece in early 2011, yet to be implemented, simplified procedures, and created a new asylum system with decentralised asylum offices. An autonomous asylum agency, rather than the police, will be responsible for the processing of asylum applications, within a 30-day period. In Turkey, authorities introduced screening of apprehended illegal migrants in order to identify those in need of protection.

Major asylum legislation in Mexico in 2010 was enacted in light of increased migration flows of people who might require special protection. For the first time, protection is guaranteed. The integration of refugees in rural areas is promoted, along with access to health care, education, employment and housing. In-country refugee status may now be granted. The law also allows for complementary protection, to be given to those who do not legally qualify as refugees but may still require protection. The law also recognises gender violence and discrimination as valid grounds for requesting refugee status.

Measures for asylum seekers who are in the system have been introduced in Australia, Austria, New Zealand and Poland. In Australia, the government pledged greater efforts to facilitate asylum seekers living in the community while their claims are assessed, rather than being held in immigration detention facilities. In Austria, from 2011, asylum seekers whose claim has been rejected by the asylum court are automatically provided with legal counselling and support, and beneficiaries of subsidiary protection can now request a permanent residence permit after five years of residence.

In New Zealand, the appeals process has been tightened; those excluded under the 1951 Geneva Convention, but who have protection status, will have their immigration status determined by the Minister of Immigration.

In July 2011, Poland amended its asylum legislation to allow resettlement in Poland of foreigners recognised as refugees by the UNHCR. Under the new regulations, the government can specify the number of and origin of refugees who can be relocated or resettled in Poland in a given year, and the amount of funds allocated to cover the costs of relocation or resettlement.

Denmark and Turkey have made it easier for asylum seekers to work while their cases are being examined. The new Danish government has announced that it will be easier for asylum seekers to work outside asylum centres, and is revising the criteria for selecting quota refugees. New regulations in Turkey in 2010 made it easier for asylum seekers to apply for work permits. In addition, residence permit fees imposed on asylum seekers have also been abolished and conditions improved for unaccompanied minors housed in institutions.

In contrast, new legislation in Finland in the spring of 2011 restricted an asylum seeker's right to work. In the future, only asylum seekers with valid travel documents will have the right to work after a three-month waiting period; for those without a valid travel document, the waiting period is six months.

Hungary and the Netherlands both tightened their policies relating to the families of asylum seekers in 2011. In the first, the definition of family was modified, so that the applicant's spouse is considered to be a family member only if the family relationship was already in existence prior to entering Hungary. Unaccompanied minor asylum seekers in the country are now placed in child protection facilities instead of reception centres. In the Netherlands, family members joining refugees will no longer be granted asylum status automatically, but will be subject to the regular family migration policy, although without income or integration requirements. Measures are also planned to return unaccompanied minors to their country of origin quickly, as long as reception is available for them locally.

The political changes in 2011 relating to the "Arab Spring" generated some flows of migrants and asylum seekers from the affected regions (see Section I.A). Italy in particular received substantial flows, which it addressed by declaring a "national state of emergency" on 12 February 2011. The main aim of this measure was to enable the Italian Department of Civil Defence to co-ordinate its migrant reception operations. It granted Tunisian citizens who entered Italy during the first months of 2011 humanitarian protection status.

5. Irregular migration and regularisation

Border control and international co-operation on border control remain a challenge

Following the rapid increase of illegal landings on the Italian shores in early 2011, Italy concluded, in April 2011, an agreement with Tunisia concerning control over departures and acceptance of direct repatriation of migrants. More than 3 500 Tunisian citizens were repatriated under this agreement by October 2011.

As the Greek-Turkish border was the main point of illegal entries into the EU in 2010,[3] Greece adopted a new law in January 2011 addressing the management of irregular migration flows. According to the new law, reception centres for newly arrived irregular migrants should be created and decentralised asylum offices. However, due to budget situation in Greece, implementation of these measures was postponed. In Turkey, where a high number of illegal migrants (around 60 000 annually) and a growing number of traffickers are apprehended, the capacity to process these cases is limited.

Several OECD countries implemented particular changes aimed at decreasing irregular migration. Austria's revision of the Alien Act in 2011 increased the possibilities of detention of asylum seekers, deprivation of subsidiary protection, and restriction of mobility for newly-arrived asylum seekers. Finland strengthened the security regime by introducing biometric features in residence permits and biometric residence cards. In Israel the Ministry of Justice accelerated plans for the construction of a large reception centre so that asylum seekers would not be released.

Another OECD region highly exposed to illegal border-crossing is the southern Mexican border. Mexico's response includes laws to combat human trafficking, such as the 2007 Act to Prevent and Punish Human Trafficking or the 2011 Migration Act, which increase sanctions and broaden the coverage of related crimes. A new institution, a Special Public Attorney for Crimes of Violence against Women and Human Trafficking, was created to address the problem. Federal and state governments in Mexico have signed agreements with the most affected Central American countries in order to exchange information and co-ordinate actions against trafficking and smuggling.

At the international level, Mexico joined the "Blue Heart" campaign led by the United Nations Office on Drugs and Crime to raise awareness on human trafficking and signed the Global Plan of Action to Combat Trafficking in Persons (September 2010) launched by the United Nations. Mexico also adopted a co-operation agreement with the United Nations Office on Drugs and Crime (UNODC). The medium-term strategy (2008-11) established a regional office for Mexico, Central America and the Caribbean and provides an operational framework for the Office's work. However, human smuggling and trafficking continues to be a major issue of concern in the region.

New amnesties and regularisation initiatives seem to subside

In July 2011, the Polish Parliament passed an Act on legalisation of the stay of some foreigners on the territory of Poland, which will give an opportunity to foreigners who have been staying in Poland illegally since at least 2007 to regularise their status. This Act amounts to the third regularisation in Poland (following 2003 and 2007). The regularisation, open during the first half of 2012, does not condition application on any economic requirements. It can lead to granting of residence permit and work permit for a two-year period. Mexico also provided for a regularisation of foreigners, with 1 800 receiving permits in 2011.

Sanctions against employers and sponsors introduced as a tool to combat illegal employment of foreigners and increase foreign workers' protection

Australia, Canada and the United States have recently focused on sanctions against employers and sponsors engaged in illegal employment. The Canadian government introduced changes to the Live-in Caregiver Program in April 2010, and further changes to the broader Temporary Foreign Worker Program in April 2011, with the aim to improve protections for temporary workers, reinforce employer compliance with program requirements and reinforce the temporary nature of work under the program. The changes will result in denying access to the program to employers who do not abide by the terms of their job offers. In Australia, concern centres on the horticulture industry, alongside construction and hospitality. The government commissioned an independent review of sanctions for illegal employment of foreign workers. The major change proposed by the report is to introduce civil penalties (or fines) for employers.

6. EU legislation and other forms of intergovernmental and international co-operation

EU legislation continues to influence the migration policies of its Member States, as well as that of neighbouring countries in the EU accession process. The new EU member countries, notably Romania and Bulgaria, continue to work to harmonise their legislative frameworks with the EU regulations. The more long-standing member countries also continuously transpose the new EU regulations into their legislative frameworks. The two most frequent issues in this regard have been recently the transposition of the so-called EU Blue Card Directive[4] (the year 2011 was the deadline for its transposition), and harmonisation of national legal systems with the EU regulations pertaining to the stay of EEA nationals in the EU. The third common legislative issue across the EU member countries was the application of transitional measures for access to the national labour markets of Bulgarian and Romanian nationals. Neighbouring and associated countries were also influenced in their migration agendas by the EU regime.[5]

Main developments in immigration policy at the EU level in 2011

Among prominent pieces of the EU legislation in the field of international migration is the so-called EU Blue Card Directive (stipulating the conditions of entry and residence of non-EU/EFTA nationals for the purposes of highly qualified employment). The main objective of the directive is to improve the ability to attract highly qualified workers from non-EU/EFTA countries. The directive applies to highly qualified non-EU/EFTA nationals seeking admission to a member country for more than three months for the purpose of employment, as well as to their family members. The entry is conditioned by the existence of a work contract or a binding job offer with a salary of at least 150% the average gross annual salary paid in the member country concerned (member countries may lower the salary threshold to 120% for certain professions where there is a particular need for foreign workers). After two years of legal employment, the Blue Card holders may receive equal treatment with nationals as regards access to any highly qualified employment. After 18 months of legal residence, they may move to another member country to take up highly qualified employment, subject to the limits set by the member country on the number of non-nationals accepted (see Box I.1).

> ### Box I.1. **Implementation of EU Blue Card Directive**
>
> The EU has been recently less successful in attracting highly skilled foreign workers than, for example, Australia or Canada. Attracting skilled workers is viewed as a means to maintain and increase competitiveness and compensate population ageing. The EU Blue Card Directive was the first of five legislative proposals presented by the Commission in its policy plan on legal migration of non-EU/EFTA country nationals in December 2005.
>
> The directive entered into force in June 2009 and it supposed to be transposed into the member state legislation by 19 June 2011. Given that the directive has implications for both employment legislation and that governing stay and residence of foreign workers (including their family members), its full transposition generally requires amendments of multiple laws and the related regulations and procedures. Besides its complexity, some member countries encounter difficulties with transposition on other grounds, such as jurisdiction (for example, in Belgium the issuance of stay permits is the responsibility of regional authorities while access to the labour market is under the jurisdiction of federal authorities). Furthermore, in some EU member countries the Blue Card co-exists with other national schemes for attracting highly skilled or skilled migrants (for example, in the Czech Republic with the Green Card scheme and in Austria with the recently introduced Red-White-Red Card scheme). The Netherlands implemented the EU Blue Card as a separate purpose of stay, alongside its existing Highly Skilled Migrant Programme.
>
> The complexity of amending legislation, the overlap with existing measures, and the poor labour market situation delayed implementation in a number of member countries, which did not comply with the transposition deadline and were found by the European Commission to be hindering highly skilled people from coming to the EU for work in July 2011 the Commission sent letters of formal notice, the first step of the infringement procedure, to Germany, Italy, Malta, Poland, Portugal and Sweden concerning their failure to notify the Commission of measures taken to implement the Directive. Three of them (Italy, Malta and Portugal) did not signal any such measures within the set deadline (two months) while the others (Germany, Poland and Sweden) replied but indicated that new implementing legislation would not enter into force until next year. The Commission sent reasoned opinions to these six member countries in October 2011 requesting them to comply with the rules of the Blue Card Directive. Another group of member countries – including Austria and Greece – had been also warned by the Commission in July 2011, and in February 2012 they were issued with the reasoned opinions requesting them to bring their laws into line with EU legislation. Malta, Romania and Luxembourg, although late in implementing the Blue Card Directive, by February 2012 had applied the Directive in national legislation.
>
> Starting from 2013, data will be collected on the number of foreigners to whom an EU Blue Card has been issued. Starting from 2014, reports on the application of the directive and proposals for any changes deemed necessary will be provided to the European Parliament and the Council every three years.

In December 2011, the European Single Permit Directive[6] was approved. The directive requires EU member countries to merge work and residence permits into a single document, and to establish a standard procedure for issuance of this document. It also accords permit-holders equal treatment to nationals in a number of areas, including employment, access to education and training, and access to public goods and services, although some restrictions are admitted. The directive is to be transposed into national legislation by the end of December 2013.

Two draft directives, regarding seasonal workers and intra-corporate transfers of non-EU/EFTA nationals, have been in discussion since 2010, but have not yet been accepted by the Council of the European Union.

Transitional measures for Romania and Bulgaria

EU/EFTA member countries have the right to apply restrictions to workers from the new EU member countries for a transitional period of up to seven years following their accession. The restrictions cannot concern the right to travel, only the right to work as employed person. After the first two years the member countries must inform the European Commission in case they want to extend the period of application of transitional measures for another three years. Afterwards the countries can continue to apply restrictions for another two years if they inform the Commission of serious disturbances in their labour market.

Since May 2011, restrictions within this transitional regime are only possible for nationals of Bulgaria and Romania. Both countries joined the EU on 1 January 2007, thus the period 2009-11 fell into the second phase of transitional measures. The right to apply restrictions was in 2011 exercised by the following member states: Austria, Germany, Belgium, France, Luxembourg, Ireland, Italy, Malta, the Netherlands and the United Kingdom. Italy lifted them in 2012.

All of the above countries provided more favourable conditions to nationals from Bulgaria and Romania compared with non-EU/EFTA nationals, for example by allowing for a simplified procedure for obtaining the permit or by easing the conditions for certain skilled professions and professions in which there are labour shortages. For example, Belgium issues work permits without a labour market test for low-qualified jobs in which there are labour shortages. France has a simplified procedure for 150 professions for which the permit is issued regardless of the labour market situation. Luxembourg introduced a simplified procedure for work in horticulture, viticulture, hotels and catering, and certain jobs in financial sector. Germany waived the labour market test for professions requiring professional training. Malta and Austria grant work permits for professions requiring qualified or experienced labour and for occupations exhibiting labour shortages. Several countries waived the work permit requirement for certain types of professions or jobs (for example Germany for seasonal work, professional in-firm training and university educated skilled workers working in their field of qualification). The United Kingdom and the Netherlands require work permits, but both allow for exemptions under certain conditions, such as labour shortage or certain categories of employment. Spain, which had lifted labour market restrictions, was granted permission to reimpose them on Romanian workers until 31 December 2012 due to serious disturbances on its labour market. Switzerland can continue to apply the transitional measures until 2016. In Norway, where unemployment is relatively low, the Norwegian government proposed a bill in January 2012 to fully open its labour market for Bulgarian and Romanian workers.

Bilateral agreements for labour migration, training, recognition, etc.

Several OECD countries concluded bilateral agreements aimed at facilitating legal labour migration with other countries. In a bid to boost the Japanese economy, the government initiated a new system of mutual recognition of some occupations (*e.g.* architects) to assist the expansion of Japanese construction companies in Asia. The list of applicable countries is now under consideration. The Canadian province of Quebec concluded an agreement with France on mutual recognition of regulated professions. New Zealand concluded two new Working Holiday Schemes, with Turkey and the Slovak Republic. Israel concluded bilateral agreements for regulating the migration of foreign workers in agriculture and construction with Thailand and Sri Lanka. The agreements aim at ensuring rotation of workers and reducing illegal fee-taking. Italy concluded a new bilateral agreement on labour migration with Egypt, Moldova, Albania and Sri Lanka.

7. Integration and citizenship policies

A common trend across the OECD is that of increased attention to integration and naturalisation policies. Given the varied immigration situation in the OECD countries, recent integration-related initiatives ranged from initial awareness-raising (mainly in the new EU member countries) to the refinement of well-established integration systems (in other OECD countries long exposed to large scale immigration). In some countries with more developed integration policy frameworks, a trend toward mainstreaming of integration policies occurred.

Trend towards mainstreaming integration measures

In Sweden, introduction of new arrivals is governed by a new Act focusing on labour market integration, in force since December 2010. Co-ordination of new arrivals was passed from municipalities to the Public Employment Service. A uniform public allowance scheme applies to newly arrived migrants, with eligibility conditional on active participation in the introductory measures. A civic orientation program and a new Introduction guide are also meant to assist the new immigrants in their integration efforts. An intra-departmental government working group was established in May 2011 to develop a new national integration strategy, with emphasis on general measures for the whole population based on needs and not on country of origin, with supplemental targeted support for new arrivals during the first two years. The government intends to present the new integration strategy and concrete policy proposals alongside the Budget Bill in autumn 2012. Finally, the Swedish government announced an objective of increasing ethnic and cultural diversity among public-sector employees.

Integration also received a new impetus in Finland where a new Act on the promotion of Integration entered into force in September 2011. When granted residence permits, all immigrants will be provided with information about the Finnish society and their rights and obligations. All immigrants will be also entitled to a needs assessment for language training and an integration plan. A new project entitled "Participative Integration in Finland" will be implemented by testing various integration training models in order to determine the most effective ways for integration including the labour market integration of immigrants.

Several other European OECD countries carried out large-scale studies and reviews on integration issues. Denmark changed immigration and integration laws, announcing a national integration survey, along with measures that include removing the dependence of social-benefit entitlements on the length of stay, and stipulating targets to raise the number of immigrants employed by 2020. In Switzerland, a wide consultation process regarding integration policies was launched towards the end of 2011 at the level of cantons and municipalities. The results should feed into the Parliamentary discussion and the adoption of new integration legislation. In Germany, the National Integration Plan adopted in 2007 received wide follow-up through a broad participatory process of consultations and discussions. Since December 2010, these discussions were further facilitated through 11 national dialogue forums led by federal ministries and agencies, providing inputs for the new National Action Plan on Integration presented to the public in early 2012. Norway released three committee reports in the course of 2010-11, related to the integration agenda and covering the following areas: Welfare and Migration, Better Integration, and Diversity in Education. The reports drew attention, among other issues, to social exclusion of immigrants, labour market integration, and living conditions among the immigrant population. The Norwegian government is in the process of preparing a White Paper for Parliament on integration and inclusion of immigrants and their children, based on the three reports and devoted to the issues of multilingual children, immigrant youth and adults in the education system, welfare and migration, and better integration.

A new multicultural policy for Australia was launched in February 2011. An Australian Multicultural Council was created to champion multiculturalism and provide advice to the government on multicultural affairs. Likewise, a national anti-racism partnership was announced by the government and tasked with developing anti-racism strategy to be put into effect in 2012. Other initiatives in the area of integration included a new longitudinal survey of refugees and other migrants.

Integration programmes

Canada introduced in 2010 a new approach to integration program funding, moving from separate programs (such as Language Instruction for Newcomers to Canada, Immigration Settlement and Adaptation Program) to one single program. The new approach allows for a range of services to be covered by a single funding agreement, thus simplifying the administrative procedures for immigrant-serving organisations and allowing them to tailor their programs to best suit newcomers' needs.

In Italy, the use of an Integration Agreement was approved in July 2011.It requires all foreigners receiving a first permit to stay in Italy for more than one year to acquire, in the course of two years, a basic knowledge of Italian language and civic principles. A one-year extension is possible. A negative score of points in the contract may prevent renewal of the residence permit. A language examination scheme was already approved in December 2009. Passing the language test is necessary for obtaining a long-term residence permit.[7] In June 2010, a plan for integration into social security systems was approved by the government, concerning the tools and actions to be adopted in areas such as education, labour market, housing, access to services, and measures in relation to minors. Other measures taken in Italy include setting a ceiling for the number of foreign-born non-citizen students per school class, and using housing policy to prevent the creation of mono-ethnic residential enclaves.

In Portugal, a Second National Plan for the Integration of Immigrants for 2010-13 entered into force in 2010 (following the First National Integration Plan 2007-09). The second plan includes 90 measures and adds two new areas for action – promotion of diversity and interculturalism and protection of elderly migrants). Protection of poor and unemployed migrants also received greater attention in the second plan.

In November 2010, Luxembourg adopted a National Action Plan for Integration for 2010-14. Two-year Integration Contracts were introduced. An information campaign was launched in 2010 and 2011 which aimed at increasing the registration of foreign residents in electoral lists for the communal elections held in October 2011.

Korea also pays increasing attention to the integration of foreigners, with special focus on foreign women coming to Korea for marriage, and their families. The key ministries involved in the integration process signed an agreement on co-operation for supporting adaptation of marriage migrants to Korean society, and agreed to share information and to provide guidelines about all support programmes.

Initial policies for integration

In the Slovak Republic, the first comprehensive concept of integration of foreigners, approved by the government in 2009, was followed-up in 2011 by a number of concrete tasks for government agencies. These included merging the current migration office and a part of the alien police into a new Immigration and Naturalisation Office, with comprehensive responsibility for tasks ranging from issuing entry visas to foreigners, issuing residence permits, and overseeing integration and naturalisation. First steps towards establishing a national integration framework were also undertaken in Poland. The inter-ministerial committee on migration – an advisory body to the prime minister – announced provisions about access to education for immigrants' children (including the undocumented), and the possibility to grant a year of language assistance at school to immigrant children who do not understand the Polish language.

Mexico's new framework migration law grants immigrants a series of rights, including rights to health care and education, which were not guaranteed under previous legislation.

In the context of the economic downturn in Japan, foreign residents of Japanese descent face increasing difficulties in leading their daily lives. In August 2010, the Government approved a Basic Policy for Foreign Residents of Japanese Descent, based on recognition of the need for measures aimed at preventing their exclusion from the Japanese society. Integration policy was further supported by an Action Plan, adopted in March 2011, to promote the acceptance of foreigners as members of Japanese society.

Initial steps towards developing integration policies were undertaken in Lithuania, where inter-ministerial discussion was initiated on the possibility of creation of institutions responsible for migrants´ integration. In Bulgaria, the 2011 strategy of the government placed the integration of immigrants among national priorities.

Language training

Language training makes an important part of integration programs in most OECD countries. Recent changes in the field include raising language requirements in terms of passing levels for the tests, adding new reading and comprehension modules to the language tests, and expanding the possibilities for language education for various groups of immigrants, notably labour migrants and school children.

Language training received increased attention in several member countries. France introduced … a new requirement for acquiring nationality: passing a language test at the B2 level (or higher) of the Common European Framework (CEF) of Reference for Languages. In Luxembourg, a "linguistic leave" of 200 hours was introduced for salaried employees who work in the country for at least six months, in order to allow them to study Luxembourgish.

In the Netherlands, the pass score on the spoken Dutch component of the civic integration examination abroad was raised from A1 minus to the A1 level in the CEF, and a reading and comprehension skills test was added to the examination.

Assessment and recognition of foreign qualifications

The assessment and recognition of foreign qualifications gained importance with increasing efforts of countries to attract skilled migrants, and the need for better integration of foreigners through labour market participation. New initiatives in this area have been established in Sweden and Germany. In Sweden, where a special government agency dealing with validation issues was created in 2009, a joint working group comprising the Ministry of Finance, Ministry of Industry, and Employers' Association was established to discuss the validation of skills and its impact on labour market outcomes. In Germany, a new law on the recognition of foreign qualifications, providing for the right to an assessment procedure, entered into force in April 2012. In emigration countries the issue of validation of skills of own nationals prior to departure gained importance. Lithuania, for example, provides for the validation of qualifications before leaving for medical personnel.

Other integration measures

While in the field of integration policies various national integration programs, strategies and action plans constitute the main frameworks, a prominent vehicle at the implementation level is the integration contract (or integration agreement) concluded between the immigrant and the recipient country authority. Some new developments were recorded in OECD countries with regard to this integration tool. In the framework of its new integration law, Spain introduced the institution of integration report, which is not compulsory for the migrants, but is meant to provide assistance and make the integration process easier. Luxembourg introduced integration contracts for migrants older than 16 years who intend to stay in the country, including both newcomers and foreigners already residing in Luxembourg. Migrants are provided with an orientation session by the public administration and are followed by the same person during a 2-year period. The integration process includes civics courses and language courses of choice.

Citizenship and naturalisation policies

Several OECD countries opened up new possibilities to acquire citizenship.

Finland amended its Nationality Act in September 2011 with the aim of promoting social cohesion of resident foreign nationals. The procedure for acquiring citizenship became more flexible – the required period of residence was shortened from six years to five years, and temporary residence in Finland can be taken into account.

Greece's Act on citizenship and naturalisation, passed in March 2010, lowered the residence requirement for naturalising from ten to seven years. A precondition is EU long-term migrant status, for which immigrants can apply after five years of legal stay. Following the adoption of the new act, the authorities are required to reply to applicants within a certain time frame and to justify their decision. Changes also concern children of immigrants. Children born in Greece of foreign parents can become Greek citizens by a simple declaration of their parents, provided that both parents have been living in Greece legally for at least five years. Children who were born abroad of foreign parents but who have completed at least six years of schooling in Greece and live in Greece may also naturalise through a simple declaration by their parents, provided that both parents have been living in Greece legally for at least five years. Foreign parents of children who became Greek citizens are entitled to a renewable five-year permit, regardless of their employment situation.

An amendment of the Hungarian Citizenship Act that entered into force in August 2010 allows for naturalisation on preferential terms for ethnic Hungarians who either prove that their ascendant was a Hungarian citizen or demonstrate their ethnic origin through the knowledge of the Hungarian language (they do not have to prove the means for livelihood and residence in Hungary, neither they have to pass the basic constitutional studies exam). However, this simplified naturalisation procedure does not automatically guarantee Hungarian passport or electoral rights in Hungary – the former has to be requested through a separate procedure and the latter requires permanent residence in the country.

In November 2010 the Israeli government adopted a decision to bring the remnants of the Falash Mura community from Ethiopia to Israel. This decision stipulates that any member of the Falash Mura community who appears in the list of registered Falash Mura awaiting immigration in Gondar, which was compiled in 2007 and updated in 2010, may immigrate to Israel, with 200 people admitted monthly over three years starting in March 2011.[8]

8. Conclusion

Migration policies have long been a political issue. Economic crises put pressure on the national labour markets and social systems, and influenced the perception of migration by both the general public and authorities. In several countries, this development resulted in a policy shift towards more restrictive immigration policies, as new governments in 2010-11 tightened controls over the immigration process and restricted the possibilities for long term immigration for migrants with poor employment prospects.

Migration policies as a factor of economic development also remain. 2011 witnessed many labour immigration schemes maintained, often with a more selective approach, giving less attention to "quantity" and more to the presumed "quality" of immigrants. High-skilled and shortage-sector labour migration is viewed favourably by a majority of member countries, and concern over maintaining global competitiveness increasingly drives admission policies.

However, as the recession has unfolded, lack of demand from employers has reduced their need to import skills and some governments became more restrictive and selective towards foreign recruitment. Many governments recently reviewed their skills shortage lists and temporary work programmes and subjected employers to more scrutiny. Points systems for admission have become more demand-driven, with supply-driven channels, where they exist, becoming increasingly restrictive. Investors and entrepreneurs are welcome, but these flows are very small.

More favourable conditions for immigration of skilled workers from non-EU/EFTA countries to the EU were effectuated by the implementation of the EU Blue Card Directive, even if other national schemes for recruitment of skilled workers were in place in most countries.

Irregular immigration continues to be a source of concern, notably around the Mexican border and several areas in Europe where illegal entries into the Schengen area are concentrated (such as Italy's Lampedusa Island and the Greek-Turkish border).

Integration of immigrants continues to be a top priority for immigration policy of OECD countries. Integration-related initiatives that were adopted varied from country to country, covering a wide array of policies – ranging from the establishment of comprehensive national strategies to fine-tuning and refining of the existing action plans and integration programs. The focus also oscillates between the groups of established migrants and the newly arrived ones. A common trend is the prioritisation of labour market integration and strengthening educational aspects, including language training. An increasing trend in efforts to improve labour market participation of immigrants is also a greater emphasis on recognition of foreign skills and qualifications.

Notes

1. Eleven constitutional articles were amended and constitutional rank was granted to human rights treaties ratified by Mexico. The constitutional term "individual rights" was replaced by "human rights and guarantees". Amended constitutional articles now explicitly mention the right to request asylum and refuge (Article 11) and the right to a prior hearing for foreigners who are subject to expulsion (Article 33).

2. The statistical data for Israel are supplied by and under the responsibility of the relevant Israeli authorities. The use of such data by the OECD is without prejudice to the status of the Golan Heights, East Jerusalem and Israeli settlements in the West Bank under the terms of international law.

3. According to FRONTEX, the EU agency tasked to co-ordinate the operational co-operation among the member states in the field of border security.

4. Council Directive 2009/50/EC of 25 May 2009.

5. For example, the codification of the Asylum Act and the Alien Act in Turkey planned by end 2012, lifting of the geographical limitation on the 1951 Geneva Convention by Turkey, and the relationship between FYROM and Greece are considered in the respective association negotiations.

6. Directive 2011/98/EU of the European Parliament and of the Council of 13 December 2011.

7. By October 2011, 69 000 tests were taken (with a 70% pass rate).

8. The updated list includes 1 900 households with a total of 7 800 people.

References

OECD (2011), *International Migration Outlook 2011*, OECD Publishing, Paris.

PART II

Renewing the skills of ageing workforces: The role of migration*

> *Part II examines the role which different demographic groups (youth, new immigrants, persons of prime working age and older persons) have played in changes in the educational attainment of the labour force and in changes in the distribution of occupations.*

* The OECD acknowledges the financial support of the European Commission for the analysis included in this chapter.

1. Introduction

As is well known, the next decade will see significant demographic change in the working-age population and labour force in OECD countries. The 8.6% increase in the working-age population (20-64-year-olds) observed on average over the period 2000-10 is expected to drop to barely 2% over the 2010-20 decade, even assuming a continuation of pre-crisis migration levels. Almost half of OECD countries will see declines in their working-age populations over the coming decade.

How will labour markets and enterprises adapt to the changing demographic landscape? Will labour and skill shortages materialise? What role will international migration play in filling them?

The 2008-09 recession and the slow recovery thereafter do not seem an opportune time to be considering prospects for international labour migration, given the extensive labour market slack which persists in many countries as a result of the economic crisis. Nonetheless, the demographic shift underway is so large and persistent that it is important to consider what contribution international migration can be expected to make to the evolution in the distribution of the workforce by educational attainment and by occupation in the future. For this, it is useful to cast a look back at the recent past, in particular the 2000-10 decade. Persons aged 55-64 in the year 2010, almost 40% of whom were already retired and who represented almost half of retirees over the 2000-10 decade, constitute the first cohort of baby-boomers born in the ten years after the second World War.[1]

Discussions concerning the ageing workforce are often phrased in terms of a replacement problem, with smaller youth cohorts entering the workforce as large baby-boom cohorts retire. The implication is that international migration will be needed to offset this imbalance, in support of economic growth, both to maintain the size of the labour force and to ensure an adequate supply of skills to respond to the continuing expected growth in high-skilled jobs.[2]

But how appropriate is the replacement model as a picture of what will happen over the next ten years and to assess the extent and nature of future skill needs that will have to be filled by recruitment from abroad? We know, for example, that young workers are on average more educated than their retiring forebears, but will there be fewer of them, and if so, does this mean that more highly educated migrants will need to be recruited? What precisely has been the role of international migration in labour force and occupational renewal over the recent past?

This part aims to provide some contextual data on, and exploratory analysis of, these issues. It attempts to do so by a decomposition of educational and occupational change according to the contribution to change of new entrants, prime-age workers, retiring workers and in particular, immigrants. The objective is to get a clearer picture of the demographic imbalance question that is central to discussions of ageing, to see how it is playing out in practice and where immigrants fit into the picture. As will be seen, the picture is not quite so simple as sometimes portrayed.

The first section of this part outlines the general methodological approach that will be followed for the analyses in the rest of the chapter. This is followed by a brief section which considers the relation between the presence of immigrants in the labour market and labour demand. The following section decomposes the change in the educational attainment of the labour force over the period from 2000 to 2010 by demographic group. The same approach is then used to examine the components of change in the distribution of occupations, which underwent considerable change over the decade. The final section summarises and concludes.

2. Main findings

- The educational attainment of new entrants into the labour force was much higher than that of retiring workers over the period 2000-10. New immigrants had educational levels that were between those of new entrants and retirees, with proportionally more highly educated workers among new immigrants than retirees, but more low-educated workers than among new entrants.

- Not only were new entrants to the labour force more educated over the period 2000-10, there were more of them. There were close to three highly educated new entrants for every retiring one in both Europe and the United States, and the reverse situation held for the low-educated.

- Immigrants represented 47/70% of the increase in the labour force in the United States and Europe, respectively, over the decade, but 21/14% respectively of the increase in the highly educated labour force. They are thus playing a more significant role in maintaining the size of the labour force than in its up-skilling in most countries.

- The composition of occupational change over the decade mirrored that observed for the educational attainment of the labour force. Young new entrants into strongly growing occupations (most of which were highly skilled) far outnumbered retirees over the past decade. Likewise, retirees from strongly declining occupations greatly outnumbered new entrants. Indeed, over 40% of net occupational change took place through the entry and exit of young and older workers.

- New immigrants represented 15% of entries into strongly growing occupations in Europe over the decade and 22% in the United States. They are thus playing a significant role in the most dynamic sectors of the economy, even under conditions when most migration has not been demand-driven.

- At the same time immigrants represented 24/28%, respectively, of entries into the most strongly declining occupations in Europe and the United States.

- Almost half of low-skilled jobs on average are taken up by immigrants, with considerable variation across countries. In some countries, the immigrant share is very high, which risks creating a segmented labour market, as low-skilled jobs become the exclusive domain of immigrants.

- In countries where labour migration has been more significant, the contribution of migrants to the up-skilling of the workforce and to growing occupations has been more significant.

- A demographic imbalance model of labour force change and occupational change seems inappropriate in the face of the large differences in educational attainment between entry and exit cohorts and in entry and exit from growing and declining occupations.

The potential need for immigrants in the ageing context thus cannot be assessed on the basis of demographic imbalances alone, but must take into account changes in the nature of employment, which appear to be more dynamic than changes in the age composition of the population and labour force.

3. General methodological approach

The analyses presented in this chapter examine change (in educational attainment, in the occupational distribution, in the levels of skills) through a *demographic accounting framework*. Succinctly, the *net* change over a period for a particular characteristic is decomposed into that due to young workers, new immigrants, prime-age workers and older workers, where the age-related components of change are estimated by comparing the situation of so-called "pseudo age-cohorts" in 2000 and 2010, respectively (see Annex II.A1 for the details). The pseudo-cohort approach implicitly includes the effects of emigration and mortality, which cannot be observed directly.[3]

In addition, since characteristics are observed at two points in time, abstraction is made of multiple changes that may have occurred over the period. A worker may change jobs if not occupation several times in the intervening period, but the only jobs and occupations that are observed are those at the beginning and end of the time period, which are the ones which enter into the net change calculations. Note also that with the pseudo-cohort approach, much of the change observed for young workers and older workers will be due to workforce entry and retirement, respectively. For the age-groups considered, these largely predominate over occupational change in the net change calculations. This means in practice that the contributions to change in the labour force and in occupations due to young and older workers are always positive, respectively negative for the labour force and for every occupation. For example, on average across countries, the net changes in employment for young workers and older workers amount to approximately 87% and 80% of employment for an entry cohort (aged 25-34 in the year 2010) and an exit cohort (aged 45-54 in the year 2000), respectively. For the prime-age group, on the other hand, the net change measure may hide a considerable amount of movement which is not visible, because it is offsetting, as new hires replace persons who quit or are laid off. The data used for the analyses are taken from the European Union labour force survey for European countries, from the American Community Survey for the United States and from the Survey of Labour Income and Dynamics (SLID) for Canada.

4. The role of immigrants in the labour market

Before delving into the empirical data, it is useful to consider first the relation between labour demand and the presence of new immigrants in the labour market. This question is of particular interest because of the fact that most arriving immigrants have not ostensibly been recruited from abroad by employers for specific jobs for which there has been an identified or tested labour need, but have arrived for family or humanitarian reasons or through unauthorised channels. Many have entered the labour market, either upon arrival or later, and been hired into jobs, of which the skill level may or may not always have been commensurate with their formal qualifications. They are not unique in this respect; some young persons entering the labour market are in the same situation. But some immigrants arrive with little knowledge of the destination-country language and with qualifications and experience acquired abroad in a different economic context that may not easily be transferable to the labour markets and workplaces of destination countries.

Still, many immigrants, especially those arriving under free-circulation regimes or through unauthorised means, may nonetheless arrive in response to knowledge about job opportunities transmitted through the media or by migrant networks, in particular friends and relatives in destination countries. There may even be specific jobs awaiting them upon arrival.

The same applies to the non-labour migrants who enter the labour market every year but were admitted under another type of residence permit. A study covering immigrant entries into the labour force over the 2004-06 period in France, for example, showed that 90% of the entries consisted of non-labour migrants, at a time when direct recruitment accounted for less than 5-10% of total immigrant inflows in France (Léger, 2008). More than three-quarters of non-labour migrant entries into the labour force occurred during the year following arrival.

The statistics and results presented in this chapter will reflect the impact of a mix of migrants in the labour market, with persons who were not specifically recruited by employers being in the majority in many countries. If the incidence of labour migration increases in the near-to-medium term, one can expect some shift in the impact of migration in general, as more workers arrive for specific jobs and relatively fewer as general entrants into a labour market, searching for work along with other domestic suppliers. In this respect, the experience of labour migration countries may be an instructive guide to what the future holds for countries expecting to increase their labour migration in the following decades.

5. The demography of changes in the educational attainment of the labour force

The labour force has increased by about 0.9 percentage points per year on average between 2000 and 2010, an amount that is expected to decline to less than 0.2 percentage points per year over the coming decade. The demographic composition of this change is portrayed in Table II.1, applying the decomposition methodology described in Annex II.A1. The labour force renewed itself by about a quarter over the period, from inflows (new entrants and immigrants) replacing outflows (retirees). Immigrants on average accounted for about 19% of the inflows, with contributions far above average in Ireland (34%), Luxembourg (57%), Spain (40%) and Switzerland (40%).

The inflows of young resident workers into the labour force have exceeded the outflows of older workers by about 5% of the labour force on average. With total growth in the labour force at 11% over the period, this means that immigrants have accounted for over 57% of the total labour force growth over the period, although their share of entries into the labour force has been considerably lower (less than 25%). In a number of countries (Switzerland, Italy, Luxembourg and the United Kingdom), all or almost all of the growth in the labour force has come from the arrival of new immigrants.

As educational attainment in origin countries has been increasing, so also has been that of immigrants arriving legally in OECD countries. But the immigrant population also includes a significant proportion of low-educated persons in a number of countries, with many persons in this group having arrived through family reunification or formation or having fled war zones or persecution in their countries of origin. Low levels of education have also been characteristic of unauthorised migration in the United States and of labour migration in southern Europe. In most other countries, legal long-term labour migration by

Table II.1. **Contributions to growth in the labour force by demographic group, 2000-10**
Percentages

	Total growth of the labour force (A + B + C + D)	Young workers (new entrants) (A)	New immigrants (B)	Prime-age workers (C)	Older workers (retirees) (D)	Net turnover (see Notes)	Replacement surplus (entrants of younger + retirement of older) (A + D)
Austria	11	22	6	–1	–17	23	5
Belgium	10	24	8	–4	–17	27	7
Canada	21	22	12	–1	–11	23	11
Switzerland	13	19	12	–1	–17	25	1
Czech Republic	3	21	1	3	–21	23	0
Germany	5	27	3	–2	–23	27	3
Denmark	–1	18	2	–2	–20	21	–2
Estonia	5	26	1	–1	–20	24	6
Spain	30	25	17	2	–14	29	11
Finland	2	19	2	0	–19	20	1
France	10	26	3	1	–20	25	6
Greece	10	22	5	1	–19	23	4
Hungary	5	22	1	2	–20	23	2
Ireland	24	25	13	–2	–12	26	13
Italy	6	17	6	0	–18	21	–1
Luxembourg	23	20	26	–5	–18	35	2
Netherlands	8	21	2	–2	–14	19	8
Norway	10	21	5	–1	–16	21	5
Portugal	8	22	4	0	–19	23	4
Sweden	12	24	6	2	–20	26	4
United Kingdom	9	24	11	–5	–20	30	4
United States	13	20	6	–1	–13	20	7
OECD average	**11**	**22**	**7**	**–1**	**–18**	**24**	**5**

Notes: The contribution of each group is the net change in the labour force for the group divided by the total number of persons in the labour force in 2000. Net turnover is half the sum of the absolute values of the individual contributions. It understates total turnover, because some entries and exits within the prime-age group and more generally as a result of in- and out-migration of residents may be offsetting. Data for Germany and the United Kingdom on the composition of growth by demographic group are based on 2005-10 change, adjusted to agree with the observed change in the labour force for the period 2000-10.
Sources: European countries: European Labour Force Surveys (Eurostat); United States: American Community Survey; Canada: Survey of Labour and Income Dynamics.
StatLink http://dx.doi.org/10.1787/888932616999

low-educated persons has been more limited. Table II.2 provides a general overview of average education attainment levels of entrants to, and exits from, the labour force in 2010 across OECD and EU member countries, excluding youth under 25 in education. On average overall, the differences between new entrants and retiring older workers was very large, with the percentage of young new entrants having low attainment levels being 31 percentage points lower than retiring older workers and the percentage of new entrants having high attainment levels being 22 percentage points higher. The improvement in attainment levels in the labour force across generations in the countries of southern Europe and Ireland was especially large, with declines in the labour force with low attainment of about 50 points. Canada is the only country which did not see double-digit reductions across generations in the percentage of the labour force with low attainment levels, but the percentage of such workers among retirees was already relatively low in that country.

At the other end of the attainment spectrum, almost all countries have seen double-digit increases in the per cent of young workers with tertiary attainment levels compared to retirees, with generally at least 20 percentage point increases. Thus in general, the difference in attainment levels between incoming and outgoing labour force cohorts is quite large.

Table II.2. **Educational attainment of the labour force, new entrants, new immigrants and retirees, 2000-10**

	Low attainment			Medium attainment			High attainment			Immigrants compared to new entrants		
	Older workers (retirees)	Young workers (new entrants)	New immigrants	Older workers (retirees)	Young workers (new entrants)	New immigrants	Older workers (retirees)	Young workers (new entrants)	New immigrants	Low attainment	Medium attainment	High attainment
	Per cent of all retirees	Percentage points +/– retirees		Per cent of all retirees	Percentage points +/– retirees		Per cent of all retirees	Percentage points +/– retirees		Percentage points +/– new entrants		
Denmark	..	..	..	..	..	..	27	+20	+8	..	..	–12
Canada	16	–10	–8	35	–10	–10	49	+19	+18	+2	–	–1
Czech Republic	18	–14	–7	73	–4	–8	10	+18	+15	+7	–4	–3
United States	19	–15	+11	52	–2	–14	29	+18	+3	+26	–12	–14
Norway	..	..	..	..	..	..	26	+21	+10	..	..	–11
Germany	26	–16	+2	52	+14	–17	22	+2	+15	+18	–31	+14
Switzerland	26	–19	–7	62	–7	–29	13	+26	+36	+12	–22	+10
Austria	28	–20	–4	60	+11	–10	11	+9	+14	+16	–21	+5
Sweden	29	–18	+3	42	+10	–19	29	+9	+17	+21	–29	+8
Hungary	29	–20	–17	55	+1	–8	16	+19	+25	+2	–9	+6
United Kingdom	30	–28	–14	53	–2	+4	17	+30	+9	+14	+6	–20
Netherlands	33	–19	–2	47	–5	–15	20	+24	+17	+18	–10	–7
Finland	42	–36	–7	32	+20	+13	27	+17	–6	+29	–7	–23
France	44	–32	–8	39	+3	–9	17	+29	+17	+24	–12	–12
Luxembourg	45	–32	–31	40	+9	–17	15	+23	+48	+1	–26	+25
Belgium	49	–37	–19	28	+11	+4	23	+25	+15	+18	–7	–11
Ireland	58	–56	–47	27	+8	+12	14	+48	+35	+9	+4	–13
Italy	65	–52	–23	25	+34	+22	10	+18	+1	+29	–12	–17
Greece	66	–52	–10	23	+19	+11	11	+33	–	+42	–9	–33
Spain	80	–51	–38	6	+16	+30	14	+35	+8	+13	+13	–27
Portugal	89	–54	–43	5	+27	+35	6	+27	+7	+11	+9	–20
OECD average	**42**	**–31**	**–14**	**40**	**+8**	**–1**	**19**	**+22**	**+15**	**+16**	**–9**	**–7**

Notes: See Table II.1. "Low" here refers to less than upper secondary attainment, "medium" to upper secondary and post-secondary non-tertiary, "high" to tertiary. The second and third columns of each attainment level give the difference between the percentage of persons in the attainment level within the group compared to the corresponding percentage within the retiring cohort. Data on low and medium attainment for Denmark and Norway were unusable because of breaks in the attainment series.
Sources: European countries: European Labour Force Surveys (Eurostat); United States: American Community Survey; Canada: Survey of Labour and Income Dynamics. StatLink http://dx.doi.org/10.1787/888932617018

In most countries, the attainment levels of new immigrant entries into the workforce were also higher than those of retiring cohorts, but not to the same extent as young resident entrants. The United States and, to a lesser extent, Finland are the only countries which saw immigrant entries into the labour force of lower attainment levels than those of retiring cohorts. The picture is much more diverse when one compares new immigrants to resident new entrants, however (last three columns). With few exceptions (Canada, Hungary, Luxembourg and to a lesser extent Ireland and the Czech Republic), there are proportionally many more new immigrants with low attainment levels than young new entrants, on average 16 percentage points more. This is generally mirrored by relatively fewer new immigrants at high attainment levels than among new entrants. The exceptions are the German-speaking countries, Hungary and Sweden, which received proportionally more highly educated immigrants and Canada and the Czech Republic, where the percentage of highly educated new immigrants is about the same as among young new entrants.

These results by themselves would point to a labour market role for new immigrants that may not resemble that for young new entrants, with their generally much higher attainment levels.

6. The composition of changes in the educational attainment of the labour force

The results above, however, concern the distribution of attainment levels in the labour force among demographic groups. They tell us little about volumes, that is about the relative numbers of entrants, new immigrants and retirees, and possible demographic imbalances resulting from large retiring cohorts compared with declining youth cohorts.

To get a clearer picture of the possible imbalances, we proceed to the decomposition of the total absolute change in the labour force by attainment level over the 2000 to 2010 period. The changes recorded represent a mix of two developments, namely increases in average attainment levels and changes in labour force participation. As noted earlier, the latter changes, for young and older workers, reflect essentially labour force entry and retirement, respectively. Note that changes attributable to prime-age workers either entering or leaving the labour force, emigrating or who have deceased appear implicitly as increases or declines in educational attainment levels of the prime-age labour force.[4] The objective is to see more clearly the contributions of various demographic groups to the evolution of educational attainment in the labour force. This hopefully provides more focused information than estimates of differences in stock levels, which are strongly affected by the inertia of the large numbers of persons whose educational attainment remains unchanged.

Figure II.1 gives the result for Europe as a whole and for the United States, as well as for a selected number of countries. The results show the composition of change in the educational attainment of the labour force over the period 2000-10. The number of young workers entering the labour force with high levels of educational attainment is much larger than that of retiring older workers, with, for example, almost three young workers at a high education level entering the labour force for each retiring worker at this level. Some of the increase in attainment has been occurring in tertiary high-level technical and vocational qualifications, forms of education which were less common decades ago than is currently the case. For low attainment, the situation is the reverse; there are three retiring workers for every entry.

That some upgrading in the educational attainment of the work-force was occurring was evident. It is the difference relative to the retiring cohort that is noteworthy. In Europe, the overall increase in the number of persons in the labour force with tertiary attainment has been on the order of 50% over the past decade, while the decline in workers with less than upper secondary has been about 20%. Workers with medium education levels have increased by about 7%. In the United States, where tertiary education levels reached high levels earlier than in Europe, the increase in the tertiary-educated labour force was about 28%. Persons in the labour force with mid-range education increased by 10%, while those with low education declined by 9%.

New immigrants were found more often in medium- and low-education levels than in high. They accounted for about 14% of the increase in high-educated workers in Europe and 20% in the United States. While low-educated workers have declined in numbers, immigrants accounted for almost 40% of the new workers at this education level in Europe and 70% in the United States.

Figures II.2a through II.2c give, for all countries, the general picture of changes in the labour force by educational attainment level and source over the 2000-10 decade. The strong increase in tertiary attainment levels among new entries compared with retiring cohorts (Figure II.2a) is seen universally. Indeed, it may even be underestimated, because a certain proportion of increases in the prime-age groups consists of late completers, that is, persons completing a first tertiary degree after the age of 24. The average ratio of young

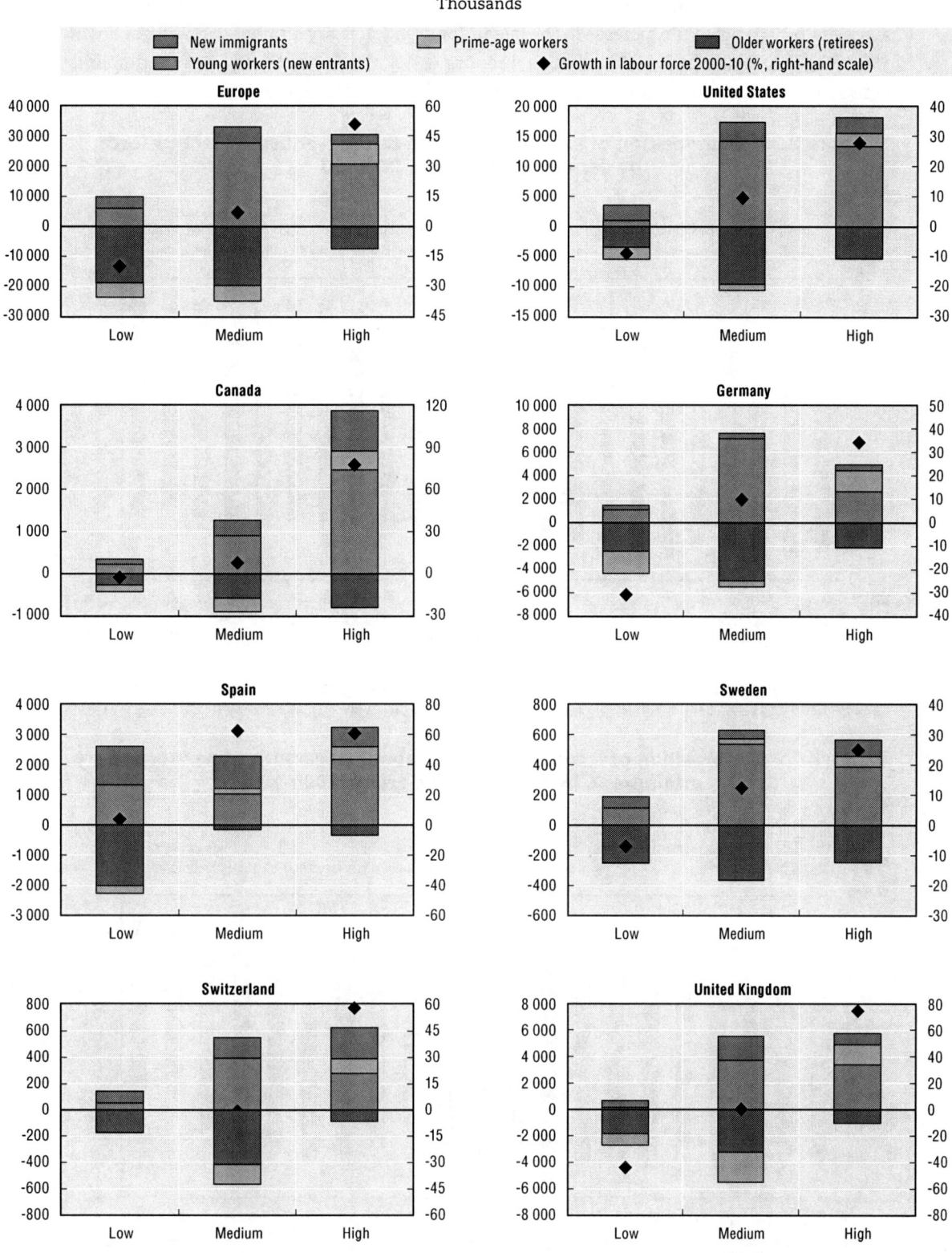

II. RENEWING THE SKILLS OF AGEING WORKFORCES: THE ROLE OF MIGRATION

Figure II.1. **Changes in the educational attainment of the labour force, 2000-10, by source**
Thousands

- New immigrants
- Young workers (new entrants)
- Prime-age workers
- Older workers (retirees)
- ◆ Growth in labour force 2000-10 (%, right-hand scale)

Sources: European countries: European Labour Force Surveys (Eurostat); United States: American Community Survey; Canada: Survey of Labour and Income Dynamics.

StatLink ᔍᖇᔕ http://dx.doi.org/10.1787/888932615574

entrants to retiring older workers is more than 3.5 which hardly suggests a replacement problem at this early juncture of ageing, at least in terms of educational attainment levels. The share of immigrants in the increase in the labour force with tertiary attainment averages about 15%, with especially high levels for Luxembourg (68%) and Switzerland (46%) and shares between 20 and 30% in Austria, Belgium, Spain and the United Kingdom.

Figure II.2a. **Composition of the change in the tertiary-educated labour force, by demographic group, 2000-10**
Percentages

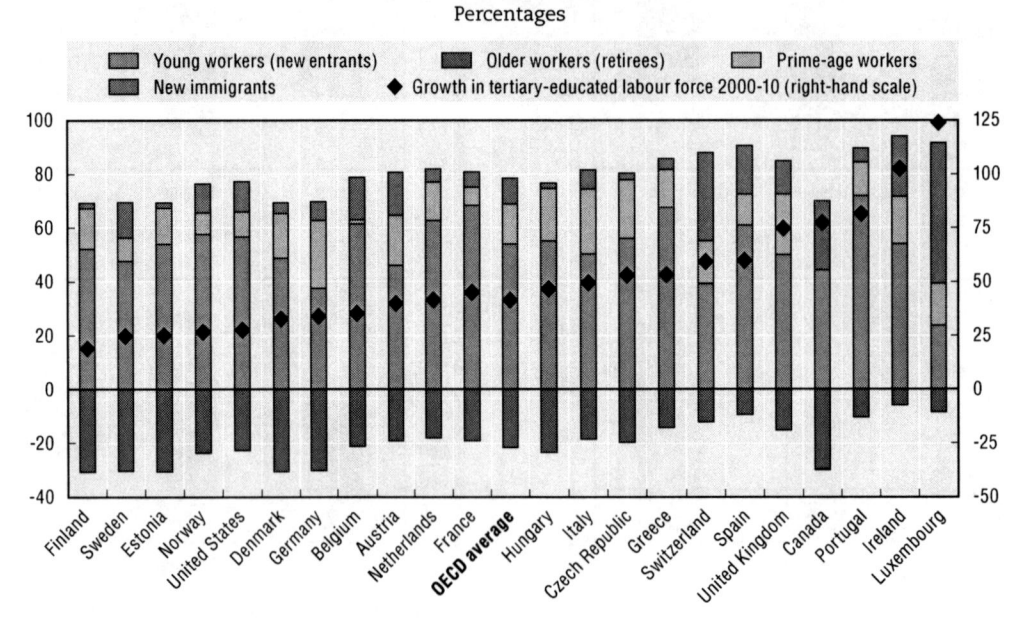

Sources: European countries: European Labour Force Surveys (Eurostat); United States: American Community Survey; Canada: Survey of Labour and Income Dynamics. StatLink http://dx.doi.org/10.1787/888932615593

Figure II.2b. **Composition of the change in the labour force with upper secondary attainment, by demographic group, 2000-10**
Percentages

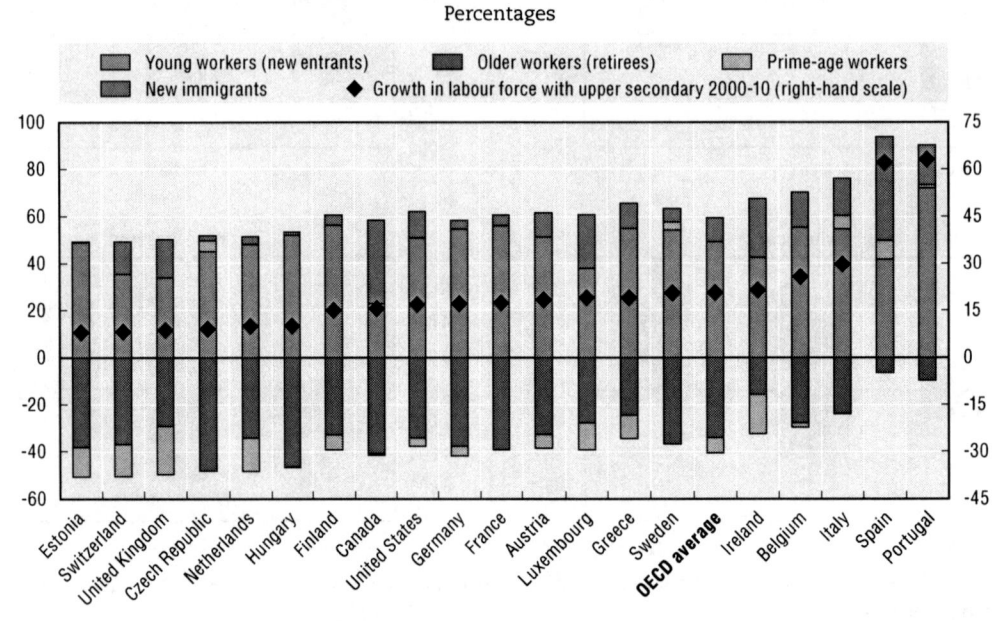

Sources: European countries: European Labour Force Surveys (Eurostat); United States: American Community Survey; Canada: Survey of Labour and Income Dynamics. StatLink http://dx.doi.org/10.1787/888932615612

Figure II.2c. **Composition of the change in the labour force with less than upper secondary education, by demographic group, 2000-10**
Percentages

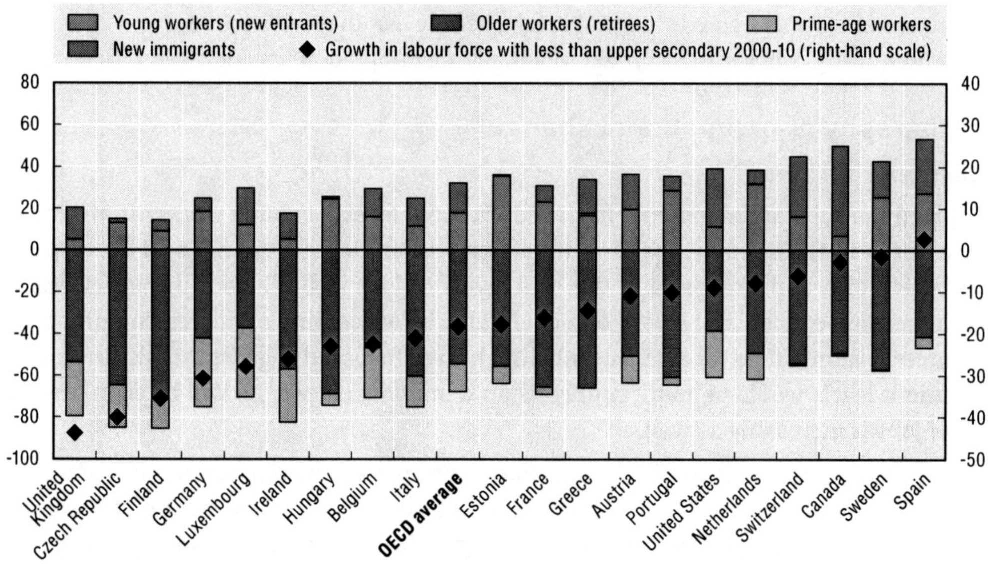

Sources: European countries: European Labour Force Surveys (Eurostat); United States: American Community Survey; Canada: Survey of Labour and Income Dynamics.
StatLink http://dx.doi.org/10.1787/888932615631

Note that there is no obvious relation between the extent of replacement of older workers by younger ones and the share of immigrants in the increase in tertiary attainment levels. By contrast, there are relatively few entries of low-educated workers into the labour force compared with retirements of such workers, with entries representing on average about 40% of retirements (Figure II.2c). As for the high-educated, entries of young mid-educated workers also tend to outnumber retirements, except in a few countries, in particular, Switzerland and the Czech Republic. On average there are about one and one-half entering mid-educated workers for every retiring one. The role of migration in the evolution of the low- and mid-educated workforces (Figures II.2b and II.2c) is more evident than was the case for the highly educated, but again, there is no obvious relationship between a "replacement deficit" and the extent of entering low- and mid-educated immigrants.

There is some selectivity in favour of high-skilled migrants in a number of countries which have seen considerable labour migration over the past decade, namely Ireland, Luxembourg and Switzerland, but most of these movements have occurred in the context of free-circulation rather than discretionary migration from non-EU countries, where employers recruit workers from abroad in response to labour market needs and where the declared needs of employers are generally verified by destination country administrations.

On the other hand, in the "new" migration countries of southern Europe, which have had substantial labour migration over the past decade as well as being open to lower-skilled migration, the increases in the labour force have come largely from lower-educated labour migrants. However, not all of these have been recruited from abroad; many have been unauthorised and later regularised, or been hired within the country after arrival under a non-work status.

In summary then, the past decade saw the replacement of retiring labour force cohorts by much more highly educated new entrants. The most highly educated were far more numerous than those retiring, which by itself would not suggest a problem with the supply of highly educated workers. Immigrants added to this number over the decade, representing about 15% of tertiary-educated entries into the labour force. This rich supply of skills among entrants does not exclude the possibility of skill shortages in certain areas, however. In most countries, immigrants had educational attainment levels that were somewhere in between entry and retiring cohorts, in a context in which most migration was non-discretionary.

7. The demography of occupational change

Background

Given the substantial increase in the educational levels of young workers entering the labour force in OECD countries, one might expect analogous changes to occur in the distribution of occupations and in the skill levels of jobs in the labour market. However, with increasing educational levels, one could also be witnessing an increasing proportion of entrants overqualified for available jobs. Such a result would suggest that the increase in attainment levels would be more supply- than demand-induced. As will be seen, the skill level of jobs is increasing as well.

The trends in the composition of employment have shown a continuous process of skill upgrading between 1950 and 2010 (Handel, 2010). The occupational distribution of employment has changed: shifting first from agricultural to production jobs, and later to professional, associate professionals and technical jobs.

Thus, there is little doubt that there has been an increase in job skill demands in OECD countries in the last decades. The increase in the demand for high-skilled workers has been interpreted for a long time as the result mostly of technological change (see Autor and Katz, 1999 for a review of the literature on skill-biased technological change, SBTC).

However, parallel to this increase in employment in higher skilled occupations, there has been as well an increase in lower-skilled occupations and a decrease in middle-skilled occupations. This phenomenon of *job polarization* has been observed in several OECD countries. Acemoglu and Autor (2010) describe the simultaneous increase in the share of employment in high-skill, high-wage occupations and low-skill, low-wage occupations in the United States and in the European Union. The authors argue that to describe the changes in the employment distribution a complex framework is necessary with "interactions among worker skills, job tasks, evolving technologies and shifting trading opportunities".

Several factors might explain *job polarisation*, Autor, Levy and Murnane (2003) suggested a *routinisation hypothesis*: middle-skilled and manual jobs are substituted by technological improvements and the relative demand for jobs with non-routine tasks increases. Non-routine tasks include not only abstract tasks which require high educational levels, but also non-routine manual tasks, as in many service occupations such as elderly care, security services, etc.

Other factors such as the increase in offshoring and outsourcing, in themselves partly facilitated by technological change, and changes in labour market institutions could be partly responsible for the reduction in the number of jobs in certain occupations. Goos, Manning and Salomons (2009, 2010) suggest that the *routinisation* of tasks is the main factor explaining the observed job polarisation of employment, abetted by offshoring. Labour market institutions affecting relative wages seem to play a smaller role in the process.

Michaels, Natraj and van Reenen (2010) have presented evidence that the observed job polarization is based on ICT technological change that increases the relative demand for high-educated workers and decreases the relative demand for middle-educated workers.

The extent of occupational change over the decade 2000-10

How much occupational change is there? The amount of change observed will depend on how fine the viewing lens is; the greater the magnifying power, the more movement one will observe. The occupation data used for the analyses to follow generally apply the International Standard Classification of Occupations (ILO, 1988), which classifies occupations up to four-digit level (390 occupations). However, for the analyses carried out here, the two-digit classification (27 groups)[5] has been used. It represents an appropriate compromise between fine resolution, on the one hand, and sampling variability, on the other, given that change is being measured at the level of the individual occupation.

The time period used for the analysis (2000-10) includes the recent economic crisis and the sluggish recovery of 2009-10. In practice, this means that the changes observed may in part be cyclical in character, in that some declines may reflect the rise in unemployment among persons in certain occupational groups.

Table II.3 lists the occupations in European countries and the United States and the growth rates observed over the period 2000-10, as well as the share of employment by occupation for all workers and for immigrants. For European countries, among the thirteen occupations with growth rates over 15% over the period, only three do not fall into a higher skill category, namely agricultural, fishery and related labourers, personal and protective

Table II.3. **Growing and declining occupations, 2000-10**

Percentages
European countries

ISCO88 code		Average growth 2000-10	Average share of employment 2010 (all workers)	Average share of employment 2010 (immigrants)
24	Other professionals	52	5.8	5.4
21	Physical, mathematical and engineering science professionals	50	3.9	4.1
32	Life science and health associate professionals	43	3.0	2.4
33	Teaching associate professionals	39	1.5	1.0
11	Legislators and senior officials	28	0.2	0.2
34	Other associate professionals	36	8.9	6.0
12	Corporate managers	29	4.2	3.5
51	Personal and protective services workers	25	9.9	12.1
31	Physical and engineering science associate professionals	22	4.0	2.8
22	Life science and health professionals	22	2.2	2.4
92	Agricultural, fishery and related labourers	22	0.5	1.0
23	Teaching professionals	21	4.6	3.0
91	Sales and services elementary occupations	21	6.4	13.6
42	Customer services clerks	12	2.1	1.7
52	Models, salespersons and demonstrators	10	5.5	5.2
93	Labourers in mining, construction, manufacturing and transport	6	2.5	4.3
83	Drivers and mobile-plant operators	5	4.0	3.8
71	Extraction and building trades workers	–1	5.4	7.0
13	General managers	–3	3.3	3.1
41	Office clerks	–6	8.6	5.5
81	Stationary-plant and related operators	–11	0.9	0.9
72	Metal, machinery and related trades workers	–12	4.7	3.9
61	Market-oriented skilled agricultural and fishery workers	–16	3.3	1.3
82	Machine operators and assemblers	–19	2.6	3.5
74	Other craft and related trades workers	–29	1.7	1.8
73	Precision, handicraft, printing and related trades workers	–31	0.6	0.5
	All occupations	9	100.0	100.0

Note: ISCO88: International Standard Classification of Occupations, 1988 version.

Table II.3. **Growing and declining occupations, 2000-10** (cont.)

Percentages
United States

SOC code		Average growth 2000-10	Average share of employment 2010 (all workers)	Average share of employment 2010 (immigrants)
39	Personal care and service occupations	37	3.6	4.4
31	Healthcare support occupations	35	2.5	2.8
37	Building and grounds cleaning and maintenance occupations	31	4.0	8.3
29	Healthcare practitioners and technical occupations	27	5.5	5.0
35	Food preparation and serving related occupations	26	5.7	8.2
21	Community and social service occupations	21	1.7	1.0
33	Protective service occupations	20	2.3	1.1
25	Education, training, and library occupations	18	6.3	3.9
13	Business and financial operations occupations	16	4.7	3.6
11	Management occupations	12	9.7	7.4
15	Computer and mathematical occupations	8	2.5	3.4
45	Farming, fishing, and forestry occupations	8	0.7	2.1
41	Sales and related occupations	6	11.2	9.0
53	Transportation and material moving occupations	4	6.1	6.8
27	Arts, design, entertainment, sports, and media occupations	4	1.9	1.5
19	Life, physical, and social science occupations	1	0.9	1.2
23	Legal occupations	0	1.0	0.5
47	Construction and extraction occupations	–2	5.1	7.7
17	Architecture and engineering occupations	–6	1.8	2.0
43	Office and administrative support occupations	–6	13.6	9.1
49	Installation, maintenance, and repair occupations	–17	3.2	2.6
51	Production occupations	–25	5.9	8.4
	All occupations	6	100.0	100.0

Note: SOC – Standard Occupational Classification.
Sources: European countries: European Labour Force Surveys (Eurostat); United States: American Community Survey.

StatLink ⟶ http://dx.doi.org/10.1787/888932617037

services workers and sales and services elementary occupations. Occupations which declined by at least 15% concern workers in the trades and in manufacturing-related jobs or skilled agricultural and fishery workers.

In the United States, the picture appears less clear-cut. Although there is no skill or credential level associated with occupational groups in the US occupational classification, one can more or less distinguish occupational groups which on the whole seem highly skilled from those which are lesser skilled. They are those numbered from 11 to 29 in Table II.3, for which the per cent of workers with tertiary qualifications varies from about 55% to 85%. This is comparable to the groups consisting of professionals, senior officials and managers in European countries (ISCO major groups 11 to 26), for which the per cent of workers with tertiary attainment varies between 55 and 90%.[6]

Among occupational groups with growth rates over 15% in the United States, 5 out of the 9 appear lesser skilled, with healthcare practitioners and technical occupations and education, training and library occupations being the two which appear to group more highly skilled occupations. Among the strongly declining occupational groups are installation, maintenance and repair occupations (–17%) and production occupations (–25%).

Over the decade from 2000 to 2010, the occupational distribution in OECD countries changed by approximately 10 percentage points on average (Figure II.3), that is, it would require a reallocation of 10% of employed persons from the occupational distribution observed in 2010 in order to make it identical to that observed in the year 2000.

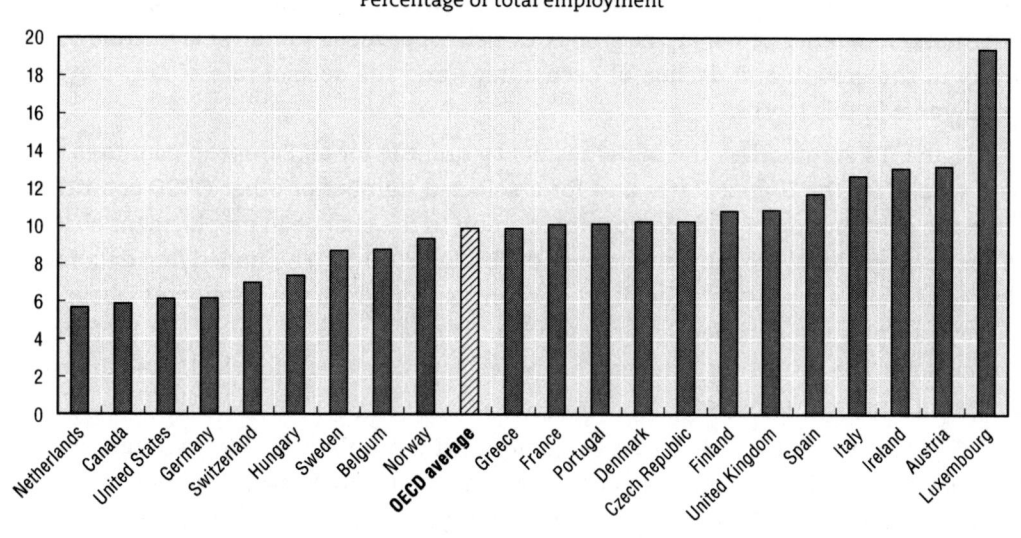

Figure II.3. **Total change in the distribution of employment by occupation, 2000-10**
Percentage of total employment

Notes: The statistic shown here is the index of dissimilarity between the distributions in the years 2000 and 2010, respectively. It is estimated as half of the sum of the absolute values of the difference in the share of workers in each occupation in 2000 and 2010. It can be interpreted as the percentage of workers in 2010 who would have to be reallocated to other occupations to make the 2010 distribution coincide with that for 2000.

Sources: European countries: European Labour Force Surveys (Eurostat); United States: American Community Survey; Canada: Survey of Labour and Income Dynamics. *StatLink* http://dx.doi.org/10.1787/888932615650

As is evident from the figure, many of the countries which have seen high levels of labour migration over the decade, such as Ireland, Italy, Luxembourg, Spain and the United Kingdom, have also seen more occupational change. But this is not the case everywhere. For example, Greece, Switzerland and the United States also saw significant labour migration, but show less occupational change.

10% of the occupational distribution does not seem like a very large amount. By way of contrast, the net turnover in the labour force[7] for the four demographic groups over the period amounted to 24% of the 2000 labour force (see Table II.2). A 10% change in the occupational distribution in the face of 24% turnover would indeed be significant, if all of the change were occurring through entry and exit. But some occurs also in the prime-age workforce, as workers change occupations, by applying skills and experience acquired in one occupation to another, by means of educational upgrading or through training.

8. Demographic components of occupational change

For the purpose of the analyses in this section, the occupational groups for each country have been divided into *quintiles*, where the quintile designation is based on the growth in employment in the occupation over the period 2000-10. Each quintile thus contains approximately 20% of total 2010 employment for each country.[8] The occupational change occurring within each quintile is then decomposed into components in the usual way, namely, that attributable to young workers, to immigrants who entered over the 2000-10 period, to prime-age workers and to older workers. Because a high proportion of the change observed for young and older workers, respectively, reflects entry and retirement, the young-worker and older-worker groups will sometimes be referred to as "new entrants" and "retirees" in what follows.

The grouping into growth quintiles makes it simpler to examine more closely a number of questions of particular interest, with respect to recent immigrants, but provides information for other demographic groups as well. Of particular interest is the role of each group in the growth and decline of occupations and the special role, if any, played by immigrants in this regard.

Figure II.4 summarises the initial results by quintile for all European countries taken as a whole, for the United States and for a selected number of other OECD countries. It gives the contribution of each demographic group to the change in employment observed in each occupational growth quintile over the period 2000-10. The underlying data for the figures as well as similar data for all other countries for which the immigrant labour force survey samples are sufficiently large to support this kind of analysis can be found in Annex II.A1. The results for European countries as a whole and for the United States are similar in a number of respects.

The first thing to note is that, in general, the number of older workers leaving particular occupations becomes smaller as one moves from strongly declining to strongly growing occupations. Conversely, the number of young worker entries increases as one passes from declining to growing occupations. Indeed, the balance between the entry of young workers and the exit of older workers accounts on average in Europe, the United States and Canada for from 35% to 60% of the net change in employment in each of the occupational growth quintiles (Table II.4). In other words, a considerable amount of net occupational change occurs through generational change in the workforce, that is, through the entry of young workers and the exit of older workers. That some of this should be the case was to be expected; that the correspondence between change and entry and exit should be so strong was less so. The data suggest that jobs in declining occupations are often suppressed following the retirement of their incumbents and that jobs for which many young workers are hired are often new ones. Note, however, that the patterns for individual countries may not always be so clear-cut.

Accompanying the general pattern observed for young and older workers is the movement out of declining occupations and into growing occupations on the part of prime-age workers. This subsumes a number of different phenomena in addition to occupational mobility, namely mortality and emigration, persons leaving employment after resignation or layoff, and movements into employment by the unemployed or inactive, in particular women re-entering the workforce after an absence. Occupational change by prime-age workers and occupational entries by young workers are both strong predictors of the direction of occupational change in general (correlations with occupational growth of 0.80 and 0.85, respectively, across occupations).[9] The change by older workers (including retirement) is a weaker covariate (0.62) and occupational entries of immigrants weaker still (0.35).

The particular character of immigrant occupational entry (an equal distribution across quintiles in the United States and a strong presence in the lowest quintile in Europe) may well be associated with the lower average level of educational attainment of this group or with the nature of the skills which they bring with them to their new country of residence. New immigrants may lack the language proficiency of the native-born and may have qualifications and experience which are not recognised by employers or are not easily transferable to a different working environment.

Figure II.4. **Demographic components of net occupational change by occupational growth quintile, 2000-10**

Thousands

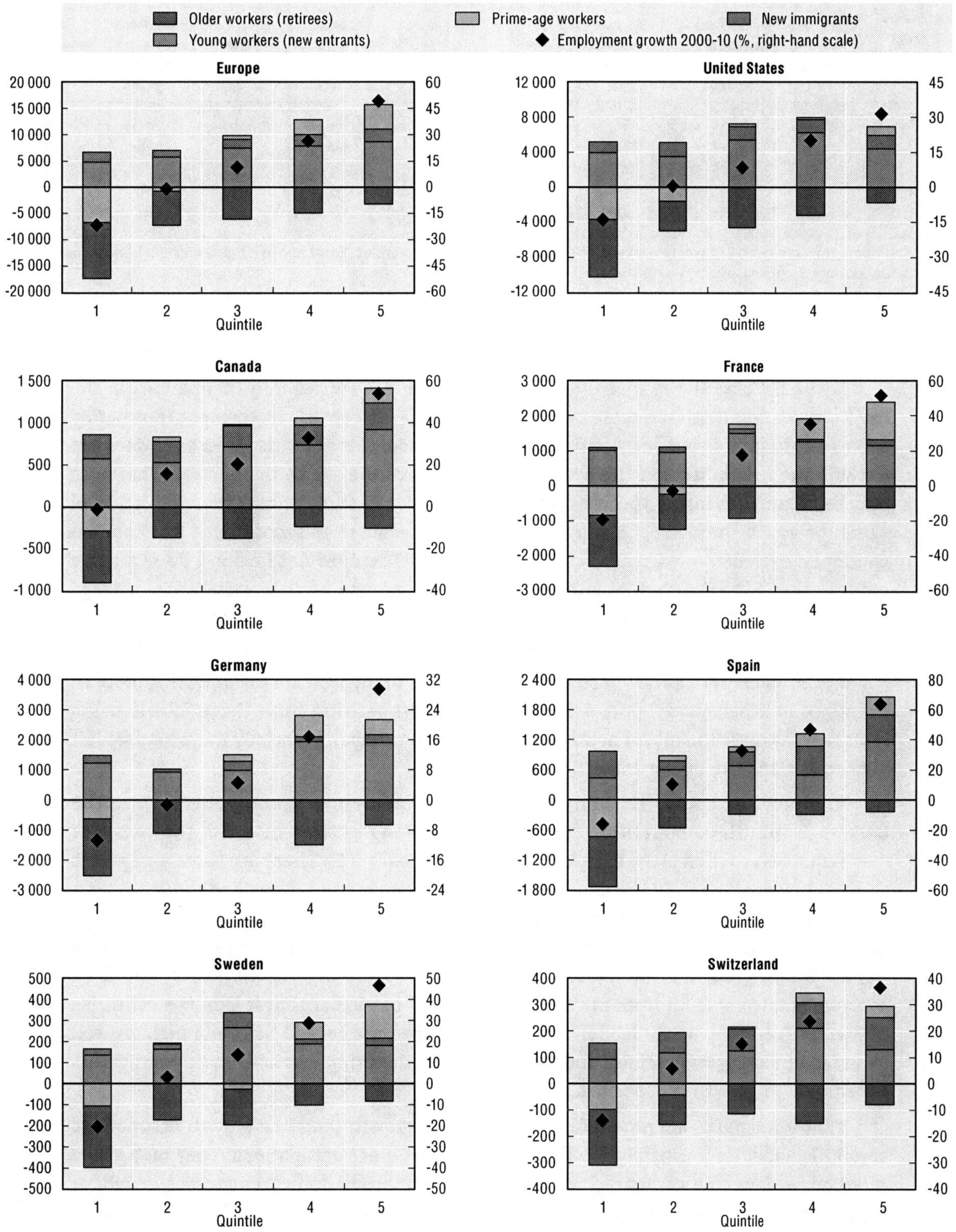
Older workers (retirees)
Young workers (new entrants)
Prime-age workers
Employment growth 2000-10 (%, right-hand scale)
New immigrants
Europe
United States
Canada
France
Germany
Spain
Sweden
Switzerland
Quintile

Sources: European countries: European Labour Force Surveys (Eurostat); United States: American Community Survey; Canada: Survey of Labour and Income Dynamics.

StatLink http://dx.doi.org/10.1787/888932615669

Table II.4. **Occupational entry and exit and occupational growth and decline, 2000-10**
Percentages

Occupational growth quintile	European countries			United States			Canada		
	Growth 2000-10	Contribution of entry-exit to employment growth	Share of entry-exit in net employment growth	Growth 2000-10	Contribution of entry-exit to employment growth	Share of entry-exit in net employment growth	Growth 1998-2008	Contribution of entry-exit to employment growth	Share of entry-exit in net employment growth
1	-22	-12	55	-14	-7	52	-1	-1	96
2	-1	-2	291	1	1	123	16	5	34
3	12	4	36	9	3	31	20	12	57
4	26	10	37	20	13	64	33	20	61
5	49	22	44	31	16	51	54	31	58

Notes: Entry here refers to entries of young workers, exit to retirement of older workers. Entry and exit figures shown here are net of some occupational change occurring among young and older workers.
Sources: European countries: European Labour Force Surveys (Eurostat); United States: American Community Survey; Canada: Survey of Labour and Income Dynamics.

StatLink ▸ http://dx.doi.org/10.1787/888932617056

Figure II.4 also shows that there are many more net entries into occupations in the top 2 growth quintiles than there are retirements. The concept of replacement thus hardly seems pertinent for these occupations, although the surplus of entries over exits does not exclude the possibility that the occupations may nevertheless be in shortage. Shortages may be regional, in highly specific occupations or fields of study or may involve high-level skills for which the domestic supply is limited. A recourse to recruitment from abroad cannot be excluded in particular cases, but the evidence does not favour a demographic explanation for expected labour needs arising because of the retirement of large baby-boom cohorts. The changing nature of labour demand, and in particular of occupations would appear to weigh heavily in the balance.

At the same time as new jobs are being created, many jobs are disappearing (bottom quintile). In other words, only a fraction of workers retiring from these jobs is being replaced. For these the role of new immigrants may be crucial, especially if the jobs are not viewed as attractive by the domestic workforce.

In almost all countries, immigrants are less numerous among entries into the bottom 2 quintile occupations than they are among entries into the top two, but somewhat less so than is the case for new entrants (Table II.5). There are some exceptions to this, however, namely the Czech Republic, Denmark, the Netherlands and Norway, where immigrants enter less often into high-growth occupations than into low-growth ones. Since the top quintiles are the growing ones, one would of course necessarily expect some groups to be overrepresented there, but that immigrants would be overrepresented was far from pre-ordained. Note in particular that it is in the countries of Southern Europe, where labour migration over the past decade has been high, as well as in Luxembourg, Switzerland and the United Kingdom that one sees more immigrants entering high-growth occupations.

That immigrants are more often entering high-growth than low-growth occupations says little about their contribution to the evolution of these occupations. They may play a relatively minor role compared with the more numerous domestic sources of labour supply, which include former migrants as well as young workers and prime-age workers. Indeed in some countries (France, Germany, the Netherlands, Sweden), the role of immigrants was not especially important over the past decade, accounting for less than

Table II.5. **Entries of new immigrants into growing and declining occupations, 2010**

	Share of immigrant entries				New immigrant share of all entries		
	In growing occupations A	In declining occupations B	Difference A-B	Difference for young resident workers	In growing occupations C	In declining occupations D	Difference C-D
	Percentages		Percentage points		Percentages		Percentage points
Denmark	34	44	−10	30	10	30	−20
Norway	41	50	−9	22	12	27	−14
Netherlands	36	42	−6	13	6	10	−4
Czech Republic	42	47	−5	18	3	7	−5
Ireland	41	42	−1	55	29	82	−53
Canada	42	40	2	16	22	31	−9
United States	41	39	2	14	20	28	−8
Sweden	31	29	2	8	9	15	−6
France	40	37	2	7	5	10	−5
Austria	40	37	3	16	12	24	−12
Finland	38	30	8	14	4	6	−2
Belgium	46	37	9	8	20	24	−4
Germany	42	32	10	24	8	14	−6
United Kingdom	47	37	11	15	22	32	−10
Portugal	47	34	12	38	10	24	−14
Greece	52	34	18	24	17	25	−8
Switzerland	50	31	19	19	34	40	−5
Spain	53	34	19	25	33	43	−10
Hungary	60	32	27	24	3	4	−1
Luxembourg	60	30	30	20	50	58	−7
Italy	59	24	35	11	22	22	0
Average, new immigrants	45	36	9	20	17	26	−10
Average, young resident workers (detail by country not shown)	49	29	20				

Notes: Growing occupations are in the top two growth quintiles, declining occupations in the bottom 2 quintiles. Entries include those of new immigrant and resident young workers plus net occupational change by prime-age workers (when positive).
Sources: European countries: European Labour Force Surveys (Eurostat); United States: American Community Survey; Canada: Survey of Labour and Income Dynamics.

StatLink ⟶ http://dx.doi.org/10.1787/888932617075

10% of the movements into high-growth occupations. Again, it is in the same countries noted above (southern Europe, Luxembourg, Switzerland, the United Kingdom) that the contribution of immigrants to high-growth occupations becomes more significant, ranging from 20% to as high as 50% of the change observed (in Luxembourg).

Changes in employment by occupation 2000-10

The picture for individual occupations is shown in Figure II.5a on average for European countries and in II.5b for the United States. The movement out of declining occupations (largely through retirement) by older workers, the movement into growing occupations by prime-age and young workers and entries by immigrants in both growing and declining occupations are evident. In both figures, the strong immigrant presence in particular lower-skilled occupations (sales and service elementary occupations, agricultural fishery and related labourers in European countries; farming, fishing and forestry occupations and building and ground cleaning and maintenance in the United States) are also evident. For neither the European countries nor the United States does immigrant entry into specific occupations appear to be related closely to occupational growth or decline or to a replacement deficit due to the retirement of older workers, at least not at the occupational

Figure II.5a. **Contribution of different demographic groups to occupational growth, average over European countries, 2000-10**

Percentages

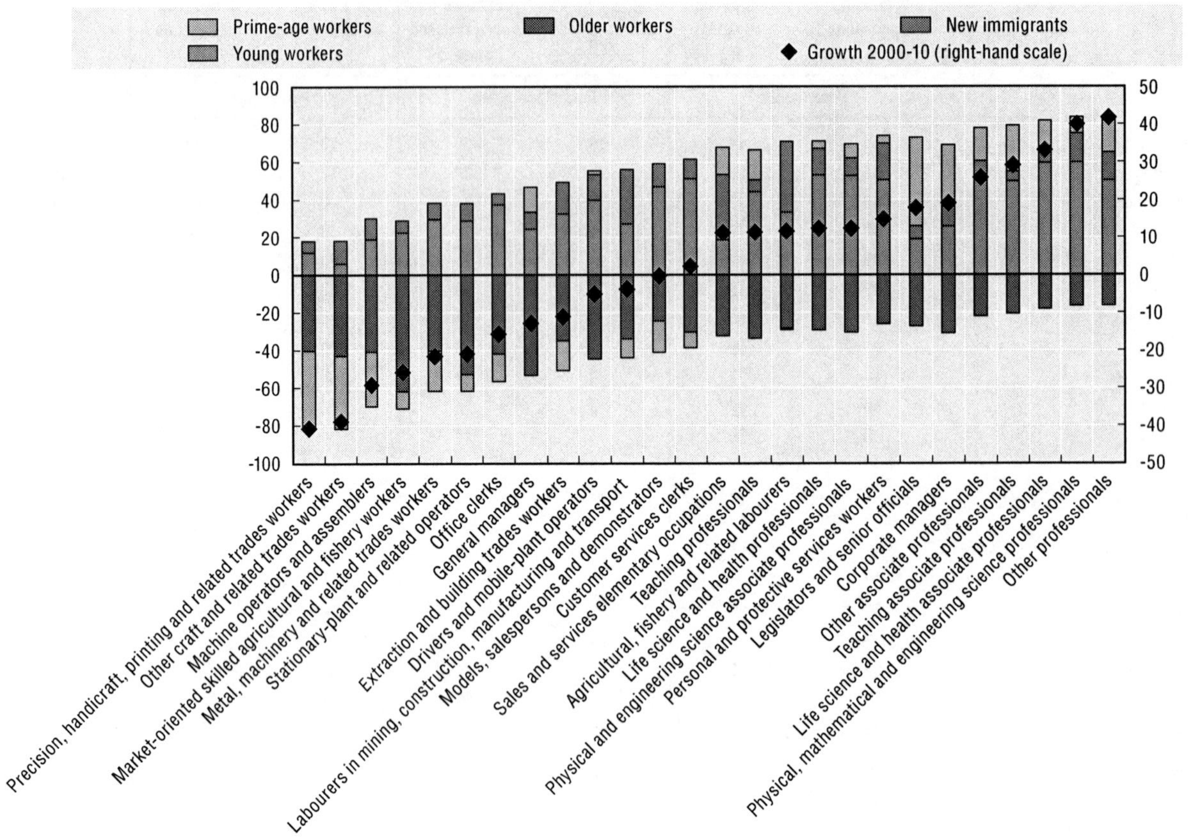

Sources: European Labour Force Surveys (Eurostat).

StatLink ᐅ http://dx.doi.org/10.1787/888932615688

level examined here. The strong growth of highly skilled occupations across the board evident in European countries appears to be less present in the United States, where architecture and engineering occupations, for example, have actually declined and where occupations in the life, physical and social sciences show scarcely any increase over the period 2000-10.

In summary then, the past decade has seen considerable occupational change, in particular movement away from trades and manufacturing professions and towards professional and other skilled occupations, especially in Europe. In the United States, the movement seems to be less polarised, with some high-skilled occupations declining or not growing. A significant part of net occupational change appears to occur towards the beginning and end of working life as older workers leave or retire from declining occupations and younger workers enter growing ones. Entries of young workers into growing occupations far outnumber the retirement of older workers from these. For declining occupations, the situation is the reverse.

Immigrants have been significant players in the growth and decline of occupations but have not been as present in entries into high-growth occupations as natives, and in particular young workers. Although more numerous among entries into growing than declining occupations, they are proportionally more present in declining or slower-growing occupations.

Figure II.5b. **Contribution of various demographic groups to occupational growth, United States, 2000-10**
Percentages

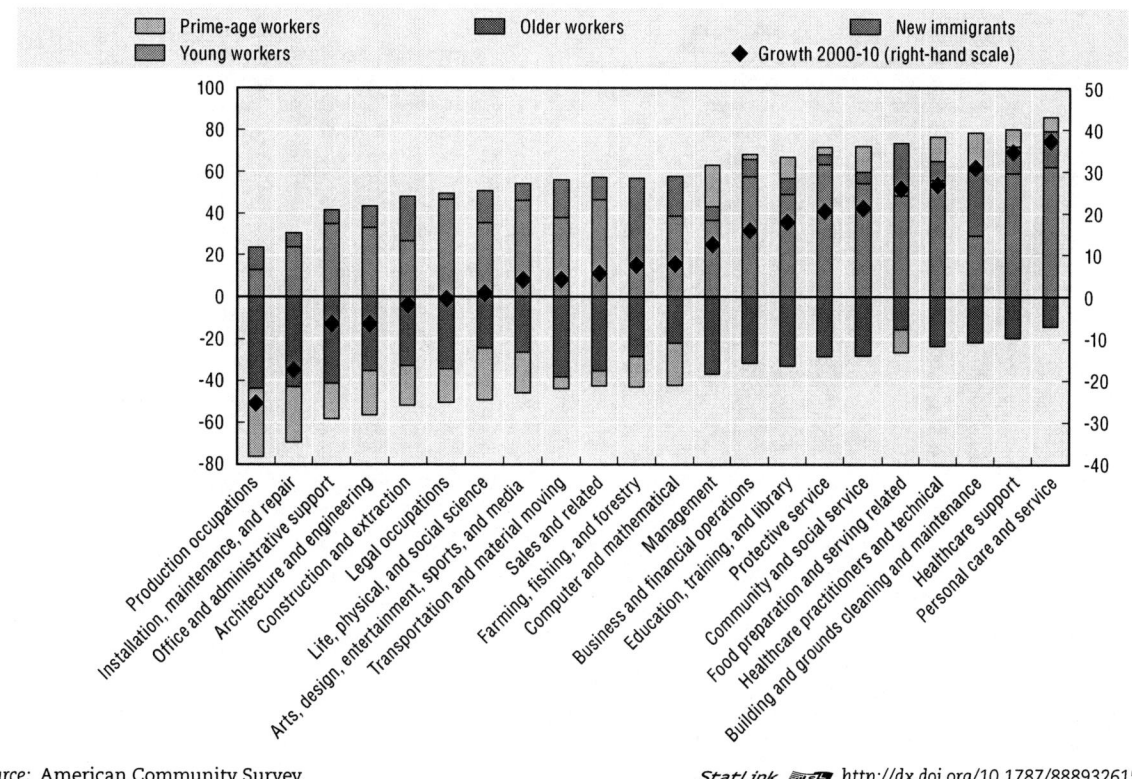

- Prime-age workers
- Young workers
- Older workers
- New immigrants
- ◆ Growth 2000-10 (right-hand scale)

Source: American Community Survey.

StatLink http://dx.doi.org/10.1787/888932615707

These results raise a number of questions. Firstly, if there is (and perhaps continues to be) such a large surplus of new entrants over retirees in growing occupations, will skill shortages still develop to the extent expected? How significant will recruitment from abroad actually have to be? The existence of a surplus is no guarantee that shortages will not emerge, if the hiring of immigrants into growing occupations over the past decade is any indication, but to project or identify shortages on the basis of analyses of demographic imbalances alone seems problematical. The evolution of the economy and of occupations would appear to be far more important factors for projecting labour needs than demographic trends *per se*.

Secondly, new immigrants account for a significant proportion of entries into declining occupations. Are they filling a real need here, for example, by taking up occupations abandoned by domestic workers and which would otherwise go begging, or are they providing cheap labour to firms that are on the decline? The answers to these questions may affect the extent to which migration channels for lesser-skilled jobs need to be opened up over the next decade.

The evolution of occupational and job skill levels

It was noted above that growing occupations in European countries on average tend to be the highly skilled ones, that is, professional, technicians and associate professionals, with some growth as well in low-skilled occupations. Although the picture for individual occupations is mixed in the United States, the aggregate result is fairly similar. Table II.6 summarises the growth rates by occupational skill level and country for the period 2000

Table II.6. **Employment growth, by occupational skill level, 2000-10**
Percentages

European countries	Employment growth 2000-10					Contributions to total employment growth				
	Professionals, senior officials and managers (A)	Technicians and associate professionals (B)	Clerks, service workers, skilled trades, machinery operators (C)	Elementary occupations (D)	All workers (A + B + C + D)	Professionals, senior officials and managers (E)	Technicians and associate professionals (F)	Clerks, service workers, skilled trades, machinery operators (G)	Elementary occupations (H)	All workers (E + F + G + H)
Austria	11	61	–4	39	11	2	9	–3	3	11
Belgium	28	10	1	–6	9	8	1	1	–1	9
Switzerland	29	16	0	15	10	6	3	0	1	10
Czech Republic	–3	39	1	–36	5	0	7	1	–3	5
Germany	21	14	–2	9	7	4	3	–1	1	7
Denmark	8	17	–6	–16	0	2	4	–3	–2	0
Spain	38	58	7	17	19	7	6	4	2	19
Finland	8	8	–2	9	3	2	1	–1	1	3
France	42	21	–5	35	11	8	4	–3	3	11
Greece	25	41	–7	44	7	6	3	–4	3	7
Hungary	18	–2	–7	11	0	3	0	–4	1	0
Ireland	22	42	2	–4	10	7	2	1	0	10
Italy	5	33	–8	32	4	1	6	–5	3	4
Luxembourg	83	54	–11	–9	22	18	10	–5	–1	22
Netherlands	12	8	2	6	7	4	1	1	1	7
Norway	18	22	5	–16	10	3	5	3	–1	10
Portugal	16	24	–5	–10	0	2	2	–3	–1	0
Sweden	31	17	–2	22	10	7	3	–1	1	10
United Kingdom	3	56	–6	39	6	1	5	–3	3	6
OECD average	22	28	–2	9	8	5	4	–1	1	8
OECD average (excluding Luxembourg)	18	27	–2	11	7	4	4	–1	1	7

Sources: European Labour Force Surveys (Eurostat).

United States	Employment growth 2000-10				Contributions to total employment growth			
	High-skilled	Medium-skilled	Lower-skilled	All workers	High-skilled	Medium-skilled	Lower-skilled	All workers
	13	–2	26	6	5	–1	2	6

Source: American Community Survey.

StatLink http://dx.doi.org/10.1787/888932617094

to 2010. The professionals group increased by 22% on average over the period, associate professionals by 28%. Occupations at mid-range skill levels, including clerks, office workers, skilled trades and machinery operators, actually declined by 2% on average, while elementary occupations grew by 9%. In the United States, the skilled group progressed by 13%, middle-skill occupations declined by 2% and low-skilled ones increased by 26%.[10] The trend is thus towards an increase at the extremes of the skill distribution and a loss of jobs in the middle, a pattern consistent with that described in Acemoglu and Autor (2011).

The situation is not entirely uniform across countries, however. The mid-range occupations progressed in a number of countries, in particular Spain and Norway, while elementary occupations declined in Belgium, the Czech Republic, Denmark, Luxembourg, Norway and Portugal.

The increase in elementary occupations is especially large in some countries, ranging from 22% in Sweden to 39% in Austria and the United Kingdom. These occupations are not especially numerous, however; their contribution to the total employment growth observed over the period of 8% was approximately 1% on average across countries.

This provides the general picture for the economy as a whole. How have the skill levels of jobs held by immigrants evolved over the past decade? We have seen that immigrants are relatively more present among movements into growing occupations and that the latter *on average* tend to be highly skilled. One might be tempted to conclude that new immigrants are finding jobs in highly skilled occupations. Although some are, the distribution of skill levels among recent immigrants is significantly below that of young workers entering or changing jobs (Figure II.6). On average, there is a 20-point difference between recent immigrants and young workers in the percentage taking on highly skilled jobs (managers, professionals and associated professionals). This apparent contradiction is due to the fact that growing occupations also include agricultural, fishery and related labourers and sales and services elementary occupations and that many recent immigrants have found jobs in these occupations.

Figure II.6. **Differences in the distribution of occupational skills of workers entering or changing jobs (2000-10) by skill level, new immigrants compared to young resident workers**

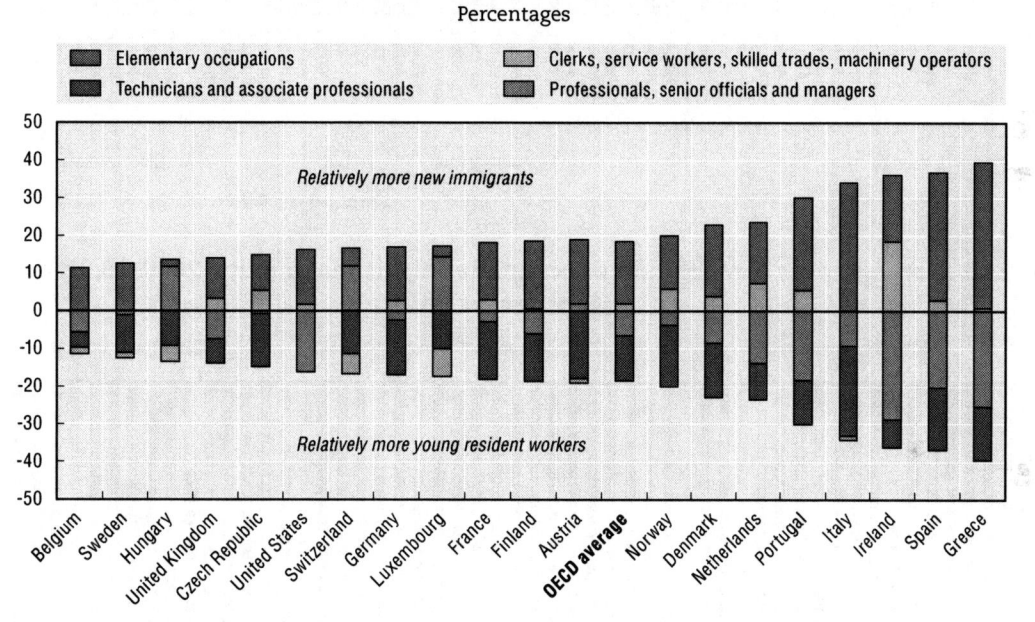

Percentages

Sources: European countries: European Labour Force Surveys (Eurostat); United States: American Community Survey.
StatLink ⟶ http://dx.doi.org/10.1787/888932615726

Only in Hungary, Luxembourg and Switzerland does one find relatively more recent immigrants in highly skilled jobs (professionals, senior officials and managers) than young workers entering such jobs. In all other countries, there are relatively fewer recent immigrants taking on skilled jobs than young workers, ranging from 10 percentage points less in Belgium and Sweden to over 35-40 percentage points less in southern Europe and Ireland. Likewise, the greater specialisation of immigrant in low-skilled jobs is evident in almost all countries, the immigrant percentage in entries into low-skilled jobs exceeding that of the young workers by 18 percentage points on average.

Finally, Figures II.7a and II.7b summarise the situation comprehensively with regard to entries and exits into jobs by occupational skill level and demographic group. In most countries, new immigrants are entering elementary occupations proportionally more than

Figure II.7a. **Skill level composition of occupational entries or exits, 2000-10, by demographic group**
Percentages

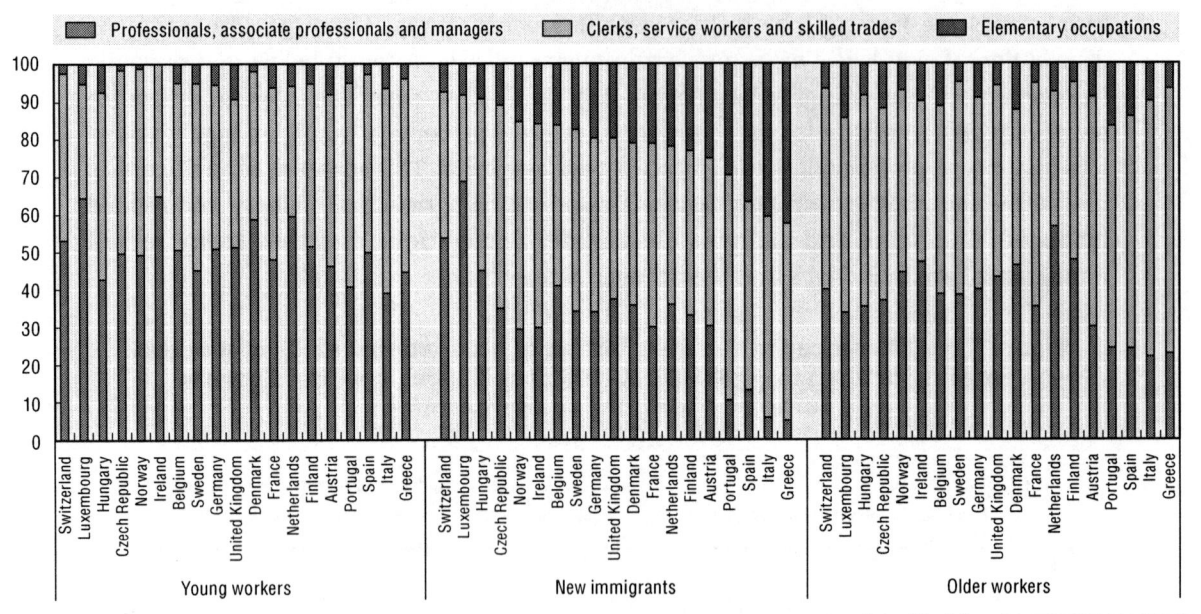

Figure II.7b. **Demographic composition of occupational entries or exits, 2000-10, by skill level**
Percentages

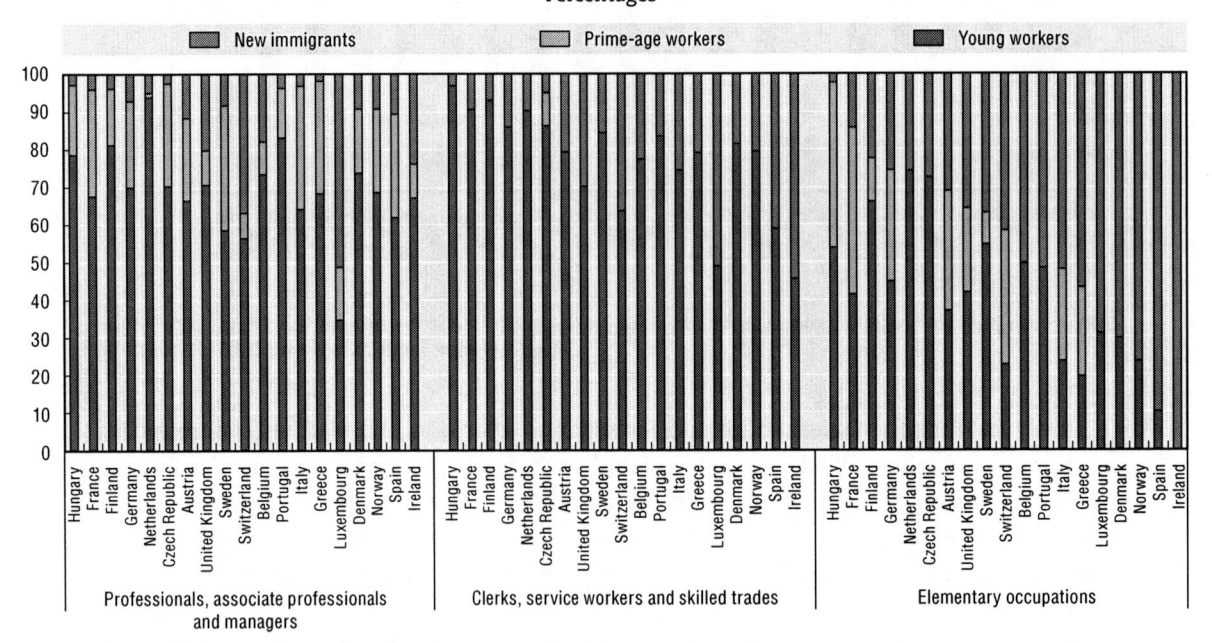

Note: In most countries, the number of prime-age workers in mid-skill jobs actually declined over the 2000-10 period, which is why they do not appear in the central panel and in for some countries in the right-hand panel.
Source: European Labour Force Surveys (Eurostat).

young workers and their presence in these occupations is often substantial. There are only a few countries where this is less the case, namely Luxembourg, Switzerland, the Czech Republic and Hungary. In the countries of southern Europe, some 30% or more of arriving immigrants over the period 2000-10 entered elementary occupations. These countries are also those which have shown the greatest increase in the share of high-skilled jobs among young workers compared with older workers over the decade. Indeed, there is a moderately strong positive correlation association (0.68) between the extent of job upskilling among young workers entering the labour force over the period 2000-10 and the incidence of new immigrants taking on low-skilled jobs.[11]

Low-skilled jobs are becoming more and more "reserved" for immigrants, as is evident from Figure II.7b, which shows that on average across countries, half of low-skilled jobs are being filled by immigrants. The proportion, however, ranges from less than 15% in France and Hungary to over 90% in Spain and Ireland.

9. Conclusion

The objective of this chapter was to examine the role of demography in educational and occupational change, in order to obtain some insight into the role which immigrants have played and can be expected to play in the future as labour markets respond to the retirement of baby-boomers and the entry of smaller youth cohorts into working life.

The past ten years have seen the entry of youth cohorts which are much more educated on average than older retiring cohorts. Attainment levels of arriving immigrants entering the labour force, on the other hand, have tended to be somewhere in between. Over a third on average are highly educated, but almost the same proportion have less than upper secondary attainment. This reflects at one and the same time the preference for highly educated labour migrants in most countries, but also the preponderance of family and humanitarian migrants in inflows, many of whom have low educational attainment levels. Immigrants have accounted for significant proportions of labour force entries of low-educated persons in many countries, while their contribution to the growth of the high-educated labour force is generally significant only in countries which have seen high levels of labour migration.

Not only have young entrants been more highly educated, there were many more of them than retiring highly educated workers. On the face of it then, this does not seem to suggest an upcoming skill deficiency, but ageing is still in its early phase and one needs to look more closely at how occupations are changing.

Over the past decade, the upskilling of jobs has gone hand-in-hand with increasing levels of educational attainment. Generally, high-skilled occupations have grown strongly, low-skilled occupations somewhat less so, while medium-skilled occupations have declined or stagnated.

In growing occupations, there were several entrants for every retirement, while at the other end of the spectrum, the reverse was generally the case. New immigrants contributed 16% of entries into growing occupations and 26% of entries into declining occupations.

In strongly growing occupations, the large surplus of new entrants over retirees means that many of the jobs were newly created ones, for which there appeared to be no shortage of domestic candidates, among both new entrants and prime-age workers. But many new immigrants were also hired into these jobs, indicating that domestic sources were not sufficient to satisfy all of the needs. At the same time, new immigrants replaced only a fraction of retiring workers in declining occupations. Many of the jobs were cut after their incumbents retired.

In other words a surplus of entrants over retirees does not obviate the need for labour migrants, nor does a significant deficit imply a major shortfall of workers that must be filled through recruitment from abroad. The labour and skill shortages to come are not a simple function of demographic imbalances in the labour force but depend significantly on the changing nature of demand for particular skills and the extent to which these can be filled from existing sources of supply. In a sense this is obvious, but the scale of ongoing and future demographic change is large and the prospect of a drop in the labour force and perhaps even in the size of the economy, has tended to dominate discussions in this area, to the neglect of the dynamics of occupational change.

The links between occupational growth and decline, demographic imbalance and the need for immigrant workers are thus far from obvious. This is all the more the case since many immigrants have arrived as a result of family and humanitarian reasons rather than having been directly recruited from abroad by employers. Their lesser-or-greater presence in certain occupations may thus reflect in many cases less a response to needs that could not be filled by resident workers, such as is generally the case for labour migrants, than a fortuitous match between whatever skills they brought with them and available jobs in a labour market where there were many other players.

For some immigrants, low levels of education constrained their occupational choices to lesser-skilled jobs and for others, the education and work experience earned abroad made them sometimes ill-prepared to compete with the skills of recently graduated young workers and of prime-age workers already having made their way in the labour market.

The analyses presented here illustrate that the labour market is highly dynamic. The focus of many analyses of ageing has emphasised the demographic imbalances and the consequences this is having and will have on the size of the workforce and on skill needs. The objective of this analysis was to focus more precisely on the impact of ageing on the educational attainment of the labour force and on occupational change, and the role of labour migration in this dynamic process.

What emerges is that labour market change is more rapid than demographic change and many future jobs are likely to be significantly different from those held by cohorts which will be retiring over the next twenty years. International migrants frequently will not be replacing retiring baby-boomers, but rather responding to the labour and skill requirements of a forever changing labour market.

Notes

1. It is on average about one third larger than the previous ten-year age cohort.
2. Although the term "high-skilled" here is used in reference to jobs, it will also generally be used synonymously with "highly educated", since for new hires, it is generally the case that high-skilled jobs require some form of tertiary education or equivalent qualification. Likewise the term "lower-skilled" or "low-skilled" will generally be used to mean "lower educated" or "low-educated", despite the fact that in every country there exists a proportion of highly educated persons who are working in lower-skilled jobs. When the distinction between education level and skill level needs to be made, it will be clear from the context.
3. Some persons who leave a particular occupation, for example, consist of persons who died or left the country over the observed period. The essential point is that they are no longer in the labour force or employed in their occupation at the end of the period. Likewise, some who enter an occupation are native-born expatriates who return from abroad; they also are not identified specifically.

4. The group representing school completers excludes some persons who obtained a first tertiary degree after the age of 25. Persons in this situation show up in the estimates for the prime-age group.

5. Two groups are excluded, namely subsistence agricultural and fishery workers (sub-major group 62) and the armed forces (major group 0).

6. The tertiary attainment share of employment in an occupational group drops off strongly thereafter in the United States, to 30%, whereas the category of associate professionals and technicians in European countries shows tertiary attainment percentages ranging from 33 to 50%. Occupations in these groups would appear to be included in the highly educated 1-to-10 numbered group in the United States.

7. A measure of turnover would in principle show how much the composition of the labour force has changed due to entry and exit. The measure given here (net turnover) is an approximation which underestimates the total turnover (see note to Table II.3).

8. The number of persons employed per quintile is not exactly 20% because the requirement that an occupational group be entirely within a quintile creates some imbalance in the quintile sizes.

9. The correlations are calculated, across occupations, between the rate of growth of the occupation and the contribution of each demographic group to the total growth.

10. Because the US Standard Occupational Classification does not include a skill classification for occupations, for the purpose of the analysis presented here, skill levels were assigned to occupations on the basis of the educational attainment of the incumbents. High-skilled occupations were defined to be those for which at least 55% of the holders had a tertiary qualification and mid-skilled those among the remaining for which at least 70% of persons employed had at least upper secondary education.

11. Luxembourg is an outlier and has been excluded from the calculation.

References

Acemoglu, D. and D.H. Autor (2011), Chapter 12 – "Skills, Tasks and Technologies: Implications for Employment and Earnings", in: O. Ashenfelter and D. Card (eds.), *Handbook of Labor Economics*, Vol. 4, Part B, pp. 1043-1171, Amsterdam: Elsevier.

Autor, D.H. and L.F. Katz (1999), "Changes in the Wage Structure and Earnings Inequality", in O. Ashenfelter and D. Card (eds.), *Handbook of Labor Economics*, Vol. 3A, pp. 1463-1555. Amsterdam: Elsevier.

Autor, D.H., F. Levy and R.J. Murnane (2003), "The Skill-Content of Recent Technological Change: An Empirical Investigation", *Quarterly Journal of Economics*, No. 118, Vol. 4, pp. 1279-1333.

Firpo, S., N.M. Fortin and T. Lemieux (2011), "Occupational Tasks and Changes in the Wage Structure", *IZA Discussion Paper* No. 5542.

Goos, M., A. Manning and A. Salomons (2009), "Job Polarization in Europe", *American Economic Review*, Vol. 99, No. 2, pp. 58-63.

Goos, M., A. Manning and A. Salomons (2010), "Explaining Job Polarization in Europe: The Roles of Technology, Globalization and Institutions", *CEP Discussion Papers dp1026*, Centre for Economic Performance, LSE.

Handel, M. (2010), "Trends in job skill demands in OECD countries", mimeo ("New skills for new jobs" project), OECD.

Léger, J.-F. (2008), "Les entrées annuelles des ressortissants des pays tiers sur le marché de l'emploi de 2004 à 2006", *Infos Migrations* No. 1, October 2008, Ministère de l'Immigration, de l'Intégration, de l'Identité nationale et du Développement solidaire, France.

Michaels, G., A. Natraj and J. van Reenen (2010), "Has ICT Polarized Skill Demand? Evidence from Eleven Countries over 25 years", *NBER Working Paper* No. 16138.

OECD (2011), *Education at a Glance – OECD Indicators*, OECD Publishing, Paris.

ANNEX II.A1

Methodology for estimating the components of demographic change

The components of demographic change identified in this part are derived using some basic demographic accounting methods, applied to changes in educational attainment, in the labour force and in the distribution of employment by occupation.

Roughly speaking, the method rests on the following general equality concerning the measure of change in a particular characteristic between time t1 and time t2:

$\Delta(T) = E + I + \Delta(PA) - R,$

where $\Delta(T)$ = the total change observed in the characteristic over the period,

E = new non-immigrant entrants over the period,

I = new immigrants who arrived over the period,

$\Delta(PA)$ = change in the prime-age group over the period,

and R = retirees over the period.

This amounts approximately to change = inflows – outflows, except that one allows for internal change in the stocks as well as distinguishing between internal inflows (new entrants) and external ones (immigration). External outflows (deaths and emigration) are included implicitly in each of the four components and are essentially netted out.

For almost all countries, the decomposition is applied to change over the period 2000-10 and is based on labour force survey data. We will describe the method in general for changes in the labour force, before explaining a number of technicalities resulting from its application to specific cases. The basic components are as follows

- New entrants = the labour force 15-34 in 2010, less persons 15-24 who were already in the labour force in the year 2000. This approximates young persons who entered the labour force over the period.
- Retirees = the labour force 45+ in 2000 less the labour force 55+ in 2010. Temporary withdrawals and re-entries prior to definitive retirement are implicitly netted out.
- Prime-age workers = the labour force 35-54 in 2010, less the labour force 25-44 in 2000.
- New immigrants = immigrants in 2010 with duration of residence of 10 years or less. Note that this implies that this group has to be excluded from all the other components above involving 2010 data, to avoid double-counting.

As can be verified, the net change in the labour force 15 years of age and older is the sum of these four components, and the sum is perfectly additive, modulo non-response.

The decomposition of change described above can be applied to each educational attainment level within the labour force. However, new entrants now have a more precise meaning, namely persons who completed their education over the period and entered the labour force, provided one excludes persons still in education from the calculation. The change for prime-age workers represents educational upgrading for this group as well as, implicitly, loss due to emigration or death.

New entrants are now estimated as follows: persons 15-24 not in education in 2010 + (persons 25-34 in 2010 – persons 15-24 not in education in 2000), for each educational attainment level.

The first term consists of persons who in principle have completed their education by 2010. For the second term, not all persons 25-34 have completed their education. However, since it is tertiary attainment that is of interest, it is assumed that persons 25-34 who are still in education will already have at least a first tertiary degree. The tertiary attainment levels of those who do not (and there are some) will show up as educational upgrading among persons who are 25-44 in 2000 and 35-54 in 2010. This is not ideal, but it is difficult to take into account sensibly situations in which a first tertiary degree is completed without interruption at a late age.

From the population of persons 25-34 in 2010, one subtracts persons from the same cohort who had already completed their education in 2000, namely persons 15-24 not in education.

This kind of decomposition can be carried out for various characteristics, in particular occupation or sector, and by gender, to provide an indication of the demographics of change for each of these characteristics.

ANNEX II.A2

Table II.A2.1. Decomposition of growth in the labour force by educational attainment and source, 2000-10
Thousands

	Young workers	New Immigrants	Older workers	Prime-age workers	Still in education	Residual	Net change in the labour force	2000 labour force
Austria	850	243	−642	−46	14	0	420	3 864
Low	71	60	−183	−47	9	0	−89	811
Medium	605	121	−386	−69	5	0	276	2 467
High	174	61	−73	70	0	0	233	586
Belgium	1 057	351	−757	−190	−7	31	484	4 411
Low	128	105	−370	−189	−4	9	−321	1 418
Medium	413	111	−209	−13	−3	9	309	1 585
High	516	134	−178	13	0	12	496	1 408
Canada	3 602	−1 637	1 422	−25	284	0	3 646	11 071
Low	233	−263	117	−158	138	0	67	2 512
Medium	912	−574	354	−318	100	0	474	4 606
High	2 456	−800	950	451	46	0	3 104	3 953
Czech Republic	1 074	55	−1 087	131	−29	0	144	5 123
Low	39	6	−192	−60	−5	0	−212	530
Medium	740	35	−791	76	−25	0	36	3 989
High	295	13	−104	114	1	0	320	605
Denmark	510	59	−563	−47	13	71	43	2 804
Low	..	..	..	..	..	..	..	..
Medium	..	..	..	..	..	..	..	..
High	239	21	−149	81	3	29	222	681
Estonia	165	3	−128	−9	0	2	33	654
Low	18	0	−28	−4	−1	0	−14	82
Medium	82	1	−64	−21	0	1	−2	379
High	65	2	−37	16	1	1	49	194
Finland	515	45	−490	−10	−51	0	9	2 663
Low	26	16	−204	−44	−30	0	−236	662
Medium	266	20	−155	−30	−14	0	86	1 163
High	222	9	−131	64	−6	0	158	837
France	6 665	750	−5 117	188	82	55	2 625	25 752
Low	802	270	−2 268	−129	−9	10	−1 323	8 198
Medium	2 834	226	−1 998	14	57	22	1 156	11 363
High	3 029	254	−851	303	34	23	2 792	6 191
Germany	10 857	1 323	−9 509	−671	−215	452	2 236	39 390
Low	1 080	366	−2 436	−1 919	−565	224	−3 250	9 467
Medium	7 143	457	−4 946	−528	321	154	2 601	21 766
High	2 634	499	−2 127	1 776	29	73	2 885	8 158
Greece	1 006	247	−842	25	−36	0	400	4 617
Low	142	138	−558	9	−10	0	−279	1 946
Medium	424	82	−191	−75	−26	0	214	1 795
High	440	26	−93	92	1	0	465	876

Table II.A2.1. **Decomposition of growth in the labour force by educational attainment and source, 2000-10** (cont.)

Thousands

	Young workers	New Immigrants	Older workers	Prime-age workers	Still in education	Residual	Net change in the labour force	2000 labour force
Hungary	906	29	–826	93	–21	0	182	4 074
Low	86	3	–241	–19	–2	0	–173	750
Medium	504	14	–451	0	–18	0	48	2 665
High	317	12	–134	112	0	0	307	659
Ireland	417	219	–199	–26	–39	1	374	1 694
Low	11	25	–116	–52	–20	0	–152	582
Medium	148	86	–55	–59	–18	1	104	701
High	258	108	–28	84	–1	0	422	411
Italy	4 072	1 467	–4 280	110	–68	33	1 332	23 642
Low	535	617	–2 801	–684	–48	19	–2 362	11 267
Medium	2 412	693	–1 063	251	–27	12	2 277	9 503
High	1 125	156	–417	543	7	3	1 417	2 872
Luxembourg	36	47	–32	–9	–1	0	40	181
Low	5	7	–15	–13	–1	0	–17	61
Medium	18	11	–13	–5	0	0	10	82
High	14	30	–5	9	0	0	48	38
Netherlands	1 696	158	–1 088	–128	–4	41	675	8 028
Low	233	50	–361	–91	–39	16	–193	2 478
Medium	715	51	–511	–210	2	16	64	3 605
High	748	58	–216	173	33	9	805	1 945
Norway	478	120	–357	–12	13	0	243	2 330
Low	..	..	..	..	..	..	..	..
Medium	..	..	..	..	..	..	..	..
High	225	43	–92	31	–10	0	196	732
Portugal	1 093	199	–911	22	–24	0	379	5 201
Low	384	92	–811	–48	–27	0	–410	4 078
Medium	347	81	–47	7	1	0	388	631
High	362	26	–52	63	2	0	401	493
Spain	4 519	2 988	–2 508	355	–174	0	5 180	17 909
Low	1 326	1 275	–2 012	–251	–69	0	269	9 720
Medium	1 018	1 070	–157	190	–66	0	2 056	3 407
High	2 175	644	–340	415	–39	0	2 855	4 782
Sweden	1 035	239	–862	105	74	10	600	4 349
Low	112	75	–250	–2	48	3	–13	917
Medium	537	55	–365	36	28	4	295	2 147
High	386	109	–247	71	–3	3	319	1 285
Switzerland	728	482	–673	–42	–6	9	497	3 971
Low	52	92	–173	–3	–19	2	–49	812
Medium	396	156	–415	–151	8	3	–3	2 233
High	280	234	–86	113	5	3	549	926
United Kingdom	7 273	3 174	–6 068	–1 613	–295	21	2 493	28 583
Low	171	521	–1 816	–881	–147	8	–2 144	4 577
Medium	3 717	1 816	–3 220	–2 256	–214	8	–148	17 688
High	3 385	837	–1 032	1 524	66	6	4 785	6 319
United States	28 456	8 318	–18 337	–823	–31	0	17 584	138 831
Low	1 027	2 495	–3 442	–2 003	–1 460	0	–3 384	21 454
Medium	14 153	3 142	–9 551	–983	1 047	0	7 808	71 074
High	13 276	2 681	–5 345	2 164	383	0	13 159	46 303

Notes: Components of change for Germany and the United Kingdom are based on 2005-10 data, which have been "decadised" to agree with net change in the labour force observed over the period 2000-10. Data on low and medium attainment for Denmark and Norway were unusable because of breaks in series. See Annex II.A1 for a description of the decomposition methodology. Some change estimates, in particular those smaller than 5 thousand, may not be significantly different from zero.

Sources: European countries: European Labour Force Surveys (Eurostat); United States: American Community Survey; Canada: Survey of Labour and Income Dynamics.

StatLink ⟶ http://dx.doi.org/10.1787/888932617113

Table II.A2.2. **Decomposition of occupational change (2000-10) by growth quintile and source**
Thousands

		Young workers	New immigrants	Prime-age workers	Older workers	Net change in employment 2000-10	2000 level employment
Austria		809	220	−26	−589	413	3 671
	1	103	40	−187	−196	−240	1 019
	2	156	42	−112	−144	−58	872
Quintile	3	160	49	36	−173	71	873
	4	181	49	61	−70	220	600
	5	209	40	177	−5	420	307
Belgium		932	284	−148	−712	356	4 078
	1	198	61	−242	−262	−245	1 372
	2	135	43	−22	−121	35	646
Quintile	3	192	50	6	−156	92	756
	4	152	61	9	−84	138	640
	5	255	69	100	−88	336	663
Canada		3 471	1 330	45	−1 837	3 009	13 968
	1	575	282	−283	−613	−40	3 387
	2	526	249	57	−365	467	2 970
Quintile	3	714	246	17	−371	606	2 972
	4	737	234	83	−235	819	2 494
	5	919	319	172	−253	1 158	2 145
Czech Republic		978	53	195	−1 013	213	4 657
	1	74	12	−119	−293	−326	1 149
	2	239	13	−48	−262	−58	1 218
Quintile	3	179	6	81	−214	52	893
	4	218	14	123	−129	226	752
	5	269	8	159	−116	320	645
Germany		6 956	1 093	806	−6 535	2 320	36 101
	1	1 223	245	−628	−1 900	−1 059	9 866
	2	926	100	−2	−1 101	−77	5 933
Quintile	3	985	293	226	−1 218	286	6 154
	4	1 930	176	714	−1 488	1 331	7 907
	5	1 892	279	496	−828	1 839	6 241
Denmark		448	94	−57	−549	−63	2 702
	1	32	15	−87	−192	−232	744
	2	65	27	−32	−130	−70	649
Quintile	3	120	21	−5	−99	37	510
	4	117	14	10	−66	75	472
	5	114	18	57	−61	128	327
Spain		3 175	2 100	81	−2 364	2 993	15 359
	1	301	530	−728	−1 006	−902	4 817
	2	566	182	96	−556	288	3 082
Quintile	3	662	279	100	−282	758	2 387
	4	493	569	257	−287	1 031	2 217
	5	1 154	540	357	−232	1 819	2 858
Finland		468	36	20	−443	81	2 355
	1	59	7	−111	−161	−206	714
	2	98	4	−19	−99	−16	473
Quintile	3	86	12	45	−88	56	491
	4	108	4	43	−62	92	398
	5	117	9	61	−33	155	280

Table II.A2.2. **Decomposition of occupational change (2000-10) by growth quintile and source** (cont.)

Thousands

		Young workers	New immigrants	Prime-age workers	Older workers	Net change in employment 2000-10	2000 level employment
France		5 881	590	747	-4 657	2 560	22 847
	1	1 017	76	-830	-1 463	-1 200	6 279
	2	962	145	-228	-1 008	-129	4 720
Quintile	3	1 490	133	145	-916	851	4 833
	4	1 265	62	586	-667	1 246	3 540
	5	1 148	174	1 074	-604	1 791	3 475
Greece		798	209	66	-806	267	4 057
	1	69	26	-56	-336	-297	1 167
	2	147	45	-25	-162	5	861
Quintile	3	172	30	17	-133	85	752
	4	178	36	44	-92	166	652
	5	233	72	86	-83	308	625
Hungary		730	27	34	-795	-4	3 760
	1	87	5	-120	-216	-244	1 044
	2	123	3	3	-158	-29	689
Quintile	3	134	2	-2	-139	-5	667
	4	221	10	56	-192	94	921
	5	165	6	97	-89	179	440
Ireland		267	212	-84	-227	169	1 664
	1	3	42	-98	-103	-155	529
	2	16	47	-20	-41	2	302
Quintile	3	80	35	-10	-36	70	350
	4	79	50	3	-23	109	259
	5	89	37	42	-25	143	223
Italy		3 520	1 245	15	-3 996	784	20 024
	1	433	163	-1 045	-1 442	-1 890	5 513
	2	624	135	-245	-855	-340	4 203
Quintile	3	1 030	209	107	-977	369	4 968
	4	698	333	287	-447	871	2 967
	5	736	405	910	-276	1 775	2 373
Luxembourg		33	46	-7	-32	39	181
	1	6	5	-13	-16	-18	68
	2	4	8	-5	-7	0	43
Quintile	3	6	4	1	-4	7	22
	4	11	9	7	-4	23	29
	5	5	18	4	-1	27	19
Netherlands		1 547	141	-160	-1 076	452	7 819
	1	200	23	-221	-320	-318	1 918
	2	354	36	-83	-231	77	1 971
Quintile	3	234	32	56	-201	120	1 323
	4	350	28	19	-176	220	1 385
	5	409	22	69	-148	352	1 221
Norway		479	112	-4	-354	233	2 262
	1	47	35	-81	-159	-158	713
	2	104	20	1	-75	51	430
Quintile	3	70	11	6	-36	51	285
	4	144	31	19	-61	132	542
	5	113	15	52	-23	157	292

Table II.A2.2. **Decomposition of occupational change (2000-10) by growth quintile and source** (cont.)

Thousands

		Young workers	New immigrants	Prime-age workers	Older workers	Net change in employment 2000-10	2000 level employment
Portugal		864	158	−123	−916	−18	4 971
	1	55	41	−187	−290	−381	1 336
	2	118	13	−39	−214	−123	1 192
Quintile	3	195	30	−42	−170	13	912
	4	225	64	64	−162	192	946
	5	272	9	81	−81	281	585
Sweden		936	181	111	−817	411	4 115
	1	135	30	−106	−291	−232	1 126
	2	164	23	5	−172	20	686
Quintile	3	266	71	−28	−167	142	1 021
	4	189	23	79	−103	188	653
	5	182	35	161	−84	293	630
Switzerland		676	440	−54	−666	395	3 875
	1	93	61	−98	−211	−154	1 105
	2	117	76	−42	−113	39	683
Quintile	3	125	83	7	−114	102	675
	4	210	98	36	−150	194	824
	5	130	121	42	−79	215	589
United Kingdom		5 003	1 989	−632	−4 673	1 687	27 155
	1	651	452	−1 755	−1 736	−2 388	8 768
	2	844	275	46	−1 041	124	5 183
Quintile	3	1 237	323	11	−922	650	5 289
	4	1 075	529	409	−628	1 385	4 349
	5	1 195	409	658	−345	1 916	3 565
United States		23 567	7 323	−3 711	−19 504	7 676	130 490
	1	3 931	1 245	−3 663	−6 538	−5 024	36 460
	2	3 521	1 584	−1 612	−3 368	125	23 045
Quintile	3	5 423	1 513	309	−4 622	2 623	30 698
	4	6 262	1 474	238	−3 207	4 767	23 788
	5	4 429	1 508	1 017	−1 769	5 185	16 499

Notes: Quintiles represent in principle 20% of 2010 employment. In practice, the percentage may deviate from 20 because of the requirement that an occupation must be entirely contained with one quintile. See Annex II.A1 for a description of the decomposition methodology. Some of the change estimates shown, in particular those less than 5 thousand, may not be statistically significant from zero.

Sources: European countries: European Labour Force Surveys (Eurostat); United States: American Community Survey; Canada: Survey of Labour and Income Dynamics.

StatLink http://dx.doi.org/10.1787/888932617132

PART III

The changing role of Asia in international migration

> Part III looks at emerging issues around migration within Asia and from Asia to OECD countries, asking three key questions: will OECD countries continue to be able to attract and retain skilled migrants from the region? Will Asian destination countries manage the transition from restrictive policies to selective policies, as well as the challenges posed by the integration of immigrants? To what extent will consolidated models for managing labour migration in the region continue to function effectively? It begins with an overview of Asian migration, then looks at the competitive challenge Asian countries are presenting as migration destinations, and considers the specific difficulties in managing low-skilled and family migration faced by OECD and non-OECD Asian countries.

1. Introduction

Migration in, from and to Asia is of growing importance to OECD countries and will likely become more important in the future.[1] Asia contains most of the world's population and has recently become the motor of global economic growth and is likely to remain so for the next decade.

OECD countries have long-standing migration ties with Asia. In recent years, Asia has provided a large part of the more skilled migration inflows to OECD countries, even as competition to attract skilled and talented workers intensifies. The skilled migration and the employer-driven labour migration favoured in many OECD countries are particularly reliant on flows from Asia. A number of apparent trends, however, are transforming migration dynamics *in* the region, with implications for OECD countries in and outside the region.

Most Asian countries are undergoing a transition to low-fertility, higher-educated societies. While the region will provide a large proportion of the world's low and high-skilled workers in upcoming years, it will also start to compete to attract migrants, draw returning migrants, and subtract skilled workers from OECD countries.

The distinct challenges faced by Asian countries in managing labour migration, in negotiating with other countries, and with addressing integration will affect their relationship with OECD countries. The integration of Asian countries into the global economy, where they are both partners and competitors, will affect patterns of mobility and the use of migration as a human resource strategy in OECD countries.

This part addresses three key questions. First, in light of the rapid development of many Asian countries, and their smaller, better educated, higher-earning youth populations, will OECD countries be able to compete to attract and retain skilled migrants from the region? Second, can Asian destination countries of migrants manage the transition from *restrictive* policies to *selective* policies, with the consequent challenges for integration of immigrants? And finally, to what extent will consolidated models for managing labour migration in the region continue to function effectively?

The third section of the part, following the main findings, provides an overview of the importance of Asian migration to the OECD and within Asia. The fourth section looks at the challenge OECD countries are facing of competing with Asian countries to attract highly skilled migrants. The fifth section examines the specific difficulties in managing low-skilled and family migration faced by OECD and non-OECD Asian countries. The part then looks at the priorities in origin countries of migrants in Asia, before concluding with a discussion of future issues.

2. Main findings

- Migrants from Asia account for 17% of all migrants over age 15 in OECD countries in the mid-2000s, and 30% of migration inflows in 2010.
- Asia provides a large part of skilled migration to OECD countries, with India and China playing an especially predominant role. Asian migrants are, on average, better educated than other migrants, and, for recent migrants, than natives of OECD countries.

- A large and growing share of the international students in OECD countries are from Asia, although more and more are studying within the region and many are returning from OECD countries after study.

- While the emigration rate from the region to the OECD is low (0.6%), due to the enormous population in Asia, for some countries it is higher (the Philippines, 4.4%), and it is higher for the tertiary-educated (3.8%), with the poorest countries seeing the highest emigration rates of the tertiary-educated.

- A number of key socio-demographic and economic changes are occurring in the region which will affect migration in the future: fertility has fallen and is below the replacement rate in a number of countries; many countries are in a period of "demographic dividend" with few older and few younger people relative to the working-age population; and youth cohorts are increasingly educated. As Asia develops, it is producing more skilled workers. It is also fostering conditions that not only make migration less attractive for Asian workers, but even draw skilled workers from other parts of the world. It is thus uncertain whether OECD countries will be able to rely on this steady stream of skilled workers from Asia in the future.

- The policies to attract and retain skilled workers in a number of Asian non-member economies are converging with those common in the OECD, although some have not yet revised their policy.

- Specific policies to encourage return migration have had little success, yet the booming local economies have attracted quite a large number of return migrants.

- Mobility within the region is facilitated through bilateral agreements for low-skilled labour migration and increasing bilateral and multilateral agreements to facilitate the mobility of skilled workers.

- Management of less-skilled migration in the region is difficult because of a large surplus of labour and limited opportunities, leading to frequent rent-taking and raising migration costs for the less educated to a significant portion of expected overseas earnings. Some schemes, such as Korea's Employment Permit System, have succeeded in reducing the costs of migration and the risk of exploitation. Other countries in the region are contemplating this experience as a model.

- Currently, most of the temporary foreign workers from the region are working in the Gulf countries, with Malaysia, Chinese Taipei, Singapore and Hong Kong, China, the main destinations within the region. Policies towards low-skilled workers are generally restrictive, with limited duration of stay and measures to discourage their employment. Irregular migration is more common in recent destination countries bordering origin countries.

- Marriage migration is the main form of family reunification in Asian countries, with men from more developed economies marrying women from less developed economies. Problems with the integration of marriage migrants and their children are driving the development of integration policies in some cases. Profound changes in the marriage market in Asia – due to a growing marriage deficit exacerbated by a prenatal gender selection favouring males – can be expected in upcoming decades, with implications for migration.

3. The importance of Asian migration to the OECD and within the region

Asia is the origin of a growing share of migrants in OECD countries. Within the region, however, growth in migrant stocks is occurring at a lower rate than in the rest of the world. The region's share of the world migrant stock fell from 14.7% in 2000 to 12.9% in 2010, equivalent to almost 28 million migrants.

Asian migration to the OECD: An overview

In the mid-2000s, there were 15.5 million emigrants over the age of 15 from Asian countries living in OECD countries (Table III.1). Migrants from Asia accounted for about 17% of all those born abroad in the OECD, and more in major receiving countries: 33% in Canada; 29% in the United Kingdom; 28% in Australia; and 19% in the United States. Further, international migration from the area to the OECD is primarily directed to just a few destinations: the United States, to which half of all those born in the region and living in the OECD in 2005/2006 had migrated; Canada (14%); the United Kingdom (10%); and Australia (8%).

The distribution of migrants from Asia reflects, to some extent, economic and geopolitical factors such as long-lasting historical ties. This is reflected in the main destination countries for specific Asian origin countries. The United States first received Chinese migrants in the 19th century, then from the Philippines from the time of its administration of that country, from Korea especially after restrictions were lifted in 1965, and lastly from Viet Nam following 1975. The United Kingdom is, for reasons related to

Table III.1. **Migrant stock of persons born in Asia (including Japan and Korea) living in OECD countries, 2005/06**

Country of residence	Population aged 15 and over	Share among total immigrant population	Share of high-educated among Asian migrants
	Thousands	Percentages	
United States	7 760	20	52
Canada	2 143	35	52
United Kingdom	1 557	29	39
Australia	1 155	28	42
Japan	546	42	25
France	436	7	30
Italy	266	9	7
Netherlands	264	18	25
New Zealand	225	29	37
Germany	222	2	19
Korea	179	78	32
Spain	119	3	18
Sweden	99	9	25
Switzerland	93	6	32
Denmark	70	19	18
Norway	68	21	16
Belgium	63	5	31
Austria	61	6	20
Ireland	44	8	59
Czech Republic	43	8	13
Israel	34	2	31
Other	71	5	13
Total	**15 518**	**31**	**40**

Information on data for Israel: http://dx.doi.org/10.1787/888932315602.
Source: DIOC 2005/06.   StatLink http://dx.doi.org/10.1787/888932617151

historical ties, the main destination for migrants from Pakistan and Bangladesh, and a leading destination for Indians. For Indonesia, most emigrants are in the Netherlands. France is the second destination for emigrants from Cambodia and Laos, after the United States, and also has a large community from Viet Nam. Afghans are principally in Germany.

Yet recent years have seen the range of destination countries for Asian immigrants to the OECD expand beyond those to which they historically migrated. Southern European countries attracted large numbers of immigrants for employment in the late 1990s and early 2000s, and Asian countries were included in this. Asia has become an increasingly important source for international students, with growing numbers coming to Japan, Korea and Australia, some of whom stay on after finishing their studies. Canada's selection system for skilled migrants attracted increasing numbers of Asians in the past two decades, as did other programmes such as its live-in caregiver and its investor schemes. This was especially true for residents of Hong Kong, China, in the mid- to late-1990s. Migration for family formation – or "marriage migration" – increased, towards Korea, Japan and some Scandinavian countries. Bilateral agreements for labour migration with Korea, and investor programmes in the Czech Republic, also created new channels from some Asian countries.

Migration from Asia was a major and growing component of migration flows to OECD countries over the course of the 2000s: it rose from 27.3% to 31.3% of total flows (Table III.2). In absolute terms, total legal flows to OECD countries from non-OECD countries in the region rose from 2000 to 2008 from 950 000 to 1.49 million. In 2010 they reached 1.55 million. Migration from the region reacted less to the global economic crisis than that from other regions.

Table III.2. **Inflows from Asia to OECD countries, by country of origin, 2000-10**

Origin	2000	2002	2004	2006	2007	2008	2009	2010
	Thousands							
China	283	334	369	506	522	534	464	507
India	114	161	194	206	213	216	227	252
Indonesia	29	33	27	31	27	32	23	25
Philippines	165	196	212	172	168	158	164	167
Viet Nam	52	64	66	82	88	98	77	88
Other Asia	309	319	359	453	431	454	480	507
Total Asian non-OECD	**951**	**1 107**	**1 227**	**1 450**	**1 450**	**1 492**	**1 435**	**1 546**
Japan	35	41	38	36	33	30	36	32
Korea	59	63	58	70	73	81	80	76
Total Asian OECD	94	104	97	106	106	111	116	108
Total Asia	**1 045**	**1 211**	**1 323**	**1 556**	**1 556**	**1 603**	**1 550**	**1 654**
Total all migration flows	3 834	4 357	4 868	5 428	5 809	5 689	5 209	5 278
As a share of all migration (%)	*27.3*	*27.8*	*27.2*	*28.7*	*26.8*	*28.2*	*29.8*	*31.3*

Source: OECD, International Migration Database.

StatLink http://dx.doi.org/10.1787/888932617189

Flows to OECD countries in the period 2006-10 largely reflected prior migration patterns. China, India and the Philippines have been leading source countries for migrants to the OECD for the past decade, consistently ranking in the top ten, with China and India usually leading the list. Flows from China to the OECD topped 500 000 in 2010, a decline from a record peak of 542 000 in 2008. China accounted for almost 10% of total flows to the OECD in 2010.

India was in third place for total flows to OECD countries in 2010, after Romania, with 252 000 migrants (4.8% of all migration). Flows were at roughly the same level as previous years. The Philippines ranked fifth among origin countries in 2010, with 167 000 migrants, (3.2% of all flows). Migration flows from the OECD Asian countries, of 108 000 in 2010, represented only 6.5% of total flows from Asia.

Asian migrants are more educated than other migrants, more are women and more have come recently

Migration from Asia to OECD countries is associated with more educated migrants, more recently arrived migrants, and more women (Table III.3). About 3 million – or 1 in 5 – of the Asian migrants living in OECD countries in 2005/2006 had arrived since the year 2000. The proportion of recent migrants was slightly higher among those from Asia than among those from other regions, reflecting the increasing share of flows from Asia in the first half of the 2000s.

Nearly half the migrants from Asia are highly educated (49%), and this proportion has in general been rising since 2000. This rate is about twice that of migrants from other regions, and is substantially higher than that of the native-born. Recent Asian migrants tend to be even more highly educated: 56% of Asian men who migrated within the previous five years had some tertiary education, and 52% of Asian women. The stock of high-educated Asian migrants in OECD countries rose sharply between 2000 and 2005/2006 (*e.g.* +67% for Indians). However, there is a significant variation according to both country of origin and country of destination. To some extent, this reflects the overall education level in the country of origin and the selectivity in the country of destination. Some of the main OECD destinations for Asian migrants are Australia, Canada and New Zealand, all of which apply selective criteria, favouring high-skilled migration. The United States also attracts the highly skilled, through labour and student migration – but also family migration, where no selective criteria are applied. As the education levels of spouses are positively correlated, family members accompanying or joining selected migrants are also likely to be highly educated.

Table III.3. **Migrants from Asia in OECD countries by place of birth, gender, education level, and recent migration, 2005/06**

Thousands

	OECD Asian migrants		Non-OECD Asian migrants		Other migrants	
	All migrants					
	Men	Women	Men	Women	Men	Women
Emigrant population	333	511	6 748	7 492	36 626	37 261
Low-educated (%)	11	14	21	25	38	39
Highly-educated (%)	51	45	49	45	25	25
Gender (%)	38	41	47	53	50	50
Share of recent migrants	49	41	20	20	18	17
	Recent migrants only					
	Men	Women	Men	Women	Men	Women
Emigrant population	164	212	1 319	1 493	6 608	6 508
Low-educated (%)	9	9	19	22	38	35
Highly-educated (%)	61	58	55	51	27	29
Gender (%)	44	56	47	53	50	50

Source: DIOC 2005/06.   StatLink http://dx.doi.org/10.1787/888932617170

Recent destination countries for Asian immigrants – especially those, such as Italy, where no selection was made on the basis of education – have attracted migrants with proportionally lower education. Countries with past historical ties also have proportionately fewer educated migrants. For example, less than 30% of Indonesians in the Netherlands are highly educated, compared with more than 50% of Indonesians in Canada and the United States. Finally, the educational level may also reflect the epoch of migration, with older migrants tending to be less educated; this is the case, for example, among the Indonesian-born in the Netherlands.

The percentage of *recent emigrants* from the region – those with less than five years stay in the host country – was about 18% in 2000 and 20% in 2005/06. In 2005/2006, about 29% of Indian and 24% of Chinese migrants were a recent migrant. The figure was 22% for Bangladeshi and Pakistani migrants, 17% for the Philippines and 9% for Viet Nam. The proportion of recent migrants was slightly higher among women overall. For Thailand, for example, this reflects the increasing feminization of flows through family formation. For Nepal and Bangladesh, it also reflects the effect of family reunification in migration channels where the migration pioneers were men.

Overall, migration from the region to OECD comprises slightly more women (about 53% of the total), although the gender composition of the migrant population varies by country of origin, and reflects the determinants of flows (Table III.A1.1). The high share of women among migrants from Thailand, for example (67%), is related to the frequency of international marriages with men in OECD countries. This is particularly evident for some of the main destination countries – Australia, Japan and Sweden, for example. For the Philippines, from which 61% of migrants are women, labour demand in disproportionately female occupations – especially nursing and care – play an important role. Some countries tend to have more male emigrants: Nepal (61%), Pakistan and Bangladesh (56%), India (53%). For Pakistan and Bangladesh, this reflects to some extent the large proportion of men among recent migrants to new destination countries (Italy and Spain, particularly) where demand for labour in specific sectors such as construction and agriculture has been more male-oriented.

Emigration rates from Asia to OECD countries are higher for the highly educated

While migrants from Asia comprise a large share of migration to OECD countries, for the region as a whole the *emigration rate* is very low. For those over 15 years of age in 2005/06, the emigration rate was less than 0.6% (Figure III.1). However, the rate varies by place of birth, with very low rates in large countries such as China and Indonesia (0.2%). One of the highest emigration rates is recorded for the Philippines, with 4.4% of its population in the OECD, and 5.9% of its female population over 15 years of age.

Across the region – as is generally the case around the world – the emigration rate to OECD countries is higher for the highly educated than for the low educated. For non-member economies in the region, the overall emigration rate for the highly educated is 3.8%, while for the medium and low-skilled it is 0.3%. Again, there is a wide range among origin countries. Some of the highest emigration rates for the tertiary educated are in poor countries such as Cambodia (43%), Laos (26%) and Papua New Guinea (19%).[2] Emigration rates for highly-educated women are systematically higher than for men, except for Bangladesh.

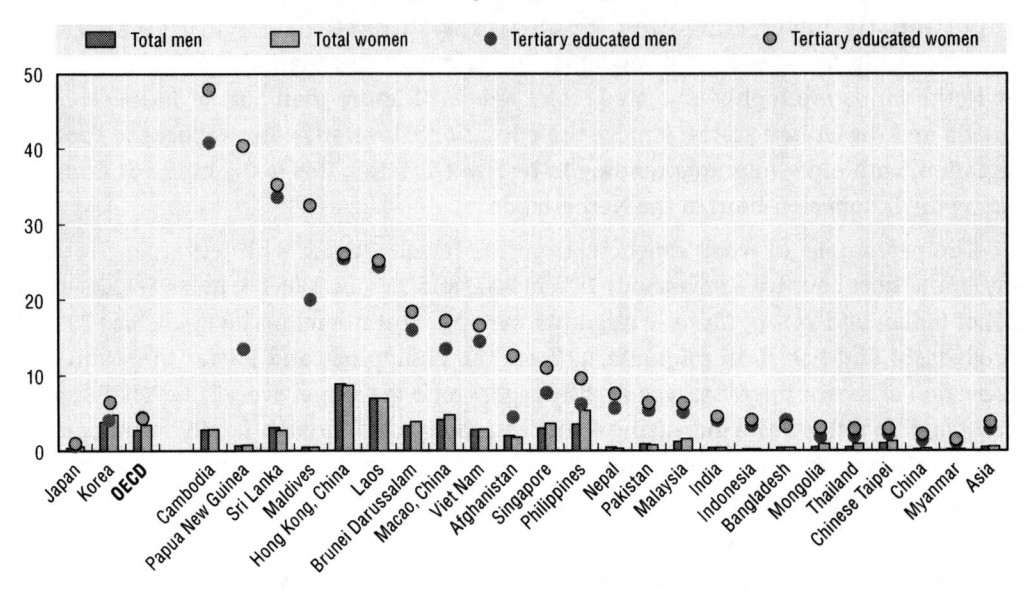

III. THE CHANGING ROLE OF ASIA IN INTERNATIONAL MIGRATION

Figure III.1. **Emigration rates to OECD countries, by place of birth and gender, total and tertiary educated, 2005/2006**

Source: DIOC 2005/06; Barro and Lee (2010).   StatLink ᕮᔐᖷ http://dx.doi.org/10.1787/888932615783

Underlying factors of migration from non-OECD Asian countries

The non-OECD Asian countries, with 3.6 billion inhabitants, represented 53% of the world population in 2010, and produced 16.6% of the world GDP. Since 1990, Asia has represented more than half (53%) of world population growth and 22% of world economic growth. GDP in these countries increased by 311% over the two decades, compared with 55% for the rest of the world. Asian countries rode through the recent economic crisis much better than most OECD countries. The growth rates in China and India, especially, remained robust in the late 2000s, and second-tier Asian economies, such as Malaysia, Thailand and Viet Nam, continued to grow. Wages in these countries rose an average of 8% through the 2000s, compared with wage growth rates of less than 1% in developed countries.

Population and economic growth in Asia has been faster in non-member economies. The OECD countries in the region, Japan and Korea, at 2.5% of the world population in 2010, represented only a marginal contribution to world population growth over the period but contributed about 5% and 3%, respectively, to world GDP growth.

Within the region, wide differences in wages between countries have induced incentives for migration, that may increase due to persisting differences in growth rates between countries. While fertility rates have fallen across the region, most countries are in a period of demographic transition, with burgeoning cohorts of young workers providing an excess labour supply which increases pressure to move abroad. Rapidly rising education levels in certain economies have led to less willingness to work in unskilled and manual labour, and increased demand for services such as domestic work.

Fertility rates have been falling in almost all Asian countries (Figure III.2), and a number of countries have seen fertility rates drop below replacement rate. China is the most noteworthy example, where decades of a one-child policy have led to smaller birth cohorts and one of the most rapidly aging populations. Other countries where the number of young people entering the working-age population is already shrinking, and expected to diminish further in upcoming years, are Japan, Korea and Singapore. Both Thailand and Viet Nam have fertility rates which have recently fallen below replacement level.

III. THE CHANGING ROLE OF ASIA IN INTERNATIONAL MIGRATION

Figure III.2. **Total fertility rate, by Asian region, 1970-2010**

■ Eastern Asia   ■ Southern Asia   ■ South-Eastern Asia

Source: UNESA, World Population Policies 2009, unweighted averages.

StatLink ᴀᴢᴘ http://dx.doi.org/10.1787/888932615802

The number of working-age individuals has increased at all educational levels, but overall the average educational level has increased. A number of these Asian economies are benefitting from a "demographic dividend" which occurs during a demographic transition: the elderly population is still small, and shrinking youth cohorts reduce the number of children (Figure III.3). While this is associated with economic growth in most economies, it also places pressure to create employment at different skill levels and may increase pressures to migrate where opportunities are insufficient.

Figure III.3. **Age structure of the population in Asian and OECD economies, 2010**
Age groups in the population

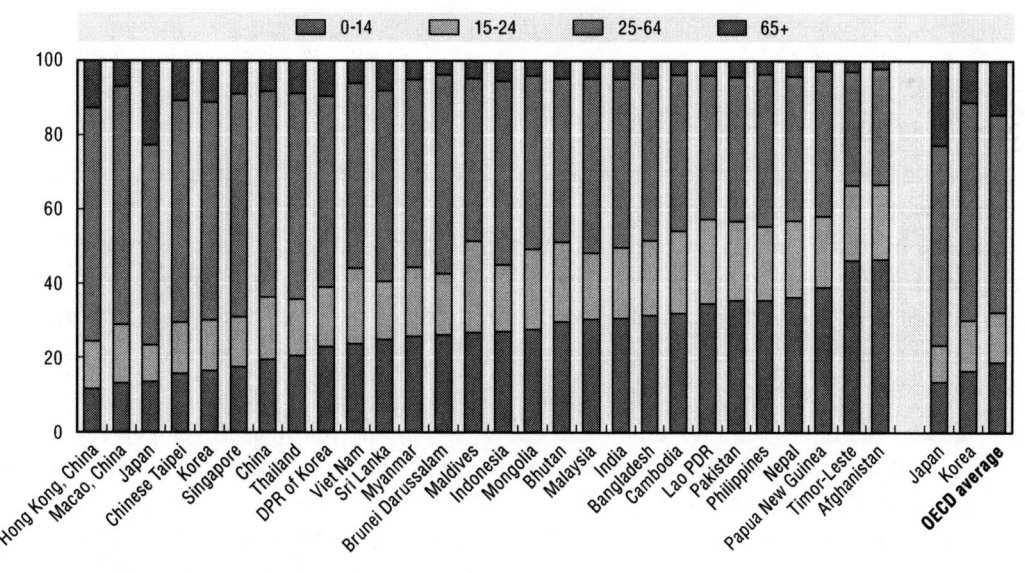

■ 0-14   ■ 15-24   ■ 25-64   ■ 65+

Source: UNESA, World Population Policies 2010.

StatLink ᴀᴢᴘ http://dx.doi.org/10.1787/888932615821

III. THE CHANGING ROLE OF ASIA IN INTERNATIONAL MIGRATION

Educational attainment is increasing overall

Figure III.4 shows the distribution of population by education level. In a number of economies, the adult population is highly educated: tertiary education rates are about 35% in Korea and Japan, and about 25% in the Philippines. In the most developed economies, tertiary education rates for young people 25-29 are very high, reaching 71% in Korea and Chinese Taipei. Upper-middle-income countries also have high and growing rates of highly educated residents. The proportion of young people in this age bracket with tertiary education is 36% in the Philippines, 28% for Malaysia, 25% for Thailand, 22% for Sri Lanka, and 15% in China. Limited opportunities for high-skilled workers in some developing countries however push them to seek employment abroad.

Figure III.4. **Educational structure of the population aged 15 and over in Asian economies, 2010**

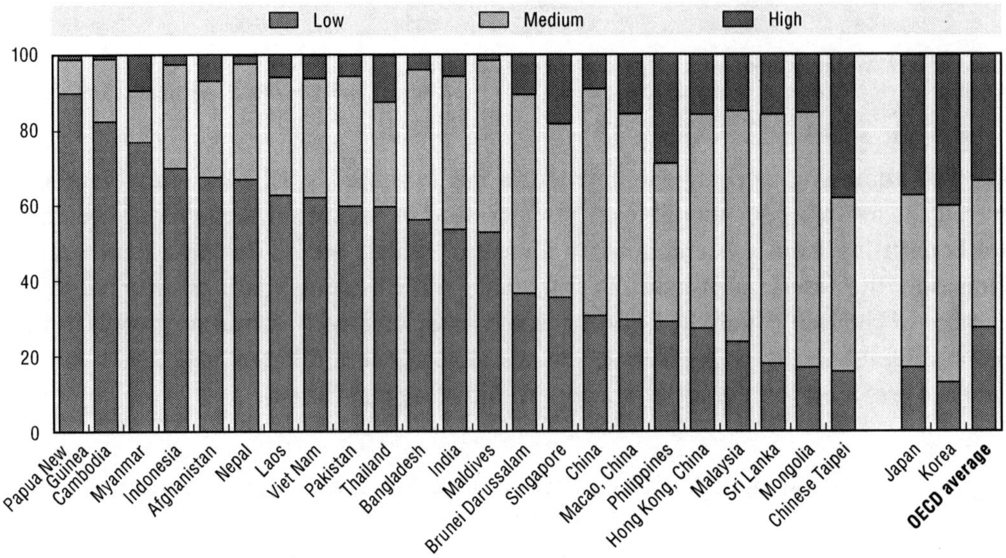

Source: Barro and Lee (2010).   StatLink http://dx.doi.org/10.1787/888932615840

Intra-Asia labour migration

While labour migration to both Japan and Korea has increased in the past two decades, foreign workers still make up a very low proportion of total employment – 2.1% in Korea, and 1.3% in Japan – much lower than in non-member Asian economies receiving labour migrants. Further, in these two countries, the systems in place for governing labour migration have evolved separately and distinctly from those in other Asian countries. Exchange of information and experience remain however essential to respond to existing policy challenges (see Box III.1).

In non-member Asian destination economies, labour shortages developed rapidly in the late 1980s, especially in low-skilled productive industries, as education levels for the native population rose. Recruitment of low-skilled workers for temporary stay began in Singapore as early as the 1970s and Chinese Taipei from 1989. Malaysia, which long employed Indonesians in its plantations, saw the expansion of low-skilled labour migration in other sectors from the 1990s as well. Asian OECD countries began to employ foreign workers as well, Japan in the early 1990s, and Korea from 1994. Thailand and the Maldives are more recent destination countries.

> **Box III.1. The ADBI-OECD Roundtable on Labour Migration in Asia**
>
> Since 2011, the Asian Development Bank Institute (ADBI) and the OECD have organised an annual Roundtable on Labour Migration in Asia. Participants in the three-day discussion are drawn from the government authorities responsible for labour migration management – outgoing or incoming – from non-member economies including Bangladesh, India, Indonesia, Laos, Malaysia, Pakistan, the Philippines, China, Sri Lanka, Chinese Taipei, Thailand and Viet Nam. OECD countries are represented (Australia, Japan, Korea, Turkey, Canada) along with International Organisations including the ILO, ADB and the World Bank, and expert researchers. Both immigration and emigration economies exchange perspectives and identify migration and policy trends. The inaugural Roundtable, held in January 2011, focused on Recent Trends and Prospects in the Postcrisis Context. The second Roundtable, in January 2012, was on Managing Migration to Support Inclusive and Sustainable Growth. This part draws on the contributions of participants in the Roundtable.
>
> Note: More information, including Roundtable programmes and presentations, is available at *www.adbi.org*.

Migration to Asian OECD countries is limited

Relative to other OECD countries, Japan and Korea have proportionally limited inflows of migrants, reflecting the recent history of migration flows to these countries and policies which remain restrictive for permanent migration of less skilled workers. In Japan, permanent-type inflows – most of which were from Asia – were the lowest, after Mexico, among OECD countries in 2010, at less than 0.05% of the population; family migration comprised more than 42% of inflows. Temporary flows were also around 0.1% of the population, and largely comprised trainees staying no more than several years. In Korea, permanent-type inflows – including foreign workers, who comprised more than two-thirds of the inflow – were 0.3% of the population, below the OECD average of 0.5%. In recent years, a large part of permanent flows to these countries have been migrants admitted under ethnic-priority schemes. Such schemes, which grant foreign descendents or members of the main national ethnic group access, are not unusual in OECD countries: Greece, Germany, Hungary, Finland and Israel[3] have all granted residence to foreigners on this basis, although in most cases – except Israel – it is less important than in Asian OECD countries.

Migration to non-member Asian economies is mostly for employment and intra-regional

Migration to non-member Asian economies comes almost entirely from other countries in the region, and in most countries where flows are reported, it is largely related to employment.

While statistics on permanent migration, or family migration, are generally lacking, for a number of economies in the region figures are available on the stock of authorised labour migrants. These figures vary widely according to destination (Table III.4). Brunei Darussalam and the Maldives have the highest proportion of foreign workers, exceeding 40% of total employment. Singapore follows; the share of foreign workers in its labour force rose from 3% to 35% between 1970 and 2010, to reach almost 1.2 million non-Singapore workers.

Table III.4. **Foreign workers, total and as percentage of total employment in different Asian economies, 2010 or most recent year, by selected sectors**

	Number of foreign workers	As a share of total employment
	Thousands	Percentages
Brunei Darussalam	88	46.3
Manufacturing/Mining/Oil	16	69.3
Construction	32	88.8
Non-government services	35	56.8
Maldives	74	40.5
Construction	12	45.7
Tourism	32	48.9
Singapore	1 157	36.0
Manufacturing	166	44.6
Construction	190	60.5
Services	313	21.6
Domestic work	196	94.1
Malaysia	1 941	16.7
Manufacturing	671	20.9
Construction	301	39.5
Agriculture, fishing	500	35.9
Service	227	3.6
Hong Kong, China	275	7.5
Chinese Taipei	404	3.8
Manufacturing	198	6.7
Construction	4	0.5
Agriculture, fishing	8	1.5
Health and social services	193	47.0
Thailand	1 335	3.5
Construction	223	10.5
Agriculture, fishing	360	2.1
Domestic work	130	31.7
Korea	507	2.1
Manufacturing		6.0
Construction		9.1
Restaurants		5.0
Housekeeping		16.3
Japan	694	1.1
Manufacturing	265	2.5
Restaurant and hotels	75	1.9

Notes: Brunei Darussalam – 2008, Maldives – 2010, for sector distributions 2009. Singapore – mid-2011 for the total, and 2006 for the sector breakdowns, except for domestic work, February 2011. Malaysia – 2009, excludes 242 700 "other" foreign workers from sector counts and denominator. Chinese Taipei – June 2011: Health and Social services includes Home nursing, which accounts for almost all the foreign employment. Thailand – 2010, adding legal and registered foreign workers. Korea – Totals refer to 2010. Percentages by sector refer to 2008. Other estimates put the total proportion at 2.9%. Japan – October 2011. Hong Kong, China – March 2010. Foreign workers include Foreign domestic helpers (273 600) and Supplementary labour scheme (1 600).

Sources: Brunei Darussalam – Dept of Econ. Planning and Development, Prime Minister's Office. Maldives – Maldives Monetary Authority, Ministry of Human Resources, Youth and Sports for sector distributions. SNG – Comprehensive Labour Force Survey, MOM. Malaysia – Department of the Treasury. Chinese Taipei – NSO. Thailand – Department of Employment, Ministry of Labour. Korea – *Korea Immigration Statistics*, Nho and Hur (2010). Japan – MHLW, NSO. Hong Kong, China – Immigration Dept. of Hong Kong, China; *China Statistical Yearbook 2011*.

StatLink http://dx.doi.org/10.1787/888932617208

After Singapore, the second major Asian receiving country is Malaysia. Its agricultural sector, especially its plantations, has long drawn on foreign workers and remains dependent on their labour (36% of employment in the sector in 2010). It was, however, the high growth rate over the past decade (an average of 4.7% annually), that led to increased migration in a broader range of sectors, including manufacturing and household work.

In terms of sectors, construction and manufacturing are reliant on foreign workers in a number of Asian countries. In Brunei Darussalam, Singapore, the Maldives and Malaysia, foreign workers represent a large share of construction employment. While some countries do not report the number of foreign workers in domestic employment, they comprise most of employment in Singapore, and a large part in Thailand and Korea. In Chinese Taipei, half of home-nursing employees are foreign workers. India does not publish comparable figures on foreign workers, although estimates of the number of undocumented foreigners are as high as 18 million.

Almost all of the foreign workers in these countries are from Asia. While stock data are not available by destination country, a number of Asian countries managing outward labour migration – which largely concerns the less skilled – provide information on destinations of workers (Table III.5). These figures suggest intraregional flows of about 1 million workers annually. Malaysia is the principal destination in most cases, and Indonesia, the Philippines and Nepal the main countries of origin.

For most Asian countries, however, the main destination of outgoing foreign workers – over 3 million annually – is not other Asian destinations, but the countries of the Gulf Co-operation Council (Table III.A1.2).

Table III.5. **Foreign workers from selected Asian countries, by destination, 2010-11**

Thousands

Destination	Source country								
	Nepal	Bangladesh	Indonesia	Sri Lanka	Thailand	India	Pakistan	Philippines	Viet Nam
Year	2010/11	2010	2011	2010	2011	2010	2008	2010	2010
Brunei Darussalam		2	11		3	1	66	8	
Chinese Taipei			76		48			37	28
Hong Kong, China			50		3		22	101	
Malaysia	106	1	134	4	4	21	2	10	12
Singapore		39	48	1	11		16	70	
Non-OECD Asia	107	42	323	10	78	21	2	264	49
Japan	1	0	2	0	9	–	45	6	5
Korea	4	3	11	5	11	–	2	12	9
OECD Asia	4	3	14	5	20	–	2	18	14
Gulf Co-operation Council	241	287	204	228	18	610	421	661	8
OECD non-Asia	1	7	19	2	23	0	4	73	0
MENA[1]	1	37	5	16	3	4	1	22	0
Other	0	15	15	1	5	6	1	82	14

Notes: Figures are for overseas workers whose departure is recorded by the government agencies in the origin country. Coverage of individual departures for employment may be partial or limited to employment under bilateral agreements. Some countries (e.g. India) do not record departures for employment to OECD countries. Data for Indonesia include both formal and informal placements. Sailors are excluded from the data for most countries.
1. MENA refers to Middle East and North Africa, according to the World Bank definition; for this table, MENA excludes OECD member and GCC countries.
Sources: Nepal – Dept. Foreign Employment. Bangladesh – BMET. Indonesia – BNP2TKI. Sri Lanka – SLBFE. Thailand – Office of Overseas Employment Administration, DOE. India – MOIA. Pakistan – Bureau of Emigration and Overseas Employment. Philippines – POEA. Viet Nam – MoLISA. StatLink http://dx.doi.org/10.1787/888932617227

III. THE CHANGING ROLE OF ASIA IN INTERNATIONAL MIGRATION

4. Can OECD countries continue to compete with Asia for highly skilled migrants?

A number of non-OECD Asian countries with high growth rates have become consolidated destinations for labour migration in the past decades, even as Asia has been the source of many of the high-skilled migrants to OECD countries. A number of developments in the region raise the possibility that more skilled migrants will move within the region, and that more skilled migrants will be attracted from elsewhere in the world.

Asia has been a main and preferred source for high-skilled migrants to OECD countries

Asians are overrepresented in employer-driven and selective migration

Skilled migration channels to the OECD have drawn heavily on Asia as a source region (Figure III.5). These skilled migration streams vary among countries, between temporary or permanent streams, and between those requiring a job offer and those selecting candidates.

Figure III.5. **Share of Asian recipients of selected permanent and temporary skilled worker visas/permits in selected OECD countries, 2009-11**
Percentage of total permits/visas

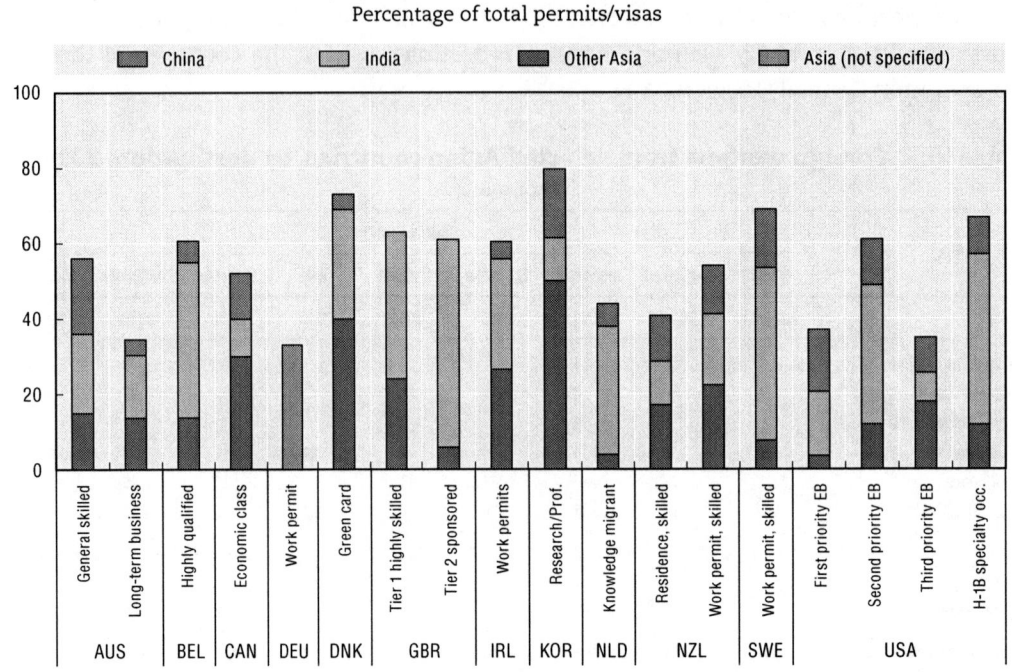

Notes: United States: Fiscal year 2010, H-1B initial employment. Canada: Other Asia includes all of Asia-Pacific. Australia: General Skilled July 2010-June 2011, Other Asia category includes Malaysia, Sri Lanka, Nepal, Philippines and Korea only; Long-term Business, July 2009-June 2010 primary applicants only, Other Asia category includes Japan, Korea, the Philippines, Malaysia, Myanmar, and Viet Nam only. United Kingdom: 2009. Denmark: 2010. Germany: 2010. Sweden: Permits for workers in SSYK occupational classification 1 and 2. New Zealand: 2010-11. Permanent residence for professionals and managers, work permits for skilled workers. Korea: Arrivals with E-3 (Research) and E-5 (Professional) visas, 2010. Korea, Netherlands: Other Asia category contains Japan only.

Sources: National governments.

StatLink ⟶ http://dx.doi.org/10.1787/888932615859

Asians, for example, are among the main recipients of the United States' "First Priority" Green Cards, issued to those with extraordinary ability, outstanding researchers, and top executives. Chinese and Indians each received about one in six of these visas. Asians also received 61% of the "Second Priority" Green Cards, issued to those with post-graduate degrees or outstanding ability who have a qualifying job offer, with Indians receiving 37% of the total. 35% of the Third Preference visas went to Asians. Citizens of Korea and Japan together received 7, 10 and 9%, respectively of these three visa categories. The employment-based Green Cards have been subject to a ceiling by nationality, and high demand kept Indians and Chinese in long queues relative to most other nationalities. Indians are the main recipients of temporary "specialty occupation" H1-B visas – 45% in 2010.

In Canada, in 2010, the three top source countries for economic immigrants were the Philippines (17%), China (12%) and India (10%). India accounted for 21%, and China 20%, of visas granted in 2010-11 under the Economic Class. Sri Lanka, Malaysia, the Philippines and Nepal comprised a further 15% of recipients. In the United Kingdom, in 2009, non-OECD Asians represented more than two-thirds of entries under the Tier 1 channel for highly skilled foreigners and the Tier 2 channel for those with a qualifying job offer.

Other OECD countries' labour migration channels are used disproportionately by Asians. In 2010, 73% of the recipients of Denmark's provisional "Green Card" for qualified foreigners with university degrees came from just four Asian countries: Pakistan, India, Bangladesh and China. These countries comprised almost three out of five entries to Denmark under its salary-based scheme, as well. In Belgium, Asian citizens received about three in five of all permits issued to highly qualified migrants in 2010.

Regarding the occupations of migrants from the region, they play an important role in health care professions (see Box III.2) and in science, technology, engineering and mathematics (STEM). In the United States, for example, in 2001-02, Asian-born immigrants were more than twice as likely to work in STEM professions as natives.

Box III.2. **Asian health professionals in OECD countries**

The region is a major source for health care professionals in OECD countries. In 2000, out of about 400 000 foreign-born doctors in OECD countries, 127 000 (32%) were from Asia. Out of 710 000 nurses, 180 000 (25%) were from Asia. One country supplies most of these nurses: there were more than 110 000 Philippine-born nurses in OECD countries in 2000.

The emigration rate for health care professionals varies across countries. The Philippines, where training in health care professions is often a precursor to emigration, the emigration rate reaches 26% for doctors and 47% for nurses. In Malaysia, another traditional origin country, it is 23% and 20%, respectively.

Asian-born workers account for more than 6% of the life-science and health workers in OECD countries. The figures are higher for certain countries: one in eight workers in life science and health professional occupations in the United Kingdom and in Australia, and more than 7% of the workforce in these professions in Ireland and New Zealand, and healthcare practitioners in the United States.

Box III.2. **Asian health professionals in OECD countries** (cont.)

Table III.6. **Share of native-born, foreign-born Asians and other foreign-born in life science and health professional occupations**

	Native-born	Foreign-born Asians		Foreign-born other	
	Share 2005/06	Share 2005/06	Change in share 2000-05/06	Share 2005/06	Change in share 2000-05/06
Australia	66.6	12.3	44.9	21.1	5.8
Austria	85.1	2.6	604.8	12.3	-13.4
Denmark	89.2	2.7	399.2	8.0	17.6
France	83.8	2.5	266.6	13.7	-1.3
Ireland	76.9	9.6	92.6	13.5	10.2
Netherlands	89.6	3.2	173.3	7.2	-21.2
New Zealand	68.4	7.5	51.3	24.1	4.3
Sweden	84.5	3.3	483.8	12.2	-6.2
Switzerland	63.3	2.9	190.0	33.9	29.9
United Kingdom	70.6	13.2	19.6	16.2	5.9
United States	84.6	7.3	30.6	8.1	5.0
Total above countries, weighted average	83.4	7.3	33.3	9.3	2.4
Total above countries, non-weighted average	78.4	6.1	70.6	15.5	5.5

Notes: "Life science and health professionals" correspond to the ISCO category 22. Data for the US are based on the classification of the US Census Bureau Occupation codes "healthcare practitioner and technical occupations".
Source: DIOC 2005/06.

StatLink ⟶ http://dx.doi.org/10.1787/888932617246

Asian migrants have better labour market outcomes than other migrants

Migrants from Asia have a higher employment rate (62%, on average in 2005/2006) in OECD countries than migrants from other regions (58%). Much of this difference lies in their overall higher education level. In fact, men from Asia with tertiary education have an employment level (80%) comparable to that of other tertiary-educated male migrants (78%) and natives (79%). A larger difference is visible for women: both Asian and non-Asian tertiary-educated women have lower employment rates than tertiary-educated native-born women, about 65% compared with 73%. The employment rates for low-educated Asian women are similar to those for other migrants – about one in three – but there are fewer low-educated women among migrants from Asia to OECD countries.

Asians predominate among international students

The region is a major and growing source for international students in OECD countries. From 2004 to 2009, the number of international students from the region increased from 753 000 to 1.07 million, an increase of 42%, almost twice the rate of increase for other international students. The increase was due to non-OECD nationals studying in OECD countries, for whom the rate of increase was 56%. The number of Chinese students rose from 215 000 to 368 000, and the number of Indians from 114 000 to 180 000.

III. THE CHANGING ROLE OF ASIA IN INTERNATIONAL MIGRATION

Three countries, the United States, Australia and the United Kingdom, account for half of all international students and three-quarters of Asian international students (Figure III.6). While the United States remains the main destination, with 405 000 international students from the region, other countries accept a proportionately larger number of students: in Australia, Asian students comprised 16% of total enrolment, and 6% in the United Kingdom (Figure III.7). International students represent an important target for universities in these countries, where education is a major export industry.

Figure III.6. **International students from Asia (including Japan and Korea) in OECD countries, 2009**

Thousands, and percentage change from enrolment in 2004

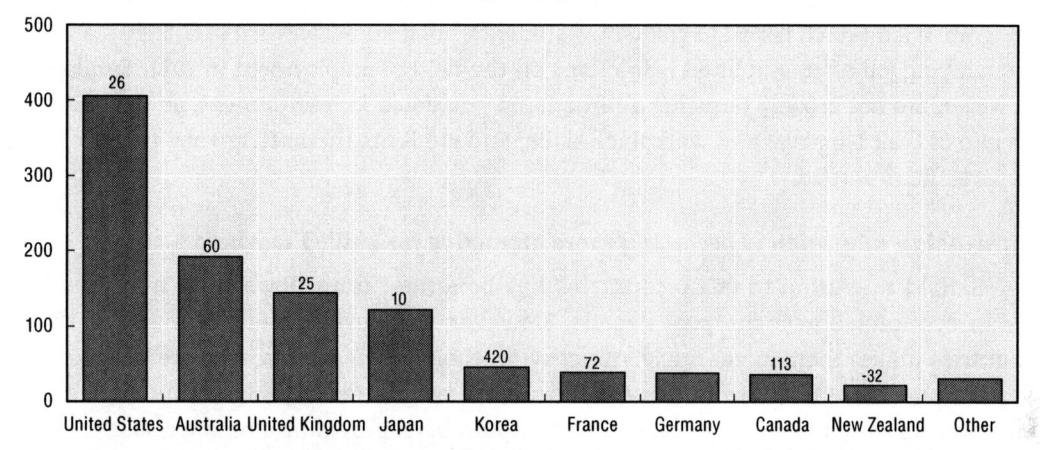

Note: For Germany, percentage change is not available as there is no comparable data for 2004. For "Other", the countries in the category are different in 2004 and 2009.
Source: UNESCO-OECD-Eurostat (UOE) Database.

StatLink http://dx.doi.org/10.1787/888932615878

Figure III.7. **International tertiary education students from Asia (incl. Japan and Korea) in OECD countries, 2009, as a percentage of international students and of all students**

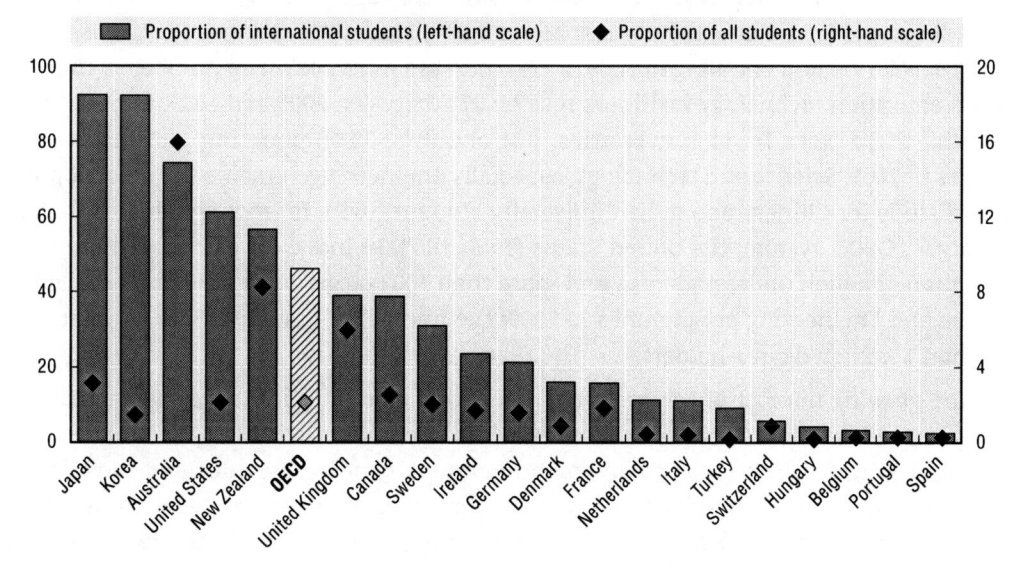

Source: UNESCO-OECD-Eurostat (UOE) Database.

StatLink http://dx.doi.org/10.1787/888932615897

INTERNATIONAL MIGRATION OUTLOOK 2012 © OECD 2012

Student migration from non-member Asian economies is also directed towards Japan and, increasingly, Korea. Both countries have a policy of increasing the number of international students. Japan, which set its goal at 300 000 students, has seen less increase in enrolment from Asia in the past five years, as most of the increase occurred between 1999 and 2003. Korea, in contrast, has seen sharp growth in the number of international students, especially from China, which accounted for 87% of its 45 000 international students in 2009. The Korean government aims to have 100 000 students, and figures for enrolment in 2011 – 88 000 – suggest it is approaching that goal. In both countries, international students may be authorised to work, and many do so; the restrictions on the maximum work hours for students are difficult to enforce. Both countries have implemented provisions for graduating students to remain. Japan allows graduates up to six months to seek qualifying employment. Korea does not grant a job-search period to graduating students, but does allow them to change status for a qualifying job offer, and lifted restrictions on the field of employment in 2011. Employers, however, are not broadly targeting international graduates for recruitment, as they may be unsure of their language and workplace skills, and students themselves may prefer career opportunities abroad.

Intra-Asian migration is becoming more attractive for skilled workers

Skilled migration to OECD countries has benefited from flows from non-member Asian economies over the past decade. However, the development of many of these countries makes them increasingly attractive for their own residents, who are less likely to depart, and more likely to return for those who have already emigrated. Science and engineering students are increasing quickly in numbers, providing a broader base for R&D and innovation in the region. The region is attracting more international students. More students and skilled workers are returning from OECD countries, in response to rising wages and more opportunities at home. These trends are starting to be reflected in the bilateral and multilateral agreements negotiated within the region.

Asia is producing more science and engineering graduates

The higher education systems in Asian countries, especially in China and India, are expanding rapidly. In China, the number of university students continues to increase, with more than 6.4 million enrolling in 2009, a 27% increase from 2005. The number of Chinese higher-education technology institutes rose by 27% between 2005 and 2009, to over 1 000. In India, there were fewer universities, but about 2 900 engineering and technology colleges in 2009. Science and technology, especially engineering, remains the most popular field of study for Chinese and Indian university students, with far more graduates than in the largest OECD system, the United States (Table III.7). In India, for example, there were more than 4 million undergraduates and more than 500 000 graduate students enrolled in Science and Engineering programmes in 2009; the number of graduates was estimated at less than 1 million degree-holders.

The growing number of science and engineering graduates in Asia suggests that the region could become a new pole for innovation to compete with OECD countries as a location for high value-added production and employment for the educated. However, a simple comparison of the reported number of science graduates, especially when compared with figures on science and engineering graduates in OECD countries, may overestimate this potential. The official statistics on engineering graduates in China, for example, cover many degrees which would not be considered in OECD countries, and for

Table III.7. **Engineering and science graduates for selected countries, 2009**

	Engineering		Science	
	Undergraduates	Graduates	Undergraduates	Graduates
Australia	13	5	20	7
Canada	14	6	23	7
China	164	131	52	42
France	41	13	35	22
Germany	44	6	57	11
India (2010)	440	..	520	..
Japan	94	35	19	12
Korea	74	15	33	5
United Kingdom	29	20	52	22
United States	95	53	157	54

Notes: For China, figures exclude undergraduate enrolment in non-degree specialised programmes. For OECD countries, Undergraduates represents tertiary type A first degree. Graduates represent tertiary type A second degree and advanced research programmes. Engineering includes Engineering and engineering trades (ISC 52), Manufacturing and processing (ISC 54) Architecture and building (ISC 58). Science includes Life sciences (ISC 42), Physical sciences (ISC 44), Mathematics and statistics (ISC 46) and Computing (ISC 48).
Sources: China: *Chinese Statistical Yearbook 2010*, India: NASSCOM. OECD countries: *UNESCO/OECD/EUROSTAT (UOE) Database*.

StatLink http://dx.doi.org/10.1787/888932617265

both countries the training in many cases may not be comparable (Gereffi et al., 2008). Many graduates in India and China are not considered employable in the field of study. For example, an Indian HR screening company found that of 40 000 final-year engineering students taking its standardised test, only a small fraction had the language and quantitative skills sought by companies (Aspiring Minds, 2010). The same firm found that the proliferation of technical colleges was also associated with lower quality of graduates.

University enrolment in China may also be approaching its peak. The number of Chinese students sitting for the annual National College Entrance Examination has been falling since 2008, and was about 9.3 million in 2011. As university places have not been reduced, selectivity has declined.

In addition to training in Asia, Asian students are an increasing proportion of engineering graduate students in OECD countries, often compensating for falling enrolment of residents. In graduate engineering programmes in Canada, for example, international enrolments grew by 36.6% between 2006 and 2009, more than making up the decline in Canadian enrolment. Their contribution to innovation in OECD countries depends on how many of them remain and how many return to Asia.

Intra-Asian international student enrolment is rising

Asian higher education is not only expanding, it is also taking a small but rapidly growing share of international students. Several non-member Asian economies attract a large number of students from within the region, especially Singapore and Malaysia. Singapore had 86 000 international students in 2008,[4] while Malaysia had 87 000 international students in 2010, half of whom were from Asia, with the largest groups coming from Iran (12 000), China and Indonesia (10 000 each). Both Singapore and Malaysia see international students as a source of economic growth, especially for the contribution their tuition makes to the public and private university systems. In these countries, OECD universities are also opening local campuses. In 2010, there were nine campuses of foreign universities in Singapore, and five in Malaysia.

China has also been attracting growing numbers of international students, with 107 000 degree-programme students in 2010, a 15% increase from the previous year, although the comparability of the degrees is limited. China has a stated objective of reaching a half-million international students by 2020. Other Asian economies also attract a growing number of students. Hong Kong, China, had more than 10 000 international university students in 2010, almost all from within Asia, with numbers rising annually. Chinese Taipei has also seen a sharp increase in recent years, with the number of international students in degree programmes doubling from 5 000 to 10 000 between 2007 and 2011, and the total number of students approaching 50 000. The Ministry of Education has set a target of 130 000 international students by 2020, in part to compensate for expected declines in the local youth cohorts entering university. Education costs are generally lower than in OECD countries, and Asian countries may attract students who would have otherwise studied – and perhaps remained – in OECD countries.

Rising wages and growing opportunities make Asian countries attractive for the high-skilled

Asia's growth rate has outstripped that of the developed world over the past decade and is likely to continue to grow much more rapidly over the upcoming decades. According to projections by Maddison (2008), non-member Asian economies represented 31% of global GDP in 2003, but will represent 47% of GDP in 2030. Over the same period, the share of OECD countries will fall from 54% of world GDP to 41%. Other OECD projections (OECD, 2012) put China and India as increasing from 11% and 3% of global GDP[5] to 25% and 7%, respectively. The same projections see China, India and Indonesia maintaining growth rates well above those of OECD countries for decades to come.

It is not just a shift in total GDP which will occur, but also the expansion of the middle class in Asian countries. Middle-class consumption in OECD countries is expected to increase by just 9% over the next decade, while middle class consumption in Asia is expected to more than double (Figure III.8). China and India alone are projected to see their middle-class consumption rise from 6.6% of the global total to 22.3%. Rising salaries in these countries (real wages in China grew by more than 10% annually over the past decade) will make emigration less attractive for many professionals, and attract more intraregional migration. It may, however, also allow more people to migrate or to study abroad.

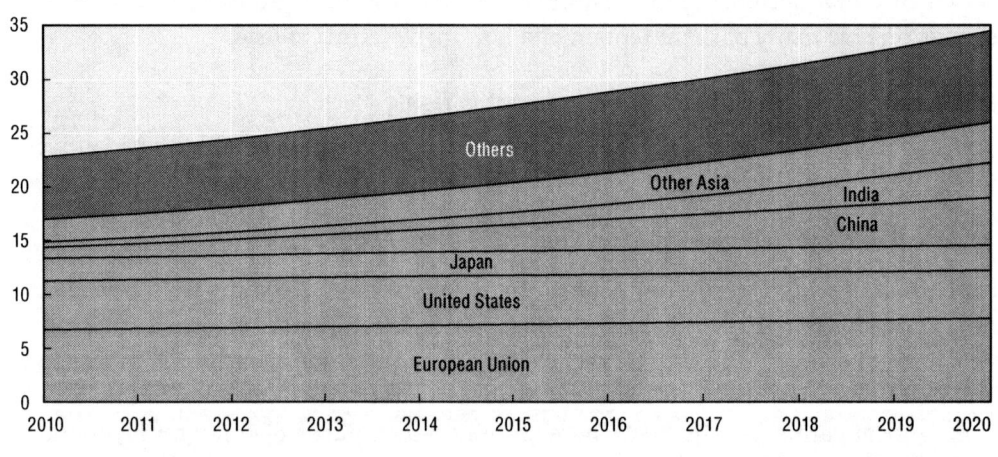

Figure III.8. **Global middle class consumption, in 2005 USD PPP, 2010-20**

Source: Kharas (2010).   StatLink http://dx.doi.org/10.1787/888932615916

Much of this growth will occur as China and India move up the value chain, although the rate at which progress will be made is not clear. The transition in both China and India to onshore technologically advanced services is likely to be a long process (Coe, 2008). Coe cites infrastructure, English-language skills, property rights, intellectual property rights enforcement, and rule of law in China as obstacles to moving up the value chain. The conditions in China for outsourcing lag far behind India (Van Welsum, 2006).

More recent analysis (OECD, 2010) suggests that despite increasing investment in R&D, China's R&D intensity – especially in industry – remains far below that in OECD countries and China is not reaping the same benefits in terms of innovation as OECD countries do. While the pace of progress is unclear, Asian countries are moving up the value chain and integrating into the global R&D infrastructure. The expansion of R&D brings more opportunities for employment of the highly skilled, as well as intracorporate mobility within the multinational corporations involved in investment in R&D infrastructure.

Free trade agreements, trade in services, and intra-Asian ICTs increase the mobility of skilled workers…

Most agreements on international labour migration in Asia are *bilateral*, reflecting the wide variety of national priorities in the area of labour migration management. One important regional body, the Association of Southeast Asian Nations (ASEAN),[6] has addressed international migration since the 2000s, although it lacks a standing ministerial body specifically addressing labour migration. It adopted a Plan of Action in 2002 on co-operation in immigration, largely devoted to border control procedures.

ASEAN decided in 2007 to achieve a regional Economic Community (AEC) by 2015. In the blueprint for achieving the AEC, five pillars are identified, the fifth of which is the free flow of skilled labour. The objective is to facilitate the issuance of visas and employment passes for ASEAN professionals and skilled labour, engaged in cross-border trade and investment-related activities. Skilled labour has so far been defined as seven professions: engineers, architects, nurses, doctors, dentists, accountants and surveyors. The facilitation of the free flow of skilled labour has been agreed through a consensus process, rather than through a vote by individual countries, avoiding reluctance from potential future receiving countries.

The achievement of free movement, even for this restricted list of professions, is subject to a number of conditions, most notably the recognition of professional qualifications, and will require time. While mutual recognition arrangements (MRAs) have been signed among ASEAN countries, implementation has yet to occur, and may represent an obstacle to free movement. For example, the Philippines restricts the practice of professions to its own nationals, and would have to pass a law specifying exemptions for ASEAN countries. Current licensing requirements for these professions vary among countries.

Another multilateral body in the region is APEC (Asia Pacific Economic Co-operation) which concentrates on trade and investment. In order to facilitate travel by businesspeople in the region, APEC introduced a "Business card" in 1999. The card substitutes a visa for extended visits (two-three months) in a three-year period, issued to high-level executives and business people in firms with trade and investments in APEC countries. The card applies to up to 18 countries – the United States and Canada do not participate. There were more than 88 000 cards in circulation in 2010, a four-fold increase since 2006.

Increasing facilitation of mobility within the region will grant more local opportunities to skilled workers, possibly subtracting from the flows towards OECD countries.

... as does the development of bilateral agreements between Asian countries

Bilateral agreements between Asian countries also facilitate the mobility of high-skilled workers. While most bilateral agreements for skilled workers in Asia have focused on less skilled workers, agreements for mobility of the skilled are starting to appear. Japan's Economic Partnership Agreements (EPAs) with the Philippines and with Indonesia, which are first and foremost agreements on trade, also include provisions on labour migration of health care workers. Japan's EPAs with India and Thailand also contain reference to labour migration. India assigns a high priority to ensuring that Free Trade Agreements open opportunities for its skilled service providers to work in other countries.

Bilateral agreements on co-operation or mutual recognition may also indirectly affect labour migration. The proposed mutual recognition agreement on higher education between Malaysia and China, for example, moves in this direction.

Asian OECD countries have introduced policies to encourage high-skilled migration

Both Japan and Korea have recently introduced facilitations for skilled migrants, allowing faster access to permanent residence. In 2012, Japan introduced a "points-based system" allowing permanent residence after five instead of 10 years to those who meet certain salary, experience, education, age and language-ability requirements. The scheme is open to academic researchers, high-skilled technical specialists and management/ business professionals. As an employment offer is required, the scheme does not introduce a new channel for skilled migration, but provides several facilitations for foreigners who would have in any case already been able to obtain a permit under the current system.

Since 2010, Korea has introduced a points-scheme for skilled foreigners who are already resident in Korea. Points are awarded based on their age, academic qualifications, Korean-language proficiency, and income. Additional points are attributed for social integration courses and work experience. The points-scheme grants accelerated access to extended residence status (the F-2 permit), and acquisition of permanent residence after three instead of five years. Here as well, the scheme is not meant to open a new channel for migration, but to facilitate the stay of skilled workers who already have residence.

Asian non-OECD countries are adopting policies to attract high-skilled migration

There has been a convergence in OECD countries around certain strategies to attract and retain skilled workers, and these strategies are being adopted in many non-member Asian economies. Provisions for international students to stay after graduation are appearing. The introduction of points-based selection systems for admitting qualified foreigners, are also being imitated.

Barriers, such as language and qualification barriers, and employer reluctance to recruit from abroad or even from among graduating international students, have limited the impact of these measures in Asian OECD countries. A number of non-member Asian economies, however, face fewer barriers, and may be better positioned to benefit from policies favouring skilled immigration. The use of the English language – and, in some Asian countries, Chinese – in both universities and the workplace reduces barriers. The expansion of mutual recognition agreements for education and professional qualifications facilitates movement. Active recruitment policies and simple and transparent permit regimes, along with relatively favourable prospects for growth, suggest that non-member Asian economies will increasingly benefit from policy convergence in this area.

A mostly open door for skilled workers

Most non-member Asian economies do not place specific obstacles to the recruitment of skilled workers, and several (Singapore, Chinese Taipei, Malaysia) have specific policies to support their immigration. Singapore grants permits to qualified employees, with several categories according to qualifications and salary level, and allows accompanying family and transition to permanent residence. Malaysia has introduced a permit open to qualified workers with several years experience to acquire a 10-year permit granting labour market mobility; qualified workers may also apply for permanent residence.

Singapore draws heavily on its skilled migration programme, with 176 000 permit-holders in 2010.[7] The relative contribution of skilled migration is much lower in Malaysia and Chinese Taipei, with 32 000 skilled workers ("expatriates") in Malaysia and 27 000 skilled workers in Chinese Taipei in 2010. In Hong Kong, China, a special scheme introduced in 2006 uses a points system, the "Quality Migrant Admission Scheme", to issue visas to qualifying skilled migrants; the annual quota of 1 000 visas, however, has been undersubscribed. Hong Kong, China, also admits more than 20 000 foreign qualified professionals annually.

These economies also allow international students to remain if they find employment. In addition, Singapore grants graduating students up to one year to find qualifying employment, and Malaysia sets aside up to 1 000 work permits annually for graduates in ITC. Hong Kong, China, since 2008, has annually granted more than 3 000 non-local graduates a 12-month job-search permit. Most of the non-local graduates, who are largely Chinese, receive this permit.

China, in contrast, has no official policy for attracting skilled foreigners. The current legal framework for issuing residence permits, put in place in 1996, has not been modified to reflect China's new role in the world economy. While the categories admitted appear relatively few and restrictive, the complex procedure has not represented a barrier for mobility of skilled foreigners working for short periods in China. In principle, recruitment of foreign employees is contingent on the employer receiving an employment permit, which is only issued if the position "has special requirements, for which there is a temporary shortage of suitable candidates inside China and which does not violate relevant state regulations". In practice, this restricts permits to a temporary duration, and imposes a qualifications threshold, considering foreign workers only if they are "experts". The requirement that employers hold Foreign Employment Licenses, issued by municipal Labor and Social Security Bureaus, has not been an obstacle to the employment of foreign experts. Nonetheless, recent figures on the number of permit-holders in China suggest that China's economic growth has not led to a boom in the number of foreign experts holding permits. At the end of 2010, the number of foreigners holding an Alien Employment Permit was 231 700, up from 180 000 in 2006. The enormous expansion of international trade and the growth of the Chinese economy is not reflected in these figures, which show a largely stable stock of foreign workers.[8] The official statistics do not cover undeclared and irregular foreign workers, including those working under business visas or other visas which do not allow employment. The 2010 Chinese Census also counts only 1 million foreigners, of whom more than half were from China's Special Autonomous Regions and Chinese Taipei.

Policies for returning overseas nationals are in place…

A number of Asian countries have put in place specific policies to attract skilled workers back from overseas.

Tax exemptions on foreign income are a common incentive. Malaysia offers a two-year tax holiday on foreign income. China, India, the Philippines and Singapore also offer different forms of tax exemptions for foreign income.

A second strategy is to offer salary top-ups or cash grants to returning experts. The "Hundred Talents" programme of the Chinese Academy of Sciences (CAS) grants overseas Chinese studying abroad in science and technology financial support and employment opportunities in domestic research institutes, and other regional authorities offer cash grants to returning entrepreneurs. China has put in place a range of policies to attract educated Chinese home from abroad, to invest or to bring back technology (Zweig, 2006). India has a programme offering a five-year salary top-up to academics who return to an Indian institution. Singapore focuses on medical professionals, with a pre-employment grant to attract overseas-trained Singaporean doctors to return home since 2010.

Recognition of foreign qualifications is another area for support to returnees. The Philippines offers a programme for returning professionals, who may acquire recognition of their qualifications through certification rather than examination.

Finally, a number of countries offer additional services to returnees, especially those related to families and residency. The Chinese programme includes housing assistance and children and spouse settlement. Non-citizens of Indian origin may acquire "Overseas Citizenship of India", which allows them to work in India. The Philippines allows reacquisition of nationality. Malaysia offers accelerated permanent residence for spouses.

Despite these incentives, return programmes often have low participation. Malaysia only attracted 400 returnees in ten years, although a government agency (Returning Experts Programme), claimed almost 600 returning experts in 2011. Evaluation is difficult, as it is rarely clear how many expatriates would have returned in the absence of these programmes.

… but opportunities are drawing Asians home from OECD countries

Increasingly, migrants from Asia are returning to their country of origin from OECD countries. In some cases, this is part of the process for students who have gone abroad to study. For China, the main sending country for international students, the number of returning students is particularly high: more than 186 000 in 2011, according to official Chinese statistics (Figure III.9). This was also the first year in which the number of returning students was more than half the number of outgoing students.

Some traditional destinations, such as the United States, have seen the highly-qualified less likely to remain after graduation. According to the National Science Board (2010), the proportion of science and engineering doctorate students from China, India, Korea and Chinese Taipei – planning on staying in the United States fell between 2000/2003 and 2004/2007. While this may reflect fewer possibilities to obtain a visa to stay in the United States, it also testifies to the growing opportunities at home.

Return migration from OECD countries has helped fuel growth in non-OECD Asian economies. Almost one in three companies in Chinese Taipei's Hsinchu Science-based Industrial Park, for example, which produces semiconductors and accounted for 10% of exports in 2007, was founded by a returnee from the United States, and returnees accounted for more than 5% of the total workforce (Chiu and Hou, 2007). Return migration

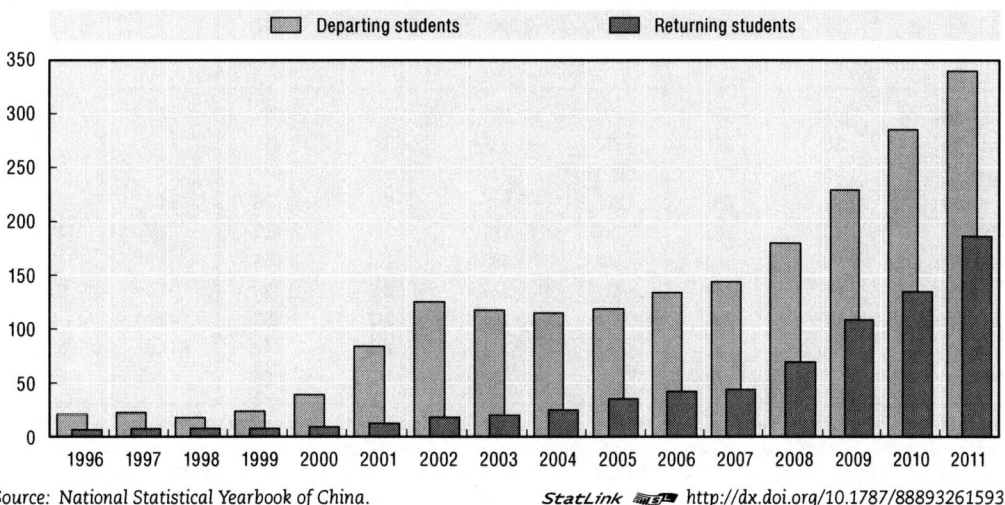

Figure III.9. **Inflows and outflows of Chinese students, 1996-2011**

Source: National Statistical Yearbook of China. StatLink http://dx.doi.org/10.1787/888932615935

has contributed to the development of advanced technology in India as well; half of the leading Indian software firms in 2000 were founded by non-resident Indians returning from the United States (Hunger, 2004).

Looking forward, OECD countries will face more competition for skilled Asian workers, even as the total pool of skilled workers increases. Real wage growth in the region is likely to continue to outstrip that in OECD countries, and although parity is a long way off in most countries, improving conditions for professionals, along with more opportunities as advanced industries expand, will give the region greater weight as a destination as well as an origin for skilled workers.

5. Key challenges for managing low-skilled and family migration

While different countries' policies to attract and retain skilled migrants tend to converge around the same objectives and measures cited above, a number of Asian economies face complex challenges of managing low-skilled labour migration and family migration. Management concerns finding means to protect the local labour market, channel irregular flows into legal schemes, and reduce rent-taking. It also focuses on ensuring the rotational and temporary nature of labour schemes. Family migration, on the other hand, is a relatively new phenomenon, driven by marriage migration in a number of economies, with implications for integration policies.

Management of low-skilled labour migration in Asian non-OECD countries

Asia contains some of the most important origin countries for labour migrants. Table III.8 shows the placement of workers, or overseas employment outflows, by origin country for 2005-10. For most countries, these outflows comprise unskilled employment, with the most qualified workers not subject to the overseas employment management schemes. Intra-Asian migration is a predominant part of flows in Indonesia, Thailand and Viet Nam, but represents only a minimal part of flows from Pakistan, India and Sri Lanka. Flows peaked in 2008 with almost 5 million outgoing workers from these countries. The Philippines is the largest origin country in absolute terms. Relative to the total active population, outflows are small for China and India (Figure III.10). For Sri Lanka, Nepal and the Philippines, however, annual outflows are equivalent to more than 3% of the total active population.

III. THE CHANGING ROLE OF ASIA IN INTERNATIONAL MIGRATION

Table III.8. **Outflows of overseas workers, 2005-10, by origin country**

Origin country	2005	2006	2007	2008	2009	2010	% women	% within Asia
	\multicolumn{6}{c	}{Thousands}		
Bangladesh	253	382	833	875	475	391	7.1	11.5
China	343	351	372	427	395	411	..	..
India	549	677	809	849	610	641	..	3.2
Indonesia	..	680	697	645	632	576	64.3	58
Nepal	..	205	249	220	294	355	2.9	31.4
Pakistan	142	183	287	432	404	365	..	1
Philippines	740	788	811	974	1 092	1 124	54.5	23.6
Sri Lanka	231	202	218	250	247	266	49.1	5.8
Thailand	140	161	162	162	148	144	17.8	60.5
Viet Nam	71	79	85	87	73	86	..	62.9

Notes: Figures are for overseas workers whose departure is recorded by the government agencies in the origin country. Coverage of individual departures for employment may be partial or limited to employment under bilateral agreements. Some countries (e.g. India) do not record departures for employment to OECD countries. Data for Indonesia include both formal and informal placements. Sailors are excluded from the data for most countries. China: "labour service co-operation". Nepal: data for fiscal years. Gender and destination ratio is for most recent year available (2011 for Indonesia and Thailand, 2008 for Pakistan, 2010 for other countries).
Sources: Nepal – Dept. Foreign Employment. Bangladesh – BMET. Indonesia – BNP2TKI. Sri Lanka – SLBFE. Thailand – Office of Overseas Employment Administration, DOE. India – MOIA. Pakistan – Bureau of Emigration and Overseas Employment. Philippines – POEA. Viet Nam – MoLISA. China – Ministry of Commerce.

StatLink http://dx.doi.org/10.1787/888932617284

Figure III.10. **Outflow of overseas workers relative to the size of the active population, Asian countries**

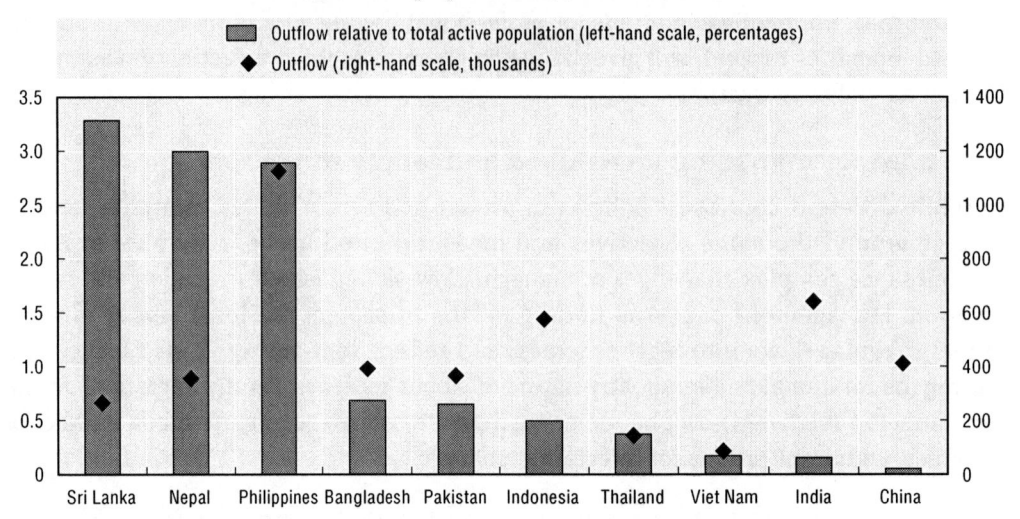

Notes: For Philippines and Thailand, active populations are annual average for 2010. For India, active population is estimated. Bangladesh – economically active population is provisional based on 2005-06 Labour Force Survey. Viet Nam – active population is preliminary for 2010.
Sources: Outflows: see Table III.8. Active population: Sri Lanka: Labour Force Survey Annual Report 2010, NSO. Nepal: 2008 NLFS NSO. Philippines: NSO. Bangladesh: *Statistical Yearbook of Bangladesh 2010*, NSO. Pakistan: Labour Force Survey 2009-10, NSO. Indonesia: NSO. Thailand: NSO. Viet Nam: NSO. India: Report on Employment and Unemployment Survey (2009-10), Labour Bureau Government of India. China: *Statistical Yearbook 2010*, NSO.

StatLink http://dx.doi.org/10.1787/888932615954

Most intra-Asian managed migration has been low-skilled. From Sri Lanka, for example, in 2009, 46% of departing workers were housemaids, and a further 20% were unskilled. Only 6% were clerical, mid-level and professional workers. From Indonesia, the government estimated that almost 70% of its overseas workers in 2011 – including irregular workers – were housemaids. From Pakistan, in 2007, 50% of workers officially departing for overseas employment were unskilled, and less than 12% highly skilled or qualified. From Bangladesh, only 1% departed for skilled employment.

China also sends unskilled workers abroad through "foreign labour service co-operation", managed by the Chinese Ministry of Commerce. There were more than 400 000 deployments of contract workers in 2010, with more than 800 000 Chinese working abroad. About half of the deployments were contracted for projects, and half through recruitment agencies for a foreign employer.

Destination economies do not allow low-skilled labour migrants to settle

The migration model for migration of low-skilled from Asian countries is different from the prevailing model in most OECD countries. Today, low-skilled labour migration in Asia remains predominantly *temporary* and *rotational*, with limits on the duration of stay and on the permanent settlement rights of labour migrants. For low-skilled workers, stay is limited to 12 years in Chinese Taipei,[9] to six years in Singapore[10] and to five years in Malaysia, although the latter grants the possibility of returning after a period at home. Receiving economies in Asia have maintained these restrictions on settlement by low-skilled foreigners even as the numbers have grown, in the belief that demand is not structural, and in the hope of avoiding challenges related to integration.

Even as the number of low-skilled foreign workers increases, most countries see this form of migration as potentially harmful to the chances of local low-skilled workers to enter employment. A number of Asian receiving economies have therefore adopted measures not only to limit the number of low-skilled workers but also to increase employment costs as a means of discouraging employers from recruiting them. Increasing employment cost may also be seen as a means of discouraging continued investment in low-productivity activities sustainable only with low-cost foreign workers, or as a means of encouraging employers to hire local low-skilled workers.

Singapore's levy system, meant to encourage employers to hire Singaporean workers and to favour capital-intensive and higher-productivity activities, stands out in Asia for its complexity as well as the relative size of employer fees. Singapore applies a "dependency ceiling" to employers according to the sector, the skill level of the worker, and the proportion of the workforce comprising foreign workers. The levy can reach USD 350 per month for unskilled workers in services, representing at least 25% of salary costs, and even higher for construction workers; for maids, it is USD 280, which may exceed the monthly salary for some of the 200 000 domestic workers in the country. The levy system induces employers to favour workers with certified skills, raising the value of skill certification in origin countries and leading to training centres aimed specifically at the Singapore market.

Other economies receiving foreign workers have attempted to increase the cost or limit use of foreign workers through other mechanisms. Hong Kong, China, imposes a minimum wage for foreign domestic workers (about USD 485 in 2011).[11] Chinese Taipei imposes a monthly "employment stability fee" of USD 70-80 as a levy on foreign workers, which represents about 15% of habitual wages. Chinese Taipei also imposes a ceiling on the percentage of foreign workers in employers' workforces. The ceiling varies according to the industry, from 10 to 35%. Malaysia also imposes a foreign worker levy, which ranges from USD 10 monthly (for domestic and agricultural workers) to USD 35 (for manufacturing, construction and tourism) and USD 50 for other service workers.

Most OECD countries test labour market shortages by requiring employers to offer the job locally and holding them to prevailing or minimum wage conditions. Increasing employment costs of foreign workers, as a means of encouraging the employment of local workers, is rarely used, although strict recruitment criteria and initial hiring fees are frequent. Only one OECD country, Israel, applies such an employment levy on foreign workers, and it has not had great success in attracting local low-skilled workers into occupations which have become dependent on foreign workers (OECD, 2011). In part, this is due to the high rents earned by employers, and in part to poor enforcement of wage and working conditions, which allow employers to pay low wages illegally. Employment subsidies for hiring local workers have been unsuccessful in agriculture and nursing, and have only had limited success in construction, highlighting the difficulty in attracting natives back to occupations which have become dependent on foreign workers. Estonia, rather than impose a levy, grants the cost to the worker, by requiring that the wage paid to foreign workers include a 24% premium relative to the average wage in the occupation.

Irregular migration is widespread

The drivers of irregular labour migration are both the limited availabilities for legal migration into low-skilled employment in the receiving country, and the cost and complexity of legal channels. As a result of limits on legal channels, and high costs imposed on workers, some non-OECD Asian countries have difficulty regulating immigration for employment, and undocumented migration remains a challenge (Abella, 2008). Enforcement at entry and the workplace and regularisations are the main policy responses by Asian countries to reduce illegal employment of low-skilled foreigners. Undocumented labour migration comprises a range of forms of migration, which Hugo (2011) describes in terms of the degree to which they are voluntary, from individual movement, to mediated movement, to misleading promises, to bonded labour and to kidnapping. Irregular migration to a country may involve a mix of all these forms of migration, complicating efforts to combat them. Further, from the perspective of migrants, illegal channels may be cheaper or more reliable than legal ones, especially where governments are not trusted and legal channels are costly and lengthy.

In contrast to most OECD countries, *illegal border crossing* is the principal channel for intraregional irregular migration between non-member Asian countries, especially for major channels of migration such as that along land borders between India and Bangladesh and Nepal, and sea and land borders between Malaysia and Indonesia, as well as more recently the land border between Thailand, Myanmar, Laos and Cambodia (Table III.9). Tourist visas may also be used to enter a country and overstay; this appears common between Indonesia and Malaysia, for example (Azizah, 2005).

Table III.9. **Estimated stocks of undocumented workers in selected Asian economies**

	Year	Estimate	Coverage
Chinese Taipei	2011	33	Overstaying non-Chinese workers
India	2001	17 400	Stock of undocumented Bangladeshis and Nepalis
Japan	2011	78	Overstayers
Korea	2009	181	Overstayers
Malaysia	2011	2 500	Applications for regularisation
Thailand	2009	700	Undocumented (post-regularisation)

Note: The figure for India includes all Bangladeshis entering between 1972-2001.
Sources: Korea: Immigration Service; Japan: Immigration Bureau, Ministry of Justice; Chinese Taipei: Labour Affairs Council; Thailand: Ministry of Labour; Malaysia: Hugo (2011); India: Das (2010), citing Report of the Group of Ministers on National Security (2000), and NIDS (2010). *StatLink* http://dx.doi.org/10.1787/888932617303

Regularisations as a means for managing low-skilled labour migration in non-OECD Asian countries

Non-member Asian countries have attempted to deal with irregular migration through regularisations (Box III.3), which consist in granting undocumented foreigners without work or residence rights some form of legal status. Regularisations of undocumented foreigners usually involve specific eligibility criteria related to employment and/or

---

Box III.3. Regularisations in Thailand and Malaysia

A number of Asian countries have implemented regularisations in the past two decades, especially Thailand and Malaysia. Thailand held its first regularisation in 1992 and has repeated the exercise since then, with regularisation becoming the primary means for managing labour migration. While the first regularisations were held in specific regions, for specific nationalities, and specific sectors of employment, eligibility has broadened over the years (Sciortino and Punpuing, 2009). As the permit issued has generally been for only one year, often most of the participants are re-regularising labour migrants who had previously participated in a scheme. The numbers involved have been comparable to the largest regularisation in OECD countries: more than half a million in the 2001 round, and more than a million in the 2009 round. Recent regularizations have required registration by the worker and then later sponsorship by an employer willing to meet conditions. Employment is restricted to manual labour and to domestic work. Most of the regularized have been citizens of Myanmar (87% in 2010), with the remainder split between citizens of Laos and Cambodia.

In 2009, Thailand, in an attempt to escape from the cycle of regularisations, introduced a new procedure, requiring those regularized in the past and wishing to renew their permits to undergo "National Verification" (NV), which requires obtaining a document issued by the home-country authorities. Permits issued to workers with NV are valid for two years and renewable for two more years, although sector and employer restrictions remain. While NV is available in Thailand itself for Cambodians and Laotians, Burmese must return home to receive their documents, exposing them to higher costs, risks of extortion and arrest for political reasons (Vasuprasat, 2010), so fewer than 5% of Burmese undertook NV in the first phase, compared with more than 50% for Laotian and Cambodian workers.

In parallel with the registration system for undocumented labour migrants, Thailand has attempted to introduce bilateral agreements with neighbouring countries for the management of labour migrants. These Memoranda of Understanding have not been competitive with irregular channels, with the stock of workers under the agreements reaching about 43 000 in 2010, compared with 1.15 million workers through regularisation.

The second Southeast Asian country to repeatedly use regularizations is Malaysia, which even prior to industrialisation had undocumented workers from Indonesia in its plantations and domestic sector. Malaysia has periodically increased its enforcement measures and expelled workers, often in conjunction with amnesties under which undocumented labour migrants were allowed to leave voluntarily without penalty and without facing a re-entry ban. In mid-2004, for example, an estimated 400 000 left or were expelled, out of a stated target of 600 000. Many later returned to Malaysia.

Malaysia introduced a new regularisation programme in mid-2011, called the "6-P Programme" for the Malay terms for registration, amnesty, legalization, enforcement, monitoring and deportation. All workers, including those holding a legal status, had to register with their biometric information. In Peninsular Malaysia, in addition to 1 million legal workers, about 1.3 million undocumented workers registered. Malaysia restricts employment of low-skilled labour migrants to manufacturing, construction, agriculture, and a limited number of service sector jobs, including domestic work, and the regularisation revealed the level of recourse to foreign workers outside these sectors. About 25% of the undocumented workers were employed in sectors in which foreign workers were not allowed, especially in services. in the 6-P regularisation, Indonesia was not the only origin country of irregular migrants: about 280 000 Nepalis and 270 000 Bangladeshis registered.

duration of stay. The application period often coincides with changes to policy meant to address the causes of irregular migration, and with stepped-up efforts to identify and expel undocumented workers who did not participate in the regularisation.

In addition to regularisations, amnesties may also be offered, allowing undocumented workers to return home on their own without incurring a re-entry ban and without facing criminal charges or forced deportation, or permission to stay for a limited period. Korea offered such an amnesty during its transition from one labour scheme to another.

Enforcement of measures to combat illegal migration is generally confined to the destination country, as most origin countries are reluctant to impose restrictions on the exit of their own citizens. Still, co-operation can be facilitated between source and destination countries, particularly in the area of readmission. Bilateral negotiations often focus on facilitated readmission in exchange for labour market access.

Most Asian non-member economies to which labour migration is significant impose restrictions on labour migrants – especially low-skilled labour migrants – which would not be permissible in most OECD countries due to the non-discriminatory application of labour law and to the framework of family and individual rights prevailing in OECD countries. The principal incompatibility lies in the extended duration of work permits during which no family reunification is allowed, and the exclusion of permanent residence for long-time foreign workers. Singapore, for example, limits low-skilled workers to temporary stay exceeding a decade for some categories, with no family reunification allowed, and, for some categories of workers, restrictions are placed on marriage with residents, and pregnancy leads to expulsion.

Management of low-skilled labour migration in Asian OECD countries

Asian OECD countries have experimented with several different models for international recruitment, according to labour market demand and identified shortages, but also as a concession to requests from origin countries in bilateral negotiations.

In both Japan and Korea, industrial trainee programmes expanded in the 1990s, with firms using trainees, largely from other Asian countries, in low-skill occupations under the framework of partnership agreements. Japan developed its technical internship and industrial trainee programme in certain sectors, such as agriculture, fisheries, textiles and small manufacturing, where local workers were difficult to find. A semi-public agency (JITCO) manages the trainee programme, which brings workers from 15 origin countries (14 in Asia) with which bilateral agreements have been signed. Since 1993, those entering as trainees may stay in Japan for up to three years, with the same employer, and are covered by Japanese labour law for the entire period. Some training is provided prior to departure, and the trainee programme is based on the idea of skills transfer, with a certain level of skill necessary to extend the traineeship beyond the first year. There were more than 49 000 participants entering the scheme in 2011.

Korea's EPS system as a consolidated practice

The model with the broadest application in a single country is that of bilateral agreements signed by Korea with 15 countries under its Employment Permit System (EPS). To some extent, this model is similar to those which prevailed in Europe in the post-war period, where employers shared in the costs of recruitment and there was a strong involvement of public employment authorities in the receiving countries (OECD, 2004). The programme has become well-known in Asia and has been recognised as a good and transferable practice. The following section reviews its salient features.

Korea also operated an Industrial Trainee System (ITS) since 1994, when labour shortages in production and manual occupations became acute. ITS was run through private agencies, considered foreigners as trainees and not workers, and restricted them to larger employers. High rents were often taken for entry, labour law was not always respected, and trainees often violated the terms of sponsorship and stay. As the labour shortage in lower-skill occupations persisted, especially in smaller enterprises, the Korean authorities decided to substitute the ITS with a government-to-government (G2G) temporary labour migration scheme, the EPS, introduced in August 2004. The ITS was eliminated in 2007.

The EPS is co-ordinated by the Korean Human Resource Development (HRD) service, which works with origin-country government agencies in the framework of bilateral agreements. A Korean-language test is offered, and successful candidates, who meet other requirements, may enrol in the roster of candidates, which exceeds the national quota. The Korean government authority selects candidates based on their characteristics, and employers may choose from among several candidates. The objective evaluation criteria and the fact that the sending agency cannot promise employment have helped reduced rent-taking in the country of origin, and fees for mandatory training courses have dropped significantly compared with those under the ITS. The agreements do not commit Korea to accepting a fixed number of workers, and recruitment may be suspended from countries where procedures are not respected, candidates are not accurately described, or if workers are overstaying. The country of origin is thus a partner in working for the success of the scheme.

The EPS is well-known in countries of origin: more than 435 000 aspirant workers in 15 countries have taken the Test of Proficiency in Korean (TOPIK) since 2007. In addition to the TOPIK, selected workers must undergo pre- and post-departure training, with training costs pre-departure borne by the employee and post-arrival training by the Korean employers, who may benefit from subsidies. EPS workers are treated as employees and have the same legal rights as Korean workers and are protected under the Korean labour law.

The EPS is meant to be a temporary and rotational programme to prevent permanent settlement in Korea, so family reunification is not allowed. When introduced, the maximum working period in Korea was three years, with renewal and reauthorization required for employers and workers each year. As the first group of workers reached their maximum stay in 2009, the duration was extended to 58 months for workers staying with the same employer. At the end of the stay, workers must leave Korea for at least six months before they may re-enter under the EPS; however, not all workers may come back to Korea. For 2012, a quota of 11 000 was imposed for qualifying participants returning to Korea after a mandatory end-of-contract trip home. With almost 70 000 workers reaching their maximum stay in 2012, even accounting for expected overstay rates of about 20-30%, most workers will not be able to come back to Korea under the programme.

The 2009 extension, and the imposition of a quota for return, underlines the challenge of maintaining a temporary and rotational programme, especially when employees are largely concentrated in small and medium-sized enterprises. Employers are reluctant to replace trusted workers who have learned the language and the practices of the workplace, with whom they have formed relationships or who have received additional training. To encourage return, HRD Korea also offers subsequent publicly-funded vocational training in a number of fields applicable in origin countries; it offered such training to 720 workers in 2012. HRD Korea also offers counselling, orientation and support services for workers in the programme.

Some facilitations are available for workers who re-enrol in the EPS after a first period in Korea and who complied with the programme rules. First, they are exempt from training and may take a special TOPIK exam, more difficult than the standard exam but offered more frequently. For workers who spent their entire first contract with the same small firm, for which they are considered essential, no tests are imposed and they may return after only three months abroad to their employer. For qualifying younger, tertiary-educated and better-paid workers, status-change to a regular work permit is allowed.

The EPS represented a novel policy, one which has effectively reduced many of the main problems which plague labour migration management for the low-skilled in Asian countries. For origin countries, the fees paid by workers were reduced and their satisfaction and protection increased. For Korea, overstay and employer abuse were curtailed. Largely for its success in reducing recruitment fees paid by workers, it received a 2011 UN Public Service Award for "Preventing and Combating Corruption in the Public Service". Both Korea and origin countries consider the EPS a "good practice" (ILO, 2008). The programme has certainly raised the profile of Korea as a destination country for labour migrants.

Ethnic migration channels have been used for labour migration

Both Japan and Korea have opened channels for labour migration to foreigners of national origin abroad. Japan first allowed foreigners of Japanese origin from certain countries in South America and the Philippines to come to Japan with a sponsor – an employer or family member – in the 1990s. The programme targeted descendents of Japanese immigrants who had left several generations previously. Most came from Brazil and Peru, and were recruited to work for manufacturing subcontractors. Most did not have Japanese-language skills, and were among the first to lose their jobs in the 2008 crisis. Many were unable to find other employment and left Japan. The number of these immigrants peaked in 2007 at almost 400 000, but fell to less than 300 000 by 2010.

In 2005, the Korean government introduced a Special visa for "Visit and Employment" (the H-2 visa), as a separate channel in its EPS scheme. Ethnic Koreans, largely from China, are able to come to Korea and, following training, seek employment. Ethnic Koreans are restricted to employment in a broad range of sectors, including service sectors such as restaurants and domestic work and personal care, although limits are placed on construction-sector work. The ceiling for H-2 workers was set at 303 000 in 2011 and 2012, with the stock of legal visa holders close to this limit. As in the general EPS programme, stay is limited to less than five years, although visa-holders may reapply to return to Korea within the ceiling.

Japan's bilateral agreements for healthcare worker migration in Economic Partnership Agreements

Starting in the mid-2000s, Japan has included channels for labour migration by health professionals, specifically nurses and institutional care workers, in Economic Partnership Agreements (EPAs) signed with other Asian countries.

Under agreements with Indonesia and the Philippines, which came into force in 2008, nurses and care workers must be trained in the home country, and are selected jointly by public Japanese and origin-country bodies. Language training prior to arriving in Japan is required, as is continued language training once in Japan. Participants have three to four years to pass the national licensing exam for nursing or carework, after which they may stay if they find employment in their sector. Those who do not pass the test must return home. The numbers foreseen in the programme are capped: in 2011, 200 nurses and 300 careworkers were allowed from each country. The actual number of entries has been lower than the cap, with fewer than 1 200 total in both categories arriving in the first three years. Of these, few remain, due to a very low pass rate (overall, 19 out of 650 nurses) associated with insufficient language skills.

The budget devoted to the support of nurses and care workers under the EPA reflects the priority assigned to the success of the EPA as a whole. Receiving institutions have received a subsidy since 2010, and in 2011 the budget for language training was more than USD 1 million, with the cost per candidate estimated at USD 10 000.

Labour migration by service providers also continues to be a point in the negotiation of EPAs by Japan. The EPA signed between Japan and India in 2011 contained a provision for eventually accepting nurses and careworkers, but also provisions for contractual service suppliers to be employed directly by Japanese employers, for renewable periods of three years. The EPA with Thailand also identified careworkers and spa therapists as occupations for future negotiation, and the EPA with Viet Nam included nurses and careworkers. The difficulties in transforming the current agreements into a labour migration channel suggest that regardless of the success of origin-country pressure in including such provisions, and the willingness of Japanese authorities to invest in the measures, insufficient demand and other structural factors such as language and training challenges will continue to limit the magnitude of labour migration flows under the EPAs.

Irregular migration in Asian OECD countries

Irregular migration to Asian OECD countries is not associated with illegal border crossing, as they have well-controlled entry points. The focus of enforcement is more on overstay or visa misuse, and evidence suggests it has been effective in both countries. The rise in undocumented foreigners in Japan in the early 2000s was in part related to abuse of the visa for entertainers, and the decision by Japanese authorities to suspend recognition of "certified" entertainers from the Philippines led to a sharp decline in entries and consequent overstay in this visa category. Finally, restricted visas, such as trainee visas, have been sometimes linked to violation of conditions, overstay and illegal employment. Korea's ITS was associated with a sharp increase in the number of undocumented migrants as trainees left their sponsors. This was one major factor leading to the programme's elimination in 2007 (Hur, 2010). Overall, Asian OECD countries have lower levels of irregular migration compared with regular labour migration flows than non-member Asian economies and many other OECD countries.

Family migration is driven by marriage with citizens and not reunification with migrants

Family-based migration is one of the main channels of migration within the OECD, representing 45% of total permanent-type flows in 2010. The main forms of family migration are accompanying family, for the family members entering with a migrant; family reunification, where spouses, children and, in some cases, other relatives migrate to join an immigrant; and family formation, where a citizen marries a foreigner. While many OECD countries do not separate family formation from family reunification in their statistics, it is often a significant part of family migration. In Asian OECD countries, it is the main form of family migration, and one of the main components of permanent-type flows.

Defining "marriage migration"

"Marriage migration" in this analysis refers to family formation with a native. This occurs around the world, is frequent in OECD countries and increases with the internationalisation of marriage markets (*e.g.* rising tourism, intermediation, international study). However, there are some challenges related to measurement of the phenomenon. Couples whose marriage takes place abroad may not appear in marriage statistics, but will appear in immigration statistics.

The discussion of "marriage migration" here focuses on marriages between one spouse from less developed countries and the other spouse from more developed economies, often arranged through mediated channels with the involvement of formal or informal matchmaking actors. The analysis here focuses on the Asian economies where marriage migration is prevalent, notably Chinese Taipei, Korea, Japan and Singapore. In almost all cases, it is men in the destination country marrying women from less developed countries.

The trend in increasing marriages with foreigners first occurred in Japan, in the late 1980s, with rising numbers of Japanese men marrying Korean, Chinese and Filipina women (Figure III.11). This expanded in the 1990s to include Thai women. In the mid-2000s, more than 6% of Japanese men married women from China or the Philippines, the main origin countries for brides. The percentage of marriages with women from these two countries has since declined slightly, to under 5% in 2010. In Chinese Taipei, the phenomenon began in the late 1980s, and remains high: of men who married in 2010, one in eight married a bride from a less developed economy. In Korea, the international marriage phenomenon began in the mid 1990s and peaked, at 14%, in 2005, before declining to 11% in 2010, when one in 12 Korean grooms married a bride from a less developed country.

International marriage migration represents a large part of permanent migration inflows into Japan and Korea. In Japan, it accounted for almost one-fourth of permanent inflows in the mid to late 2000s. In Korea, outside of the temporary labour migration programmes, it represented more than half of permanent flows in 2010.

Figure III.11. **Proportion of marriages involving a foreign bride and a foreign spouse in Japan, Korea, Chinese Taipei and Singapore, 1998-2010**

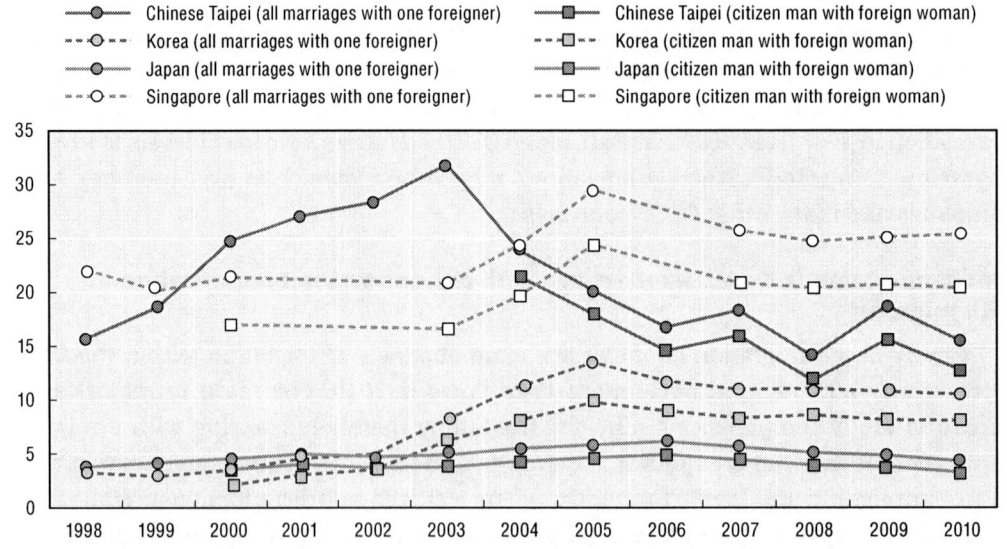

Notes: Singapore: Marriages between citizen with non-residents; Marriages between citizen groom with non-resident brides. Chinese Taipei: About three-quarters of non-citizen brides are from mainland China.
Sources: National statistical services.

Factors driving marriage migration

In addition to cultural aspects – a tradition of arranged marriages, social pressure to marry – several trends have contributed to driving marriage migration.

The first is the dramatic change in *local* marriage markets, especially for men living in rural areas or those with low education or income levels. Marriage migration was in fact initially largely driven by men from rural areas, and those with a lower socio-economic status, although it also has come to involve older divorced or widowed men (Lee, 2011). This is related to increasing education among women, who prefer to seek employment in urban areas. The difficulty of pursuing a career and maternity at the same time – limited public childcare, unequal division of labour in the household, and a professional culture incompatible with childrearing – also contributes to delayed marriage among educated women.

The second factor is the "marriage deficit" due to shrinking youth cohorts. Men generally marry younger women, and the birth cohorts have been shrinking in these economies. The marriage deficit is already visible in Singapore and Chinese Taipei. In Korea, the marriage deficit, which has not been sufficient to explain the recourse to international marriage, will also become a factor over the next decade. Similarly, cohorts of marriage-age men in China are still larger than cohorts of marriage-age women, so the marriage deficit in China has yet to transition. In the next decade, however, a wide deficit in the ratio of marriage-age women to marriage-age men will open, with implications for the marriage market.

Along with a general reduction in the size of birth cohorts, the marriage deficit can be exacerbated by the effect of *pre-natal gender selection*. The usual gender ratio at birth is about 1.05 males per female, but strong traditional preferences for male children and the introduction of ultrasound technology have led to pre-natal gender selection and a gender ratio at birth favouring males in a number of economies (Table III.10). The effects of this are already notable in Chinese Taipei, where gender disparity at birth has expanded the "marriage gap" for the current generation, and makes the marriage market even more competitive for men. While policy changes and public information campaigns in some countries have lowered the gender ratio at birth, especially in Korea, other countries, such as Viet Nam and India, have seen the ratio of males at birth increase in recent years. The marriage market in upcoming decades will likely be affected by these trends, potentially increasing marriage migration.

Table III.10. **Sex ratio at birth (SRB) or for 0-4 age cohort, selected Asian economies, 1990-2010**

	1990/91	1995	2000/01	2005	2009/10
Bangladesh	102.9	103.3	108.5	104.4	104.5
China (SRB)	111.3	115.6	116.9	122.7	119.5
India	107.6	108.7	108.7	108.7	108.7
Korea (SRB)	116.5	112.4	111.5	109.1	107.5
Pakistan	104.3	104.4	104.4	104.3	104.3
Philippines	104.9	104.9	105	105	105.1
Chinese Taipei (SRB)	110.3	107.9	109.4	109	109
Thailand	104.3	104.9	105.6	105.5	106
Viet Nam (SRB 2005-10)	103.7	104.2	104.4	105.6	111.2

Sources: Bangladesh: Age: 0-4, Bangladesh Bureau of Statistics, except for 2005-10, UNESA WPP: The 2010 Revision; China: National Bureau of Statistics of China; India: UNESA; Korea: Korea Statistical Information Service; Pakistan: UNESA; Philippines: Age UNESA; Chinese Taipei: Department of Household Registration Affairs, MOI; Thailand: UNESA; Viet Nam: UNESA except 2005, 2010 SRB, General Statistics Office of Viet Nam.

StatLink http://dx.doi.org/10.1787/888932617322

The organisation of families in East Asia also affects marriage migration. Eldercare has traditionally fallen disproportionately on families, where women, including daughters-in-law, are often expected to assume responsibility as carers. Immigration for care-work is restricted in these countries, and marriage migration may in some cases be a strategy by individuals or families in the destination country to ensure care for elderly parents, or for the disabled. In countries which place restrictions on international recruitment for live-in care workers, this may be a means to circumvent such restrictions, or a means to save on wages (Wang and Hsaio, 2009).

Finally, for the migrant, marriage migration is often the simplest and least expensive – if not the only – means for migration from rapidly developing countries in Southeast Asia to developed East Asian economies. In Chinese Taipei, for example, Chinese are excluded from labour migration and marriage is an accessible alternative. As elsewhere, marriage may also be a solution for temporary residents unable to extend their legal stay on a work or other permit.

Channels through which marriage migration in Asia occurs

Outside of Asia, marriage migration may reflect tourism and other opportunities for meetings through technology and globalisation, but the role of formal intermediation is more common in Asia.

Co-ethnic marriage migration preceded inter-ethnic marriage migration, and continues to make up a large part of marriage migration in Korea, with ethnic Koreans from China, and in Chinese Taipei, with mainland Chinese. Japanese-Koreans account for many of the international marriages with people of Korean origin in Japan, and *vice versa*.[12] Marriage migration has, however, expanded beyond co-ethnic marriage in these countries, and mediation has become more common.

In some cases, temporary migrants – international students, entertainers, or temporary workers – married locals, establishing the first links in a migration chain. The increase in marriages between foreign women and local men in Korea and Japan in the mid-2000s, for example, was related to changes in the programmes in place in these countries. In Japan, a sharp rise in entertainment visas issued to Filipino women contributed to an increase in marriages in 2005-06 (Lee, 2011). In Korea, the number of international marriages with Chinese women peaked in 2005, with the introduction of a new Visiting Employment visa for ethnic Koreans from China and other countries which provided an alternative to marriage migration.

Matchmaking across international boundaries is also facilitated through commercial agencies. In many cases, agencies which previously conducted domestic matchmaking expanded to include international matchmaking. Initially treated as a private matter, the increasing number of marriages and agencies, and the fact that these flows represented a large part of permanent migration flows into countries with little immigration, drew more institutional attention (Box III.4).

Implications for integration

The increase in marriage migration has represented the first and least controversial impetus for the development of integration policies in these receiving countries. These policies have concentrated on the cultural, linguistic and labour market integration of marriage migrants.

> **Box III.4. Managed marriage migration – agencies and regulations**
>
> Institutions in receiving economies have supported marriage migration. In some cases, local authorities in rural areas, concerned over depopulation, have supported matchmaking and mediation with origin countries, organising matchmaking tours and facilitating administrative procedures.
>
> Private agencies tend to be small, often with local partners in origin countries, and sometimes build on relationships established by prior marriage migrants. There were 1 250 registered agencies in Korea in 2010, and almost 4 000 in Japan in 2006. Agencies organise tours to origin countries and arrange introductions, often in groups.
>
> Governments in Korea and Chinese Taipei have reacted to concern over the role of commercial agencies. To better regulate these agencies and to reduce false advertising, in 2007 Korea imposed an advertising ban and the requirement for agencies to register with local governments. In 2010, it took the further step of requiring that the local resident using an agency provide full documentation on marital status, health, employment and criminal records, to be translated by the agency and provided to prospective spouses. The Korean Ministry of Gender Equality and Family provides training for agencies, and pre-departure orientation for brides in Viet Nam, Cambodia, Mongolia and the Philippines. Since 2011, Korean men applying for a spouse visa for a bride from Cambodia, China, Mongolia, the Philippines, Thailand, Uzbekistan and Viet Nam, must undergo a course on international marriage before the visa is issued.
>
> Chinese Taipei introduced a screening system to restrict marriage migration in 2004, ostensibly to reduce trafficking, with a resulting decline in the number of international migrants. It banned commercial agencies outright in 2009.
>
> Matchmaking agencies are illegal in the Philippines, Viet Nam and Cambodia, although these regulations are easily flouted. The Philippines requires potential brides to attend pre-departure counseling organised by the Commission on Filipinos Overseas before they are issued a passport for departure with a spousal visa. Courses are provided for specific destinations, principally certain OECD countries as well as Chinese Taipei. In Viet Nam, the government established a required channel for marriage migration, through the Viet Nam Women's Union, and imposed limits in 2005 on the age difference between spouses, health requirements for the foreign spouse, and set a basic level of shared language. The Viet Nam Women's Union also signed a Memorandum of Understanding with the Korean Ministry of Gender Equality and Family, focusing on pre-departure orientation and post-arrival support, integration and rights. In Cambodia, international arranged marriages, considered comparable to human trafficking, were temporarily suspended in 2008. In 2011, an age and income limit was imposed on foreign men wishing to marry Cambodian women.

Various concerns have focused on the difficult integration of marriage migrants and the poor outcomes of their children, whether from previous marriages or born in the country of arrival. Compared with non-Asian OECD countries, where neither marriage migrants nor their children have traditionally been a target of specific labour market integration policies, much greater concern is apparent in Asia. In most OECD countries, the performance of children with one native-born parent is largely similar to that of children of two native-born parents. The results for the 2009 Programme of International Student Assessment (PISA) found that there was no significant difference in reading scores for children of a foreign-born mother and a native-born father, or *vice versa*, when compared with children of two native-born parents. While labour market outcomes for children of one native-born parent and one foreign-born parent tend to be poorer than those of two native-born parents, they are generally much better than those of children of two foreign-born parents (OECD, 2008). Although Korea (and Japan) did not have a sufficient sample of these children for a comparison in PISA, national evidence suggests that the children of marriage migrants have not only poorer performance, but also a much lower school enrolment rate.[13]

To some extent, this reflects the socio-economic characteristics of couples in marriage migration, where the man tends to be poorer than average, and the foreign bride has a lower level of education than her peers. In Korea, less than 20% have a post-secondary education compared with 60% of Korean women (Choi, 2010). Half of these families earn only the minimum wage. While they are more likely to co-habit with their in-laws than Korean or ethnic-Korean couples,[14] child-rearing is largely the mother's responsibility, and childcare is not generally available, so children often arrive at school with poor Korean-language skills. Supplementary private education is common in Korea, but marriage migrant families are poorer and have less access to it in comparison with native families, further limiting their school outcomes. One institutional response has been to offer additional hours of schooling at the secondary-school level, and separate schools for children of marriage migrants, but little has been available for young children.[15]

Future challenges

The implications for migration in the region are significant. The next few decades will see expanding marriage deficits in a number of countries, especially China. Pressure in the marriage market has led to increased marriage migration in a number of countries already, and this could be expected to involve additional countries. The present origin countries of marriage migrants face their own demographic transitions, some with similar looming marriage deficits, and have already shown a reluctance to accept organised international matchmaking. Further, as the impact on local marriage markets is felt and cases of abuse come to the attention of policymakers, the reaction has been negative in countries of origin, where marriage migration brings remittances but is often treated as morally dubious and consequently regulated. Concern over the education and labour market integration outcomes of marriage migrants and their children mean that marriage migration will also play a large role in guiding integration policy choices.[16]

6. Key priorities for origin countries in Asia

In origin countries, policy priorities have converged around several objectives in recent years. Most origin countries still have an excess of labour, especially less skilled labour, and favour migration to traditional destinations of employment in the region and in the Gulf countries, as well as to newer destinations in developed countries offering higher salaries, to relieve pressure on labour markets and to bring remittances. In addition, origin countries have generally placed a priority on sending more skilled workers abroad, as the returns in terms of remittances are much higher, and workers are better able to exert their rights, making issues of worker protection much less problematic. Origin countries also seek to find a balance between pushing for labour rights and protection of their citizens in receiving countries, on the one hand, and ensuring on the other hand that their recruiters do not favour workers from other, less protective, countries.

Countries face the trade-off between promoting less-skilled migration and protecting their citizens working abroad

Origin countries are faced with a double challenge: on the one hand, they seek to increase opportunities for their citizens to work abroad, and compete with other origin countries as a source for workers; and on the other hand they seek to ensure that their citizens who work abroad receive good working and salary conditions and are protected from abuse and exploitation. These two objectives are not always compatible. In democracies, however, as labour migration increases, origin-country governments are pushed to pursue both objectives, as voters become more sensitive. This balance has been particularly difficult to maintain in the case of domestic workers, with a number of countries imposing temporary deployment bans on domestic workers to certain destinations, especially the Gulf countries.

One of the priorities for origin countries in Asia is to increase remittance inflows by increasing not only the number of their workers employed abroad but also the salaries earned by these workers. Whether the result of government policy or independent of policy decisions, remittance inflows to Asian countries have been increasing rapidly in the past decade, parallel to the increase in the number of immigrants (Box III.5). Total inflows of officially recorded remittances reached almost USD 190 billion in 2010, compared with just over USD 40 billion in 2000. Remittances to countries in the region are expected to top USD 200 billion in 2011, with the increase driven by Pakistan (+26%) and China (+8%).

> Box III.5. **Remittance flows have been large and growing, especially within the region**
>
> Remittances constitute an important source of capital for a number of Asian economies. Remittance inflows in 2010 in Nepal represented around 20% of GDP, in Philippines and Bangladesh around 10% of GDP and in Sri Lanka almost 7% of GDP. Separate estimations of bilateral remittance data (World Bank, 2011b) show that almost half (47.6%) of the remittance inflows to non-OECD Asian countries come from OECD countries outside of Asia, followed by inflows from other non-OECD Asian countries (22.8%) and Gulf countries (22.6%) (Table III.11). Asia is the main recipient (82%) of remittances from the GCC countries. Almost the totality of remittance outflows from Asian countries is intra-Asian (93% of total outflows goes to other Asian countries). Japan and Korea represent only 3.4% and 1.1% of total remittance inflows, respectively. Korea, however, began the past decade as a net recipient of remittances, but is now a net supplier of remittances and the main remittance origin country in the region.
>
> Table III.11. **Estimated remittance flows, by origin and receiving country and region, 2010**
> USD million
>
> | Receiving region | Sending region | | | | | |
> |---|---|---|---|---|---|---|
> | | Non-OECD Asian countries | GCC | Japan | Korea | Other OECD (non-Asia) | Other |
> | Non-OECD Asian | 39 579 | 39 182 | 5 938 | 1 912 | 82 752 | 4 334 |
> | Gulf Co-operation Council (GCC) | 6 | 10 | 1 | 0 | 157 | 96 |
> | Japan | 135 | 0 | 0 | 30 | 1 443 | 298 |
> | Korea | 7 | 0 | 785 | 0 | 1 863 | 81 |
> | Non-Asian OECD | 766 | 141 | 376 | 89 | 111 439 | 12 766 |
> | Other | 40 | 8 433 | 1 296 | 1 | 88 999 | 33 482 |
>
> Source: Estimates by World Bank (2011b). StatLink http://dx.doi.org/10.1787/888932617341
>
> India and China were the main remittance recipients in 2010, receiving each over USD 50 billion. The other two main recipients were the Philippines (USD 21 billion) and Bangladesh (USD 11 billion). Remittance outflows have also gained importance during this period, albeit their volume is smaller, around USD 34 billion in 2010 (compared with USD 9 billion in 2000).

> **Box III.5. Remittance flows have been large and growing, especially within the region** *(cont.)*
>
> For a number of countries in the region, the estimated increase in remittances has been even greater. China has multiplied the amount of remittances received in 2000 by almost twelve by 2010, Pakistan by nine, Viet Nam by eight and Indonesia by six. This increase in remittance inflows is related to the rise in the number of immigrants, but also to the higher educational attainment of recent migrants together with improvements in remittance statistics. For example, the number of high-educated Pakistani migrants increased from 202 000 to 311 000 between 2000 and 2005/6, and the trend towards more high-educated migration has continued, and this has led to higher remittance amounts (Kock and Sun, 2011). The incentives to remit might have increased as well in 2010 and 2011 in countries that have seen a sharp depreciation of their currencies, such as India and Bangladesh. The outlook for 2012-14 is that remittance inflows to Asian countries will continue to grow steadily at an annual rate of over 7% (World Bank, 2011a).
>
> In light of the contribution of remittances, one focus of governments has been on reducing the costs of remittances; at the G8 summit in 2009, participating countries pledged to reduce the cost of remittances from 10% to 5% by 2014 (the "5 × 5 Objective"). Among the solutions proposed are to increase transparency by publishing transaction commissions and to shift to partner banks over cash-to-cash transactions.

One means to increase opportunities for employment abroad while protecting workers is through bilateral agreements – which reserve a role for public authorities, in selection or administration of the scheme. The presence of movement of natural persons in the EPAs signed by a number of origin countries with Japan, for example, testifies to the priority of this issue, as does the interest in origin countries in joining and remaining partners in Korea's EPS scheme.

The model for bilateral labour migration agreements – pre-departure training, randomised selection to reduce the risk of rent-taking, mechanisms to protect workers abroad and to encourage their circularity – appears consolidated, although it may not be suited to migration of more skilled workers.[17] Recognition agreements may help transfer the model to the movement of skilled workers, although the broader non-equivalence of education between origin and destination countries may prove to be a greater obstacle than can be resolved in a recognition agreement. Further, the hiring practices for skilled workers, with individual evaluation of candidates, are less conducive to institutional intermediation than recruitment of largely substitutable unskilled and less skilled workers.

Bilateral agreements may be signed between origin and receiving countries to protect workers rather than to facilitate labour migration. Countries have been, in general, reluctant to use the best-known UN convention, the International Convention on the protection of the rights of all migrant workers and members of their families (ICRMW), as a means to protect their citizens working abroad (see Box III.6), preferring to work through bilateral agreements.

The Philippines has been the most successful origin country in Asia to conclude bilateral labour agreements, with 12 agreements with receiving countries, and one with an origin country (Indonesia) in 2007. Under Filipino law, deployment is only allowed to those countries where the rights of Filipino migrant workers are protected. In the absence of sufficient labour laws or efforts to protect migrants in general, the existence of a bilateral agreement is considered a form of protection. However, the Philippines has not signed agreements with the largest countries receiving its nationals (*e.g.* Saudi Arabia, Singapore).[18]

> **Box III.6. Asian countries and the International Convention on the protection of the rights of migrant workers**
>
> The International Convention on the protection of the rights of all migrant workers and members of their families (ICRMW), adopted by the United Nations General Assembly in 1990, establishes minimum standards that States parties should apply to migrant workers and members of their families, reinforcing and completing a series of other measures already taken by the United Nations, and extends them to irregular migrants. No major migration-receiving country has signed the Convention, as it runs counter to many prevailing regulations, such as the right to mobility, to union membership, equal access to public services, or extension of full protection to irregular migrants. Countries of origin of migrants have also been reluctant to sign the ICRMW.
>
> Bangladesh, the Philippines and Sri Lanka, the only Asian countries to ratify the ICRMW, did so for very different reasons.* The Philippines was the first Asian country to ratify the Convention, in a context characterized by widely-publicised cases of Filipino workers being mistreated abroad. The Philippines' own Migrant Workers' Act obliges it to protect its workers abroad, and the ICRMW adds pressure for better conditions for workers in certain countries. Sri Lanka, in contrast, did not experience internal pressure to sign the Convention, has placed reserves on certain articles, and has not implemented it in national law. Bangladesh ratified the ICRMW only in 2011, officially to enhance the country's image and show that Bangladesh is concerned over its migrants abroad.
>
> The disinterest in the Convention as a tool for managing labour migration agreements with origin countries springs from its limited applicability, from the complexity and cost of implementation, and as far as origin countries are concerned from the risk that receiving countries will close access to their labour markets for their nationals. As the countries where most Asian migrants are going have not signed the Convention, its impact in the region is limited. The convention brings reporting and pre-departure training requirements which may be burdensome for governments with little administrative capacity. Further, as with other negotiations with receiving countries, origin countries wish to remain competitive.
>
> * Only a few Asian countries are party to the convention: Philippines (1995), Sri Lanka (1996), Timor-Leste (2004) and Bangladesh (2011). Cambodia and Indonesia (2004) have both signed it but have not ratified it.

The Philippines has also imposed, since 2006, its own contractual requirements on overseas workers: for example, household service workers (maids) must be paid at least USD 400 monthly. Ensuring respect of these conditions is, however, extremely difficult, especially in the absence of co-operation from the receiving country and the strong demand of Filipinos to work as maids abroad even at salaries well below the minimum.

The Indonesian experience with bilateral agreements is indicative of the difficulties countries face in imposing salary requirements on receiving countries. While Indonesia signed a Memorandum of Understanding with Malaysia in 2006, it suspended authorisation of labour migration for household work in 2009, citing insufficient protection of its citizens, especially in terms of respecting contractual conditions. It was not until December 2011 that Indonesia reauthorised its citizens to go back to Malaysia for domestic work, after the Malaysian government agreed to contractual conditions including a rest day and restrictions on employers' ability to hold workers' passports. Indonesia applies a minimum wage for its domestic workers which varies according to the destination country, from USD 210 in Saudi Arabia to 360 in Singapore and 460 in Hong Kong, China. Sri Lanka sets a minimum wage at USD 225. Finally, Bangladesh also imposes a minimum salary on its departing domestic workers, set at USD 200. Malaysia exempts foreign domestic workers from application of its own minimum-wage law, but has accepted, as part of the recent re-opening with Indonesia, to apply the minimum wage to Indonesians.

The threat of facing a deployment ban may not necessarily push destination governments to improve working conditions for foreign workers. Destinations must also ensure they are not shunned by the most qualified domestic workers, those with some education and language skills. The expansion of a mandatory rest day, for example, from Chinese Taipei to Hong Kong, China, and, this year, to Singapore, reflects this response from recruiting countries.

In addition to bilateral agreements for labour migration and workers rights, social security schemes in the country of employment can also affect mobility and the ability of migrant workers to exercise their rights (Pasadilla, 2011).

Origin countries would like to lower migration costs…

The organisation of labour migration in Asia is distinct from that in other regions due to the level of involvement of private fee-taking intermediaries, which result in costs of migration which are very high relative to total earnings abroad, especially for low-skilled labourers and domestic workers. While international labour migration always has costs, including costs of information, documents, required procedures, and fees for visas and certification, workers expect higher earnings abroad to more than offset migration costs (Sjaastad, 1962).

Martin (2011) underlines how Asian labour migrants are subject to high costs in a 4-stage recruitment process. In the first stage, information deficits in origin countries lead workers to pay rents to recruiters' sub-agents. In the second stage, contract negotiation with the licensed recruiter, additional costs for certification and required medical checks and documents may be applied. In the third stage, the worker obtains documents or takes a pre-departure course from public agencies, requiring time or bribes. Finally, the fourth stage is departure, with a valid visa and passport; if there are irregularities, workers may pay to avoid control.

One factor affecting the cost of low-skilled migration costs is the permit regime in the main destination countries for low-skilled labour, the GCC countries. Foreigners must have a local sponsor to enter, work and depart at the end of their stay. Sponsorship allows foreign workers to obtain a visa, and has led to the creation of a market in real and false offers of employment, where sponsorship is sold to intermediaries who sell it on to the worker. Enforcement of existing rules requiring employers to bear recruitment costs is difficult, as has been seen in some OECD countries – *e.g.* in Israel, where rent-taking by employers and false employment offers ("visa-floating") were frequent problems in its temporary labour migration system (OECD, 2011). In destination countries where sponsorship systems are not in place, or where employer rent-taking is less common, low-skill migrants still pay large fees to find work, due to rent-taking opportunities built into the official migration infrastructure in the origin country (see Box III.7).

For labour migrants with specific and special skills, and especially those with recognised certification, intermediation fees are generally absorbed by the employer, and in any case are a small fraction of total earnings. The large number of low-skilled workers competing for a limited number of opportunities for employment abroad, however, drives up the value of the low-skilled jobs for workers, leading to high rents. Martin (2011) estimates that these costs are about one-third of total earnings for low-skilled labourers earning USD 250 a month during a typical 24-36 month contract in the GCC countries or other intra-regional Asian destinations.

> **Box III.7. Rent-taking for low-skilled migration from Asian countries**
>
> Rent-taking is built into the migration infrastructure for low-skilled migration in most origin countries in Asia.
>
> Bangladesh, a growing player in intraregional and international labour migration, is one such example. The public Bangladesh Overseas Employment and Services handles the tiny fraction of skilled workers, but all others pass through private recruitment agencies, both licensed and unlicensed. Migrants paid an average of about USD 3 100 to go abroad to work, of which 90% went to intermediaries, agencies and other helpers (IOM Dhaka, 2010). A number of actors work in the recruitment chain. Recruiters in the capital pay commissions to sub-agents in villages, from which most low-skilled migrants come. Sub-agents may be trusted locals, who accompany the workers through contract and emigration procedures. Labour migrants are not allowed to leave without approval by the public Bureau of Manpower Employment and Training, which requires a short training course. Agents, however, often obtain certificates through paying rents to officials.
>
> The Philippines government attempts to manage labour migration by its citizens closely, through the Philippines Overseas Employment Agency (POEA), created in 1982. The POEA regulates private agencies, which mediate most recruitment, and is responsible for enforcing a limit on recruitment fees to one month's salary. Agencies must post bonds and are legally responsible, along with the foreign employer, for the contracts they mediate. The system has not entirely eliminated illegal fees, since the demand for employment opportunities abroad remains high. A 2007 survey of Filipina domestic workers found that more than half had paid illegally high fees of USD 1 200-2 000 (MFMFW, 2007)
>
> Labour migrants have gone abroad from Thailand since the 1970s, with private employment agencies handling most of the placements until recently. While agencies are licensed, there is little oversight, high fees are frequently charged, and the use of double contracts (a false contract is shown to the Thai authorities, while a contract with lower wage and worse conditions is signed with the employer) is common (Chantavanich et al., 2010). While service fees and recruitment fees are limited by law – to several multiples of monthly wages, for contracts over a year – actual costs are often higher. Employment in Chinese Taipei, where wages are relatively high and permits are few, may cost almost USD 7 000 and even seasonal berry-picking in Sweden almost USD 3 000. Agencies commonly pay brokers in receiving countries for job openings, passing the cost onto migrants. The share of employment agency mediation in placement fell from 70% in 1999 to less than 40% in 2007, as more workers used – or claimed – direct recruitment to save on placement fees. The government requires workers – including those directly hired – to receive approval from the Department of Employment for labour migration.
>
> The recruitment model of local sub-agents is frequent in other major origin countries, such as Indonesia and Viet Nam. Sub-agents are a challenge for enforcement of legislation on fees, since they often operate in cash and outside of any regulatory framework.

... while maintaining a key role for public institutions in managing labour migration

Governments in origin countries maintain a strong institutional control over exiting labour migrants, through an agency (in the Philippines, Indonesia, Pakistan and Sri Lanka) or ministry (in India and Indonesia) responsible for migration. Public management of outgoing labour migration is a means for improving the protection of migrants, monitoring their movements and certifying their skills, but also a revenue stream, as fees and pre-departure training may be imposed on migrants. Governments are also responsible for regulating private agencies, who play the principal role in matching supply and demand, and policing unlicensed recruiters and sub-agents, who also play a key role in matching, especially for low-skilled employment. In the Philippines, for example, the POEA regulates the international recruitment industry, assists Overseas Filipino Workers (OFWs) pre- and at departure, and protects workers when abroad. The Philippines also has a Commission on Overseas Filipinos (CFO), responsible for diaspora relations and migration and development; the CFO provides pre-departure training to permanent emigrants, including marriage migrants.

The institutional role in managing labour migration has tended to increase in recent years, with the expansion of pre-departure requirements in a number of countries. While fee-based mandatory services increase migration costs, the main target for cost reduction in sending countries remains private recruitment costs and transaction fees for remittances, rather than fees related to maintaining or expanding the institutional infrastructure for migration governance.

The shared interest in increasing migration, improving protection and reducing costs has also led to regional dialogue. The Colombo Process is a Regional Consultation Process, underway since 2003, bringing together most of the origin countries of labour migrants in Asia, to improve the management of overseas employment and its impact on development. As with other consultation process, it is primarily focused on sharing information and good practices.

... and increasing skilled migration

Most origin countries in Asia, from which organised labour migration is largely low-skilled, see increased outmigration of skilled workers as a positive development and a policy objective, as higher skilled workers, compared with low-skilled labour migrants of similar duration of stay, have the potential to remit more, and represent less of a concern in terms of the need for protection.

Skilled migration is not limited to professionals, and may include trades and other qualified workers. For example, in the Philippines, which has the most developed system for managing expatriate workers, the POEA is largely responsible for tracking and supporting the deployment of Philippines citizens working overseas (OFWs). As the overall strategy of the Philippines is to increase the skill level of its labour migrants, some effort to ensure the qualifications of workers is made. OFWs are required to prove their skill level prior to departure, from accredited skills-testing centres, or from higher-education bodies. Certification of skills is meant to ensure that Filipinos are perceived as more productive than those from countries with no trusted verification, and to increase their attractiveness for recruiters. In Indonesia, the government has an objective of reducing migration by the less-educated, and has set a deadline of 2017 after which the minimum qualification for working abroad will be secondary education. Indonesia hopes to not only ensure that workers are able to avoid abuse, but also to prevent workers from being sent back to Indonesia for lack of skills.

Overseas employment in the region is heavily dependent on demand from GCC countries, where the opportunities for skilled and semi-skilled labour migration have been put into question by the trend towards favouring local employment and imposing quotas on foreign employment in private-sector businesses. Saudi Arabia's "Saudization" rules, for example, impose limits on the number of foreign workers in private sector firms and the duration of stay. Similar quotas in other GCC countries may reduce demand for skilled and semi-skilled labour from Asia, and origin countries are seeking new destinations.

The increasing level of education among youth cohorts, noted above, means that for most Asian countries the risk of brain drain is not a primary policy concern, and the issue does not temper interest in increased skilled migration abroad.

7. Conclusion

This part has reviewed some of the emerging issues and key challenges in international migration in Asia. Asia has long been a major player in international migration, but its role is changing as more Asian countries become both sources and destinations for intraregional migration, and this will have implications for migration outside the region. OECD countries have benefitted from Asian migration, which has supplied skilled workers who have had, in most cases, good labour market outcomes. In addition, enrolment of Asians is a large component of international study in OECD countries, and many of these students have stayed on.

It is not so obvious that OECD countries will be able to rely on this steady stream of skilled workers in the future. As Asia develops, it will produce more skilled workers, but also foster the conditions for them to remain, and attract skilled workers from other parts of the world. The policies to attract and retain skilled workers in a number of Asian non-member economies are converging with those common in the OECD, although some, like China, have not yet revised their policy to reflect their new role in international mobility.

Low-skilled migration represents another area where practice is evolving. Future demand in developed countries will not only be restricted to highly skilled occupations. Asian origin countries, where the workforce already contemplates employment abroad and where the institutional infrastructure for negotiating and implementing bilateral agreements is already in place, are looking forward to meeting these needs. While most OECD countries have, since the 1970s, largely abandoned large-scale international recruitment through bilateral agreements, a model has nonetheless developed in Asia, with the Korea EPS as the main example. From the point of view of countries recruiting low-skilled labour, the Korean model may be a solution to issues of rent-taking, language skills, and international matching – issues which were secondary during the epoch of guest-worker programmes in European OECD countries, and for which few other successful models are evident. If bilateral agreements for less skilled labour are resuscitated in other OECD countries, this evolution will have to be taken into account, as well as origin-country concerns over worker protection and the cost of migration. In any case, bilateral agreements which work well for the low-skilled appear less applicable to skilled migration, especially towards OECD countries.

Origin countries have also become willing to jeopardise labour migration channels with receiving countries over the protection of their workers, even going so far as to implement deployment bans. Some non-member Asian destination economies, faced with strong domestic demand on the one hand, and an interest in increasing the cost of foreign workers to discourage their recruitment on the other, have become more willing to improve wage and working conditions. Despite the labour surplus in a number of countries in the region, then, conditions may improve even for less skilled labour migrants. As labour market slack persists in many OECD countries and wages increase in faster-growing Asian economies, incentives to migration may diminish for some categories of workers, notably the most highly skilled.

Still, the region will have a surplus of low-skilled labour in the near future. As demand for low-skilled labour is unlikely to grow enormously in the short-term, especially with restrictive policies in place in destination countries, gains in market share by one country of origin will come at the expense of other countries. Many countries look to the Philippines as a model of how to integrate surplus labour into the global labour market – in different sectors, towards different destinations, and at different skill levels – while protecting their rights. Yet the Philippines' successful overseas employment system has created a structural dependency on migration and remittances.

As the growth in demand for low-skilled migration remains limited in GCC and OECD destination countries as well as within Asia, there will be little scope to increase significantly the supply of this type of migrants. Many Asian sending countries, including the Philippines, have decided to address this challenge by increasing the skill level of their emigrants without much concern, so far, about the risk of brain drain, including in sensitive sectors such as health and education.

While demography does not necessarily determine the nature and magnitude of migration flows, the profound demographic transition underway in Asian countries has already begun to affect migration in the region, and will likely determine part of future movements. One feature specific to Asia is the marriage deficit and changing marriage market, which may affect migration in many directions, as women migrate for marriage and unmarried men seek to improve their position in the marriage market through migration.

Finally, destination countries in the region have opened opportunities for settlement for the highly skilled. Settlement – or at least longer duration of stay – is also becoming more frequent for less skilled migrants. Increased acquisition of permanent residence through marriage or other means is likely to be accompanied by integration challenges. Several Asian countries have adopted measures to support the integration of immigrants and their children, but more comprehensive strategies might be needed in the future to address this emerging policy challenge.

Notes

1. This part covers Asian economies ranging from South Asia to East and Southeast Asia, two Special Autonomous Regions of China, and Chinese Taipei. The part covers two Asian OECD countries (Japan and Korea) and three countries with which the OECD has enhanced engagement (China, India and Indonesia). Individual economies in the region vary considerably in terms of their state of development and their growth rates. In addition to Japan and Korea, several wealthy city states (Singapore and two Special Autonomous Regions of China, Hong Kong and Macao), and a small oil-rich sultanate (Brunei), the region contains the world's most populous countries (China and India), one of its fastest developing middle-income countries (Malaysia), and some of its poorest countries (Afghanistan, Cambodia, Laos and Nepal).

2. This may reflect the limited opportunities for tertiary education in these countries, since many of those born in the country who have a tertiary education will have studied and remained abroad.

3. The statistical data for Israel are supplied by and under the responsibility of the relevant Israeli authorities. The use of such data by the OECD is without prejudice to the status of the Golan Heights, East Jerusalem and Israeli settlements in the West Bank under the terms of international law.

4. These figures include students at all levels, including non-tertiary and short-term study. Singapore does not publish figures on international students in universities. Based on reported figures for total enrolment, and considering that international students comprised 18% of university enrolment in 2011, with a cap imposed at 20%, there are about 12 000 international students in Singapore universities.

5. Nominal USD GDP at market exchange rates in 2010.

6. ASEAN Community: Brunei Darussalam, Cambodia, Indonesia, Laos, Malaysia, Myanmar, Philippines, Singapore, Thailand, Viet Nam.

7. This permit class includes the skilled workers in P, Q and PE Passes, but not the less-skilled S Pass, work permits and domestic workers.

8. A decade earlier, in 2001, there were 250 000 invited foreign experts, of which 105 000 long-term experts. An additional 70 000 foreign workers in other categories were registered at the end of 2002.

9. Chinese Taipei extended the maximum stay from nine to twelve years in 2012.

10. Singapore allows qualified and experienced tradespeople to stay for up to 18 years.

11. Hong Kong, China, imposed a USD 50 monthly "Employees Retraining Levy" in 1992 on foreign workers, extended in 2003 to foreign domestic helpers, with funds destined to retrain local workers. More than USD 600 million were collected in the first five years, but employers – especially those of domestic helpers – complained of the burden, and the levy was suspended in 2008 and is now due to be reinstated in 2013.

12. While Chinese brides accounted for almost 7% of all marriages by Korean men in Korea in 2005, this had fallen to 3% in 2010, while the proportion of brides from Viet Nam, Philippines, Cambodia and Mongolia rose above 4%. In 2004, in Chinese Taipei, 16% of all marriages were with foreigners not from Mainland China, while less than 10% were with mainland Chinese (some of the marriage migrants from other countries were, however, ethnic Chinese). The proportion has since diminished, with mainland Chinese representing 10% of marriages and other foreigners representing 4% of marriages in 2010.

13. According to Korean Parliamentary Inspection Policy Reports (2008, 2010), the enrolment rates in elementary, middle and high school were 85%, 84% and 71%, compared with 97%, 95% and 89% for the general student population. 70% of the children of marriage migrants enrolled in high school were failing.

14. 42% of Cambodian wives and 35% of Vietnamese wives co-habit with their in-laws, compared with 12% for local couples and co-ethnic couples, according to Lee (2010).

15. The Korean Ministry of Education, Science and Technology announced the opening of 26 special pre-schools for these children in 2012, providing language support in the six months before starting regular schooling.

16. Korea began to develop an official policy for integration of marriage migrants in the mid-2000s. The term "multicultural family" was adopted in 2006, and integration of marriage migrants is one of the central objectives of the 2008 First [5-year] Basic Plan for Immigration Policy.

17. Sri Lanka signed such an agreement with Italy in 2011, focusing on semi-skilled workers.

18. The Philippines and Indonesia faced a 6-month recruitment ban in Saudi Arabia due to insistence on minimum wage and working conditions for domestic workers, although Saudi Arabia finally agreed to the conditions in 2012. Indonesia has suspended domestic workers from going to Saudi Arabia in the past over concern over contractual issues, but also in reaction to execution of its labour migrants.

References

Abella, M. (2008), "Challenges to Governance of Labour Migration in Asia Pacific", paper presented at PECC-ABAC Conference on International Labor Mobility, Seoul, Korea.

Aspiring Minds (2010), "National IT/ITeS Employability Study", Gurgaon, India.

Azizah, K. (2005), "Illegal Immigrants and the State in Sabah: Conflicting Interests and the Contest of Will", in Proceedings of Seminar on State Responses to the Presence and Employment of Foreign Workers in Sabah, Universiti Malaysia Sabah, Sabah, pp. 1-35.

Barro, R. and J.-W. Lee (2010), "A New Data Set of Educational Attainment in the World, 1950-2010", NBER Working Paper No. 15902.

Chantavanich S., S. Laodumrongchai and P. Vangsiriphisal (2010), "Understanding the Recruitment Industry in Thailand", Asian Research Center for Migration, Bangkok.

Chiu, L.-C. and J. Hou (2007), "Determinants of Highly-Skilled Migration – Taiwan's Experiences", Chung-Hua Institution for Economic Research, *Working Paper Series* No. 2007-1, Taipei.

Choi, K.-S. (2010), "Medium- and Long-term Effects of Immigrant or Foreign Labor Force Entering the Domestic Labor Market", *Policy Analysis Series* 2010-18, Korea Development Institute 2010, pp. 24-25.

Coe, D.C. (2008), "Globalisation and Labour Markets: Policy Issues Arising from the Emergence of China and India", OECD Social, Employment and Migration Working Papers No. 63, OECD Publishing, Paris.

Das, P. (2010), "India's Border Management: Select Documents", Institute for Defence Studies and Analyses, New Delhi.

Gereffi, G., V. Wadhwa, B. Rissing and R. Ong (2008), "Getting the Numbers Right: International Engineering Education in the United States, China and India", *Journal of Engineering Education*, pp. 13-25.

Hugo, G. (2011), "Irregular International Migration in Asia", background paper for the OECD, unpublished.

Hunger, U. (2004), "Indian IT Entrepreneurs in the US and in India: An Illustration of the Brain Gain Hypothesis", *Journal of Comparative Policy Analysis*, Vol. 6, No. 2, pp. 99-109, August 2004.

Hur, J.-J. (2010), "The Economics and Governance of Korea's Migrant Worker Policy", presented at the IPS and World Bank Labor Mobility and Development Conference, Singapore, 1-2 June 2010.

ILO (2008), "Decent Work for Migrants through Decent Talks by Countries: Improving the Management of Labour Migration to Korea through Bilateral Cooperation", Bangkok.

IOM Dhaka (2010), "Final Report on the Bangladesh Household Remittance Survey 2009", www.iom.org.bd/publications/The%20Bangladesh%20Household%20Remittance%20Survey%202009%20.pdf.

Kharas, H. (2010), "The Emerging Middle Class in Developing Countries", OECD *Development Centre Working Paper* No. 285, OECD Publishing, Paris.

Kock, U. and Y. Sun (2011), "Remittances in Pakistan – Why they have gone up, and why aren't they coming down?", IMF Working Paper WC/11/200.

Lee, H.K. (2010), "Characteristics of international marriage couples and families", in Statistics Korea. *Korean Social Trends 2010*: 47-55 (in Korean).

Lee, H.K. (2011), "Marriage Migration in Asian Countries", background paper for the OECD, unpublished.

Maddison, A. (2008), *Chinese Economic Performance in the Long Run, 960-2030 AD*, 2nd Edition, Development Centre Studies, OECD Publishing, Paris.

Martin, P.L. (2011), "Migration Costs in Asia", background paper for the OECD, unpublished.

MFMFW (2007), "Overcharging by Recruitment Agencies and Burdensome Philippine Government Fees Eat Up Wages and Remittances of Filipino Migrant Workers – Survey Report on Recruitment Fees, Wages and Remittances of Filipino Migrant Workers in Hong Kong – 2007", Mission For Migrant Workers, Hong Kong.

Ministry of Home Affairs of India (2000), "Border Management, Reforming the National Security System – Recommendations of Group of Ministers", Ministry of Home Affairs of India.

National Science Board (2010), *Science and Engineering Indicators 2010*, Arlington, VA: National Science Foundation (NSB 10-01).

Nho, Y. and J.-J. Hur (2010), "The Impact of Temporary Immigration of Unskilled Workers on Firm Performances: Evidences from the Korean Small-Medium Business Sector", Presented at the IPS and World Bank Labor Mobility and Development Conference, Singapore, 1-2 June 2010.

NIDS (2010), "Nepal Migration Year Book 2009", Nepal Institute of Development Studies, Kathmandu.

OECD (2004), *Migration for Employment – Bilateral Agreements at a Crossroads*, OECD Publishing, Paris.

OECD (2007), "Immigrant Health Workers in the Broader Context of Highly Skilled Migration", in *International Migration Outlook*, pp. 161-228, OECD Publishing, Paris.

OECD (2008), *Jobs for Immigrants – Vol. 2: Labour Market Integration in Belgium, France, the Netherlands and Portugal*, OECD Publishing, Paris.

OECD (2010), *OECD Economic Survey of China*, OECD Publishing, Paris.

OECD (2011), "International Migration in Israel", in *International Migration Outlook*, OECD Publishing, Paris.

OECD (2012), "Long-Term Growth Scenarios", paper prepared for Working Party No. 1 on Macroeconomic and Structural Policy Analysis ECO/CPE/WP1(2012)5.

Pasadilla, G.O. (2011), "Social Security and Labor Migration in ASEAN", *ADBI Research Policy Brief* 34, ADBI, Tokyo.

Sciortino, R. and S. Punpuing (2009), *International Migration in Thailand 2009*, International Organization for Migration, Thailand Office, Bangkok.

Sjaastad, L.A. (1962), "The Costs and Returns of Human Migration", *The Journal of Political Economy*, Vol. 70, No. 5. Part 2: Investment in Human Beings. pp. 80-93.

United Nations, Department of Economic and Social Affairs, Population Division (2009), *Trends in International Migrant Stock: The 2008 Revision*.

Van Welsum, D. and T.-T. Xu (2007), "Is China the New Centre for Offshoring of IT and ICT-Enabled Services?", *Working Paper* DSTI/ICCP/IE(2006)10/FINA, OECD Publishing, Paris.

Vasuprasat, P. (2010), *Agenda for labour migration policy in Thailand: Towards long-term competitiveness*, ILO Bangkok.

Wang, H.-Z. and H.H.M. Hsaio (2009) (eds.), *Cross-Border Marriages with Asian Characteristics*, Academia Sinica, Taipei.

World Bank (2011a), "Outlook for Remittance Flows 2012-14", *Migration and Development Brief*, No. 17, World Bank, Washington, DC.

World Bank (2011b), *Migration and Remittances Factbook 2011*, World Bank, Washington, DC.

Zweig, D. (2006), "Learning to Compete: China's Efforts to Encourage a Reverse Brain Drain", in Kuptsch, C. and E.F. Pang (eds.): *Competing for Global Talent*, International Institute for Labour Studies, Geneva.

ANNEX III.A1

Supplementary tables

Table III.A1.1. **Migrants from Asia in OECD countries by place of birth, gender, education level, and recent migration, 2005/06**

Place of birth	Gender	All migrants					Recent migrants only			
		Recent	Emigrant population	Gender distribution	Low-educated	Highly-educated	Emigrant population	Gender distribution	Low-educated	Highly-educated
		Percentage	Thousands	Percentages			Thousands	Percentages		
Afghanistan	Men	21	142	55	41	26	30	50	54	17
	Women	25	117	45	49	21	29	50	63	12
Bangladesh	Men	21	222	56	33	44	46	53	33	44
	Women	23	176	44	43	30	41	47	36	36
Brunei Darussalam	Men	12	5	48	15	51	1	44	51	16
	Women	14	5	52	20	51	1	56	40	23
Bhutan	Men	13	1	59	44	30		60	1	73
	Women	12	1	41	29	45		40	12	63
China	Men	24	1 254	46	24	47	299	46	19	51
	Women	24	1 470	54	27	43	355	54	20	50
Hong Kong, China	Men	8	277	48	15	56	22	48	22	39
	Women	8	300	52	18	52	24	52	17	42
Indonesia	Men	12	153	45	14	45	18	40	9	51
	Women	14	183	55	21	39	26	60	16	50
India	Men	28	1 469	53	14	67	417	53	11	74
	Women	28	1 306	47	20	59	363	47	16	68
Japan	Men	26	229	38	7	58	59	41	5	68
	Women	22	377	62	9	52	83	59	5	61
Korea[1]	Men	15	717	43	13	49	105	43	12	58
	Women	14	934	57	17	42	128	57	11	57
Laos	Men	3	126	49	35	22	4	39	51	16
	Women	5	130	51	47	17	6	61	59	10
Sri Lanka	Men	17	227	52	27	37	39	48	27	40
	Women	20	206	48	31	31	42	52	33	30
Macao, China	Men	9	8	43	22	44	1	72	60	14
	Women	3	11	57	21	45		28	11	31
Maldives	Men	65	1	55	11	67		52	3	85
	Women	74		45	4	76		48	3	82
Myanmar	Men	27	38	48	23	45	10	48	40	27
	Women	27	41	52	28	44	11	52	43	33
Mongolia	Men	18	5	37	16	51	1	25	34	41
	Women	30	9	63	18	45	3	75	31	32
Malaysia	Men	21	109	44	10	61	23	45	8	54
	Women	21	137	56	13	56	28	55	9	47

Table III.A1.1. **Migrants from Asia in OECD countries by place of birth, gender, education level, and recent migration, 2005/06** (cont.)

Place of birth		All migrants					Recent migrants only			
		Recent	Emigrant population	Gender distribution	Low-educated	Highly-educated	Emigrant population	Gender distribution	Low-educated	Highly-educated
	Gender	Percentage	Thousands	Percentages			Thousands	Percentages		
Nepal	Men	46	38	61	13	54	17	55	14	51
	Women	59	24	39	24	36	14	45	22	32
Pakistan	Men	23	472	56	30	44	110	58	29	49
	Women	22	371	44	41	33	80	42	36	39
Philippines	Men	17	966	39	13	49	164	39	18	52
	Women	17	1 536	61	14	53	256	61	15	58
Papua New Guinea	Men	12	13	45	14	37	2	46	10	44
	Women	12	15	55	22	42	2	54	24	57
Singapore	Men	21	55	46	13	54	11	45	5	59
	Women	21	65	54	19	52	14	55	10	59
Thailand	Men	17	113	33	22	36	19	25	33	41
	Women	25	234	67	35	32	59	75	37	39
Timor-Leste	Men	4	6	50	54	14		38	83	6
	Women	7	6	50	51	13		62	74	9
Chinese Taipei	Men	14	195	44	6	72	27	41	11	64
	Women	16	247	56	8	68	38	59	8	62
Viet Nam	Men	7	855	49	29	30	59	38	32	19
	Women	11	903	51	38	25	98	62	38	16
OECD Asian migrants	Men	17	946	42	11	51	164	44	9	61
	Women	16	1 311	58	14	45	212	56	9	58
Non-OECD Asian migrants	Men	20	6 748	47	21	49	1 319	47	19	55
	Women	20	7 492	53	25	45	1 493	53	22	51
Other migrants	Men	18	36 626	50	38	25	6 608	50	38	27
	Women	17	37 261	50	39	25	6 508	50	35	29

1. Korea includes North and South Korea, as well as not specified categories.
Source: DIOC 2005/06.

StatLink http://dx.doi.org/10.1787/888932617360

Table III.A1.2. **Migration flows from Asian countries by destination, 2010 or most recent year**
Thousands

Country of origin	Nepal	Bangladesh	Indonesia	Sri Lanka	Thailand	India	Pakistan	Philippines	Viet Nam
Destination	2010/11	2010	2011	2010	2011	2010	2008	2010	2010
Bahrain	4.6	21.8	..	7.1	1.1	15.1	5.9	15.4	..
Kuwait	15.2	0.0	2.7	48.1	2.8	37.7	6.3	87.8	..
Oman	2.4	42.6	7.3	6.4	0.4	105.8	37.6	11.0	..
Qatar	103.0	12.1	16.6	53.6	3.4	45.8	10.2	53.0	0.3
Saudi Arabia	71.1	7.1	137.6	70.9	0.6	275.2	138.5	293.0	2.7
United Arab Emirates	44.5	203.3	39.8	42.2	9.6	130.9	222.1	201.2	5.2
GCC countries	**240.8**	**287.0**	**204.0**	**228.3**	**17.8**	**610.4**	**420.5**	**661.5**	**8.3**
Japan	0.6	0.0	2.4	0.1	9.3	..	0.0	5.9	4.9
Korea	3.7	2.7	11.2	5.3	11.0	..	2.3	11.7	8.6
OECD-Asia countries	**4.3**	**2.7**	**13.7**	**5.4**	**20.3**	**0.0**	**2.3**	**17.6**	**13.5**
Brunei Darussalam	0.0	2.2	10.8	0.0	3.4	0.0	0.1	7.9	..
Chinese Taipei	0.0	0.0	75.6	0.0	47.8	..	0.0	36.9	28.5
Hong Kong, China	0.1	0.0	50.3	0.3	2.8	..	0.0	101.3	..
Malaysia	105.9	0.9	133.9	3.7	4.3	20.6	1.8	9.8	11.7
Singapore	0.0	39.1	47.5	1.0	11.5	..	0.0	70.3	..
Non-OECD Asia	**107.4**	**42.2**	**323.0**	**10.2**	**77.9**	**20.8**	**2.1**	**263.5**	**49.3**
OECD Non-Asia	**1.0**	**6.9**	**19.5**	**2.0**	**22.9**	**0.0**	**4.0**	**73.4**	**..**
MENA countries	**0.7**	**36.7**	**5.4**	**16.4**	**2.9**	**3.9**	**1.3**	**21.6**	**..**
Non-OECD Europe	**0.2**	**0.0**	**0.3**	**2.8**	**0.9**	**0.0**	**0.1**	**4.5**	**..**
Others	0.2	15.3	15.2	1.4	5.0	6.2	1.5	81.6	14.5

Notes: Figures are for overseas workers whose departure is recorded by the government agencies in the origin country. Coverage of individual departures for employment may be partial or limited to employment under bilateral agreements. Some countries (*e.g.* India) do not record departures for employment to OECD countries. Data for Indonesia include both formal and informal placements. Sailors are excluded from the data for most countries. GCC refers to the Gulf Co-operation Council (Bahrain, Kuwait, Oman, Qatar, Saudi Arabia, and United Arab Emirates). 1. MENA refers to Middle East and North Africa, according to the World Bank definition; for this table, MENA excludes OECD member and GCC countries.

Sources: Nepal – Dept. Foreign Employment. Bangladesh – BMET. Indonesia – BNP2TKI. Sri Lanka – BFE. Thailand – Office of Overseas Employment Administration, DOE. India – MOIA. Pakistan – Bureau of Emigration and Overseas Employment. Philippines – POEA. Viet Nam – MoLISA.

StatLink ⟶ http://dx.doi.org/10.1787/888932617379

PART IV

Country notes: Recent changes in migration movements and policies

Australia

In 2010-11, Australia's combined migration and humanitarian programmes totalled 182 500, slightly higher than the 2009-10 figure, and the second highest level on record after 2008-09. 92% of places came under the migration programme – 62% through the skill stream and 30% through the family stream – and 8% through the humanitarian programme. For the first time, China was the main source of new migrants to Australia, accounting for an 18% share of the 2010-11 Migration Program, up from a 10% share a decade ago. In addition, over 34 500 New Zealand permanent settlers came under the Trans-Tasman Travel Arrangement, 41% more than in 2009-10. For 2011-12, the overall size of the migration and humanitarian programmes is set at 199 750 places, comprising 125 850 skilled migration, 58 600 family, and 13 750 humanitarian places.

The Australian economy, which experienced a mild downturn during the global financial crisis of 2008-09, made a quick recovery during 2010 and rising global demand for commodities led to regional labour shortages. Business Long Stay visas grew by 33% in 2010-11, after a 33% fall in the previous year. The Working Holiday Maker programme grew by 6% in 2010-11, returning to its 2008-09 levels. Conditions surrounding the small Pacific Season Worker Pilot Scheme were eased in 2010: workers may now stay for four months, and more regions, employers and partner countries are eligible. Visas issued under the scheme increased fivefold, albeit remaining below 500, and are expected to increase in 2011-12.

Inflows of international students continued to drop in 2010-11, with a 7% decrease in visa grants compared to 2009-10. The number of students from abroad fell 21%, while student visas granted to temporary migrants already resident in Australia increased 11%. Stricter checks on applications from selected countries, increased financial requirements, and the appreciation of the Australian dollar all contributed to the decline. A review of the student visa programme, released in September 2011, contained a number of recommendations, including: streamlined visa processing for university enrolment, with lower up-front fund requirements; a requirement that applicants prove that they are both a genuine student and a temporary entrant to Australia; and post-study work rights for certain students, tied to course duration. A first set of recommendations were implemented in November 2011.

The number of asylum seekers arriving in Australia by boat (largely on Christmas Island) decreased by 11% compared to 2009-10, to 4 730 new arrivals. Figures for 2010-11 and 2009-10 have, however, been much higher than in previous years, leading the government to explore new possibilities to discourage such inflows.

Net overseas migration declined from a peak of 315 700 for the year ending December 2008 to 167 000 just over two years later. In May 2011, the first-ever Population Strategy was released, emphasising the role of migration in supporting regional growth. The 2011-12 Budget introduced three new migration initiatives to aid the process of structural adjustment to potentially sustained high levels of the terms of trade and the Australian dollar. For major new resource projects, developers may recruit overseas labour under Enterprise Migration Agreements, which will specify the type, number and visa duration for temporary foreign workers. Regional Migration Agreements, in partnership with employers, unions, and local and state governments as well as the federal government, will be introduced for regions where there is an overall shortage of workers, regardless of skill level. First-priority visa processing under the migration programme will be granted to applicants under the Regional Sponsored Migration Scheme.

In July 2011, a government report estimated that illegal employment of foreigners accounted for less than 1% of total employment, and proposed broader sanctions for employers hiring unauthorised workers.

Reform to the skilled migration programme is ongoing. A new points test for General Skilled Migration took effect from July 2011. The government has also announced the introduction from July 2012 of a new two-step regime for skilled migration ("Skill-Select"). Applicants must first submit an electronic expression of interest for a skilled migration visa. In the second step, according to the number of visas available, a sub-set will be invited to apply. Only those invited to apply will be legally entitled to a decision, which will favour efficient processing.

For further information:
www.immi.gov.au

Recent trends in migrants' flows and stocks
AUSTRALIA

Migration flows (foreigners) National definition	2000	2005	2009	2010	Average		Level ('000)
					2001-05	2006-10	2010
Per 1 000 inhabitants							
Inflows	5.6	7.9	10.1	9.3	6.8	9.3	206.7
Outflows	0.5	0.7	0.8	0.8	0.6	0.7	18.3

Migration inflows (foreigners) by type	Thousands		% distribution	
Permit based statistics (standardised)	2009	2010	2009	2010
Work	51.7	46.5	23.4	22.3
Family (incl. accompanying family)	119.6	121.3	54.1	58.0
Humanitarian	14.9	14.6	6.7	7.0
Free movements	33.0	24.4	14.9	11.7
Others	1.8	2.2	0.8	1.0
Total	221.0	209.0	100.0	100.0

Inflows of top 10 nationalities as a % of total inflows of foreigners

2000-2009 annual average / 2010

United Kingdom, China, New Zealand, India, South Africa, Philippines, Sri Lanka, Malaysia, Korea, Viet Nam

Temporary migration	2005	2009	2010	Average
				2006-10
Thousands				
International students	116.7	227.9	158.2	176.2
Trainees	7.0	5.3	3.7	5.4
Working holiday makers	104.4	187.7	175.7	153.2
Seasonal workers	..	0.1	0.1	0.1
Intra-company transfers	..	6.0	6.0	5.1
Other temporary workers	71.6	126.7	91.1	114.8

Inflows of asylum seekers	2000	2005	2009	2010	Average		Level
					2001-05	2006-10	2010
Per 1 000 inhabitants	0.7	0.2	0.3	0.4	0.3	0.2	8 246

Components of population growth	2000	2005	2009	2010	Average		Level ('000)
					2001-05	2006-10	2010
Per 1 000 inhabitants							
Total	12.3	14.3	19.8	..	12.8	..	..
Natural increase	6.3	6.5	7.2	..	6.0	..	..
Net migration	5.8	6.7	12.7	..	6.0	..	..

Stocks of immigrants	2000	2005	2009	2010	Average		Level ('000)
					2001-05	2006-10	2010
Percentage of the total population							
Foreign-born population	23.0	24.2	26.4	26.8	23.6	25.8	5 994
Foreign population	..	..	..	..	..	..	

Naturalisations	2000	2005	2009	2010	Average		Level
					2001-05	2006-10	2010
Percentage of the foreign population	..	..	..	..	..	..	95 284

Labour market outcomes	2000	2005	2009	2010	Average	
					2001-05	2006-10
Employment/population ratio						
Native-born men	..	79.9	78.8	79.2	78.8	80.0
Foreign-born men	..	74.6	75.1	77.0	73.2	76.3
Native-born women	..	67.0	69.0	68.5	65.6	68.9
Foreign-born women	..	58.0	59.5	60.3	55.5	59.7
Unemployment rate						
Native-born men	..	4.9	5.6	5.3	6.0	4.7
Foreign-born men	..	5.2	6.5	5.1	6.1	5.0
Native-born women	..	5.2	5.0	5.2	5.8	4.8
Foreign-born women	..	5.5	6.9	6.1	6.4	5.8

Macroeconomic indicators	2000	2005	2009	2010	Average		Level
					2001-05	2006-10	2010
Annual growth in %							
Real GDP	2.1	3.1	2.3	2.5	3.5	2.7	
GDP/capita (level in USD)	0.8	1.6	0.3	0.7	2.2	0.8	40 719
Employment (level in thousands)	2.6	3.5	0.7	2.7	2.1	2.4	11 305
Percentage of the labour force							
Unemployment	6.2	5.0	5.6	5.2	5.9	4.8	

Notes and sources are at the end of the part.

StatLink http://dx.doi.org/10.1787/888932615992

Austria

In 2010, according to national statistics, the total inflow of foreign nationals to Austria was 98 300, up 7% over 2009, when there had been a decline related to the economic crisis. At the same time, outflows remained fairly stable at 66 400, leading to net immigration of foreign nationals of 31 900, 24% higher than in 2009.

One third of all new immigrants to Austria came from countries outside the European Economic Area (EEA) and Switzerland, a higher share than in 2009. Another third came from the EU15, 16% from the EU10 and 21% from Romania and Bulgaria. Germany remained the main origin country, making up one quarter of total inflows. Immigration of Germans has been diminishing in importance, in favour of the countries that entered the European Union (EU) in 2004 and 2007. In contrast, the inflows of third country citizens were similar to those in 2009, although immigration of citizens from Serbia and Montenegro more than tripled. Taken together, the successor countries of the former Yugoslavia accounted for 11% of new immigrants, and Turkey 4%.

The total permanent inflows of third-country nationals was 16 200 in 2010. Family migration of family members of Austrian or EEA-citizens, which is not subject to quotas, accounted for almost two-thirds of this. Among the 4 400 persons who acquired residence permits under the quota system, only about 610 were admitted under the key worker scheme, while the remainder were mostly family members of third-country nationals.

The inflow of temporary migrants continued to decline slightly in 2010 to 16 700. The slow decline is due to fewer third-country national seasonal workers, as demand is increasingly filled by nationals from new EU member countries. Seasonal workers, however, still comprise two-thirds of temporary inflows. Seasonal labour migration of less than 6 months is not subject to permits, and is regulated by special work-visas. The second major group was international students from outside the EEA whose share rose to 21%. The total number of temporary residence permits acquired by third-country nationals rose slightly to 6 200.

The number of asylum seekers rose from 2007 to reach 15 800 in 2009. In 2010 the numbers declined again to 11 000. Inflows started to climb again from mid-2011, and the total for 2011 was 14 400. The main countries of origin continued to be Afghanistan and the Russian Federation, followed by Pakistan, Somalia and Iraq. The acceptance rate in 2010 was about 18%.

Following a comprehensive revision of the Alien Law, in January 2010, several amendments were implemented tightening asylum legislation. In addition, in July 2011 a one-week mobility restriction outside the asylum reception centre was introduced for newly arrived asylum seekers. From October 2011, asylum seekers who have had their claim rejected by the asylum court are automatically provided with legal counselling and support by one of the NGOs designated to provide those services. Beneficiaries of subsidiary protection can now request a permanent residence permit after five years of residence.

In July 2011, Austria reformed its system for the management of skilled migration. Under the so-called "Red-White-Red-Card" scheme (RWR card), two new permits were introduced that combine residence and work titles. The RWR card grants one year of residence and work with a specific employer. After this initial period, if the applicant has been continuously employed for ten months, free labour market access can be obtained through acquisition of a RWR card-*plus*. The reform also introduces a criteria-based system for the selection of candidates for the RWR card. In a points-based system, candidates are selected based on their score in categories such as qualification, work experience, age or language skills. The system is three-tiered. A supply-driven tier grants a 6-month job-search visa to very highly qualified workers who can subsequently obtain the RWR-card. Two demand driven-tiers target so-called "key workers", who have to pass a wage threshold and a labour market test; and workers in shortage occupations. Family members of those with RWR cards or EU Blue Cards are granted unlimited labour market access through the RWR card-*plus* if they can prove basic German language skills (family members of the "very highly qualified" are exempt from this requirement). Finally, graduates of Austrian universities receive a six-month job-search visa, with which they may obtain an RWR card without the points assessment if they find an adequate job above a wage threshold. By the end of November 2011, about 500 RWR Cards had been issued, 11% of which went to former international students. The scheme for skilled workers in shortage occupations will, however, not be introduced before May 2012.

For further information:

www.bmi.gv.at
www.bmask.gv.at
www.migration.gv.at/en/
www.statistik.at/web_en/statistics/population/index.html

Recent trends in migrants' flows and stocks
AUSTRIA

Migration flows (foreigners) National definition	2000	2005	2009	2010	Average 2001-05	Average 2006-10	Level ('000) 2010
Per 1 000 inhabitants							
Inflows	8.1	11.9	11.0	11.7	11.2	11.0	98.3
Outflows	5.5	6.1	7.9	7.9	6.0	7.1	66.4

Migration inflows (foreigners) by type Permit based statistics (standardised)	Thousands		% distribution	
	2009	2010	2009	2010
Work	0.6	0.6	1.2	1.4
Family (incl. accompanying family)	10.0	11.1	22.0	24.1
Humanitarian	5.0	4.7	10.9	10.3
Free movements	29.9	29.3	65.4	63.7
Others	0.2	0.2	0.5	0.5
Total	45.7	45.9	100.0	100.0

Temporary migration	2005	2009	2010	Average 2006-10
Thousands				
International students	3.2	3.1	3.5	3.0
Trainees	0.4	..	..	..
Working holiday makers	..	..	..	..
Seasonal workers	11.4	11.7	10.5	11.3
Intra-company transfers	0.2	0.1	0.2	0.1
Other temporary workers	6.3	2.4	2.6	2.9

Inflows of top 10 nationalities as a % of total inflows of foreigners

2000-2009 annual average / 2010

- Germany
- Romania
- Serbia
- Hungary
- Turkey
- Poland
- Slovak Republic
- Bulgaria
- Bosnia and Herzegovina
- Russian Federation

Inflows of asylum seekers	2000	2005	2009	2010	Average 2001-05	Average 2006-10	Level 2010
Per 1 000 inhabitants	2.3	2.7	1.9	1.3	3.7	1.6	11 012

Components of population growth	2000	2005	2009	2010	Average 2001-05	Average 2006-10	Level ('000) 2010
Per 1 000 inhabitants							
Total	2.5	6.4	2.4	3.5	5.7	3.6	29
Natural increase	0.2	0.4	-0.1	0.2	0.3	0.2	2
Net migration	2.2	5.4	2.5	3.3	4.9	3.4	28

Stocks of immigrants	2000	2005	2009	2010	Average 2001-05	Average 2006-10	Level ('000) 2010
Percentage of the total population							
Foreign-born population	10.4	14.5	15.5	15.7	14.1	15.2	1 316
Foreign population	8.7	9.7	10.7	11.1	9.4	10.4	928

Naturalisations	2000	2005	2009	2010	Average 2001-05	Average 2006-10	Level 2010
Percentage of the foreign population	3.5	4.5	0.9	0.7	5.0	1.5	6 135

Labour market outcomes	2000	2005	2009	2010	Average 2001-05	Average 2006-10
Employment/population ratio						
Native-born men	76.2	76.2	77.7	77.9	75.3	78.3
Foreign-born men	76.1	71.1	72.5	73.5	73.4	73.7
Native-born women	59.9	63.5	68.4	67.9	61.5	67.1
Foreign-born women	58.3	54.2	57.5	59.8	56.8	57.0
Unemployment rate						
Native-born men	4.3	3.9	3.9	3.8	4.1	3.4
Foreign-born men	8.7	10.8	10.7	8.8	9.8	9.0
Native-born women	4.2	4.6	3.9	3.6	4.1	3.9
Foreign-born women	7.2	10.5	8.2	7.6	8.5	8.6

Macroeconomic indicators	2000	2005	2009	2010	Average 2001-05	Average 2006-10	Level 2010
Annual growth in %							
Real GDP	3.7	2.4	-3.8	2.3	1.7	1.5	
GDP/capita (level in USD)	3.4	1.7	-4.1	2.0	1.1	1.1	40 017
Employment (level in thousands)	0.6	2.2	-0.3	0.5	0.6	1.4	4 096
Percentage of the labour force							
Unemployment	3.5	5.2	4.8	4.4	4.4	4.4	

Notes and sources are at the end of the part.

StatLink http://dx.doi.org/10.1787/888932616011

Belgium

The most recent data on the stock of foreigners in Belgium are from 31 December 2009, when the foreign population of 1.06 million represented 9.8% of the total population of Belgium. At the same date, the foreign-born population was 1.5 million (14% of the total population). Since 2008, the principal country of origin of the foreign-born has been Morocco, followed by France, the Netherlands and Italy.

The number of first-time work permits issued to migrant workers in 2010 (that is to say, all foreigners coming to Belgium to work), was close to the 2009 level. From around 25 000 first time permits awarded in 2008, the number fell to 13 000 in 2009 and 2010, as citizens of new EU member countries were exempted from permit requirements on 1 May 2009. Only Bulgarian and Romanian nationals were still required to apply for a work permit, although they benefit from the accelerated procedure applied for jobs considered to be in shortage. These two countries comprised half of all first permits issued in 2010.

The number of Bulgarians and Romanians in the labour force – including self-employed and unemployed as well as the employed – increased by 24% in the course of 2010. The number of Polish citizens in the labour force – the largest single group of foreigners – increased by 20% in 2010, and overall the foreign labour force increased by 9%.

The number of highly skilled workers entering for work-related reasons has been steady since 2007, at between 7 500 and 7 900 annually. The highly skilled now comprise a greater share of total entries for employment, as permits for less skilled employment were largely issued to European citizens no longer subject to permit requirements. In 2009 and 2010, over half of the permits issued to highly skilled workers went to Indian, Japanese or US citizens.

In 2009, there were 32 800 naturalisations, a decrease of 13% compared with 2008. Morocco and Turkey still remain the two main countries of origin of naturalised Belgians, comprising 30% of all naturalisations in 2009. Italy, the Russian Federation and Democratic Republic of the Congo follow, comprising a further 14% of acquisitions of nationality.

Just over 17 000 applications for asylum – covering around 22 800 person – were received in Belgium in 2009. This figure is 16% more than for 2008, but remains close to the average for the past twenty years. In 2010, one in six asylum seekers was from Iraq or the Russian Federation. The number of favourable decisions granting refugee status exceeded 2 100 in 2010, with the main recipients (270) coming from Guinea.

A Royal Order adopted in March 2011 clarified and harmonised employment legislation and legislation governing the right of residence. The Order makes the legislation clearer and increases its legal certainty. For example, the concept of spouse has been broadened to include registered partners. To comply with EU Directives 2004/38 on the right of free movement and 2003/86 on the right to family reunification, registered partners and spouses are placed on an equal footing with regard to access to the labour market.

For further information:

www.emploi.belgique.be
www.ibz.be
www.dofi.fgov.be
http://statbel.fgov.be/

Recent trends in migrants' flows and stocks
BELGIUM

Migration flows (foreigners) National definition	2000	2005	2009	2010	Average 2001-05	Average 2006-10	Level ('000) 2010
Per 1 000 inhabitants							
Inflows	5.6	7.4	9.5	10.4	6.8	9.4	113.6
Outflows	3.5	3.7	4.6	..	3.3	..	50.8

Migration inflows (foreigners) by type Permit based statistics (standardised)	Thousands 2009	Thousands 2010	% distribution 2009	% distribution 2010
Work	7.4	6.6	19.6	18.3
Family (incl. accompanying family)	14.2	13.0	37.8	36.2
Humanitarian	1.9	2.1	5.0	5.9
Free movements	14.2	14.2	37.7	39.6
Others	..	..	..	..
Total	37.7	35.9	100.0	100.0

Inflows of top 10 nationalities as a % of total inflows of foreigners

(2000-2008 annual average; 2009)
France, Poland, Morocco, Netherlands, Romania, Spain, Italy, Germany, Bulgaria, Turkey

Temporary migration	2005	2009	2010	Average 2006-10
Thousands				
International students	..	..	..	..
Trainees	..	0.2	0.2	0.3
Working holiday makers	..	..	..	..
Seasonal workers	2.7	4.8	6.2	11.1
Intra-company transfers	..	..	..	..
Other temporary workers	2.8	0.7	6.2	8.5

Inflows of asylum seekers	2000	2005	2009	2010	Average 2001-05	Average 2006-10	Level 2010
Per 1 000 inhabitants	4.2	1.5	1.6	2.0	1.8	1.4	21 755

Components of population growth	2000	2005	2009	2010	Average 2001-05	Average 2006-10	Level ('000) 2010
Per 1 000 inhabitants							
Total	2.4	6.3	8.0	..	4.8	..	..
Natural increase	1.0	1.4	2.1	..	1.0	..	..
Net migration	2.5	4.5	5.8	..	4.0	..	..

Stocks of immigrants	2000	2005	2009	2010	Average 2001-05	Average 2006-10	Level ('000) 2010
Percentage of the total population							
Foreign-born population	10.3	12.1	13.9	..	11.4	..	..
Foreign population	8.4	8.6	9.8	10.2	8.3	9.5	1 119

Naturalisations	2000	2005	2009	2010	Average 2001-05	Average 2006-10	Level 2010
Percentage of the foreign population	6.9	3.6	3.2	..	4.9	..	..

Labour market outcomes	2000	2005	2009	2010	Average 2001-05	Average 2006-10
Employment/population ratio						
Native-born men	70.8	69.3	68.1	68.5	69.1	68.9
Foreign-born men	62.2	61.2	61.4	61.4	59.9	61.8
Native-born women	53.8	56.0	58.2	58.7	54.1	57.7
Foreign-born women	37.3	39.7	43.4	45.0	38.0	42.8
Unemployment rate						
Native-born men	4.2	6.5	6.4	6.7	5.5	6.0
Foreign-born men	14.7	15.7	16.3	16.9	15.8	15.8
Native-born women	7.4	8.4	7.0	7.1	7.1	7.3
Foreign-born women	17.5	18.9	16.1	17.3	16.8	17.0

Macroeconomic indicators	2000	2005	2009	2010	Average 2001-05	Average 2006-10	Level 2010
Annual growth in %							
Real GDP	3.7	1.7	–2.8	2.3	1.6	1.2	
GDP/capita (level in USD)	3.4	1.2	–3.6	1.4	1.1	0.4	37 676
Employment (level in thousands)	2.0	1.4	–0.1	0.8	0.8	1.1	4 571
Percentage of the labour force							
Unemployment	6.9	8.5	7.9	8.3	7.8	7.8	

Notes and sources are at the end of the part.

StatLink ⟶ http://dx.doi.org/10.1787/888932616030

Bulgaria

The 2011 census data confirmed that Bulgaria has been a net emigration country since 1992. Over the twenty-year period, emigration represented a 6% loss in the total population, and a 10% loss considering only the active population. High emigration levels were accompanied by natural decrease, related to low fertility rates, which contributed a further 12% to total population loss in the same period.

Declared immigration remains low, with 3 500 registered immigrants in 2010, a slight increase over 2009 (3 300). The stock of foreign permanent residents was about 37 000, or 0.5% of the population.

In 2010, only 300 new work permits were issued to foreigners by the National Employment Service, compared with 700 in 2009 and 1 450 in the peak year of 2008. Most permits are issued to workers involved in projects by foreign contractors, mainly in construction, and 80% of permits were granted to Turkish nationals. Work permit issuance remained low in the first half of 2011.

The number of foreign students, in contrast, continued to increase in 2010. Almost 5 900 new resident permits for the purpose of study were issued, 62% to Turkish nationals.

The number of asylum seekers has decreased significantly in recent years, from the record high of almost 2 900 applications in 2002. In 2010, asylum applications grew by 20% compared with 2009, to around 1 000. The principal nationalities of asylum seekers in Bulgaria are Afghanistan, Iraq, Armenia, the Former Yugoslav Republics and Iran.

Figures on declared emigration show an increase from 19 000 in 2009 to 27 700 in 2010. However, actual outflows are considered to be much greater, based on immigration statistics of the main destination countries. Spain, the most important destination country in recent years, recorded 10 400 Bulgarians entering in 2010, 7% more than in 2009. Outflows of Bulgarian citizens from Spain also increased in 2010, to 7 600 from almost 5 000 in the previous year (+52%). The number of Bulgarians in Spain increased by 14 500 in 2010, and a further 13 000 in 2011. There are no consistent data for Greece, the second main destination of Bulgarian immigrants in recent years, but it seems that the stock increased less in 2010 than in previous years.

Out of the 15 bilateral employment agreements signed since 1991, only three were operating in 2010, respectively with France, Germany and Switzerland. The total number of mediated employment contracts was 1 000, 10% less than in 2009. Most of those contracts are with Germany.

Emigration is mainly of short-term nature. According to the 2011 census, 73% of all Bulgarians who emigrated in the period 2001-11 resided abroad less than five years. Despite the worsening economic situation in Bulgaria, return migration increased in 2010. According to official statistics there were about 23 800 return migrants in 2010 compared with fewer than 15 300 in 2008, although net migration of Bulgarians remained negative.

In July 2011, the Bulgarian government adopted a new National Migration, Asylum and Integration Strategy for the period 2011-20. The new strategy aims primarily at the full implementation of the Schengen *acquis*, so that Bulgaria may accede to the Schengen area. Another objective of the strategy is the introduction of labour migration policies in response to demographic and economic needs of the country. Priorities under the new strategy are effective prevention of illegal migration, better regulation of legal immigration, and encouraging return of highly skilled Bulgarian migrants. Highly skilled workers become the main target group of migration policy.

The new strategy also includes a new focus on migrant integration, with integration measures for legally resident foreigners. Among the initiatives already implemented in 2010-11 is the establishment of information centres in the three largest cities to provide support measures to newly arrived foreigners.

The main amendments to the regulation of the entry and stay of foreigners in Bulgaria in the period 2010-11 were related to the transposition of the EU Blue Card and long-term residents' directives, as well as measures to comply with the Schengen visa code. Repatriation rules were also tightened. For the first time, the entry and stay of long-term residents for the purpose of study was regulated under specific provisions.

Procedural changes in application for citizenship were introduced in 2011 to avoid abuse of the system for ethnic Bulgarians. A draft law abolishing dual nationality was introduced in Parliament, but failed to pass.

In 2011 Bulgaria signed readmission agreements with Bosnia and Herzegovina, and Moldova. Readmission agreements with Georgia, the Russian Federation and Serbia are under negotiation.

For further information:

www.nsi.bg/Index_e.htm
www.aref.government.bg
www.government.bg/cgi-bin/e-cms/vis/vis.pl?s=001&p=0136&g

Recent trends in migrants' flows and stocks
BULGARIA

Migration flows (foreigners) National definition	2000	2005	2009	2010	Average		Level ('000)
					2001-05	2006-10	2010
Per 1 000 inhabitants							
Inflows	0.5	2.0	2.9	..	1.5	..	..
Outflows	..	..	..	..	..	..	..
Migration inflows (foreigners) by type	**Thousands**		**% distribution**				
Permit based statistics (standardised)	2009	2010	2009	2010			
Work	..	..	..	..			
Family (incl. accompanying family)	..	..	..	..			
Humanitarian	..	..	..	..			
Free movements	..	..	..	..			
Others	..	..	..	..			
Total	..	..	..	..			
Temporary migration	2005	2009	2010	Average 2006-10			
Thousands							
International students	2.1	..	..	2.7			
Trainees	..	..	..	..			
Working holiday makers	..	..	..	..			
Seasonal workers	..	..	..	..			
Intra-company transfers	..	..	..	..			
Other temporary workers	0.6	0.7	0.3	0.9			
Inflows of asylum seekers	2000	2005	2009	2010	Average		Level
					2001-05	2006-10	2010
Per 1 000 inhabitants	0.2	0.1	0.1	0.1	0.2	0.1	1 025
Components of population growth	2000	2005	2009	2010	Average		Level ('000)
					2001-05	2006-10	2010
Per 1 000 inhabitants							
Total	-5.1	-5.5	-5.6	-7.8	-10.9	-5.6	-59
Natural increase	-5.1	-5.5	-3.6	-4.6	-5.6	-4.5	-35
Net migration	0.0	0.0	-2.1	-3.2	-5.3	-1.1	-24
Stocks of immigrants	2000	2005	2009	2010	Average		Level ('000)
					2001-05	2006-10	2010
Percentage of the total population							
Foreign-born population	..	..	..	..	..	..	..
Foreign population	..	..	..	0.5	..	..	37
Naturalisations	2000	2005	2009	2010	Average		Level
					2001-05	2006-10	2010
Percentage of the foreign population	..	..	..	..	..	..	14 979
Labour market outcomes	2000	2005	2009	2010	Average		
					2001-05	2006-10	
Employment/population ratio							
Native-born men	..	..	66.9	63.0	..	65.4	
Foreign-born men	..	..	54.6	52.2	..	57.7	
Native-born women	..	..	58.4	56.4	..	57.3	
Foreign-born women	..	..	50.6	47.5	..	54.3	
Unemployment rate							
Native-born men	..	..	7.1	11.0	..	7.8	
Foreign-born men	..	..	7.9	0.0	..	9.1	
Native-born women	..	..	6.6	9.5	..	7.7	
Foreign-born women	..	..	11.0	0.0	..	9.5	
Macroeconomic indicators	2000	2005	2009	2010	Average		Level
					2001-05	2006-10	2010
Annual growth in %							
Real GDP	5.4	6.4	-5.5	0.1	5.5	2.7	
GDP/capita (level in USD)	4.3	6.9	-4.9	0.9	6.6	3.2	12 668
Employment (level in thousands)	..	2.4	-3.1	-6.1	1.3	0.4	3 010
Percentage of the labour force							
Unemployment	16.4	10.1	6.8	10.2	14.7	7.7	

Notes and sources are at the end of the part.

StatLink http://dx.doi.org/10.1787/888932616049

Canada

Canada admitted about 281 000 permanent migrants in 2010, an 11% increase over the previous year, and the largest number since 1957. As in previous years, the top sending countries were the Philippines (13%), India (11%) and China (11%), although the order changed from 2009. China, despite a 4% increase in new permanent residents, fell from the top source country in 2009 to third in 2010. The Philippines jumped into top place recording a 34% increase over 2009, while India rose to second with a 16% increase. In 2010, most permanent migrants (61%) entered Canada for family-related reasons (this includes the spouses and dependents of economic principal applicants). Labour migrants accounted for roughly one-quarter of long-term inflows, and one out of eight permanent migrants acquired a residence permit on humanitarian grounds.

Canada admitted 384 000 temporary residents in 2010, slightly more than in 2009. The number of temporary foreign workers remained stable, representing 47% of all temporary migrants. Within the group, however, growth was recorded in managerial and professional occupations while lower-skilled groups all declined. The main sending country for temporary workers remained the United States. The number of international students rose almost 13% from 2009 levels and accounted for 25% of temporary flows. In addition, the Youth Exchange Program has grown five-fold over the last ten years (from 11 000 to 56 000).

Canada received almost 24 700 refugees in 2010, half through government resettlement programmes and private sponsors. These included 4 000 Iraqi and 1 400 Bhutanese refugees. The remaining refugees were successful asylum seekers, mainly from Colombia, Haiti, and Sri Lanka. In 2010, asylum claims fell by about 30% from 2009, mainly due to a reinstated visa requirement for the Czech Republic and a new visa requirement for Mexicans.

The number of naturalisations has been declining continuously since 2006. In 2010, 143 600 persons were granted Canadian citizenship, a decrease of 8% compared with 2009. India, China and the Philippines were the top three source countries for new Canadian citizens in 2010.

Following the 2008 *Action Plan for Faster Immigration* aimed at accelerating processing and reducing the backlog of applications from skilled workers, four sets of Ministerial Instructions amending admission procedures were issued. The first, in November 2008, established eligibility criteria for skilled workers to have their applications considered using an occupation filter. The second, in June 2010, set caps (annual cap of 20 000 in total and 1 000 per priority occupation) on new applications to be considered under a new priority occupation scheme and introduced a language testing requirement for all permanent economic migrants. The third was introduced in June 2011, to deal with a persistent backlog by further reducing the annual skilled worker cap to 10 000 in total and 500 per prioritised occupation as well as introducing an annual intake cap of 700 for immigrant investors and placing a moratorium on immigrant entrepreneur applications. The fourth, on 5 November 2011, suspended the acceptance of sponsorship applications for parents and grandparents for up to 24 months. These instructions also allow up to 1 000 foreign nationals per year currently studying at the PhD level or recently graduated to apply as a skilled worker.

The Canadian government has since 2010 changed temporary worker programmes to improve protections and reinforce employer compliance. Changes to the Live-in Caregiver Program were implemented in April 2010, and in April 2011 to the Temporary Foreign Worker Program. Temporary foreign workers may stay in Canada only for a limited time, encouraging use of permanent residence pathways if applicable, and departure if not. Transitions from temporary to permanent resident status are facilitated through avenues including the Canadian Experience Class, the Federal Skilled Worker Program and the Provincial Nominee Program.

In 2010, Canada changed its integration programme funding to a "Modernized Approach", uniting separate programmes for settlement programming. Newcomer services are covered by a single funding agreement, simplifying the administrative process for immigrant-serving organisations, and allowing them to tailor their offerings to suit newcomers' needs. Since introduction, the use of settlement services by newcomers has increased by 8%.

An evaluation of the Federal Skilled Worker Program (FSWP) 2002-08 was published by CIC in 2010. While identifying several critical issues with the current selection system (principally, fraudulent employment offers), the evaluation showed that skilled workers with prior employment offers performed better, and that the 2002 changes led to selection of more highly educated workers, with better language proficiency, and more diversification of both origin countries and occupation.

For further information:

www.cic.gc.ca

Recent trends in migrants' flows and stocks
CANADA

Migration flows (foreigners) National definition	2000	2005	2009	2010	Average 2001-05	Average 2006-10	Level ('000) 2010
Per 1 000 inhabitants							
Inflows	7.4	8.1	7.5	8.2	7.6	7.6	280.7
Outflows	..	..	..	..	..	..	..

Migration inflows (foreigners) by type	Thousands		% distribution	
Permit based statistics (standardised)	2009	2010	2009	2010
Work	64.0	76.6	25.4	27.3
Family (incl. accompanying family)	154.7	170.6	61.3	60.8
Humanitarian	33.4	33.4	13.2	11.9
Free movements	..	..	..	..
Others	0.1	0.1	0.0	0.0
Total	252.2	280.7	100.0	100.0

Inflows of top 10 nationalities as a % of total inflows of foreigners
(2000-2009 annual average; 2010)
Philippines, India, China, United Kingdom, United States, France, Iran, United Arab Emirates, Morocco, Korea

Temporary migration	2005	2009	2010	Average 2006-10
Thousands				
International students	56.7	66.8	76.7	65.9
Trainees	..	..	..	..
Working holiday makers	28.0	45.3	50.0	40.0
Seasonal workers	20.3	23.4	23.9	23.8
Intra-company transfers	6.8	10.1	13.6	10.3
Other temporary workers	62.4	90.4	85.5	88.7

Inflows of asylum seekers	2000	2005	2009	2010	Average 2001-05	Average 2006-10	Level 2010
Per 1 000 inhabitants	1.1	0.6	1.0	0.7	1.0	0.9	22 543

Components of population growth	2000	2005	2009	2010	Average 2001-05	Average 2006-10	Level ('000) 2010
Per 1 000 inhabitants							
Total	9.7	9.9	11.9	11.1	9.9	11.4	381
Natural increase	3.6	3.5	4.2	4.0	3.5	4.1	136
Net migration	6.5	7.0	7.7	7.2	7.1	7.4	244

Stocks of immigrants	2000	2005	2009	2010	Average 2001-05	Average 2006-10	Level ('000) 2010
Percentage of the total population							
Foreign-born population	17.4	18.7	19.6	19.9	18.1	19.4	6 778
Foreign population	..	..	..	..	..	..	

Naturalisations	2000	2005	2009	2010	Average 2001-05	Average 2006-10	Level 2010
Percentage of the foreign population	..	..	..	..	..	..	143 562

Labour market outcomes	2000	2005	2009	2010	Average 2001-05	Average 2006-10
Employment/population ratio						
Native-born men	77.4	..	74.0	74.3	..	..
Foreign-born men	77.0	..	73.9	74.5	..	..
Native-born women	66.0	..	70.7	70.5	..	..
Foreign-born women	59.6	..	63.4	63.3	..	..
Unemployment rate						
Native-born men	5.7	..	9.3	8.6	..	..
Foreign-born men	6.1	..	10.7	10.0	..	..
Native-born women	6.2	..	6.4	6.6	..	..
Foreign-born women	8.7	..	9.6	9.9	..	..

Macroeconomic indicators	2000	2005	2009	2010	Average 2001-05	Average 2006-10	Level 2010
Annual growth in %							
Real GDP	5.2	3.0	−2.8	3.2	2.5	1.2	
GDP/capita (level in USD)	4.3	2.0	−3.9	2.0	1.5	0.1	39 070
Employment (level in thousands)	2.5	1.3	−1.6	1.4	1.8	1.1	17 045
Percentage of the labour force							
Unemployment	6.8	6.7	8.3	8.0	7.3	7.0	

Notes and sources are at the end of the part.

StatLink http://dx.doi.org/10.1787/888932616068

Chile

According to national estimations based on Census data, almost 370 000 foreign-born persons were living in Chile in 2010, which represents an increase of around 20 000 compared with the previous year and twice the number of immigrants registered in 2002. Most immigrants in Chile are from other South American countries, with 61% from neighbouring countries. Over the past few years, Peru has replaced Argentina as the main country of origin. Between 2002 and 2009, the number of immigrants from Peru has more than tripled, from 38 000 to 131 000. They now account for 37% of the migrant population, followed by Argentines (17%), Bolivians (6%), Ecuadorians (5%) and Colombians (4%).

Despite the increase in the stock of migrants over the past years, Chile is still a country with more expatriates abroad than immigrants. In 2004, the latest year for which figures are available, about 860 000 Chileans were living outside the country. Overall, 50% of Chilean emigrants settled in Argentina. The other principal destinations, especially for the migrants of the 1970s, were Australia, Canada and Sweden.

Estimates based on the 2002 Census data and on projections on the number of resident permits granted since then, suggest that more than half of all migrants who were living in Chile in 2010 entered the country after 1996. This is particularly the case for migrants from Peru, Colombia and Ecuador, while inflows from Bolivia were also important prior to the second half of the 1990s.

In 2011, there were 71 600 applications for temporary residence visa and 20 400 for permanent residence in Chile.

The numbers of asylum seekers in Chile is low compared with other OECD countries and declined further in 2011, from 560 applications in 2009, to 260 in 2011, most from Colombia. In April 2010, a new Law for the Protection of Refugees was implemented which establishes the legal framework for the protection of refugees and incorporates the country's obligations under the 1951 Convention and the 1967 Protocol of the *United Nations relating to the Status of Refugees*. The new legislation includes universal and regional definitions of refugees; sets out guarantees and obligations for refugees; and regularises procedures and guidelines for determining refugee status.

According to national estimates, about 5% of the total immigrant population was in an irregular situation in 2009, the majority from Peru (72%). To address this issue, Chile has held regularisation programmes, in 1998 and in 2007/2008, with more than 40 000 beneficiaries of each regularisation.

In April 2011, a law entered into force which provides for the recognition of human trafficking and smuggling as penal crimes and entitles foreigners who have been victims of such crimes to submit an application for temporary residence in Chile for a minimum period of six months. In this period they are allowed to exercise legal actions against the authors of the crimes or initiate proceedings to regularise their residence status in the country. The law excludes the forced repatriation of those victims who apply for residence. Several procedural measures to facilitate the legalisation process for this group of immigrants have also been introduced.

In February 2011, Chile launched a modernisation plan aimed at substantially improving the procedures for the issuance of temporary residence permits and at reducing processing times for applications. Measures carried out under this plan include, among others, studies about possible reforms of the system for granting residence permits and projects for joint migration management by various public services, including Civil Registry and Identification, Treasury, Supreme Court of Justice, Criminal Police and the Ministry of Foreign Affairs.

In the context of the modernisation plan, in 2010-11 the government appointed an interdisciplinary group to prepare a draft Migration Act which should incorporate rules in accordance with relevant international agreements signed by Chile and take into account the current dynamics of migration flows. A final draft of this act is expected to be submitted to the Congress by mid-2012.

For further information:

www.extranjeria.gov.cl/
www.minrel.gov.cl
www.interior.gov.cl

Recent trends in migrants' flows and stocks
CHILE

Migration flows (foreigners) National definition	2000	2005	2009	2010	Average 2001-05	Average 2006-10	Level ('000) 2010
Per 1 000 inhabitants							
Inflows	..	2.3	3.4	3.7	..	3.8	63.9
Outflows	..	..	..	..	..	..	..

Migration inflows (foreigners) by type	Thousands		% distribution				
Permit based statistics (standardised)	2009	2010	2009	2010			
Work	..	..	..	..			
Family (incl. accompanying family)	..	..	..	..			
Humanitarian	..	..	..	..			
Free movements	..	..	..	..			
Others	..	..	..	..			
Total	..	..	..	..			

Inflows of top 10 nationalities as a % of total inflows of foreigners

2003-2009 annual average / 2010

Peru, Colombia, Bolivia, Argentina, United States, Ecuador, China, Brazil, Dominican Republic, Spain

Temporary migration	2005	2009	2010	Average 2006-10
Thousands				
International students	..	..	..	..
Trainees	..	..	..	..
Working holiday makers	..	..	..	..
Seasonal workers	..	..	..	..
Intra-company transfers	..	..	..	..
Other temporary workers	..	..	..	..

Inflows of asylum seekers	2000	2005	2009	2010	Average 2001-05	Average 2006-10	Level 2010
Per 1 000 inhabitants	0.0	0.0	..	0.0	0.0	..	260

Components of population growth	2000	2005	2009	2010	Average 2001-05	Average 2006-10	Level ('000) 2010
Per 1 000 inhabitants							
Total	12.2	10.4	9.8	9.3	10.9	9.8	160
Natural increase	11.6	9.7	9.5	8.9	10.4	9.5	152
Net migration	0.4	0.4	0.4	0.4	0.4	0.4	6

Stocks of immigrants	2000	2005	2009	2010	Average 2001-05	Average 2006-10	Level ('000) 2010
Percentage of the total population							
Foreign-born population	..	1.5	2.1	2.2	..	1.9	369
Foreign population	..	..	..	..	..	..	..

Naturalisations	2000	2005	2009	2010	Average 2001-05	Average 2006-10	Level 2010
Percentage of the foreign population	..	..	..	..	..	..	629

Labour market outcomes	2000	2005	2009	2010	Average 2001-05	Average 2006-10	
Employment/population ratio							
Native-born men	..	..	..	..	..	..	
Foreign-born men	..	..	..	..	..	..	
Native-born women	..	..	..	..	..	..	
Foreign-born women	..	..	..	..	..	..	
Unemployment rate							
Native-born men	..	..	..	..	..	..	
Foreign-born men	..	..	..	..	..	..	
Native-born women	..	..	..	..	..	..	
Foreign-born women	..	..	..	..	..	..	

Macroeconomic indicators	2000	2005	2009	2010	Average 2001-05	Average 2006-10	Level 2010
Annual growth in %							
Real GDP	4.5	5.6	-1.7	5.2	4.2	3.3	
GDP/capita (level in USD)	3.1	4.4	-2.6	4.2	3.1	2.3	15 107
Employment (level in thousands)	..	..	..	..	..	..	..
Percentage of the labour force							
Unemployment	9.7	9.2	10.8	8.1	9.7	8.3	

Notes and sources are at the end of the part.

StatLink ⟶ http://dx.doi.org/10.1787/888932616087

Czech Republic

Immigration into the Czech Republic continued to decline in 2010, following a trend started in 2008. According to national statistics, about 30 500 immigrants entered the country in 2010, a decrease by 21% compared with the previous year (39 000). In parallel, outflows increased from almost 12 000 to almost 15 000 persons. In total, net migration declined to 15 600, about 11 700 less than in 2009.

The decline in immigration from Ukraine accounted for more than half of the decrease in the total inflow into the Czech Republic in 2010. With 3 500 inflows in 2010, Ukraine lost its longstanding position as the main origin country for immigration into the Czech Republic, preceded by the Slovak Republic and the Russian Federation, with about 5 000 and 3 700 inflows respectively. Immigration of Vietnamese also continued to decline in 2010. With inflows of about 1 400, Viet Nam fell from the fifth to seventh position in the ranking of source countries (it had been second in 2006 and 2007), preceded by Germany and the United States. In contrast to the trend observed for all other main origin countries, inflows from Germany increased in 2010, albeit remaining at modest levels (about 2 200).

The total number of foreigners holding a residence permit slightly decreased in 2010, to about 425 000, compared with 433 000 in 2009, due to a 6% decline in the number of migrants with a long-term residence permit, following a trend already visible in 2009. In contrast, the stock of permanent residents increased by almost 5% compared with 2009, reaching almost 190 000 persons. The decline in long-term residents was largely due to the decrease in the number of labour migrants, while the stock of family and business migrants continued to increase. In the context of the crisis, many foreigners who lost their job and did not find another within 60 days would have been obliged to leave the country. Many thus changed their purpose of residence as a way to stay legally in the Czech Republic. Abuse of business authorisations (the so-called "Schwarz" System) by foreign nationals (which had declined in previous years) appears to have become more frequent since 2009. In 2010, almost 91 000 foreigners held a trade license in the Czech Republic, an almost 4% increase compared with 2009. The amendment to the "Act on Residence of Foreign Nationals", which entered into force on 1 January 2011, introduced restrictions to the permit regime for the purpose of carrying out an independent economic activity, including a two-year legal residence requirement for status changes into self-employment.

The 2009 economic crisis interrupted the trend started in 1993 towards a growing share of foreign workers in the Czech labour market. From almost 7% in 2008, it decreased to 5.6% in 2009 and 5.4% in 2010. Although the programme for the voluntary return of unemployed immigrants was extended to illegal migrants in September 2009, only 221 voluntary returns were registered in 2010 (2000 in the previous phase in 2009).

The Green-Card scheme – introduced in January 2009 to facilitate labour market access to qualified workers from selected countries – remained limited, at 213 applicants in 2010.

Asylum seeking in the Czech Republic continued to decline in 2010, to less than 900, its lowest level ever. The most important source country for asylum seekers in the Czech Republic continued to be Ukraine. 125 persons obtained refugee status in the Czech Republic in 2010, mostly nationals of Myanmar, the Russian Federation and Ukraine.

Amendments to the "Act on Residence of Foreign Nationals" and to the Employment Act entered into force on 1 January 2011, transposing various EU directives (Blue Card, return, employer sanctions, as well as regulations on Visa Code and on a uniform residence permit format).

The High-Skilled Migration Programme ("Project of Selection of Qualified Foreign Workers"), in place since 2003, was terminated by Government Resolution in December 2010. This programme aimed at attracting young, qualified people to the Czech Republic by offering faster access to permanent residence. The programme covered nationals of 51 non-EU countries, and the final number of beneficiaries was about 1 800 principal applicants and 1 700 family members.

For further information:

www.mvcr.cz
www.czso.cz

Recent trends in migrants' flows and stocks
CZECH REPUBLIC

Migration flows (foreigners) National definition	2000	2005	2009	2010	Average		Level ('000)
					2001-05	2006-10	2010
Per 1 000 inhabitants							
Inflows	0.4	5.7	3.8	2.9	4.3	6.1	30.5
Outflows	0.0	2.1	0.9	1.4	2.8	1.5	14.9

Migration inflows (foreigners) by type	Thousands		% distribution	
Permit based statistics (standardised)	2009	2010	2009	2010
Work	..	..	..	..
Family (incl. accompanying family)	..	..	..	..
Humanitarian	..	..	..	..
Free movements	..	..	..	..
Others	..	..	..	..
Total	39.0	30.5	100.0	100.0

Temporary migration	2005	2009	2010	Average
				2006-10
Thousands				
International students	4.4	..	..	5.6
Trainees	..	..	..	..
Working holiday makers	..	..	..	..
Seasonal workers	..	..	..	..
Intra-company transfers	..	..	..	..
Other temporary workers	..	..	..	..

Inflows of top 10 nationalities as a % of total inflows of foreigners

2000-2009 annual average | 2010

Slovak Republic
Russian Federation
Ukraine
Germany
United States
Viet Nam
Poland
Kazakhstan
Bulgaria
Turkey

Inflows of asylum seekers	2000	2005	2009	2010	Average		Level
					2001-05	2006-10	2010
Per 1 000 inhabitants	0.9	0.4	0.1	0.1	0.9	0.2	979

Components of population growth	2000	2005	2009	2010	Average		Level ('000)
					2001-05	2006-10	2010
Per 1 000 inhabitants							
Total	-1.1	3.0	3.7	2.5	-0.3	5.4	26
Natural increase	-1.8	-0.6	1.0	1.0	-1.2	0.9	10
Net migration	0.6	3.5	2.7	1.5	1.7	4.5	16

Stocks of immigrants	2000	2005	2009	2010	Average		Level ('000)
					2001-05	2006-10	2010
Percentage of the total population							
Foreign-born population	4.2	5.1	6.4	6.3	4.7	6.2	661
Foreign population	2.0	2.7	4.1	4.0	2.4	3.9	424

Naturalisations	2000	2005	2009	2010	Average		Level
					2001-05	2006-10	2010
Percentage of the foreign population	3.6	1.0	0.4	0.3	1.9	0.5	1 495

Labour market outcomes	2000	2005	2009	2010	Average	
					2001-05	2006-10
Employment/population ratio						
Native-born men	..	73.3	73.8	73.4	..	74.2
Foreign-born men	..	71.0	74.6	79.1	..	75.7
Native-born women	..	56.4	56.7	56.3	..	57.0
Foreign-born women	..	51.3	56.8	56.2	..	55.4
Unemployment rate						
Native-born men	..	6.4	5.9	6.5	..	5.2
Foreign-born men	..	9.7	8.5	5.6	..	6.9
Native-born women	..	9.7	7.7	8.5	..	7.5
Foreign-born women	..	15.8	11.0	9.5	..	11.4

Macroeconomic indicators	2000	2005	2009	2010	Average		Level
					2001-05	2006-10	2010
Annual growth in %							
Real GDP	4.2	6.8	-4.7	2.7	4.1	2.8	
GDP/capita (level in USD)	4.3	6.5	-5.3	2.5	4.2	2.2	25 245
Employment (level in thousands)	-0.7	1.4	-1.3	-1.0	0.3	0.5	4 870
Percentage of the labour force							
Unemployment	8.9	8.0	6.7	7.3	7.9	6.2	

Notes and sources are at the end of the part.

StatLink http://dx.doi.org/10.1787/888932616106

Denmark

In 2010, the total number of new residence permits granted in Denmark was about 59 000, a slight increase compared with the corresponding figure for 2009 (57 000). 43% of residence permits were granted on the basis of EEA free movement, 26% for study (including permits granted to au pairs and interns), 18% for employment (including self-employment) and 8% for family reunification. More than 2 100 persons were granted refugee status (4% of the total number of residence permits), which was the highest level since 2004.

The number of residence permits issued in Denmark in a given year represents an approximate indication of the level of immigration that year, as Nordic nationals may enter and stay in Denmark without a residence permit, while foreign nationals may subsequently apply for – and be granted – different types of residence permits (e.g. a person granted family reunification may also be granted asylum).

In 2010 net migration to Denmark was 22 400 persons. By 1 January 2011 immigrants represented around 10% of the Danish population of 5.6 million.

Foreign-born men are more frequently unemployed than native-born men. This is particularly true for first generation immigrants of Non-Western origin, for which the unemployment rate was 8.9%, compared with 4.1% for native-born men and 4.2% for foreign-born men of Western origin. The discrepancy is even larger among women: while only 2.5% of native-born women are unemployed, the rate rises to 7.4% for foreign-born women from non-Western countries.

After ten years of centre-right coalitions, a new left coalition government came out from September 2011 elections and was appointed in October 2011. The new government abolished the Ministry of Refugees, Immigrants and Integration Affairs, which had been created in 2001, and divided its portfolio between the Social Affairs Ministry – renamed as Ministry of Social Affairs and Integration – and the Ministry of Justice.

In its official policy platform, entitled "A Denmark that stands together", the new government has announced wide-ranging reforms of migration and integration policy. According to the government programme, the points-based system for permanent residence introduced in June 2010 would be abolished and the issuance of a permanent residence permit made conditional on four requirements: at least five years residence in Denmark, three years full-time employment in the previous five years, financial self-support, and passage of a language test.

Admission requirements for family migrants would be loosened. The "attachment" requirement for the family migration of spouses or partners would be reviewed, and the length of legal residency/citizenship granting exemption from this requirement would be reduced from 28 to 26 years. The financial collateral requirement will be halved. However, the minimum age required to both partners for family migration will be restored to age 24, while the current points-system allows for younger spouses with high points scores. Revised rules concerning family reunification of children have also been announced, as has the establishment of an independent board of appeal dedicated to family reunification cases.

In addition, asylum seekers should be allowed to live and work outside the asylum centres six months after arrival. The criteria for selecting quota refugees will be revised and the Refugees Appeals Board will be expanded, with two additional members. Finally, requirements for acquiring Danish citizenship, and, especially, the citizenship test, will be adjusted in order not to exclude the lower educated. Dual citizenship will be allowed.

In the area of integration the focus remains on facilitating immigrant access to the labour market and education. Following the previous government plan "Denmark 2020", the new government has set a target of 10 000 additional immigrants in employment by the end of the decade. More broadly, the creation of the new Ministry of Social Affairs and Integration brings a different approach to integration, one which allows for differentiations among immigrants and their needs according to their social context.

The government has also announced the abolition of lower social benefit rates applied for immigrants, and the launch of a national integration survey tool for statistically monitoring developments in various aspects of the integration of immigrants, including employment, education, and acquisition and exercise of citizenship.

For further information:

www.sm.dk/Sider/Start.aspx
www.justitsministeriet.dk/english.html
www.newtodenmark.dk
www.workindenmark.dk

Recent trends in migrants' flows and stocks
DENMARK

Migration flows (foreigners) National definition	2000	2005	2009	2010	Average		Level ('000)
					2001-05	2006-10	2010
Per 1 000 inhabitants							
Inflows	4.3	3.7	5.8	6.0	3.8	5.7	33.4
Outflows	2.6	3.0	4.8	4.9	2.9	4.1	27.1

Migration inflows (foreigners) by type Permit based statistics (standardised)	Thousands		% distribution	
	2009	2010	2009	2010
Work	6.6	8.1	17.2	19.6
Family (incl. accompanying family)	6.8	7.5	17.8	18.2
Humanitarian	1.4	2.1	3.6	5.1
Free movements	21.9	21.0	57.0	50.9
Others	1.7	2.5	4.5	6.2
Total	38.4	41.3	100.0	100.0

Inflows of top 10 nationalities as a % of total inflows of foreigners

2000-2009 annual average / 2010

Poland, Romania, Germany, Philippines, Lithuania, Norway, Ukraine, Sweden, United Kingdom, Bulgaria

Temporary migration	2005	2009	2010	Average
				2006-10
Thousands				
International students	6.9	6.1	5.8	6.1
Trainees	1.9	2.2	1.6	2.6
Working holiday makers	..	..	..	..
Seasonal workers	..	..	..	..
Intra-company transfers	..	..	..	..
Other temporary workers	2.6	3.8	3.8	3.5

Inflows of asylum seekers	2000	2005	2009	2010	Average		Level
					2001-05	2006-10	2010
Per 1 000 inhabitants	2.4	0.4	0.7	0.9	1.0	0.5	4 965

Components of population growth	2000	2005	2009	2010	Average		Level ('000)
					2001-05	2006-10	2010
Per 1 000 inhabitants							
Total	3.6	3.0	5.3	5.6	2.9	5.5	31
Natural increase	1.7	1.7	1.4	1.6	1.3	1.6	9
Net migration	1.7	1.2	4.0	4.0	1.4	3.9	22

Stocks of immigrants	2000	2005	2009	2010	Average		Level ('000)
					2001-05	2006-10	2010
Percentage of the total population							
Foreign-born population	5.8	6.5	7.5	7.7	6.3	7.2	429
Foreign population	4.8	5.0	6.0	6.2	5.0	5.7	346

Naturalisations	2000	2005	2009	2010	Average		Level
					2001-05	2006-10	2010
Percentage of the foreign population	7.3	3.8	2.0	0.9	4.6	1.7	3 006

Labour market outcomes	2000	2005	2009	2010	Average	
					2001-05	2006-10
Employment/population ratio						
Native-born men	81.5	80.4	78.8	76.6	80.9	80.5
Foreign-born men	67.0	71.0	73.5	67.6	67.0	71.2
Native-born women	73.3	73.2	74.3	72.6	73.0	74.5
Foreign-born women	53.3	55.7	63.2	60.0	54.4	59.4
Unemployment rate						
Native-born men	3.7	4.2	6.4	7.7	4.1	4.6
Foreign-born men	10.7	9.0	10.0	15.1	11.3	9.5
Native-born women	4.9	4.9	5.0	6.0	4.9	4.5
Foreign-born women	6.6	10.4	9.7	12.1	9.7	9.1

Macroeconomic indicators	2000	2005	2009	2010	Average		Level
					2001-05	2006-10	2010
Annual growth in %							
Real GDP	3.5	2.4	-5.8	1.3	1.3	-0.1	
GDP/capita (level in USD)	3.2	2.1	-6.3	0.9	1.0	-0.5	40 170
Employment (level in thousands)	0.5	1.0	-3.1	-2.1	0.1	0.3	2 807
Percentage of the labour force							
Unemployment	4.3	4.8	5.9	7.2	4.9	4.8	

Notes and sources are at the end of the part.

StatLink http://dx.doi.org/10.1787/888932616125

Estonia

There were 1.32 million people living in Estonia on 1 January 2012, of which almost 16% were foreigners. The vast majority of the foreign population is longstanding and arrived in Estonia prior to 1991 as internal migrants from other parts of the Soviet Union.

After Estonia regained its independence in 1991, Estonian citizens were defined as those who were Estonian citizens prior to the 1940 occupation by the Soviet Union, and their descendants. Others had the opportunity to become naturalised Estonian citizens or apply for citizenship of their country of origin. Many did not determine their citizenship status. Estonia promotes Estonian citizenship and the number of residents with no determined citizenship has declined. In the beginning of 2012 the number of residents with undetermined citizenship was 98 000.

The economic crisis hit Estonia particularly hard, although GDP resumed positive growth in 2010. Net migration has been negative over the past few years, albeit less than in the two other Baltic countries. About 2 800 persons migrated to Estonia in 2010, 27% fewer than in 2009. According to the Estonian Labour Force Survey there were 21 600 Estonians working abroad in 2011, 500 fewer than a year earlier.

The unemployment rate for non-Estonians has been consistently higher than for Estonians. The unemployment rate in 2011 was 9.7% for Estonians and 18.2% for non-Estonians. The main explanatory factors are limited language skills and low mobility of non-Estonians. The economic crisis affected non-Estonians more, as they were disproportionately employed in the hard-hit manufacturing and construction sectors.

Since Estonia's accession to the European Union (EU) in 2004, returning Estonian citizens have accounted for a large proportion of inflows to Estonia. In 2010 this percentage reached 57% of all immigrants, 14 percentage points more than the previous year. To promote return of Estonian migrants, financial support has been offered since 1992. In 2010, the Estonian Chamber of Commerce and Industry initiated the "Talents Back Home" project, to attract back Estonians who have graduated from universities abroad, by offering them employment opportunities. The project includes a website to connect Estonians abroad with possible employers in Estonia.

In 2011, there were 9 700 decisions to grant a residence permit for foreigners or to prolong a residence permit. 37% of residence permits were granted to Russians, 31% to foreigners with no determined citizenship and 13% to Ukrainians. Family migration continues to be the most important category of migration in Estonia, comprising about a third of all residence permits issued annually. In 2011, 3 000 residence permits were issued on the grounds of family reunification.

In 2011, 18% of residence permits were issued for employment. Estonia operates a system of quotas for labour migration. The quota for the respective calendar year is set annually by the government within a ceiling of 0.1% of the population. In 2010, the quota was only 82% utilised. For 2011, the quota was set at 1 008 persons (0.075% of the population). The quota was utilised by the end of August 2011 due to a sharp rise in applications for employment as board members of Estonian companies. Estonia receives few asylum seekers (30 in 2010 and 70 in 2011).

In June 2011, changes to the Aliens Act came into effect providing for the transposition of the EU Blue Card directive. The adoption of the Blue Card was accompanied by a debate, initiated by the Estonian Employers' Confederation, over opening the Estonian labour market to foreign workers by lowering the minimum salary threshold not only for highly skilled workers but also less-skilled in short-term employment. However, in the context of the crisis, the Estonian government declined to implement this change.

Since 2010 Estonia has offered a free introduction programme to newly arrived third-country nationals. It consists of three modules: civic education, Estonian language training, and professional training courses, where necessary.

For further information:

www.politsei.ee/en/
www.tootukassa.ee/?lang=en
www.stat.ee/en
www.meis.ee/tagasiranne-eng
www.sisekaitse.ee/eass/the-academy/emn/

Recent trends in migrants' flows and stocks
ESTONIA

Migration flows (foreigners) *National definition*	2000	2005	2009	2010	Average		Level ('000)
					2001-05	2006-10	2010
Per 1 000 inhabitants							
Inflows	..	0.7	1.7	0.9	..	1.3	*1.2*
Outflows	..	0.5	0.5	0.5	..	0.4	*0.6*

Migration inflows (foreigners) by type	Thousands		% distribution		
Permit based statistics (standardised)	2009	2010	2009	2010	
Work	..	..	..	..	
Family (incl. accompanying family)	..	..	..	..	
Humanitarian	..	..	..	..	
Free movements	..	..	..	..	
Others	..	..	..	..	
Total	..	..	..	..	

Inflows of top 10 nationalities as a % of total inflows of foreigners

2004-2008 annual average; 2009

Russian Federation, Finland, Ukraine, Germany, Latvia, China, Sweden, United States, Italy, France

Temporary migration	2005	2009	2010	Average
				2006-10
Thousands				
International students	..	..	..	..
Trainees	..	..	..	..
Working holiday makers	..	..	..	..
Seasonal workers	..	..	..	..
Intra-company transfers	..	..	..	..
Other temporary workers	..	..	..	..

Inflows of asylum seekers	2000	2005	2009	2010	Average		Level
					2001-05	2006-10	2010
Per 1 000 inhabitants	0.0	0.0	0.0	0.0	0.0	0.0	*30*

Components of population growth	2000	2005	2009	2010	Average		Level ('000)
					2001-05	2006-10	2010
Per 1 000 inhabitants							
Total	-3.7	-2.1	-0.2	0.0	-3.3	-0.7	*0*
Natural increase	-3.9	-2.2	-0.2	0.0	-3.4	-0.7	*0*
Net migration	..	..	..	..	..	..	*..*

Stocks of immigrants	2000	2005	2009	2010	Average		Level ('000)
					2001-05	2006-10	2010
Percentage of the total population							
Foreign-born population	18.5	17.5	16.6	16.3	17.9	16.7	*218*
Foreign population	21.0	19.0	16.4	..	19.6	..	*..*

Naturalisations	2000	2005	2009	2010	Average		Level
					2001-05	2006-10	2010
Percentage of the foreign population	..	2.7	0.7	0.5	1.9	..	*1 184*

Labour market outcomes	2000	2005	2009	2010	Average	
					2001-05	2006-10
Employment/population ratio						
Native-born men	62.2	66.1	63.5	61.6	65.4	68.1
Foreign-born men	70.5	73.4	68.8	60.8	70.8	72.6
Native-born women	57.1	61.4	62.4	61.0	58.7	63.7
Foreign-born women	57.7	65.6	67.0	58.0	60.7	67.3
Unemployment rate						
Native-born men	15.3	8.9	17.3	19.4	10.6	10.8
Foreign-born men	13.4	9.4	17.7	23.6	12.2	12.5
Native-born women	11.8	6.3	10.5	13.4	9.0	7.7
Foreign-born women	11.1	11.4	12.3	22.2	13.2	10.5

Macroeconomic indicators	2000	2005	2009	2010	Average		Level
					2001-05	2006-10	2010
Annual growth in %							
Real GDP	10.0	8.9	-14.3	2.3	7.2	0.4	
GDP/capita (level in USD)	10.5	9.1	-14.2	2.3	7.5	0.5	*20 383*
Employment (level in thousands)	..	2.0	-9.2	-4.2	1.2	-1.1	*571*
Percentage of the labour force							
Unemployment	13.6	7.9	13.9	16.8	10.1	9.4	

Notes and sources are at the end of the part.

StatLink http://dx.doi.org/10.1787/888932616144

Finland

According to national statistics, the number of foreigners living in Finland at the end of 2011 was 183 000, or about 3.4% of the population, with the largest groups represented by Estonians (33 900) and Russians (29 600).

In 2010, according to national statistics, 25 600 persons moved to Finland, which is 4% less than in 2009. Out of these entries, foreign nationals accounted for 18 200, roughly the same level as in 2009. Main countries of origin of immigrants continued to be Estonia (3 900), the Russian Federation (2 300), Iraq (1 100), and Somalia (1 000). Preliminary statistics show that 21 000 people moved to Finland during January-September 2011, a slight increase compared to the corresponding period of the previous year (19 800).

The number of residence permit applications increased for all application types in 2010. The number of applications based on family ties increased 25% over 2009, to 10 600. The number of residence permit applications for employment purposes increased by 14% in 2010. Out of the total 16 300 residence permits issued in 2010, 34% were granted on the grounds of family ties, 28% for study and 18% for employment. The distribution of the 17 700 permits in 2011 saw fewer family permits (32%) and more study permits (31%) than in 2010.

In 2010 a total of 4 000 persons, including 330 unaccompanied minors, sought asylum in Finland, a decline of 33% compared with 2009. Asylum seeking fell further in 2011, to 3 100.

The new Finnish government formed in June 2011 included integration of immigrants and the prevention of discrimination in its programme. The new immigration policy is meant to support the building of a pluralistic society and to enhance Finland's international competitiveness. Measures to be implemented aim at increasing the employment rate of immigrants, making integration policy more effective, accelerating the processing of asylum applications, and fighting discrimination. Labour market supervision will be increased to ensure equal rights to all employees. From January 2012, the Ministry of Employment and Economy is responsible for integration matters, with the exception of nationality issues and the promotion of good ethnic relations, which remain, with all other migration issues, under the responsibility of the Ministry of Interior.

An *Act on the Promotion of Integration*, adopted under the previous government, entered into force on 1 September 2011. The Act expands the scope of integration measures, especially at the early stages. Under the new Act, all immigrants – and not, as previously, only the registered unemployed – will be provided with basic information on Finnish society and their rights and obligations, when granted a residence permit. Immigrants are also entitled to a needs-assessment regarding language training and a possible integration plan. New models of integration training will be studied, to find the most effective ways to bring immigrants into the labour market or support the integration of those who are already in the labour market.

The *Nationality Act* was reformed in September 2011, providing a more flexible process for the acquisition of citizenship. The required period of residence to apply for Finnish nationality was shortened from six to five years and temporary residence in Finland will be partially taken into account.

A new law on the reception of humanitarian migrants also came into force in September 2011. It separates financial support to persons applying for international protection and to beneficiaries of temporary protection, from the general social benefit system.

The specific return migration system for Ingrian Finns will end after a transition period of five years from July 2011. From July 2016, Ingrian Finns who want to move to Finland will have to apply under the general migration channels.

As of January 2012, Finland implemented the EU Blue Card Directive, for the issuance of residence permits for highly skilled migrants from outside the EU with at least one year of employment in the area where high skills are required, conditional on an above-average salary.

Amendments concerning biometric features in residence permits entered into force in January 2012. Since then, applicants must apply in person for a residence permit. Biometric residence cards are meant to prevent and combat illegal immigration and illegal residence by creating a reliable link between the residence permit and its holders.

For further information:

www.migri.fi/netcomm/?language=EN
www.intermin.fi

Recent trends in migrants' flows and stocks
FINLAND

Migration flows (foreigners) National definition	2000	2005	2009	2010	Average 2001-05	Average 2006-10	Level ('000) 2010
Per 1 000 inhabitants							
Inflows	1.8	2.4	3.4	3.4	2.1	3.3	18.2
Outflows	0.8	0.5	0.8	0.6	0.5	0.7	3.1

Migration inflows (foreigners) by type Permit based statistics (standardised)	Thousands 2009	Thousands 2010	% distribution 2009	% distribution 2010
Work	1.6	1.1	8.8	5.8
Family (incl. accompanying family)	6.3	6.2	35.0	34.3
Humanitarian	3.0	3.2	16.6	17.4
Free movements	6.5	7.1	35.8	39.0
Others	0.7	0.7	3.7	3.6
Total	18.1	18.2	100.0	100.0

Inflows of top 10 nationalities as a % of total inflows of foreigners

2000-2009 annual average / 2010

Estonia, Russian Federation, Iraq, Somalia, Sweden, Thailand, China, India, Afghanistan, Germany

Temporary migration	2005	2009	2010	Average 2006-10
Thousands				
International students	..	4.3	4.5	4.2
Trainees	..	..	..	..
Working holiday makers	..	..	..	..
Seasonal workers	12.2	12.5	12.0	12.7
Intra-company transfers	..	..	..	..
Other temporary workers	6.5	10.0	9.0	10.2

Inflows of asylum seekers	2000	2005	2009	2010	Average 2001-05	Average 2006-10	Level 2010
Per 1 000 inhabitants	0.6	0.7	1.1	0.7	0.6	0.7	4 018

Components of population growth	2000	2005	2009	2010	Average 2001-05	Average 2006-10	Level ('000) 2010
Per 1 000 inhabitants							
Total	1.9	3.6	4.5	4.5	2.9	4.4	24
Natural increase	1.5	1.9	1.9	1.9	1.6	2.0	10
Net migration	0.4	1.7	2.6	2.4	1.3	2.4	13

Stocks of immigrants	2000	2005	2009	2010	Average 2001-05	Average 2006-10	Level ('000) 2010
Percentage of the total population							
Foreign-born population	2.6	3.4	4.4	4.6	3.1	4.1	248
Foreign population	1.8	2.2	2.9	3.1	2.0	2.7	168

Naturalisations	2000	2005	2009	2010	Average 2001-05	Average 2006-10	Level 2010
Percentage of the foreign population	3.4	5.2	2.4	2.8	4.3	3.3	4 334

Labour market outcomes	2000	2005	2009	2010	Average 2001-05	Average 2006-10
Employment/population ratio						
Native-born men	71.2	71.2	69.6	69.5	71.0	71.3
Foreign-born men	49.9	61.7	67.7	66.2	64.9	68.2
Native-born women	65.3	68.0	68.2	67.5	67.4	68.5
Foreign-born women	39.0	49.7	59.8	55.1	50.8	57.2
Unemployment rate						
Native-born men	10.3	9.3	8.7	8.8	10.0	7.7
Foreign-born men	36.6	22.4	16.1	18.4	20.8	15.2
Native-born women	12.0	9.4	7.4	7.4	10.0	7.4
Foreign-born women	21.3	22.7	14.7	15.8	22.6	16.0

Macroeconomic indicators	2000	2005	2009	2010	Average 2001-05	Average 2006-10	Level 2010
Annual growth in %							
Real GDP	5.3	2.9	-8.4	3.7	2.6	1.1	
GDP/capita (level in USD)	5.1	2.6	-8.8	3.3	2.4	0.6	36 477
Employment (level in thousands)	1.7	1.5	-2.9	-0.5	0.6	0.4	2 438
Percentage of the labour force							
Unemployment	9.8	8.4	8.3	8.4	8.9	7.5	

Notes and sources are at the end of the part.

StatLink http://dx.doi.org/10.1787/888932616163

France

Permanent immigration excluding freedom of movement (nationals of Romania, Bulgaria and third countries do not benefit from freedom of movement) reached a level of roughly 137 000 entries in 2010, an 8% increase over 2009. This increase was driven by an 8% rise in family reunification, to 84 000, while humanitarian and labour migration flows were stable. In part the increase reflects the entries with a "long-stay visa constituting a residence permit" (*Visa de long séjour valant titre de séjour*, VLS-TS) in 2009, some of whom were not registered until 2010.

Most permits issued for permanent residence went to citizens from Africa (62%), and especially North Africa (34%, principally Algeria and Morocco). Asia was the second-ranking region of origin (18%). Over two-thirds of the new temporary work permits (excluding seasonal permits) were granted to immigrants already living in the country under other immigration categories, more than half as students. In 2010, 15 000 new temporary work permits were issued, including 8 000 new seasonal work permits.

In 2010, 65 000 permits (89% of which were VLS-TS) were granted to foreign students, an increase of approximately 28% over the previous year. The main countries of origin were China (10 500), Morocco (5 700), the United States (5 600), Algeria (3 900) and Tunisia (3 000).

The number of asylum-seekers has been rising constantly for four years. In 2010, more than 48 000 asylum requests were recorded, about 14% more than in the previous year. Nearly 10% of the applications were from Serbia and Montenegro. The other countries were, in order of ranking, the Democratic Republic of the Congo, the Russian Federation, Sri Lanka, and China. In 2010, as in 2009, approximately 15 000 persons were granted protection by France, including 4 600 accompanying minors and 2 450 persons who received subsidiary protection.

The number of persons receiving assistance for voluntary departures rose in 2010 to 4 000 (38% higher than in 2009), its highest level ever. In addition, 9 700 persons qualified for humanitarian repatriation, including 8 000 Romanians. 16 000 expulsions were carried out in 2010, out of 73 500 ordered.

In 2009, 101 000 persons signed compulsory "Welcoming and Integration Contracts", a slight increase over the previous year.

In 2010, 140 000 acquisitions of citizenship were recorded. Most were by decree (95 500). The number for reasons of marriage (22 000) was higher than the previous year (16 400), as 2009 figures were influenced by legislative changes which increased the required length of marriage before application for French citizenship.

The worsening employment situation led the government to set an objective of reduced immigration for employment, except for temporary and seasonal workers, the highly qualified and intra-corporate transfers. In light of that objective, the government issued instructions to the prefectures on 31 May 2011, indicating strict controls when evaluating applications for work permits, especially for status changes, less qualified employment, and from students offered their first job. A new set of instructions issued on 12 January 2012 loosened the criteria for issuing work permits to students who have successfully completed at least a masters-level degree programme. Expulsion orders issued to students under the previous instructions were suspended pending re-examination of their applications.

A new immigration law was adopted on 16 June 2011, transposing three European directives into French law (the so-called "Return Directive", the European Blue Card Directive and the directive providing for minimum standards on sanctions and measures against employers of illegally staying third-country nationals). In addition, the new law directly conditions stay and acquisition of nationality on respect of the Welcoming and Integration Contract. The residence requirement for naturalisation may be reduced to two years for those who clearly meet the criterion of assimilation. A "Charter of Rights and Duties of the French Citizen" must be signed at the moment of naturalisation. Some of the rules for acquiring a residence permit, especially the temporary permit of stay for health reasons, have been made stricter.

On 11 August 2011, the list of shortage occupations applied to those outside of the free movement zone was cut back, from 30 to 14 occupations. A single list, which provides exemption from the labour market test, is valid for all of France.

For further information:

www.immigration.gouv.fr
www.ofii.fr/
www.ofpra.gouv.fr

Recent trends in migrants' flows and stocks
FRANCE

Migration flows (foreigners) National definition	2000	2005	2009	2010	Average		Level ('000)
					2001-05	2006-10	2010
Per 1 000 inhabitants							
Inflows	1.6	2.2	2.0	2.2	2.1	2.1	136.0
Outflows	..	..	..	..	..	..	..

Migration inflows (foreigners) by type	Thousands		% distribution	
Permit based statistics (standardised)	2009	2010	2009	2010
Work	22.5	22.9	12.6	11.9
Family (incl. accompanying family)	76.6	82.8	42.8	42.9
Humanitarian	10.4	10.3	5.8	5.4
Free movements	54.0	58.5	30.2	30.3
Others	15.3	18.5	8.6	9.6
Total	178.7	193.1	100.0	100.0

Inflows of top 10 nationalities as a % of total inflows of foreigners

2000-2009 annual average / 2010

Algeria, Morocco, Tunisia, Turkey, Mali, Haiti, China, Senegal, Cameroon, Dem. Rep. of the Congo

Temporary migration	2005	2009	2010	Average
				2006-10
Thousands				
International students	46.2	50.7	65.2	51.2
Trainees	0.6	0.6	0.6	0.6
Working holiday makers	..	..	..	..
Seasonal workers	16.2	8.0	7.8	12.7
Intra-company transfers	1.0	0.7	1.0	1.0
Other temporary workers	6.5	3.5	4.7	5.0

Inflows of asylum seekers	2000	2005	2009	2010	Average		Level
					2001-05	2006-10	2010
Per 1 000 inhabitants	0.7	0.8	0.7	0.8	0.9	0.6	48 074

Components of population growth	2000	2005	2009	2010	Average		Level ('000)
					2001-05	2006-10	2010
Per 1 000 inhabitants							
Total	6.9	7.1	5.2	5.4	7.1	5.6	337
Natural increase	4.1	4.0	4.1	4.2	3.9	4.3	262
Net migration	1.2	1.6	1.1	1.2	1.6	1.2	75

Stocks of immigrants	2000	2005	2009	2010	Average		Level ('000)
					2001-05	2006-10	2010
Percentage of the total population							
Foreign-born population	7.4	8.1	..	..	7.8	..	..
Foreign population	..	..	..	6.0	..	..	3 769

Naturalisations	2000	2005	2009	2010	Average		Level
					2001-05	2006-10	2010
Percentage of the foreign population	4.6	..	3.6	3.8	..	..	143 275

Labour market outcomes	2000	2005	2009	2010	Average	
					2001-05	2006-10
Employment/population ratio						
Native-born men	69.8	69.6	68.8	68.4	70.2	69.0
Foreign-born men	66.7	67.1	65.5	66.4	66.7	66.7
Native-born women	56.6	59.9	61.3	61.1	58.8	61.0
Foreign-born women	45.6	48.2	50.6	49.7	48.0	50.0
Unemployment rate						
Native-born men	7.7	7.5	8.2	8.4	7.0	7.6
Foreign-born men	14.5	12.5	14.2	13.7	13.2	13.3
Native-born women	11.3	9.0	8.8	8.9	9.3	8.4
Foreign-born women	19.7	16.8	14.3	16.0	16.1	14.9

Macroeconomic indicators	2000	2005	2009	2010	Average		Level
					2001-05	2006-10	2010
Annual growth in %							
Real GDP	3.7	1.8	-2.7	1.5	1.6	0.7	
GDP/capita (level in USD)	3.0	1.1	-3.3	0.9	0.9	0.1	34 148
Employment (level in thousands)	2.7	0.7	-0.9	0.2	0.8	0.6	25 694
Percentage of the labour force							
Unemployment	8.5	8.9	9.1	9.4	8.4	8.5	

Notes and sources are at the end of the part.

StatLink http://dx.doi.org/10.1787/888932616182

Germany

Total inflows of foreigners in Germany were 683 500 in 2010, an increase by 13% over 2009. In the same period, outflows of foreigners decreased by 8%, to just under 530 000, leading to a net inward migration of foreigners of almost 154 000 in 2010, a fivefold increase on the corresponding figure for 2009. Net migration of German nationals, however, was negative 26 000 in 2010. The main origin countries of arriving foreigners remained Poland (17%) and Romania (11%), followed by Bulgaria (6%) and Hungary, which replaced Turkey in the fourth position.

All major categories of immigration flows grew in 2010, with the highest relative increases recorded for family migration and free mobility, both up by 14% compared with the 2009 levels. Permanent-type labour migration from non-EU countries – which is essentially highly skilled – remained very limited in international comparison, at 20 000, 2 000 more than in 2009.

Following the expiration of the transitional arrangements for labour migration from Central and Eastern European countries which joined the European Union (EU) in 2004 (EU8), since 1 May 2011 workers from those countries have been granted unrestricted access to the German labour market. A substantial increase in the inflows from the EU8 was recorded in the first month of application of free movement rules. While April 2011 saw around 4 500 entries from the EU8, their number more than doubled in May 2011, to 10 200 entries. Inflows from EU8 countries subsided after the May 2011 spike, but remain well above the 2010 levels.

The Federal Employment Agency, approved a total of almost 11 400 work authorisations for third-country nationals in 2010. Half of those authorised held a degree from a German institution. By the end of 2010, around 185 000 foreign students were enrolled in German universities. The main country of origin of those students was China (12%), followed by the Russian Federation (5%), Bulgaria and Poland (4% each).

The government adopted, in June 2011, the "Concept for Securing the Skilled Labour Base". The five-pronged strategy aims at sustaining the supply of skilled workers in Germany in the medium and long term, in light of the decline in the working-age population. The main pillar of the strategy is the activation of the domestic labour force. The improvement of the labour market integration of migrants already living in the country is one of the key objectives.

The "Law to improve the assessment and recognition of foreign professional qualifications", due to come into force in April 2012, is meant to improve the labour market integration of persons with foreign professional qualifications. The law entitles holders of a foreign qualification in one of 350 specified occupations (mostly requiring vocational qualifications) to the right, within three months from application, to have their credentials assessed in terms of equivalence with German degrees. The assessment procedure has been standardised and foreign qualifications are evaluated exclusively in terms of "essential differences" with the German equivalent, while the applicant's nationality is no longer relevant. The new recognition act covers immigrants residing in Germany and potential immigrants abroad who may seek recognition before arrival. An estimated 285 000 current residents hold foreign qualifications eligible for evaluation. Eleven regional contact points are being established to provide basic information and support in finding the appropriate recognition authority.

The "Concept for Securing the Skilled Labour Base" also aims to attract skilled workers from abroad through managed migration in response to labour market needs. One measure is the establishment of a "positive list" of shortage professions granting exemption from the labour market test. The list, reviewed by the Federal Employment Agency every six months on the basis of a job monitoring system, initially included doctors as well as mechanical, automotive and electrical engineers, with several other occupations added in 2012. An additional measure is a proposal to lower the salary threshold for the issuance of permanent residence permits to highly qualified specialists and executive staff with exceptional professional experience, from EUR 66 000 annually to EUR 48 000 (prior to 2009, it stood at EUR 88 000).

Finally, implementation of the EU Blue Card Directive is expected to be approved by the Parliament in the first half of 2012. According to the law, highly qualified persons from outside the European Economic Area (EEA), with a minimum annual salary of EUR 44 000, will be allowed to obtain a residence permit in Germany without being subject to the labour market test. The threshold will be further lowered to EUR 33 000 for workers having qualifications in shortage occupations.

For further information:

www.bmas.bund.de
www.bmi.bund.de
www.bamf.de
www.integrationsbeauftragte.de
www.destatis.de

Recent trends in migrants' flows and stocks
GERMANY

Migration flows (foreigners) National definition	2000	2005	2009	2010	Average		Level ('000)
					2001-05	2006-10	2010
Per 1 000 inhabitants							
Inflows	7.9	7.0	7.4	8.4	7.6	7.3	683.5
Outflows	6.8	5.9	7.1	8.2	6.1	6.8	670.6

Migration inflows (foreigners) by type Permit based statistics (standardised)	Thousands		% distribution	
	2009	2010	2009	2010
Work	18.0	20.1	9.0	9.0
Family (incl. accompanying family)	48.2	54.9	23.9	24.7
Humanitarian	11.1	11.8	5.5	5.3
Free movements	120.7	133.3	59.9	59.9
Others	3.4	2.4	1.7	1.1
Total	201.4	222.4	100.0	100.0

Inflows of top 10 nationalities as a % of total inflows of foreigners

Poland, Romania, Bulgaria, Hungary, Turkey, Italy, Serbia, United States, China, Russian Federation (2000-2009 annual average vs 2010)

Temporary migration	2005	2009	2010	Average 2006-10
Thousands				
International students	55.8	60.9	66.4	58.6
Trainees	2.6	4.8	4.8	4.8
Working holiday makers	..	..	..	..
Seasonal workers	329.8	294.8	296.5	295.9
Intra-company transfers	3.6	4.4	5.9	5.2
Other temporary workers	63.6	32.2	33.9	37.5

Inflows of asylum seekers	2000	2005	2009	2010	Average		Level
					2001-05	2006-10	2010
Per 1 000 inhabitants	1.0	0.4	0.3	0.5	0.7	0.3	41 332

Components of population growth	2000	2005	2009	2010	Average		Level ('000)
					2001-05	2006-10	2010
Per 1 000 inhabitants							
Total	1.2	−0.8	..	..	0.4	..	..
Natural increase	−0.9	−1.7	..	..	−1.5	..	..
Net migration	2.0	1.0	..	..	1.9	..	..

Stocks of immigrants	2000	2005	2009	2010	Average		Level ('000)
					2001-05	2006-10	2010
Percentage of the total population							
Foreign-born population	12.5	12.6	12.9	13.0	..	12.9	10 591
Foreign population	8.9	8.2	8.2	8.3	8.6	8.2	6 754

Naturalisations	2000	2005	2009	2010	Average		Level
					2001-05	2006-10	2010
Percentage of the foreign population	2.5	1.7	1.4	1.5	2.0	1.6	101 570

Labour market outcomes	2000	2005	2009	2010	Average	
					2001-05	2006-10
Employment/population ratio						
Native-born men	73.8	72.6	76.4	76.7	72.3	75.9
Foreign-born men	66.3	64.9	71.7	72.9	65.3	70.4
Native-born women	59.6	63.2	68.5	68.3	61.1	66.5
Foreign-born women	46.6	49.1	55.7	55.7	47.9	53.3
Unemployment rate						
Native-born men	6.9	10.2	7.2	6.7	9.0	7.5
Foreign-born men	12.9	18.4	13.6	12.4	15.8	14.0
Native-born women	8.0	9.8	6.5	5.9	8.7	7.3
Foreign-born women	12.1	16.8	11.8	10.7	13.8	13.0

Macroeconomic indicators	2000	2005	2009	2010	Average		Level
					2001-05	2006-10	2010
Annual growth in %							
Real GDP	3.1	0.7	−5.1	3.7	0.6	1.3	
GDP/capita (level in USD)	2.9	0.7	−4.8	3.8	0.5	1.5	37 411
Employment (level in thousands)	1.7	−0.1	0.0	0.5	−0.2	0.8	40 552
Percentage of the labour force							
Unemployment	7.5	10.6	7.4	6.8	9.0	7.9	

Notes and sources are at the end of the part.

StatLink http://dx.doi.org/10.1787/888932616201

Greece

Data on immigration in Greece are not consistently available, but the principal sources available suggest a decline in the stock of immigrants in 2010, and an even sharper decrease in 2011. According to LFS data, in the fourth quarter of 2010 there were 810 000 foreigners living in Greece, a 4% decrease over the corresponding figures for 2009. According to the Ministry of Citizen Protection (former Ministry of Interior) permit data, the stock of non-EU permit holders (non-seasonal) at the end of 2010 stood at 567 000, a decrease by 20 000 compared with the previous year. Preliminary figures for the end of 2011 suggest that the total number of permit holders was down by 100 000. In 2010, the largest groups of non-EU citizens with permits were from Albania (491 000), Ukraine (20 500), Georgia (16 500), and Pakistan (16 300). The largest groups of EU nationals in Greece come from Bulgaria and Romania.

The fall in the stock of registered immigrants is related to the severe economic crisis in Greece: the average unemployment rate stood at 18.2% in July 2011, up 6% higher over one year, and since 2009, the unemployment level of non-EU immigrants has been higher than that of Greek nationals. While the crisis has hit all sectors of the Greek economy hard in the last two years, sectors employing many immigrants, such as construction, have seen employment loss since 2008. Fewer permit holders may not mean that immigrants left Greece, since some, unable to meet employment and welfare payment requirements for permit renewal, may have lost their legal status and remained in the country.

In 2010, according to official figures, about 133 000 migrants were apprehended illegally crossing into Greece (by land and sea), a slight increase compared with 2010. The number fell in 2011 (81 000 apprehensions in the first ten months). Since 2010, most apprehensions have occurred at the land border with Turkey.

According to UNHCR, the number of asylum seekers in Greece fell from 15 900 in 2009 to 10 300 in 2010. This was partly due to an increased backlog after the 2009 reforms of the asylum procedure – abolition of the appeal system and transfer of the responsibility for status determination to local police – and UNHCR's subsequent withdrawal from assistance in the process. In addition, a number of other European countries halted the return of asylum seekers to Greece under the Dublin Convention, citing inadequate reception facilities and access to asylum. The main origin countries of asylum seekers in 2010 were Pakistan, Georgia and Bangladesh.

In January 2011, the Greek parliament approved a new law reforming the asylum system. The law transfers refugee status determination from the police to a new civilian body, re-establishes an appeals system, and creates a first reception system and new decentralised asylum offices. The latter two measures have yet to be funded. The new law also transposed the EU "Return" directive, creating, among other changes, two separate agencies, one for asylum and one for First Reception of irregular migrants. A new stay permit for exceptional reasons may now be granted to irregular migrants who have lived in Greece for 12 years, and at least 10 years preceding the application, and can demonstrate special ties with the country – such as having studied in a Greek school, being a family member of a Greek citizen, speaking the Greek language, or past legal stay.

Acquisition of the EU long term resident status, a prerequisite for naturalisation under the March 2010 citizenship law, became easier in 2011: immigrants may now prove knowledge of Greek language and history by passing a test, without having to attend a special state-run course as under previous legislation. The 2011 law also granted local voting rights to foreigners with at least five years residence and a long-term permit. About 12 000 non-EU nationals participated in November 2010 local elections.

In the context of the reorganisation of local and regional government in 2010, Councils for Migrant Integration were introduced at the municipal level, as consultative bodies on issues of concern to the local migrant population. These councils are composed of members of the municipal councils and social stakeholders, including migrants.

For further information:

www.statistics.gr
www.ypakp.gr
www.yptp.gr

Recent trends in migrants' flows and stocks
GREECE

Migration flows (foreigners) National definition	2000	2005	2009	2010	Average 2001-05	Average 2006-10	Level ('000) 2010
Per 1 000 inhabitants							
Inflows	..	..	3.0	2.0	..	..	23.0
Outflows	..	..	1.4	4.2	..	..	47.1

Migration inflows (foreigners) by type	Thousands		% distribution				
Permit based statistics (standardised)	2009	2010	2009	2010			
Work	..	..	..	..			
Family (incl. accompanying family)	..	..	..	..			
Humanitarian	..	..	..	..			
Free movements	..	..	..	..			
Others	..	..	..	..			
Total	..	..	..	..			

Temporary migration	2005	2009	2010	Average 2006-10
Thousands				
International students	..	..	..	..
Trainees	..	..	..	..
Working holiday makers	..	..	..	..
Seasonal workers	..	..	..	..
Intra-company transfers	..	..	..	..
Other temporary workers	..	..	..	..

Inflows of asylum seekers	2000	2005	2009	2010	Average 2001-05	Average 2006-10	Level 2010
Per 1 000 inhabitants	0.3	0.8	1.4	0.9	0.6	1.5	10 273

Components of population growth	2000	2005	2009	2010	Average 2001-05	Average 2006-10	Level ('000) 2010
Per 1 000 inhabitants							
Total	2.5	3.8	..	..	3.5	..	..
Natural increase	−0.2	0.3	..	..	0.0	..	..
Net migration	2.7	3.5	..	..	3.5	..	..

Stocks of immigrants	2000	2005	2009	2010	Average 2001-05	Average 2006-10	Level ('000) 2010
Percentage of the total population							
Foreign-born population	..	..	..	..	..	..	..
Foreign population	2.8	5.0	7.4	7.1	4.3	6.4	810

Naturalisations	2000	2005	2009	2010	Average 2001-05	Average 2006-10	Level 2010
Percentage of the foreign population	..	..	2.3	..	..	..	..

Labour market outcomes	2000	2005	2009	2010	Average 2001-05	Average 2006-10
Employment/population ratio						
Native-born men	71.3	73.5	72.7	70.2	72.5	73.0
Foreign-born men	78.1	82.6	80.5	76.7	81.8	82.1
Native-born women	41.6	45.7	48.7	47.8	43.9	48.0
Foreign-born women	45.0	50.2	51.1	51.2	47.8	50.4
Unemployment rate						
Native-born men	7.5	6.2	6.5	9.4	6.4	6.4
Foreign-born men	9.5	6.7	10.4	15.2	7.4	8.2
Native-born women	17.0	15.4	13.2	16.2	15.3	13.4
Foreign-born women	21.4	15.6	14.5	17.7	18.3	14.7

Macroeconomic indicators	2000	2005	2009	2010	Average 2001-05	Average 2006-10	Level 2010
Annual growth in %							
Real GDP	4.5	2.3	−3.2	−3.5	4.0	0.3	
GDP/capita (level in USD)	4.1	1.9	−3.6	−3.7	3.7	0.0	28 430
Employment (level in thousands)	1.4	1.3	−1.1	−2.7	1.3	0.1	4 389
Percentage of the labour force							
Unemployment	11.4	9.9	9.5	12.5	10.2	9.4	

Notes and sources are at the end of the part.

StatLink http://dx.doi.org/10.1787/888932616220

Hungary

Hungary is a not a major destination for international migrants. The stock of foreign nationals is comparably small and makes up only 2% of the overall population. By January 2011 it stood at 209 000 persons. It is estimated that up to 40% of these are ethnic Hungarians from neighbouring countries.

Long-term migration to Hungary (as defined by residence of at least one year) continued to decline in 2010, to 23 900, 6% less than in 2009 and 32% less than the record level observed in 2008. This trend reflects the economic crisis, which hit Hungary hard from 2009-10. Outflows of foreign nationals peaked at around 6 000 in 2010. Net long-term migration thus amounted to about 17 800, a decrease of 10% compared with 2009.

Romania has been, by far, the most important country of origin of immigrants over the past decade, although its share in long-term inflows declined from 50% in 2001/2002 to 27% in 2010. At the same time, the share of nationals from the EU15 rose from less than 10% during the first half of the decade, to 21% in 2010. After Romania, the other main countries of origin for long-term migration were Germany (10%), Ukraine (7%), the Slovak Republic and China (both accounting for about 5% of total inflow).

As a consequence of the economic downturn and the worsening employment situation, only some 24 500 work permits were issued by the National Employment Office in 2010, a decrease of 13% compared with the 2009 figure, which was already almost half of the 2007 level. Two thirds of the work permits were issued to immigrants from neighbouring countries. The number of residence permits issued by the Office of Immigration and Nationality for the purpose of "gainful employment" increased by 14%, to roughly 16 000. Family migrants obtained almost 4 700 permits, 9% more than in the previous year. The number of permits for students also increased, to about 11 200, 14% more than in 2009.

The 2 100 persons seeking asylum in Hungary in 2010 represented half the number of 2009. This was mainly due to a sharp decline (more than 70%) in the number of asylum seekers from Serbia and Kosovo, a decline that might be related to the December 2009 implementation of the EU visa exemption agreement with Serbia, the Former Yugoslav Republic of Macedonia (FYROM) and Montenegro. The main origin countries of asylum seekers remained Afghanistan (700 applicants) and Kosovo (380). However a new phenomenon is the emergence of applicants from the West Bank and Gaza Strip (220).

Following amendments to the Asylum Act in 2010, Hungary changed its reception system of unaccompanied minors by conferring a major role to child-protection facilities. From May 2011, unaccompanied minors are placed in specific child-protection facilities outside reception centres. While Hungarian legislation exempts third-country family members of a recognised refugee from general maintenance requirements for family reunification, the Act on the Entry and Stay of Foreigners was amended in 2010 to exclude family members of beneficiaries of subsidiary protection from this exemption.

About 6 000 persons were apprehended for attempted or actual illegal border crossing at the borders with Ukraine, Serbia and Romania in 2009. The number of border apprehensions decreased by 21% in 2010. The EU Return directive was transposed into Romanian legislation in 2010, and amendments to the Act on the Entry and Stay of third country-nationals entered into force in April 2011, providing for harmonisation with the Community Visa Code.

About 5 500 foreign nationals acquired Hungarian citizenship in 2010, a slight decrease over 2009 (5 800). Nearly 90% of the new citizens came from neighbouring countries, in particular from Romania (60%), followed by Ukraine (15%) and Serbia and Montenegro (12%). An amendment to the Hungarian citizenship law introducing a simplified and preferential naturalisation procedure for persons of Hungarian descent came into effect in January 2011.

Various projects in the field of migrant integration were carried out in 2010, largely supported by the European Integration Fund. The main focus was on integration of migrant children through education. Other initiatives included the introduction of language course opportunities for adults, and media campaigns for strengthening intercultural dialogue and consciousness about immigration in the Hungarian society.

For further information:
http://portal.ksh.hu
www.bmbah.hu/
http://mfa.gov.hu/kum/en/bal
https://magyarorszag.hu/

Recent trends in migrants' flows and stocks
HUNGARY

Migration flows (foreigners) National definition	2000	2005	2009	2010	Average 2001-05	Average 2006-10	Level ('000) 2010
Per 1 000 inhabitants							
Inflows	2.0	2.5	2.6	2.4	2.1	2.6	*23.9*
Outflows	0.2	0.3	0.6	0.6	0.3	0.5	*6.0*

Migration inflows (foreigners) by type Permit based statistics (standardised)	Thousands 2009	Thousands 2010	% distribution 2009	% distribution 2010
Work	..	..	..	..
Family (incl. accompanying family)	..	..	..	..
Humanitarian	..	..	..	..
Free movements	..	..	..	..
Others	..	..	..	..
Total	..	..	..	..

Inflows of top 10 nationalities as a % of total inflows of foreigners

2000-2009 annual average / 2010

Romania, Germany, Ukraine, Slovak Republic, China, United States, Serbia, Austria, Turkey, Korea

Temporary migration	2005	2009	2010	Average 2006-10
Thousands				
International students	..	..	..	..
Trainees	..	..	..	..
Working holiday makers	..	..	..	..
Seasonal workers	..	..	..	..
Intra-company transfers	..	..	..	..
Other temporary workers	..	..	..	..

Inflows of asylum seekers	2000	2005	2009	2010	Average 2001-05	Average 2006-10	Level 2010
Per 1 000 inhabitants	0.8	0.2	0.5	0.2	0.4	0.3	*2 104*

Components of population growth	2000	2005	2009	2010	Average 2001-05	Average 2006-10	Level ('000) 2010
Per 1 000 inhabitants							
Total	-2.2	-2.2	-1.7	-2.8	-2.4	-1.8	*-28*
Natural increase	-3.7	-3.9	-3.4	-4.0	-3.7	-3.4	*-40*
Net migration	1.7	1.7	1.7	1.2	1.3	1.6	*12*

Stocks of immigrants	2000	2005	2009	2010	Average 2001-05	Average 2006-10	Level ('000) 2010
Percentage of the total population							
Foreign-born population	2.9	3.3	4.1	4.5	3.1	3.9	*451*
Foreign population	1.1	1.5	2.0	2.1	1.3	1.9	*209*

Naturalisations	2000	2005	2009	2010	Average 2001-05	Average 2006-10	Level 2010
Percentage of the foreign population	4.9	6.9	3.1	3.1	4.9	3.8	*6 086*

Labour market outcomes	2000	2005	2009	2010	Average 2001-05	Average 2006-10	
Employment/population ratio							
Native-born men	62.6	63.0	60.9	60.2	63.0	62.3	
Foreign-born men	69.4	72.3	74.0	69.2	72.0	72.4	
Native-born women	49.4	50.9	49.7	50.4	50.3	50.5	
Foreign-born women	49.8	54.3	59.2	62.4	49.8	57.5	
Unemployment rate							
Native-born men	7.3	7.1	10.4	11.7	6.4	8.9	
Foreign-born men	3.5	3.0	8.6	7.6	2.4	5.8	
Native-born women	5.8	7.4	9.8	10.8	5.7	8.9	
Foreign-born women	4.8	6.4	9.6	7.4	6.5	7.9	

Macroeconomic indicators	2000	2005	2009	2010	Average 2001-05	Average 2006-10	Level 2010
Annual growth in %							
Real GDP	4.2	4.0	-6.8	1.3	4.2	-0.1	
GDP/capita (level in USD)	4.5	4.2	-6.7	1.5	4.4	0.0	*20 545*
Employment (level in thousands)	1.6	0.0	-2.3	0.0	0.2	-0.5	*3 756*
Percentage of the labour force							
Unemployment	6.5	7.3	10.1	11.2	6.2	8.8	

Notes and sources are at the end of the part.

StatLink http://dx.doi.org/10.1787/888932616239

Ireland

Migration in Ireland continues to be affected by the country's severe economic crisis. Between 2007 and 2011, net migration fell from +1.6% to −0.8% of total population. Three years after Irish employment levels peaked in the third quarter of 2007, the country had lost almost 290 000 jobs, a decline of 14%, and the unemployment rate exceeded 14%. Migrant inflows to Ireland decreased sharply from 110 000 in the year prior to April 2007 (FY 2007) to 31 000 in FY 2010. A slight increase in immigration was observed in FY 2011, when 42 000 inflows were recorded.

The 2011 increase in inflows was mainly due to returning Irish nationals (171 000 compared with 133 000 in FY 2010). Immigration from new EU member countries also increased, by 55% compared with FY 2010, to 9 000, but remained at one-fifth of 2007 levels. Inflows from non-EEA countries also increased (+61%), albeit remaining at much smaller levels than those of the period 2002-04.

Outflows increased in recent years as Irish nationals left and immigrants returned home. Outward migration has continued to increase steadily from 29 000 in FY 2005 to 76 000 in FY 2011, with more Irish than EU8 citizens leaving since 2010. Over 40 000 Irish left in FY 2011. Citizens of the new EU member states accounted for less than 20% of all outflows in FY 2011.

There were less than 2 000 applications for asylum in FY 2010, the lowest level since 1996. The 2011 figure was about 33% lower. The 2003 Immigration Act and the 2004 Irish Nationality and Citizenship Act, which withdrew birthright citizenship, may have contributed to the decline in asylum applications.

Fewer employment permits were issued, with all categories of permit except for spouses and dependants falling during 2010. Initial trends for 2011 show an overall decrease in both new permits and renewals. New employment permits may only be issued to highly skilled, highly paid positions; non-EEA nationals already legally resident in the country on employment permits; or for officially recognised shortages of a particular type or qualification. From June 2010, non-EEA doctors recruited to certain positions within the Irish Public Health Service are exempt from a labour-market test and no longer require a permit to work.

Measures taken during 2009 to facilitate migrants' stay and economic activity continued to be implemented during 2010. As of August 2010, certain current or former Green Card holders may work without renewing their employment permit for two years. As of November 2010, those holding work permits (including spousal and dependent permits) and work authorisations/visas for at least five consecutive years are granted one-year renewable stay and are exempt from employment permit requirements at renewal.

A revised Immigration, Residence and Protection Bill published in June 2010 sets out a legislative framework for the management of inward migration to Ireland. Among other rules, it requires foreign nationals unlawfully in the country to leave. It sets out statutory processes for applying for a visa, entry, residence and deportation.

A five-year international education strategy framework, published in 2010, sets a target of 38 000 international students in higher education (+50%) by 2015. In January 2011, the length of stay for non-EEA students in Ireland was capped according to the type of course followed (two years for language or non-degree programmes; five years for degree programmes). Non-EEA student permission will be limited to seven years in total.

In June 2011 the first Irish Short-Stay Visa Waiver Programme was launched under a governmental "Jobs Initiative", with the aim of increasing tourism. The waiver, valid until October 2012, allows travel to Ireland on a valid UK visa for tourists, business persons and long-term residents who have lawfully entered the United Kingdom. Nationals of sixteen "emerging" economies are included under the Programme including, China, certain Gulf States, India, the Russian Federation, Belarus, Ukraine and Turkey.

In June 2011 a number of measures aimed at simplifying and fastening the processing of naturalisation applications were introduced, together with citizenship ceremonies. A flexible system of fees for applications was also introduced in 2011, together with improved recognition of the position of civil partners.

For further information:

www.inis.gov.ie
www.entemp.ie/labour/workpermits
www.ria.gov.ie

Recent trends in migrants' flows and stocks
IRELAND

Migration flows (foreigners) National definition	2000	2005	2009	2010	Average 2001-05	Average 2006-10	Level ('000) 2010
Per 1 000 inhabitants							
Inflows	7.3	16.0	8.7	3.9	11.1	13.9	17.4
Outflows	..	..	10.5	8.4	..	7.5	37.6

Migration inflows (foreigners) by type Permit based statistics (standardised)	Thousands		% distribution	
	2009	2010	2009	2010
Work	3.1	2.8	7.9	16.3
Family (incl. accompanying family)	9.0	1.9	23.1	11.0
Humanitarian	0.4	0.2	0.9	0.9
Free movements	26.5	12.5	68.1	71.8
Others	..	..	..	..
Total	38.9	17.4	100.0	100.0

Temporary migration	2005	2009	2010	Average 2006-10
Thousands				
International students	..	..	..	..
Trainees	..	..	..	..
Working holiday makers	..	..	..	..
Seasonal workers	..	..	..	..
Intra-company transfers	..	..	..	..
Other temporary workers	..	..	..	..

Inflows of asylum seekers	2000	2005	2009	2010	Average 2001-05	Average 2006-10	Level 2010
Per 1 000 inhabitants	2.9	1.0	0.6	0.8	2.0	0.8	3 405

Components of population growth	2000	2005	2009	2010	Average 2001-05	Average 2006-10	Level ('000) 2010
Per 1 000 inhabitants							
Total	14.5	23.1	4.0	..	18.7	..	..
Natural increase	6.1	8.2	10.1	..	8.0	..	..
Net migration	8.4	16.3	−6.3	..	11.0	..	..

Stocks of immigrants	2000	2005	2009	2010	Average 2001-05	Average 2006-10	Level ('000) 2010
Percentage of the total population							
Foreign-born population	8.7	12.6	17.2	17.3	10.8	16.2	773
Foreign population	..	..	..	..	..	..	..

Naturalisations	2000	2005	2009	2010	Average 2001-05	Average 2006-10	Level 2010
Percentage of the foreign population	..	..	..	..	..	..	6 387

Labour market outcomes	2000	2005	2009	2010	Average 2001-05	Average 2006-10	
Employment/population ratio							
Native-born men	75.8	75.8	66.0	63.7	75.4	71.4	
Foreign-born men	75.2	78.8	67.7	65.0	75.6	74.8	
Native-born women	53.1	58.0	57.6	56.4	55.7	58.5	
Foreign-born women	54.9	57.7	56.1	54.1	55.6	59.1	
Unemployment rate							
Native-born men	4.4	4.5	14.4	16.6	4.5	9.4	
Foreign-born men	5.4	6.0	18.2	19.7	5.9	11.7	
Native-born women	4.1	3.5	7.2	8.9	3.6	5.6	
Foreign-born women	6.1	6.0	11.7	13.0	5.4	8.6	

Macroeconomic indicators	2000	2005	2009	2010	Average 2001-05	Average 2006-10	Level 2010
Annual growth in %							
Real GDP	9.3	5.3	−7.0	−0.4	4.9	0.0	
GDP/capita (level in USD)	7.9	3.0	−7.5	−0.6	3.1	−1.5	40 458
Employment (level in thousands)	4.8	4.7	−8.8	−3.8	2.9	−1.0	1 844
Percentage of the labour force							
Unemployment	4.3	4.3	11.7	13.5	4.4	8.0	

Notes and sources are at the end of the part.

StatLink http://dx.doi.org/10.1787/888932616258

Israel*

The foreign-born population still accounts for about 26% of total population in Israel, although migration flows have been relatively low in the past decade. In 2010, there were 16 600 new permanent immigrants to Israel, an increase of 14% over 2009 and a rate of 2 immigrants per thousand residents. The uptick in permanent immigration to Israel continued in 2011, with 12 500 entries of permanent immigrants recorded in the first 8 months of the year, 1 500 more than in the corresponding period for 2010. The main countries from which immigrants arrived were the United States, the Russian Federation and Ethiopia, with a share of about 17% each, followed by France (11%) and Ukraine (9%).

While permanent immigration is generally limited to entries under the Law of Return (Jews and their family members) and family reunification with an Israeli citizen, Israel has a large temporary labour migration programme for employment in specific low-skill sectors or in specialist jobs. In 2010, there were 32 000 new entries for employment under this programme, an increase of about 20% from 2009. The main origin countries were Thailand (24%), the Philippines (18%), the former Soviet Union countries (18%), India (10%), China and Nepal (5% each).

As of June 2011, the stock of legal foreign workers was about 74 000, although an additional 15 000 workers had lost their legal status and remained in Israel. Most of the temporary foreign workers are employed in the caregiving sector (52 500), in agriculture (24 000) and construction (8 000). There were also an estimated 95 000 individuals who had entered with a tourist visa and illegally overstayed, many of whom are assumed to have entered the labour force.

Israel also admits Palestinian workers for employment, on a temporary renewable basis. By October 2011, there were about 25 000 Palestinian workers holding regular work permits and another 5 000 with seasonal work permits. The 2011 quota for Palestinian workers was set at 30 000, 5 000 more than in 2010.

The years 2010-11 saw continuous increase in the number of migrants illegally crossing the border from Egypt into Israel. From 1 000 in 2006, their stock reached 33 000 at the end of 2010, and 41 000 in November 2011. Most are Eritreans (61%) or Sudanese (25%), who are not generally granted access to the asylum process in Israel, but who receive a tolerated temporary status (residence permit without permission to work).

The government aims to reduce the number of foreign workers in agriculture and construction. While the quota for foreign workers in agriculture remained unchanged from 2010 to 2011, at 26 000, between 2012 and 2016 it will be gradually reduced to 18 900. The quota for foreign construction workers will remain at 8 000 until July 2014, and end in 2016. An agreement between the government and the builders' association includes provisions for bilateral agreements for recruitment of foreign construction workers and for expanding training of Israeli construction workers. In the period 2009-10, more than 30 000 new Israeli workers entered the construction sector, a trend which continued in 2011. At the same time, the number of African asylum seekers with residence permits working in agriculture increased. No quota is applied to the home care sector, although steps have been taken to encourage the employment of Israelis in this sector.

After a pilot scheme with Sri Lanka in 2010, in 2011 Israel signed its first bilateral agreements for employment in agriculture with Thailand and Sri Lanka. Bilateral agreements for the employment of foreign workers in the construction sector are being negotiated with Bulgaria, Romania, and Sri Lanka. Bilateral agreements are also meant to combat illegal fee-taking by mediation agencies.

A government resolution in February 2010 contained a commitment to develop a new framework law for immigration. Parliamentary discussions on the new framework are still ongoing and a draft law is expected for mid-2012.

For further information:

www.cbs.gov.il
www.moit.gov.il/NR/exeres/
8CD0F279-80FA-43A6-934B-35B28B0CDE1F.htm
www.piba.gov.il
www.knesset.gov.il/mmm/heb/MMM_Results.asp?CatId=9
www.knesset.gov.il/mmm/heb/MMM_Results.asp?CatId=10
www.moia.gov.il/

---

* The statistical data for Israel are supplied by and under the responsibility of the relevant Israeli authorities. The use of such data by the OECD is without prejudice to the status of the Golan Heights, East Jerusalem and Israeli settlements in the West Bank under the terms of international law.

Recent trends in migrants' flows and stocks
ISRAEL

Migration flows (foreigners) National definition	2000	2005	2009	2010	Average 2001-05	Average 2006-10	Level ('000) 2010
Per 1 000 inhabitants							
Inflows	9.6	3.1	1.9	2.2	4.3	2.3	16.6
Outflows	..	..	..	..	..	..	..

Migration inflows (foreigners) by type	Thousands		% distribution	
Permit based statistics (standardised)	2009	2010	2009	2010
Work	..	..	..	..
Family (incl. accompanying family)	0.1	..	0.8	..
Humanitarian	..	..	..	..
Free movements	..	..	..	..
Others	14.5	..	99.2	..
Total	14.6	..	100.0	..

Inflows of top 10 nationalities as a % of total inflows of foreigners
(2000-2009 annual average; 2010)
Former USSR, United States, France, Ethiopia, United Kingdom, Argentina, Canada, Brazil, South Africa, Belgium

Temporary migration	2005	2009	2010	Average 2006-10
Thousands				
International students	..	..	..	..
Trainees	..	..	..	..
Working holiday makers	..	..	..	..
Seasonal workers	..	..	..	..
Intra-company transfers	..	..	..	..
Other temporary workers	29.4	26.6	32.3	31.7

Inflows of asylum seekers	2000	2005	2009	2010	Average 2001-05	Average 2006-10	Level 2010
Per 1 000 inhabitants	1.0	0.1	0.1	0.2	..	0.5	1 448

Components of population growth	2000	2005	2009	2010	Average 2001-05	Average 2006-10	Level ('000) 2010
Per 1 000 inhabitants							
Total	37.4	28.8	18.1	18.9	30.1	..	143
Natural increase	27.7	26.4	16.3	16.5	27.0	..	127
Net migration	9.8	2.4	1.8	2.4	3.1	..	19

Stocks of immigrants	2000	2005	2009	2010	Average 2001-05	Average 2006-10	Level ('000) 2010
Percentage of the total population							
Foreign-born population	31.1	28.1	25.1	24.5	29.5	25.9	1 869
Foreign population	..	..	..	..	..	..	..

Naturalisations	2000	2005	2009	2010	Average 2001-05	Average 2006-10	Level 2010
Percentage of the foreign population	..	..	..	..	..	..	..

Labour market outcomes	2000	2005	2009	2010	Average 2001-05	Average 2006-10
Employment/population ratio						
Native-born men	..	..	60.4	61.5	..	..
Foreign-born men	..	..	68.8	69.3	..	..
Native-born women	..	..	54.5	55.5	..	..
Foreign-born women	..	..	59.2	60.5	..	..
Unemployment rate						
Native-born men	..	..	7.8	7.0	..	..
Foreign-born men	..	..	7.5	6.9	..	..
Native-born women	..	..	8.1	7.2	..	..
Foreign-born women	..	..	6.6	5.3	..	..

Macroeconomic indicators	2000	2005	2009	2010	Average 2001-05	Average 2006-10	Level 2010
Annual growth in %							
Real GDP	9.3	4.9	0.8	4.8	2.1	4.2	
GDP/capita (level in USD)	6.4	3.1	−1.1	2.9	0.1	2.3	28 596
Employment (level in thousands)	4.0	3.9	2.0	3.5	2.4	3.3	2 937
Percentage of the labour force							
Unemployment	8.8	9.0	7.6	6.6	9.9	7.2	

Notes and sources are at the end of the part.
Information on data for Israel: http://dx.doi.org/10.1787/888932315602.   StatLink http://dx.doi.org/10.1787/888932616277

Italy

Permanent immigration to Italy remains at high levels. According to data from the population register, as of 1 January 2011 the stock of foreign residents had increased by 8% on an annual basis, to reach 4.57 million persons. Foreign residents accounted for 7.5% of the entire Italian population. The increase in the stock of foreign population in 2010 was mainly due to the 424 000 arrivals from abroad, up 4% compared with 2009.

Romanian citizens accounted for almost a quarter of all new enrolments of foreign residents in 2010. Their number rose 9% compared with 2009 to reach 969 000 persons, comprising the main group of foreign residents. As EU citizens, Romanians and Bulgarians are not subject to residence permits and had largely unrestricted labour market access; the remaining restrictions were lifted in 2012. At the end of 2010, the other leading groups of foreigners resident in Italy were Albanians (483 000) and Moroccans (452 000).

The number of residence permits granted to non-EU citizens rose by 16.4% in 2010 compared with the previous year, to 599 000, 62% of which were issued for more than 12 months. Most of the permits were granted for the purpose of employment – both subordinate and seasonal – (359 000) and family reunification (179 000). In 2011, 331 000 first permits were issued, with 141 000 for family reunification and 119 000 for employment.

Entry of non-EU citizens for employment is governed by annual quotas. In 2009, the non-seasonal quota was limited to 10 000 places for training and apprenticeships. However, that year a regularisation was held for home and care workers. 295 000 applications were filed, most (233 000) of which had been accepted by October 2011, accounting for about half of the employment permits issued in 2010-11. By 2010, there were 710 000 foreigners legally employed in home care and domestic services. In December 2010 a non-seasonal quota was set to 98 000 entries, of which 52 080 reserved for immigrants from countries with which Italy has signed migration agreements, 30 000 for the domestic and care sector, 4 000 for those who completed training courses in their country of origin, and 11 500 for status changes. About 430 000 applications were filed. Of those applications, only 58 000 had been processed as of 10 October 2011. The seasonal quota for 2010 was set at 80 000, with 21 400 permits issued. A new seasonal quota was set in 2011 to 60 000, and in 2012 at 35 000.

In 2011, landings of illegal migrants on the coasts of Italy increased dramatically due to political change in Tunisia and Libya. By August 2011, almost 60 300 illegal migrants were intercepted along the Italian coasts, mainly of Sicily, compared with 4 400 in all of 2010. Many applied for asylum. In the first half of 2011, 23 800 asylum requests were filed, exceeding the 2010 total (10 050). Almost 25% were filed by Tunisians. Of the 11 300 asylum applications reviewed in 2010, 14% resulted in refugee status and 24% in a permit for humanitarian reasons or subsidiary status.

Tunisians illegally entering Italy in early 2011 were granted humanitarian protection status. On 5 April 2011 a bilateral agreement on co-operation against illegal migration was signed with the new Tunisian government, which led to 3 500 Tunisians readmitted by October 2011. A memorandum signed with Libya's NTC (National Transitional Council) on 17 June 2011 confirmed the co-operation in migration management. In 2011 Italy also started to sign "new generation" bilateral agreements in the field of labour migration aimed at better matching supply and demand through the creation of lists of emigration candidates and the strengthening of vocational training systems in partner countries. The first agreements were concluded with Egypt, Moldova, Albania and Sri Lanka with negotiations ongoing with ten other countries.

As of 10 March 2012 all foreigners applying for a first residence permit for more than one year must sign an Integration Contract and commit to acquire a basic knowledge of the Italian language and civic principles. The required number of points should be achieved in two years, although the contract may be extended for one year. Points may also be lost for violations of certain terms; if the points drop to zero or below, the residence permit may not be renewed and an expulsion order issued. As of 2011, long-term residence is granted only to immigrants who pass an Italian language test. By 10 October 2011, 69 000 tests had been taken, with a 70% pass rate.

The new government formed in November 2011 set the reform of citizenship law – pending in Parliament since December 2009 – amongst its priorities, especially with regards to regulations concerning Italian-born foreigners.

For further information:

www.interno.it/
www.istat.it/
www.lavoro.gov.it/lavoro/

Recent trends in migrants' flows and stocks
ITALY

Migration flows (foreigners) National definition	2000	2005	2009	2010	Average		Level ('000)
					2001-05	2006-10	2010
Per 1 000 inhabitants							
Inflows	3.4	4.9	6.8	7.1	5.0	7.1	424.5
Outflows	0.2	0.3	0.5	0.5	0.2	0.4	32.8

Migration inflows (foreigners) by type	Thousands		% distribution	
Permit based statistics (standardised)	2009	2010	2009	2010
Work	130.0	134.2	35.2	40.5
Family (incl. accompanying family)	115.1	94.8	31.2	28.6
Humanitarian	9.6	4.3	2.6	1.3
Free movements	109.6	93.5	29.7	28.2
Others	4.7	4.9	1.3	1.5
Total	369.0	331.7	100.0	100.0

Inflows of top 10 nationalities as a % of total inflows of foreigners

Temporary migration	2005	2009	2010	Average 2006-10
Thousands				
International students	31.7	34.5	36.8	35.3
Trainees	..	..	..	..
Working holiday makers	0.4	0.4	0.4	0.4
Seasonal workers	84.2	34.7	27.7	53.3
Intra-company transfers	..	..	..	..
Other temporary workers	..	..	..	..

Inflows of asylum seekers	2000	2005	2009	2010	Average		Level
					2001-05	2006-10	2010
Per 1 000 inhabitants	0.3	0.2	0.3	0.2	0.2	0.3	10 052

Components of population growth	2000	2005	2009	2010	Average		Level ('000)
					2001-05	2006-10	2010
Per 1 000 inhabitants							
Total	0.7	4.9	4.9	4.7	6.2	6.3	286
Natural increase	−0.2	−0.2	−0.3	−0.4	−0.3	−0.2	−26
Net migration	0.9	5.2	5.2	5.2	6.5	6.5	312

Stocks of immigrants	2000	2005	2009	2010	Average		Level ('000)
					2001-05	2006-10	2010
Percentage of the total population							
Foreign-born population	..	..	8.0	..	..	..	..
Foreign population	2.4	4.6	7.1	7.6	3.5	6.4	4 570

Naturalisations	2000	2005	2009	2010	Average		Level
					2001-05	2006-10	2010
Percentage of the foreign population	0.7	0.8	1.0	0.9	0.7	1.0	40 223

Labour market outcomes	2000	2005	2009	2010	Average	
					2001-05	2006-10
Employment/population ratio						
Native-born men	67.4	69.2	67.7	66.7	69.0	68.6
Foreign-born men	82.4	79.9	77.3	76.1	82.8	79.7
Native-born women	39.3	45.1	45.9	45.7	43.1	46.1
Foreign-born women	40.5	47.6	50.2	49.5	46.8	50.4
Unemployment rate						
Native-born men	8.4	6.2	6.6	7.4	6.9	6.0
Foreign-born men	6.5	6.8	9.4	10.0	5.7	7.3
Native-born women	14.9	9.7	8.8	9.2	11.5	8.5
Foreign-born women	21.2	14.5	13.0	13.3	15.5	12.4

Macroeconomic indicators	2000	2005	2009	2010	Average		Level
					2001-05	2006-10	2010
Annual growth in %							
Real GDP	3.7	0.9	−5.5	1.8	1.0	−0.2	
GDP/capita (level in USD)	3.6	0.2	−6.1	1.3	0.4	−0.8	31 895
Employment (level in thousands)	1.9	0.7	−1.5	−0.7	1.2	0.3	22 884
Percentage of the labour force							
Unemployment	10.1	7.7	7.8	8.4	8.4	7.2	

Notes and sources are at the end of the part.

StatLink http://dx.doi.org/10.1787/888932616296

Japan

Inflows of foreign nationals reached 287 000 in 2010 (excluding temporary visitors), a decrease of almost 10 000 compared with 2009. The number of new entrants with the status of residence for the purpose of work, declining since 2005, fell a further 8% in 2010, to 52 500. The most important category of entry for employment remained "entertainers" (28 600). Entries of intra-company transferees remained at the same level as in 2009 (5 000), while the inflow of skilled workers decreased by 33%, to less than 4 000.

International students account for many temporary migrants, although fewer arrived in 2010 compared with 2009 (–4% to 63 500). About 80% come from Asia, especially China and Korea. According to the Japan Student Services Organization (JASSO), the total number of foreign students in May 2011 was 138 000, a 3% decrease compared with the previous year.

The number of incoming trainees supported by the Japanese International Training Cooperation Organization peaked at more than 100 000 in 2007 and 2008, before falling by 20% in 2009 and a further 36% in 2010, to 51 700 – roughly half the 2007 level – due to the economic downturn. The number of status changes from trainee to technical intern also decreased in 2010, to less than 50 000. In July 2010, the New Technical Intern Training Programme was launched in order to improve compliance with employment laws and protect trainees from abuse.

Since October 2007, business owners must provide notification of the employment situation of foreign workers. According to the result of notification, there were 686 000 foreign workers in Japan at the end of October 2011, an increase of 22% since October 2009. Almost half of them (around 320 000) were foreign nationals working in Japan with the status of residence based on civil status or position. Total employment of this group increased 8% from October 2010. On the other hand, employment of technical interns and trainees (about 130 000), and students permitted to work part-time (93 000) was slightly lower than one year earlier.

The number of resident foreigners declined by 2.4% in 2010 compared with the previous year, to 2 134 000, about 1.7% of the population. The largest nationalities are Chinese (32%), Koreans (27%) and Brazilians (11%). The number of Brazilians in Japan fell by more than 14% in 2009 and a further 14% in 2010.

The number of overstayers has been falling for almost two decades and in the course of 2010 fell by 15%, to 78 500. The government attributes part of this decline to greater enforcement and border control fingerprinting since 2007. Although Japan does not offer regularisation, the Ministry of Justice issued more than 6 300 case-by-case special permissions to stay in 2010, a 37% increase compared with 2009.

Measures to facilitate immigrants' labour market integration were introduced in the context of the economic downturn. Since 2009, support measures targeted at foreign residents of Japanese descent include Japanese language courses aimed at facilitating the re-employment of unemployed foreigners of Japanese ancestry. The "Basic Policy on Measures for Foreign Residents of Japanese Descent", established in August 2010, was followed by the Action Plan in March 2011.

The fourth Basic Plan for Immigration Control approved in March 2010 includes strategies to favour highly qualified immigration to Japan. The New Growth Strategy launched in June 2010 introduced a preferential immigration channel for highly skilled foreigners through a points-based system, and the structure of the points-based system was announced in early 2012. The Strategy also sets a target of doubling the number of foreign students in Japan, by facilitating the application procedure and access to employment during their studies and after graduation. International graduates of vocational schools in Japan are now allowed to apply for a working visa in Japan even after returning to their origin countries.

In November 2010 restrictions on working years for foreign nurses and dentists holding Japanese professional licenses were eliminated. A medical-care visa for foreign nationals is now available for visitors receiving long-term medical treatment in Japan. The Basic Plan for Immigration Control also includes measures related to stricter border and residence control.

On 9 July 2012, the new system of residence management enacted in July 2009 will be fully implemented, including the issuance of a residence card to medium and long-term residents with resident status under the Immigration Control Act and the extension of the maximum length of residence status from three to five years.

For further information:

www.immi-moj.go.jp/english
www.mhlw.go.jp/english/index.html
www8.cao.go.jp/teiju-portal/eng/index.html

Recent trends in migrants' flows and stocks
JAPAN

Migration flows (foreigners) National definition	2000	2005	2009	2010	Average		Level ('000)
					2001-05	2006-10	2010
Per 1 000 inhabitants							
Inflows	2.7	2.9	2.3	2.2	2.8	2.5	287.1
Outflows	1.7	2.3	2.1	1.9	2.1	1.8	242.6

Migration inflows (foreigners) by type	Thousands		% distribution	
Permit based statistics (standardised)	2009	2010	2009	2010
Work	23.4	19.3	35.7	34.6
Family (incl. accompanying family)	27.5	21.9	42.1	39.3
Humanitarian	0.5	0.4	0.8	0.7
Free movements	..	..	..	..
Others	14.1	14.1	21.5	25.4
Total	65.5	55.7	100.0	100.0

Inflows of top 10 nationalities as a % of total inflows of foreigners

(2000-2009 annual average; 2010)

China, Korea, United States, Philippines, Viet Nam, Thailand, Indonesia, Chinese Taipei, United Kingdom, India

Temporary migration	2005	2009	2010	Average 2006-10
Thousands				
International students	41.5	66.1	63.5	56.3
Trainees	83.3	80.5	51.7	85.8
Working holiday makers	4.7	6.5	7.5	6.6
Seasonal workers	..	..	..	..
Intra-company transfers	4.2	5.2	5.8	6.2
Other temporary workers	110.2	41.6	38.4	46.9

Inflows of asylum seekers	2000	2005	2009	2010	Average		Level
					2001-05	2006-10	2010
Per 1 000 inhabitants	0.0	0.0	0.0	0.0	0.0	0.0	1 203

Components of population growth	2000	2005	2009	2010	Average		Level ('000)
					2001-05	2006-10	2010
Per 1 000 inhabitants							
Total	0.5	0.4	..	..	0.8	..	..
Natural increase	1.8	0.0	..	..	0.7	..	..
Net migration	0.3	0.0	..	..	-0.1	..	..

Stocks of immigrants	2000	2005	2009	2010	Average		Level ('000)
					2001-05	2006-10	2010
Percentage of the total population							
Foreign-born population	..	..	..	..	..	..	..
Foreign population	1.3	1.6	1.7	1.7	1.5	1.7	2 133

Naturalisations	2000	2005	2009	2010	Average		Level
					2001-05	2006-10	2010
Percentage of the foreign population	1.0	0.8	0.7	0.6	0.8	0.6	13 072

Labour market outcomes	2000	2005	2009	2010	Average	
					2001-05	2006-10
Employment/population ratio						
Native-born men	..	..	..	..	..	..
Foreign-born men	..	..	..	..	..	..
Native-born women	..	..	..	..	..	..
Foreign-born women	..	..	..	..	..	..
Unemployment rate						
Native-born men	..	..	..	..	..	..
Foreign-born men	..	..	..	..	..	..
Native-born women	..	..	..	..	..	..
Foreign-born women	..	..	..	..	..	..

Macroeconomic indicators	2000	2005	2009	2010	Average		Level
					2001-05	2006-10	2010
Annual growth in %							
Real GDP	2.9	1.9	-6.3	4.0	1.3	0.2	
GDP/capita (level in USD)	2.7	1.9	-6.2	4.1	1.2	0.2	33 751
Employment (level in thousands)	-0.2	0.4	-1.6	-0.4	-0.3	-0.3	62 564
Percentage of the labour force							
Unemployment	4.7	4.4	5.1	5.1	5.0	4.4	

Notes and sources are at the end of the part.

StatLink http://dx.doi.org/10.1787/888932616315

Korea

By the end of 2010, the foreign population in Korea stood at around 1 261 000 persons, an increase of 8% (92 200) compared with the previous year. Foreign residents represented 2.5% of the total population. Citizens of China account for a half of total foreign population, followed by citizens of the United States (127 000) and Vietnamese (103 000).

Almost 50% of the stock of foreign residents consists of workers in low-skilled jobs (513 600 in 2010). Most are recruited through the Employment Permit System (EPS), a temporary low-skilled work permit scheme, and the Working Visit (H-2) scheme, which allows ethnic Koreans who are nationals of China and CIS countries to stay and seek work in Korea. In 2010, the stock of low-skilled workers under the Employment Permit System increased by 17% compared with 2009, to 220 300. Over the same period, the number of ethnic Koreans under Working Visit visa decreased by 6%, to 286 600.

The number of foreign workers admitted under the EPS and Working Visa is subject to quotas set by the Foreign Policy Committee. The quota for EPS was set, respectively, at 34 000 for 2010, 48 000 for 2011, and 57 000 for 2012, reflecting the economic recovery. Of the 2012 quota, 11 000 visas are set aside for qualifying repeat participants returning to the same employer. Around 40 500 foreign workers entered Korea under EPS in 2010. Most of the permits for low-skilled workers are allocated to the manufacturing sector, followed by agriculture and livestock sectors. H-2 permits are issued as long as the total number of permit-holders does not exceed a ceiling set at 303 000.

The total number of highly skilled workers and professionals increased by 7% in 2010, compared with 2009, to almost 44 300.

The stock of foreign students continued to increase in 2010, to 87 500 from 81 000 in 2009 (+8%), and has more than tripled since 2005. Marriage migrants also increased over the period, to 141 600 (+13%). Marriage migrants first came from China and the Philippines, but countries of origin now include Viet Nam, Cambodia, Mongolia and Thailand. In 2010, marriage migrants were mainly from China (48%), Viet Nam (35%), Japan (7%), and the Philippines (5%).

Ethnic Koreans – almost all from China – may enter with a variety of visas apart from the Working Visa. Other visa categories include Overseas Koreans, family visitors, residents and permanent residents. They totalled 477 000 persons in 2010, an increase of 11% compared with 2009. Since December 2009, overseas Koreans who meet the requirements for acquiring Korean nationality can be granted permanent residence status (F-5). This measure was implemented to reduce the demand for naturalisation among overseas Koreans. The number of overseas Koreans holding F-5 visas jumped from 1 000 in 2009 to 20 600 in 2010. Another measure was enforced in order to attract ethnic Koreans into shortage occupations. Ethnic Koreans having worked at the same workplace for a long time – especially in manufacturing, agriculture and livestock – can now be granted Overseas Korean status (F-4). As a consequence, the number of F-4 visa-holders increased by 68% from 2009 to 2010, to 85 000.

The number of naturalisations decreased by 35% in 2010 compared with 2009, to 17 300. 6% of naturalisations were recovering of Korean nationality.

The number of overstaying foreign nationals continued to decline after the record-high level of 2007 (223 500). In 2010 it stood at around 168 500, down 5.3% from 2009. The decrease in overstaying is the result of active government policies, including law enforcement, facilitations for voluntary return, and larger opportunities for Korean employers to lawfully recruit low-skilled workers from abroad through the EPS.

Since 2010, professionals legally resident in Korea for at least one year and able to meet the requirements set in a points-based system (PBS) are eligible for residence status (F-2). Points under the PBS are awarded mainly for academic qualifications, Korean language proficiency, income and age. Foreign professionals granted F-2 status are allowed a wide range of employment activities, with permits extended to their family members. For foreigners obtaining F-2 status through the PBS, permanent residence is possible after five years. International students graduating from Korean universities are also now allowed to seek qualifying employment, regardless of the field of study.

For further information:

www.immigration.go.kr
www.eps.go.kr
www.kostat.go.kr
www.moj.go.kr

Recent trends in migrants' flows and stocks
KOREA

Migration flows (foreigners) National definition	2000	2005	2009	2010	Average		Level ('000)
					2001-05	2006-10	2010
Per 1 000 inhabitants							
Inflows	3.7	5.3	4.8	5.8	3.9	5.9	293.1
Outflows	1.9	5.5	4.8	3.9	3.3	4.1	196.1

Migration inflows (foreigners) by type Permit based statistics (standardised)	Thousands		% distribution	
	2009	2010	2009	2010
Work	103.0	106.9	74.7	68.1
Family (incl. accompanying family)	26.5	31.2	19.2	19.9
Humanitarian	0.1	0.0	0.1	0.0
Free movements	..	..	..	..
Others	5.1	15.5	3.7	9.9
Total	137.9	156.9	100.0	100.0

Inflows of top 10 nationalities as a % of total inflows of foreigners

(2000-2009 annual average; 2010)
China, United States, Viet Nam, Philippines, Uzbekistan, Thailand, Canada, Mongolia, Indonesia, Japan

Temporary migration	2005	2009	2010	Average 2006-10
Thousands				
International students	9.0	15.8	16.8	15.2
Trainees	4.4	11.4	11.8	11.9
Working holiday makers	0.3	0.3	0.5	0.3
Seasonal workers	..	..	..	..
Intra-company transfers	8.4	..	..	8.4
Other temporary workers	24.7	27.2	27.1	31.1

Inflows of asylum seekers	2000	2005	2009	2010	Average		Level
					2001-05	2006-10	2010
Per 1 000 inhabitants	0.0	0.0	0.0	0.0	0.0	0.0	425

Components of population growth	2000	2005	2009	2010	Average		Level ('000)
					2001-05	2006-10	2010
Per 1 000 inhabitants							
Total	..	..	..	..	..	..	..
Natural increase	..	..	..	..	..	..	215
Net migration	..	..	..	..	..	..	..

Stocks of immigrants	2000	2005	2009	2010	Average		Level ('000)
					2001-05	2006-10	2010
Percentage of the total population							
Foreign-born population	..	..	..	..	..	..	..
Foreign population	0.4	1.1	1.9	2.0	0.8	1.7	1 003

Naturalisations	2000	2005	2009	2010	Average		Level
					2001-05	2006-10	2010
Percentage of the foreign population	..	3.5	3.0	1.9	1.8	1.8	17 323

Labour market outcomes	2000	2005	2009	2010	Average	
					2001-05	2006-10
Employment/population ratio						
Native-born men	..	..	..	..	..	..
Foreign-born men	..	..	..	..	..	..
Native-born women	..	..	..	..	..	..
Foreign-born women	..	..	..	..	..	..
Unemployment rate						
Native-born men	..	..	..	..	..	..
Foreign-born men	..	..	..	..	..	..
Native-born women	..	..	..	..	..	..
Foreign-born women	..	..	..	..	..	..

Macroeconomic indicators	2000	2005	2009	2010	Average		Level
					2001-05	2006-10	2010
Annual growth in %							
Real GDP	8.8	4.0	0.3	6.2	4.5	3.8	
GDP/capita (level in USD)	7.9	3.7	0.0	5.9	4.0	3.5	29 101
Employment (level in thousands)	4.3	1.3	-0.3	1.4	1.6	0.8	23 829
Percentage of the labour force							
Unemployment	4.4	3.7	3.6	3.7	3.6	3.4	

Notes and sources are at the end of the part.

StatLink http://dx.doi.org/10.1787/888932616334

Lithuania

From 2009 to 2010, Lithuania saw a drop in total immigration and a sharp increase in emigration parallel with steadily worsening labour market conditions. After falling 30% on an annual basis in 2009, total inflows declined by a further 20% in 2010, to 5 200 entries, including returning Lithuanian citizens, who represented 80% of the total inflow. The number of registered departures increased from 22 000 in 2009 to 83 600 in 2010. The 2010 figure was five times higher than the corresponding figures for 2004 and 2005. This increase may, however, include many previous emigrants who only now reported their departures, as deregistration from the population register became mandatory, to avoid compulsory health insurance payments. While unemployment levels have fallen in 2011, emigration continues, albeit at a lower level: in 2011, 53 900 departures were recorded. Official figures only reflect emigrants who leave the country for a period longer than one year and report their departure. According to estimations based on census data, undeclared emigration accounted, on average, for more than a half of total outflows in the period 2001-10. In 2010 the net migration rate (based on the national registry) in Lithuania was –23.7 per 1 000 inhabitants, the lowest in the European Union (EU). Provisional data for 2011 suggest net migration of –11.8 per 1 000 inhabitants.

Since Lithuania has joined the EU in 2004, most emigration has been toward other EU countries. Outflows to the EU accounted for 84% of the total in 2010 (up from 60% in 2009). The two main destination countries were the United Kingdom (almost 50% of total outflows) and Ireland (16%). The number of Lithuanians going to Norway, the third destination (6% of total outflows), increased from 500 in 2009 to almost 5 000 in 2010. Germany (4.5%) and Spain (4%) followed. The share of outflows to the Russian Federation, Belarus and Ukraine dropped from 19% in 2009 to 4% in 2010.

Labour flows represent the bulk of outflows from Lithuania. Growing unemployment, especially among youth (35% in 2010), can partly explain increasing emigration trends. In 2010, emigrants aged 20-34 represented 55% of total outflow. With migration disproportionately involving young people, growing demographic imbalances and labour shortages are expected to arise in the future. However, due to the economic crisis, the Lithuanian government suspended most of the initiatives to facilitate the immigration of foreign workforce, and the Global Lithuania Strategy adopted in October 2011 to address return migration issues focused largely on maintaining cultural ties with the Diaspora.

Inflows of foreigners decreased by 36% in 2010 compared with the previous year, to around 1 000. The main origin countries were Belarus, the Russian Federation and Ukraine. Limited demand, especially in construction and transport, led to a decrease in the number of work permits issued since the second half of 2008. The total number of work permits issued in 2010 (including renewals) was 1 800, only a quarter of the corresponding figure for 2008. Preliminary data for 2011 show a slight increase, due to recovery in the transport sector. Taken together, nationals from Belarus and Ukraine accounted for more than half of the work permits delivered in 2010, followed by China and the Russian Federation.

In March 2011, simplified admission procedures, already applying to full-time students and workers with occupations in the shortage list, were extended to all foreign students and workers. The new procedure allows them to enter the country on a national D visa without having to wait for the issuance of a temporary residence permit. The Shortage Occupation List was reduced from seven occupations in the first half of 2010, to four occupations in 2011. There were 60 occupations on the list in 2008.

In February 2011, the programme for the Internationalisation of Higher Education in Lithuania was approved to increase academic mobility of students and teachers. Measures foreseen under the programme include facilitated migration procedures. Privileged relations on education with CIS countries are also foreseen.

In the second half of 2011, visa facilitations were accorded to Belarus citizens through the elimination of consular fees and the issuance of local traffic documents.

A new Law on the legal Status of Aliens was submitted to Parliament in 2011. Among the main amendments proposed are: facilitated conditions for family reunification for foreign entrepreneurs and highly skilled workers; tighter controls for the issuance/renewal of permits for migrant entrepreneurs; faster issuance of residence permits; and issuance of a residence permit without a requirement to obtain a work permit for foreign workers in approved professions.

For further information:

www.migracija.lt/index.php?–484440258
www.stat.gov.lt/lt/en

Recent trends in migrants' flows and stocks
LITHUANIA

Migration flows (foreigners) National definition	2000	2005	2009	2010	Average 2001-05	Average 2006-10	Level ('000) 2010
Per 1 000 inhabitants							
Inflows	..	0.6	0.5	0.3	0.9	0.6	1.1
Outflows	..	0.7	1.7	1.2	..	1.0	3.8

Migration inflows (foreigners) by type	Thousands		% distribution				
Permit based statistics (standardised)	2009	2010	2009	2010			
Work	..	..	..	..			
Family (incl. accompanying family)	..	..	..	..			
Humanitarian	..	..	..	..			
Free movements	..	..	..	..			
Others	..	..	..	..			
Total	..	..	..	..			

Inflows of top 10 nationalities as a % of total inflows of foreigners

2001-2009 annual average / 2010

Belarus, Russian Federation, Ukraine, United States, Bulgaria, India, Turkey, Spain, Moldova, Poland

Temporary migration	2005	2009	2010	Average 2006-10
Thousands				
International students	..	..	..	..
Trainees	..	..	..	..
Working holiday makers	..	..	..	..
Seasonal workers	..	..	..	..
Intra-company transfers	..	..	..	..
Other temporary workers	..	..	..	..

Inflows of asylum seekers	2000	2005	2009	2010	Average 2001-05	Average 2006-10	Level 2010
Per 1 000 inhabitants	0.1	0.0	0.1	0.1	0.1	0.1	373

Components of population growth	2000	2005	2009	2010	Average 2001-05	Average 2006-10	Level ('000) 2010
Per 1 000 inhabitants							
Total	-7.2	-6.5	-6.2	-25.7	-4.9	-9.5	-84
Natural increase	-1.4	-3.9	-1.6	-2.0	-3.2	-2.8	-6
Net migration	-5.8	-2.6	-4.6	-23.7	-1.7	-6.7	-78

Stocks of immigrants	2000	2005	2009	2010	Average 2001-05	Average 2006-10	Level ('000) 2010
Percentage of the total population							
Foreign-born population	7.1	..	6.5	6.4	..	6.5	208
Foreign population	1.0	1.0	1.1	1.0	..	1.2	34

Naturalisations	2000	2005	2009	2010	Average 2001-05	Average 2006-10	Level 2010
Percentage of the foreign population	..	1.3	0.6	0.5	..	0.7	162

Labour market outcomes	2000	2005	2009	2010	Average 2001-05	Average 2006-10	
Employment/population ratio							
Native-born men	61.1	65.7	59.3	56.6	64.0	63.2	
Foreign-born men	60.6	76.6	64.3	64.5	69.4	71.6	
Native-born women	58.6	59.4	60.6	58.7	58.3	60.7	
Foreign-born women	52.5	59.7	63.3	60.5	58.1	64.0	
Unemployment rate							
Native-born men	18.5	8.2	17.3	21.6	13.1	11.0	
Foreign-born men	17.8	10.8	18.1	20.2	13.9	11.2	
Native-born women	13.5	8.1	10.5	14.5	11.8	8.0	
Foreign-born women	21.4	16.6	11.8	18.3	18.1	10.6	

Macroeconomic indicators	2000	2005	2009	2010	Average 2001-05	Average 2006-10	Level 2010
Annual growth in %							
Real GDP	3.3	7.8	-14.7	1.3	7.8	1.0	
GDP/capita (level in USD)	4.0	8.5	-14.3	2.8	8.3	1.8	16 581
Employment (level in thousands)	-4.8	2.9	-6.9	-4.9	1.2	-1.9	1 320
Percentage of the labour force							
Unemployment	16.4	8.3	13.7	17.8	12.4	9.5	

Notes and sources are at the end of the part.

StatLink http://dx.doi.org/10.1787/888932616353

Luxembourg

Luxembourg, one of the faster-growing countries in Europe, had 512 000 inhabitants on 1 January 2011, 43% of whom were foreign nationals.

In 2010, about 17 000 migrants entered Luxembourg. This represents a 16% increase over the inflows in 2009. Portugal remained the leading country of origin, contributing more than a quarter of inflows. Neighbouring countries follow: France (18%), Belgium (6%) and Germany (5%). 9 300 foreigners left Luxembourg in 2010, yielding net migration of 7 700 people.

Luxembourg has seen negative net migration of its own nationals for many years now, related to the higher cost of housing in the Grand Duchy than in neighbouring countries. Some Luxembourg citizens move across the border and continue to work in Luxembourg. According to the Housing Observatory (*Observatoire de l'habitat*), these cross-border moves occur most frequently among employed people 25-34 years of age.

In 2010, employment in Luxembourg rose at a faster pace than in 2009 (total employment rose 1.5% in 2010, compared with 1% in 2009). Employment rose both among residents and among cross-border workers, although growth was less for the latter. The number of cross-border workers at the end of December 2010 was almost 150 000, up 3% over December 2009.

Luxembourg received 770 new asylum-seekers in 2010, a 55% increase from 2009. About 20% of the asylum-seekers arriving in 2010 were originally from Kosovo and 19% were from Serbia. 2011 saw a sharp increase in asylum applications, with 1 800 filed in the first eight months of the year, primarily from asylum seekers holding the nationality of Serbia or the Former Yugoslav Republic of Macedonia (FYROM).

The number of acquisitions of Luxembourg citizenship increased sharply following the entry into force, on 1 January 2009, of a new citizenship law which introduced dual citizenship. From 1 200 acquisitions (options and naturalisations) in 2008, the number increased to 4 000 in 2009 and 4 300 in 2010. Of these naturalisations, 31% involved Portuguese citizens and 17% citizens of countries of the former Yugoslavia.

The grand ducal regulation of 2 September 2011 defined the conditions for application and implementation of the Welcome and Integration Contract (CAI). The optional 2-year Contract is offered to all foreign newcomers aged 16 or older who wish to settle in Luxembourg. By signing the Contract, the foreigner commits to participating in a half-day orientation session on information on daily life in Luxembourg, a 6-hour civics course and language training. The language training offered under the CAI costs participants EUR 5/hour, and is available in Luxembourgish, French or German. The choice to study one or more of the official languages of Luxembourg is left to the immigrant based on his or her personal and professional needs. The minimum objective of the course is to acquire beginner-level language knowledge (A1 in the Common European Framework), so that the largest possible number of participants may achieve a result by the end of the training. Literacy education and a meeting with a social worker may also be offered, if necessary.

While voluntary, the Welcome and Integration Contract provides some benefits for signatories. Participation in the civics course provides an exemption from the mandatory course for acquisition of Luxembourg nationality and is also taken into account in applications for permanent residence. Signatories also have priority access to national integration measures.

Two European directives were transposed into Luxembourg legislation in the latter half of 2011: the "Return" directive, and the "Blue Card" directive. Regarding the latter, recipients must have a diploma of higher education or five years specialised professional experience, and an employment contract of at least 12 months duration. The salary threshold for acquisition of the Blue Card was set in 2012 at EUR 66 560, or EUR 53 250 for high-skill shortage occupations.

For further information:

www.mae.lu
www.statistiques.public.lu
www.olai.public.lu
www.men.public.lu

Recent trends in migrants' flows and stocks
LUXEMBOURG

Migration flows (foreigners) National definition	2000	2005	2009	2010	Average 2001-05	Average 2006-10	Level ('000) 2010
Per 1 000 inhabitants							
Inflows	24.7	29.8	29.7	31.5	26.9	31.7	15.8
Outflows	16.1	15.5	14.7	15.2	16.6	16.2	7.7

Migration inflows (foreigners) by type Permit based statistics (standardised)	Thousands 2009	Thousands 2010	% distribution 2009	% distribution 2010
Work	..	..	..	..
Family (incl. accompanying family)	..	..	..	..
Humanitarian	..	..	..	..
Free movements	..	..	..	..
Others	..	..	..	..
Total	..	..	..	..

Inflows of top 10 nationalities as a % of total inflows of foreigners

2000-2009 annual average / 2010

Portugal, France, Belgium, Germany, Italy, United Kingdom, Poland, United States, Romania, Spain

Temporary migration	2005	2009	2010	Average 2006-10
Thousands				
International students	..	..	..	..
Trainees	..	..	..	..
Working holiday makers	..	..	..	..
Seasonal workers	..	..	..	..
Intra-company transfers	..	..	..	..
Other temporary workers	..	..	..	..

Inflows of asylum seekers	2000	2005	2009	2010	Average 2001-05	Average 2006-10	Level 2010
Per 1 000 inhabitants	1.4	1.7	1.0	1.5	2.5	1.1	744

Components of population growth	2000	2005	2009	2010	Average 2001-05	Average 2006-10	Level ('000) 2010
Per 1 000 inhabitants							
Total	12.8	17.0	17.1	19.3	12.2	17.4	10
Natural increase	4.3	3.9	3.8	4.1	3.6	3.8	2
Net migration	8.2	13.1	13.3	15.2	8.6	13.6	8

Stocks of immigrants	2000	2005	2009	2010	Average 2001-05	Average 2006-10	Level ('000) 2010
Percentage of the total population							
Foreign-born population	33.2	35.0	36.9	37.6	33.8	36.7	189
Foreign population	37.7	41.5	43.8	44.1	39.5	43.6	221

Naturalisations	2000	2005	2009	2010	Average 2001-05	Average 2006-10	Level 2010
Percentage of the foreign population	0.4	0.5	1.9	2.0	0.4	1.1	4 311

Labour market outcomes	2000	2005	2009	2010	Average 2001-05	Average 2006-10
Employment/population ratio						
Native-born men	73.2	68.8	69.2	68.4	69.9	68.2
Foreign-born men	78.1	80.1	78.1	78.9	80.2	78.3
Native-born women	46.5	50.5	54.4	52.8	48.5	52.1
Foreign-born women	55.3	58.3	60.3	62.4	56.8	61.2
Unemployment rate						
Native-born men	1.4	3.0	3.0	2.5	2.2	2.7
Foreign-born men	2.5	4.2	5.9	5.2	3.5	5.3
Native-born women	3.0	4.5	3.6	3.6	3.3	4.2
Foreign-born women	3.3	7.5	8.8	6.5	6.4	7.2

Macroeconomic indicators	2000	2005	2009	2010	Average 2001-05	Average 2006-10	Level 2010
Annual growth in %							
Real GDP	8.4	5.4	-5.3	2.7	3.6	1.9	
GDP/capita (level in USD)	7.0	3.8	-7.1	0.8	2.3	0.2	86 226
Employment (level in thousands)	4.2	1.7	1.2	1.8	1.7	2.1	224
Percentage of the labour force							
Unemployment	2.6	4.7	5.7	6.0	3.6	5.0	

Notes and sources are at the end of the part. StatLink http://dx.doi.org/10.1787/888932616372

Mexico

The number of foreign-born residents in Mexico rose 13% from 2009 to 2010, from 860 000 to 961 000. Since 2000, the foreign-born population has doubled, although most of the foreign-born are Mexican citizens, as inflows of foreigners over the past decade have been more limited. Permanent immigration of foreigners to Mexico increased by almost 10% in 2010 compared with 2009, to around 26 000 persons. The top origin countries were the United States, (4 000 immigrants), followed by Colombia, Cuba, Guatemala and China, (about 2 000 immigrants each). The number of seasonal workers entering Mexico in 2010 decreased by 10% on an annual basis, to 27 400, almost all from Guatemala.

These movements are small relative to the population of Mexico and to emigration of Mexican nationals, mostly to the United States. The recession and increased border control have led, however, to a decline in the migration of Mexicans. According to estimates based on the Mexican labour force survey, annual outflows from Mexico have been declining since 2006. In 2010, they fell 44% after falling 16% in 2009 and 22% in 2008. The decline continued in 2011.

Attempts to cross the border with the United States continued to decline in 2010, as evidenced by the drop in apprehensions of Mexicans by the US authorities, which fell from 503 000 in 2009 to 404 000 in 2010. Removals or deportations of Mexicans, on the other hand, remained at the 2009 level, at 282 000. 45% of all Mexicans expelled from the United States in 2010 had a criminal record. The rate of irregular migrants sent back to Mexico has started to decline since September 2011, following a US policy change.

Mexico is a transit country for irregular migrants from Central American countries directed to the United States; here, too, the flow has decreased steadily since 2005. In 2010 it was estimated at 140 000, 30% of the 2005 estimate. The same factors explain the decline of transit migration as Mexican emigration: lower labour demand in the United States; increased cost of cross-border smuggling; increasing risks and rising violence affecting migrants; and a relative increase in employment opportunities in Mexico.

Kidnapping and violence against migrants has increased in recent years as drug cartels have moved into human trafficking. Legal and enforcement measures have been strengthened to deal with the issue. Mexico signed a regional plan with Central American countries to co-ordinate co-operation, exchange information, educate migrants, and dismantle cartels involved in human trafficking.

Remittance flows to Mexico picked up in 2010-11 after a sharp decline in 2008 and 2009. From USD 22.1 billion in 2009 and USD 22.6 billion in 2010, the World Bank estimates USD 24 billion for 2011, below the peak level of 2007. While partly a consequence of the economic recovery in the United States, the increase is also likely related to the depreciation of the peso against the dollar in late 2011 and consequent greater purchasing power of remittances.

Mexico adopted its first Migration Law in May 2011, replacing the 1994 General Law on Population. The new law establishes the conditions for entry and stay of persons in the national territory and addresses the social, economic and cultural integration of immigrants in Mexico. The number of categories of migration is reduced, to limit the margins for discretion by immigration authorities. The Migration Law defines regularisation procedures for undocumented migrants. It also doubles prison sentences for human trafficking and violence against migrants. Sanctions may be increased if the author of the crime is a public official. The Mexican government is still preparing the regulation that will fully implement the new law.

The Law on Refugees and Complementary Protection also entered into force in January 2011. Among the main changes introduced are the acceptance of asylum applications after entry, the creation of the status of complementary protection and the recognition of gender violence and discrimination as valid grounds for asylum.

A constitutional reform implemented in July 2011 improves the legal regime for immigrants. Human rights are now recognised as Mexico's fundamental rights. The reformed constitution explicitly states the right of any person to request asylum and refugee status. In addition, it grants foreign citizens subject to expulsion the right to a prior hearing, and limits the maximum detention period, eliminating discretionary expulsion without a legal basis or judicial sentence.

For further information:

www.inm.gob.mx/index.php/page/ Estadisticas_Migratorias

www.inegi.org.mx/Sistemas/temasV2/ Default.aspx?s=est&c=17484.

Recent trends in migrants' flows and stocks
MEXICO

Migration flows (foreigners) National definition	2000	2005	2009	2010	Average 2001-05	Average 2006-10	Level ('000) 2010
Per 1 000 inhabitants							
Inflows	0.1	0.1	0.2	0.2	0.1	0.1	26.2
Outflows	..	..	..	..	..	..	..

Migration inflows (foreigners) by type	Thousands		% distribution		
Permit based statistics (standardised)	2009	2010	2009	2010	
Work	..	14.4	..	54.4	
Family (incl. accompanying family)	..	8.9	..	33.9	
Humanitarian	..	0.2	..	0.8	
Free movements	..	..	..	..	
Others	..	2.9	..	10.9	
Total	23.9	26.4	100.0	100.0	

Inflows of top 10 nationalities as a % of total inflows of foreigners

(2007-2009 annual average; 2010)
United States, Colombia, Cuba, Guatemala, China, Venezuela, Honduras, Argentina, Spain, Peru

Temporary migration	2005	2009	2010	Average 2006-10
Thousands				
International students	5.1	..	4.6	5.8
Trainees	..	..	..	..
Working holiday makers	..	..	..	..
Seasonal workers	45.5	30.7	28.6	30.1
Intra-company transfers	..	..	..	..
Other temporary workers	..	..	..	..

Inflows of asylum seekers	2000	2005	2009	2010	Average 2001-05	Average 2006-10	Level 2010
Per 1 000 inhabitants	0.0	0.0	0.0	0.0	0.0	0.0	1 039

Components of population growth	2000	2005	2009	2010	Average 2001-05	Average 2006-10	Level ('000) 2010
Per 1 000 inhabitants							
Total	..	..	..	..	..	..	834
Natural increase	19.6	14.5	13.1	12.8	16.0	13.5	1 389
Net migration	-6.4	-5.6	-5.2	-5.1	-5.6	-5.2	-555

Stocks of immigrants	2000	2005	2009	2010	Average 2001-05	Average 2006-10	Level ('000) 2010
Percentage of the total population							
Foreign-born population	0.5	0.6	0.8	0.9	..	0.7	961
Foreign population	..	..	0.2	..	..	..	..

Naturalisations	2000	2005	2009	2010	Average 2001-05	Average 2006-10	Level 2010
Percentage of the foreign population	..	..	..	..	..	..	2 150

Labour market outcomes	2000	2005	2009	2010	Average 2001-05	Average 2006-10	
Employment/population ratio							
Native-born men	..	..	..	..	..	..	
Foreign-born men	..	..	..	..	..	..	
Native-born women	..	..	..	..	..	..	
Foreign-born women	..	..	..	..	..	..	
Unemployment rate							
Native-born men	..	..	..	..	..	..	
Foreign-born men	..	..	..	..	..	..	
Native-born women	..	..	..	..	..	..	
Foreign-born women	..	..	..	..	..	..	

Macroeconomic indicators	2000	2005	2009	2010	Average 2001-05	Average 2006-10	Level 2010
Annual growth in %							
Real GDP	6.6	3.3	-6.3	5.6	1.9	1.8	
GDP/capita (level in USD)	4.7	2.3	-7.0	4.7	0.8	0.9	15 200
Employment (level in thousands)	2.2	0.6	0.5	1.1	1.5	1.4	43 845
Percentage of the labour force							
Unemployment	2.6	3.6	5.5	5.4	3.2	4.4	

Notes and sources are at the end of the part.

StatLink http://dx.doi.org/10.1787/888932616391

Netherlands

Inflows to the Netherlands rose by 5% in 2010 to 154 400, the highest figure in three decades. 30% of these entries were Dutch nationals. Outflows also increased, to 91 400. Out of the emigrants, 56% were Dutch nationals. Overall net migration decreased slightly compared with 2009, with a surplus of 33 100 after correction for unreported emigration.

Immigration to the Netherlands has increased steadily since 2005. The main reason for this trend is the growth in immigration from the new EU countries which joined the European Union (EU) in 2004 and 2007. Inflows from those countries further increased by 15% in 2010, to almost 28 000, representing 18% of the total inflow of foreigners. The main origin countries of new immigrants remained Poland (14 500) and Germany (9 700). China (4 500) replaced the United Kingdom as the third most important sending country. Altogether, EU27 countries made up for more than half of the total inflows of foreign nationals (60 900).

The Netherlands received 13 300 new asylum applications in 2010, a decrease by 10% compared with 2009. Almost a quarter of new applicants in 2010 came from Somalia. Iraq and Afghanistan followed as main origin countries of asylum seekers.

In 2010, 13 600 temporary work permits (TWVs) were issued to migrants from outside the EU25, the same level as in 2009. TWVs issued to Bulgarians and Romanians decreased from 4 200 in 2009 to 3 600 in 2010. In an attempt to reduce unemployment of Dutch citizens by lowering the number of labour migrants, in 2011 the government restricted the issuance of TWV to exceptional cases.

The new coalition government formed in October 2010 has made reducing immigration and tightening integration requirements one of its policy priorities. Initiatives focused on family migrants, who in 2009 accounted for almost half of all immigrants from "non Western countries" in the Netherlands. Regulation of family migration had already been tightened in 2010, when the minimum age required for family reunification was raised from 18 to 21 for both partners in a couple, and prospective family migrants required to prove greater integration pre-requisites prior to admission to the Netherlands. After taking office, the new government proposed to further increase the minimum age for partners to 24 years and the minimum income requirement from 100% to 120% of the minimum wage. In addition, in September 2011, the Minister for Immigration and Asylum announced new measures, including: the limitation of family reunification to the "core family" – i.e. spouses or registered partners and underage children – and the introduction of a one-year waiting period for family reunification for partners. During this period, the partner abroad is expected to strengthen his/her integration pre-requisites before entering the Netherlands. The length of continued independent stay for immigrants to be entitled to have their partner join them from abroad will be increased from three to five years.

Other measures announced include the criminalisation of illegal residence for adult immigrants, punishable by a minimum of four months imprisonment or a fine, and a lower threshold (on a so-called "sliding scale" of violations) for revocation of residence permits.

On 1 April 2011, the pass score on the Spoken Dutch component of the civic integration examination abroad was raised from A1-minus to A1, and a Reading and Comprehension Skills test was added to the examination.

Concern about possible fraud by users of the Highly Skilled Migrants Scheme, especially compliance with the minimum salary requirement, led to a ministerial investigation on the issue in 2010. The investigation found that, despite some abuse of the regulation, no structural change of the Highly Skilled Migrants Scheme was necessary. However, some amendments were adopted to limit abuse, focusing on better supervision on the payment of salaries to foreign nationals. Payment of salaries to bank accounts outside the Netherlands are restricted, and benefits such as housing and transportation no longer count in meeting the salary threshold.

The "Modern Migration Policy" bill approved by the Parliament in July 2010 is expected to enter into force by mid-2012. The core of the new policy consists in a simplification of procedures for economic migration and increased responsibility of the party requesting the migrant to come to the Netherlands (e.g. an employer or an education institution), who will be given the status of an independent sponsor.

For further information:

www.ind.nl/EN/
www.cbs.nl/en-GB/default.htm

Recent trends in migrants' flows and stocks
NETHERLANDS

Migration flows (foreigners) *National definition*	2000	2005	2009	2010	Average		Level ('000)
					2001-05	2006-10	2010
Per 1 000 inhabitants							
Inflows	5.7	3.9	6.3	6.6	4.7	5.7	110.2
Outflows	1.3	1.5	2.1	2.4	1.4	2.0	40.2

Migration inflows (foreigners) by type	Thousands		% distribution		
Permit based statistics (standardised)	2009	2010	2009	2010	
Work	10.9	10.4	12.2	10.9	
Family (incl. accompanying family)	19.8	20.8	22.1	21.7	
Humanitarian	9.6	10.0	10.7	10.5	
Free movements	49.2	54.4	55.0	56.9	
Others	..	..	..	..	
Total	89.5	95.6	100.0	100.0	

Inflows of top 10 nationalities as a % of total inflows of foreigners

2000-2009 annual average / 2010

Poland, Germany, China, United Kingdom, Bulgaria, Turkey, United States, India, Spain, France

Temporary migration	2005	2009	2010	Average
				2006-10
Thousands				
International students	10.9	10.0	10.4	10.1
Trainees	9.9	4.5	4.5	10.9
Working holiday makers	..	..	..	..
Seasonal workers	..	..	..	..
Intra-company transfers	..	..	..	..
Other temporary workers	46.1	13.7	13.6	33.4

Inflows of asylum seekers	2000	2005	2009	2010	Average		Level
					2001-05	2006-10	2010
Per 1 000 inhabitants	2.8	0.8	0.9	0.8	1.1	0.8	13 333

Components of population growth	2000	2005	2009	2010	Average		Level ('000)
					2001-05	2006-10	2010
Per 1 000 inhabitants							
Total	7.7	1.8	5.4	4.9	4.3	3.9	81
Natural increase	4.2	3.2	3.1	2.9	3.6	3.0	48
Net migration	3.4	-1.7	2.1	2.0	0.4	0.7	33

Stocks of immigrants	2000	2005	2009	2010	Average		Level ('000)
					2001-05	2006-10	2010
Percentage of the total population							
Foreign-born population	10.1	10.6	11.1	11.2	10.6	10.9	1 869
Foreign population	4.2	4.2	4.4	4.6	4.3	4.4	760

Naturalisations	2000	2005	2009	2010	Average		Level
					2001-05	2006-10	2010
Percentage of the foreign population	7.7	4.1	4.1	3.6	5.0	4.0	26 275

Labour market outcomes	2000	2005	2009	2010	Average	
					2001-05	2006-10
Employment/population ratio						
Native-born men	84.0	81.5	83.5	81.2	83.1	82.9
Foreign-born men	69.9	69.5	74.8	71.7	70.1	73.0
Native-born women	65.6	68.6	73.5	71.1	67.9	71.7
Foreign-born women	48.8	52.4	59.3	57.8	52.2	56.7
Unemployment rate						
Native-born men	1.8	3.6	2.9	3.9	2.7	2.9
Foreign-born men	5.4	10.8	7.2	8.8	7.9	7.6
Native-born women	3.0	4.4	3.0	4.0	3.3	3.4
Foreign-born women	7.6	10.0	6.4	8.2	7.9	7.9

Macroeconomic indicators	2000	2005	2009	2010	Average		Level
					2001-05	2006-10	2010
Annual growth in %							
Real GDP	3.9	2.0	-3.5	1.7	1.3	1.5	
GDP/capita (level in USD)	3.2	1.8	-4.0	1.2	0.8	1.1	42 175
Employment (level in thousands)	2.2	0.4	-0.6	-0.3	0.2	0.8	8 514
Percentage of the labour force							
Unemployment	2.9	5.1	3.7	4.4	3.9	3.8	

Notes and sources are at the end of the part.

StatLink http://dx.doi.org/10.1787/888932616410

New Zealand

In total, net migration in 2010/11 was positive, although it fell to 3 900 from 16 500 the previous year, as more New Zealanders left and fewer returned. New Zealand citizens who had previously held off migrating during uncertain economic times and those leaving Christchurch after the 22 February 2011 earthquake, contributed to the increase in departures in 2010/11. Most went to Australia, which had a net gain of New Zealanders of 30 500 in 2010/11, up from 16 700 in 2009/10.

Permanent residence approvals, 40 700, were lower than in the previous year, due to a decrease in the number of skilled migrants. Since 2006/07, the planning level has remained unchanged at 45 000-50 000 approvals per year.

Immigration from the two largest source countries of permanent residents (the United Kingdom and China) declined by 16% and 11%, to 6 400 and 5 300 respectively, followed by India, South Africa, and the Philippines. While immigration of South Africans and Filipinos has also decreased in number, immigration from India increased both in absolute and relative terms.

The annual number of temporary workers grew on average by 9% in the decade to 2010/11, although growth in the immigration of temporary workers decreased 5% between 2008/09 and 2009/2010. In 2010/11 immigration of temporary workers increased again 5% annually, to 137 000. Despite the overall increase, the number of people admitted under the Essential Skills Policy has continued to decrease, down 3% to 22 300. The Essential Skills Policy facilitates the entry of temporary workers to fill shortages where suitable New Zealand citizens or residents are not available.

Admissions for seasonal work, which are subject to a labour market test, increased by 2% in 2010/11. Similarly, non-labour market tested categories also increased – by 8% for the Working Holiday Schemes and by 16% for the Study to Work Policy. This latter programme allows applicants who completed a course or qualification in New Zealand that would qualify for points under the Skilled Migrant Category to obtain a work visa for 12 or 24 months. The growth in the Study to Work Policy reflects the increase in Indian international students, who typically have a high rate of transition to work post-study.

A new Immigration Act came into force in November 2010. Implementation of the Immigration Act has included the introduction of interim visas, granted automatically to immigrants whose visa expires before a decision can be made on their application for a new temporary visa. This bridging visa allows applicants to remain in New Zealand and is valid for six months or until the application has been processed. The conditions of interim visas (right to work, study or visitor rights) depend on the expired visa and the visa requested. Sponsorship regulations were changed, requiring sponsors to guarantee maintenance, accommodation and repatriation (or deportation) costs; making sponsorship a condition of visa issuance rather than application; and introducing eligibility criteria for sponsors, who now may include organisations and government agencies. The new Immigration Act also established an Immigration and Protection Tribunal, administered by the Ministry of Justice and responsible for hearing appeals regarding visas, deportation and refugee claims. Whenever possible, the Tribunal will consider all grounds for appeal together in a single decision.

In 2011, a visitor's visa was introduced for visiting academics, as was a special policy for victims of human trafficking, and Working Holiday Schemes were established with Turkey and the Slovak Republic. The Migrant Investment policies, revised in 2009, were further reviewed, resulting in a shorter residence requirement for Investor Plus migrants, a reduction in the extension available for Investor Category migrants to transfer funds, and an expanded list of acceptable investments.

The Student Policy was reviewed in parallel with a review of the pathways to work and residence available to international students. Changes resulting from both reviews, announced in mid-2011, aim to improve the labour market outcomes and integration of former international students. These changes, to be implemented in April 2012, include limiting student work rights, both during their studies and post-study, to those studying higher level qualifications. Higher level qualifications will also receive more points for residence under the Skilled Migrant Category.

For further information:

www.immigration.govt.nz/
www.dol.govt.nz/research/
www.immigration.govt.nz/migrant/general/generalinformation/immigrationact/
www.investmentnow.govt.nz/index.html

Recent trends in migrants' flows and stocks
NEW ZEALAND

Migration flows (foreigners) National definition	2000	2005	2009	2010	Average 2001-05	Average 2006-10	Level ('000) 2010
Per 1 000 inhabitants							
Inflows	9.8	13.1	10.1	10.2	11.7	10.8	44.3
Outflows	4.0	7.4	5.5	6.0	6.8	5.4	26.3

Migration inflows (foreigners) by type	Thousands		% distribution	
Permit based statistics (standardised)	2009	2010	2009	2010
Work	11.6	12.1	24.5	25.4
Family (incl. accompanying family)	28.8	28.6	60.8	60.0
Humanitarian	3.1	2.8	6.6	5.9
Free movements	3.9	4.1	8.2	8.7
Others	..	..	..	..
Total	47.5	47.7	100.0	100.0

Inflows of top 10 nationalities as a % of total inflows of foreigners

2000-2009 annual average / 2010

United Kingdom, China, South Africa, India, Philippines, Fiji, Samoa, United States, Korea, Sri Lanka

Temporary migration	2005	2009	2010	Average 2006-10
Thousands				
International students	70.0	73.4	74.9	71.9
Trainees	1.8	1.3	1.4	1.2
Working holiday makers	29.0	40.9	44.8	38.9
Seasonal workers	2.9	7.8	7.7	7.6
Intra-company transfers	..	..	..	..
Other temporary workers	44.2	37.4	30.9	44.1

Inflows of asylum seekers	2000	2005	2009	2010	Average 2001-05	Average 2006-10	Level 2010
Per 1 000 inhabitants	0.4	0.1	0.1	0.1	0.2	0.1	340

Components of population growth	2000	2005	2009	2010	Average 2001-05	Average 2006-10	Level ('000) 2010
Per 1 000 inhabitants							
Total	5.6	11.4	12.7	10.5	14.4	10.8	47
Natural increase	7.7	7.5	7.9	8.2	7.1	8.0	36
Net migration	-2.9	1.7	4.9	2.3	5.2	2.6	10

Stocks of immigrants	2000	2005	2009	2010	Average 2001-05	Average 2006-10	Level ('000) 2010
Percentage of the total population							
Foreign-born population	17.2	20.3	22.7	23.2	19.1	22.2	1 013
Foreign population	..	..	..	..	..	..	

Naturalisations	2000	2005	2009	2010	Average 2001-05	Average 2006-10	Level 2010
Percentage of the foreign population	..	..	..	..	..	..	15 173

Labour market outcomes	2000	2005	2009	2010	Average 2001-05	Average 2006-10	
Employment/population ratio							
Native-born men	..	..	78.8	76.6	..	..	
Foreign-born men	..	..	73.5	67.6	..	..	
Native-born women	..	..	74.3	72.6	..	..	
Foreign-born women	..	..	63.2	60.0	..	..	
Unemployment rate							
Native-born men	..	..	6.4	7.7	..	..	
Foreign-born men	..	..	10.0	15.1	..	..	
Native-born women	..	..	5.0	6.0	..	..	
Foreign-born women	..	..	9.7	12.1	..	..	

Macroeconomic indicators	2000	2005	2009	2010	Average 2001-05	Average 2006-10	Level 2010
Annual growth in %							
Real GDP	2.5	3.2	0.8	2.3	3.8	1.4	
GDP/capita (level in USD)	1.8	2.1	-0.4	1.1	2.4	0.3	29 871
Employment (level in thousands)	1.9	3.0	-1.1	0.7	3.0	0.9	2 181
Percentage of the labour force							
Unemployment	6.1	3.8	6.2	6.5	4.7	4.9	

Notes and sources are at the end of the part.

StatLink http://dx.doi.org/10.1787/888932616429

Norway

In 2010, the total inflow of persons to Norway increased by 13% compared with 2009, to reach the record level of 73 900, representing a migration rate of 15 per thousand inhabitants. 88% of entries were foreigners and 12% Norwegians. The increase in 2010 was mainly due to more inflows from Lithuania (+105%), Sweden (+26%) and Poland (+8%). Poles continue to be the largest immigrant group, with 11 350 immigrants, followed by Swedes (7 600). Lithuanians, with 6 550 inflows, remained third. Overall, 64% of immigrants came from EU member countries, and 38% from the new members in Central and Eastern Europe. Emigration of foreigners also reached a record level in 2010, at 22 500. Net migration of all foreign nationals was 42 600, close to the 2008 peak.

Labour migration had increased in 2008, fell in 2009 and increased in 2010. Almost 24 000 persons from outside the Nordic countries immigrated to Norway primarily for employment, an increase of 45% over the previous year. More than half of these immigrants came from Poland (7 600) or Lithuania (4 800). EEA-nationals no longer need to apply for a residence permit, but must register with the police within three months. Labour immigration remained at a high level in 2011.

The number of permits issued to skilled workers from non-EEA countries increased from 2 600 in 2009 to 2 800 in 2010, still below its 2008 peak of 3 400. Main origin countries of foreign skilled workers granted permits in 2010 were India, China, the Philippines, the United States and the Russian Federation. In 2011 the number of permits peaked at 3 500 with the same main source countries.

The total number of new family-related permits granted dropped from 18 100 in 2009 to 10 000 in 2010, as permit requirement for nationals from EEA countries and Switzerland were abolished and a system of registration introduced. There were more than 11 500 EEA-registrations based on family-ties in 2010. Altogether, non-Nordic family-related immigration rose from 2009 through 2011. In 2010, 44% of new family permits issued to non-EEA nationals were granted to persons who came to live with a Norwegian citizen, and one in three for marriage or partnership. Most family migrants from non-EEA countries came from Thailand, the Philippines and Somalia. Major EEA-countries were Poland, Lithuania and Germany.

Norway accepts refugees for resettlement; the quota was 1 200 in both 2010 and 2011. The number of asylum seekers fell from 17 200 in 2009 to 10 100 in 2010 and 9 100 in 2011. The main countries of origin of asylum seekers in 2010 were Eritrea, Somalia and Afghanistan; the number from Somalia increased by 59% in 2011. The decline in applications since 2009 may reflect restrictive measures implemented since 2008, especially increased return of persons whose asylum request was rejected. In 2010, the number of forced returns increased by almost 40% and reached 4 600, while the number of voluntary assisted returns also increased, to 1 500. During 2011, total returns exceeded 6 500, of which 1 800 were voluntary assisted.

During 2010, almost 12 000 persons participated in the introduction programme for new immigrants, compared with 10 000 in 2009. More than 30 000 persons participate in language training each year, and more than 25 000 take the voluntary language tests. Of all these approximately 70% pass the tests.

Since 2010, several expert committees appointed by the government have reviewed aspects of migration and integration policy. The report submitted by the Welfare and Migration Committee in May 2011 points to the importance of increasing labour market participation among the immigrant population, to the level of Norwegians. Among the measures suggested to achieve this goal are stronger focus on labour market training in the introduction programme and coverage of more immigrant groups. Changes in the Introduction Act were adopted in June 2011. In addition, for persons granted a residence permit after January 2012, Norwegian language training has been extended to 600 compulsory hours, with up to 2 400 additional optional hours.

The action plan against forced marriages implemented in the period 2008-11 will be strengthened with a new action plan for 2012. Based on documentation and proposals in three committee reports – "Multitude and Mastering. Multilingual children, youth and adults in the education system", "Better Integration. Goals, Strategies and Measures", and "Welfare and Migration" – the government is preparing a new White Paper on integration and inclusion of immigrants and their children in Norway.

For further information:

www.ssb.no/innvandring_en/
www.udi.no/

Recent trends in migrants' flows and stocks
NORWAY

Migration flows (foreigners) National definition	2000	2005	2009	2010	Average		Level ('000)
					2001-05	2006-10	2010
Per 1 000 inhabitants							
Inflows	6.2	6.8	11.7	13.3	6.2	11.4	*65.1*
Outflows	3.3	2.7	3.8	4.6	3.0	3.4	*22.5*

Migration inflows (foreigners) by type	Thousands		% distribution		
Permit based statistics (standardised)	2009	2010	2009	2010	
Work	2.7	2.8	5.5	5.1	
Family (incl. accompanying family)	9.2	10.1	18.9	18.0	
Humanitarian	6.2	5.3	12.8	9.5	
Free movements	30.4	37.7	62.8	67.4	
Others	..	..	..	..	
Total	48.5	55.9	100.0	100.0	

Inflows of top 10 nationalities as a % of total inflows of foreigners

2000-2009 annual average | 2010

Poland, Sweden, Lithuania, Germany, Latvia, Philippines, Eritrea, Iceland, Somalia, United Kingdom

Temporary migration	2005	2009	2010	Average
				2006-10
Thousands				
International students	4.3	5.8	7.7	5.9
Trainees	0.3	0.3	0.1	0.3
Working holiday makers	0.1	0.1	0.1	0.1
Seasonal workers	22.7	10.9	31.0	30.0
Intra-company transfers	0.2	0.3	0.3	0.4
Other temporary workers	2.1	1.5	1.3	1.9

Inflows of asylum seekers	2000	2005	2009	2010	Average		Level
					2001-05	2006-10	2010
Per 1 000 inhabitants	2.4	1.2	3.6	2.1	2.7	2.2	*10 064*

Components of population growth	2000	2005	2009	2010	Average		Level ('000)
					2001-05	2006-10	2010
Per 1 000 inhabitants							
Total	5.6	7.4	12.2	12.7	5.9	11.7	*62*
Natural increase	3.3	3.5	4.3	4.1	3.0	3.9	*20*
Net migration	2.0	3.9	8.1	8.6	2.9	7.9	*42*

Stocks of immigrants	2000	2005	2009	2010	Average		Level ('000)
					2001-05	2006-10	2010
Percentage of the total population							
Foreign-born population	6.8	8.2	10.9	11.6	7.6	10.2	*569*
Foreign population	4.1	4.8	6.9	7.6	4.5	6.3	*369*

Naturalisations	2000	2005	2009	2010	Average		Level
					2001-05	2006-10	2010
Percentage of the foreign population	5.3	5.9	3.8	3.6	4.8	4.1	*11 903*

Labour market outcomes	2000	2005	2009	2010	Average	
					2001-05	2006-10
Employment/population ratio						
Native-born men	82.3	78.8	78.8	77.8	79.7	79.3
Foreign-born men	74.6	67.0	74.0	72.7	71.9	73.9
Native-born women	74.6	72.9	75.3	74.3	73.8	74.7
Foreign-born women	63.5	59.8	66.5	64.8	62.7	65.8
Unemployment rate						
Native-born men	3.4	4.0	3.1	3.5	3.9	2.9
Foreign-born men	6.8	12.5	8.5	9.8	9.7	7.9
Native-born women	3.2	3.9	2.4	2.5	3.7	2.5
Foreign-born women	5.3	8.5	4.9	7.0	7.4	5.8

Macroeconomic indicators	2000	2005	2009	2010	Average		Level
					2001-05	2006-10	2010
Annual growth in %							
Real GDP	3.3	2.6	-1.7	0.7	2.2	0.8	
GDP/capita (level in USD)	2.6	1.9	-2.8	-0.6	1.6	-0.3	*57 231*
Employment (level in thousands)	0.4	0.6	-0.6	0.0	0.2	1.9	*2 508*
Percentage of the labour force							
Unemployment	3.4	4.6	3.2	3.6	4.2	3.1	

Notes and sources are at the end of the part.

StatLink ⟶ http://dx.doi.org/10.1787/888932616448

Poland

Registered migration inflows to Poland decreased by 12% in 2010, to around 15 200. Outflows also fell, by 6%, to about 17 400. Outflow from Poland recorded by the Central Population Register reflects permanent emigration, that is, Polish citizens who deregister. 2010 was the fourth consecutive year of decline in registered outflows, which were three times smaller than in the peak year 2006.

Estimations by the Central Statistical Office, on the basis of different data sources, including the 2011 National Census, suggest that almost 2 million Polish citizens were staying abroad for longer than two months by the end of 2010. Labour Force Survey (LFS) data indicate that the number of long-term Polish emigrants stabilised, while the number of short-term emigrants plummeted back to 2004 levels in the third quarter of 2010. Poland now appears to be in a phase of post-accession emigration, with stabilisation of outflow for settlement abroad and intensification of return migration.

According to LFS estimations on the stock of foreign citizens aged over 14 residing in Poland (50 000 in the first quarter of 2010 and 44 000 one year later), the foreign population is marginal compared to a total population of 38 million.

Data indicate increasing foreign employment in Poland, mostly in agriculture, construction, retail and wholesale trade. The number of work permits issued in Poland exceeded 35 000 in 2010 (20% more than in 2009). Preliminary figures for 2011 indicate a further increase. More than one third of work permits were granted to Ukrainians, and almost one fifth to Chinese. Viet Nam, Nepal, Belarus and Turkey followed as the other main countries of origin.

In addition to work permits, the number of work visas issued – mostly to Ukrainian nationals – on the basis of a simplified procedure increased from 22 000 in 2007 to 180 000 in 2010. Under this procedure – extended indefinitely from 2010 – residents of Belarus, Georgia, Moldova, the Russian Federation and Ukraine may work in Poland without a work permit for up to six months during a year on the basis of a declaration by their Polish employer. Data for the first half of 2011 indicate continuing increase: 164 000 employer declarations were recorded by June 2011. Since July 2011, employers have been required to provide greater detail on employment of foreigners as a measure to improve monitoring of the system and to reduce abuse.

After having reached its highest level ever in 2009, at 10 600, the number of asylum seekers dropped by 38% in 2010, to 6 500. As in 2009, most asylum seekers in Poland came from the Russian Federation (73%) and Georgia (17%). The largest group of Russian applicants is originated from Chechenia. Prior to 2009, most received subsidiary protection or tolerated status, but the number of Russian citizens granted subsidiary protection in Poland decreased sharply in 2010, to 170 from 2 260 in 2009.

In 2011 the Polish Parliament passed the Act on Legalisation of Stay of Foreigners. A regularisation will be held in the first half of 2012, open to foreigners who have been living continuously in Poland illegally at least since the end of 2007 (since January 2010 for specific groups of asylum applicants). The 2012 regularisation is Poland's third, after 2003 and 2007, and the most liberal, as it is not conditional on any economic requirement. Successful applicants will be granted a 2-year stay permit allowing working in Poland without a work permit but only on the basis of an employment contract.

In July 2011, the inter-ministerial Committee on Migration adopted the "Polish migration policy – current state of play and further actions" which sets out recommendations for a new migration policy for Poland. The document, expected to form the basis for a new Foreigners Act but awaiting approval by the Council of Ministers, recommends a broader set of migration categories (including workers with needed skills, self-employed, students and researchers, as well as immigrants of Polish descent); a clear pathway for regularisation for irregular migrants; and a strategy for integration through better Polish language knowledge among immigrants.

Since 2008, Poland has signed Local Border Traffic Agreements (LBTA) with non-EU neighbouring countries. Under the LBTA, permits allowing for visa-free border crossing and maximum 60 days stay in the area can be issued to persons who are able to prove that they lived in the border region for no less than three years. Only the LBTA with Ukraine has entered into force (July 2009), leading to greater border mobility and stimulating regional enterprise creation. The LBTA with Belarus, signed in November 2010, has not yet been ratified, while a LBTA encompassing the entire Kaliningrad district signed by Polish and Russian authorities on December 2011 should come into force by mid-2012.

For further information:

www.udsc.gov.pl/
www.stat.gov.pl
www.mpips.gov.pl

Recent trends in migrants' flows and stocks
POLAND

Migration flows (foreigners) National definition	2000	2005	2009	2010	Average 2001-05	Average 2006-10	Level ('000) 2010
Per 1 000 inhabitants							
Inflows	0.4	1.0	1.1	1.1	0.8	1.0	41.1
Outflows	..	..	..	..	..	..	..

Migration inflows (foreigners) by type Permit based statistics (standardised)	Thousands 2009	Thousands 2010	% distribution 2009	% distribution 2010
Work	..	..	..	..
Family (incl. accompanying family)	..	..	..	..
Humanitarian	..	..	..	..
Free movements	..	..	..	..
Others	..	..	..	..
Total	..	..	..	..

Inflows of top 10 nationalities as a % of total inflows of foreigners

2000-2009 annual average / 2010

Ukraine, Belarus, Viet Nam, China, Germany, Russian Federation, Armenia, India, Turkey, Korea

Temporary migration	2005	2009	2010	Average 2006-10
Thousands				
International students	..	..	..	..
Trainees	..	..	..	..
Working holiday makers	..	..	..	..
Seasonal workers	..	..	..	..
Intra-company transfers	..	..	..	..
Other temporary workers	..	..	..	..

Inflows of asylum seekers	2000	2005	2009	2010	Average 2001-05	Average 2006-10	Level 2010
Per 1 000 inhabitants	0.1	0.2	0.3	0.2	0.2	0.2	6 534

Components of population growth	2000	2005	2009	2010	Average 2001-05	Average 2006-10	Level ('000) 2010
Per 1 000 inhabitants							
Total	-0.2	-0.4	0.8	..	-0.5	..	..
Natural increase	0.3	-0.1	0.9	..	-0.1	..	..
Net migration	-0.5	-0.3	0.0	..	-0.4	..	..

Stocks of immigrants	2000	2005	2009	2010	Average 2001-05	Average 2006-10	Level ('000) 2010
Percentage of the total population							
Foreign-born population	..	..	..	..	..	..	..
Foreign population	..	..	0.1	..	..	..	..

Naturalisations	2000	2005	2009	2010	Average 2001-05	Average 2006-10	Level 2010
Percentage of the foreign population	..	..	4.1	5.9	..	..	2 926

Labour market outcomes	2000	2005	2009	2010	Average 2001-05	Average 2006-10
Employment/population ratio						
Native-born men	..	59.0	66.2	65.6	..	64.6
Foreign-born men	..	35.9	54.2	59.3	..	50.9
Native-born women	..	47.0	52.8	53.1	..	51.5
Foreign-born women	..	24.0	39.4	43.7	..	35.0
Unemployment rate						
Native-born men	..	16.9	7.9	9.4	..	9.2
Foreign-born men	..	-	-	12.1	..	8.8
Native-born women	..	19.4	8.7	10.1	..	10.5
Foreign-born women	..	-	-	11.1	..	9.2

Macroeconomic indicators	2000	2005	2009	2010	Average 2001-05	Average 2006-10	Level 2010
Annual growth in %							
Real GDP	4.3	3.6	1.6	3.9	3.1	4.7	
GDP/capita (level in USD)	4.3	3.7	1.5	3.9	3.1	4.7	19 883
Employment (level in thousands)	-1.5	2.3	0.4	0.6	-0.6	2.5	15 961
Percentage of the labour force							
Unemployment	16.1	17.7	8.2	9.6	18.9	9.7	

Notes and sources are at the end of the part.

StatLink http://dx.doi.org/10.1787/888932616467

Portugal

Exact data on migration flows for Portugal continue to be difficult to obtain, because available sources combine different categories (e.g. new entries and status changes) and do not capture some inflows, especially that of EU nationals. However, estimates based on new long-term visas and residence permits suggest that overall migration inflows declined 12% in 2010, to 30 000. Portuguese emigration has been on the rise since the mid-decade. Estimates suggest more than 70 000 departures per year, more than half of whom are under 29 years of age.

The number of long-term visas issued to citizens from non-EEA countries continued to decline in 2010, to less than 15 000, the lowest level since 2003. Study visas have become the most significant category, accounting for about 47% of total long-term visas, followed by family visas (about 25%), and work visas (16%). The share of work visas decreased from 2009 (20%), below the 3 800 annual indicative quota set by the government. Immigration from lusophone countries – in particular from Cape Verde and Brazil – re-gained importance. Most visas were issued to citizens from the lusophone countries of Africa (PALOP) (42%), Brazil (23%) and China (7%). The number of long-term visas issued to non-EU Eastern European immigrants has kept the declining trend already observed in 2008 and 2009, mirroring the reduction of employment opportunities in the context of the economic crisis.

Between 2009 and 2010, the number of new residence permits issued in Portugal continued to decline, from 61 400 to 50 700. This figure comprises EU and non-EU foreigners, and includes status changes and regularisations according to the case-by-case procedure. Brazilians, although fewer than in previous years, still represent the largest group of recipients of residence permits (32%), followed by Romanians (12%) and Cape Verdeans (8%).

The total stock of foreign population with a valid residence permit declined 2% in 2010, to 448 000. Brazilians accounted for 27% of the total, followed by Ukrainians (11%) and Cape Verdeans (10%). The latter two groups represent a shrinking share of the total foreign population due to both naturalisations (particularly important among Cape Verdean and other PALOP citizens), and growing re-emigration/return migration of Ukrainians and other Eastern Europeans.

Data from the 2011 Census show that net migration over the decade, at +182 000, was half the level of the preceding decade from 1991-2000.

The share of foreigners in the Portuguese labour force declined slightly in 2009, to 5.7%, with more than half employed in construction, hospitality, and low-skilled services.

Despite a slight increase in the number of asylum applications (from 140 in 2009 to 160 in 2010), Portugal remains one of the countries which receive the lowest number of asylum applications in the OECD.

No major changes occurred in migration policies in Portugal in 2010, after comprehensive reforms in 2006 (Nationality Law), in 2007 (Foreigners Law) and in 2008 (Asylum Law). Following the reform of the Nationality Law, the number of naturalisations kept a high level, though decreasing from around 29 000 in 2009 to 24 500 in 2010. Naturalised people are predominantly from Brazil and the PALOP, in particular Cape Verde, Guinea-Bissau and Angola, but also from Ukraine and Moldova.

Integration of immigrants remains a policy priority. The Second National Plan for the Integration of Immigrants (2010-13) entered into force in 2010. The First National Integration Plan (2007-09) established government priorities in the domain of immigrant integration and included 122 measures addressing a wide range of areas, such as housing, education, health, social security, racism, information society, training or labour. The assessment of this first plan showed two main outcomes, improvement of public services dealing with immigrants and facilitation of immigrants' access to rights. Overall, objectives were considered to be 80% achieved. Taking into account the results of this evaluation as well as the evolution of immigrant communities and the present social and economic situation, the new integration plan reduces the number of measures to 90 but adds two new domains of action, promotion of diversity and protection of elderly immigrants. It also aims to improve the protection of impoverished and unemployed immigrants.

For further information:

www.imigrante.pt
www.sef.pt
www.acidi.gov.pt

Recent trends in migrants' flows and stocks
PORTUGAL

Migration flows (foreigners) National definition	2000	2005	2009	2010	Average 2001-05	Average 2006-10	Level ('000) 2010
Per 1 000 inhabitants							
Inflows	1.6	2.7	3.2	2.8	6.1	2.8	30.0
Outflows	0.0	0.0	..	..	0.0	..	..

Migration inflows (foreigners) by type	Thousands		% distribution	
Permit based statistics (standardised)	2009	2010	2009	2010
Work	18.3	10.9	30.5	21.9
Family (incl. accompanying family)	19.9	17.5	33.3	35.3
Humanitarian	0.0	0.1	0.0	0.1
Free movements	18.0	18.0	30.0	36.3
Others	3.7	3.1	6.2	6.3
Total	59.9	49.5	100.0	100.0

Inflows of top 10 nationalities as a % of total inflows of foreigners

(2000-2009 annual average; 2010)
Romania, Cape Verde, Brazil, United Kingdom, Spain, Bulgaria, Sao Tome and Principe, China, Germany, Italy

Temporary migration	2005	2009	2010	Average 2006-10
Thousands				
International students	4.1	5.0	5.4	5.0
Trainees	..	..	..	..
Working holiday makers	..	..	..	..
Seasonal workers	..	..	..	..
Intra-company transfers	..	..	..	..
Other temporary workers	7.7	3.4	3.4	4.5

Inflows of asylum seekers	2000	2005	2009	2010	Average 2001-05	Average 2006-10	Level 2010
Per 1 000 inhabitants	0.0	0.0	0.0	0.0	0.0	0.0	160

Components of population growth	2000	2005	2009	2010	Average 2001-05	Average 2006-10	Level ('000) 2010
Per 1 000 inhabitants							
Total	6.1	3.9	1.0	−0.1	6.0	1.3	−1
Natural increase	1.5	0.2	−0.5	−0.5	0.6	−0.2	−5
Net migration	4.6	3.6	1.4	0.4	5.5	1.4	4

Stocks of immigrants	2000	2005	2009	2010	Average 2001-05	Average 2006-10	Level ('000) 2010
Percentage of the total population							
Foreign-born population	5.1	6.3	6.3	6.3	6.6	6.2	669
Foreign population	2.0	4.1	4.3	4.2	4.1	4.2	448

Naturalisations	2000	2005	2009	2010	Average 2001-05	Average 2006-10	Level 2010
Percentage of the foreign population	0.4	0.2	6.5	5.4	0.3	3.8	24 478

Labour market outcomes	2000	2005	2009	2010	Average 2001-05	Average 2006-10	
Employment/population ratio							
Native-born men	76.2	73.1	70.8	69.7	75.1	72.2	
Foreign-born men	75.5	78.1	74.8	74.3	78.7	77.2	
Native-born women	60.2	61.2	61.2	60.8	61.2	61.4	
Foreign-born women	65.1	67.3	65.6	64.5	66.3	66.5	
Unemployment rate							
Native-born men	3.1	7.0	9.0	10.2	5.0	8.0	
Foreign-born men	6.0	8.3	13.2	12.7	7.3	9.8	
Native-born women	4.9	9.1	10.5	12.0	6.9	10.2	
Foreign-born women	6.9	10.4	13.0	17.2	8.9	13.0	

Macroeconomic indicators	2000	2005	2009	2010	Average 2001-05	Average 2006-10	Level 2010
Annual growth in %							
Real GDP	3.9	0.8	−2.9	1.4	0.8	0.5	
GDP/capita (level in USD)	3.4	0.3	−3.0	1.4	0.2	0.3	25 432
Employment (level in thousands)	2.3	0.1	−2.7	−1.4	0.4	−0.6	4 953
Percentage of the labour force							
Unemployment	4.0	7.7	9.5	10.8	5.9	8.7	

Notes and sources are at the end of the part.

StatLink http://dx.doi.org/10.1787/888932616486

Romania

Romania's migration pattern is mainly characterised by emigration, especially following accession to the European Union on 1 January 2007. The number of Romanians working abroad in 2010 is estimated to be around 3 million persons. However, data on emigration of Romanian citizens or persons born in Romania is limited.

Officially registered emigration captures only a small fraction of actual outflows. The number of newly registered permanent emigrants in 2010 was about 7 900, down 23% from 2009. A better approximation of actual emigration is provided by the statistics of the main destination countries. For example, the Romanian population residing in Italy increased by around 80 000 (to a total of 969 000) in 2010, and the corresponding increase in Spain was 33 000 (to a total of almost 864 300).

The National Agency for Employment mediates temporary labour emigration through bilateral employment agreements. Only five out of 13 agreements signed are currently operating: with Germany for seasonal workers and students, and with France and Switzerland for the exchange of trainees. By far the largest number of mediated employment contracts relates to Germany, as restrictions on labour market access for Romanian workers are still in force. Further, when Spain reintroduced transitional arrangements for Romanian workers in August 2011, the bilateral employment agreement for employment in agriculture regained relevance. In 2010, the number of mediated employment contracts remained roughly stable compared with 2009, at 110 100, 1 000 less than in 2009 but still more than double the 2008 figure.

According to the Romanian Office for Immigration, the immigrant population in Romania increased by 10% from 2009 to 2010, to a total of 97 400, representing less than 5% of the total population. Around 60% of those immigrants were non-EU citizens, mainly from Moldova (18%), Turkey (9%) and China (7%).

In light of the economic downturn, the Romanian government tried to regulate immigration inflows by reducing the quota for work authorisations, to 8 000 in both 2009 and 2010 compared with 15 000 in 2008. Actual admissions in 2009 and 2010 were, however, well below that figure. According to the Romanian Office for Immigration, 4 200 work permits were issued in 2009, a decrease of over 60% compared with the previous year. A further decrease was recorded in 2010, when almost 3 000 permits were issued, representing less than 40% of the quota allotted. The work permits were mainly granted for permanent workers (77%) and posted workers (13%). Most immigrant workers come from Turkey (21%) and China (18%). The 2011 quota for work authorisations was set at 5 500.

In 2010, almost 890 asylum applications were submitted in Romania, a slight increase compared with the 2009 figure (830). The main origin countries of applicants were Afghanistan, Moldova and Pakistan. Preliminary data for 2011 suggest a further increase in asylum applications.

In the second half of 2011, several amendments to the law on foreigners were approved, which adapt Romanian legislation to the EU framework on migration and to the Schengen *acquis*. Romania's admission to the Schengen system, originally foreseen for March 2011, has been postponed.

The new legislation transposes a number of EU directives – namely the "Blue Card", "Employer Sanctions", "Return" and "Long-Term Residents" directive, the directives on family reunification and on posted workers, as well as the regulation on a common Visa Code. Other changes concern the implementation of EU legislation in the area of free movement, with the extension of the rights already recognised to EEA citizens also to Swiss citizens, and the abolition of the obligation of registering for EU citizens and their family members.

In addition, the new legislation provides for the issuance of a personal identification number to all foreigners in Romania – including asylum seekers – for the access to social security services (including health, education and social assistance benefits) and the fulfilment of legal obligations

Other changes include tighter requirements for the issuance of business visas and simpler procedures for the issuance of work authorisations. Amendments were also introduced to the immigration regime for posted workers, with the creation of a special visa and the reinstatement of the labour market test for posted workers who wish to continue working permanently for the same employer. Status change from study to work is now facilitated, conditional on a full-time employment contract in the same domain as prior studies.

Romania's National Strategy for Immigration for the period 2011-14 was adopted in May 2011, with its main objectives being: promoting legal immigration, strengthening control over irregular immigration, developing a national asylum system, and integrating foreign residents.

For further information:

www.insse.ro/cms/rw/pages/index.ro.do
www.mai.gov.ro/engleza/english.htm
http://ori.mai.gov.ro

Recent trends in migrants' flows and stocks
ROMANIA

Migration flows (foreigners) National definition	2000	2005	2009	2010	Average 2001-05	Average 2006-10	Level ('000) 2010
Per 1 000 inhabitants							
Inflows	0.5	0.2	0.4	0.3	0.2	0.4	7.1
Outflows	..	..	..	..	..	..	..

Migration inflows (foreigners) by type Permit based statistics (standardised)	Thousands 2009	Thousands 2010	% distribution 2009	% distribution 2010
Work	..	..	..	..
Family (incl. accompanying family)	..	..	..	..
Humanitarian	..	..	..	..
Free movements	..	..	..	..
Others	..	..	..	..
Total	..	..	..	..

Inflows of top 10 nationalities as a % of total inflows of foreigners
- 2005-2009 annual average
- 2010

Moldova, Italy, Germany, United States, Turkey, China, Hungary, Canada, France, Syria

Temporary migration	2005	2009	2010	Average 2006-10
Thousands				
International students	..	..	..	..
Trainees	..	..	..	..
Working holiday makers	..	..	..	..
Seasonal workers	..	..	..	..
Intra-company transfers	..	..	..	..
Other temporary workers	..	..	..	..

Inflows of asylum seekers	2000	2005	2009	2010	Average 2001-05	Average 2006-10	Level 2010
Per 1 000 inhabitants	0.1	0.0	0.0	0.0	0.1	0.0	887

Components of population growth	2000	2005	2009	2010	Average 2001-05	Average 2006-10	Level ('000) 2010
Per 1 000 inhabitants							
Total	-1.1	-2.2	-1.7	-2.3	-7.4	-1.8	-48
Natural increase	-0.9	-1.9	-1.6	-2.2	-2.2	-1.8	-48
Net migration	-0.2	-0.3	-0.1	0.0	-5.3	-0.1	-1

Stocks of immigrants	2000	2005	2009	2010	Average 2001-05	Average 2006-10	Level ('000) 2010
Percentage of the total population							
Foreign-born population	..	..	..	..	..	..	..
Foreign population	..	..	0.3	0.3	..	0.2	58

Naturalisations	2000	2005	2009	2010	Average 2001-05	Average 2006-10	Level 2010
Percentage of the foreign population	..	..	..	..	..	..	..

Labour market outcomes	2000	2005	2009	2010	Average 2001-05	Average 2006-10
Employment/population ratio						
Native-born men	..	63.7	65.2	65.7	..	65.2
Foreign-born men	..	76.2	78.1	82.8	..	..
Native-born women	..	51.5	52.0	52.0	..	52.4
Foreign-born women	..	–	59.6	56.1	..	..
Unemployment rate						
Native-born men	..	8.1	8.0	8.2	..	7.8
Foreign-born men	..	–	–	–	..	..
Native-born women	..	6.8	6.2	6.9	..	6.0
Foreign-born women	..	–	–	–	..	..

Macroeconomic indicators	2000	2005	2009	2010	Average 2001-05	Average 2006-10	Level 2010
Annual growth in %							
Real GDP	2.9	4.2	-7.1	-1.3	5.7	2.5	
GDP/capita (level in USD)	3.4	4.4	-6.9	-1.1	6.5	2.7	11 893
Employment (level in thousands)	..	0.2	-0.9	0.2	-2.0	0.4	8 822
Percentage of the labour force							
Unemployment	6.8	7.2	6.9	7.3	7.2	6.7	

Notes and sources are at the end of the part.

StatLink http://dx.doi.org/10.1787/888932616505

Russian Federation

The most recent data on the stock of foreign-born persons in the Russian Federation date back to the 2002 Census, which counted 12 million foreign-born persons, about 8.3% of the total population. Many of these people were born in other republics of the former Soviet Union (FSU) before its dissolution. Close to 90% held Russian nationality; only 1.4 million were foreigners.

Permanent-type migration inflows from the FSU have averaged less than 200 000 annually since the year 2000. According to data from the central Statistical Office, Rosstat, between 2007 and 2009 there were about 280 000 inflows per year. Over the same period, there were on average 40 000 annual outflows to FSU countries. However, due to double-counting of immigrants changing status, the actual volume of inflows is estimated to be smaller, at around 220 000 per year. In 2010 inflows from the FSU declined further to 192 000, leading to a net migration of 158 000 persons. This was the result of the tightening of naturalisation rules since mid-2009.

In July 2009 an amendment to citizenship legislation came into force abolishing the simplified procedure which previously allowed most applicants from the former USSR to acquire Russian nationality within the first year of residence in the country on a temporary permit. According to the new law, applications for Russian citizenship cannot be filed until at least one year on a temporary residence permit (TRP) and an additional five years on a permanent residence permit (PRP). While most simplified procedures for specific groups of immigrants remained unchanged, nationals of Belarus, Kazakhstan and Kyrgyzstan, who could previously apply for citizenship immediately, must obtain residence documents and wait for a period of almost two years as of November 2011.

Between 2007 and 2009, about 370 000 persons were granted Russian citizenship annually, 60% of whom used the simplified procedure abolished in 2009. The number of naturalisations thus decreased sharply in 2010, to 111 000. A larger share of naturalisations were granted through simplified procedures for nationals of Belarus, Kazakhstan and Kyrgyzstan: from 22% in 2006-09 to 54% in 2010.

In 2010, the main origin countries of immigrants were Kazakhstan (28 000), Ukraine (27 500) and Uzbekistan (24 000). Traditional destination countries of emigration from the Russian Federation are Germany, the United States and Israel, although outflows of Russians towards those countries are constantly decreasing. In 2010, 3 700 persons left for Germany, 1 500 to the United States and fewer than 1 000 to Israel.

Labour migration flows remain significant in the Russian Federation in spite of the crisis. In 2010, 863 000 foreign workers were hired on the basis of a work permit, 18% less than in 2009. Almost a third were Uzbek citizens, followed by Tajiks (135 000) and Chinese (117 000). Since mid-2010, a "patent" (license) system has been implemented in the Russian Federation which allows labour migrants from visa-free countries to legally stay and work in private households in the country, upon the payment of a monthly tax (RUB 1000). The license card and the tax payment receipt replace a work permit. The number of licenses issued grew rapidly in 2011 (from 157 000 in 2010 to 677 000 in the first nine months of 2011). In 2010, almost half of patent holders were Uzbek citizens, followed by nationals of Tajikistan (16%) and Kyrgyzstan (7%).

The quota for visa-free labour migration was set at 1 940 000 for 2010 and 1 750 000 for 2011. As in previous years, actual inflows were below the quota, at 1 170 000 in 2010 and around 1 million in the first ten months of 2011. Despite liberalisation in legislation for labour migration, the number of irregular labour migrants remains high and is estimated at about 5-6 million (at the seasonal peak).

Since July 2010, a simplified procedure has been implemented to attract highly qualified specialists. Under this procedure, foreign workers earning at least RUB 2 million per year are granted, with their dependents, a 3-year residence permit. The salary threshold is halved for high-level professors and researchers. About 10 000 such permits had been issued by October 2011, 93% to citizens of countries subject to visas.

Following the enlargement of the Customs Union in 2011, Kazakh citizens are allowed to work in the Russian Federation without a work permit. A law on the legal status of migrant workers and their family members was adopted in mid-2011, aimed at providing social security to CIS migrant workers and their family members.

For further information:

www.fms.gov.ru/useful/formvisa/index_eng.php
www.montreal.mid.ru/migration_01.html
www.fms.gov.ru/useful/migrate/index_eng.php
www.gks.ru/wps/wcm/connect/rosstat/rosstatsite.eng/figures/population/

Recent trends in migrants' flows and stocks
RUSSIAN FEDERATION

Migration flows (foreigners) National definition	2000	2005	2009	2010	Average 2001-05	Average 2006-10	Level ('000) 2010
Per 1 000 inhabitants							
Inflows	2.5	1.2	2.0	1.4	1.1	1.7	191.7
Outflows	1.0	0.5	0.2	0.2	0.7	0.3	33.6

Migration inflows (foreigners) by type Permit based statistics (standardised)	Thousands 2009	Thousands 2010	% distribution 2009	% distribution 2010
Work	42.7	67.3	14.3	25.5
Family (incl. accompanying family)	192.6	138.0	64.4	52.3
Humanitarian	5.5	1.5	1.8	0.6
Free movements	..	..	..	..
Others	58.3	57.1	19.5	21.6
Total	299.0	263.9	100.0	100.0

Inflows of top 10 nationalities as a % of total inflows of foreigners

Temporary migration	2005	2009	2010	Average 2006-10
Thousands				
International students	..	34.4	37.3	35.5
Trainees	..	..	..	..
Working holiday makers	..	..	..	..
Seasonal workers	..	..	..	..
Intra-company transfers	..	..	..	..
Other temporary workers	..	1 009.6	795.7	1 077.9

Inflows of asylum seekers	2000	2005	2009	2010	Average 2001-05	Average 2006-10	Level 2010
Per 1 000 inhabitants	0.0	0.0	0.0	0.0	0.0	0.0	3 889

Components of population growth	2000	2005	2009	2010	Average 2001-05	Average 2006-10	Level ('000) 2010
Per 1 000 inhabitants							
Total	-4.0	-5.0	0.1	-0.6	-4.9	..	..
Natural increase	-6.5	-5.9	-1.8	-1.7	-6.1	..	..
Net migration	1.6	0.8	1.7	1.1	0.5	..	..

Stocks of immigrants	2000	2005	2009	2010	Average 2001-05	Average 2006-10	Level ('000) 2010
Percentage of the total population							
Foreign-born population	..	..	..	..	..	..	..
Foreign population	..	..	..	..	..	..	..

Naturalisations	2000	2005	2009	2010	Average 2001-05	Average 2006-10	Level 2010
Percentage of the foreign population	..	..	..	..	..	..	111 298

Labour market outcomes	2000	2005	2009	2010	Average 2001-05	Average 2006-10
Employment/population ratio						
Native-born men	..	..	..	..	..	..
Foreign-born men	..	..	..	..	..	..
Native-born women	..	..	..	..	..	..
Foreign-born women	..	..	..	..	..	..
Unemployment rate						
Native-born men	..	..	..	..	..	..
Foreign-born men	..	..	..	..	..	..
Native-born women	..	..	..	..	..	..
Foreign-born women	..	..	..	..	..	..

Macroeconomic indicators	2000	2005	2009	2010	Average 2001-05	Average 2006-10	Level 2010
Annual growth in %							
Real GDP	10.0	6.4	-7.9	4.0	6.1	3.6	
GDP/capita (level in USD)	10.5	6.9	-7.8	4.1	6.6	3.9	19 880
Employment (level in thousands)	3.4	1.3	-2.3	0.7	0.9	0.5	69 804
Percentage of the labour force							
Unemployment	10.5	7.6	8.4	7.5	8.3	7.1	

Notes and sources are at the end of the part.

StatLink http://dx.doi.org/10.1787/888932616524

Slovak Republic

In 2010, immigration to the Slovak Republic increased only modestly on an annual basis, remaining roughly at the same level as in 2009, when immigration, which had been steadily rising since 2004, was interrupted by the economic crisis. According to national statistics, the inflow of foreign nationals in 2010 was 6 400, compared with 6 300 in the previous year. Despite restored GDP growth – up to 4% from –4.7% in 2009 – the labour market situation continued to worsen and the unemployment rate continued to grow in 2010, reaching 14.4%.

Recorded outflows continued to increase, from about 2000 in 2009 to 2500 in 2010. However, these figures – based on administrative data – do not accurately capture outflows. In contrast, Labour Force Survey data on Slovaks working abroad indicate not only that there has been a decline in emigration, but that there has even been significant return migration. From 170 000 Slovaks working abroad at the end of 2008, by the second quarter of 2010 the number decreased to about 130 000. Figures for the second quarter of 2011 indicate a further 10% decrease. The number of Slovak workers in the main destination country, the Czech Republic, fell from 53 500 in the second quarter of 2010 to 44 300 in the second quarter of 2011. Over the same period, the number of Slovak workers in the United Kingdom fell from 10 800 to 10 300 (half of the 2008 level), while the number of Slovak workers in Austria increased from 23 500 to 25 700.

Inflows have traditionally been from nearby European countries. In 2010, the Czech Republic remained the main origin country. Over the same period, inflows from Hungary and Romania, respectively the second and third origin country, continued to decrease.

The total number of registered immigrants increased from about 58 300 in 2009 to more than 62 500 in 2010. EEA nationals account for more than 80% of the population with permanent permits, while non-EEA nationals account for almost all residents with a temporary permit.

There were about 16 600 registered foreign workers at the end of 2010, an increase of 18% compared with the previous year. This increase was largely attributable to more registered foreign workers from EEA countries (mainly Romania, the Czech Republic, Poland, Hungary and Germany), whose number rose from 11 300 in 2009 to 13 700 in 2010; fewer than 3 000 nationals from third countries hold a work permit. Altogether, foreign workers account only for a small fraction of the labour force in the Slovak Republic (0.8% in 2010).

Illegal migration to the Slovak Republic, as well as asylum seeking, continued to decline. The number of asylum seekers fell from 800 in 2009 to 540 in 2010 and preliminary figures for 2011 suggest further decline. In 2010, the largest groups of applicants came from Afghanistan, Georgia, the Russian Federation, India and Moldova.

In 2010, the Act on the Stay of Foreigners was amended. Among the main changes, more flexibility has been provided for some categories of foreign workers and foreign students, notably in terms of granting and extending their temporary stay in the Slovak Republic.

In November 2011, the Government approved a comprehensive national migration policy document entitled "Migration Policy of the Slovak Republic with Horizon 2020". As the previously adopted "Concept of Migration Policy of the Slovak Republic" (2005), the new document mainly brings national legislation on migration and asylum in line with the EU framework. Legal migration measures are focused on attracting the highly skilled, through the introduction of a Slovak card modelled on the EU Blue card, and those able to fill labour shortages, through the implementation of a shortage list. The document also calls for a plan on return migration and specific programmes to facilitate the economic integration of Slovaks returning from abroad. The document also creates an Immigration and Naturalisation Office, an independent office within the Ministry of Interior in charge of the implementation of all aspects of the national migration policy. The Policy document is being followed by action plans for its implementation.

For further information:

www.minv.sk
www.employment.gov.sk

Recent trends in migrants' flows and stocks
SLOVAK REPUBLIC

Migration flows (foreigners) National definition	2000	2005	2009	2010	Average		Level ('000)
					2001-05	2006-10	2010
Per 1 000 inhabitants							
Inflows	0.9	1.4	2.7	2.3	1.1	2.6	12.7
Outflows	..	0.2	0.6	0.5	..	0.5	2.9

Migration inflows (foreigners) by type Permit based statistics (standardised)	Thousands		% distribution	
	2009	2010	2009	2010
Work	..	..	..	..
Family (incl. accompanying family)	..	..	..	..
Humanitarian	..	..	..	..
Free movements	..	..	..	..
Others	..	..	..	..
Total	..	..	..	..

Inflows of top 10 nationalities as a % of total inflows of foreigners

2003-2009 annual average / 2010

Ukraine, Czech Republic, Hungary, Romania, Serbia, Korea, China, Viet Nam, Russian Federation, Poland

Temporary migration	2005	2009	2010	Average 2006-10
Thousands				
International students	..	..	..	..
Trainees	..	..	..	..
Working holiday makers	..	..	..	..
Seasonal workers	..	..	..	..
Intra-company transfers	..	..	..	..
Other temporary workers	..	..	..	..

Inflows of asylum seekers	2000	2005	2009	2010	Average		Level
					2001-05	2006-10	2010
Per 1 000 inhabitants	0.3	0.7	0.2	0.1	1.6	0.3	541

Components of population growth	2000	2005	2009	2010	Average		Level ('000)
					2001-05	2006-10	2010
Per 1 000 inhabitants							
Total	0.7	0.8	2.3	1.9	-0.5	1.7	10
Natural increase	0.4	0.2	1.5	1.3	0.0	0.8	7
Net migration	0.3	0.6	0.8	0.6	0.4	0.9	3

Stocks of immigrants	2000	2005	2009	2010	Average		Level ('000)
					2001-05	2006-10	2010
Percentage of the total population							
Foreign-born population	..	..	..	..	..	..	..
Foreign population	0.5	0.5	1.2	1.3	0.5	0.9	68

Naturalisations	2000	2005	2009	2010	Average		Level
					2001-05	2006-10	2010
Percentage of the foreign population	..	6.3	0.5	0.4	..	1.8	239

Labour market outcomes	2000	2005	2009	2010	Average	
					2001-05	2006-10
Employment/population ratio						
Native-born men	..	64.6	67.5	65.2	..	67.6
Foreign-born men	..	67.1	72.4	74.5	..	73.2
Native-born women	..	51.0	52.8	52.4	..	53.0
Foreign-born women	..	37.7	50.6	38.9	..	49.9
Unemployment rate						
Native-born men	..	15.5	11.4	14.3	..	11.3
Foreign-born men	..	-	-	8.9	..	8.7
Native-born women	..	17.2	12.9	14.6	..	13.2
Foreign-born women	..	-	-	16.7	..	13.1

Macroeconomic indicators	2000	2005	2009	2010	Average		Level
					2001-05	2006-10	2010
Annual growth in %							
Real GDP	1.4	6.7	-4.9	4.2	4.9	4.8	
GDP/capita (level in USD)	1.3	6.6	-5.1	3.9	5.0	4.6	23 252
Employment (level in thousands)	-1.4	2.2	-2.7	-2.1	1.1	0.9	2 317
Percentage of the labour force							
Unemployment	18.8	16.2	12.1	14.4	18.0	12.1	

Notes and sources are at the end of the part.

StatLink http://dx.doi.org/10.1787/888932616543

Slovenia

At the beginning of 2011, just under 230 000 foreign-born persons were living in Slovenia, representing 11% of the total population. Almost all – more than 86% – of the foreign-born population is originating from the successor countries of the former Yugoslavia, with Bosnia and Herzegovina (42%), Croatia (21%), Serbia (11%) and the Former Yugoslav Republic of Macedonia – FYROM (3%) being the main origin countries of foreign-born. 58% of the foreign-born are men, while the foreign population is evenly divided between men and women.

12 700 foreigners migrated to Slovenia in 2010, a sharp decrease from 27 400 in 2009. This was due to the reduction of the annual quota for the issuance of work permits for migrants from outside the European Economic Area (from 24 000 in 2009 to 12 000 in 2010) due to the economic downturn. More than one third of all immigrants in 2010 were citizens of Bosnia and Herzegovina. A further 15% were from Kosovo, 9% from the FYROM, 8% from Serbia and 7% from Croatia. Most immigration is temporary labour migration, in particular for construction, and almost all work permits issued are tied to a specific employer.

A total of 9 700 first residence permits were issued in 2010. Approximately, 60% of those permits were issued for work purposes, and 8% for study. By the end of 2010, the total population with a valid residence permit reached 88 000 persons.

According to official data based on deregistration from registers, about 3 900 Slovene citizens emigrated from Slovenia in 2010, roughly the same level as in 2009 (3 700). Almost 20% of Slovenian citizens in 2010 were headed to Germany, followed by Austria (14%), and Croatia (12%). Return migration of Slovene citizens was about 2 700 in 2009, just 200 less than in 2009. In 2010, outflows of foreign nationals from Slovenia were around 12 000, a decrease by 20% compared with the record high registered in 2009, but still the second highest level since 1999.

Slovenia is not a major destination of asylum seekers, with 120 applications filed in 2010. In November 2010, amendments to the International Protection Act entered into force which extend judicial protection for asylum seekers and facilitate their access to the Slovenian labour market. Asylum seekers are now entitled to free legal aid from the first instance of the procedure. After submission of the asylum request, applicants must now wait 9 – rather than 12 – months for access to the labour market. The new law also accelerates the procedure for refugee status determination. Particular attention is devoted to the issue of unaccompanied minors. In 2010, an inter-departmental working group was set up at the initiative of the Ministry of the Interior to deal with this issue.

A new Aliens Act was adopted in July 2011, which has transposed into the Slovenian legislation various EU directives (namely the EU Blue Card, Return and Employers Sanctions directives). The new law has also broadened the scope of family members eligible for family reunification to *de-facto* and same-sex partners.

The 2009 Decree on Restrictions and Prohibition of Employment and Work of Aliens, introduced in response to the severe economic crisis, limited labour migration from non-EEA countries, including through measures aimed at tackling abuses in work and residence permit issuance procedures. As a consequence, work and residence permit abuse dropped following the introduction of these measures.

With Slovenia's entry into the Schengen area, border controls were reinforced, associated with a decline in irregular migration. About 650 irregular migrants were apprehended at the border in 2010, almost half the 2008 level and the lowest number since Slovenia's independence in 1991. Since March 2011, a system for the issuance of biometric residence permits has been established in Slovenia.

Finally, in December 2009, the Slovene government adopted the Strategy for Economic Migrations for 2010-20. The strategy recognises active economic migration policy as a fundamental tool to respond to labour shortages expected to arise in the context of ageing population. The strategy focuses on migration of highly skilled workers, with particular attention to international students and researchers.

For further information:

www.mnz.gov.si/en/
www.stat.si/eng/index.asp
www.infoforeigners.si

Recent trends in migrants' flows and stocks
SLOVENIA

Migration flows (foreigners) National definition	2000	2005	2009	2010	Average 2001-05	Average 2006-10	Level ('000) 2010
Per 1 000 inhabitants							
Inflows	2.6	6.6	13.4	6.2	4.4	11.2	12.7
Outflows	1.0	3.3	7.4	5.9	2.5	5.6	12.0

Migration inflows (foreigners) by type Permit based statistics (standardised)	Thousands 2009	Thousands 2010	% distribution 2009	% distribution 2010
Work	..	..	..	..
Family (incl. accompanying family)	..	..	..	..
Humanitarian	..	..	..	..
Free movements	..	..	..	..
Others	..	..	..	..
Total	..	..	..	..

Inflows of top 10 nationalities as a % of total inflows of foreigners

2000-2009 annual average / 2010

Bosnia and Herzegovina, Serbia, Former Yug. Rep. of Mac., Croatia, Bulgaria, Italy, Ukraine, Germany, United Kingdom, Russian Federation

Temporary migration	2005	2009	2010	Average 2006-10
Thousands				
International students	..	..	..	..
Trainees	..	..	..	..
Working holiday makers	..	..	..	..
Seasonal workers	..	..	..	..
Intra-company transfers	..	..	..	..
Other temporary workers	..	..	..	..

Inflows of asylum seekers	2000	2005	2009	2010	Average 2001-05	Average 2006-10	Level 2010
Per 1 000 inhabitants	4.6	0.8	0.1	0.1	0.6	0.2	246

Components of population growth	2000	2005	2009	2010	Average 2001-05	Average 2006-10	Level ('000) 2010
Per 1 000 inhabitants							
Total	..	..	..	..	..	..	3
Natural increase	..	..	..	..	..	..	4
Net migration	..	..	..	..	..	..	-1

Stocks of immigrants	2000	2005	2009	2010	Average 2001-05	Average 2006-10	Level ('000) 2010
Percentage of the total population							
Foreign-born population	..	..	..	11.2	..	..	229
Foreign population	2.1	2.4	4.0	4.0	2.3	3.5	83

Naturalisations	2000	2005	2009	2010	Average 2001-05	Average 2006-10	Level 2010
Percentage of the foreign population	..	..	..	..	..	..	..

Labour market outcomes	2000	2005	2009	2010	Average 2001-05	Average 2006-10
Employment/population ratio						
Native-born men	66.7	70.2	71.0	69.6	68.8	71.4
Foreign-born men	66.7	72.7	70.9	70.3	70.1	72.1
Native-born women	58.2	61.3	64.1	62.8	59.6	63.2
Foreign-born women	61.3	61.6	61.0	59.8	61.9	61.3
Unemployment rate						
Native-born men	6.6	6.2	5.9	7.4	5.8	5.3
Foreign-born men	10.0	6.2	7.5	9.4	6.7	6.3
Native-born women	7.1	7.1	5.8	6.9	6.5	6.1
Foreign-born women	7.9	7.8	7.2	9.8	8.8	8.0

Macroeconomic indicators	2000	2005	2009	2010	Average 2001-05	Average 2006-10	Level 2010
Annual growth in %							
Real GDP	4.3	4.0	-8.0	1.4	3.6	1.9	
GDP/capita (level in USD)	4.0	3.8	-8.9	1.0	3.5	1.5	26 928
Employment (level in thousands)	2.0	0.6	-1.5	-1.5	1.1	0.4	966
Percentage of the labour force							
Unemployment	6.7	6.5	5.9	7.2	6.4	5.6	

Notes and sources are at the end of the part.

StatLink http://dx.doi.org/10.1787/888932616562

Spain

Migration inflows to Spain continued to decrease in 2010, although at a much lower rate compared with 2009. Around 431 000 entries were recorded, 8% less than in 2009 (470 000) and 40% less than in 2008 (690 000). In parallel, migration outflows continued to increase, from 290 000 in 2009 to almost 340 000 in 2010. Those trends, the consequence of the economic downturn which hit Spain particularly hard, led to a net inflow of less than 95 000 in 2010, almost half the 2009 level.

The stock of foreigners with residence permits fell during the first half of 2010, but has continued to grow since, reaching 5.25 million at the end of 2011. While the number of non-EU nationals (*Regimen General*) fell by 160 000 in 2010, it increased by 153 000 in 2011. The number of EU nationals (*Regimen Comunitario*) continued to increase throughout the period.

By mid-2011, foreigners with a permanent residence permit (under non-EU regime) accounted for 65% of the total, up from about 43% at the end of 2009. The increase in the share of foreign permanent residents is due to the fact that the numerous beneficiaries of the 2005 regularisation acquired the five years residence necessary to obtain the permanent permit under the general regime.

The employment situation of immigrants in Spain has deteriorated sharply with the economic crisis. According to the Labour Force Survey, at the end of 2010, the total number of unemployed in Spain was 4.7 million, of which one million were foreigners. The unemployment rate of foreigners climbed to 32% by mid-2011.

Data available for mid-2011 indicate 72 000 fewer employed in the first six months of 2011. During that period, the foreign active population continued to shrink, although not enough to offset employment loss.

The crisis does not seem to create a greater volume of illegal employment of foreigners; their illegal employment has even slightly declined in the last two years. However, discrepancy between LFS and Social Security data suggest that there were no fewer than 600 000 illegal foreign workers in mid-2011, representing 25% of employed foreigners.

About 12 000 applications for the assisted return programme were approved between November 2008 and December 2010. The programme, set up in 2008, provides unemployed foreigners entitled to unemployment benefits an advance payment on benefits if they return home. Eligibility is restricted to citizens of non-EU countries maintaining bilateral agreements on Social Security with Spain. Moreover, since 2003, fewer than 13 000 migrants have returned under the separate Plan de Retorno Social for refugees, irregular migrants, failed asylum seekers, etc.

The implementing regulations of the 2009 Immigration Act were approved in April 2011. For the first time, the basic principles of the country's migration policy are stated by Organic Law, as is the objective of migrant integration. Specific relevance is given to the "integration effort" of migrants as an added value that can replace the lack of compliance with other formal residence requirements. Regional governments may require an "integration effort report" only if no other residence requirements are imposed. While the spirit of this regulation was to facilitate residence authorisation/renewal for migrants with the highest integration potential, regional interpretations vary. The new law clarifies procedures and requirements for labour migration, as well as transposing various EU directives.

The Immigration Act created a Sector Conference on Immigration to co-ordinate actions implemented by various public administrations on immigration, and clarify the relative competences of the various local authorities.

In September 2011, the second Strategic Plan for Citizenship and Integration (PECI II) was approved. Among its main elements are a strategy against racism and xenophobia, and the training of social and institutional actors. Integration measures foreseen in the Plan include labour-market oriented measures, education and training initiatives, and initiatives for community living and social cohesion.

In a context of growing unemployment, Spain reintroduced, on 22 July 2011, transitional measures regulating the access of Romanian citizens to the Spanish labour market, to prevent further large inflows of Romanian workers.

Finally, the newly elected Spanish government, in 2011, reorganised its ministries, with the Ministry of Labour and Immigration becoming the Ministry of Employment and Social Security, while maintaining a General Secretariat for Immigration and Emigration.

For further information:

http://extranjeros.meyss.es/es/index.html
www.meyss.es/es/estadisticas/index.htm
www.ine.es/inebmenu/mnu_migrac.htm

Recent trends in migrants' flows and stocks
SPAIN

Migration flows (foreigners) National definition	2000	2005	2009	2010	Average		Level ('000)
					2001-05	2006-10	2010
Per 1 000 inhabitants							
Inflows	8.2	15.7	10.2	9.4	12.3	14.7	431.3
Outflows	..	1.1	6.3	7.3	..	5.2	336.7

Migration inflows (foreigners) by type Permit based statistics (standardised)	Thousands		% distribution	
	2009	2010	2009	2010
Work	102.2	89.8	30.6	29.9
Family (incl. accompanying family)	82.5	56.1	24.7	18.7
Humanitarian	0.3	0.6	0.1	0.2
Free movements	144.9	149.8	43.4	49.9
Others	4.1	3.7	1.2	1.2
Total	334.0	300.0	100.0	100.0

Inflows of top 10 nationalities as a % of total inflows of foreigners

Legend: 2000-2009 annual average; 2010

Romania, Morocco, Pakistan, Colombia, China, United Kingdom, Italy, Paraguay, Brazil, Ecuador (scale 0 to 20)

Temporary migration	2005	2009	2010	Average 2006-10
Thousands				
International students	29.9	44.5	46.9	41.1
Trainees	..	..	..	..
Working holiday makers	..	..	..	..
Seasonal workers	7.0	1.9	1.8	14.1
Intra-company transfers	1.2	0.9	0.7	1.1
Other temporary workers	33.8	3.4	9.2	40.1

Inflows of asylum seekers	2000	2005	2009	2010	Average		Level
					2001-05	2006-10	2010
Per 1 000 inhabitants	0.2	0.1	0.1	0.1	0.2	0.1	2 744

Components of population growth	2000	2005	2009	2010	Average		Level ('000)
					2001-05	2006-10	2010
Per 1 000 inhabitants							
Total	10.6	16.6	..	..	15.6	..	..
Natural increase	0.9	1.8	..	..	1.5	..	..
Net migration	8.9	15.0	..	..	14.0	..	..

Stocks of immigrants	2000	2005	2009	2010	Average		Level ('000)
					2001-05	2006-10	2010
Percentage of the total population							
Foreign-born population	4.9	11.1	14.4	14.5	8.9	13.7	6 660
Foreign population	3.4	9.5	12.5	12.4	7.4	11.9	5 731

Naturalisations	2000	2005	2009	2010	Average		Level
					2001-05	2006-10	2010
Percentage of the foreign population	1.3	1.1	1.4	2.2	0.9	1.6	123 721

Labour market outcomes	2000	2005	2009	2010	Average	
					2001-05	2006-10
Employment/population ratio						
Native-born men	70.8	74.6	67.7	65.6	73.0	71.6
Foreign-born men	75.4	79.6	61.1	60.0	78.6	71.0
Native-born women	41.0	50.0	52.3	52.0	45.7	52.9
Foreign-born women	45.7	59.2	54.9	53.8	54.1	57.1
Unemployment rate						
Native-born men	9.4	6.8	15.1	17.3	7.5	10.6
Foreign-born men	11.8	9.1	29.8	31.1	10.6	19.0
Native-born women	20.4	11.9	17.1	19.1	14.8	13.9
Foreign-born women	20.0	13.8	24.1	26.7	16.3	19.5

Macroeconomic indicators	2000	2005	2009	2010	Average		Level
					2001-05	2006-10	2010
Annual growth in %							
Real GDP	5.0	3.6	-3.7	-0.1	3.3	0.9	
GDP/capita (level in USD)	4.2	1.9	-4.4	-0.4	1.7	-0.3	31 888
Employment (level in thousands)	5.6	4.8	-6.8	-2.3	4.0	-0.5	18 457
Percentage of the labour force							
Unemployment	10.8	9.2	18.0	20.1	10.4	13.2	

Notes and sources are at the end of the part.

StatLink http://dx.doi.org/10.1787/888932616581

Sweden

After reaching a record high in 2009 (102 000), immigration to Sweden declined slightly in 2010, to 98 800. As in 2009, the largest component of the inflow was returning Swedish citizens (20 000, 7% more than 2009), followed by citizens from Somalia (7 000), Iraq and Poland (each at around 4 500). The inflows from Iraq halved compared with 2009, as a result of fewer asylum applications. Total emigration increased by one-fourth, to almost 49 000 persons, although the increase is partly due to the harmonisation of population registers with the actual population. Individuals with an unknown residence for more than two years were deregistered and counted in the emigration figures. Overall net migration decreased to 53 000 persons.

Since December 2008, recruitment of labour from non-EEA countries has been greatly facilitated. The number of new non-seasonal labour migrants to Sweden has increased steadily since 2009. In 2010 it was 9 500, almost three times higher than in 2008. The reform also led to more accompanying family members receiving permits. Family members of labour migrants are in general allowed labour market access. The number of family permits jumped from 580 in 2008, to 3 760 in 2009 and 5 100 in 2010, half of which were issued to people of working age. The number of seasonal workers – largely Thai – doubled from 2008 to 2009, to 7 300, but fell to 4 500 in 2010 and to 2 800 in 2011. India and China are the main origin countries for other work permit holders.

Since December 2008, refused asylum seekers may receive a residence permit for work if employed for at least six months. By the end of May 2011, about 1 060 were granted permits under this provision.

International student numbers, rising until 2010, were affected by the imposition of tuition fees in 2011, with fewer students applying and accepted. According to the Swedish National Agency for Higher Education, applications for master's level programmes fell from 96 000 in 2010 to 28 000 in 2011, and admitted applicants fell from 19 100 to 8 100. In international programmes, where applications fell from 43 700 to 7 900, admitted applicants fell from 5 400 to 1 900.

Sweden, one of the main EU countries of destination for asylum seekers, received about 32 000 applications for asylum in 2010, one-third more than in 2009. This increase was driven by the large inflow of asylum seekers from Serbia (6 300), mainly belonging to minority groups, after the abolition of visa requirements in late 2009. Serbia became the main country of origin of asylum seekers, followed by Somalia (5 500), Afghanistan (2 300), and Iraq (2 000). Out of 6 000 asylum applications filed by Serbian nationals, 40 individuals were granted permits.

Between 2000 and 2010 the number of unaccompanied minors – mostly boys between the age of 15 and 17 – requesting asylum increased from less than 500 to over 2 000 annually. In the second half of 2010, about 1 400 applied, 60% of whom were from Afghanistan, followed by Somalia (12%) and Iraq.

A new Act on the introduction of new arrivals of refugees, others in need of protection and their family members entered into force on 1 December 2010. The Act assigns the Public Employment Service (PES) responsibility and a co-ordinating role for their integration. According to the PES, in the first six months of implementation, 4 100 eligible new arrivals received approval for an individual introduction plan. A PES monitoring report found shortcomings in the new system, including burdensome co-ordination and local difficulty in providing appropriate accommodation and childcare services, especially in areas with many job openings.

In May 2011, the Government set up an intra-departmental working group to develop a follow-up national integration strategy to the one which ended in 2010. The new strategy will focus on employment-related measures and policy goals that address general needs rather than those of a specific population. General measures will be complemented by targeted support during the first two years for new arrivals. The strategy and concrete policy proposals are expected to be presented by the government in the third quarter of 2012.

In March 2011, the Parliamentary Committee on Circular Migration and Development presented its final report to the Government. The final report contains proposals for legislative changes and other recommendations aimed at facilitating increased back-and-forth mobility between Sweden and migrants' countries of origin, in order to promote its positive development effects.

The Government has commissioned an enquiry concerning citizenship issues, which shall lead to a final report on the citizenship law in April 2013. Proposals are expected on various issues, including the symbolic significance of Swedish citizenship, the content and organisation of citizenship ceremonies, as well as possible initiatives that can favour citizenship as an incentive for integration.

For further information:

www.migrationsverket.se/info/start_en.html
www.sweden.gov.se/sb/d/8281

Recent trends in migrants' flows and stocks
SWEDEN

Migration flows (foreigners) National definition	2000	2005	2009	2010	Average 2001-05	Average 2006-10	Level ('000) 2010
Per 1 000 inhabitants							
Inflows	4.8	5.6	8.9	8.4	5.3	8.8	79.0
Outflows	1.4	1.7	2.0	2.4	1.6	2.2	22.1

Migration inflows (foreigners) by type Permit based statistics (standardised)	Thousands 2009	Thousands 2010	% distribution 2009	% distribution 2010
Work	2.7	3.7	3.8	5.7
Family (incl. accompanying family)	34.7	25.5	48.7	39.6
Humanitarian	11.1	12.1	15.6	18.7
Free movements	22.8	23.1	31.9	35.9
Others	..	..	..	..
Total	71.3	64.4	100.0	100.0

Inflows of top 10 nationalities as a % of total inflows of foreigners
(2000-2009 annual average; 2010): Somalia, Iraq, Poland, Denmark, China, Iran, Thailand, Finland, Turkey, Germany

Temporary migration	2005	2009	2010	Average 2006-10
Thousands				
International students	10.8	16.7	17.6	14.2
Trainees	0.6	0.7	0.5	0.6
Working holiday makers	..	..	..	..
Seasonal workers	0.5	7.3	4.5	3.6
Intra-company transfers	..	..	..	..
Other temporary workers	4.8	11.5	12.9	10.4

Inflows of asylum seekers	2000	2005	2009	2010	Average 2001-05	Average 2006-10	Level 2010
Per 1 000 inhabitants	1.8	1.9	2.6	3.4	2.9	3.1	31 823

Components of population growth	2000	2005	2009	2010	Average 2001-05	Average 2006-10	Level ('000) 2010
Per 1 000 inhabitants							
Total	2.5	4.0	9.1	8.1	3.7	8.0	75
Natural increase	−0.3	1.0	2.4	2.8	0.5	2.1	26
Net migration	2.8	3.0	6.8	5.3	3.1	5.9	50

Stocks of immigrants	2000	2005	2009	2010	Average 2001-05	Average 2006-10	Level ('000) 2010
Percentage of the total population							
Foreign-born population	11.3	12.5	14.4	14.8	12.0	13.9	1 385
Foreign population	5.3	5.1	6.4	6.8	5.2	6.0	633

Naturalisations	2000	2005	2009	2010	Average 2001-05	Average 2006-10	Level 2010
Percentage of the foreign population	8.8	7.8	5.1	5.5	7.2	6.2	32 457

Labour market outcomes	2000	2005	2009	2010	Average 2001-05	Average 2006-10
Employment/population ratio						
Native-born men	75.8	76.2	75.6	76.6	76.6	77.0
Foreign-born men	59.6	63.7	66.7	67.3	64.7	67.5
Native-born women	73.2	72.6	72.8	73.5	73.9	73.7
Foreign-born women	54.7	58.4	58.0	56.0	58.8	57.9
Unemployment rate						
Native-born men	5.1	7.0	7.5	7.4	5.5	6.2
Foreign-born men	13.5	15.1	16.2	15.9	12.8	13.8
Native-born women	4.3	6.9	6.9	6.8	4.9	6.2
Foreign-born women	11.2	13.7	14.5	16.7	10.8	14.0

Macroeconomic indicators	2000	2005	2009	2010	Average 2001-05	Average 2006-10	Level 2010
Annual growth in %							
Real GDP	4.5	3.2	−5.0	6.1	2.7	1.6	
GDP/capita (level in USD)	4.3	2.7	−5.8	5.2	2.3	0.9	39 326
Employment (level in thousands)	2.2	0.4	−2.1	1.0	0.4	0.9	4 545
Percentage of the labour force							
Unemployment	6.7	7.7	8.3	8.4	6.7	7.2	

Notes and sources are at the end of the part.

StatLink http://dx.doi.org/10.1787/888932616600

Switzerland

In 2010, long-term immigration flows to Switzerland remained at levels similar to 2009, with a slight rise from 132 000 to 134 200 individuals. This is about 14% lower than the pre-crisis level in 2008. Inflows rose 6% to 142 400 in 2011. Citizens of EU/EFTA countries continue to comprise the majority (67%) of migration flows. Germany and Portugal are the main countries of nationality of immigrants, respectively 23% and 9.6% of inflows in 2010, although fewer immigrated than in 2009. Immigration of Italian citizens (7.5% of the total) has been increasing since 2007. Outflows of foreigners from Switzerland increased 20% in 2010 compared with 2009, and remained at the same level in 2011. The stock of foreigners resident in Switzerland rose 3.3% in 2010 and 4.1% in 2011, to 1.77 million.

More than 61% of immigration from the EU/EFTA in 2010 was for employment, while the main reason for migration from third countries was for family reunification. EU/EFTA citizens comprised 88% of the inflow of workers (55 700 out of 63 000) in 2010, the same proportion as in previous years.

Since 1 May 2011, citizens of Central and Eastern European countries joining the EU in 2004 (EU8) have benefitted from the same access to the Swiss labour market as nationals, as foreseen in the protocol to the Free Movement of Persons Agreement. For Bulgaria and Romania, restrictions remain in place until 2014 for dependent workers and for service providers in certain sectors such as landscaping, construction, cleaning and security. These restrictions may be extended until 2016 if there are disturbances in the labour market.

Prior to liberalisation, the number of authorisations for employment issued to EU8 citizens – both long and short term – had been declining, and were below the quotas established. Long-term authorisations spiked in May 2011, at about 1 000, compared with an average of less than 200 for previous months, but have fallen since to an average of 600 monthly. The 2010-11 quotas for Bulgarians and Romanians were, in contrast, largely exhausted, with the long-term quota (523) fully used and the short-term quota (4 987) more than 90% used. Quotas were slightly higher in 2011-12 (684 and 6 355, respectively), with monthly quotas again largely exhausted.

A number of studies released in 2010-11 indicated that foreigners having immigrated to Switzerland since 2002 under free-mobility agreements with the EU have a higher education level and better labour market outcomes than other immigrants. Nonetheless, the increase in migration flows related to free mobility have raised concerns in public opinion, especially regarding its impact on employment of locals, on infrastructure, transportation, the housing market, urban planning, education, integration and public safety. A high-level interdepartmental working group was established by the government to bring a global approach to these issues and produce a report.

In 2010, the number of asylum seekers fell slightly compared with 2009, from 16 000 to 15 600. Nigeria (2 000 applications) was the largest single nationality of asylum seekers, followed by Eritrea (1 800) and Sri Lanka (900). 2011 saw a sharp increase, to 22 500, related to the crises in North Africa. Eritrea was the main nationality of asylum seekers (3 400), followed by Tunisia (2 600).

In 2010, 39 300 foreigners obtained Swiss nationality. Most were nationals of the EU/EFTA (36.1%) or other European countries (41.4%). In 2011, the figure was 36 800, with the decline due to fewer naturalisations under the ordinary procedure in cantons and communes. The main nationalities were Serbian, Italian and German.

In May 2010, the Swiss Federal Council adopted a proposed revision of the asylum law, currently under discussion in Parliament. At the same time, the Federal Department of Justice was instructed to prepare a complementary report on measures for improving asylum application processing times, with the approaches used in the Netherlands, Norway and the United Kingdom serving as models. In the draft law, special attention is devoted to preventing abuse. Legal protection accorded to asylum seekers will be improved.

A proposed comprehensive revision of the citizenship law was adopted by the Federal Council and sent to Parliament in 2011. The draft law aims to harmonise cantonal and local residence requirements, and contains a number of procedural changes aimed at greater transparency and more effective processing. The draft law also reduces the requisite period of residence for naturalisation from twelve to eight years.

For further information:

www.bfm.admin.ch/bfm/en/home.html
www.bfs.admin.ch/bfs/portal/en/index/themen/01/07.html

Recent trends in migrants' flows and stocks
SWITZERLAND

Migration flows (foreigners) National definition	2000	2005	2009	2010	Average 2001-05	Average 2006-10	Level ('000) 2010
Per 1 000 inhabitants							
Inflows	12.2	12.7	17.1	17.2	13.3	17.4	*134.2*
Outflows	7.8	6.7	7.1	8.4	6.7	7.4	*65.5*

Migration inflows (foreigners) by type Permit based statistics (standardised)	Thousands		% distribution	
	2009	2010	2009	2010
Work	2.7	2.4	2.4	2.1
Family (incl. accompanying family)	18.4	21.7	16.0	18.8
Humanitarian	5.4	6.7	4.7	5.8
Free movements	86.0	82.1	74.9	71.4
Others	2.3	2.3	2.0	2.0
Total	114.8	115.0	100.0	100.0

Inflows of top 10 nationalities as a % of total inflows of foreigners

2000-2009 annual average | 2010

Germany, Portugal, France, Italy, United Kingdom, United States, Spain, Austria, Brazil, India

Temporary migration	2005	2009	2010	Average 2006-10
Thousands				
International students	8.6	11.1	12.4	10.8
Trainees	0.3	0.1	0.0	0.1
Working holiday makers	..	..	..	..
Seasonal workers	..	..	..	..
Intra-company transfers	..	..	..	..
Other temporary workers	101.6	86.5	92.4	97.2

Inflows of asylum seekers	2000	2005	2009	2010	Average 2001-05	Average 2006-10	Level 2010
Per 1 000 inhabitants	2.5	1.4	2.1	1.7	2.5	1.8	*13 521*

Components of population growth	2000	2005	2009	2010	Average 2001-05	Average 2006-10	Level ('000) 2010
Per 1 000 inhabitants							
Total	5.5	5.9	10.5	..	7.1	..	..
Natural increase	2.2	1.6	2.0	..	1.5	..	..
Net migration	2.8	4.8	8.5	..	5.7	..	..

Stocks of immigrants	2000	2005	2009	2010	Average 2001-05	Average 2006-10	Level ('000) 2010
Percentage of the total population							
Foreign-born population	21.9	23.8	26.3	26.6	23.1	25.6	*2 075*
Foreign population	19.3	20.3	21.7	22.1	20.0	21.3	*1 720*

Naturalisations	2000	2005	2009	2010	Average 2001-05	Average 2006-10	Level 2010
Percentage of the foreign population	2.1	2.6	2.7	2.3	2.4	2.7	*39 314*

Labour market outcomes	2000	2005	2009	2010	Average 2001-05	Average 2006-10	
Employment/population ratio							
Native-born men	..	85.1	84.5	85.3	86.1	85.6	
Foreign-born men	..	80.5	84.1	82.8	82.8	83.0	
Native-born women	..	73.1	75.9	75.1	72.9	74.9	
Foreign-born women	..	63.0	67.6	66.6	64.3	66.0	
Unemployment rate							
Native-born men	..	2.7	3.0	3.1	2.7	2.5	
Foreign-born men	..	7.8	6.2	7.2	6.3	6.2	
Native-born women	..	3.7	3.4	3.6	3.3	3.2	
Foreign-born women	..	9.7	7.8	8.8	8.1	8.5	

Macroeconomic indicators	2000	2005	2009	2010	Average 2001-05	Average 2006-10	Level 2010
Annual growth in %							
Real GDP	3.6	2.6	-1.9	2.7	1.3	2.0	
GDP/capita (level in USD)	3.0	2.0	-3.0	2.9	0.5	1.3	*46 622*
Employment (level in thousands)	0.9	0.5	0.6	0.2	0.4	1.4	*4 359*
Percentage of the labour force							
Unemployment	2.6	4.3	4.3	4.5	3.6	3.9	

Notes and sources are at the end of the part.

StatLink http://dx.doi.org/10.1787/888932616619

Turkey

Statistics on migration flows in Turkey are limited to certain categories. There is no direct and reliable data source on total flows in and out of the country.

Administrative information on labour emigration flows is provided by the Ministry for Labour and Social Security (MLSS). The number of contract workers sent abroad by the Turkish Employment Office decreased from 2009 to 2010 by 8%, to 54 800. The two main destinations of Turkish contract workers were the Middle East (34 000) and the Commonwealth of Independent States (19 000).

Information on labour migration inflows to Turkey is also provided by the MLSS. In 2010, there were 9 300 new permits, the same as in the previous year. More than half the work permits were issued to foreigners with a tertiary qualification. There are no available statistics for inflows of students or family migration.

While no figures are available for the total number of residence permits in 2010, in 2009, there were 163 000 permit-holders. Of these, 11% were for employment and 17% for study, with most of the others ethnic Turks from nearby countries living with relatives in Turkey. The leading nationalities of resident foreigners were Azerbaijan (11%), the Russian Federation and Bulgaria (8% each) and Germany (6%). Among the 17 500 work-permit holders, the main nationalities were the Russian Federation (11%), Germany (7%) and the United States (6%). The number of international students in Turkish universities exceeded 21 000 in 2011.

The number of irregular migrants apprehended fell by half from 2008 to 2009, to 34 300, and remained at that level in 2010 32 700). Of those apprehended in Turkey, about two-thirds were overstaying workers, and the rest had entered illegally. One factor reducing illegal stay may be the elimination of visa requirements for citizens of Syria, Iran, Lebanon, Morocco, Tunisia, Libya and Jordan. Citizens of many other countries, including Iraq, are able to obtain visas at the Turkish border. Readmission agreements with most of these countries are still under negotiation.

The inflow of asylum seekers increased from 7 800 in 2009 to 9 200 in 2010, below the 2008 level (13 000). In 2010, 40% of applicants came from Iraq and 31% from Iran. Most asylum seekers were transiting Turkey on their way to Europe.

In the context of the economic crisis, remittances have fallen by around 35%, from USD 1.4 billion in 2008 to USD 930 million in 2009. A further decrease by 11% was recorded in 2010, when remittances stood at USD 830 million, according to the Bank of Turkey. They now represent less than 0.1% of GDP.

Migration policy developments in Turkey are closely related to the negotiations and legislative requirements for admission to the European Union. Developments in 2010 included an amendment to the implementing regulation of the law on Work permits for Foreigners, softening the conditions for asylum seekers to apply for work permits, and the provision of increased penal sentences for human smugglers. The Draft Law on Foreigners and International Protection was prepared. This law combines the two separate laws originally planned (the Law on Aliens and the Law on Asylum) to provide a comprehensive legal framework for migration and asylum in Turkey.

The conclusion of readmission agreements with the European Commission as well as with non-EU countries constitutes a substantive issue in view of the harmonisation of Turkish law on migration and asylum with the EU *acquis*. In 2010-11, Turkey concluded readmission agreements with Pakistan and the Russian Federation. A draft text of the EC-Turkey readmission agreement was prepared in 2010 and negotiations concluded by the end of February 2011, without acceptance from the Turkish side.

Finally, since 2008, Turkey has devoted growing attention to border management issues. In 2010, visa procedures were modernised through the implementation of online processing and the introduction of biometric security measures. The modernisation of Turkish border crossing points, required for the implementation of EU integrated border management, continued over the period 2009-10. A co-ordination board for integrated border management (IBM) was established. Turkey continued its negotiations to conclude a working arrangement with European Union's border management agency, FRONTEX. The Turkish Ministry of the Interior and the Greek Ministry for Citizen Protection signed joint declarations in 2010 and ordered stricter border control on the Aegean Sea and Turkish-Greek land borders. However, IBM issues and the transfer of border security control from Turkish military to civilian command continue to be debated between Turkey and the European Union.

For further information:

www.iskur.gov.tr
www.tuik.gov.tr
www.nvi.gov.tr/English,En_Html.html

Recent trends in migrants' flows and stocks
TURKEY

Migration flows (foreigners) National definition	2000	2005	2009	2010	Average 2001-05	Average 2006-10	Level ('000) 2010
Per 1 000 inhabitants							
Inflows	..	..	..	0.4	..	..	29.9
Outflows	..	..	..	..	..	..	..

Migration inflows (foreigners) by type Permit based statistics (standardised)	Thousands 2009	Thousands 2010	% distribution 2009	% distribution 2010
Work	..	..	..	..
Family (incl. accompanying family)	..	..	..	..
Humanitarian	..	..	..	..
Free movements	..	..	..	..
Others	..	..	..	..
Total	..	..	..	..

Inflows of top 10 nationalities as a % of total inflows of foreigners (2010): Azerbaijan, Afghanistan, Russian Federation, Germany, United States, Iran, Kazakhstan, Turkmenistan, Iraq, United Kingdom

Temporary migration	2005	2009	2010	Average 2006-10
Thousands				
International students	..	..	..	..
Trainees	..	..	..	..
Working holiday makers	..	..	..	..
Seasonal workers	..	..	..	..
Intra-company transfers	..	..	..	..
Other temporary workers	..	..	..	..

Inflows of asylum seekers	2000	2005	2009	2010	Average 2001-05	Average 2006-10	Level 2010
Per 1 000 inhabitants	0.1	0.1	0.1	0.1	0.1	0.1	9 226

Components of population growth	2000	2005	2009	2010	Average 2001-05	Average 2006-10	Level ('000) 2010
Per 1 000 inhabitants							
Total						..	..
Natural increase	13.8	12.3	11.3	..	12.9	..	..
Net migration	..	..	..	..	..	..	..

Stocks of immigrants	2000	2005	2009	2010	Average 2001-05	Average 2006-10	Level ('000) 2010
Percentage of the total population							
Foreign-born population	2.0	..	..	..	..	..	..
Foreign population	0.4	..	..	..	..	..	..

Naturalisations	2000	2005	2009	2010	Average 2001-05	Average 2006-10	Level 2010
Percentage of the foreign population	..	..	..	..	..	..	..

Labour market outcomes	2000	2005	2009	2010	Average 2001-05	Average 2006-10
Employment/population ratio						
Native-born men	..	..	64.6	66.7	..	66.8
Foreign-born men	..	..	61.9	64.5	..	65.0
Native-born women	..	..	24.2	26.1	..	24.2
Foreign-born women	..	..	26.4	27.8	..	29.1
Unemployment rate						
Native-born men	..	..	12.7	10.5	..	10.0
Foreign-born men	..	..	14.7	12.4	..	10.6
Native-born women	..	..	12.8	11.6	..	10.4
Foreign-born women	..	..	16.6	14.1	..	11.5

Macroeconomic indicators	2000	2005	2009	2010	Average 2001-05	Average 2006-10	Level 2010
Annual growth in %							
Real GDP	6.8	8.4	-4.8	9.0	4.7	3.3	
GDP/capita (level in USD)	5.3	7.1	-5.9	7.6	3.3	2.0	15 666
Employment (level in thousands)	-2.1	2.2	0.4	6.0	0.6	2.4	23 094
Percentage of the labour force							
Unemployment	6.9	10.4	13.7	11.7	10.2	11.2	

Notes and sources are at the end of the part.

StatLink http://dx.doi.org/10.1787/888932616638

United Kingdom

According to ONS estimates published in November 2011, total inflows to the United Kingdom in 2010 were 591 000, an increase of 4% compared with 2009. Over the same period, outflows decreased by 8%, to 339 000. Total net migration rose by 27%, to 252 000, the highest figure ever recorded. A net outflow of 43 000 UK nationals was compensated by a net inflow of 294 000 non-UK nationals. Net migration increased for all foreign groups except for EU15 citizens.

The number of persons granted settlement in the United Kingdom in 2010, excluding EEA and Swiss nationals, reached the record level of 241 000, a 24% increase compared with the previous year. This was due to large numbers of grants on a discretionary basis (82 300), mainly under measures aimed at clearing the backlog of unresolved cases, especially for asylum. The largest group (84 300) was granted settlement for work-related reasons (including dependants). This record number reflects the high numbers admitted in work-related categories five years earlier who became eligible for settlement. The number of family-related grants was slightly lower (–4%) than the record level of 2009, and stood at 69 200. Around 195 000 immigrants were granted citizenship in 2010, a slight decrease compared with 2009. Half of the citizenship grants were on the grounds of residence.

The number of asylum applications received in 2010 from main applicants decreased by over 25% compared with 2009, to under 18 000. The figure rose somewhat in 2011, to 19 800. The leading nationality of asylum seekers in 2010 was Iran (10%), followed by Afghanistan, Zimbabwe, Pakistan and Sri Lanka.

In Tier 1 of the Points-Based System (PBS), for highly skilled migrants, 33 000 visas were issued in 2010 (of which 49% to main applicants), 3% fewer than in 2009. Of those visas issued in 2010, 20% were issued to those of Indian nationality. 40 000 visas were issued to main applicants in PBS Tier 2, the employer-driven skilled migration stream, in 2010, up from 36 000 in 2009. Provisional figures for 2011 show a decrease in PBS Tier 2 visas issued compared with 2010. Intra-corporate transferees comprise a growing share of Tier 2 visas, comprising 73% of main applicant out-of-country visas in 2010 and 78% in 2011.

The main policy developments stem from the May 2010 election of a new coalition government intent on sharply reducing net migration. New caps implemented from April 2011 limited the number of those admitted under Tiers 1 and 2 to 21 700. Tier 1 is limited to "exceptional talent", endorsed by an appropriate designated body. The quota has been set at 1 000 annual entries through 2012. Investors and entrepreneurs are quota-exempt. Tier 2 is limited to 20 700 permits and requires graduate level education and a job offer from an employer with a certificate of sponsorship. The monthly quotas available have not been fully used. Intra-corporate transfers are exempt from the quota, but salary thresholds were raised for this category. Following review by the Migration Advisory Committee, in November 2011 the Shortage Occupation List for Tier 2 was reduced, with 29 occupations removed and several added. The new list represents less than 1% of employment in the United Kingdom, about $1/_5$ of the coverage of the first list published in 2008. In March 2012, further changes to the system were announced. Tier 2 is now limited to six years stay, and salary criteria for settlement have also been raised.

In July 2011, restrictions were imposed on work entitlements and on rights to bring dependants for students (Tier 4). Course requirements were imposed on sponsoring institutions, although a streamlined application process was created for "low risk" nationals sponsored by highly trusted sponsors. The Post-Study Work route in Tier 1 ended in April 2012, and students who graduate from a university must qualify for Tier 2 to remain. Their sponsors are exempt from the labour market test, but all other conditions must be met. However, a new Graduate Entrepreneurs route in Tier 1 – with a quota of 1 000 visas annually – has been created for graduating students with innovative ideas but who do not qualify for the Tier 1 Entrepreneurship route. The Graduate Entrepreneur route grants them two years to meet the regular requirements.

In April 2012, restrictions were also placed on duration of stay for certain temporary workers (Tier 5) and overseas domestic workers. An English language requirement for migrants seeking to enter or remain in the United Kingdom as the spouse of a UK citizen or permanent resident was introduced in 2010.

For further information:

www.ukba.homeoffice.gov.uk

www.ons.gov.uk/ons/taxonomy/index.html?nscl=International+Migration

www.homeoffice.gov.uk/science-research/research-statistics/migration/migration-statistics1/

Recent trends in migrants' flows and stocks
UNITED KINGDOM

Migration flows (foreigners) National definition	2000	2005	2009	2010	Average 2001-05	Average 2006-10	Level ('000) 2010
Per 1 000 inhabitants							
Inflows	6.4	7.9	7.7	8.1	7.3	8.2	498.0
Outflows	2.7	2.9	3.7	3.3	2.8	3.7	203.0

Migration inflows (foreigners) by type	Thousands		% distribution				
Permit based statistics (standardised)	2009	2010	2009	2010			
Work	142.4	137.3	37.9	33.1			
Family (incl. accompanying family)	107.4	109.3	28.6	26.4			
Humanitarian	3.1	4.9	0.8	1.2			
Free movements	75.7	72.2	20.1	17.4			
Others	47.3	90.6	12.6	21.9			
Total	375.9	414.3	100.0	100.0			

Inflows of top 10 nationalities as a % of total inflows of foreigners

2000-2009 annual average | 2010

India, Poland, Pakistan, China, Australia, United States, Ireland, Lithuania, France, Sri Lanka

Temporary migration	2005	2009	2010	Average 2006-10
Thousands				
International students	124.0	209.0	234.0	179.4
Trainees	..	..	..	..
Working holiday makers	56.6	5.1	0.6	24.6
Seasonal workers	15.7	21.0	6.0	15.3
Intra-company transfers	..	..	..	..
Other temporary workers	202.6	88.0	81.6	137.7

Inflows of asylum seekers	2000	2005	2009	2010	Average 2001-05	Average 2006-10	Level 2010
Per 1 000 inhabitants	1.4	0.5	0.5	0.4	1.0	0.5	22 645

Components of population growth	2000	2005	2009	2010	Average 2001-05	Average 2006-10	Level ('000) 2010
Per 1 000 inhabitants							
Total	3.6	6.2	7.0	6.6	4.7	6.6	409
Natural increase	1.2	2.3	3.7	3.9	1.6	3.4	246
Net migration	2.4	3.8	3.3	2.6	3.1	3.1	163

Stocks of immigrants	2000	2005	2009	2010	Average 2001-05	Average 2006-10	Level ('000) 2010
Percentage of the total population							
Foreign-born population	7.9	9.4	11.3	11.5	8.7	10.7	7 056
Foreign population	4.0	5.1	7.1	7.4	4.6	6.7	4 524

Naturalisations	2000	2005	2009	2010	Average 2001-05	Average 2006-10	Level 2010
Percentage of the foreign population	3.7	5.7	4.9	4.5	4.7	4.2	195 046

Labour market outcomes	2000	2005	2009	2010	Average 2001-05	Average 2006-10	
Employment/population ratio							
Native-born men	78.3	77.9	74.8	74.5	78.1	76.2	
Foreign-born men	71.1	72.4	75.1	74.8	72.3	76.3	
Native-born women	65.7	67.0	66.3	65.7	66.6	66.6	
Foreign-born women	53.1	56.0	57.4	58.0	54.8	57.2	
Unemployment rate							
Native-born men	5.9	4.7	8.7	8.7	5.0	6.9	
Foreign-born men	9.6	7.4	8.9	8.8	7.7	7.7	
Native-born women	4.6	3.7	6.1	6.6	3.9	5.3	
Foreign-born women	7.8	7.1	8.9	9.0	6.8	8.3	

Macroeconomic indicators	2000	2005	2009	2010	Average 2001-05	Average 2006-10	Level 2010
Annual growth in %							
Real GDP	4.5	2.1	−4.4	2.1	2.9	0.5	
GDP/capita (level in USD)	4.1	1.4	−5.0	1.5	2.4	−0.1	35 715
Employment (level in thousands)	1.2	1.0	−1.6	0.3	0.9	0.2	29 035
Percentage of the labour force							
Unemployment	5.5	4.9	7.6	7.9	5.0	6.4	

Notes and sources are at the end of the part.

StatLink http://dx.doi.org/10.1787/888932616657

United States

Permanent immigration to the United States declined 8% in the US Fiscal Year (FY) 2010 with more than 1.04 million beneficiaries. The previous year had seen a 2% increase. Employment-based (EB) preference immigrant admissions grew 5% in FY2010, to 148 000, as a result of an increase that year in the annual limit for the EB categories. Most immigrants granted permanent residence based on employment were family members of principal workers, and 92% were already in the United States on a temporary visa.

Humanitarian migration, comprising resettled ("quota") refugees and those receiving asylum inside the United States, decreased in FY2010. The number of quota refugees admitted to the United States decreased slightly from 74 600 in FY2009 to 73 300 in FY2010. The main origin countries continued to be Iraq, Burma and Bhutan. 21 100 individuals were granted asylum status, of which a third were Chinese (32%).

Issuances of visas for purposes of temporary work and study increased slightly. In FY2010, the number of visa issuances for H-1B specialty occupation workers reversed from the sharp drop registered in 2009. While temporary H-1B visas are subject to an annual cap of 85 000, exemptions allow more visas to be issued each year: 117 400 were issued in FY2010, 7 000 more than in FY2009. Visa issuances under the uncapped temporary/seasonal agricultural worker programme (H-2A) fell 8%, to 56 000, as a stricter wage requirement and labour market test were imposed in March 2010. Issuance of H-2B visas, reserved for temporary/seasonal, non-agricultural workers, increased slightly in FY2010 compared with FY2009, albeit remaining below the 66 000 annual cap, with 47 000 visas issued.

The number of student visas (F-1) rose in FY 2010 to 385 000, 54 000 more than the previous year and the highest level in ten years. On the other hand, total J-1 visa (educational and cultural exchange programmes) issuances peaked at 360 000 in FY2008 and dropped to 320 000 in FY2010. The decline was partly due to a recession-related drop in the J-1 Summer Work-Travel Programme (SWT), under which foreign students may work in the United States for several months, primarily in seasonal and tourism-related jobs. The SWT shrank from 150 000 in FY2008 to less than 100 000 in FY2009, before rising in FY2010 to 120 000. Following complaints about this programme, the State Department announced stricter management.

In FY2010 the official estimate of undocumented immigrants remained unchanged from the FY2009 level, at 10.8 million, 1 million fewer than pre-crisis in 2007. Increased border and workplace enforcement, but especially shrinking employment opportunities due to the downturn, continued to deter inflows. Border apprehensions have been falling for a decade, and fell 36% from FY2008 to FY2010. The decline appears to be driven primarily by decreased entries. Nevertheless, a record 400 000 undocumented foreigners were removed from the United States in 2011.

Specific legislative proposals considered by Congress largely focused on illegal migration. The DREAM Act, a regularisation for undocumented high school graduates who came to the United States as children and who have at least two years of either military service or college attendance, was approved by the US House of Representatives in December 2010, but failed to achieve the number of votes in the US Senate needed to advance. The Secure Visas Act, a bill that would clarify the exercise of the US Government's authority to refuse or revoke a visa, as well as expand on-site review of all visa applications before adjudication at certain visa-issuing posts, was placed on the House of Representatives voting calendar in March 2012.

The existing "E-Verify" electronic employment-eligibility verification system is a temporary, voluntary programme due to sunset by the end of September 2012. A bill to establish a permanent, mandatory national electronic verification system is under review.

Restrictive bills for local control of illegal immigration were adopted or discussed in several US states, some of which were challenged in court at the federal level.

Reforms of some of the permanent immigrant visa categories were also discussed in Congress. In July 2011, a bill was introduced to eliminate the Diversity Visa programme (i.e. the "visa lottery"), reflecting concerns over its vulnerability to fraud and misuse. Congress is also debating several bills to expand the scope of the EB-5 immigrant investor visa category. Finally, the Fairness for High-Skilled Immigrants Act of 2011, which would remove the cap on the share of EB visas available each year that may be granted to nationals of a given country, was approved by the House of Representatives in November 2011 and is being considered by the Senate.

For further information:

www.dhs.gov/ximgtn/
www.foreignlaborcert.doleta.gov/
www.dol.gov/compliance/laws/comp-ina.htm
www.ice.gov

Recent trends in migrants' flows and stocks
UNITED STATES

Migration flows (foreigners) National definition	2000	2005	2009	2010	Average		Level ('000)
					2001-05	2006-10	2010
Per 1 000 inhabitants							
Inflows	3.0	3.8	3.7	3.4	3.4	3.7	1 042.6
Outflows	..	..	..	..	..	..	..
Migration inflows (foreigners) by type	Thousands		% distribution				
Permit based statistics (standardised)	2009	2010	2009	2010			
Work	65.6	67.0	5.8	6.4			
Family (incl. accompanying family)	825.9	772.4	73.1	74.1			
Humanitarian	177.4	136.3	15.7	13.1			
Free movements	..	..	..	..			
Others	61.4	66.3	5.4	6.4			
Total	1 130.2	1 041.9	100.0	100.0			
Temporary migration	2005	2009	2010	Average 2006-10			
Thousands							
International students	237.9	331.2	385.2	325.9			
Trainees	1.8	2.1	1.8	2.6			
Working holiday makers	88.6	116.4	118.2	128.3			
Seasonal workers	31.9	60.1	55.9	53.7			
Intra-company transfers	65.5	64.7	74.7	76.1			
Other temporary workers	266.1	209.8	217.6	251.2			
Inflows of asylum seekers	2000	2005	2009	2010	Average		Level
					2001-05	2006-10	2010
Per 1 000 inhabitants	0.1	0.1	0.1	0.1	0.2	0.1	42 971
Components of population growth	2000	2005	2009	2010	Average		Level ('000)
					2001-05	2006-10	2010
Per 1 000 inhabitants							
Total	10.5	9.2	7.9	7.5	9.2	8.7	2 327
Natural increase	5.7	5.7	5.6	5.2	5.7	5.8	1 608
Net migration	4.6	3.2	2.4	2.3	3.3	2.6	719
Stocks of immigrants	2000	2005	2009	2010	Average		Level ('000)
					2001-05	2006-10	2010
Percentage of the total population							
Foreign-born population	10.7	12.1	12.5	12.9	11.6	12.6	39 917
Foreign population	6.3	7.3	6.9	7.0	7.1	7.2	21 581
Naturalisations	2000	2005	2009	2010	Average		Level
					2001-05	2006-10	2010
Percentage of the foreign population	4.1	2.8	3.4	2.9	2.7	3.4	619 913
Labour market outcomes	2000	2005	2009	2010	Average		
					2001-05	2006-10	
Employment/population ratio							
Native-born men	77.2	73.3	69.1	68.2	74.1	71.4	
Foreign-born men	82.0	81.7	77.5	77.4	80.8	80.2	
Native-born women	68.4	65.3	63.2	62.2	66.3	64.5	
Foreign-born women	57.7	56.4	57.4	57.4	57.1	58.3	
Unemployment rate							
Native-born men	4.5	6.3	10.7	10.9	6.5	7.9	
Foreign-born men	4.5	5.1	10.1	10.0	5.8	7.0	
Native-born women	4.2	5.2	8.1	8.7	5.2	6.0	
Foreign-born women	5.5	5.2	9.2	9.5	6.5	6.5	
Macroeconomic indicators	2000	2005	2009	2010	Average		Level
					2001-05	2006-10	2010
Annual growth in %							
Real GDP	4.2	3.1	-3.5	3.0	2.4	0.7	
GDP/capita (level in USD)	3.0	2.1	-4.4	2.2	1.4	-0.2	46 588
Employment (level in thousands)	2.5	1.8	-3.8	-0.6	0.7	-0.4	139 069
Percentage of the labour force							
Unemployment	4.0	5.1	9.3	9.6	5.4	6.8	

Inflows of top 10 nationalities as a % of total inflows of foreigners

2000-2009 annual average — 2010

Mexico, China, India, Philippines, Dominican Republic, Cuba, Viet Nam, Haiti, Colombia, Korea

Notes and sources are at the end of the part.

StatLink http://dx.doi.org/10.1787/888932616676

SOURCES AND NOTES OF THE COUNTRY TABLES OF PART IV

Migration flows of foreigners

OECD countries and the Russian Federation: sources and notes are available in the Statistical Annex (metadata related to Table A.1 and B.1).

Bulgaria: Number of new permanent and long-term residence permits granted (*Source*: Ministry of the Interior); Lithuania: Arrivals and departures of residents (*Source*: Department of Statistics of the Government of the Republic of Lithuania); Romania: *Source*: Permanent residence changes (*Source*: Romanian Statistical Yearbook).

Long-term migration inflows of foreigners by type (standardised inflows)

The statistics are based largely on residence and work permit data and have been standardised, to the extent possible (*cf. www.oecd.org/migration/imo*).

Temporary migration

Based on residence or work permit data. Data on temporary workers generally do not cover workers who benefit from a free circulation agreement.

Inflows of asylum seekers

United Nations High Commission for Refugees (*www.unhcr.org/statistics*).

Components of population growth

OECD countries: *Labour Force Statistics*, OECD, 2010; Italy, United Kingdom, Bulgaria, Lithuania and Romania: Eurostat.

Total population
Foreign-born population

National sources and Secretariat estimates (*cf. www.oecd.org/els/migration/foreignborn* for more information on methods of estimation). Sources and notes of national sources are provided in the Statistical Annex (see metadata for Tables A.4 and B.4).

Foreign population

National sources. Exact sources and notes for the OECD countries are given in the Statistical Annex (metadata related to Tables A.5 and B.5).

Lithuania: Residents' Register Service (Ministry of the Interior); Romania: Ministry of the Interior.

Naturalisations

National sources. Exact sources and notes for the OECD countries are given in the Statistical Annex (metadata related to Tables A.6 and B.6). Bulgaria and Lithuania: Ministry of the Interior.

Labour market outcomes

European countries: Labour Force Surveys (Eurostat) ; Australia, Canada: Labour Force Surveys (annual averages); United States: Current Population Survey, March supplement.

Macroeconomic and labour market indicators

Real GDP and GDP per capita

Annual National Accounts – Comparative tables at the price levels and PPPs of 2005 (OECD).

Employment and unemployment

OECD Employment Outlook, OECD, 2012.

STATISTICAL ANNEX

List of Tables

Inflows and outflows of foreign population 290
    A.1. Inflows of foreign population into selected OECD countries and the Russian Federation 292
    B.1. Inflows of foreign population by nationality 293
    A.2. Outflows of foreign population from selected OECD countries 310

Inflows of asylum seekers 315
    A.3. Inflows of asylum seekers into OECD countries and the Russian Federation . 316
    B.3. Inflows of asylum seekers by nationality 317

Stocks of foreign and foreign-born populations 335
    A.4. Stocks of foreign-born population in OECD countries and the Russian Federation 336
    B.4. Stock of foreign-born population by country of birth 338
    A.5. Stocks of foreign population by nationality in OECD countries and the Russian Federation 356
    B.5. Stock of foreign population by nationality 358

Acquisitions of nationality 374
    A.6. Acquisitions of nationality in OECD countries and the Russian Federation .. 375
    B.6. Acquisitions of nationality by country of former nationality 376

STATISTICAL ANNEX

Introduction

Most of the data published in this annex have been provided by national correspondents of the continuous reporting system on migration appointed by the OECD Secretariat with the approval of the authorities of member countries. Consequently, these data are not necessarily based on common definitions. Countries under review in this annex are OECD countries for which data are available, as well as the Russian Federation. The continuous reporting system on migration has no authority to impose changes in data collection procedures. It is an observatory which, by its very nature, has to use existing statistics. However, it does play an active role in suggesting what it considers to be essential improvements in data collection and makes every effort to present consistent and well-documented statistics.

The purpose of this annex is to describe the "immigrant" population (generally the foreign-born population). The information gathered concerns the flows and stocks of the total immigrant population as well as the acquisition of nationality. These data have not been standardised and are therefore not fully comparable across countries. In particular, the criteria for registering persons in population registers and the conditions for granting residence permits, for example, vary across countries, which means that measurements may differ greatly even if the same type of source is being used.

In addition to the problem of the comparability of statistics, there is the difficulty of the very partial coverage of unauthorised migrants. Part of this population may be counted in censuses. Regularisation programmes, when they exist, make it possible to identify and enumerate a far from negligible fraction of unauthorised immigrants after the fact. In terms of measurement, this makes it possible to better measure the volume of the foreign-born population at a given time, even if it is not always possible to determine the year these immigrants entered the country.

Each series in the annex is preceded by an explanatory note concerning the data presented. A summary table then follows (Series A, giving the total for each destination country), and finally the tables by nationality or country of birth, as the case may be (Series B). At the end of each series, a table provides the sources and notes for the data presented in the tables for each country.

General comments

- The tables provide annual series covering the period 2000-10.
- The Series A tables are presented in alphabetical order by the name of the country. In the other tables, nationalities or countries of birth are ranked by decreasing order of frequency for the last year available.

- In the tables by country of origin (Series B) only the 15 main countries are shown. "Other countries" is a residual calculated as the difference between the total foreign or foreign-born population and the sum for all countries indicated in the table. For some countries, data are not available for all years and this is reflected in the residual entry of "Other countries". This must be borne in mind when interpreting changes in this category.

- There is no table by nationality for the series on outflows of the foreign population (Series A.2). These statistics, as well as data by gender are available online (*www.oecd.org/migration/imo*).

- The rounding of data cells may cause totals to differ slightly from the sum of the component cells.

- The symbol ". ." used in the tables means that the data are not available.

- Note on Israel: The statistical data for Israel are supplied by and under the responsibility of the relevant Israeli authorities. The use of such data by the OECD is without prejudice to the status of the Golan Heights, East Jerusalem and Israeli settlements in the West Bank under the terms of international law.

- Note on Cyprus by Turkey: The information in this document with reference to "Cyprus" relates to the southern part of the Island. There is no single authority representing both Turkish and Greek Cypriot people on the Island. Turkey recognizes the Turkish Republic of Northern Cyprus (TRNC). Until a lasting and equitable solution is found within the context of the United Nations, Turkey shall preserve its position concerning the "Cyprus issue".

- Note on Cyprus by all the European Union Member States of the OECD and the European Commission: The Republic of Cyprus is recognised by all members of the United Nations with the exception of Turkey. The information in this document relates to the area under the effective control of the Government of the Republic of Cyprus.

Inflows and outflows of foreign population

OECD countries seldom have tools specifically designed to measure the inflows and outflows of the foreign population, and national estimates are generally based either on population registers or residence permit data. This note describes more systematically what is measured by each of the sources used.

Flows derived from population registers

Population registers can usually produce inflow and outflow data for both nationals and foreigners. To register, foreigners may have to indicate possession of an appropriate residence and/or work permit valid for at least as long as the minimum registration period. Emigrants are usually identified by a stated intention to leave the country, although the period of (intended) absence is not always specified.

In population registers, departures tend to be less well recorded than arrivals. Indeed, the emigrant who plans to return to the host country in the future may be reluctant to inform about his departure to avoid losing rights related to the presence on the register. Registration criteria vary considerably across countries; in particular the minimum duration of stay for individuals to be registered ranges from three months to one year, which poses major problems of international comparisons. For example, in some countries, register data cover many temporary migrants, in some cases including asylum seekers when they live in private households (as opposed to reception centres or hostels for immigrants) and international students.

Flows derived from residence and/or work permits

Statistics on permits are generally based on the number of permits issued during a given period and depend on the types of permits used. The so-called "settlement countries" (Australia, Canada, New Zealand and the United States) consider as immigrants persons who have been granted the right of permanent residence, and this right is often granted upon arrival. Statistics on temporary immigrants are also published in this annex for these countries. In the case of France, the permits covered are those valid for at least one year (excluding students). Data for Portugal include temporary migrants.

Another characteristic of permit data is that flows of nationals are not recorded. Some flows of foreigners may also not be recorded, either because the type of permit they hold is not included in the statistics or because they are not required to have a permit (freedom of movement agreements). In addition, permit data do not necessarily reflect physical flows or actual lengths of stay since: i) permits may be issued overseas but individuals may decide not to use them, or delay their arrival; ii) permits may be issued to persons who have in fact been resident in the country for some time, the permit indicating a change of status.

Flows estimated from specific surveys

Ireland provides estimates based on the results of Quarterly National Household Surveys and other sources such as permit data and asylum applications. These estimates are revised periodically on the basis of census data. Data for the United Kingdom are based on a survey of passengers entering or exiting the country by plane, train or boat (International Passenger Survey). One of the aims of this survey is to estimate the number and characteristics of migrants. The survey is based on a random sample of approximately one out of every 500 passengers. The figures were revised significantly following the latest census in each of these two countries, which seems to indicate that these estimates do not constitute an "ideal" source either. Australia and New Zealand also conduct passenger surveys which enable them to establish the length of stay on the basis of migrants' stated intentions when they enter or exit the country.

Table A.1. Inflows of foreign population into selected OECD countries and the Russian Federation

Thousands

	2000	2001	2002	2003	2004	2005	2006	2007	2008	2009	2010
Australia											
Permanent	107.1	127.9	119.1	123.4	146.4	161.7	176.2	189.5	203.9	222.6	206.7
Temporary	224.0	245.1	240.5	244.7	261.6	289.4	321.6	368.5	420.0	474.8	504.7
Austria	66.0	74.8	86.1	93.3	104.2	98.0	82.9	91.7	94.8	91.8	98.3
Belgium	57.3	66.0	70.2	68.8	72.4	77.4	83.4	93.4	106.0	102.7	113.6
Canada											
Permanent	227.5	250.6	229.0	221.3	235.8	262.2	251.6	236.8	247.2	252.2	280.7
Temporary	254.2	268.5	247.9	228.3	228.2	229.6	250.1	279.9	313.8	382.1	383.9
Chile	..	..	..	29.8	32.1	38.1	48.5	79.4	68.4	57.1	63.9
Czech Republic	4.2	11.3	43.6	57.4	50.8	58.6	66.1	102.5	77.8	40.0	30.5
Denmark	22.8	24.6	21.5	18.4	18.7	20.1	24.0	31.4	37.0	32.0	33.4
Estonia	..	..	..	..	0.8	1.0	1.5	2.0	1.9	2.2	1.2
Finland	9.1	11.0	10.0	9.4	11.5	12.7	13.9	17.5	19.9	18.1	18.2
France	91.9	106.9	124.2	136.4	141.6	135.9	135.1	128.9	136.0	126.2	136.0
Germany	648.8	685.3	658.3	601.8	602.2	579.3	558.5	574.8	573.8	606.3	683.5
Greece	..	..	..	..	..	..	..	..	..	33.5	23.0
Hungary	20.2	20.3	18.0	19.4	22.2	25.6	23.6	22.6	35.5	25.6	23.9
Iceland	2.5	2.5	1.9	1.4	2.5	4.7	7.1	9.3	7.5	3.4	3.0
Ireland	27.8	32.7	39.9	42.4	41.8	66.1	88.9	89.5	67.6	38.9	17.4
Israel	60.2	43.6	33.6	23.3	20.9	21.2	19.3	18.1	13.7	14.6	16.6
Italy	192.6	172.8	161.9	424.9	394.8	282.8	254.6	515.2	496.5	406.7	424.5
Japan	345.8	351.2	343.8	373.9	372.0	372.3	325.6	336.6	344.5	297.1	287.1
Korea	185.4	172.5	170.9	178.3	188.8	266.3	314.7	317.6	311.7	242.8	293.1
Luxembourg	10.8	11.1	11.0	12.6	12.2	13.8	13.7	15.8	16.8	14.6	15.8
Mexico	6.4	8.1	5.8	6.9	8.5	9.2	6.9	6.8	15.1	23.9	26.2
Netherlands	91.4	94.5	86.6	73.6	65.1	63.4	67.7	80.3	103.4	104.4	110.2
New Zealand	37.6	54.4	47.5	43.0	36.2	54.1	49.8	46.8	46.9	43.6	44.3
Norway	27.8	25.4	30.8	26.8	27.9	31.4	37.4	53.5	58.8	56.7	65.1
Poland	15.9	21.5	30.2	30.3	36.9	38.5	34.2	40.6	41.8	41.3	41.1
Portugal	15.9	151.4	72.0	31.8	34.1	28.1	22.5	32.6	32.3	33.8	30.0
Russian Federation	359.3	193.5	184.6	129.1	119.2	177.2	186.4	287.0	281.6	279.9	191.7
Slovak Republic	4.6	4.7	4.8	4.6	7.9	7.7	11.3	14.8	16.5	14.4	12.7
Slovenia	5.3	6.8	7.7	8.0	8.6	13.3	18.3	27.5	28.1	27.4	12.7
Spain	330.9	394.0	443.1	429.5	645.8	682.7	803.0	920.5	692.2	469.3	431.3
Sweden	42.2	43.8	47.3	47.1	46.7	50.6	78.9	82.6	82.0	82.4	79.0
Switzerland	87.4	101.4	101.9	94.0	96.3	94.4	102.7	139.7	157.3	132.4	134.2
Turkey	..	..	..	..	..	..	..	..	..	..	29.9
United Kingdom	379.0	370.0	418.0	411.0	500.0	469.0	513.0	500.0	505.0	471.0	498.0
United States											
Permanent	841.0	1 058.9	1 059.4	703.5	957.9	1 122.4	1 266.3	1 052.4	1 107.1	1 130.8	1 042.6
Temporary	1 249.4	1 375.1	1 282.6	1 233.4	1 299.3	1 323.5	1 457.9	1 606.9	1 617.6	1 419.2	1 517.9

Notes: For details on definitions and sources, refer to the metadata at the end of Table A.2.
Information on data for Israel: http://dx.doi.org/10.1787/888932315602.

StatLink http://dx.doi.org/10.1787/888932617398

Table B.1. Inflows of foreign population by nationality
Thousands
AUSTRALIA (PERMANENT)

	2000	2001	2002	2003	2004	2005	2006	2007	2008	2009	2010	Of which: Women 2010 (%)
United Kingdom	11.8	13.2	14.6	18.6	25.7	26.2	30.9	30.7	31.7	33.3	26.7	48
China	8.1	8.3	9.1	9.4	12.5	15.2	17.3	21.1	20.7	22.9	25.0	55
New Zealand	31.6	42.3	21.6	16.4	18.7	22.4	23.8	28.3	34.5	33.0	24.4	49
India	4.6	5.8	7.6	8.2	11.3	12.8	15.2	19.8	22.7	25.3	23.5	51
South Africa	6.2	6.8	7.2	5.9	7.1	5.7	4.8	5.4	6.9	11.3	11.1	50
Philippines	3.6	3.4	3.4	3.6	4.4	4.8	5.4	6.1	7.1	8.9	10.3	58
Sri Lanka	1.5	1.8	2.4	2.3	2.1	3.0	3.3	3.8	4.8	5.3	5.8	48
Malaysia	2.0	2.5	2.6	3.9	5.1	4.7	4.8	4.8	5.1	5.4	4.9	53
Korea	0.8	1.5	2.0	2.3	2.8	3.5	4.0	4.2	5.0	5.2	4.3	55
Viet Nam	1.7	1.9	2.5	3.0	2.5	2.5	2.9	3.4	3.0	3.3	3.9	65
United States	1.8	2.3	2.6	2.5	3.0	3.0	2.9	2.8	3.0	3.1	3.2	53
Afghanistan	0.9	0.5	0.7	1.0	1.3	3.5	3.5	2.6	2.0	2.0	3.2	28
Ireland	1.0	1.1	1.0	1.2	1.6	1.6	1.8	1.9	2.0	2.7	3.0	42
Iraq	2.0	1.3	1.3	2.9	1.8	3.3	5.1	2.5	2.6	4.4	2.9	50
Myanmar	0.2	0.3	0.3	0.3	0.3	0.5	0.8	1.8	2.6	3.2	2.7	51
Other countries	29.3	34.9	40.1	42.0	46.2	49.1	49.8	50.4	50.0	53.4	51.9	
Total	**107.1**	**127.9**	**119.1**	**123.4**	**146.4**	**161.7**	**176.2**	**189.5**	**203.9**	**222.6**	**206.7**	**52**

Note: For details on definitions and sources, please refer to the metadata at the end of Table A.2.

StatLink http://dx.doi.org/10.1787/888932617512

Table B.1. Inflows of foreign population by nationality
Thousands
AUSTRIA

	2000	2001	2002	2003	2004	2005	2006	2007	2008	2009	2010	Of which: Women 2010 (%)
Germany	7.5	10.2	9.2	10.9	13.2	14.7	15.9	17.9	19.2	17.6	17.8	46
Romania	1.9	2.4	4.8	5.7	5.5	5.1	4.5	9.3	9.3	9.3	11.5	51
Serbia	6.5	6.3	9.9	10.5	11.6	11.7	7.4	6.4	6.1	6.2	8.5	43
Hungary	2.4	3.0	2.6	2.8	3.2	3.4	3.6	4.5	5.2	5.8	6.5	51
Turkey	7.1	7.8	11.3	10.4	8.2	7.7	4.9	5.2	5.0	4.8	4.3	41
Poland	3.4	3.5	3.0	3.4	7.0	6.8	5.7	5.3	4.4	3.8	4.2	44
Slovak Republic	1.9	2.5	2.5	2.6	3.5	3.6	3.5	3.6	4.9	4.0	4.1	63
Bulgaria	0.7	0.9	1.5	1.7	1.7	1.4	1.2	2.2	2.5	2.6	3.2	51
Bosnia and Herzegovina	3.9	6.0	4.9	5.4	5.4	4.6	3.2	3.0	2.9	2.4	2.5	40
Russian Federation	0.9	0.9	1.8	4.0	6.8	4.0	2.5	2.2	3.0	2.4	2.2	57
Italy	1.3	1.7	1.4	1.5	1.4	1.4	1.5	1.7	1.8	2.0	2.2	39
Croatia	4.8	6.1	3.8	3.4	3.3	2.8	2.5	2.3	2.0	1.9	1.9	46
United States	0.9	0.9	1.0	1.1	1.3	1.4	1.5	1.6	1.7	1.6	1.7	50
Iran	2.5	1.1	1.0	1.2	1.0	1.0	2.2	2.0	1.7	1.9	1.6	49
Former Yug. Rep. of Macedonia	0.9	1.4	1.8	1.6	1.6	1.4	0.9	0.9	1.0	0.9	1.4	43
Other countries	19.4	20.2	25.7	27.2	29.5	27.0	22.1	23.5	24.1	24.6	24.5	
Total	**66.0**	**74.8**	**86.1**	**93.3**	**104.2**	**98.0**	**82.9**	**91.7**	**94.8**	**91.8**	**98.3**	**47**

Note: For details on definitions and sources, please refer to the metadata at the end of Table A.2.

StatLink http://dx.doi.org/10.1787/888932617512

Table B.1. Inflows of foreign population by nationality
Thousands
BELGIUM

	2000	2001	2002	2003	2004	2005	2006	2007	2008	2009	2010	Of which: Women 2009 (%)
France	8.1	8.0	8.1	8.2	9.5	10.4	11.6	12.3	14.1	12.3	..	51
Poland	1.1	2.9	2.4	2.1	3.5	4.8	6.7	9.4	9.0	9.9	..	58
Morocco	5.7	7.1	8.5	8.4	8.0	7.1	7.5	7.8	8.2	9.1	..	54
Netherlands	7.2	8.2	8.4	8.5	8.8	10.1	11.5	11.4	11.7	8.8	..	46
Romania	0.7	1.0	1.0	1.0	1.4	2.3	3.1	5.5	6.8	6.1	..	46
Spain	1.4	1.5	1.5	1.5	1.6	1.8	1.8	1.9	2.8	3.6	..	46
Italy	2.6	2.4	2.3	2.3	2.3	2.5	2.6	2.7	3.7	3.6	..	45
Germany	3.0	2.9	3.0	2.9	3.3	3.3	3.3	3.4	3.8	3.4	..	52
Bulgaria	0.3	0.4	0.5	0.5	0.7	0.9	0.8	2.6	3.9	3.3	..	49
Turkey	2.8	3.0	3.9	3.8	3.2	3.4	3.0	3.2	3.2	3.1	..	51
Portugal	1.3	1.3	1.6	1.8	1.9	1.9	2.0	2.3	3.2	2.9	..	40
United States	2.8	2.9	2.7	2.5	2.6	2.4	2.6	2.5	2.6	2.7	..	54
United Kingdom	3.2	2.7	2.5	2.5	2.4	2.2	2.0	2.0	2.4	1.9	..	45
India	0.7	0.9	1.0	1.1	1.2	1.3	1.5	1.6	2.1	1.8	..	37
China	0.8	1.3	2.1	1.6	1.4	1.2	1.5	1.2	1.3	1.3	..	57
Other countries	15.7	19.5	20.8	20.0	20.6	21.8	22.0	23.6	27.4	29.1	..	
Total	**57.3**	**66.0**	**70.2**	**68.8**	**72.4**	**77.4**	**83.4**	**93.4**	**106.0**	**102.7**	**113.6**	**52**

Note: For details on definitions and sources, please refer to the metadata at the end of Table A.2.

StatLink http://dx.doi.org/10.1787/888932617512

Table B.1. Inflows of foreign population by nationality
Thousands
CANADA (PERMANENT)

	2000	2001	2002	2003	2004	2005	2006	2007	2008	2009	2010	Of which: Women 2010 (%)
Philippines	10.1	12.9	11.0	12.0	13.3	17.5	17.7	19.1	23.7	27.3	36.6	56
India	26.1	27.9	28.8	24.6	25.6	33.1	30.8	26.1	24.5	26.1	30.3	50
China	36.8	40.4	33.3	36.3	36.4	42.3	33.1	27.0	29.3	29.0	30.2	53
United Kingdom	4.6	5.4	4.7	5.2	6.1	5.9	6.5	8.1	9.2	9.6	9.5	45
United States	5.8	5.9	5.3	6.0	7.5	9.3	10.9	10.5	11.2	9.7	9.2	50
France	4.4	4.5	4.0	4.2	5.1	5.5	5.0	5.6	6.4	7.4	6.9	43
Iran	5.6	5.7	7.9	5.7	6.1	5.5	7.1	6.7	6.0	6.1	6.8	49
United Arab Emirates	3.1	4.5	4.4	3.3	4.4	4.1	4.1	3.4	4.7	4.6	6.8	48
Morocco	2.6	4.0	4.1	3.2	3.5	2.7	3.1	3.8	3.9	5.2	5.9	47
Korea	7.6	9.6	7.3	7.1	5.3	5.8	6.2	5.9	7.2	5.9	5.5	53
Pakistan	14.2	15.4	14.2	12.4	12.8	13.6	12.3	9.5	8.1	6.2	5.0	52
Colombia	2.2	3.0	3.2	4.3	4.4	6.0	5.8	4.8	5.0	4.2	4.8	52
Haiti	1.7	2.5	2.2	1.9	1.7	1.7	1.7	1.6	2.5	2.1	4.6	57
Iraq	1.4	1.6	1.4	1.0	1.1	1.3	1.0	1.6	2.6	4.6	4.5	51
Bangladesh	2.7	3.4	2.6	1.9	2.4	3.9	3.8	2.7	2.7	1.9	4.4	50
Other countries	98.5	104.1	94.6	92.4	100.2	104.0	102.5	100.4	100.0	102.3	109.6	
Total	**227.5**	**250.6**	**229.0**	**221.3**	**235.8**	**262.2**	**251.6**	**236.8**	**247.2**	**252.2**	**280.7**	**51**

Note: For details on definitions and sources, please refer to the metadata at the end of Table A.2.

StatLink http://dx.doi.org/10.1787/888932617512

Table B.1. Inflows of foreign population by nationality
Thousands
CHILE

	2000	2001	2002	2003	2004	2005	2006	2007	2008	2009	2010	Of which: Women 2010 (%)
Peru	..	..	..	12.9	15.6	20.0	28.6	53.2	39.0	27.6	27.7	55
Colombia	..	..	..	1.0	1.1	1.7	2.4	3.3	4.4	5.3	7.2	54
Bolivia	..	..	..	1.3	1.4	1.6	1.9	6.0	4.5	3.6	5.8	50
Argentina	..	..	..	4.9	4.3	4.1	3.5	3.0	3.7	3.9	3.8	36
United States	..	..	..	1.6	1.3	1.5	1.5	1.5	2.1	2.2	2.9	39
Ecuador	..	..	..	2.0	1.8	1.9	2.2	3.1	3.1	2.7	2.5	50
China	..	..	..	0.5	0.6	0.7	0.7	0.9	1.3	1.3	1.3	33
Brazil	..	..	..	0.7	0.8	0.8	1.1	1.2	1.2	1.1	1.3	50
Dominican Republic	..	..	..	0.1	0.1	0.1	0.2	0.3	0.0	0.6	1.0	73
Spain	..	..	..	0.5	0.5	0.5	0.6	0.6	0.7	0.8	0.9	39
Uruguay	..	..	..	0.6	0.7	0.7	0.8	0.9	1.0	0.7	0.8	41
Venezuela	..	..	..	0.4	0.4	0.4	0.4	0.6	0.6	0.7	0.7	53
Paraguay	..	..	..	0.2	0.2	0.3	0.4	0.6	0.7	0.7	0.7	60
Mexico	..	..	..	0.3	0.3	0.4	0.5	0.5	0.7	0.7	0.7	45
Haiti	..	..	..	0.0	0.0	0.0	0.1	0.1	0.1	0.3	0.7	25
Other countries	..	..	..	2.8	2.9	3.4	3.6	3.5	5.3	5.0	5.8	
Total	..	..	..	**29.8**	**32.1**	**38.1**	**48.5**	**79.4**	**68.4**	**57.1**	**63.9**	**50**

Note: For details on definitions and sources, please refer to the metadata at the end of Table A.2.

StatLink http://dx.doi.org/10.1787/888932617512

Table B.1. Inflows of foreign population by nationality
Thousands
CZECH REPUBLIC

	2000	2001	2002	2003	2004	2005	2006	2007	2008	2009	2010	Of which: Women 2010 (%)
Slovak Republic	1.0	2.4	13.0	23.7	15.0	10.1	6.8	13.9	7.6	5.6	5.1	49
Russian Federation	0.4	0.7	2.4	1.8	2.0	3.3	4.7	6.7	5.8	4.1	3.7	55
Ukraine	1.1	2.8	10.7	15.5	16.3	23.9	30.2	39.6	18.7	8.1	3.5	57
Germany	0.1	0.2	0.8	0.8	1.3	1.4	0.8	1.9	4.3	2.0	2.0	13
United States	0.1	0.1	0.7	0.9	0.7	1.4	1.8	1.7	2.2	2.5	1.7	52
Viet Nam	0.3	2.2	5.7	3.6	4.5	4.9	6.4	12.3	13.4	2.3	1.4	54
Poland	0.1	0.4	1.7	1.6	1.8	1.3	0.9	2.3	1.2	0.9	0.7	42
Kazakhstan	0.1	0.1	0.2	0.2	0.2	0.4	0.5	1.0	0.7	0.8	0.7	..
Bulgaria	0.1	0.2	0.7	0.6	0.7	0.8	0.8	1.1	1.0	0.6	0.6	38
Turkey	..	..	..	0.1	0.6	0.2	0.4	0.4	0.4	0.4	0.5	..
China	..	..	..	0.5	0.5	0.8	1.4	1.0	0.9	0.6	0.5	57
Romania	0.0	0.2	0.3	0.4	0.3	0.4	0.4	0.9	0.6	0.5	0.4	30
Austria	..	..	..	0.3	0.4	0.4	0.1	0.2	0.5	0.4	0.4	18
Korea	..	..	..	0.7	0.4	0.1	0.2	0.5	0.7	0.3	0.4	48
Moldova	0.0	0.2	0.8	1.2	1.0	1.7	2.4	3.4	3.3	1.3	0.4	54
Other countries	0.9	1.7	6.5	5.6	5.2	7.4	8.4	15.5	16.4	9.7	8.7	
Total	**4.2**	**11.3**	**43.6**	**57.4**	**50.8**	**58.6**	**66.1**	**102.5**	**77.8**	**40.0**	**30.5**	**46**

Note: For details on definitions and sources, please refer to the metadata at the end of Table A.2.

StatLink http://dx.doi.org/10.1787/888932617512

Table B.1. Inflows of foreign population by nationality
Thousands
DENMARK

	2000	2001	2002	2003	2004	2005	2006	2007	2008	2009	2010	Of which: Women 2010 (%)
Poland	0.3	0.4	0.4	0.4	0.7	1.3	2.5	4.3	6.5	3.4	2.9	46
Romania	0.1	0.2	0.2	0.2	0.2	0.3	0.3	0.8	1.4	1.5	2.0	40
Germany	0.8	0.9	0.8	0.8	1.0	1.3	1.9	3.0	3.0	2.2	1.9	51
Philippines	0.2	0.2	0.2	0.2	0.4	0.5	0.8	1.3	1.7	1.8	1.8	94
Lithuania	0.4	0.4	0.4	0.3	0.5	0.6	0.8	0.7	1.1	1.3	1.5	44
Norway	1.3	1.2	1.3	1.3	1.2	1.2	1.4	1.4	1.4	1.3	1.4	62
Ukraine	0.3	0.3	0.4	0.5	0.6	0.9	1.3	1.8	1.8	1.4	1.2	40
Sweden	0.9	0.8	0.7	0.8	0.8	0.9	1.2	1.3	1.3	1.1	1.1	55
United Kingdom	0.8	0.8	0.7	0.7	0.7	0.7	0.9	0.9	1.0	0.9	1.0	37
Bulgaria	0.1	0.1	0.1	0.1	0.1	0.1	0.1	0.3	0.7	0.9	0.9	38
India	0.2	0.2	0.2	0.3	0.4	0.5	0.5	0.9	1.0	0.8	0.9	36
Iceland	0.8	0.8	1.1	1.0	1.1	1.1	1.1	1.2	1.1	1.0	0.9	53
United States	0.5	0.6	0.5	0.5	0.6	0.6	0.7	0.8	0.9	0.7	0.9	51
Latvia	0.3	0.2	0.2	0.2	0.2	0.2	0.3	0.4	0.4	0.7	0.9	51
Thailand	0.6	0.7	0.5	0.4	0.5	0.5	0.5	0.6	0.7	0.7	0.8	84
Other countries	15.3	16.8	13.7	10.6	9.7	9.3	9.9	12.0	13.0	12.4	13.2	
Total	**22.8**	**24.6**	**21.5**	**18.4**	**18.7**	**20.1**	**24.0**	**31.4**	**37.0**	**32.0**	**33.4**	**50**

Note: For details on definitions and sources, please refer to the metadata at the end of Table A.2.

StatLink http://dx.doi.org/10.1787/888932617512

Table B.1. Inflows of foreign population by nationality
Thousands
ESTONIA

	2000	2001	2002	2003	2004	2005	2006	2007	2008	2009	2010	Of which: Women 2010 (%)
Russian Federation	..	..	..	..	0.2	0.2	0.3	0.4	0.4	0.5	0.4	52
Finland	..	..	..	..	..	..	..	..	..	0.3	..	..
Ukraine	..	..	..	..	..	..	..	..	..	0.2	..	..
Germany	..	..	..	..	..	..	..	..	..	0.1	..	..
Latvia	..	..	..	..	..	..	..	..	..	0.1	..	..
China	..	..	..	..	..	..	..	..	..	0.1	..	..
Sweden	..	..	..	..	..	..	..	..	..	0.1	..	..
United States	..	..	..	..	..	..	..	..	..	0.1	..	..
Italy	..	..	..	..	..	..	..	..	..	0.1	..	..
France	..	..	..	..	..	..	..	..	..	0.1	..	..
Other countries	..	..	..	..	0.5	0.7	1.1	1.5	1.5	0.6	0.8	
Total	..	..	..	..	**0.8**	**1.0**	**1.5**	**2.0**	**1.9**	**2.2**	**1.2**	**41**

Note: For details on definitions and sources, please refer to the metadata at the end of Table A.2.

StatLink http://dx.doi.org/10.1787/888932617512

STATISTICAL ANNEX

Table B.1. **Inflows of foreign population by nationality**
Thousands
FINLAND

	2000	2001	2002	2003	2004	2005	2006	2007	2008	2009	2010	Of which: Women 2010 (%)
Estonia	0.7	1.1	1.2	1.1	1.7	1.9	2.5	2.9	3.0	3.2	3.9	48
Russian Federation	2.5	2.5	2.0	1.7	1.9	2.1	2.1	2.5	3.0	2.3	2.3	60
Iraq	0.2	0.3	0.3	0.1	0.3	0.1	0.1	0.4	0.5	0.9	1.1	27
Somalia	0.2	0.3	0.3	0.2	0.2	0.4	0.3	0.6	0.6	0.8	1.0	45
Sweden	0.7	0.7	0.6	0.7	0.7	0.7	0.7	0.7	0.9	0.8	0.7	36
Thailand	0.2	0.3	0.3	0.4	0.4	0.4	0.4	0.6	0.6	0.6	0.6	85
China	0.2	0.3	0.4	0.4	0.4	0.6	0.5	0.7	1.0	0.8	0.6	58
India	0.2	0.2	0.2	0.2	0.3	0.4	0.5	0.5	0.6	0.6	0.5	40
Afghanistan	0.2	0.3	0.4	0.2	0.3	0.3	0.3	0.2	0.2	0.2	0.3	36
Germany	0.2	0.2	0.2	0.2	0.3	0.3	0.4	0.5	0.4	0.3	0.3	50
United States	0.2	0.2	0.2	0.2	0.2	0.3	0.3	0.3	0.3	0.3	0.3	33
Turkey	0.1	0.2	0.3	0.3	0.2	0.3	0.4	0.3	0.4	0.4	0.3	33
Viet Nam	0.1	0.1	0.1	0.0	0.1	0.2	0.2	0.3	0.3	0.3	0.3	61
United Kingdom	0.2	0.3	0.3	0.3	0.3	0.3	0.3	0.4	0.3	0.3	0.3	23
Nepal	0.0	0.0	0.0	0.0	0.0	0.1	0.1	0.2	0.2	0.2	0.3	20
Other countries	3.1	4.0	3.1	3.4	4.1	4.5	4.8	6.4	7.5	5.9	5.6	
Total	**9.1**	**11.0**	**10.0**	**9.4**	**11.5**	**12.7**	**13.9**	**17.5**	**19.9**	**18.1**	**18.2**	**46**

Note: For details on definitions and sources, please refer to the metadata at the end of Table A.2.

StatLink http://dx.doi.org/10.1787/888932617512

Table B.1. **Inflows of foreign population by nationality**
Thousands
FRANCE

	2000	2001	2002	2003	2004	2005	2006	2007	2008	2009	2010	Of which: Women 2010 (%)
Algeria	12.4	15.0	23.4	28.5	27.9	24.8	25.4	23.1	22.3	20.0	19.1	..
Morocco	17.4	19.1	21.8	22.6	22.2	20.0	19.2	17.9	19.2	15.5	18.0	..
Tunisia	5.6	6.6	7.8	9.4	8.9	8.0	8.2	7.8	7.9	7.5	9.5	..
Turkey	6.6	6.9	8.5	8.6	9.1	8.9	8.3	7.6	7.7	6.2	5.6	..
Mali	1.5	1.7	2.0	2.6	2.6	2.5	2.9	2.8	4.6	5.6	5.0	..
Haiti	1.8	2.2	2.1	2.7	3.1	3.2	2.8	2.4	2.2	2.3	4.7	..
China	1.8	2.3	1.9	2.4	2.9	2.8	4.3	3.7	4.0	4.1	4.6	..
Senegal	2.0	2.3	2.5	2.6	2.5	2.5	2.7	2.6	3.1	3.2	3.8	..
Cameroon	1.8	2.4	2.9	3.4	4.1	4.3	4.4	3.9	3.7	3.8	3.6	..
Dem. Rep. of the Congo	1.1	1.4	1.8	1.7	1.8	2.4	1.8	2.0	2.4	3.4	3.5	..
Côte d'Ivoire	1.8	2.2	2.8	3.4	4.0	3.8	3.6	3.4	3.4	3.3	3.4	..
Russian Federation	1.2	1.4	1.9	2.4	2.9	3.0	2.5	2.3	3.0	2.9	3.2	..
Romania	1.2	1.5	1.5	1.6	1.8	1.7	1.9	2.4	3.7	2.5	2.7	..
United States	2.6	2.6	2.4	2.3	2.6	2.4	2.3	2.0	2.3	2.2	2.7	..
Sri Lanka	1.3	2.1	1.7	1.4	1.6	1.8	1.1	1.9	2.4	2.6	2.4	..
Other countries	31.8	37.1	39.4	40.7	43.6	44.0	43.7	43.1	44.1	41.0	44.3	
Total	**91.9**	**106.9**	**124.2**	**136.4**	**141.6**	**135.9**	**135.1**	**128.9**	**136.0**	**126.2**	**136.0**	..

Note: For details on definitions and sources, please refer to the metadata at the end of Table A.2.

StatLink http://dx.doi.org/10.1787/888932617512

STATISTICAL ANNEX

Table B.1. Inflows of foreign population by nationality
Thousands
GERMANY

	2000	2001	2002	2003	2004	2005	2006	2007	2008	2009	2010	Of which: Women 2010 (%)
Poland	74.3	79.0	81.6	88.2	125.0	147.7	151.7	140.0	119.9	112.0	115.6	34
Romania	24.2	20.1	24.0	23.8	23.5	23.3	23.4	42.9	48.2	57.3	75.5	39
Bulgaria	10.4	13.2	13.2	13.4	11.6	9.1	7.5	20.5	24.1	29.2	39.8	37
Hungary	16.1	17.0	16.5	14.3	17.4	18.6	18.6	22.2	25.2	25.3	29.3	24
Turkey	50.0	54.7	58.1	49.8	42.6	36.0	29.6	26.7	26.7	27.2	27.6	38
Italy	33.2	28.8	25.0	21.6	19.6	18.3	17.7	18.2	20.1	22.2	23.9	37
Serbia	33.0	28.3	26.4	22.8	21.7	17.5	10.9	2.2	7.0	9.1	19.1	40
United States	16.5	16.0	15.5	14.7	15.3	15.2	16.3	17.5	17.5	17.7	18.3	46
China	14.7	19.1	18.5	16.1	13.1	12.0	12.9	13.6	14.3	15.4	16.2	50
Russian Federation	32.7	35.9	36.5	31.8	28.5	23.1	16.4	15.0	15.1	15.7	16.1	63
France	15.3	13.5	12.7	12.3	12.5	12.3	13.6	13.8	13.0	12.9	13.3	49
India	6.5	8.9	9.4	9.2	9.1	8.4	8.9	9.4	11.4	12.0	13.2	30
Greece	17.4	16.2	15.0	12.1	10.2	9.0	8.2	8.0	8.3	8.6	12.3	38
Spain	8.8	8.7	8.5	7.7	7.6	7.1	8.2	8.6	7.8	9.0	10.7	48
Croatia	14.4	14.1	13.1	11.6	10.5	9.3	8.3	8.4	8.7	9.1	10.2	26
Other countries	314.3	340.1	310.9	275.2	255.6	230.0	217.0	210.2	208.3	225.8	244.9	
Total	**648.8**	**685.3**	**658.3**	**601.8**	**602.2**	**579.3**	**558.5**	**574.8**	**573.8**	**606.3**	**683.5**	**40**

Note: For details on definitions and sources, please refer to the metadata at the end of Table A.2.

StatLink http://dx.doi.org/10.1787/888932617512

Table B.1. Inflows of foreign population by nationality
Thousands
HUNGARY

	2000	2001	2002	2003	2004	2005	2006	2007	2008	2009	2010	Of which: Women 2010 (%)
Romania	8.9	10.6	10.3	9.6	12.1	8.9	7.9	6.7	10.0	7.1	6.6	43
Germany	0.8	0.8	0.3	0.4	0.1	3.9	0.7	0.7	3.2	2.7	2.4	44
Ukraine	2.4	2.5	2.1	2.6	3.6	2.1	3.7	2.9	4.1	1.9	1.6	42
Slovak Republic	1.0	0.5	0.5	0.4	0.1	1.6	0.6	0.7	1.3	1.2	1.2	58
China	1.1	0.4	0.1	0.7	0.8	0.5	1.4	1.9	1.5	1.3	1.1	40
United States	0.4	0.5	0.4	0.5	0.4	0.4	0.6	0.4	1.2	1.3	1.1	46
Serbia	1.8	1.0	0.4	0.7	1.6	1.1	2.4	4.4	4.1	1.2	1.0	44
Austria	0.2	0.1	0.1	0.1	0.0	0.8	0.4	0.3	0.7	0.7	0.6	34
Turkey	0.1	0.1	0.1	0.1	0.2	0.1	0.3	0.3	0.7	0.5	0.5	36
Korea	..	..	..	..	..	0.1	0.4	0.3	0.3	0.3	0.4	34
Iran	..	..	..	..	..	0.2	0.4	0.2	0.5	0.5	0.4	43
Russian Federation	0.3	0.3	0.3	0.3	0.3	0.2	0.4	0.3	0.4	0.5	0.4	62
France	0.2	0.2	0.2	0.2	0.0	0.7	0.1	0.0	0.4	0.4	0.3	45
United Kingdom	0.1	0.2	0.3	0.4	0.1	0.7	0.1	0.1	0.4	0.3	0.3	35
Netherlands	0.1	0.1	0.1	0.1	0.0	0.4	0.0	0.0	0.3	0.4	0.3	38
Other countries	4.6	4.0	3.2	3.9	4.5	5.0	6.5	7.7	6.5	5.5	5.5	
Total	**20.2**	**20.3**	**18.0**	**19.4**	**22.2**	**25.6**	**23.6**	**22.6**	**35.5**	**25.6**	**23.9**	**44**

Note: For details on definitions and sources, please refer to the metadata at the end of Table A.2.

StatLink http://dx.doi.org/10.1787/888932617512

Table B.1. Inflows of foreign population by nationality
Thousands
ICELAND

	2000	2001	2002	2003	2004	2005	2006	2007	2008	2009	2010	Of which: Women 2010 (%)
Poland	0.4	0.4	0.3	0.1	0.2	1.5	3.3	5.6	3.9	1.2	0.8	47
Lithuania	0.1	0.2	0.1	0.0	0.1	0.2	0.4	0.6	0.4	0.2	0.3	47
Germany	0.2	0.2	0.1	0.1	0.1	0.3	0.3	0.3	0.3	0.2	0.2	58
United States	0.1	0.1	0.1	0.1	0.1	0.1	0.2	0.1	0.1	0.1	0.1	43
Latvia	0.0	0.0	0.0	0.0	0.0	0.1	0.2	0.2	0.3	0.2	0.1	57
United Kingdom	0.1	0.1	0.1	0.0	0.1	0.1	0.1	0.1	0.1	0.1	0.1	33
France	0.0	0.0	0.0	0.0	0.0	0.0	0.0	0.1	0.1	0.1	0.1	50
Spain	0.0	0.0	0.0	0.0	0.0	0.0	0.0	0.0	0.1	0.1	0.1	38
China	0.0	0.0	0.0	0.1	0.1	0.4	0.2	0.1	0.1	0.1	0.1	40
Denmark	0.2	0.2	0.1	0.1	0.2	0.2	0.2	0.2	0.1	0.1	0.1	47
Sweden	0.1	0.1	0.1	0.1	0.1	0.1	0.1	0.2	0.1	0.1	0.1	51
Italy	0.0	0.0	0.0	0.0	0.2	0.1	0.1	0.1	0.1	0.1	0.1	26
Philippines	0.2	0.1	0.1	0.1	0.1	0.2	0.1	0.1	0.1	0.1	0.1	54
Thailand	0.1	0.1	0.1	0.1	0.1	0.1	0.1	0.1	0.1	0.0	0.0	90
Canada	0.0	0.0	0.0	0.0	0.0	0.0	0.1	0.1	0.1	0.0	0.0	40
Other countries	0.9	0.9	0.7	0.6	1.2	1.2	1.6	1.4	1.6	0.8	0.8	
Total	**2.5**	**2.5**	**1.9**	**1.4**	**2.5**	**4.7**	**7.1**	**9.3**	**7.5**	**3.4**	**3.0**	**49**

Note: For details on definitions and sources, please refer to the metadata at the end of Table A.2.

StatLink http://dx.doi.org/10.1787/888932617512

Table B.1. Inflows of foreign population by nationality
Thousands
ISRAEL

	2000	2001	2002	2003	2004	2005	2006	2007	2008	2009	2010	Of which: Women 2010 (%)
Former USSR	50.8	33.6	18.5	12.4	10.1	9.4	7.5	6.5	5.6	6.8	7.0	55
United States	1.2	1.2	1.5	1.7	1.9	2.0	2.2	2.1	2.0	2.5	2.5	50
France	1.2	1.0	2.0	1.8	2.0	2.5	2.4	2.3	1.6	1.6	1.8	51
Ethiopia	2.2	3.3	2.7	3.0	3.7	3.6	3.6	3.6	1.6	0.2	1.7	50
United Kingdom	0.3	0.3	0.3	0.3	0.4	0.4	0.6	0.6	0.5	0.7	0.6	49
Argentina	1.1	1.4	5.9	1.4	0.5	0.4	0.3	0.3	0.2	0.3	0.3	53
Canada	0.2	0.1	0.1	0.2	0.2	0.3	0.2	0.2	0.3	0.3	0.3	50
Brazil	0.2	0.2	0.2	0.2	0.2	0.3	0.2	0.3	0.2	0.2	0.2	51
South Africa	0.2	0.2	0.2	0.1	0.1	0.1	0.1	0.1	0.3	0.3	0.2	49
Belgium	0.1	0.1	0.1	0.1	0.1	0.1	0.1	0.1	0.1	0.1	0.2	48
Mexico	0.1	0.1	0.0	0.1	0.1	0.1	0.1	0.1	0.1	0.1	0.1	51
Australia	0.1	0.1	0.0	0.1	0.1	0.1	0.1	0.1	0.1	0.1	0.1	44
Turkey	0.1	0.1	0.1	0.1	0.1	0.1	0.1	0.1	0.1	0.1	0.1	55
Peru	0.1	0.1	0.1	0.1	0.1	0.4	0.2	0.2	0.1	0.1	0.1	50
Germany	0.1	0.1	0.1	0.1	0.1	0.1	0.1	0.1	0.1	0.1	0.1	58
Other countries	2.3	1.8	1.8	1.7	1.3	1.4	1.5	1.5	0.9	1.0	1.2	
Total	**60.2**	**43.5**	**33.6**	**23.3**	**20.9**	**21.2**	**19.3**	**18.1**	**13.7**	**14.6**	**16.6**	**52**

Notes: For details on definitions and sources, please refer to the metadata at the end of Table A.2.
Information on data for Israel: http://dx.doi.org/10.1787/888932315602.

StatLink http://dx.doi.org/10.1787/888932617512

STATISTICAL ANNEX

Table B.1. Inflows of foreign population by nationality
Thousands
ITALY

	2000	2001	2002	2003	2004	2005	2006	2007	2008	2009	2010	Of which: Women 2010 (%)
Romania	19.3	..	16.5	78.4	66.1	45.3	39.7	271.4	174.6	105.6	92.1	60
Ukraine	2.7	..	3.6	44.2	35.0	15.7	14.8	15.5	24.0	22.6	30.4	81
Morocco	20.1	..	15.3	40.8	34.8	26.1	21.8	23.5	37.3	33.1	30.0	45
Moldova	1.2	..	2.2	16.3	11.9	9.3	7.8	13.0	22.0	16.8	26.6	74
China	..	..	10.0	14.2	19.3	14.7	13.6	9.7	12.8	16.8	22.9	48
Albania	32.0	..	24.5	49.3	38.8	28.4	23.1	23.3	35.7	27.5	22.6	52
India	4.7	..	4.8	8.5	9.0	7.2	6.3	7.1	12.5	12.8	15.2	29
Peru	5.0	..	3.0	9.2	10.0	5.4	4.9	4.5	7.2	10.4	12.2	63
Pakistan	3.3	..	3.4	5.3	7.5	6.5	4.1	3.5	5.7	7.9	10.8	39
Philippines	6.7	..	3.9	6.9	8.1	5.5	4.4	4.0	7.8	10.0	10.7	58
Bangladesh	3.5	..	3.7	6.7	8.4	5.8	5.6	5.2	9.3	8.9	9.7	27
Egypt	4.0	..	2.9	6.4	11.6	5.6	5.0	3.7	5.3	8.0	9.3	24
Senegal	4.7	..	1.7	8.5	5.3	2.9	2.3	2.3	4.8	4.9	8.9	28
Brazil	2.6	..	2.8	5.5	5.2	8.8	10.2	11.9	12.6	9.7	8.6	64
Poland	4.8	..	3.2	11.2	11.8	10.4	11.8	19.1	12.3	9.1	7.2	76
Other countries	78.0	..	60.5	113.5	112.0	85.3	79.2	97.5	112.6	102.7	107.4	
Total	**192.6**	**172.8**	**161.9**	**424.9**	**394.8**	**282.8**	**254.6**	**515.2**	**496.5**	**406.7**	**424.5**	**56**

Note: For details on definitions and sources, please refer to the metadata at the end of Table A.2.
StatLink http://dx.doi.org/10.1787/888932617512

Table B.1. Inflows of foreign population by nationality
Thousands
JAPAN

	2000	2001	2002	2003	2004	2005	2006	2007	2008	2009	2010	Of which: Women 2010 (%)
China	75.3	86.4	88.6	92.2	90.3	105.8	112.5	125.3	134.2	121.2	107.9	..
Korea	24.3	24.7	22.9	21.9	22.8	22.7	24.7	28.1	30.0	27.0	27.9	..
United States	24.0	20.6	21.5	21.5	21.3	22.1	22.2	22.8	24.0	23.5	22.7	..
Philippines	74.2	84.9	87.2	93.4	96.2	63.5	28.3	25.3	21.0	15.8	13.3	..
Viet Nam	3.8	4.7	5.3	6.6	6.5	7.7	8.5	9.9	12.5	10.9	11.9	..
Thailand	6.6	6.8	5.9	6.6	7.1	9.0	8.7	9.0	10.5	9.9	10.9	..
Indonesia	9.9	10.6	9.7	11.1	10.7	12.9	11.4	10.1	10.1	7.5	8.3	..
Chinese Taipei	..	..	..	..	..	..	4.5	4.9	5.5	5.4	6.6	..
United Kingdom	7.0	6.7	6.6	6.6	6.3	6.3	6.6	5.8	6.0	5.3	5.8	..
India	..	..	..	..	..	..	4.9	5.8	5.7	4.6	4.9	..
Brazil	45.5	29.7	22.7	33.4	32.2	33.9	27.0	22.9	14.4	3.0	4.7	..
Germany	..	..	..	..	..	..	4.7	4.9	4.8	4.5	4.3	..
France	..	..	..	..	..	..	3.8	4.2	4.5	3.9	4.0	..
Russian Federation	6.4	6.3	6.6	7.7	7.1	6.2	5.0	4.2	4.5	4.5	3.5	..
Austria	..	..	..	..	..	..	1.1	0.9	1.4	1.0	3.1	..
Other countries	68.7	69.7	66.9	73.1	71.4	82.2	51.7	52.6	55.2	49.0	47.5	
Total	**345.8**	**351.2**	**343.8**	**373.9**	**372.0**	**372.3**	**325.6**	**336.6**	**344.5**	**297.1**	**287.1**	..

Note: For details on definitions and sources, please refer to the metadata at the end of Table A.2.
StatLink http://dx.doi.org/10.1787/888932617512

Table B.1. Inflows of foreign population by nationality
Thousands
KOREA

	2000	2001	2002	2003	2004	2005	2006	2007	2008	2009	2010	Of which: Women 2010 (%)
China	66.6	70.6	60.0	57.7	72.6	119.3	163.4	183.8	164.3	121.4	155.3	49
United States	14.7	16.2	19.0	17.1	17.7	18.8	19.4	21.1	24.8	28.2	28.3	49
Viet Nam	7.6	..	3.2	6.8	8.0	18.2	20.2	21.3	23.8	16.4	22.9	57
Philippines	13.4	7.8	8.1	10.2	10.2	16.7	17.9	12.3	9.2	8.9	9.1	58
Uzbekistan	5.5	3.8	3.9	7.0	..	..	..	4.9	9.3	4.6	8.6	25
Thailand	8.0	6.7	6.8	7.2	9.7	13.7	15.8	10.6	8.6	6.0	6.9	45
Canada	..	4.2	5.3	5.3	5.6	5.8	5.9	6.4	6.6	6.7	6.5	53
Mongolia	4.8	4.9	..	..	5.1	8.3	9.8	8.8	8.2	5.4	5.4	46
Indonesia	7.9	7.2	10.0	9.3	5.2	10.3	6.9	5.2	9.7	3.3	5.3	13
Japan	7.2	8.0	8.5	7.3	7.7	8.6	7.8	7.7	6.6	6.2	4.7	67
Sri Lanka	..	..	..	..	..	..	..	2.5	4.8	1.7	4.2	3
Cambodia	..	..	..	..	..	..	..	1.9	3.4	2.6	3.7	50
Bangladesh	..	..	..	..	..	..	..	1.0	2.2	1.4	2.9	5
Nepal	..	..	..	..	..	..	..	0.8	2.4	2.6	2.7	16
Russian Federation	7.5	8.0	9.5	10.8	6.6	6.2	5.2	..	..	3.1	2.6	60
Other countries	42.1	35.2	36.4	39.6	40.4	40.6	42.4	29.1	27.6	24.4	24.0	
Total	**185.4**	**172.5**	**170.9**	**178.3**	**188.8**	**266.3**	**314.7**	**317.6**	**311.7**	**242.8**	**293.1**	**47**

Note: For details on definitions and sources, please refer to the metadata at the end of Table A.2.

StatLink http://dx.doi.org/10.1787/888932617512

Table B.1. Inflows of foreign population by nationality
Thousands
LUXEMBOURG

	2000	2001	2002	2003	2004	2005	2006	2007	2008	2009	2010	Of which: Women 2010 (%)
Portugal	2.2	2.3	2.8	3.9	3.5	3.8	3.8	4.4	4.5	3.8	3.8	41
France	2.3	2.1	1.9	1.9	2.0	2.2	2.5	2.8	3.2	2.7	2.9	43
Belgium	1.3	1.5	1.3	1.1	1.0	1.0	0.9	0.9	1.0	1.0	1.2	42
Germany	0.6	0.7	0.6	0.7	0.8	0.8	0.9	1.0	1.1	1.0	1.0	48
Italy	0.6	0.6	0.5	0.5	0.5	0.6	0.6	0.6	0.8	0.7	0.8	38
United Kingdom	0.5	0.5	0.4	0.3	0.3	0.4	0.4	0.4	0.5	0.4	0.4	47
Poland	0.1	0.1	0.1	0.1	0.2	0.3	0.3	0.4	0.5	0.4	0.4	50
United States	0.3	0.2	0.1	0.3	0.2	0.3	0.3	0.3	0.3	0.3	0.3	50
Romania	0.1	0.0	0.0	0.0	0.1	0.1	0.1	0.3	0.3	0.2	0.3	61
Spain	0.2	0.2	0.2	0.2	0.2	0.2	0.2	0.2	0.2	0.2	0.3	44
Serbia	..	..	..	..	0.1	0.3	0.2	0.4	0.3	0.1	0.3	50
Brazil	0.0	0.0	0.1	0.1	0.1	0.1	0.2	0.2	0.2	0.2	0.2	70
Netherlands	0.2	0.2	0.2	0.2	0.2	0.2	0.3	0.2	0.3	0.2	0.2	35
Cape Verde	0.1	0.1	0.2	0.1	0.1	0.2	0.1	0.2	0.2	0.2	0.2	49
China	0.1	0.1	0.1	0.1	0.1	0.1	0.1	0.1	0.1	0.1	0.1	58
Other countries	2.3	2.5	2.5	3.1	3.0	3.5	3.0	3.5	3.5	3.0	3.5	
Total	**10.8**	**11.1**	**11.0**	**12.6**	**12.2**	**13.8**	**13.7**	**15.8**	**16.8**	**14.6**	**15.8**	**45**

Note: For details on definitions and sources, please refer to the metadata at the end of Table A.2.

StatLink http://dx.doi.org/10.1787/888932617512

Table B.1. Inflows of foreign population by nationality
Thousands
MEXICO

	2000	2001	2002	2003	2004	2005	2006	2007	2008	2009	2010	Of which: Women 2010 (%)
United States	..	..	..	..	..	..	..	1.4	2.2	2.9	4.0	42
Colombia	..	..	..	..	..	..	..	0.3	1.1	1.9	2.3	55
Cuba	..	..	..	..	..	..	..	0.3	1.0	1.7	1.8	52
Guatemala	..	..	..	..	..	..	..	0.1	1.0	2.1	1.8	59
China	..	..	..	..	..	..	..	0.6	1.3	2.0	1.7	43
Venezuela	..	..	..	..	..	..	..	0.3	0.7	1.3	1.7	55
Honduras	..	..	..	..	..	..	..	0.0	0.8	1.4	1.5	57
Argentina	..	..	..	..	..	..	..	0.5	0.9	1.4	1.4	43
Spain	..	..	..	..	..	..	..	0.3	0.6	0.9	1.0	34
Peru	..	..	..	..	..	..	..	0.2	0.4	0.7	0.8	47
Canada	..	..	..	..	..	..	..	0.2	0.4	0.6	0.7	46
El Salvador	..	..	..	..	..	..	..	0.1	0.5	0.8	0.7	58
France	..	..	..	..	..	..	..	0.2	0.4	0.5	0.6	38
Italy	..	..	..	..	..	..	..	0.2	0.3	0.5	0.6	29
Brazil	..	..	..	..	..	..	..	0.2	0.3	0.4	0.5	60
Other countries	..	..	..	..	..	..	..	2.0	3.4	4.8	5.0	
Total	**6.4**	**8.1**	**5.8**	**6.9**	**8.5**	**9.2**	**6.9**	**6.8**	**15.1**	**23.9**	**26.2**	**48**

Note: For details on definitions and sources, please refer to the metadata at the end of Table A.2.

StatLink http://dx.doi.org/10.1787/888932617512

Table B.1. Inflows of foreign population by nationality
Thousands
NETHERLANDS

	2000	2001	2002	2003	2004	2005	2006	2007	2008	2009	2010	Of which: Women 2010 (%)
Poland	1.3	1.4	1.6	1.5	4.5	5.7	6.8	9.2	13.3	12.7	14.5	47
Germany	4.9	5.1	5.1	4.8	5.3	5.9	7.2	7.5	9.0	8.7	9.8	57
China	1.8	2.8	3.4	3.8	3.0	3.0	2.9	3.4	4.2	4.3	4.5	53
United Kingdom	5.9	5.9	4.8	4.1	3.6	3.2	3.6	4.0	4.7	4.4	4.4	40
Bulgaria	0.3	0.3	0.4	0.5	0.4	0.4	0.5	4.9	5.2	4.3	4.3	50
Turkey	4.5	4.8	5.4	6.2	4.1	3.1	2.8	2.4	3.3	3.5	3.7	40
United States	3.4	3.1	3.0	2.5	2.3	2.5	3.1	3.2	3.4	3.1	3.3	52
India	0.7	0.7	0.6	0.6	0.6	1.2	2.0	2.5	3.5	3.1	3.2	37
Spain	1.3	1.4	1.4	1.3	1.3	1.3	1.4	1.5	2.3	2.6	3.1	50
France	2.2	2.2	2.0	1.9	1.8	1.8	2.0	2.2	3.0	2.9	2.9	48
Italy	1.5	1.5	1.4	1.3	1.2	1.4	1.6	1.9	2.6	2.6	2.8	38
Romania	0.6	0.7	0.6	0.7	0.6	0.5	0.7	2.3	2.4	2.2	2.6	56
Hungary	0.5	0.5	0.4	0.4	0.6	0.6	0.6	1.0	1.7	2.2	2.4	50
Belgium	2.0	1.8	1.8	1.7	1.5	1.4	1.7	1.8	2.1	2.0	2.1	50
Portugal	1.2	1.4	1.5	1.4	1.2	1.0	1.4	1.8	2.4	2.4	2.0	38
Other countries	59.6	60.9	53.0	40.9	33.3	30.4	29.6	30.6	40.2	43.5	44.7	
Total	**91.4**	**94.5**	**86.6**	**73.6**	**65.1**	**63.4**	**67.7**	**80.3**	**103.4**	**104.4**	**110.2**	**50**

Note: For details on definitions and sources, please refer to the metadata at the end of Table A.2.

StatLink http://dx.doi.org/10.1787/888932617512

Table B.1. Inflows of foreign population by nationality
Thousands
NEW ZEALAND

	2000	2001	2002	2003	2004	2005	2006	2007	2008	2009	2010	Of which: Women 2010 (%)
United Kingdom	5.0	6.8	6.6	8.2	8.7	17.1	13.0	11.3	9.5	7.8	7.5	50
China	4.3	7.9	7.6	5.9	4.0	5.6	6.8	5.6	7.4	5.8	5.6	55
South Africa	3.5	4.8	3.3	2.4	2.4	4.5	3.6	4.0	4.7	5.2	4.6	50
India	4.3	7.4	8.2	4.8	3.1	3.5	3.7	3.9	3.2	3.2	4.0	47
Philippines	1.0	1.3	1.6	0.9	0.8	1.1	1.7	3.7	3.6	3.4	3.9	53
Fiji	2.2	3.6	2.3	2.5	2.3	2.6	2.7	2.8	3.2	3.3	3.0	50
Samoa	2.5	2.0	1.2	2.2	1.6	2.6	2.1	1.9	2.2	2.0	1.6	46
United States	0.8	1.0	1.0	1.1	1.0	2.1	1.6	1.3	1.2	1.2	1.1	55
Korea	1.1	2.4	2.4	1.6	1.5	2.1	2.1	1.0	0.8	0.9	1.1	54
Sri Lanka	0.7	0.9	0.7	0.3	0.2	0.3	0.3	0.4	0.6	0.6	0.8	47
Tonga	0.9	0.8	0.7	2.4	1.2	1.1	1.2	0.9	0.9	0.8	0.8	44
Malaysia	1.0	2.1	1.2	1.0	0.5	0.6	0.7	0.6	0.7	0.6	0.7	53
Germany	0.4	0.4	0.3	0.4	0.4	0.8	0.7	0.8	0.7	0.7	0.7	55
Canada	0.3	0.4	0.3	0.3	0.3	0.5	0.5	0.4	0.4	0.5	0.5	57
Ireland	..	..	..	..	..	..	0.4	0.4	0.3	0.3	0.5	51
Other countries	9.5	12.5	10.1	9.0	8.0	9.6	8.5	7.8	7.6	7.5	8.0	
Total	**37.6**	**54.4**	**47.5**	**43.0**	**36.2**	**54.1**	**49.8**	**46.8**	**46.9**	**43.6**	**44.3**	**52**

Note: For details on definitions and sources, please refer to the metadata at the end of Table A.2.

StatLink http://dx.doi.org/10.1787/888932617512

Table B.1. Inflows of foreign population by nationality
Thousands
NORWAY

	2000	2001	2002	2003	2004	2005	2006	2007	2008	2009	2010	Of which: Women 2010 (%)
Poland	0.2	0.4	0.7	0.6	1.6	3.3	7.4	14.2	14.4	10.5	11.3	34
Sweden	3.5	3.1	2.9	2.7	2.4	2.7	3.4	4.4	5.7	6.0	7.6	45
Lithuania	0.1	0.2	0.3	0.3	0.5	0.8	1.3	2.4	2.9	3.2	6.6	39
Germany	1.0	1.1	1.2	1.2	1.4	1.7	2.3	3.8	4.3	2.8	2.7	46
Latvia	0.1	0.1	0.2	0.1	0.1	0.2	0.3	0.5	0.6	1.1	2.3	40
Philippines	0.4	0.5	0.6	0.6	0.6	0.8	1.1	1.6	1.8	1.7	2.1	87
Eritrea	0.0	0.1	0.1	0.1	0.1	0.3	0.3	0.4	0.8	1.7	2.0	46
Iceland	0.5	0.5	0.6	0.4	0.3	0.3	0.3	0.3	0.3	1.6	1.7	44
Somalia	1.5	1.1	2.2	1.7	1.2	1.1	1.2	1.6	1.2	1.3	1.6	46
United Kingdom	0.8	0.9	0.8	0.6	0.9	0.8	1.0	1.1	1.2	1.3	1.5	31
Afghanistan	0.5	0.9	1.1	1.4	0.7	0.8	0.6	0.6	0.8	1.4	1.4	27
Denmark	1.9	2.0	2.1	1.7	1.6	1.5	1.5	1.5	1.3	1.3	1.4	39
Romania	0.1	0.2	0.2	0.2	0.2	0.2	0.2	0.6	1.1	1.1	1.3	42
Thailand	0.5	0.6	0.9	0.9	1.1	1.1	1.1	1.2	1.3	1.3	1.2	86
Estonia	0.1	0.1	0.2	0.1	0.1	0.2	0.2	0.4	0.5	0.5	1.0	35
Other countries	16.3	13.7	16.9	14.4	15.0	15.4	15.4	19.0	20.4	20.0	19.4	
Total	**27.8**	**25.4**	**30.8**	**26.8**	**27.9**	**31.4**	**37.4**	**53.5**	**58.8**	**56.7**	**65.1**	**45**

Note: For details on definitions and sources, please refer to the metadata at the end of Table A.2.

StatLink http://dx.doi.org/10.1787/888932617512

Table B.1. Inflows of foreign population by nationality
Thousands
POLAND

	2000	2001	2002	2003	2004	2005	2006	2007	2008	2009	2010	Of which: Women 2010 (%)
Ukraine	3.4	4.8	6.9	8.4	10.2	9.8	9.6	9.4	10.3	10.1	10.3	..
Belarus	0.8	1.3	2.7	2.5	2.4	2.4	2.3	2.6	3.1	3.2	2.9	..
Viet Nam	1.2	1.1	1.2	1.3	2.2	1.9	1.7	1.8	2.8	3.0	2.4	..
China	0.4	0.4	0.5	0.4	0.5	0.6	0.4	0.7	1.2	2.0	2.3	..
Germany	0.7	1.1	1.6	1.5	2.2	6.1	4.6	6.7	2.9	1.7	1.8	..
Russian Federation	1.1	1.6	2.0	2.1	2.1	1.9	1.8	1.6	1.8	1.6	1.6	..
Armenia	0.7	0.6	0.7	1.0	2.0	1.5	1.3	1.4	1.6	1.6	1.4	..
India	0.3	0.4	0.5	0.6	0.7	0.7	0.7	0.7	1.0	1.1	1.2	..
Turkey	0.2	0.3	0.6	0.6	0.5	0.6	0.7	0.7	0.9	1.0	1.1	..
Korea	0.3	0.3	0.3	0.3	0.3	0.4	0.5	0.9	1.1	1.0	1.1	..
United States	0.5	0.7	1.2	1.0	1.0	0.8	0.9	0.9	1.0	1.0	1.0	..
Nigeria	0.1	0.1	0.1	0.1	0.2	0.2	0.3	0.6	0.6	0.7	0.6	..
Japan	0.1	0.3	0.2	0.3	0.3	0.5	0.5	0.6	0.8	0.7	0.6	..
Chinese Taipei	..	..	..	..	..	..	..	..	..	0.7	0.6	..
Italy	0.2	0.3	0.5	0.5	0.7	0.7	0.3	0.7	0.5	0.6	0.5	..
Other countries	5.8	8.1	11.3	9.7	11.6	10.5	8.5	11.4	12.1	11.5	11.8	
Total	**15.9**	**21.5**	**30.2**	**30.3**	**36.9**	**38.5**	**34.2**	**40.6**	**41.8**	**41.3**	**41.1**	..

Note: For details on definitions and sources, please refer to the metadata at the end of Table A.2.

StatLink http://dx.doi.org/10.1787/888932617512

Table B.1. Inflows of foreign population by nationality
Thousands
PORTUGAL

	2000	2001	2002	2003	2004	2005	2006	2007	2008	2009	2010	Of which: Women 2010 (%)
Romania	..	7.8	3.2	0.9	0.8	0.8	0.6	0.2	5.3	8.1	6.0	..
Cape Verde	2.1	9.1	5.9	3.4	3.1	3.5	3.3	4.1	3.5	3.3	3.5	..
Brazil	1.7	26.6	14.7	6.7	14.4	9.5	6.1	5.0	3.5	2.9	3.4	..
United Kingdom	0.8	0.9	1.0	0.9	1.2	1.0	0.8	3.9	2.7	2.2	1.8	..
Spain	1.1	1.4	0.9	0.7	0.6	0.6	0.3	1.4	1.3	1.5	1.7	..
Bulgaria	..	1.8	1.3	0.6	0.3	0.3	0.3	0.1	0.9	1.5	1.4	..
Sao Tome and Principe	0.6	2.6	1.6	0.8	0.9	0.7	0.6	0.8	0.7	1.0	1.1	..
China	0.4	3.9	1.0	0.6	0.8	0.3	0.5	1.0	1.3	1.3	1.1	..
Germany	0.8	0.7	0.7	0.6	0.6	0.5	0.3	1.6	1.1	1.1	1.0	..
Italy	0.3	0.3	0.4	0.4	0.4	0.3	0.1	1.0	1.0	1.0	1.0	..
Guinea-Bissau	1.6	5.1	2.6	1.3	1.0	1.1	1.3	1.6	1.6	0.8	0.9	..
France	0.7	0.6	0.6	0.5	0.5	0.4	0.2	0.8	0.7	0.7	0.7	..
Angola	2.5	7.6	4.7	2.1	1.1	1.2	0.4	0.4	0.6	0.5	0.6	..
Moldova	..	10.1	4.0	1.4	1.7	1.8	2.1	2.0	1.7	0.9	0.5	..
Ukraine	..	45.5	17.5	4.1	1.9	1.6	1.5	2.0	1.3	0.9	0.4	..
Other countries	3.3	27.4	11.8	6.7	4.9	4.7	4.0	6.7	5.2	6.0	4.9	
Total	**15.9**	**151.4**	**72.0**	**31.8**	**34.1**	**28.1**	**22.5**	**32.6**	**32.3**	**33.8**	**30.0**	..

Note: For details on definitions and sources, please refer to the metadata at the end of Table A.2.

StatLink http://dx.doi.org/10.1787/888932617512

Table B.1. Inflows of foreign population by nationality
Thousands
RUSSIAN FEDERATION

	2000	2001	2002	2003	2004	2005	2006	2007	2008	2009	2010	Of which: Women 2010 (%)
Kazakhstan	124.9	65.2	55.7	29.6	40.2	51.9	38.6	40.3	40.0	38.8	27.9	53
Ukraine	74.7	36.5	36.8	23.4	17.7	30.8	32.7	51.5	49.1	45.9	27.5	51
Uzbekistan	40.8	24.9	25.0	21.5	14.9	30.4	37.1	52.8	43.5	42.5	24.1	42
Kyrgyzstan	15.5	10.7	13.1	6.9	9.5	15.6	15.7	24.7	24.0	23.3	20.9	51
Armenia	16.0	5.8	6.8	5.1	3.1	7.6	12.9	30.8	35.2	35.8	19.9	44
Tajikistan	11.0	6.7	6.0	5.3	3.3	4.7	6.5	17.3	20.7	27.0	18.2	27
Azerbaijan	14.9	5.6	5.6	4.3	2.6	4.6	8.9	21.0	23.3	22.9	14.5	36
Moldova	11.7	7.6	7.6	6.4	4.8	6.6	8.6	14.1	15.5	16.4	11.8	47
Georgia	20.2	9.7	7.1	5.5	4.9	5.5	6.8	10.6	8.8	7.5	5.2	48
Belarus	10.3	6.5	6.8	5.3	5.7	6.8	5.6	6.0	5.9	5.5	4.9	53
Germany	1.8	1.6	2.0	2.7	3.1	3.0	2.9	3.2	3.1	2.6	2.6	51
Turkmenistan	6.7	4.4	4.5	6.3	3.7	4.1	4.1	4.8	4.0	3.3	2.3	50
China	1.1	0.4	0.4	0.3	0.2	0.4	0.5	1.7	1.2	0.8	1.4	29
Viet Nam	..	..	..	..	0.0	0.1	0.2	0.9	0.7	1.0	0.9	..
Israel	1.5	1.4	1.7	1.8	1.5	1.0	1.1	1.1	1.0	0.9	0.8	40
Other countries	8.2	6.4	5.5	4.6	3.9	4.1	4.1	6.2	5.6	5.8	8.7	
Total	**359.3**	**193.5**	**184.6**	**129.1**	**119.2**	**177.2**	**186.4**	**287.0**	**281.6**	**279.9**	**191.7**	**45**

Note: For details on definitions and sources, please refer to the metadata at the end of Table A.2.

StatLink http://dx.doi.org/10.1787/888932617512

Table B.1. Inflows of foreign population by nationality
Thousands
SLOVAK REPUBLIC

	2000	2001	2002	2003	2004	2005	2006	2007	2008	2009	2010	Of which: Women 2010 (%)
Ukraine	..	..	..	0.7	0.7	0.6	1.0	1.2	1.8	1.6	1.3	43
Czech Republic	..	..	..	0.6	1.6	1.1	1.3	1.2	1.4	1.6	1.2	46
Hungary	..	..	..	0.1	0.3	0.4	0.5	0.8	1.1	1.1	1.1	22
Romania	..	..	..	0.0	0.1	0.1	0.4	3.0	2.3	0.8	0.9	31
Serbia	..	..	..	0.1	0.1	0.1	0.6	0.8	1.3	1.1	0.7	34
Korea	..	..	..	0.0	0.1	0.3	0.5	0.6	0.8	0.7	0.7	35
China	..	..	..	0.2	0.2	0.2	0.6	0.5	0.5	0.6	0.6	43
Viet Nam	..	..	..	0.3	0.2	0.2	0.5	0.6	1.3	0.9	0.5	38
Russian Federation	..	..	..	0.2	0.2	0.2	0.3	0.3	0.3	0.5	0.5	50
Poland	..	..	..	0.1	0.9	0.5	1.1	0.7	0.6	0.7	0.5	38
Germany	..	..	..	0.3	0.6	0.9	0.9	0.9	1.1	0.6	0.5	24
Italy	..	..	..	0.1	0.2	0.2	0.3	0.3	0.2	0.3	0.3	16
United States	..	..	..	0.3	0.2	0.3	0.3	0.3	0.3	0.3	0.3	43
Bulgaria	..	..	..	0.1	0.1	0.1	0.1	0.8	0.5	0.2	0.2	29
Austria	..	..	..	0.1	0.4	0.4	0.4	0.3	0.3	0.3	0.2	23
Other countries	..	..	..	1.5	2.2	2.1	3.1	2.6	2.7	3.1	3.1	
Total	**4.6**	**4.7**	**4.8**	**4.6**	**7.9**	**7.7**	**11.3**	**14.8**	**16.5**	**14.4**	**12.7**	**35**

Note: For details on definitions and sources, please refer to the metadata at the end of Table A.2.

StatLink http://dx.doi.org/10.1787/888932617512

Table B.1. Inflows of foreign population by nationality
Thousands
SLOVENIA

	2000	2001	2002	2003	2004	2005	2006	2007	2008	2009	2010	Of which: Women 2010 (%)
Bosnia and Herzegovina	2.0	2.4	2.5	2.1	3.0	4.3	7.9	12.5	13.0	12.9	4.4	29
Serbia	0.7	0.9	1.2	1.5	2.4	3.3	4.4	6.5	4.5	3.0	1.2	35
Former Yug. Rep. of Macedonia	0.9	1.0	1.2	1.6	1.3	1.7	2.1	3.2	3.2	3.0	1.1	41
Croatia	0.9	1.1	1.3	1.3	0.8	1.0	1.1	1.4	1.6	1.4	0.9	39
Bulgaria	0.0	0.0	0.0	0.0	0.0	0.0	0.1	0.8	0.5	0.5	0.6	25
Italy	0.0	0.1	0.1	0.1	0.0	0.2	0.2	0.3	0.3	0.3	0.3	37
Ukraine	0.2	0.2	0.3	0.2	0.3	0.4	0.4	0.5	0.4	0.4	0.3	74
Germany	0.0	0.1	0.0	0.1	0.0	0.3	0.2	0.2	0.3	0.2	0.2	42
United Kingdom	0.0	0.0	0.0	0.0	0.0	0.1	0.1	0.1	0.1	0.1	0.1	39
Russian Federation	0.1	0.1	0.1	0.1	0.1	0.1	0.1	0.1	0.1	0.2	0.1	61
Austria	0.0	0.0	0.0	0.0	0.0	0.1	0.1	0.1	0.1	0.1	0.1	34
Montenegro	..	..	..	..	..	..	..	0.1	0.1	0.1	0.1	51
Romania	0.0	0.1	0.0	0.0	0.1	0.3	0.3	0.2	0.1	0.1	0.1	53
Hungary	0.0	0.0	0.0	0.0	0.0	0.1	0.1	0.1	0.1	0.0	0.1	22
United States	0.0	0.1	0.1	0.1	0.0	0.1	0.1	0.1	0.1	0.1	0.1	47
Other countries	0.3	0.6	0.7	0.8	0.5	1.3	1.3	1.6	3.6	5.1	3.1	
Total	**5.3**	**6.8**	**7.7**	**8.0**	**8.6**	**13.3**	**18.3**	**27.5**	**28.1**	**27.4**	**12.7**	**35**

Note: For details on definitions and sources, please refer to the metadata at the end of Table A.2.
StatLink http://dx.doi.org/10.1787/888932617512

Table B.1. Inflows of foreign population by nationality
Thousands
SPAIN

	2000	2001	2002	2003	2004	2005	2006	2007	2008	2009	2010	Of which: Women 2010 (%)
Romania	17.5	23.3	48.3	55.0	103.6	108.3	131.5	197.6	71.5	52.4	62.6	52
Morocco	38.3	39.5	40.2	41.2	73.4	82.5	78.5	85.0	93.6	61.8	47.9	40
Pakistan	1.7	1.8	1.8	1.7	9.4	12.4	8.2	10.6	13.4	10.6	21.7	28
Colombia	46.1	71.2	34.2	11.1	21.5	24.9	35.6	41.7	42.2	25.6	18.1	54
China	4.8	5.2	5.7	7.5	20.3	18.4	16.9	20.4	27.2	18.6	17.4	49
United Kingdom	10.9	16.0	25.3	31.8	48.4	44.7	42.5	38.2	25.0	19.2	17.3	48
Italy	3.9	6.2	10.4	10.0	15.0	16.5	18.6	21.2	18.0	13.6	12.9	44
Paraguay	0.2	0.3	0.7	2.4	10.4	12.6	21.6	24.0	20.6	13.4	11.9	75
Brazil	4.1	4.3	4.7	7.4	16.5	24.6	32.6	36.1	27.3	14.4	11.9	62
Ecuador	91.1	82.6	89.0	72.8	17.2	15.2	21.4	30.2	37.8	18.2	11.0	48
Bulgaria	6.5	11.8	15.9	13.7	21.0	18.4	21.7	31.3	13.1	9.7	10.4	50
Peru	6.0	7.1	8.0	13.5	17.7	19.9	21.7	27.4	31.1	16.3	10.0	56
Germany	10.2	10.7	11.2	10.8	14.0	15.2	16.9	17.8	12.6	10.4	9.3	51
France	4.2	4.9	5.5	5.9	9.9	11.1	12.7	13.0	10.1	8.9	8.6	49
Dominican Republic	5.5	5.4	5.5	6.6	10.3	12.2	14.7	18.1	17.8	10.8	8.3	54
Other countries	79.9	103.6	136.9	138.1	237.3	245.6	307.8	307.9	231.0	165.4	151.8	
Total	**330.9**	**394.0**	**443.1**	**429.5**	**645.8**	**682.7**	**803.0**	**920.5**	**692.2**	**469.3**	**431.3**	**48**

Note: For details on definitions and sources, please refer to the metadata at the end of Table A.2.
StatLink http://dx.doi.org/10.1787/888932617512

Table B.1. Inflows of foreign population by nationality
Thousands
SWEDEN

	2000	2001	2002	2003	2004	2005	2006	2007	2008	2009	2010	Of which: Women 2010 (%)
Somalia	0.6	0.7	0.9	1.3	1.1	1.3	3.0	3.8	4.1	6.9	6.8	47
Iraq	6.6	6.5	7.4	5.4	2.8	2.9	10.9	15.2	12.1	8.5	4.5	51
Poland	0.6	0.8	1.1	1.0	2.5	3.4	6.3	7.5	7.0	5.2	4.4	44
Denmark	2.0	2.5	3.2	3.6	3.8	4.0	5.1	5.1	4.1	3.8	3.4	43
China	0.9	1.0	1.2	1.4	1.5	1.7	2.0	2.4	2.7	3.1	3.2	53
Iran	1.1	1.3	1.4	1.0	1.5	1.1	2.0	1.4	1.8	2.4	2.8	48
Thailand	0.8	0.9	1.2	2.0	2.1	2.1	2.3	2.5	3.1	3.0	2.8	78
Finland	3.6	3.4	3.3	3.2	2.8	2.9	2.6	2.6	2.4	2.4	2.3	54
Turkey	0.7	0.7	0.8	1.2	1.1	1.1	1.6	1.5	1.5	2.0	2.2	33
Germany	1.5	1.6	1.7	1.8	1.8	2.0	2.9	3.6	3.4	2.8	2.2	52
India	0.4	0.4	0.6	0.8	0.8	1.1	1.0	1.1	1.5	1.8	2.2	28
Norway	2.9	3.0	3.5	3.2	2.6	2.4	2.5	2.4	2.3	1.9	2.1	48
Afghanistan	0.9	1.0	1.0	1.0	1.0	0.7	1.7	0.8	1.0	1.6	1.9	33
Romania	0.3	0.3	0.4	0.3	0.3	0.4	0.3	2.6	2.5	1.8	1.7	46
Eritrea	0.1	0.1	0.2	0.2	0.3	0.6	0.8	0.8	1.2	1.4	1.6	55
Other countries	19.2	19.4	19.7	19.8	20.7	22.9	33.9	29.3	31.4	33.8	34.8	
Total	**42.2**	**43.8**	**47.3**	**47.1**	**46.7**	**50.6**	**78.9**	**82.6**	**82.0**	**82.4**	**79.0**	**46**

Note: For details on definitions and sources, please refer to the metadata at the end of Table A.2.

StatLink ▄▀▄ http://dx.doi.org/10.1787/888932617512

Table B.1. Inflows of foreign population by nationality
Thousands
SWITZERLAND

	2000	2001	2002	2003	2004	2005	2006	2007	2008	2009	2010	Of which: Women 2010 (%)
Germany	12.5	14.6	15.5	14.9	18.1	20.4	24.8	41.1	46.4	33.9	30.7	43
Portugal	4.9	4.9	9.3	12.3	13.6	12.2	12.5	15.5	17.8	13.7	12.8	41
France	6.6	6.6	6.8	6.6	6.7	6.9	7.6	11.5	13.7	10.9	11.5	44
Italy	5.4	5.6	6.1	5.6	5.7	5.4	5.5	8.4	9.9	8.5	10.1	38
United Kingdom	3.7	3.9	3.1	2.8	2.9	3.0	3.4	5.1	5.6	4.8	5.5	42
United States	3.3	3.3	2.9	2.5	2.7	2.9	3.2	..	..	..	4.0	52
Spain	1.7	1.7	1.9	1.7	1.7	1.5	1.6	2.1	2.4	2.5	3.3	47
Austria	2.0	2.5	2.6	2.0	2.3	1.9	2.0	2.8	3.2	2.8	2.6	43
Brazil	..	..	..	..	..	..	..	..	..	..	2.5	69
India	..	..	..	..	..	..	..	..	..	..	2.4	40
Serbia	6.7	7.5	7.7	6.3	5.7	4.9	4.8	5.4	4.9	2.6	2.4	47
Eritrea	..	..	..	..	..	..	..	..	..	..	2.1	37
Poland	0.6	0.7	0.7	0.6	0.7	0.8	1.3	2.1	2.4	2.1	2.0	51
Turkey	2.8	3.1	3.2	2.7	2.4	2.1	2.0	0.9	2.1	2.2	2.0	46
China	..	..	..	..	..	..	..	..	..	..	1.9	61
Other countries	37.3	46.8	42.2	35.9	34.0	32.3	34.1	44.9	48.8	48.5	38.3	
Total	**87.4**	**101.4**	**101.9**	**94.0**	**96.3**	**94.4**	**102.7**	**139.7**	**157.3**	**132.4**	**134.2**	**47**

Note: For details on definitions and sources, please refer to the metadata at the end of Table A.2.

StatLink ▄▀▄ http://dx.doi.org/10.1787/888932617512

Table B.1. Inflows of foreign population by nationality
Thousands
TURKEY

	2000	2001	2002	2003	2004	2005	2006	2007	2008	2009	2010	Of which: Women 2010 (%)
Azerbaijan	..	..	..	..	..	..	..	..	..	..	2.5	52
Afghanistan	..	..	..	..	..	..	..	..	..	..	2.2	36
Russian Federation	..	..	..	..	..	..	..	..	..	..	1.8	76
Germany	..	..	..	..	..	..	..	..	..	..	1.6	57
United States	..	..	..	..	..	..	..	..	..	..	1.5	54
Iran	..	..	..	..	..	..	..	..	..	..	1.5	40
Kazakhstan	..	..	..	..	..	..	..	..	..	..	1.4	55
Turkmenistan	..	..	..	..	..	..	..	..	..	..	1.2	47
Iraq	..	..	..	..	..	..	..	..	..	..	1.2	43
United Kingdom	..	..	..	..	..	..	..	..	..	..	1.1	51
Bulgaria	..	..	..	..	..	..	..	..	..	..	1.1	70
Kyrgyzstan	..	..	..	..	..	..	..	..	..	..	1.0	54
Ukraine	..	..	..	..	..	..	..	..	..	..	0.9	85
Syria	..	..	..	..	..	..	..	..	..	..	0.9	79
China	..	..	..	..	..	..	..	..	..	..	0.8	24
Other countries	..	..	..	..	..	..	..	..	..	..	9.1	
Total	..	..	..	..	..	..	..	..	..	..	**29.9**	**54**

Note: For details on definitions and sources, please refer to the metadata at the end of Table A.2.

StatLink http://dx.doi.org/10.1787/888932617512

Table B.1. Inflows of foreign population by nationality
Thousands
UNITED KINGDOM

	2000	2001	2002	2003	2004	2005	2006	2007	2008	2009	2010	Of which: Women 2010 (%)
India	17	16	21	30	51	47	57	55	48	64	68	..
Poland	0	2	..	..	16	49	60	88	55	32	34	..
Pakistan	9	10	7	10	21	16	31	27	17	17	30	..
China	19	18	29	31	32	22	23	21	18	22	28	..
Australia	24	34	20	21	27	20	26	18	14	12	18	..
United States	14	13	16	16	14	15	16	15	17	17	16	..
Ireland	2	0	..	..	..	..	..	..	..	11	14	..
Lithuania	..	..	..	..	..	..	..	..	..	..	13	..
France	15	16	9	21	10	..	..	..	..	14	11	..
Sri Lanka	4	2	4	6	5	6	6	..	5	7	11	..
Nigeria	6	2	2	5	9	9	9	9	11	12	10	..
Bangladesh	3	4	3	5	6	10	10	6	6	13	9	..
Malaysia	6	5	4	5	6	..	..	8	11	7	9	..
Philippines	6	12	21	12	11	10	12	13	13	12	9	..
Italy	8	1	..	..	..	..	..	..	14	8	9	..
Other countries	129	126	153	165	226	201	202	195	227	182	170	
Total	**260**	**262**	**289**	**327**	**434**	**405**	**452**	**455**	**456**	**430**	**459**	**44**

Note: For details on definitions and sources, please refer to the metadata at the end of Table A.2.

StatLink http://dx.doi.org/10.1787/888932617512

Table B.1. Inflows of foreign population by nationality
Thousands
UNITED STATES (PERMANENT)

	2000	2001	2002	2003	2004	2005	2006	2007	2008	2009	2010	Of which: Women 2010 (%)
Mexico	173.5	205.6	218.8	115.6	175.4	161.4	173.8	148.6	190.0	164.9	139.1	..
China	45.6	56.3	61.1	40.6	55.5	70.0	87.3	76.7	80.3	64.2	70.9	..
India	41.9	70.0	70.8	50.2	70.2	84.7	61.4	65.4	63.4	57.3	69.2	..
Philippines	42.3	52.9	51.0	45.3	57.8	60.7	74.6	72.6	54.0	60.0	58.2	..
Dominican Republic	17.5	21.2	22.5	26.2	30.5	27.5	38.1	28.0	31.9	49.4	53.9	..
Cuba	19.0	27.5	28.2	9.3	20.5	36.3	45.6	29.1	49.5	39.0	33.6	..
Viet Nam	26.6	35.4	33.6	22.1	31.5	32.8	30.7	28.7	31.5	29.2	30.6	..
Haiti	22.3	27.0	20.2	12.3	14.2	14.5	22.2	30.4	26.0	24.3	22.6	..
Colombia	14.4	16.6	18.8	14.7	18.8	25.6	43.2	33.2	30.2	27.8	22.4	..
Korea	15.7	20.5	20.7	12.4	19.8	26.6	24.4	22.4	26.7	25.9	22.2	..
Iraq	5.1	5.0	5.2	2.5	3.5	4.1	4.3	3.8	4.8	12.1	19.9	..
Jamaica	15.9	15.3	14.8	13.3	14.4	18.3	25.0	19.4	18.5	21.8	19.8	..
El Salvador	22.5	31.1	31.1	28.2	29.8	21.4	31.8	21.1	19.7	19.9	18.8	..
Pakistan	14.5	16.4	13.7	9.4	12.1	14.9	17.4	13.5	19.7	21.6	18.3	..
Bangladesh	7.2	7.2	5.5	4.6	8.1	11.5	14.6	12.1	11.8	16.7	14.8	..
Other countries	356.9	450.9	443.4	296.9	395.8	512.1	571.9	447.5	449.3	496.7	428.5	
Total	**841.0**	**1 058.9**	**1 059.4**	**703.5**	**957.9**	**1 122.4**	**1 266.3**	**1 052.4**	**1 107.1**	**1 130.8**	**1 042.6**	**55**

Note: For details on definitions and sources, please refer to the metadata at the end of Table A.2.

StatLink http://dx.doi.org/10.1787/888932617512

Table A.2. **Outflows of foreign population from selected OECD countries**
Thousands

	2000	2001	2002	2003	2004	2005	2006	2007	2008	2009	2010
Australia											
Permanent departures	23.4	24.1	24.9	29.9	31.6	33.6	35.2	35.2	37.8	39.8	43.7
Long-term departures	42.2	31.9	29.5	29.6	31.8	34.4	36.1	36.1	..	..	..
Austria	44.4	51.0	44.5	48.9	50.0	49.8	55.0	52.6	55.3	66.1	66.4
Belgium	35.6	31.4	31.0	33.9	37.7	38.5	39.4	38.5	44.9	49.1	50.8
Czech Republic	0.2	20.6	31.1	33.2	33.8	21.8	31.4	18.4	3.8	9.4	14.9
Denmark	14.0	14.8	14.9	15.8	15.8	16.3	17.3	17.9	19.7	26.6	27.1
Estonia	..	..	..	..	0.6	0.6	0.6	0.4	0.5	0.7	0.6
Finland	4.1	2.2	2.8	2.3	4.2	2.6	2.7	3.1	4.5	4.0	3.1
Germany	562.8	497.0	505.6	499.1	547.0	483.6	483.8	475.8	563.1	578.8	670.6
Hungary	2.2	1.9	2.4	2.6	3.5	3.3	4.0	4.1	4.2	5.6	6.0
Ireland	..	..	..	..	..	..	20.7	29.1	31.9	46.7	37.6
Japan	210.9	232.8	248.4	259.4	278.5	292.0	218.8	214.9	234.2	262.0	242.6
Korea	89.1	107.2	114.0	152.3	148.8	266.7	183.0	163.6	215.7	236.4	196.1
Luxembourg	7.0	7.6	8.3	6.9	7.5	7.2	7.7	8.6	8.0	7.3	7.7
Netherlands	20.7	20.4	21.2	21.9	23.5	24.0	26.5	29.0	30.7	35.5	40.2
New Zealand	15.6	28.6	22.4	25.4	29.0	30.6	20.5	21.4	23.0	23.6	26.3
Norway	14.9	15.2	12.3	14.3	13.9	12.6	12.5	13.3	15.2	18.4	22.5
Portugal	0.4	0.1	0.1	0.2	0.1	0.2	0.1	..	..	..	..
Slovak Republic	..	..	..	3.6	5.0	1.1	1.5	2.0	3.3	3.3	2.9
Slovenia	2.0	3.4	4.6	4.0	6.0	6.5	11.0	11.8	7.3	15.1	12.0
Spain	..	..	6.9	10.0	41.9	48.7	120.3	199.0	232.0	288.3	336.7
Sweden	12.5	12.7	14.1	15.1	16.0	15.8	20.0	20.4	19.2	18.3	22.1
Switzerland	55.8	52.7	49.7	46.3	47.9	49.7	53.0	56.2	54.1	55.2	65.5
United Kingdom	136.7	117.3	141.3	144.1	126.2	154.1	173.4	158.0	243.0	211.0	252.0

Note: For details on definitions and sources, refer to the metadata at the end of the table.

StatLink http://dx.doi.org/10.1787/888932617417

Metadata related to Tables A.1, A.2 and B.1. **Migration flows**

Country	Types of migrant recorded in the data	Other comments	Source
Australia	*Permanent migrants:* Includes offshore migration (*Settler Arrivals*) and onshore migration (people granted permanent residence while in Australia on a temporary visa). Permanent migrants include holders of a permanent visa, a temporary (provisional) visa where there is a clear intention to settle, citizens of New Zealand indicating an intention to settle and persons otherwise eligible to settle. *Temporary migrants:* Entries of temporary migrants, excluding students. Includes short and long-term temporary entrants, *e.g.* top managers, executives, specialists and technical workers, diplomats and other personnel of foreign governments, temporary business entry, working holiday makers and entertainers. *Permanent departures:* Residents who on departure state that they do not intend to return to Australia.	Data refer to the fiscal year (July to June of the year indicated).	Department of Immigration and Citizenship.
Austria	Foreigners holding a residence permit and actually staying in the country for at least 3 months.	Until 2001, data are from local population registers. Starting in 2002, they are from the central population register. The data for 2002-07 were revised to match with the results of the register-based test census of 2006.	Population Registers, Statistics Austria.
Belgium	Foreigners holding a residence permit and intending to stay in the country for at least 3 months. Outflows include administrative corrections.	Asylum seekers were formerly grouped under the category "Refugees". From 1 January 2008 on, they are classified like other migrants. This may explain some of the increase for certain nationalities between 2007 and 2008.	Population Register, Directorate for Statistics and Economic Information (DGSEI).
Canada	*Permanent migrants:* Inflows of persons who have acquired permanent resident status (including onshore). *Temporary migrants:* Inflows (first entries) of people who are lawfully in Canada on a temporary basis under the authority of a temporary resident permit. Temporary residents include foreign workers (including seasonal workers), foreign students, refugee claimants, people allowed to remain temporarily in Canada on humanitarian grounds and other individuals entering Canada on a temporary basis who are not under a work or student permit and who are not seeking protection.	Table B.1 presents the inflow of persons who have acquired permanent resident status only. Country of origin refers to country of last permanent residence.	Citizenship and Immigration Canada.
Chile	Temporary residence permits granted.		Register of permits of residence granted, *Chile Sistema B3000*, Department of Foreigners and Migration, Ministry of the Interior.
Czech Republic	Foreigners holding a permanent or a long-term residence permit or who were granted asylum in the given year.	In 2000, data include only holders of a permanent residence permit. From 2001 on, data also include refugees and long-term residence permit holders.	Register of Foreigners, Population Information System of the Ministry of the Interior and Czech Statistical Office.

Metadata related to Tables A.1, A.2 and B.1. **Migration flows** (cont.)

Country	Types of migrant recorded in the data	Other comments	Source
Denmark	Foreigners who live legally in Denmark, are registred in the Central population register, and have been living in the country for at least one year. From 2006 on, Statistics Denmark started using a new calculation on the underlying demographic data. The data from 2006 on are therefore not comparable with previous years. Outflows include administrative corrections.	Excludes asylum seekers and all those with temporary residence permits.	Central Population Register, Statistics Denmark.
Estonia			Population Register and Police and Border Guard Board (PBG), Statistics Estonia.
Finland		Includes foreign persons of Finnish origin. Excludes asylum seekers and persons with temporary residence permits.	Central Population Register, Statistics Finland.
France	The "permanent" entries consist of the first statistical registration as a permanent migrant of people coming from abroad, regularised or who changed their status from a temporary migrant. Data include entries due to labour migration (employees, non-employed holders of a "competence and talent" permit or a "scientific" permit), family migration (family reunification, members of families of French persons or refugees, families accompanying workers), refugees and other permit holders.	Excludes citizens from the European Economic Area.	French Office for Immigration and Integration (OFII), Ministry of the Interior, Overseas Territories, Local Authorities and Immigration, French Office for the Protection of Refugees and Stateless Persons (OFPRA).
Germany	Foreigners holding a residence permit and intending to stay at least one week in the country.	Includes asylum seekers living in private households. Excludes inflows of ethnic Germans. In 2008, local authorities started to purge registers of inactive records. As a result, higher emigration figures were reported from this year.	Central Population Register, Federal Statistical Office.
Greece	Initial issuance of residence permit.	Does not refer to physical inflows but to flows into legal status.	Ministry of Interior Affairs
Hungary	*Inflows:* Foreign citizens who entered Hungary in the given year and obtained a residence document according to legal regulations in effect. *Outflows*: Foreign citizens having a residence or a settlement document and who left Hungary in the given year without the intent to return, or whose permission's validity is expired and did not apply for a new one or whose permission was invalidated by authority due to withdrawal.		Office of Immigration and Nationality, Hungarian Central Statistical Office.
Iceland			Register of Migration Data, Statistics Iceland.
Ireland	Figures are derived from the quarterly National Household Survey (QNHS) series. The estimates relate to those persons resident in the country at the time of the survey and who were living abroad at a point in time twelve months earlier (B.1) or to those persons resident in the country at a point in the previous twelve month period who are now living abroad (B.2).		Central Statistics Office.
Israel	Data refer to permanent immigrants by last country of residence.	The statistical data for Israel are supplied by and under the responsibility of the relevant Israeli authorities. The use of such data by the OECD is without prejudice to the status of the Golan Heights, East Jerusalem and Israeli settlements in the West Bank under the terms of international law.	Central Bureau of Statistics.

Metadata related to Tables A.1, A.2 and B.1. **Migration flows** (cont.)

Country	Types of migrant recorded in the data	Other comments	Source
Italy	Foreigners holding a residence, work or student permit.	Excludes seasonal workers.	Population Register, ISTAT.
Japan	Foreigners holding a valid visa and intending to remain in the country for more than 90 days.	Excludes temporary visitors and re-entries.	Register of Foreigners, Ministry of Justice, Immigration Bureau.
Korea	Data refer to long-term inflows/outflows (more than 90 days).		Ministry of Justice.
Luxembourg	Foreigners holding a residence permit and intending to stay in the country for at least 3 months.		Central Population Register, Central Office of Statistics and Economic Studies (Statec).
Mexico	Number of foreigners who are issued an immigrant permit for the first time ("inmigrante" FM2).		National Migration Institute (INM).
Netherlands	Foreigners holding a residence permit and intending to stay in the country for at least four of the next six months. Outflows exclude administrative corrections, *i.e.* unreported emigration of foreigners.	Inflows exclude asylum seekers who are staying in reception centres.	Population Register, Central Bureau of Statistics.
New Zealand	*Inflows:* Residence approvals. *Outflows:* Permanent and long term departures (foreign-born persons departing permanently or intending to be away for a period of 12 months or more).		Immigration Service, Department of Labour, and New Zealand Statistics.
Norway	Foreigners holding a residence or work permit and intending to stay in the country for at least 6 months.	Asylum seekers are registered as immigrants only after having settled in a Norwegian municipality following a positive outcome of their application. An asylum seeker whose application has been rejected will not be registered as an "immigrant", even if the application process has taken a long time and the return to the home country is delayed for a significant period.	Central Population Register, Statistics Norway.
Poland	Number of permanent and "fixed-term" residence permits issued. Since 26 August 2006, nationals of European Union Member States and their family members are no longer issued residence permits in Poland. However, they still need to register their stay in Poland, provided that they are planning to stay in Poland for more than three months.	2007 data include registrations of nationals of European Union member states for the period August 2006 to December 2007.	Office for Foreigners.
Portugal	Data based on residence permits. 2001 to 2004 figures include foreigners that entered the country with Long Term Visas (Temporary Stay, Study and Work) issued in each year and also foreigners with Stay Permits yearly delivered under the 2001 programme of regularisation (126 901 in 2001, 47 657 in 2002, 9 097 in 2003 and 178 in 2004). In 2005, inflows include residence permits and long term visas issued over the year. Since 2006, figures include long term visas for non-EU25 citizens and new residence titles attributed to EU25 citizens (who do not need a visa).		Immigration and Border Control Office (SEF), National Statistical Institute (INE) and Ministry of Foreign Affairs.
Russian Federation	*Inflows:* Temporary and permanent residence permits issued. *Outflows:* Holders of a temporary or a permanent residence permit.		Federal Migration Service, Ministry of the Interior.
Slovak Republic	Until 2002, first long term and permanent residence permits. From 2003 on, data include permanent, temporary, and tolerated residents.		Register of Foreigners, Statistical Office of the Slovak Republic.

Metadata related to Tables A.1, A.2 and B.1. **Migration flows** (cont.)

Country	Types of migrant recorded in the data	Other comments	Source
Slovenia	*Inflows:* Prior to 2008, data on migration included temporary migrants. From 2008 on, immigrants are included when they register residence with the intention to live in Slovenia for a year or more. *Outflows:* Data on emigration of foreigners are estimated on the basis of the number of foreigners and natural changes in Slovenia. Includes temporary absence from Slovenia because of departure abroad for more than three months and arrivals after residing abroad temporarily.	Prior to 2008, the data on immigration of foreigners were from the Ministry of the Interior (initially from the Database on Foreigners and later from the Register of Foreigners), while data on emigrated foreigners were estimates prepared by the Statistical Office. From 2008 on, data on migration are from the Central Population Register based on the registration/deregistration of residence in Slovenia, registration of temporary departure from Slovenia and registration of return to Slovenia.	Central Population Register, Ministry of the Interior, and Statistical office of the Republic of Slovenia.
Spain	Data include information regarding registrations and cancellations due to changes of residence registered in the Municipal Registers for all foreigners, by nationality, independently of their legal status.	From 2004 on, the Residential Variation Statistics (RVS) also include registrations by omission and cancellations for undue registration of foreign nationals. Cancellations by expiration are included from 2006 on. These cancellations arise as a result of the legislative modification introduced by the Organic Law 14/2003 on foreign nationals, to Law 7/1985, Regulation of the Basis of Local Regimes.	RVS derived from Municipal Population Registers (*Padron municipal de habitantes*), National Statistical Institute (INE).
Sweden	Foreigners holding a residence permit and intending to stay in the country for at least one year.	Excludes asylum seekers and temporary workers.	Population Register, Statistics Sweden.
Switzerland	Foreigners holding a permanent or an annual residence permit. Holders of an L-permit (short duration) are also included if their stay in the country is longer than 12 months.		Register of Foreigners, Federal Office of Migration.
Turkey	Residence permits issued for the first time to foreigners intending to stay 12 months or more in the country.		General Directorate of Security, Ministry of the Interior.
United Kingdom	*Inflows:* Non-British citizens admitted to the United Kingdom. Data in Table A.1 are adjusted to include short term migrants (including asylum seekers) who actually stayed longer than one year. Data by nationality in Table B.1 on inflows are not adjusted. Statistics whose coefficient of variation exceeds 30% are not shown separately but grouped under "Other countries". *Outflows:* Non-British citizens leaving the territory of the United Kingdom.		International Passenger Survey, Office for National Statistics.
United States	*Permanent migrants:* Issues of permanent residence permits. *Temporary migrants:* Data refer to non-immigrant visas issued, excluding visitors and transit passengers (B and C visas) and crewmembers (D visas). Includes family members.	Includes persons already present in the United States who changed status. Data cover the fiscal year (October to September of the year indicated).	US Department of Homeland Security and Bureau of Consular Affairs, United States Department of State.

Data for Serbia include persons from Serbia, Montenegro and Serbia and Montenegro.

Inflows of asylum seekers

The statistics on asylum seekers published in this annex are based on data provided by the United Nations High Commission for Refugees. Since 1950, the UNHCR, which has a mission of conducting and co ordinating international initiatives on behalf of refugees, has regularly produced complete statistics on refugees and asylum seekers in OECD countries and other countries of the world (www.unhcr.org/pages/49c3646c4d6.html).

These statistics are most often derived from administrative sources, but there are differences depending on the nature of the data provided. In some countries, asylum seekers are enumerated when the application is accepted. Consequently, they are shown in the statistics at that time rather than at the date when they arrived in the country. Acceptance of the application means that the administrative authorities will review the applicants' claims and grant them certain rights during this review procedure. In other countries, the data do not include the applicants' family members, who are admitted under different provisions (France), while other countries count the entire family (Switzerland).

The figures presented in the summary table (Table A.3) generally concern initial applications (primary processing stage) and sometimes differ significantly from the totals presented in Tables B.3, which give data by country of origin. This is because the data received by the UNHCR by country of origin combine both initial applications and appeals, and it is sometimes difficult to separate these two categories retrospectively. The reference for total asylum applications remains the figures shown in summary Table A.3.

Table A.3. Inflows of asylum seekers into OECD countries and the Russian Federation

	2000	2001	2002	2003	2004	2005	2006	2007	2008	2009	2010	2011[1]
Australia	13 065	12 366	5 863	4 295	3 201	3 204	3 515	3 980	4 771	6 206	8 246	11 510
Austria	18 284	30 135	39 354	32 359	24 634	22 461	13 349	11 921	12 841	15 821	11 012	14 430
Belgium	42 691	24 549	18 805	16 940	15 357	15 957	11 587	11 115	12 252	17 186	21 755	25 980
Canada	34 252	44 038	39 498	31 937	25 750	20 786	22 873	28 342	34 800	33 970	22 543	25 350
Chile	69	81	43	87	203	380	573	756	872	..	260	..
Czech Republic	8 788	18 094	8 484	11 396	5 459	4 160	3 016	1 878	1 711	1 355	979	490
Denmark	12 200	12 512	6 068	4 593	3 235	2 260	1 918	1 852	2 360	3 819	4 965	3 810
Estonia	3	12	9	14	14	11	7	14	14	36	30	70
Finland	3 170	1 651	3 443	3 221	3 861	3 574	2 331	1 434	4 016	5 910	4 018	3 090
France	38 747	54 291	58 971	59 768	58 545	49 733	30 748	29 387	35 404	42 118	48 074	51 910
Germany	78 564	88 287	71 127	50 563	35 607	28 914	21 029	19 164	22 085	27 649	41 332	45 740
Greece	3 083	5 499	5 664	8 178	4 469	9 050	12 267	25 113	19 884	15 928	10 273	9 310
Hungary	7 801	9 554	6 412	2 401	1 600	1 609	2 117	3 425	3 118	4 672	2 104	1 690
Iceland	24	52	117	80	76	88	39	42	77	35	51	70
Ireland	10 938	10 325	11 634	7 900	4 769	4 324	4 314	3 988	3 866	2 689	3 405	1 290
Israel	6 148	456	355	..	922	909	1 348	5 382	7 738	809	1 448	..
Italy	15 564	9 620	16 015	13 455	9 722	9 548	10 348	14 053	30 324	17 603	10 052	34 120
Japan	216	353	250	336	426	384	954	816	1 599	1 388	1 203	1 870
Korea	43	39	37	86	145	412	278	717	364	324	425	1 010
Luxembourg	621	687	1 043	1 549	1 577	802	523	426	463	477	744	2 160
Mexico	277	415	257	275	404	687	480	374	317	680	1 039	..
Netherlands	43 895	32 579	18 667	13 402	9 782	12 347	14 465	7 102	13 399	14 905	13 333	11 590
New Zealand	1 551	1 601	997	841	580	348	276	245	254	336	340	310
Norway	10 842	14 782	17 480	15 959	7 945	5 402	5 320	6 528	14 431	17 226	10 064	9 050
Poland	4 589	4 529	5 170	6 909	8 079	6 860	4 430	7 205	7 203	10 587	6 534	5 190
Portugal	224	234	245	88	113	114	128	224	161	139	160	280
Russian Federation	1 467	1 684	876	737	910	960	1 170	3 369	5 418	5 701	3 889	..
Slovak Republic	1 556	8 151	9 743	10 358	11 395	3 549	2 871	2 643	910	822	541	450
Slovenia	9 244	1 511	702	1 100	1 173	1 596	518	425	238	183	246	310
Spain	7 926	9 489	6 309	5 918	5 535	5 254	5 297	7 662	4 517	3 007	2 744	3 410
Sweden	16 303	23 515	33 016	31 348	23 161	17 530	24 322	36 370	24 353	24 194	31 823	29 650
Switzerland	17 611	20 633	26 125	20 806	14 248	10 061	10 537	10 387	16 606	16 005	13 521	19 440
Turkey	5 685	5 041	3 795	3 952	3 908	3 921	4 553	7 646	12 981	7 834	9 226	16 020
United Kingdom	98 900	91 600	103 080	60 050	40 625	30 840	28 320	28 300	31 315	30 675	22 645	25 420
United States	40 867	59 432	58 439	43 338	44 972	39 240	41 101	40 449	39 362	38 080	42 971	74 020
OECD	**553 741**	**596 113**	**577 217**	**463 502**	**371 492**	**316 315**	**285 752**	**319 365**	**364 606**	**362 668**	**348 106**	**429 040**

Notes: For details on definitions and sources, refer to the metadata at the end of the Tables B.3.
Information on data for Israel: http://dx.doi.org/10.1787/888932315602.
1. Preliminary data.

StatLink http://dx.doi.org/10.1787/888932617436

Table B.3. Inflows of asylum seekers by nationality
AUSTRALIA

	2000	2001	2002	2003	2004	2005	2006	2007	2008	2009	2010
Afghanistan	1 326	2 161	53	54	116	32	21	20	52	940	1 265
China	1 215	1 176	1 083	800	822	966	1 033	1 207	1 232	1 192	1 187
Sri Lanka	451	397	219	166	125	317	324	445	422	555	589
Iran	589	559	57	75	71	101	77	84	161	312	458
Pakistan	207	132	86	63	61	103	90	145	220	260	428
India	770	650	549	604	242	173	316	349	373	213	409
Fiji	658	799	369	165	84	52	34	70	81	262	375
Iraq	2 165	1 784	148	142	66	80	188	216	199	298	373
Zimbabwe	32	36	44	37	27	22	43	94	215	351	288
Malaysia	264	261	232	184	210	170	109	145	238	231	249
El Salvador	8	7	5	2	6	0	0	2	3	2	204
Lebanon	168	191	108	90	57	56	65	75	91	115	200
Former Yug. Rep. of Macedonia	56	90	25	11	5	4	3	4	6	11	179
Indonesia	831	897	619	230	164	166	296	183	238	192	179
Nepal	103	92	73	57	40	73	36	48	33	45	161
Other countries	4 222	3 134	2 193	1 615	1 105	889	880	893	1 207	1 227	1 702
Total	**13 065**	**12 366**	**5 863**	**4 295**	**3 201**	**3 204**	**3 515**	**3 980**	**4 771**	**6 206**	**8 246**

Note: For details on definitions and sources, please refer to the metadata at the end of the tables.

StatLink http://dx.doi.org/10.1787/888932617531

Table B.3. Inflows of asylum seekers by nationality
AUSTRIA

	2000	2001	2002	2003	2004	2005	2006	2007	2008	2009	2010
Russian Federation	291	366	2 221	6 709	6 172	4 355	2 441	2 676	3 435	3 559	2 322
Afghanistan	4 205	12 955	6 651	2 357	757	923	699	761	1 382	2 237	1 582
Serbia	1 486	1 637	4 723	2 526	2 835	4 403	2 522	1 774	1 715	2 041	975
Nigeria	390	1 047	1 432	1 849	1 828	880	421	394	535	837	573
India	2 441	1 802	3 366	2 822	1 839	1 530	479	385	355	427	433
Iran	2 559	734	760	979	343	306	274	248	250	340	387
Georgia	34	597	1 921	1 525	1 731	954	564	400	511	975	370
Turkey	592	1 868	3 561	2 854	1 114	1 064	668	659	417	554	369
Iraq	2 361	2 118	4 466	1 446	232	221	380	472	490	399	336
Algeria	84	121	239	221	234	185	138	109	173	248	304
Armenia	165	1 235	2 038	1 098	414	516	350	405	360	440	278
Pakistan	624	486	359	508	575	498	110	103	106	183	276
China	91	154	779	661	663	492	212	223	236	398	217
Syria	161	137	134	153	131	77	88	166	140	279	194
Former Yug. Rep. of Macedonia	21	947	786	415	323	452	193	157	205	158	194
Other countries	2 779	3 931	5 918	6 236	5 443	5 605	3 810	2 989	2 531	2 746	2 202
Total	**18 284**	**30 135**	**39 354**	**32 359**	**24 634**	**22 461**	**13 349**	**11 921**	**12 841**	**15 821**	**11 012**

Note: For details on definitions and sources, please refer to the metadata at the end of the tables.

StatLink http://dx.doi.org/10.1787/888932617531

Table B.3. Inflows of asylum seekers by nationality
BELGIUM

	2000	2001	2002	2003	2004	2005	2006	2007	2008	2009	2010
Serbia	4 921	1 932	1 523	1 280	1 294	1 203	778	1 223	1 057	2 065	4 556
Russian Federation	3 604	2 424	1 156	1 680	1 361	1 438	1 582	1 436	1 620	1 605	1 886
Iraq	569	368	461	282	388	903	695	825	1 070	1 386	1 637
Former Yug. Rep. of Macedonia	275	667	337	194	175	97	85	59	122	201	1 631
Guinea	488	494	515	354	565	643	413	526	661	1 052	1 455
Armenia	1 331	571	340	316	477	706	381	339	461	1 099	1 266
Afghanistan	861	504	326	329	287	253	365	696	879	1 659	1 124
Dem. Rep. of the Congo	1 421	1 371	1 789	1 778	1 471	1 272	843	716	579	670	813
Syria	292	230	199	210	182	228	167	199	281	347	374
Rwanda	866	617	487	450	427	565	370	321	273	308	361
Georgia	1 227	481	313	302	211	256	232	156	222	327	336
Pakistan	655	237	177	341	308	222	160	150	150	233	325
Cameroon	417	324	435	625	506	530	335	279	367	302	289
Turkey	838	900	970	618	561	453	380	250	284	259	275
Somalia	252	179	125	128	139	113	124	168	163	216	262
Other countries	24 674	13 250	9 652	8 053	7 005	7 075	4 677	3 771	4 063	5 457	5 165
Total	**42 691**	**24 549**	**18 805**	**16 940**	**15 357**	**15 957**	**11 587**	**11 114**	**12 252**	**17 186**	**21 755**

Note: For details on definitions and sources, please refer to the metadata at the end of the tables.

StatLink http://dx.doi.org/10.1787/888932617531

Table B.3. Inflows of asylum seekers by nationality
CANADA

	2000	2001	2002	2003	2004	2005	2006	2007	2008	2009	2010
Hungary	1 936	3 895	1 180	132	162	58	48	24	288	2 440	2 300
China	1 855	2 413	2 862	1 848	1 982	1 821	1 645	1 456	1 711	1 592	1 650
Colombia	1 063	1 831	2 718	2 131	3 664	1 487	1 361	2 632	3 132	2 299	1 384
Mexico	1 310	1 669	2 397	2 560	2 918	3 541	4 948	7 028	8 069	9 296	1 299
Sri Lanka	2 822	3 001	1 801	1 270	1 141	934	907	808	1 008	824	1 200
Haiti	354	237	256	195	175	378	759	3 741	4 936	1 597	1 062
Nigeria	800	790	828	637	589	591	685	759	766	760	846
Saint Vincent and the Grenadines	96	178	459	402	322	418	375	355	498	651	710
India	1 360	1 300	1 313	1 125	1 083	844	764	554	561	502	532
Pakistan	3 088	3 192	3 884	4 257	1 006	746	652	361	403	437	526
El Salvador	269	561	305	190	194	180	244	289	587	528	511
Saint Lucia	23	67	249	294	167	218	165	131	252	366	486
Somalia	753	799	388	348	408	285	206	231	505	508	425
Afghanistan	488	463	204	151	152	264	268	308	488	445	399
United States	98	92	213	317	240	228	389	949	969	468	344
Other countries	17 937	23 550	20 441	16 080	11 547	8 793	9 452	8 239	10 627	11 257	8 869
Total	**34 252**	**44 038**	**39 498**	**31 937**	**25 750**	**20 786**	**22 868**	**27 865**	**34 800**	**33 970**	**22 543**

Note: For details on definitions and sources, please refer to the metadata at the end of the tables.

StatLink http://dx.doi.org/10.1787/888932617531

Table B.3. Inflows of asylum seekers by nationality
CHILE

	2000	2001	2002	2003	2004	2005	2006	2007	2008	2009	2010
Colombia	22	33	27	56	182	347	540	713	816	..	220
Cuba	9	4	3	1	7	1	0	4	2	..	14
Peru	8	3	0	3	2	6	6	3	8	..	5
Ghana	0	0	0	0	0	0	1	6	0	..	5
Senegal	..	..	..	..	..	..	..	..	..	..	5
Bolivia	0	0	0	0	1	0	0	2	0	..	3
Dem. Rep. of the Congo	1	3	1	0	0	9	3	3	3	..	2
Iraq	2	4	0	1	0	0	0	0	0	..	1
Ukraine	0	0	0	0	0	0	0	0	0	..	1
Nigeria	6	2	0	2	2	0	1	0	0	..	1
Haiti	0	2	0	0	1	1	3	9	17	..	1
Ecuador	0	0	0	0	1	4	14	4	19	..	1
Kenya	0	0	0	0	0	0	0	2	0	..	1
Other countries	21	30	12	24	7	12	5	10	7	..	0
Total	**69**	**81**	**43**	**87**	**203**	**380**	**573**	**756**	**872**	**..**	**260**

Note: For details on definitions and sources, please refer to the metadata at the end of the tables.

StatLink http://dx.doi.org/10.1787/888932617531

Table B.3. Inflows of asylum seekers by nationality
CZECH REPUBLIC

	2000	2001	2002	2003	2004	2005	2006	2007	2008	2009	2010
Ukraine	1 145	4 419	1 676	2 044	1 600	1 020	571	293	323	220	141
Mongolia	67	134	79	81	123	119	95	160	193	161	106
Turkey	90	58	31	11	31	33	66	213	253	69	68
Belarus	193	438	312	281	226	244	174	130	81	60	67
Russian Federation	623	642	629	4 853	1 498	278	171	99	85	66	62
Kazakhstan	103	133	66	47	44	34	236	30	80	192	57
Viet Nam	586	1 525	891	566	385	217	124	100	109	65	49
Myanmar	0	1	0	0	0	0	0	3	26	23	42
Niger	..	..	..	..	..	..	..	..	..	2	40
Kyrgyzstan	52	50	59	80	138	35	85	63	36	26	36
Armenia	274	1 019	452	49	75	56	51	37	33	23	19
Cuba	11	8	5	7	0	0	20	94	19	12	18
Syria	21	25	13	6	4	22	20	31	36	54	17
Uzbekistan	7	34	84	75	30	41	25	25	17	19	16
Dem. Rep. of the Congo	18	7	8	5	0	0	20	26	14	24	15
Other countries	5 598	9 601	4 178	3 291	1 305	2 061	1 358	575	406	339	226
Total	**8 788**	**18 094**	**8 483**	**11 396**	**5 459**	**4 160**	**3 016**	**1 879**	**1 711**	**1 355**	**979**

Note: For details on definitions and sources, please refer to the metadata at the end of the tables.

StatLink http://dx.doi.org/10.1787/888932617531

STATISTICAL ANNEX

Table B.3. **Inflows of asylum seekers by nationality**
DENMARK

	2000	2001	2002	2003	2004	2005	2006	2007	2008	2009	2010
Afghanistan	3 732	3 749	1 186	664	285	173	122	138	418	1 049	1 476
Syria	55	62	31	56	56	46	55	71	105	380	821
Iran	389	263	178	158	140	123	89	106	196	334	597
Serbia	1 647	567	1 030	750	784	375	267	90	118	271	402
Russian Federation	245	123	198	269	163	119	61	114	183	335	340
Iraq	2 605	2 099	1 045	442	217	264	507	695	543	305	237
Somalia	747	566	391	370	154	80	57	35	58	177	110
West Bank and Gaza Strip	266	184	167	153	148	0	68	53	91	0	106
Turkey	68	67	111	108	84	47	39	23	39	29	51
India	100	67	96	52	39	72	83	56	37	33	48
Algeria	22	19	97	62	50	45	15	16	38	46	46
Myanmar	3	1	5	3	1	7	2	5	9	18	41
Sudan	24	12	41	34	17	21	5	9	10	25	41
Bangladesh	24	9	12	24	21	16	14	6	14	16	32
Armenia	297	44	37	23	29	19	17	4	12	17	32
Other countries	2 781	2 437	1 443	1 425	1 047	853	517	431	489	784	585
Total	**13 005**	**10 269**	**6 068**	**4 593**	**3 235**	**2 260**	**1 918**	**1 852**	**2 360**	**3 819**	**4 965**

Note: For details on definitions and sources, please refer to the metadata at the end of the tables.
StatLink http://dx.doi.org/10.1787/888932617531

Table B.3. **Inflows of asylum seekers by nationality**
ESTONIA

	2000	2001	2002	2003	2004	2005	2006	2007	2008	2009	2010
Afghanistan	0	1	0	0	0	0	0	0	0	9	7
Russian Federation	2	0	1	4	0	4	4	3	3	5	7
Nigeria	0	0	0	0	0	0	1	0	1	1	3
Sri Lanka	0	0	0	0	0	0	0	4	0	0	3
Other countries	1	11	8	10	14	7	2	7	10	21	10
Total	**3**	**12**	**9**	**14**	**14**	**11**	**7**	**14**	**14**	**36**	**30**

Note: For details on definitions and sources, please refer to the metadata at the end of the tables.
StatLink http://dx.doi.org/10.1787/888932617531

Table B.3. **Inflows of asylum seekers by nationality**
FINLAND

	2000	2001	2002	2003	2004	2005	2006	2007	2008	2009	2010
Iraq	62	103	115	150	123	289	225	327	1 253	1 183	575
Somalia	28	18	54	91	253	321	92	82	1 176	1 169	571
Bulgaria	13	0	287	287	238	570	463	13	82	722	485
Russian Federation	289	289	272	288	215	233	176	172	208	599	436
Serbia	262	98	223	519	792	413	282	151	181	336	327
Afghanistan	31	25	27	51	166	237	97	96	249	445	265
Iran	50	56	41	47	99	79	91	79	143	159	142
Turkey	76	94	197	185	140	97	41	73	65	140	117
Romania	29	36	596	109	132	56	20	9	18	54	94
Nigeria	12	8	28	77	92	73	64	41	76	130	84
Ghana	8	2	5	15	3	11	6	9	27	52	78
Belarus	37	55	39	46	58	57	97	48	68	94	66
Georgia	2	7	11	26	93	64	35	6	13	22	61
Dem. Rep. of the Congo	27	23	53	38	48	37	38	36	31	56	47
Algeria	18	38	38	38	31	33	25	24	27	48	47
Other countries	2 226	799	1 457	1 254	1 378	1 004	572	339	399	701	623
Total	**3 170**	**1 651**	**3 443**	**3 221**	**3 861**	**3 574**	**2 324**	**1 505**	**4 016**	**5 910**	**4 018**

Note: For details on definitions and sources, please refer to the metadata at the end of the tables.

StatLink http://dx.doi.org/10.1787/888932617531

Table B.3. **Inflows of asylum seekers by nationality**
FRANCE

	2000	2001	2002	2003	2004	2005	2006	2007	2008	2009	2010
Serbia	2 053	1 591	1 629	2 704	3 812	3 997	3 047	3 122	3 257	5 313	5 843
Russian Federation	787	1 783	1 741	3 347	3 331	3 080	2 313	3 265	3 595	3 392	4 334
Dem. Rep. of the Congo	2 950	3 781	5 260	5 093	3 848	3 022	2 283	2 154	2 543	2 800	3 426
Bangladesh	1 054	825	668	956	959	860	607	960	1 249	1 441	3 145
Sri Lanka	2 117	2 000	1 992	2 129	2 246	2 071	2 145	2 159	2 322	3 129	2 864
Guinea	544	745	753	808	1 020	1 147	859	981	1 270	1 671	2 034
Haiti	1 886	2 713	1 904	1 488	3 133	5 060	1 844	677	930	1 458	2 008
China	4 968	2 948	2 869	5 330	4 196	2 590	1 214	1 286	821	1 602	1 937
Armenia	405	544	963	1 106	1 292	1 642	1 684	1 929	2 075	3 112	1 775
Turkey	3 735	5 347	6 582	7 192	4 741	3 867	2 758	2 234	2 198	2 047	1 415
Georgia	373	1 067	1 554	1 726	1 563	788	282	176	379	471	1 355
Algeria	1 818	2 933	2 865	2 794	4 209	2 018	1 127	967	978	1 118	1 171
Mauritania	1 385	2 332	2 998	2 380	1 540	1 067	548	432	719	1 214	984
Pakistan	798	600	438	756	1 046	572	393	343	325	634	893
Sudan	92	98	136	406	286	409	452	404	399	811	817
Other countries	14 810	17 984	18 735	21 553	21 323	17 543	9 192	8 298	12 344	11 905	14 073
Total	**39 775**	**47 291**	**51 087**	**59 768**	**58 545**	**49 733**	**30 748**	**29 387**	**35 404**	**42 118**	**48 074**

Note: For details on definitions and sources, please refer to the metadata at the end of the tables.

StatLink http://dx.doi.org/10.1787/888932617531

Table B.3. Inflows of asylum seekers by nationality
GERMANY

	2000	2001	2002	2003	2004	2005	2006	2007	2008	2009	2010
Serbia	11 121	7 758	6 679	4 909	3 855	5 522	3 237	2 057	1 645	2 038	6 651
Afghanistan	5 380	5 837	2 772	1 473	918	711	531	338	657	3 375	5 905
Iraq	11 601	17 167	10 242	3 850	1 293	1 983	2 117	4 327	6 836	6 538	5 555
Iran	4 878	3 455	2 642	2 049	1 369	929	611	631	815	1 170	2 475
Former Yug. Rep. of Macedonia	216	1 163	505	320	198	193	132	89	82	109	2 466
Somalia	398	262	203	257	240	163	146	121	165	346	2 235
Syria	2 641	2 232	1 829	1 192	768	933	609	634	775	819	1 490
Turkey	8 968	10 869	9 575	6 301	4 148	2 958	1 949	1 437	1 408	1 429	1 340
Russian Federation	2 763	4 523	4 058	3 383	2 757	1 719	1 040	772	792	936	1 199
Viet Nam	2 332	3 721	2 340	2 096	1 668	1 222	990	987	1 042	1 115	1 009
Pakistan	1 506	1 180	1 084	1 122	1 062	551	464	301	320	481	840
India	1 826	2 651	2 246	1 736	1 118	557	512	413	485	681	810
Nigeria	420	526	987	1 051	1 130	608	481	503	561	791	716
Georgia	801	1 220	1 531	1 139	802	493	240	181	232	560	664
Eritrea	251	299	378	556	456	367	281	335	262	346	642
Other countries	23 462	25 424	24 056	19 129	13 825	10 005	7 689	6 038	6 008	6 915	7 335
Total	78 564	88 287	71 127	50 563	35 607	28 914	21 029	19 164	22 085	27 649	41 332

Note: For details on definitions and sources, please refer to the metadata at the end of the tables.

StatLink http://dx.doi.org/10.1787/888932617531

Table B.3. Inflows of asylum seekers by nationality
GREECE

	2000	2001	2002	2003	2004	2005	2006	2007	2008	2009	2010
Pakistan	141	252	250	681	247	1 154	2 378	9 144	6 914	3 716	2 748
Georgia	1	0	8	48	323	1 897	428	1 559	2 241	2 170	1 162
Bangladesh	49	33	34	233	208	550	3 750	2 965	1 778	1 809	987
Albania	1	10	9	12	23	21	20	51	202	517	693
China	4	2	70	140	52	251	97	36	55	391	549
Afghanistan	446	1 459	1 238	561	382	458	1 087	1 556	2 287	1 510	524
Nigeria	14	33	184	444	325	406	391	390	746	780	393
Senegal	0	0	5	3	1	7	66	219	386	336	381
India	27	41	84	105	42	166	162	261	227	156	381
Iraq	1 334	1 972	2 567	2 831	936	971	1 415	5 474	1 760	886	342
Ghana	4	17	3	19	16	41	85	71	104	154	291
Syria	7	15	13	19	44	57	143	1 311	808	965	167
West Bank and Gaza Strip	36	38	60	173	75	..	..	..	..	..	150
Somalia	5	14	69	389	119	110	150	174	149	140	141
Iran	135	212	411	608	228	203	528	354	312	303	125
Other countries	879	1 401	659	1 912	1 448	2 758	1 567	1 548	1 915	2 095	1 239
Total	3 083	5 499	5 664	8 178	4 469	9 050	12 267	25 113	19 884	15 928	10 273

Note: For details on definitions and sources, please refer to the metadata at the end of the tables.

StatLink http://dx.doi.org/10.1787/888932617531

Table B.3. Inflows of asylum seekers by nationality
HUNGARY

	2000	2001	2002	2003	2004	2005	2006	2007	2008	2009	2010
Afghanistan	2 185	4 311	2 348	469	38	22	13	35	116	1 194	702
Serbia	692	214	97	112	180	243	384	911	1 604	2 325	447
West Bank and Gaza Strip	29	104	29	35	63	24	37	52	41	..	225
Georgia	27	29	91	205	288	114	175	131	165	116	68
Iran	55	144	160	170	46	25	20	14	10	87	62
Turkey	116	116	124	125	125	65	43	56	70	114	59
Somalia	152	298	213	113	18	7	42	99	185	75	51
Iraq	889	1 014	2 008	348	36	18	68	136	125	57	48
Pakistan	220	157	40	53	54	40	18	15	246	41	41
Nigeria	94	111	125	74	73	89	109	86	56	66	37
Viet Nam	65	53	182	49	105	319	406	862	42	73	37
Algeria	95	76	34	79	57	19	22	48	19	11	35
Syria	41	17	20	11	10	18	32	48	16	19	23
Russian Federation	52	40	43	105	41	37	63	51	21	27	23
Lebanon	18	10	1	1	2	1	2	5	13	18	19
Other countries	3 071	2 860	897	452	464	568	683	875	389	449	227
Total	7 801	9 554	6 412	2 401	1 600	1 609	2 117	3 424	3 118	4 672	2 104

Note: For details on definitions and sources, please refer to the metadata at the end of the tables.

StatLink http://dx.doi.org/10.1787/888932617531

Table B.3. Inflows of asylum seekers by nationality
ICELAND

	2000	2001	2002	2003	2004	2005	2006	2007	2008	2009	2010
Afghanistan	3	1	0	3	2	6	2	1	5	2	7
Iran	0	7	0	1	2	4	2	1	3	7	6
Iraq	0	0	2	3	6	0	1	1	4	2	5
Somalia	0	0	0	0	0	0	0	0	2	2	5
Former Yug. Rep. of Macedonia	0	5	1	1	0	0	0	0	0	0	4
Spain	0	0	0	0	0	0	0	0	0	0	3
Syria	2	0	0	0	0	0	0	5	1	3	2
Nigeria	0	1	3	1	7	2	1	1	5	2	2
Moldova	0	0	0	0	3	5	0	0	1	1	2
Croatia	0	0	1	1	0	1	1	0	0	0	2
Nepal	0	0	0	1	0	0	0	0	0	0	2
Other countries	19	38	110	69	56	70	32	33	56	16	11
Total	24	52	117	80	76	88	39	42	77	35	51

Note: For details on definitions and sources, please refer to the metadata at the end of the tables.

StatLink http://dx.doi.org/10.1787/888932617531

Table B.3. Inflows of asylum seekers by nationality
IRELAND

	2000	2001	2002	2003	2004	2005	2006	2007	2008	2009	2010
Nigeria	3 405	3 461	4 050	3 110	1 776	1 278	1 038	1 028	1 009	569	630
Pakistan	46	127	120	62	55	68	167	185	237	257	347
China	16	25	85	168	152	96	139	259	180	194	244
Dem. Rep. of the Congo	358	281	270	256	140	138	109	149	173	102	148
Zimbabwe	25	102	357	88	69	51	77	87	114	91	126
Ghana	106	148	293	180	64	67	88	82	104	82	118
Somalia	138	70	77	183	198	367	161	144	141	84	112
Cameroon	76	144	187	125	62	57	78	44	67	50	101
Georgia	55	97	103	133	130	151	171	174	181	88	98
Bangladesh	2	0	16	6	7	20	5	24	47	30	97
Afghanistan	7	27	7	24	106	142	88	78	79	68	92
Sudan	39	26	50	70	145	203	308	157	126	61	88
Moldova	387	549	536	244	100	100	110	133	141	86	82
Iraq	89	48	148	129	38	55	215	285	203	76	73
South Africa	143	203	183	114	45	33	38	39	75	54	71
Other countries	6 046	5 015	5 149	3 008	1 678	1 499	1 523	1 117	989	797	978
Total	10 938	10 323	11 631	7 900	4 765	4 325	4 315	3 985	3 866	2 689	3 405

Note: For details on definitions and sources, please refer to the metadata at the end of the tables.

StatLink http://dx.doi.org/10.1787/888932617531

Table B.3. Inflows of asylum seekers by nationality
ISRAEL

	2000	2001	2002	2003	2004	2005	2006	2007	2008	2009	2010
Côte d'Ivoire	0	3	50	..	74	43	91	751	507	20	289
Ghana	1	3	2	..	34	25	74	192	233	113	189
Nigeria	0	6	14	..	100	160	448	567	418	198	168
Ethiopia	80	201	140	..	316	56	13	45	495	16	148
Philippines	0	0	0	..	5	6	10	40	27	73	77
Colombia	2	17	3	..	28	23	31	67	92	40	75
Guinea	0	1	1	..	7	181	151	23	24	10	35
Liberia	2	48	23	..	61	16	36	34	8	1	27
Turkey	0	1	4	..	32	66	126	178	142	28	22
Chad	0	0	1	..	0	0	1	5	19	1	17
Mali	0	0	0	..	3	0	10	4	12	6	17
Togo	0	1	1	..	21	10	8	22	13	0	15
Dem. Rep. of the Congo	0	22	38	..	19	17	7	3	68	0	10
Niger	0	0	0	..	0	0	1	3	19	4	6
Somalia	0	0	1	..	0	2	1	8	13	1	4
Other countries	6 063	153	77	..	222	304	340	3 440	5 648	298	349
Total	6 148	456	355	..	922	909	1 348	5 382	7 738	809	1 448

Notes: For details on definitions and sources, please refer to the metadata at the end of the tables.
Information on data for Israel: http://dx.doi.org/10.1787/888932315602.

StatLink http://dx.doi.org/10.1787/888932617531

Table B.3. Inflows of asylum seekers by nationality
ITALY

	2000	2001	2002	2003	2004	2005	2006	2007	2008	2009	2010
Nigeria	57	388	594	722	930	536	830	1 336	5 673	3 991	1 385
Pakistan	92	113	1 256	787	267	411	203	176	1 143	1 362	929
Afghanistan	524	299	137	70	84	76	177	663	1 732	711	873
Turkey	4 062	1 690	730	466	323	168	175	394	501	541	854
Bosnia and Herzegovina	32	53	47	0	19	9	9	8	20	128	816
Serbia	2 417	1 526	1 769	1 510	1 991	1 704	581	1 113	282	634	948
Iraq	6 082	1 985	1 944	493	166	118	87	189	758	417	380
Ghana	8	15	33	505	62	407	530	673	1 815	991	278
Iran	182	173	84	87	70	65	50	69	149	198	269
Côte d'Ivoire	6	14	93	348	183	586	508	982	1 653	643	235
Bangladesh	88	174	374	297	342	407	283	315	1 684	1 338	222
Eritrea	33	276	927	1 230	831	1 313	2 151	2 260	2 934	890	181
Guinea	3	5	0	0	5	20	70	217	465	242	167
Senegal	12	20	0	0	26	13	16	67	131	156	162
Montenegro	0	0	0	0	0	0	0	0	0	14	153
Other countries	1 966	2 889	8 027	6 940	4 423	3 715	4 678	5 591	11 384	5 347	2 200
Total	**15 564**	**9 620**	**16 015**	**13 455**	**9 722**	**9 548**	**10 348**	**14 053**	**30 324**	**17 603**	**10 052**

Note: For details on definitions and sources, please refer to the metadata at the end of the tables.

StatLink http://dx.doi.org/10.1787/888932617531

Table B.3. Inflows of asylum seekers by nationality
JAPAN

	2000	2001	2002	2003	2004	2005	2006	2007	2008	2009	2010
Myanmar	23	23	38	111	138	212	626	500	979	568	342
Sri Lanka	6	3	9	4	9	7	27	43	90	234	171
Turkey	40	123	52	77	131	40	149	76	156	94	126
Nepal	0	0	0	1	3	5	11	4	20	29	109
India	0	9	9	12	7	0	2	2	17	59	91
Pakistan	74	47	26	12	12	10	12	27	37	92	83
Iran	17	20	19	25	18	16	27	19	38	40	35
Bangladesh	3	10	12	6	33	29	15	14	33	51	33
Nigeria	0	0	12	2	2	2	10	6	10	17	33
Uganda	0	0	0	1	1	1	2	4	16	46	21
Cameroon	0	0	15	8	11	1	5	12	29	11	20
Ethiopia	6	1	2	2	2	3	14	29	51	15	18
China	3	10	22	22	16	16	13	17	18	18	17
Ghana	0	0	0	1	1	0	0	1	4	3	13
Dem. Rep. of the Congo	0	0	0	5	0	0	4	10	14	18	13
Other countries	44	107	34	47	42	42	37	52	87	93	78
Total	**216**	**353**	**250**	**336**	**426**	**384**	**954**	**816**	**1 599**	**1 388**	**1 203**

Note: For details on definitions and sources, please refer to the metadata at the end of the tables.

StatLink http://dx.doi.org/10.1787/888932617531

Table B.3. **Inflows of asylum seekers by nationality**
KOREA

	2000	2001	2002	2003	2004	2005	2006	2007	2008	2009	2010
Pakistan	1	6	2	9	0	1	5	4	47	95	129
Kyrgyzstan	..	..	..	..	..	..	3	0	0	0	77
Bangladesh	..	1	11	6	1	9	8	23	30	41	41
Myanmar	21	..	..	21	46	50	12	23	33	32	34
Nigeria	0	0	0	0	0	26	16	100	27	16	19
Afghanistan	..	2	1	1	1	1	0	1	0	8	15
Uganda	..	..	..	1	9	46	20	50	21	15	12
Cameroon	..	3	1	0	0	4	2	2	5	10	11
China	..	3	11	10	64	145	28	29	30	19	7
Ethiopia	2	2	5	13	1	7	21	4	6	1	6
India	0	0	0	0	0	2	0	1	0	2	6
Uzbekistan	0	0	0	0	1	1	2	2	0	2	6
Iran	1	4	..	9	1	8	5	3	7	11	6
Kenya	1	0	0	0	1	3	7	3	4	2	5
Nepal	..	..	..	1	2	8	78	275	12	2	5
Other countries	17	18	6	15	18	101	71	197	142	68	46
Total	**43**	**39**	**37**	**86**	**145**	**412**	**278**	**717**	**364**	**324**	**425**

Note: For details on definitions and sources, please refer to the metadata at the end of the tables.

StatLink http://dx.doi.org/10.1787/888932617531

Table B.3. **Inflows of asylum seekers by nationality**
LUXEMBOURG

	2000	2001	2002	2003	2004	2005	2006	2007	2008	2009	2010
Serbia	269	206	495	541	361	219	207	240	233	155	302
Iraq	3	8	34	14	9	8	16	14	29	37	95
Algeria	9	16	30	81	69	39	8	11	4	11	43
Somalia	0	10	4	10	18	27	7	1	10	8	29
Iran	12	0	13	31	59	41	31	16	18	24	23
Syria	2	0	0	1	1	0	0	0	0	1	19
Turkey	3	27	8	14	3	2	3	3	2	4	18
Albania	79	34	54	66	48	33	20	16	14	26	18
Russian Federation	25	66	68	60	66	54	43	13	13	26	16
Belarus	6	0	8	55	40	16	5	8	6	15	15
Afghanistan	14	9	0	2	6	3	8	3	4	13	15
Former Yug. Rep. of Macedonia	11	68	44	23	13	0	3	5	7	6	13
Eritrea	0	0	0	0	1	2	6	0	11	11	11
Bosnia and Herzegovina	52	87	77	59	35	36	17	24	31	35	11
Dem. Rep. of the Congo	9	18	26	21	22	19	20	1	6	3	10
Other countries	134	137	182	572	827	303	129	71	75	102	106
Total	**628**	**686**	**1 043**	**1 550**	**1 578**	**802**	**523**	**426**	**463**	**477**	**744**

Note: For details on definitions and sources, please refer to the metadata at the end of the tables.

StatLink http://dx.doi.org/10.1787/888932617531

Table B.3. Inflows of asylum seekers by nationality
MEXICO

	2000	2001	2002	2003	2004	2005	2006	2007	2008	2009	2010
India	0	32	6	1	10	27	5	2	3	37	271
El Salvador	1	4	3	5	46	31	31	45	51	119	159
Honduras	0	4	7	37	67	51	39	31	55	184	135
Colombia	20	58	65	38	40	40	52	57	41	62	82
Guatemala	22	35	10	62	23	29	20	15	18	39	59
Sri Lanka	22	28	5	0	13	16	8	0	3	11	51
Cuba	24	24	50	14	26	80	65	27	7	42	42
Haiti	0	1	1	8	11	20	17	41	61	65	39
Nigeria	2	1	10	6	0	2	1	13	1	8	23
Nepal	0	0	0	0	0	10	6	0	8	0	19
Dominican Republic	0	3	0	2	3	0	0	1	1	1	16
Nicaragua	6	6	2	3	11	14	4	7	9	29	15
Pakistan	1	7	0	0	0	0	0	0	1	2	11
United States	3	2	0	3	1	1	1	2	1	4	10
Ghana	0	0	4	0	0	0	2	1	3	3	9
Other countries	176	210	94	96	153	366	229	132	54	74	98
Total	**277**	**415**	**257**	**275**	**404**	**687**	**480**	**374**	**317**	**680**	**1 039**

Note: For details on definitions and sources, please refer to the metadata at the end of the tables.

StatLink http://dx.doi.org/10.1787/888932617531

Table B.3. Inflows of asylum seekers by nationality
NETHERLANDS

	2000	2001	2002	2003	2004	2005	2006	2007	2008	2009	2010
Somalia	2 110	1 098	533	451	792	1 315	1 462	1 874	3 842	5 889	3 372
Iraq	2 773	1 329	1 020	3 473	1 043	1 620	2 766	2 004	5 027	1 991	1 383
Afghanistan	5 055	3 614	1 067	492	688	902	932	143	395	1 281	1 364
Iran	2 543	1 519	663	555	450	557	921	187	322	502	785
Armenia	812	529	417	203	247	197	280	97	208	349	611
Georgia	291	298	216	116	73	213	156	66	64	412	587
Eritrea	260	213	152	123	148	204	175	153	236	475	392
Former Yug. Rep. of Macedonia	62	187	80	30	30	14	26	2	4	7	389
China	1 406	706	534	298	285	356	318	243	563	304	302
Guinea	1 394	1 467	475	199	116	105	116	102	154	235	230
Mongolia	267	254	239	127	66	118	110	96	103	237	227
Russian Federation	1 021	918	426	245	206	285	254	81	95	151	207
Sri Lanka	975	676	294	95	76	93	147	104	216	193	197
Nigeria	282	401	550	414	223	155	243	179	97	151	168
Sudan	1 426	869	512	293	255	339	320	57	53	116	166
Other countries	23 218	18 501	11 489	6 288	5 084	5 874	6 239	1 714	2 020	2 612	2 953
Total	**43 895**	**32 579**	**18 667**	**13 402**	**9 782**	**12 347**	**14 465**	**7 102**	**13 399**	**14 905**	**13 333**

Note: For details on definitions and sources, please refer to the metadata at the end of the tables.

StatLink http://dx.doi.org/10.1787/888932617531

Table B.3. Inflows of asylum seekers by nationality
NEW ZEALAND

	2000	2001	2002	2003	2004	2005	2006	2007	2008	2009	2010
Fiji	..	44	22	19	2	12	10	10	7	45	66
Iran	..	129	101	135	88	47	29	27	28	24	43
Sri Lanka	..	97	52	23	29	6	30	25	25	30	28
China	..	68	25	56	49	19	30	26	24	20	22
South Africa	..	13	8	10	8	3	2	2	3	9	20
Saudi Arabia	..	2	5	3	8	0	3	2	3	3	16
Czech Republic	..	39	2	10	29	28	12	4	10	23	14
Iraq	..	69	31	39	12	22	35	30	33	25	11
Pakistan	..	22	21	7	9	8	11	8	3	18	8
Bangladesh	..	32	19	29	22	23	16	18	9	7	6
Egypt	..	3	1	2	2	6	0	2	4	5	6
Nepal	..	17	3	3	7	19	5	1	6	0	6
Germany	..	..	..	..	..	..	..	..	..	..	6
Zimbabwe	..	98	85	73	20	8	5	8	8	8	6
Afghanistan	..	17	4	4	0	1	0	3	2	2	5
Other countries	1 551	951	618	428	294	146	88	79	89	117	77
Total	**1 551**	**1 601**	**997**	**841**	**579**	**348**	**276**	**245**	**254**	**336**	**340**

Note: For details on definitions and sources, please refer to the metadata at the end of the tables.

StatLink http://dx.doi.org/10.1787/888932617531

Table B.3. Inflows of asylum seekers by nationality
NORWAY

	2000	2001	2002	2003	2004	2005	2006	2007	2008	2009	2010
Eritrea	51	132	269	201	110	177	316	789	1 799	2 667	1 711
Somalia	910	1 080	1 534	1 623	958	667	632	187	1 293	1 901	1 397
Afghanistan	326	603	786	2 050	1 059	466	224	234	1 363	3 871	979
Russian Federation	471	1 318	1 719	1 923	937	545	548	863	1 078	867	628
Ethiopia	96	173	325	293	148	100	143	241	354	706	505
Iraq	766	1 056	1 624	971	412	671	1 002	1 227	3 137	1 214	460
Serbia	4 188	928	2 460	2 216	859	468	369	592	681	408	454
Iran	327	412	450	621	394	279	218	222	720	574	429
Nigeria	14	27	139	241	205	94	54	108	436	582	354
China	12	19	87	118	67	49	51	40	81	71	192
Sudan	31	47	94	67	33	45	36	37	118	251	181
Algeria	72	346	468	191	103	45	37	27	100	161	133
Syria	60	57	80	97	71	79	49	49	115	278	119
Uzbekistan	4	105	206	95	51	42	52	38	148	145	108
Pakistan	220	186	216	95	48	33	26	43	38	139	99
Other countries	3 294	8 293	7 023	5 157	2 490	1 642	1 563	1 831	2 970	3 391	2 315
Total	**10 842**	**14 782**	**17 480**	**15 959**	**7 945**	**5 402**	**5 320**	**6 528**	**14 431**	**17 226**	**10 064**

Note: For details on definitions and sources, please refer to the metadata at the end of the tables.

StatLink http://dx.doi.org/10.1787/888932617531

Table B.3. Inflows of asylum seekers by nationality
POLAND

	2000	2001	2002	2003	2004	2005	2006	2007	2008	2009	2010
Russian Federation	1 153	1 490	3 048	5 581	7 182	6 244	4 018	6 668	6 647	5 726	4 795
Georgia	71	92	39	30	47	47	31	12	54	4 213	1 082
Armenia	823	635	223	104	18	27	15	22	33	147	107
Viet Nam	161	197	48	25	16	23	27	40	57	67	47
Belarus	61	74	67	58	53	82	55	62	33	37	46
Ukraine	69	144	102	85	72	84	43	26	25	36	45
Kyrgyzstan	6	4	3	10	19	16	13	7	5	13	37
Iraq	30	108	137	75	6	15	16	22	66	21	27
Pakistan	30	31	55	151	211	69	46	25	15	19	27
Afghanistan	299	415	595	251	57	6	11	9	4	14	25
Mongolia	188	240	156	27	3	4	5	10	12	15	19
Nigeria	9	26	7	15	10	10	11	18	19	23	19
Turkey	9	9	6	22	29	11	10	10	17	11	19
Bangladesh	13	12	0	4	2	5	6	23	4	13	18
India	13	43	196	235	150	36	13	35	15	16	17
Other countries	1 654	986	471	248	205	181	110	216	197	216	204
Total	**4 589**	**4 506**	**5 153**	**6 921**	**8 080**	**6 860**	**4 430**	**7 205**	**7 203**	**10 587**	**6 534**

Note: For details on definitions and sources, please refer to the metadata at the end of the tables.

StatLink http://dx.doi.org/10.1787/888932617531

Table B.3. Inflows of asylum seekers by nationality
PORTUGAL

	2000	2001	2002	2003	2004	2005	2006	2007	2008	2009	2010
Guinea	8	4	2	1	0	1	6	14	8	18	43
Colombia	2	6	3	5	8	27	6	86	26	15	16
Angola	13	45	46	10	8	9	6	5	3	4	12
Guinea-Bissau	3	1	4	1	5	6	5	1	4	5	10
Dem. Rep. of the Congo	12	10	6	3	2	7	16	11	20	5	9
Nigeria	16	3	3	2	1	1	6	2	8	9	7
Sierra Leone	52	39	34	3	2	3	4	3	1	3	7
Iran	3	4	2	0	0	0	1	2	1	4	6
Russian Federation	19	5	13	3	13	7	6	6	0	2	5
Georgia	1	0	2	6	2	5	1	0	4	2	4
Sri Lanka	6	6	8	0	1	0	0	6	26	8	4
Pakistan	5	7	0	1	5	0	1	2	0	1	4
Cuba	0	9	11	4	5	5	3	3	0	1	2
Gambia	2	13	1	1	0	1	0	0	0	2	2
Former Yug. Rep. of Macedonia	2	4	0	0	0	0	0	3	0	0	2
Other countries	79	76	110	48	61	42	67	80	60	60	27
Total	**223**	**232**	**245**	**88**	**113**	**114**	**128**	**224**	**161**	**139**	**160**

Note: For details on definitions and sources, please refer to the metadata at the end of the tables.

StatLink http://dx.doi.org/10.1787/888932617531

Table B.3. **Inflows of asylum seekers by nationality**
RUSSIAN FEDERATION

	2000	2001	2002	2003	2004	2005	2006	2007	2008	2009	2010
Afghanistan	1 088	1 300	618	500	638	674	827	2 211	2 047	1 577	1 611
Georgia	30	40	23	46	24	27	138	586	2 684	3 580	1 353
Kyrgyzstan	10	11	1	3	0	12	0	5	3	7	291
Uzbekistan	33	34	34	38	72	102	37	63	90	136	164
Dem. People's Rep. of Korea	0	0	0	0	0	1	7	11	26	59	39
Tajikistan	12	22	18	12	23	3	7	43	48	29	37
Somalia	11	4	5	4	2	4	0	0	9	9	33
Egypt	..	..	..	..	..	..	..	..	..	..	31
Ukraine	4	6	0	4	6	4	10	20	19	10	23
Cambodia	0	5	1	0	0	0	0	0	14	5	23
West Bank and Gaza Strip	0	0	0	0	0	0	0	0	31	34	20
Azerbaijan	44	12	23	21	9	5	21	31	48	4	20
Dem. Rep. of the Congo	3	11	7	4	10	7	2	34	23	11	18
Iran	0	0	0	0	0	0	0	0	5	12	16
Iraq	59	73	35	13	18	20	13	36	61	37	16
Other countries	173	166	111	92	108	101	108	329	310	191	194
Total	**1 467**	**1 684**	**876**	**737**	**910**	**960**	**1 170**	**3 369**	**5 418**	**5 701**	**3 889**

Note: For details on definitions and sources, please refer to the metadata at the end of the tables.

StatLink http://dx.doi.org/10.1787/888932617531

Table B.3. **Inflows of asylum seekers by nationality**
SLOVAK REPUBLIC

	2000	2001	2002	2003	2004	2005	2006	2007	2008	2009	2010
Afghanistan	624	4 315	1 669	627	393	109	41	67	72	51	76
Russian Federation	14	84	618	2 653	2 413	1 037	463	307	100	72	66
Georgia	0	27	58	582	989	258	209	134	119	98	63
India	380	1 111	1 611	1 653	2 969	561	727	619	88	57	44
Moldova	1	16	266	587	826	309	385	208	113	73	42
Pakistan	161	176	168	307	799	196	182	648	109	168	34
Viet Nam	0	38	220	61	155	100	63	58	41	56	32
China	0	33	1 764	1 080	1 271	280	164	96	44	39	31
Somalia	3	129	199	114	12	16	3	9	0	13	23
Ukraine	5	8	47	73	64	45	32	36	32	13	20
Armenia	15	29	102	758	144	17	14	28	22	21	12
Iran	11	109	79	182	53	9	5	2	5	10	12
Serbia	38	27	50	65	51	29	15	7	15	21	10
Algeria	4	20	25	9	11	0	2	3	2	1	9
Iraq	115	990	1 245	475	116	35	206	131	42	13	9
Other countries	185	1 039	1 622	1 132	1 129	548	360	290	106	116	58
Total	**1 556**	**8 151**	**9 743**	**10 358**	**11 395**	**3 549**	**2 871**	**2 643**	**910**	**822**	**541**

Note: For details on definitions and sources, please refer to the metadata at the end of the tables.

StatLink http://dx.doi.org/10.1787/888932617531

Table B.3. Inflows of asylum seekers by nationality
SLOVENIA

	2000	2001	2002	2003	2004	2005	2006	2007	2008	2009	2010
Serbia	397	205	121	181	413	640	243	237	74	41	33
Turkey	1 119	379	73	192	188	231	62	38	72	12	32
Afghanistan	247	66	7	2	5	6	2	12	10	11	31
Bosnia and Herzegovina	48	22	29	48	123	303	44	22	13	41	27
Nigeria	3	1	7	2	1	2	1	4	7	9	11
Iran	5 924	272	61	88	7	4	3	2	11	9	11
West Bank and Gaza Strip	5	5	1	17	7	5	11	4	0	1	10
Iraq	447	214	133	190	28	15	6	4	0	3	10
Somalia	12	4	9	1	1	0	0	0	0	0	8
Russian Federation	34	5	23	15	15	11	7	9	3	5	8
Sudan	17	11	3	0	0	2	1	0	0	0	8
Croatia	8	3	0	5	3	3	0	3	3	11	8
Algeria	172	44	67	65	19	3	0	0	2	2	6
Eritrea	0	0	0	0	0	0	0	0	0	1	4
Senegal	0	0	0	0	0	1	0	0	0	0	4
Other countries	811	280	168	294	363	370	138	90	43	37	35
Total	**9 244**	**1 511**	**702**	**1 100**	**1 173**	**1 596**	**518**	**425**	**238**	**183**	**246**

Note: For details on definitions and sources, please refer to the metadata at the end of the tables.

StatLink http://dx.doi.org/10.1787/888932617531

Table B.3. Inflows of asylum seekers by nationality
SPAIN

	2000	2001	2002	2003	2004	2005	2006	2007	2008	2009	2010
Cuba	801	2 371	1 179	125	79	78	59	83	119	84	406
Nigeria	843	1 350	1 440	1 688	1 029	726	632	680	808	458	238
Algeria	326	231	350	682	991	406	230	247	152	181	176
Guinea	23	30	46	171	228	173	23	91	98	130	166
Cameroon	16	10	24	178	72	99	83	57	71	111	156
Colombia	1 361	2 532	1 105	577	760	1 655	2 239	2 497	752	255	123
Côte d'Ivoire	13	11	45	241	110	162	236	335	500	304	119
Morocco	36	23	41	30	20	55	281	263	121	73	114
West Bank and Gaza Strip	0	0	0	0	0	0	0	70	56	59	106
Dem. Rep. of the Congo	90	118	175	274	203	170	102	141	105	114	87
Pakistan	73	32	20	20	25	7	23	23	52	57	63
Gambia	2	4	9	48	108	67	34	64	44	52	63
Iran	79	30	18	21	34	23	20	27	64	45	63
Georgia	170	99	74	55	43	38	19	14	62	36	48
Russian Federation	394	350	172	153	84	138	110	88	66	55	44
Other countries	3 699	2 298	1 611	1 655	1 749	1 457	1 206	2 982	1 447	993	772
Total	**7 926**	**9 489**	**6 309**	**5 918**	**5 535**	**5 254**	**5 297**	**7 662**	**4 517**	**3 007**	**2 744**

Note: For details on definitions and sources, please refer to the metadata at the end of the tables.

StatLink http://dx.doi.org/10.1787/888932617531

Table B.3. Inflows of asylum seekers by nationality
SWEDEN

	2000	2001	2002	2003	2004	2005	2006	2007	2008	2009	2010
Serbia	2 055	3 102	5 852	5 305	4 022	2 944	2 001	2 601	2 040	1 842	7 949
Somalia	260	525	1 107	3 069	905	422	1 066	3 349	3 361	5 874	5 553
Afghanistan	374	593	527	811	903	435	594	609	784	1 694	2 393
Iraq	3 499	6 206	5 446	2 700	1 456	2 330	8 951	18 559	6 083	2 297	1 977
Eritrea	127	151	266	641	395	425	608	878	857	1 000	1 443
Iran	739	780	762	787	660	582	494	485	799	1 144	1 182
Russian Federation	590	841	1 496	1 361	1 288	1 057	755	788	933	1 058	988
Former Yug. Rep. of Macedonia	30	420	501	470	429	158	111	101	57	86	908
Mongolia	38	259	376	342	346	326	461	519	791	753	727
Kyrgyzstan	6	63	197	241	104	83	49	37	111	153	434
Syria	335	441	541	666	411	392	433	440	551	587	421
Kazakhstan	92	150	176	247	212	127	57	100	282	185	367
Belarus	231	327	722	901	519	372	432	365	361	347	338
Nigeria	28	58	164	452	429	154	104	136	176	321	321
Libya	26	114	456	435	419	451	318	420	646	367	311
Other countries	7 873	9 485	14 427	12 920	10 663	7 272	7 888	6 983	6 521	6 486	6 511
Total	**16 303**	**23 515**	**33 016**	**31 348**	**23 161**	**17 530**	**24 322**	**36 370**	**24 353**	**24 194**	**31 823**

Note: For details on definitions and sources, please refer to the metadata at the end of the tables.

StatLink http://dx.doi.org/10.1787/888932617531

Table B.3. Inflows of asylum seekers by nationality
SWITZERLAND

	2000	2001	2002	2003	2004	2005	2006	2007	2008	2009	2010
Eritrea	82	68	203	235	180	159	1 201	1 662	2 849	1 724	1 708
Nigeria	226	289	1 062	480	418	219	209	310	988	1 786	1 597
Serbia	3 613	3 425	3 692	2 921	1 777	1 506	1 228	989	1 327	1 285	1 376
Sri Lanka	898	684	459	340	251	233	328	618	1 262	1 415	892
Afghanistan	433	530	237	218	207	238	233	307	405	751	632
Georgia	179	273	687	756	731	397	287	199	481	638	531
Iraq	908	1 201	1 182	1 444	631	468	816	935	1 440	935	501
Turkey	1 431	1 960	1 940	1 652	1 154	723	693	621	519	559	462
Former Yug. Rep. of Macedonia	64	884	1 085	337	225	142	69	67	97	62	403
Syria	156	148	221	175	127	116	161	290	388	400	387
China	64	161	394	228	70	87	475	251	272	365	333
Russian Federation	254	456	507	534	505	375	426	195	208	452	315
Algeria	477	828	1 020	836	480	186	161	132	236	300	313
Somalia	470	369	387	471	592	485	273	395	2 014	753	302
Tunisia	173	146	163	154	121	102	80	90	74	204	291
Other countries	8 183	9 211	12 886	10 025	6 779	4 625	3 897	3 326	4 046	4 376	3 478
Total	**17 611**	**20 633**	**26 125**	**20 806**	**14 248**	**10 061**	**10 537**	**10 387**	**16 606**	**16 005**	**13 521**

Note: For details on definitions and sources, please refer to the metadata at the end of the tables.

StatLink http://dx.doi.org/10.1787/888932617531

Table B.3. Inflows of asylum seekers by nationality
TURKEY

	2000	2001	2002	2003	2004	2005	2006	2007	2008	2009	2010
Iraq	1 641	982	974	342	964	1 047	722	3 470	6 904	3 763	3 656
Iran	3 860	3 385	2 505	3 092	2 029	1 716	2 297	1 685	2 116	1 981	2 881
Afghanistan	81	431	47	77	341	364	261	705	2 642	1 009	1 248
Somalia	11	25	23	183	308	473	680	1 125	647	295	448
Kyrgyzstan	0	0	1	1	5	5	0	3	4	2	246
Uzbekistan	13	24	38	24	28	24	24	42	35	38	101
Dem. Rep. of the Congo	0	4	24	7	10	12	28	76	71	41	66
West Bank and Gaza Strip	13	9	24	6	23	29	51	157	..	..	64
Sudan	7	7	2	64	28	76	113	76	156	92	48
Pakistan	1	5	9	0	6	2	3	12	9	36	42
Ethiopia	12	7	5	48	18	32	58	54	17	23	39
Syria	3	10	14	7	16	10	7	21	20	46	37
Tajikistan	0	1	0	0	0	0	1	0	0	22	37
Eritrea	0	3	11	20	18	18	57	45	76	66	33
Myanmar	1	0	1	1	3	0	0	2	20	112	33
Other countries	42	148	117	80	111	113	251	173	264	308	247
Total	**5 685**	**5 041**	**3 795**	**3 952**	**3 908**	**3 921**	**4 553**	**7 646**	**12 981**	**7 834**	**9 226**

Note: For details on definitions and sources, please refer to the metadata at the end of the tables.

StatLink http://dx.doi.org/10.1787/888932617531

Table B.3. Inflows of asylum seekers by nationality
UNITED KINGDOM

	2000	2001	2002	2003	2004	2005	2006	2007	2008	2009	2010
Iran	5 610	3 420	3 370	3 495	3 990	3 505	2 685	2 510	2 595	2 145	2 225
Pakistan	3 165	2 860	3 780	3 145	3 030	2 290	1 850	1 765	2 075	2 100	2 150
Zimbabwe	1 010	2 140	8 695	4 020	2 520	1 390	2 145	2 300	4 475	7 610	1 955
Afghanistan	5 555	8 920	8 065	2 590	1 605	1 775	2 660	2 815	3 725	3 540	1 845
Sri Lanka	6 395	5 510	3 485	810	400	480	620	1 250	1 865	1 445	1 635
China	4 015	2 400	3 725	3 495	2 410	1 775	2 030	2 185	1 615	1 585	1 375
Nigeria	835	810	1 220	1 110	1 210	1 230	990	905	1 070	910	1 150
Eritrea	505	620	1 315	1 070	1 265	1 900	2 735	1 905	2 335	1 410	770
Somalia	5 020	6 420	9 425	7 195	3 295	2 105	2 175	1 960	1 575	1 105	680
Sudan	415	390	770	1 050	1 445	990	750	400	290	255	645
India	2 120	1 850	1 975	2 410	1 485	1 000	715	600	775	715	610
Bangladesh	795	510	825	820	550	465	495	590	510	495	500
Iraq	7 475	6 680	15 635	4 290	1 880	1 595	1 315	2 075	2 040	995	495
Viet Nam	180	400	880	1 175	790	400	95	185	235	470	465
Gambia	50	65	130	100	110	110	135	135	210	400	455
Other countries	37 155	28 015	39 815	23 265	14 635	9 805	6 940	6 300	5 925	5 495	5 690
Total	**80 300**	**71 010**	**103 110**	**60 040**	**40 620**	**30 815**	**28 335**	**27 880**	**31 315**	**30 675**	**22 645**

Note: For details on definitions and sources, please refer to the metadata at the end of the tables.

StatLink http://dx.doi.org/10.1787/888932617531

STATISTICAL ANNEX

Table B.3. **Inflows of asylum seekers by nationality**
UNITED STATES

	2000	2001	2002	2003	2004	2005	2006	2007	2008	2009	2010
China	5 541	8 008	10 237	4 906	5 627	7 623	9 362	8 781	9 825	10 725	12 510
Mexico	3 669	8 747	8 775	3 955	1 763	1 581	1 673	2 551	2 713	2 295	3 879
El Salvador	1 736	1 264	640	376	1 423	1 755	2 393	3 455	2 789	2 366	2 685
Guatemala	890	1 131	1 193	2 236	1 569	1 411	1 515	2 388	1 853	1 740	2 171
Haiti	4 257	4 938	3 643	3 316	5 107	5 299	5 135	3 079	2 078	1 649	1 223
Ethiopia	1 445	1 467	1 287	890	1 118	807	1 168	1 124	1 168	1 249	1 193
Nepal	28	53	172	314	321	415	494	532	680	1 068	1 054
Honduras	43	58	59	50	603	781	986	1 096	893	850	1 030
Russian Federation	856	844	837	761	783	669	638	615	677	806	828
India	1 289	1 894	1 708	1 241	866	620	602	576	734	751	755
Colombia	2 631	7 144	7 950	4 661	3 215	2 064	1 810	1 399	910	650	623
Eritrea	253	220	246	196	213	224	282	329	420	559	595
Venezuela	0	96	259	899	1 509	1 226	954	754	709	430	584
Somalia	2 364	1 805	538	168	212	155	210	177	299	344	556
Pakistan	338	410	567	513	859	551	512	433	491	491	538
Other countries	15 527	21 353	20 293	18 856	19 784	14 059	13 367	13 160	13 123	11 710	12 747
Total	**40 867**	**59 432**	**58 404**	**43 338**	**44 972**	**39 240**	**41 101**	**40 449**	**39 362**	**37 683**	**42 971**

Note: For details on definitions and sources, please refer to the metadata at the end of the tables.

StatLink http://dx.doi.org/10.1787/888932617531

Metadata related to Tables A.3 and B.3. **Inflows of asylum seekers**

Sources for all countries: Governments, compiled by the United Nations High Commissioner for Refugees, Population Data Unit. www.unhcr.org/statistics.

Totals in Table A.3 might differ from the tables by nationality (Tables B.3) because the former totals get revised retroactively while the origin breakdown does not. Data for Table A.3 generally refer to first instance/new applications only and exclude repeat/review/appeal applications while data by origin (Tables B.3) may include some repeat/review/appeal applications.

Comments on countries of asylum:
France: From 2003 on, data include unaccompanied minors.
United Kingdom: Prior to 2003, data by nationality refer to the number of cases, and not persons. All figures are rounded to the nearest multiple of 5.
United States: Data for 2004-10 are a combination of the United States Citizenship and Immigration Service (USCIS – number of cases) affirmative asylum applications, and of the Executive Office for Immigration Review (EOIR – number of persons) defensive asylum applications, if the person is under threat of removal.

Comments on countries of origin:
Serbia: Data may include asylum-seekers from Serbia, Montenegro, Serbia and Montenegro, and/or Former Yugoslavia.

Stocks of foreign and foreign-born populations

Who is an immigrant?

There are major differences in how immigrants are defined across OECD countries. Some countries have traditionally focused on producing data on foreign residents (European countries, Japan and Korea) whilst others refer to the foreign-born (settlement countries, i.e. Australia, Canada, New Zealand and the United States). This difference in focus relates in part to the nature and history of immigration systems and legislation on citizenship and naturalisation.

The foreign-born population can be viewed as representing first-generation migrants, and may consist of both foreign and national citizens. The size and composition of the foreign-born population is influenced by the history of migration flows and mortality amongst the foreign-born. For example, where inflows have been declining over time, the stock of the foreign-born will tend to age and represent an increasingly established community.

The concept of foreign population may include persons born abroad who retained the nationality of their country of origin but also second and third generations born in the host country. The characteristics of the population of foreign nationals depend on a number of factors: the history of migration flows, natural increase in the foreign population and naturalisations. Both the nature of legislation on citizenship and the incentives to naturalise play a role in determining the extent to which native-born persons may or may not be foreign nationals.

Sources for and problems in measuring the immigrant population

Four types of sources are used: population registers, residence permits, labour force surveys and censuses. In countries which have a population register and in those which use residence permit data, stocks and flows of immigrants are most often calculated using the same source. There are exceptions, however, with some countries using census or labour force survey data to estimate the stock of the immigrant population. In studying stocks and flows, the same problems are encountered whether population register or permit data are used (in particular, the risk of underestimation when minors are registered on the permit of one of the parents or if the migrants are not required to have permits because of a free movement agreement). To this must be added the difficulty of purging the files regularly to remove the records of persons who have left the country.

Census data enable comprehensive, albeit infrequent analysis of the stock of immigrants (censuses are generally conducted every five to ten years). In addition, many labour force surveys now include questions about nationality and place of birth, thus providing a source of annual stock data. The OECD produces estimates of stocks for some countries

Some care has to be taken with detailed breakdowns of the immigrant population from survey data since sample sizes can be small. Both census and survey data may underestimate the number of immigrants, because they can be missed in the census or because they do not live in private households (labour force surveys may not cover those living in collective dwelling such as reception centres and hostels for immigrants). Both these sources may cover a portion of the unauthorised population, which is by definition excluded from population registers and residence permit systems.

Table A.4. Stocks of foreign-born population in OECD countries and the Russian Federation

Thousands and percentages

	2000	2001	2002	2003	2004	2005	2006	2007	2008	2009	2010
Australia	4 412.2	4 482.3	4 585.0	4 694.4	4 796.8	4 927.2	5 090.4	5 295.4	5 545.2	5 804.3	5 994.1
% of total population	23.0	23.1	23.3	23.6	23.8	24.2	24.6	25.1	25.8	26.5	26.8
Austria	843.0	1 112.1	1 137.4	1 141.2	1 154.8	1 195.2	1 215.7	1 246.3	1 277.1	1 292.9	1 315.5
% of total population	10.4	13.8	14.1	14.1	14.1	14.5	14.7	15.0	15.3	15.5	15.7
Belgium	1 058.8	1 112.2	1 151.8	1 185.2	1 220.1	1 268.9	1 319.3	1 380.3	1 444.3	1 504.3	..
% of total population	10.3	10.8	11.1	11.4	11.7	12.1	12.5	13.0	13.5	13.9	..
Canada	5 327.0	5 448.5	5 600.7	5 735.9	5 872.3	6 026.9	6 187.0	6 331.7	6 471.9	6 617.6	6 777.6
% of total population	17.4	17.6	17.9	18.1	18.4	18.7	19.0	19.2	19.4	19.6	19.9
Chile	..	..	184.5	223.0	235.5	247.4	258.8	290.9	317.1	352.3	369.4
% of total population	..	..	1.2	1.4	1.5	1.5	1.6	1.8	1.9	2.1	2.2
Czech Republic	434.0	448.5	471.9	482.2	499.0	523.4	566.3	636.1	679.6	672.0	661.2
% of total population	4.2	4.4	4.6	4.7	4.9	5.1	5.5	6.2	6.5	6.4	6.3
Denmark	308.7	321.8	331.5	337.8	343.4	350.4	360.9	378.7	401.8	414.4	428.9
% of total population	5.8	6.0	6.2	6.3	6.4	6.5	6.6	6.9	7.3	7.5	7.7
Estonia	252.7	249.5	245.3	242.5	239.3	235.5	228.6	226.5	224.3	221.9	217.9
% of total population	18.4	18.3	18.0	17.9	17.7	17.5	17.0	16.9	16.7	16.6	16.3
Finland	136.2	145.1	152.1	158.9	166.4	176.6	187.9	202.5	218.6	233.2	248.1
% of total population	2.6	2.8	2.9	3.0	3.2	3.4	3.6	3.8	4.1	4.4	4.6
France	4 379.6	4 467.7	4 572.8	4 689.7	4 811.2	4 926.4	5 040.5	5 147.8	5 342.3	..	..
% of total population	7.4	7.5	7.6	7.8	7.9	8.1	8.2	8.3	8.6	..	..
Germany	10 256.1	..	..	..	..	10 399.0	10 431.0	10 534.0	10 623.0	10 601.0	10 591.0
% of total population	12.5	..	..	..	..	12.6	12.7	12.8	12.9	12.9	13.0
Greece	..	1 122.9	..	..	..	..	..	..	..	..	..
% of total population	..	10.3	..	..	..	..	..	..	..	..	..
Hungary	294.6	300.1	302.8	307.8	319.0	331.5	344.6	381.8	394.2	407.3	451.4
% of total population	2.9	2.9	3.0	3.0	3.2	3.3	3.4	3.8	3.9	4.1	4.5
Iceland	16.9	18.3	19.1	19.5	20.7	24.7	30.4	35.9	37.6	35.1	34.7
% of total population	6.0	6.4	6.6	6.8	7.1	8.3	10.0	11.5	11.8	11.0	10.9
Ireland	328.7	356.0	390.0	426.5	461.8	520.8	601.7	682.0	739.2	766.8	772.5
% of total population	8.7	9.2	9.9	10.7	11.4	12.6	14.2	15.7	16.7	17.2	17.3
Israel	1 957.8	1 978.1	1 983.2	1 974.8	1 960.8	1 947.6	1 930.0	1 916.2	1 899.4	1 877.7	1 869.0
% of total population	32.2	31.8	31.3	30.6	29.8	29.1	28.3	27.6	26.9	26.2	24.5
Italy	..	2 240.0	..	..	..	..	..	..	4 375.2	4 798.7	..
% of total population	..	3.9	..	..	..	..	..	..	7.4	8.0	..
Luxembourg	145.0	144.8	147.0	152.0	155.9	161.6	166.6	172.6	180.3	182.2	188.8
% of total population	33.2	32.8	32.9	33.8	34.3	35.0	35.5	36.2	37.3	36.9	37.6
Mexico	492.6	..	..	..	..	584.5	610.1	699.3	733.7	850.1	961.1
% of total population	0.5	..	..	..	..	0.6	0.6	0.7	0.7	0.8	0.9
Netherlands	1 615.4	1 674.6	1 714.2	1 731.8	1 736.1	1 734.7	1 732.4	1 751.0	1 793.7	1 832.5	1 868.7
% of total population	10.1	10.4	10.6	10.7	10.7	10.6	10.6	10.7	10.9	11.1	11.2
New Zealand	663.0	698.6	737.1	770.5	796.7	840.6	879.5	915.0	950.0	981.3	1 013.0
% of total population	17.2	18.0	18.7	19.1	19.5	20.3	21.0	21.6	22.3	22.7	23.2
Norway	305.0	315.1	333.9	347.3	361.1	380.4	405.1	445.4	488.8	526.8	569.1
% of total population	6.8	7.0	7.4	7.6	7.9	8.2	8.7	9.5	10.3	10.9	11.6
Poland	..	775.3	776.2	..	..	..	..	..	..	..	..
% of total population	..	2.0	2.0	..	..	..	..	..	..	..	..
Portugal	522.6	651.5	699.1	705.0	714.0	661.0	651.6	648.0	648.3	672.6	669.1
% of total population	5.1	6.3	6.7	6.8	6.8	6.3	6.2	6.1	6.1	6.3	6.3

Table A.4. **Stocks of foreign-born population in OECD countries and the Russian Federation** (cont.)

Thousands and percentages

	2000	2001	2002	2003	2004	2005	2006	2007	2008	2009	2010
Russian Federation	..	..	11 976.8	..	..	..	..	..	..	..	..
% of total population	..	..	8.2	..	..	..	..	..	..	..	..
Slovak Republic	..	119.1	..	..	207.6	..	..	..	..	..	..
% of total population	..	2.2	..	..	3.9	..	..	..	..	..	..
Slovenia	..	..	170.0	..	..	..	..	..	..	..	228.6
% of total population	..	..	8.5	..	..	..	..	..	..	..	11.2
Spain	1 969.3	2 594.1	3 302.4	3 693.8	4 391.5	4 837.6	5 250.0	6 044.5	6 466.3	6 604.2	6 659.9
% of total population	4.9	6.4	8.0	8.8	10.3	11.1	11.9	13.5	14.2	14.3	14.5
Sweden	1 003.8	1 028.0	1 053.5	1 078.1	1 100.3	1 125.8	1 175.2	1 227.8	1 281.6	1 338.0	1 384.9
% of total population	11.3	11.6	11.8	12.0	12.2	12.5	12.9	13.4	13.9	14.4	14.8
Switzerland	*1 570.8*	*1 613.8*	*1 658.7*	*1 697.8*	*1 737.7*	*1 772.8*	*1 811.2*	*1 882.6*	*1 974.2*	*2 037.5*	2 075.2
% of total population	*21.9*	*22.3*	*22.8*	*23.1*	*23.5*	*23.8*	*24.2*	*24.9*	*25.8*	*26.3*	26.6
Turkey	1 278.7	..	..	..	..	..	..	..	..	..	..
% of total population	2.0	..	..	..	..	..	..	..	..	..	..
United Kingdom	*4 666.0*	4 865.0	*5 000.0*	*5 143.0*	*5 338.0*	*5 557.0*	5 757.0	6 192.0	6 633.0	6 899.0	7 056.0
% of total population	*7.9*	8.2	*8.4*	*8.6*	*8.9*	*9.4*	9.6	10.3	11.0	11.3	11.5
United States	30 273.3	31 548.1	33 096.2	33 667.7	34 257.7	35 769.6	37 469.4	38 048.5	38 016.1	38 452.8	39 916.9
% of total population	10.7	11.1	11.5	11.6	11.7	12.1	12.6	12.6	12.5	12.5	12.9

Notes: Estimates are in italic. For details on definitions and sources, refer to the metadata at the end of Tables B.4.
Information on data for Israel: http://dx.doi.org/10.1787/888932315602.

StatLink http://dx.doi.org/10.1787/888932617455

Table B.4. Stock of foreign-born population by country of birth
Thousands
AUSTRALIA

	2000	2001	2002	2003	2004	2005	2006	2007	2008	2009	2010	Of which: Women 2010 (%)
United Kingdom	1 132.6	1 126.9	1 120.0	1 118.5	1 120.8	1 125.7	1 141.0	1 157.9	1 175.4	1 189.5	1 192.9	49
New Zealand	369.1	394.1	407.4	414.9	419.9	430.0	445.1	469.0	499.9	525.9	544.2	49
China	148.0	157.0	174.2	192.2	210.6	233.8	259.2	285.8	321.0	353.3	379.8	54
India	95.7	103.6	114.5	126.4	140.6	157.9	180.1	216.1	264.5	323.2	340.6	42
Italy	242.7	238.5	236.5	234.2	231.9	229.7	227.3	224.2	220.5	217.3	216.3	48
Viet Nam	169.6	169.5	172.4	176.3	178.8	181.5	185.5	190.3	197.3	206.0	210.8	53
Philippines	110.1	112.2	116.3	121.3	126.6	132.7	140.0	148.9	160.2	171.8	177.4	63
South Africa	80.7	87.0	95.4	101.8	108.9	114.7	120.3	127.9	138.0	150.1	155.7	50
Malaysia	85.3	87.2	90.0	94.0	98.7	102.6	107.1	112.9	119.9	126.2	135.6	53
Germany	118.1	117.5	118.7	120.0	121.3	122.6	124.4	125.6	126.2	126.2	128.6	52
Greece	134.5	132.5	132.7	133.0	133.1	133.3	133.4	131.9	130.1	128.5	127.2	51
Korea	38.8	41.8	44.6	47.7	50.8	55.1	60.3	69.5	79.1	87.1	100.3	52
Sri Lanka	56.3	58.6	61.5	64.0	65.7	68.5	71.7	76.6	82.9	89.1	92.3	48
Lebanon	79.1	80.0	81.2	83.0	84.0	85.3	86.5	88.1	89.3	89.8	90.4	47
Hong Kong, China	76.7	75.2	76.8	78.8	79.9	81.5	83.2	84.1	85.2	86.3	90.3	52
Other countries	1 474.9	1 500.7	1 542.9	1 588.3	1 625.3	1 672.3	1 725.2	1 786.5	1 855.8	1 934.1	2 011.9	
Total	**4 412.2**	**4 482.2**	**4 584.9**	**4 694.3**	**4 796.8**	**4 927.2**	**5 090.4**	**5 295.4**	**5 545.2**	**5 804.3**	**5 994.1**	**50**

Note: For details on definitions and sources, please refer to the metadata at the end of the tables.
StatLink http://dx.doi.org/10.1787/888932617550

Table B.4. Stock of foreign-born population by country of birth
Thousands
AUSTRIA

	2000	2001	2002	2003	2004	2005	2006	2007	2008	2009	2010	Of which: Women 2010 (%)
Germany	126.0	140.1	142.7	148.1	155.5	163.0	169.8	178.4	187.0	192.5	198.5	54
Serbia	..	165.7	170.0	175.2	181.5	187.7	188.5	188.2	188.3	187.9	188.6	52
Turkey	110.1	126.8	135.2	142.7	147.9	152.5	154.1	155.9	157.8	159.0	159.9	47
Bosnia and Herzegovina	115.4	119.8	122.7	125.8	128.8	131.2	132.1	132.9	133.6	133.5	134.1	50
Romania	31.2	39.1	42.0	44.7	46.6	47.8	48.2	53.4	57.6	60.5	65.2	56
Poland	42.3	41.3	42.0	43.1	47.8	51.8	54.2	56.0	56.9	56.8	57.6	54
Czech Republic	..	56.7	55.4	54.6	54.2	52.9	51.5	50.2	48.9	47.3	45.9	62
Hungary	18.0	30.7	31.2	31.6	32.5	33.2	33.9	35.3	36.9	38.3	40.1	55
Croatia	54.7	33.2	34.0	34.5	35.0	35.2	35.1	35.0	34.8	34.4	34.0	53
Russian Federation	..	7.8	9.1	12.1	18.0	21.2	22.8	24.2	26.0	26.6	27.3	57
Italy	23.2	25.9	25.6	25.8	25.9	25.7	25.5	25.5	25.6	25.6	25.9	49
Slovak Republic	..	12.8	13.9	14.9	16.8	18.3	19.3	20.5	22.5	23.4	24.2	65
Former Yug. Rep. of Macedonia	..	13.0	14.3	15.4	16.4	17.3	17.6	18.1	18.6	18.9	19.4	46
Slovenia	15.9	16.8	16.6	16.4	16.4	16.2	16.0	15.8	15.7	15.4	15.3	56
Bulgaria	..	7.6	8.5	9.3	9.9	10.2	10.3	11.5	12.7	13.5	14.8	57
Other countries	306.2	274.5	274.2	247.1	221.5	230.9	236.7	245.5	254.4	259.3	264.6	
Total	**843.0**	**1 112.1**	**1 137.4**	**1 141.2**	**1 154.8**	**1 195.2**	**1 215.7**	**1 246.3**	**1 277.1**	**1 292.9**	**1 315.5**	**52**

Note: For details on definitions and sources, please refer to the metadata at the end of the tables.
StatLink http://dx.doi.org/10.1787/888932617550

Table B.4. **Stock of foreign-born population by country of birth**
Thousands
BELGIUM

	2000	2001	2002	2003	2004	2005	2006	2007	2008	2009	2010	Of which: Women 2007 (%)
Morocco	107.3	118.8	126.5	134.2	141.3	147.9	155.1	162.6	170.2	178.9	..	47
France	150.3	151.9	152.5	153.0	154.2	156.2	159.3	164.6	169.0	171.3	..	56
Netherlands	92.3	97.8	101.3	104.4	107.7	111.6	115.8	120.4	123.8	124.8	..	51
Italy	135.2	132.2	130.5	128.7	126.7	125.1	123.6	122.2	121.4	120.5	..	49
Turkey	66.5	71.6	78.6	78.6	81.0	83.8	86.4	89.0	91.4	93.6	..	48
Germany	83.7	83.4	80.1	83.3	83.5	83.6	83.6	83.8	84.2	84.1	..	55
Democratic Republic of the Congo	46.8	50.8	52.7	53.8	66.8	68.5	70.5	72.4	74.2	76.2	..	53
Poland	18.4	20.4	21.9	23.0	25.2	29.0	33.7	40.5	45.5	51.7	..	56
Russian Federation	..	..	..	14.6	17.6	25.1	29.8	30.8	34.5	39.0	..	62
Spain	37.3	37.0	36.6	36.2	35.7	35.5	35.4	35.5	36.1	37.0	..	55
Serbia	21.5	20.9	23.2	25.8	27.6	29.8	31.8	34.2	34.4	36.6	..	49
Romania	6.2	7.7	8.7	9.5	10.6	12.6	15.3	20.4	26.2	30.6	..	52
Portugal	21.2	21.3	21.7	22.3	22.8	23.3	24.0	25.0	26.5	27.5	..	50
United Kingdom	26.1	26.1	25.9	25.6	25.3	24.9	24.2	24.1	24.2	23.8	..	49
Algeria	14.0	15.1	16.0	17.0	17.7	18.5	19.4	20.3	21.2	22.4	..	44
Other countries	232.0	257.2	275.6	275.3	276.2	293.6	311.4	334.7	361.5	386.3	..	
Total	**1 058.8**	**1 112.2**	**1 151.8**	**1 185.5**	**1 220.1**	**1 268.9**	**1 319.3**	**1 380.3**	**1 444.3**	**1 504.3**	..	**52**

Note: For details on definitions and sources, please refer to the metadata at the end of the tables.

StatLink http://dx.doi.org/10.1787/888932617550

Table B.4. **Stock of foreign-born population by country of birth**
Thousands
CANADA

	2000	2001	2002	2003	2004	2005	2006	2007	2008	2009	2010	Of which: Women 2006 (%)
United Kingdom	..	606.0	..	..	..	..	579.6	..	..	..	..	53
China	..	332.8	..	..	..	..	466.9	..	..	..	..	54
India	..	314.7	..	..	..	..	443.7	..	..	..	..	50
Philippines	..	232.7	..	..	..	..	303.2	..	..	..	..	59
Italy	..	315.5	..	..	..	..	296.9	..	..	..	..	49
United States	..	237.9	..	..	..	..	250.5	..	..	..	..	57
Hong Kong, China	..	235.6	..	..	..	..	215.4	..	..	..	..	52
Germany	..	174.1	..	..	..	..	171.4	..	..	..	..	52
Poland	..	180.4	..	..	..	..	170.5	..	..	..	..	54
Viet Nam	..	148.4	..	..	..	..	160.2	..	..	..	..	52
Portugal	..	153.5	..	..	..	..	150.4	..	..	..	..	51
Pakistan	..	79.3	..	..	..	..	133.3	..	..	..	..	48
Jamaica	..	120.2	..	..	..	..	123.4	..	..	..	..	58
Netherlands	..	117.7	..	..	..	..	112.0	..	..	..	..	49
Sri Lanka	..	87.3	..	..	..	..	105.7	..	..	..	..	50
Other countries	..	2 112.4	..	..	..	..	2 503.9	..	..	..	..	
Total	..	**5 448.5**	..	..	..	..	**6 187.0**	..	..	..	..	**52**

Note: For details on definitions and sources, please refer to the metadata at the end of the tables.

StatLink http://dx.doi.org/10.1787/888932617550

Table B.4. **Stock of foreign-born population by country of birth**
Thousands
CHILE

	2000	2001	2002	2003	2004	2005	2006	2007	2008	2009	2010	Of which: Women 2010 (%)
Peru	..	..	37.9	49.1	53.7	58.4	66.1	83.4	107.6	130.9	138.5	..
Argentina	..	..	48.2	50.0	51.9	53.8	57.7	59.7	59.2	60.6	61.9	..
Bolivia	..	..	10.9	12.4	13.0	13.5	14.7	20.2	22.2	24.1	25.1	..
Ecuador	..	..	9.4	9.9	10.9	11.8	13.3	14.7	17.5	19.1	20.0	..
Colombia	..	..	4.1	4.5	5.5	6.6	7.7	9.2	10.9	12.9	14.4	..
Spain	..	..	9.1	..	..	..	..	..	..	11.0	11.3	..
Brazil	..	..	6.9	..	..	..	..	..	..	9.6	10.1	..
United States	..	..	7.8	..	..	..	..	..	..	9.7	10.0	..
Germany	..	..	5.5	..	..	..	..	..	..	6.5	6.7	..
China	..	..	1.7	..	..	..	..	..	..	4.6	5.2	..
Other countries	..	..	43.2	97.1	100.5	103.3	99.3	103.8	99.8	63.2	66.2	..
Total	..	..	**184.5**	**223.0**	**235.5**	**247.4**	**258.8**	**290.9**	**317.1**	**352.3**	**369.4**	..

Note: For details on definitions and sources, please refer to the metadata at the end of the tables.

StatLink http://dx.doi.org/10.1787/888932617550

Table B.4. **Stock of foreign-born population by country of birth**
Thousands
CZECH REPUBLIC

	2000	2001	2002	2003	2004	2005	2006	2007	2008	2009	2010	Of which: Women 2010 (%)
Slovak Republic	..	285.4	..	..	..	..	..	..	..	..	..	..
Ukraine	..	33.3	..	..	..	..	..	..	..	..	..	..
Poland	..	24.7	..	..	..	..	..	..	..	..	..	..
Viet Nam	..	14.6	..	..	..	..	..	..	..	..	..	..
Russian Federation	..	13.3	..	..	..	..	..	..	..	..	..	..
Romania	..	12.0	..	..	..	..	..	..	..	..	..	..
Germany	..	9.6	..	..	..	..	..	..	..	..	..	..
Austria	..	7.4	..	..	..	..	..	..	..	..	..	..
Hungary	..	6.2	..	..	..	..	..	..	..	..	..	..
Former Yugoslavia	..	4.8	..	..	..	..	..	..	..	..	..	..
Bulgaria	..	4.7	..	..	..	..	..	..	..	..	..	..
France	..	3.6	..	..	..	..	..	..	..	..	..	..
United States	..	2.2	..	..	..	..	..	..	..	..	..	..
Kazakhstan	..	1.8	..	..	..	..	..	..	..	..	..	..
Greece	..	1.8	..	..	..	..	..	..	..	..	..	..
Other countries	..	23.0	..	..	..	..	..	..	..	..	..	..
Total	..	**448.5**	..	..	..	..	..	..	..	..	..	..

Note: For details on definitions and sources, please refer to the metadata at the end of the tables.

StatLink http://dx.doi.org/10.1787/888932617550

Table B.4. **Stock of foreign-born population by country of birth**
Thousands
DENMARK

	2000	2001	2002	2003	2004	2005	2006	2007	2008	2009	2010	Of which: Women 2010 (%)
Turkey	29.7	30.4	30.8	30.9	30.9	31.0	31.1	31.4	31.8	32.3	32.5	48
Germany	22.7	22.6	22.5	22.5	22.6	23.0	23.9	25.8	27.8	28.2	28.5	52
Poland	10.4	10.6	10.7	10.9	11.3	12.4	14.7	18.5	24.4	25.4	26.6	51
Iraq	15.1	18.0	19.7	20.7	20.8	20.7	20.7	21.2	21.3	21.3	21.3	45
Bosnia and Herzegovina	18.0	18.1	18.1	18.2	17.9	17.7	17.6	18.0	18.0	17.9	17.8	50
Norway	13.4	13.4	13.6	13.9	14.0	14.1	14.2	14.3	14.5	14.7	14.7	65
Sweden	12.6	12.5	12.3	12.2	12.3	12.5	12.7	12.9	13.2	13.2	13.2	63
Iran	11.3	11.4	11.6	11.7	11.7	11.7	11.8	11.9	11.9	12.1	12.5	41
Former Yugoslavia	12.5	12.5	12.4	12.3	11.9	11.7	11.5	11.5	11.2	12.6	12.3	50
Lebanon	11.9	12.0	12.1	12.1	12.1	12.0	12.0	12.0	12.0	12.0	12.1	45
United Kingdom	10.5	10.6	10.6	10.7	10.7	10.8	11.1	11.4	11.8	11.8	12.1	35
Pakistan	10.3	10.5	10.6	10.7	10.6	10.6	10.5	10.6	10.8	11.2	11.7	45
Afghanistan	4.3	7.2	8.4	9.0	9.4	9.5	9.6	9.6	9.7	10.0	10.6	45
Somalia	11.8	12.2	12.3	11.8	11.2	10.7	10.4	10.4	10.2	10.1	10.1	47
Thailand	5.1	5.7	6.1	6.3	6.6	7.0	7.3	7.8	8.3	8.8	9.5	85
Other countries	108.9	114.2	119.6	124.1	129.4	135.1	141.9	151.4	164.7	172.7	183.7	
Total	**308.7**	**321.8**	**331.5**	**337.8**	**343.4**	**350.4**	**360.9**	**378.7**	**401.8**	**414.4**	**428.9**	**51**

Note: For details on definitions and sources, please refer to the metadata at the end of the tables.

StatLink http://dx.doi.org/10.1787/888932617550

Table B.4. **Stock of foreign-born population by country of birth**
Thousands
FINLAND

	2000	2001	2002	2003	2004	2005	2006	2007	2008	2009	2010	Of which: Women 2010 (%)
Former USSR	32.9	34.8	36.3	37.3	38.5	40.2	41.9	43.8	45.8	47.3	48.7	63
Sweden	28.0	28.3	28.6	28.9	29.2	29.5	29.8	30.2	30.6	31.0	31.2	48
Estonia	7.8	8.7	9.5	10.3	11.2	12.6	14.5	16.7	19.2	21.8	25.0	52
Somalia	4.1	4.3	4.6	4.7	4.8	5.1	5.3	5.8	6.4	7.1	8.1	47
Russian Federation	2.6	3.1	3.5	3.9	4.3	4.7	5.3	5.9	6.7	7.3	8.0	56
Iraq	3.2	3.5	3.8	4.0	4.3	4.4	4.4	4.8	5.3	6.2	7.2	39
China	2.1	2.4	2.7	3.1	3.5	4.1	4.6	5.3	6.0	6.6	7.0	58
Thailand	1.8	2.1	2.4	2.8	3.1	3.6	4.1	4.8	5.4	6.1	6.7	79
Former Yugoslavia	4.2	4.5	4.6	4.7	4.9	5.0	5.2	5.5	5.8	6.1	6.3	44
Germany	3.6	3.8	3.9	4.1	4.3	4.6	4.9	5.3	5.6	5.8	5.9	43
Turkey	2.2	2.4	2.6	2.9	3.1	3.4	3.7	4.1	4.5	4.9	5.1	27
United Kingdom	2.7	2.9	3.1	3.2	3.4	3.5	3.7	4.0	4.2	4.4	4.5	28
Viet Nam	2.9	2.9	3.0	3.0	3.1	3.3	3.4	3.7	4.0	4.3	4.5	55
Iran	2.1	2.3	2.5	2.7	3.0	3.2	3.4	3.6	3.8	3.9	4.1	42
United States	2.9	3.0	3.1	3.1	3.1	3.2	3.5	3.7	3.8	3.9	4.1	43
Other countries	33.1	36.1	37.9	40.3	42.7	46.3	50.1	55.5	61.7	66.6	71.7	
Total	**136.2**	**145.1**	**152.1**	**158.9**	**166.4**	**176.6**	**187.9**	**202.5**	**218.6**	**233.2**	**248.1**	**49**

Note: For details on definitions and sources, please refer to the metadata at the end of the tables.

StatLink http://dx.doi.org/10.1787/888932617550

STATISTICAL ANNEX

Table B.4. Stock of foreign-born population by country of birth
Thousands
FRANCE

	2000	2001	2002	2003	2004	2005	2006	2007	2008	2009	2010	Of which: Women 2008 (%)
Algeria	..	..	..	..	..	..	1 356.6	1 359.3	1 366.5	..	..	50
Morocco	..	..	..	..	..	..	846.9	859.0	870.9	..	..	48
Portugal	..	..	..	..	..	..	592.0	598.0	604.7	..	..	49
Tunisia	..	..	..	..	..	..	365.8	368.5	370.6	..	..	46
Italy	..	..	..	..	..	..	372.3	364.4	357.0	..	..	53
Spain	..	..	..	..	..	..	307.0	300.0	295.9	..	..	57
Turkey	..	..	..	..	..	..	237.4	243.4	246.8	..	..	46
Germany	..	..	..	..	..	..	225.6	224.6	223.5	..	..	58
Belgium	..	..	..	..	..	..	139.0	140.5	143.6	..	..	54
Viet Nam	..	..	..	..	..	..	119.6	119.8	120.1	..	..	54
Madagascar	..	..	..	..	..	..	108.5	110.7	112.5	..	..	57
Senegal	..	..	..	..	..	..	103.3	106.1	108.3	..	..	45
Poland	..	..	..	..	..	..	101.6	101.7	102.6	..	..	63
Switzerland	..	..	..	..	..	..	85.6	87.4	89.1	..	..	54
China	..	..	..	..	..	..	75.4	80.3	85.3	..	..	53
Other countries	..	..	..	..	..	..	1 873.5	1 953.6	2 031.9	..	..	..
Total	..	..	..	..	..	..	**6 910.1**	**7 017.2**	**7 129.3**	..	**7 196.5**	**50**

Note: For details on definitions and sources, please refer to the metadata at the end of the tables.
StatLink http://dx.doi.org/10.1787/888932617550

Table B.4. Stock of foreign-born population by country of birth
Thousands
GERMANY

	2000	2001	2002	2003	2004	2005	2006	2007	2008	2009	2010	Of which: Women 2010 (%)
Turkey	..	..	..	..	..	1 472	1 477	1 511	1 508	1 489	1 497	48
Poland	..	..	..	..	..	719	723	532	508	1 103	1 112	55
Russian Federation	..	..	..	..	..	1 005	875	513	445	992	977	54
Kazakhstan	..	..	..	..	..	..	340	206	140	628	696	52
Italy	..	..	..	..	..	437	431	431	433	434	420	37
Romania	..	..	..	..	..	317	318	209	168	386	372	55
Greece	..	..	..	..	..	233	229	240	232	227	231	45
Ukraine	..	..	..	..	..	..	202	193	181	228	227	58
Croatia	..	..	..	..	..	268	256	251	256	249	226	54
Former USSR	..	..	..	..	..	..	..	77	56	286	218	53
Austria	..	..	..	..	..	191	191	194	198	199	197	51
Serbia	..	..	..	..	..	..	..	334	321	209	204	52
Bosnia and Herzegovina	..	..	..	..	..	237	225	217	207	176	154	50
Netherlands	..	..	..	..	..	107	103	115	123	128	133	48
France	..	..	..	..	..	99	99	103	110	118	120	51
Other countries	..	..	..	..	..	5 314	4 962	5 403	5 737	3 749	3 807	
Total	**10 256**	..	..	..	..	**10 399**	**10 431**	**10 529**	**10 623**	**10 601**	**10 591**	**51**

Note: For details on definitions and sources, please refer to the metadata at the end of the tables.
StatLink http://dx.doi.org/10.1787/888932617550

Table B.4. **Stock of foreign-born population by country of birth**
Thousands
GREECE

	2000	2001	2002	2003	2004	2005	2006	2007	2008	2009	2010	Of which: Women 2010 (%)
Albania	..	403.9	..	..	..	..	..	..	..	..	..	46
Georgia	..	71.7	..	..	..	..	..	..	..	..	..	62
Russian Federation	..	72.7	..	..	..	..	..	..	..	..	..	61
Bulgaria	..	38.9	..	..	..	..	..	..	..	..	..	70
Romania	..	26.5	..	..	..	..	..	..	..	..	..	61
Germany	..	101.4	..	..	..	..	..	..	..	..	..	63
Pakistan	..	10.9	..	..	..	..	..	..	..	..	..	8
Bangladesh	..	4.7	..	..	..	..	..	..	..	..	..	4
Ukraine	..	16.7	..	..	..	..	..	..	..	..	..	73
Poland	..	15.5	..	..	..	..	..	..	..	..	..	58
Cyprus	..	22.5	..	..	..	..	..	..	..	..	..	53
Egypt	..	32.7	..	..	..	..	..	..	..	..	..	31
Turkey	..	76.6	..	..	..	..	..	..	..	..	..	58
Armenia	..	9.0	..	..	..	..	..	..	..	..	..	46
United States	..	23.1	..	..	..	..	..	..	..	..	..	48
Other countries	..	196.2	..	..	..	..	..	..	..	..	..	
Total	..	**1 122.9**	..	..	..	..	..	..	..	..	..	**50**

Notes: For details on definitions and sources, please refer to the metadata at the end of the tables. See notes on Cyprus in the introduction of this annex.

StatLink http://dx.doi.org/10.1787/888932617550

Table B.4. **Stock of foreign-born population by country of birth**
Thousands
HUNGARY

	2000	2001	2002	2003	2004	2005	2006	2007	2008	2009	2010	Of which: Women 2010 (%)
Romania	144.2	145.2	146.5	148.5	152.7	155.4	170.4	196.1	202.2	198.2	201.9	52
Former Yugoslavia	35.1	33.4	30.3	30.7	29.9	29.6	28.6	28.5	28.0	33.7	33.2	49
Former USSR	31.5	30.4	31.0	31.4	32.2	31.9	27.4	28.5	30.1	31.2	30.7	66
Germany	14.4	15.3	15.9	16.3	18.8	21.9	24.5	27.4	28.7	31.3	29.4	50
Former Czechoslovakia	36.0	34.6	33.3	33.4	31.4	32.6	30.4	29.6	28.5	28.5	24.1	64
Ukraine	..	..	..	..	..	..	4.9	4.9	4.6	6.5	13.4	51
China	3.5	3.6	3.8	3.9	4.2	4.5	4.7	5.0	5.4	5.6	10.9	45
Serbia	..	..	..	..	..	..	0.1	0.2	0.3	0.3	8.6	49
Austria	3.9	4.0	4.2	4.3	4.7	5.4	6.2	6.9	7.3	7.9	7.8	47
United States	2.3	2.1	2.4	2.7	3.0	3.4	4.0	4.3	4.6	5.0	6.9	45
Slovak Republic	..	..	..	..	..	..	2.1	3.0	3.2	3.3	5.7	47
United Kingdom	..	..	..	..	..	..	3.2	3.8	4.3	4.8	4.7	58
Poland	2.7	2.7	2.7	2.7	2.9	3.2	3.4	3.7	3.8	3.9	3.9	40
France	1.4	1.4	1.5	1.6	2.2	2.7	3.1	3.6	3.9	4.1	3.6	64
Italy	..	..	..	..	..	..	2.6	3.0	3.3	3.6	3.5	46
Other countries	19.8	27.4	31.2	32.4	37.0	40.9	28.8	33.3	36.1	39.3	62.8	
Total	**294.6**	**300.1**	**302.8**	**307.8**	**319.0**	**331.5**	**344.6**	**381.8**	**394.2**	**407.3**	**451.4**	**52**

Note: For details on definitions and sources, please refer to the metadata at the end of the tables.

StatLink http://dx.doi.org/10.1787/888932617550

STATISTICAL ANNEX

Table B.4. Stock of foreign-born population by country of birth
Thousands
ICELAND

	2000	2001	2002	2003	2004	2005	2006	2007	2008	2009	2010	Of which: Women 2010 (%)
Poland	1.6	1.8	2.0	2.0	2.2	3.6	6.6	10.5	11.6	10.1	9.5	46
Denmark	2.5	2.5	2.5	2.5	2.6	2.7	2.8	2.9	3.0	2.9	2.9	51
Sweden	1.7	1.7	1.7	1.7	1.7	1.8	1.8	1.9	1.9	1.8	1.8	51
United States	1.5	1.5	1.5	1.5	1.6	1.7	1.8	1.9	1.8	1.9	1.8	46
Germany	1.1	1.2	1.3	1.2	1.2	1.5	1.6	1.8	1.8	1.7	1.6	60
Lithuania	0.0	0.1	0.3	0.3	0.3	0.5	0.9	1.4	1.6	1.4	1.5	46
Philippines	0.7	0.8	0.9	1.0	1.1	1.2	1.3	1.3	1.4	1.4	1.4	66
United Kingdom	0.8	0.8	0.8	0.8	0.8	0.9	0.9	1.0	1.1	1.1	1.1	39
Thailand	0.6	0.7	0.7	0.8	0.8	0.9	1.0	1.0	1.1	1.1	1.1	73
Norway	0.9	0.9	0.9	0.9	0.9	1.0	1.0	1.0	1.0	1.0	1.0	54
Latvia	0.0	0.0	0.1	0.1	0.1	0.2	0.3	0.5	0.6	0.6	0.7	50
China	0.2	0.2	0.2	0.3	0.4	0.8	0.9	0.6	0.5	0.5	0.5	62
Viet Nam	0.2	0.3	0.3	0.4	0.4	0.4	0.4	0.4	0.5	0.5	0.5	55
Portugal	0.1	0.1	0.1	0.1	0.3	0.4	0.7	0.9	0.8	0.6	0.5	35
France	0.3	0.3	0.3	0.3	0.3	0.3	0.3	0.4	0.4	0.4	0.5	49
Other countries	4.8	5.4	5.6	5.7	6.1	6.9	7.8	8.3	8.5	8.1	8.1	
Total	**16.9**	**18.3**	**19.1**	**19.5**	**20.7**	**24.7**	**30.4**	**35.9**	**37.6**	**35.1**	**34.7**	**51**

Note: For details on definitions and sources, please refer to the metadata at the end of the tables.

StatLink http://dx.doi.org/10.1787/888932617550

Table B.4. Stock of foreign-born population by country of birth
Thousands
IRELAND

	2000	2001	2002	2003	2004	2005	2006	2007	2008	2009	2010	Of which: Women 2006 (%)
United Kingdom	..	..	242.2	..	..	..	266.1	..	..	..	..	51
Poland	..	..	2.1	..	..	..	62.5	..	..	..	..	36
United States	..	..	21.0	..	..	..	24.6	..	..	..	..	54
Lithuania	..	..	2.1	..	..	..	24.6	..	..	..	..	44
Nigeria	..	..	8.9	..	..	..	16.3	..	..	..	..	54
Latvia	..	..	2.2	..	..	..	13.9	..	..	..	..	46
Germany	..	..	8.5	..	..	..	11.5	..	..	..	..	54
China	..	..	5.6	..	..	..	11.0	..	..	..	..	47
Philippines	..	..	3.9	..	..	..	9.4	..	..	..	..	59
India	..	..	3.3	..	..	..	9.2	..	..	..	..	48
France	..	..	6.7	..	..	..	9.1	..	..	..	..	51
Romania	..	..	5.8	..	..	..	8.5	..	..	..	..	46
Slovak Republic	..	..	..	..	..	..	8.1	..	..	..	..	35
South Africa	..	..	6.1	..	..	..	7.6	..	..	..	..	50
Australia	..	..	5.9	..	..	..	6.5	..	..	..	..	51
Other countries	..	..	65.7	..	..	..	112.7	..	..	..	..	..
Total	..	..	**390.0**	..	..	..	**601.7**	..	..	..	..	**48**

Note: For details on definitions and sources, please refer to the metadata at the end of the tables.

StatLink http://dx.doi.org/10.1787/888932617550

Table B.4. Stock of foreign-born population by country of birth

Thousands

ISRAEL

	2000	2001	2002	2003	2004	2005	2006	2007	2008	2009	2010	Of which: Women 2010 (%)
Former USSR	926.5	948.4	951.6	946.9	941.0	935.1	929.1	921.7	913.8	877.5	875.4	55
Morocco	166.3	164.1	161.9	159.7	157.5	155.4	153.2	150.7	148.5	154.7	152.6	53
Ukraine	..	..	..	..	..	..	..	..	..	..	127.5	56
Russian Federation	..	..	..	..	..	..	..	..	..	..	109.5	57
Romania	124.1	120.9	117.3	113.8	110.4	106.9	103.7	100.2	96.9	96.4	93.2	56
United States	..	..	..	..	..	..	..	..	..	..	82.6	52
Ethiopia	57.4	60.5	63.0	65.8	69.4	72.8	76.1	79.4	80.8	77.4	78.9	50
Iraq	76.0	74.5	73.0	71.4	69.9	68.3	66.7	65.1	63.5	63.7	61.9	53
Poland	81.1	76.7	72.5	68.3	64.4	60.6	57.0	53.4	50.1	54.0	50.9	56
Iran	51.5	51.1	50.5	49.9	49.4	48.8	48.2	47.6	46.8	49.8	48.9	51
France	27.8	28.5	30.1	31.4	33.2	35.4	37.6	39.6	40.9	41.4	42.9	54
Argentina	32.0	33.0	38.6	39.5	38.9	38.2	37.7	37.2	36.7	37.6	37.5	53
Tunisia	..	..	..	..	..	..	..	..	..	..	30.0	54
Yemen	36.5	35.6	34.6	33.7	32.7	31.8	30.8	29.9	28.9	28.9	28.0	56
Turkey	31.0	30.3	29.6	28.9	28.2	27.5	26.9	26.2	25.6	26.1	25.6	53
Other countries	347.7	354.5	360.5	365.5	365.8	366.8	363.0	365.2	366.9	370.3	23.7	
Total	**1 957.8**	**1 978.1**	**1 983.2**	**1 974.8**	**1 960.8**	**1 947.6**	**1 930.0**	**1 916.2**	**1 899.4**	**1 877.7**	**1 869.0**	**51**

Notes: For details on definitions and sources, please refer to the metadata at the end of the tables.
Information on data for Israel: http://dx.doi.org/10.1787/888932315602.

StatLink http://dx.doi.org/10.1787/888932617550

Table B.4. Stock of foreign-born population by country of birth

Thousands

ITALY

	2000	2001	2002	2003	2004	2005	2006	2007	2008	2009	2010	Of which: Women 2009 (%)
Romania	..	86.6	..	..	..	..	..	..	678.5	847.5	..	55
Albania	..	159.2	..	..	..	..	..	..	418.9	482.4	..	48
Morocco	..	155.8	..	..	..	..	..	..	277.0	355.9	..	42
Germany	..	195.3	..	..	..	..	..	..	..	209.2	..	56
Ukraine	..	11.4	..	..	..	..	..	..	138.8	149.9	..	77
Poland	..	34.0	..	..	..	..	..	..	100.3	122.5	..	70
Philippines	..	48.3	..	..	..	..	..	..	121.0	120.0	..	60
India	..	29.3	..	..	..	..	..	..	107.0	115.9	..	42
Moldova	..	4.3	..	..	..	..	..	..	83.6	108.4	..	61
Ecuador	..	14.6	..	..	..	..	..	..	98.9	102.0	..	54
Peru	..	32.9	..	..	..	..	..	..	98.5	94.0	..	60
China	..	39.9	..	..	..	..	..	..	89.7	92.5	..	47
Tunisia	..	59.8	..	..	..	..	..	..	85.2	83.2	..	39
Egypt	..	34.7	..	..	..	..	..	..	68.8	81.5	..	32
Serbia	..	52.5	..	..	..	..	..	..	78.3	75.6	..	48
Other countries	..	1 281.5	..	..	..	..	..	..	1 931.0	1 758.2	..	..
Total	**..**	**2 240.0**	**..**	**..**	**..**	**..**	**..**	**..**	**4 375.2**	**4 798.7**	**..**	**53**

Note: For details on definitions and sources, please refer to the metadata at the end of the tables.

StatLink http://dx.doi.org/10.1787/888932617550

STATISTICAL ANNEX

Table B.4. Stock of foreign-born population by country of birth
Thousands
LUXEMBOURG

	2000	2001	2002	2003	2004	2005	2006	2007	2008	2009	2010	Of which: Women 2001 (%)
Portugal	..	41.7	..	..	..	..	..	..	..	..	..	48
France	..	18.8	..	..	..	..	..	..	..	..	..	53
Belgium	..	14.8	..	..	..	..	..	..	..	..	..	49
Germany	..	12.8	..	..	..	..	..	..	..	..	..	59
Italy	..	12.3	..	..	..	..	..	..	..	..	..	44
Serbia	..	6.5	..	..	..	..	..	..	..	..	..	46
Netherlands	..	3.3	..	..	..	..	..	..	..	..	..	49
United Kingdom	..	3.2	..	..	..	..	..	..	..	..	..	44
Cape Verde	..	2.4	..	..	..	..	..	..	..	..	..	54
Spain	..	2.1	..	..	..	..	..	..	..	..	..	52
Bosnia and Herzegovina	..	1.7	..	..	..	..	..	..	..	..	..	48
Denmark	..	1.5	..	..	..	..	..	..	..	..	..	52
United States	..	1.1	..	..	..	..	..	..	..	..	..	47
China	..	1.0	..	..	..	..	..	..	..	..	..	51
Poland	..	1.0	..	..	..	..	..	..	..	..	..	62
Other countries	..	20.6	..	..	..	..	..	..	..	..	..	..
Total	..	**144.8**	..	..	..	..	..	..	..	..	..	**50**

Note: For details on definitions and sources, please refer to the metadata at the end of the tables.
StatLink http://dx.doi.org/10.1787/888932617550

Table B.4. Stock of foreign-born population by country of birth
Thousands
MEXICO

	2000	2001	2002	2003	2004	2005	2006	2007	2008	2009	2010	Of which: Women 2010 (%)
United States	343.6	..	..	..	..	..	..	..	..	..	738.1	..
Guatemala	24.0	..	..	..	..	..	..	..	..	..	35.3	..
Spain	21.0	..	..	..	..	..	..	..	..	..	18.9	..
Cuba	6.6	..	..	..	..	..	..	..	..	..	12.1	..
Argentina	6.5	..	..	..	..	..	..	..	..	..	..	..
Colombia	6.2	..	..	..	..	..	..	..	..	..	13.9	..
Canada	5.8	..	..	..	..	..	..	..	..	..	..	..
France	5.7	..	..	..	..	..	..	..	..	..	7.2	..
Germany	5.6	..	..	..	..	..	..	..	..	..	6.2	..
El Salvador	5.5	..	..	..	..	..	..	..	..	..	..	..
Italy	3.9	..	..	..	..	..	..	..	..	..	..	..
Chile	3.8	..	..	..	..	..	..	..	..	..	..	..
Peru	3.7	..	..	..	..	..	..	..	..	..	..	..
Honduras	3.7	..	..	..	..	..	..	..	..	..	..	..
Japan	2.9	..	..	..	..	..	..	..	..	..	3.0	..
Other countries	43.9	..	..	..	..	..	..	..	..	..	126.4	..
Total	**492.6**	..	..	..	..	..	..	..	..	..	**961.1**	**49**

Note: For details on definitions and sources, please refer to the metadata at the end of the tables.
StatLink http://dx.doi.org/10.1787/888932617550

STATISTICAL ANNEX

Table B.4. Stock of foreign-born population by country of birth
Thousands
NETHERLANDS

	2000	2001	2002	2003	2004	2005	2006	2007	2008	2009	2010	Of which: Women 2010 (%)
Turkey	181.9	186.2	190.5	194.6	195.9	196.0	195.4	194.8	195.7	196.7	197.4	48
Suriname	186.5	188.0	189.0	189.7	190.1	189.2	187.8	187.0	186.7	186.8	186.2	55
Morocco	155.8	159.8	163.4	166.6	168.5	168.6	168.0	167.2	166.9	167.4	167.7	47
Indonesia	165.8	163.9	161.4	158.8	156.0	152.8	149.7	146.7	143.7	140.7	137.8	56
Germany	123.1	122.1	120.6	119.0	117.7	116.9	116.4	117.0	119.2	120.5	122.3	59
Poland	17.4	18.6	20.1	21.2	25.0	30.0	35.3	42.1	51.1	58.1	66.6	57
Former Yugoslavia	53.9	55.9	56.2	55.5	54.5	53.7	53.0	52.8	52.7	52.8	52.7	52
Belgium	46.0	46.5	46.8	47.1	47.1	47.1	47.4	47.9	48.6	49.2	50.0	56
United Kingdom	45.7	47.9	48.5	48.3	47.5	46.6	45.8	45.8	46.7	47.1	47.2	45
Former USSR	21.6	27.1	30.8	32.8	34.5	35.3	36.0	37.4	39.4	41.9	45.6	63
China	22.7	25.8	28.7	31.5	33.5	34.8	35.5	37.1	40.0	42.5	44.7	57
Iraq	33.7	36.0	35.8	36.0	35.9	35.3	34.8	35.7	38.7	40.9	41.0	41
Afghanistan	24.3	28.5	31.0	32.1	32.4	32.0	31.3	31.0	30.7	31.1	31.8	46
Iran	21.5	23.2	24.2	24.2	24.1	23.8	23.8	24.2	24.8	25.4	26.2	45
United States	21.4	22.1	22.5	22.6	22.6	22.8	23.0	23.3	24.0	24.3	24.9	51
Other countries	494.3	523.2	544.7	551.9	550.9	549.9	549.3	561.2	584.8	607.1	626.6	
Total	**1 615.4**	**1 674.6**	**1 714.2**	**1 731.8**	**1 736.1**	**1 734.7**	**1 732.4**	**1 751.0**	**1 793.7**	**1 832.5**	**1 868.7**	**52**

Note: For details on definitions and sources, please refer to the metadata at the end of the tables.
StatLink http://dx.doi.org/10.1787/888932617550

Table B.4. Stock of foreign-born population by country of birth
Thousands
NEW ZEALAND

	2000	2001	2002	2003	2004	2005	2006	2007	2008	2009	2010	Of which: Women 2006 (%)
United Kingdom	..	218.4	..	..	..	..	245.1	..	..	..	..	51
China	..	38.9	..	..	..	..	78.1	..	..	..	..	52
Australia	..	56.3	..	..	..	..	62.7	..	..	..	..	53
Samoa	..	47.1	..	..	..	..	50.6	..	..	..	..	52
India	..	20.9	..	..	..	..	43.3	..	..	..	..	48
South Africa	..	26.1	..	..	..	..	41.7	..	..	..	..	51
Fiji	..	25.7	..	..	..	..	37.7	..	..	..	..	52
Korea	..	17.9	..	..	..	..	28.8	..	..	..	..	53
Netherlands	..	22.2	..	..	..	..	22.1	..	..	..	..	47
Tonga	..	18.1	..	..	..	..	20.5	..	..	..	..	50
United States	..	13.3	..	..	..	..	18.3	..	..	..	..	50
Philippines	..	10.1	..	..	..	..	15.3	..	..	..	..	63
Cook Islands	..	15.2	..	..	..	..	14.7	..	..	..	..	52
Malaysia	..	11.5	..	..	..	..	14.5	..	..	..	..	53
Chinese Taipei	..	12.5	..	..	..	..	10.8	..	..	..	..	54
Other countries	..	144.3	..	..	..	..	175.2	..	..	..	..	..
Total	..	**698.6**	..	..	..	..	**879.5**	..	..	..	..	**51**

Note: For details on definitions and sources, please refer to the metadata at the end of the tables.
StatLink http://dx.doi.org/10.1787/888932617550

Table B.4. Stock of foreign-born population by country of birth
Thousands
NORWAY

	2000	2001	2002	2003	2004	2005	2006	2007	2008	2009	2010	Of which: Women 2010 (%)
Poland	5.9	6.2	6.7	7.0	8.3	11.2	18.0	30.8	42.7	49.5	57.1	35
Sweden	33.3	33.0	33.0	33.1	33.1	33.9	35.0	36.8	39.4	41.8	44.6	50
Germany	11.8	12.2	12.9	13.5	14.1	15.2	16.7	19.7	23.0	24.9	26.2	47
Denmark	22.0	22.1	22.3	22.3	22.2	22.3	22.3	22.5	22.6	22.7	22.9	49
Iraq	11.3	12.3	14.7	14.9	15.4	16.7	17.4	18.2	19.4	20.6	21.4	43
Somalia	7.8	8.6	10.7	12.1	12.8	13.5	14.5	16.0	16.9	18.0	19.4	47
Pakistan	13.6	14.1	14.6	14.9	15.2	15.6	15.9	16.2	16.7	17.2	17.6	48
United Kingdom	14.2	14.1	14.3	14.3	14.6	14.7	15.1	15.6	16.2	16.9	17.5	41
United States	14.7	14.6	14.6	14.6	14.5	14.6	14.8	15.2	15.7	16.0	16.3	43
Lithuania	0.4	0.5	0.8	0.9	1.3	1.9	3.0	5.0	7.3	9.9	15.6	42
Philippines	6.0	6.4	7.0	7.5	8.0	8.7	9.6	10.9	12.3	13.5	14.7	78
Russian Federation	3.9	4.7	6.0	7.5	8.9	10.1	10.9	12.2	13.1	13.8	14.6	66
Thailand	4.1	4.6	5.5	6.3	7.3	8.3	9.3	10.5	11.8	13.1	14.1	81
Iran	9.3	10.1	10.7	11.3	11.6	11.8	12.0	12.3	12.6	13.1	13.6	45
Viet Nam	11.3	11.5	11.7	11.9	12.1	12.3	12.5	12.6	12.9	13.0	13.1	53
Other countries	135.6	140.1	148.5	155.2	161.6	169.6	178.2	190.9	206.2	223.0	240.5	
Total	**305.0**	**315.1**	**333.9**	**347.3**	**361.1**	**380.4**	**405.1**	**445.4**	**488.8**	**526.8**	**569.1**	**49**

Note: For details on definitions and sources, please refer to the metadata at the end of the tables.

StatLink http://dx.doi.org/10.1787/888932617550

Table B.4. Stock of foreign-born population by country of birth
Thousands
POLAND

	2000	2001	2002	2003	2004	2005	2006	2007	2008	2009	2010	Of which: Women 2002 (%)
Ukraine	..	..	312.3	..	..	..	..	..	..	..	..	61
Belarus	..	..	105.2	..	..	..	..	..	..	..	..	60
Germany	..	..	98.2	..	..	..	..	..	..	..	..	58
Lithuania	..	..	79.8	..	..	..	..	..	..	..	..	61
Russian Federation	..	..	55.2	..	..	..	..	..	..	..	..	65
France	..	..	33.9	..	..	..	..	..	..	..	..	56
United States	..	..	8.4	..	..	..	..	..	..	..	..	59
Czech Republic	..	..	6.3	..	..	..	..	..	..	..	..	59
Austria	..	..	3.9	..	..	..	..	..	..	..	..	53
Kazakhstan	..	..	3.8	..	..	..	..	..	..	..	..	56
Serbia	..	..	3.6	..	..	..	..	..	..	..	..	53
Romania	..	..	3.4	..	..	..	..	..	..	..	..	58
Italy	..	..	3.3	..	..	..	..	..	..	..	..	45
Bosnia and Herzegovina	..	..	3.3	..	..	..	..	..	..	..	..	57
United Kingdom	..	..	2.8	..	..	..	..	..	..	..	..	41
Other countries	..	..	52.8	..	..	..	..	..	..	..	..	..
Total	..	..	**776.2**	..	..	..	..	..	..	..	..	**59**

Note: For details on definitions and sources, please refer to the metadata at the end of the tables.

StatLink http://dx.doi.org/10.1787/888932617550

Table B.4. Stock of foreign-born population by country of birth
Thousands
PORTUGAL

	2000	2001	2002	2003	2004	2005	2006	2007	2008	2009	2010	Of which: Women 2001 (%)
Angola	..	174.2	..	..	..	..	..	..	..	..	..	53
France	..	95.3	..	..	..	..	..	..	..	..	..	53
Mozambique	..	76.0	..	..	..	..	..	..	..	..	..	53
Brazil	..	49.9	..	..	..	..	..	..	..	..	..	51
Cape Verde	..	45.0	..	..	..	..	..	..	..	..	..	49
Germany	..	24.3	..	..	..	..	..	..	..	..	..	51
Venezuela	..	22.4	..	..	..	..	..	..	..	..	..	52
Guinea-Bissau	..	21.4	..	..	..	..	..	..	..	..	..	40
Spain	..	14.0	..	..	..	..	..	..	..	..	..	60
Switzerland	..	12.9	..	..	..	..	..	..	..	..	..	49
Sao Tome and Principe	..	12.5	..	..	..	..	..	..	..	..	..	54
South Africa	..	11.2	..	..	..	..	..	..	..	..	..	52
United Kingdom	..	10.1	..	..	..	..	..	..	..	..	..	50
Canada	..	7.3	..	..	..	..	..	..	..	..	..	52
United States	..	7.3	..	..	..	..	..	..	..	..	..	51
Other countries	..	67.8	..	..	..	..	..	..	..	..	..	..
Total	..	**651.5**	..	..	..	..	..	..	..	..	..	**51**

Note: For details on definitions and sources, please refer to the metadata at the end of the tables.

StatLink http://dx.doi.org/10.1787/888932617550

Table B.4. Stock of foreign-born population by country of birth
Thousands
RUSSIAN FEDERATION

	2000	2001	2002	2003	2004	2005	2006	2007	2008	2009	2010	Of which: Women 2002 (%)
Ukraine	..	..	3 560.0	..	..	..	..	..	..	..	..	52
Kazakhstan	..	..	2 585.0	..	..	..	..	..	..	..	..	53
Belarus	..	..	935.8	..	..	..	..	..	..	..	..	55
Uzbekistan	..	..	918.0	..	..	..	..	..	..	..	..	50
Azerbaijan	..	..	846.1	..	..	..	..	..	..	..	..	42
Georgia	..	..	629.0	..	..	..	..	..	..	..	..	46
Armenia	..	..	481.3	..	..	..	..	..	..	..	..	42
Kyrgyzstan	..	..	463.5	..	..	..	..	..	..	..	..	51
Tajikistan	..	..	383.1	..	..	..	..	..	..	..	..	42
Moldova	..	..	277.5	..	..	..	..	..	..	..	..	45
Turkmenistan	..	..	175.3	..	..	..	..	..	..	..	..	51
Germany	..	..	150.2	..	..	..	..	..	..	..	..	50
Latvia	..	..	102.5	..	..	..	..	..	..	..	..	51
Lithuania	..	..	86.2	..	..	..	..	..	..	..	..	50
Estonia	..	..	67.4	..	..	..	..	..	..	..	..	52
Other countries	..	..	316.0	..	..	..	..	..	..	..	..	..
Total	..	..	**11 976.8**	..	..	..	..	..	..	..	..	**50**

Note: For details on definitions and sources, please refer to the metadata at the end of the tables.

StatLink http://dx.doi.org/10.1787/888932617550

Table B.4. Stock of foreign-born population by country of birth
Thousands
SLOVAK REPUBLIC

	2000	2001	2002	2003	2004	2005	2006	2007	2008	2009	2010	Of which: Women 2004 (%)
Czech Republic	..	71.5	..	..	107.7	..	..	..	..	..	..	52
Hungary	..	17.2	..	..	22.5	..	..	..	..	..	..	60
Ukraine	..	7.1	..	..	13.3	..	..	..	..	..	..	54
Poland	..	3.4	..	..	7.2	..	..	..	..	..	..	52
Russian Federation	..	1.6	..	..	5.8	..	..	..	..	..	..	60
Germany	..	0.6	..	..	4.7	..	..	..	..	..	..	37
Former Yug. Rep. of Macedonia	..	0.1	..	..	4.6	..	..	..	..	..	..	36
Romania	..	3.0	..	..	4.4	..	..	..	..	..	..	50
Austria	..	0.7	..	..	3.9	..	..	..	..	..	..	42
United States	..	0.7	..	..	3.5	..	..	..	..	..	..	52
France	..	1.3	..	..	3.4	..	..	..	..	..	..	51
Viet Nam	..	0.6	..	..	2.4	..	..	..	..	..	..	33
United Kingdom	..	..	..	..	1.8	..	..	..	..	..	..	37
Bulgaria	..	1.0	..	..	1.7	..	..	..	..	..	..	42
China	..	..	..	..	1.6	..	..	..	..	..	..	41
Other countries	..	10.0	..	..	19.2	..	..	..	..	..	..	
Total	..	**119.1**	..	..	**207.6**	..	..	..	..	..	..	**50**

Note: For details on definitions and sources, please refer to the metadata at the end of the tables.

StatLink ᔛ http://dx.doi.org/10.1787/888932617550

Table B.4. Stock of foreign-born population by country of birth
Thousands
SLOVENIA

	2000	2001	2002	2003	2004	2005	2006	2007	2008	2009	2010	Of which: Women 2010 (%)
Bosnia and Herzegovina	..	..	..	..	..	..	..	..	..	..	96.9	38
Croatia	..	..	..	..	..	..	..	..	..	..	49.2	51
Serbia	..	..	..	..	..	..	..	..	..	..	29.2	42
Former Yug. Rep. of Macedonia	..	..	..	..	..	..	..	..	..	..	13.7	37
Other countries	..	..	..	..	..	..	..	..	..	..	39.7	
Total	..	..	**170.0**	..	..	..	..	..	..	..	**228.6**	**43**

Note: For details on definitions and sources, please refer to the metadata at the end of the tables.

StatLink ᔛ http://dx.doi.org/10.1787/888932617550

Table B.4. Stock of foreign-born population by country of birth
Thousands
SPAIN

	2000	2001	2002	2003	2004	2005	2006	2007	2008	2009	2010	Of which: Women 2010 (%)
Romania	33.0	68.6	137.8	206.4	312.1	397.3	511.0	706.2	762.2	784.8	809.4	48
Morocco	299.9	370.7	438.2	474.5	557.2	606.0	621.3	683.1	737.8	760.2	766.2	40
Ecuador	140.6	259.8	387.6	470.1	487.2	456.6	434.7	458.4	479.1	484.6	478.9	52
United Kingdom	120.0	140.6	173.6	187.5	238.2	283.7	322.0	358.3	379.3	390.0	392.6	50
Colombia	99.9	205.3	259.4	264.5	288.2	287.0	291.7	330.4	358.8	371.1	372.5	57
Argentina	84.9	118.9	191.7	226.5	260.4	271.4	273.0	290.3	295.4	291.7	285.6	49
Germany	158.0	173.0	189.4	176.9	193.1	208.9	222.1	237.9	246.7	251.0	250.9	50
France	162.5	170.6	180.2	178.1	188.7	199.4	208.8	220.2	227.1	229.7	228.0	51
Bolivia	8.4	15.5	30.6	54.4	99.5	140.7	200.7	240.9	229.4	213.9	201.5	58
Peru	47.3	59.0	72.9	88.8	108.0	123.5	137.0	162.4	188.2	197.6	197.4	54
Bulgaria	12.4	30.2	53.4	70.4	93.0	100.8	120.2	150.7	160.0	163.6	165.5	47
China	27.6	37.5	51.1	62.3	87.0	104.8	108.3	127.0	146.3	154.1	160.2	51
Venezuela	62.3	71.6	83.5	100.3	116.2	124.9	130.6	144.6	152.4	155.1	159.0	54
Portugal	62.6	67.3	71.8	71.1	80.8	93.8	111.6	136.2	148.2	148.8	146.2	40
Dominican Republic	41.1	49.9	59.1	65.8	78.0	87.1	96.7	114.7	129.7	136.8	140.7	61
Other countries	608.5	755.4	922.1	996.4	1 203.9	1 351.9	1 460.5	1 683.1	1 825.7	1 871.2	1 905.3	
Total	**1 969.3**	**2 594.1**	**3 302.4**	**3 693.8**	**4 391.5**	**4 837.6**	**5 250.0**	**6 044.5**	**6 466.3**	**6 604.2**	**6 659.9**	**49**

Note: For details on definitions and sources, please refer to the metadata at the end of the tables.
StatLink http://dx.doi.org/10.1787/888932617550

Table B.4. Stock of foreign-born population by country of birth
Thousands
SWEDEN

	2000	2001	2002	2003	2004	2005	2006	2007	2008	2009	2010	Of which: Women 2010 (%)
Finland	195.4	193.5	191.5	189.3	186.6	183.7	180.9	178.2	175.1	172.2	169.5	60
Iraq	49.4	55.7	62.8	67.6	70.1	72.6	82.8	97.5	109.4	117.9	121.8	46
Former Yugoslavia	72.0	73.3	74.4	75.1	74.6	74.0	73.7	72.9	72.3	71.6	70.8	49
Poland	40.1	40.5	41.1	41.6	43.5	46.2	51.7	58.2	63.8	67.5	70.3	57
Iran	51.1	51.8	52.7	53.2	54.0	54.5	55.7	56.5	57.7	59.9	62.1	47
Bosnia and Herzegovina	51.5	52.2	52.9	53.9	54.5	54.8	55.5	55.7	56.0	56.1	56.2	51
Germany	38.2	38.9	39.4	40.2	40.8	41.6	43.0	45.0	46.9	47.8	48.2	53
Denmark	38.2	38.9	39.9	40.9	41.7	42.6	44.4	45.9	46.2	46.0	45.5	47
Norway	42.5	43.4	44.5	45.1	45.0	44.8	44.7	44.6	44.3	43.8	43.4	56
Turkey	31.9	32.5	33.1	34.1	35.0	35.9	37.1	38.2	39.2	40.8	42.5	45
Somalia	13.1	13.5	14.0	14.8	15.3	16.0	18.3	21.6	25.2	31.7	37.8	50
Thailand	10.4	11.2	12.4	14.3	16.3	18.3	20.5	22.9	25.9	28.7	31.4	78
Chile	26.8	27.2	27.3	27.5	27.7	27.8	28.0	28.0	28.1	28.3	28.4	50
Lebanon	20.0	20.2	20.5	20.8	21.1	21.4	22.7	23.0	23.3	23.7	24.1	45
China	8.2	9.0	9.8	10.9	11.9	13.3	14.5	16.0	18.3	21.2	24.0	61
Other countries	315.1	326.4	337.1	348.6	362.3	378.4	401.5	423.5	450.0	480.6	508.9	
Total	**1 003.8**	**1 028.0**	**1 053.5**	**1 078.1**	**1 100.3**	**1 125.8**	**1 175.2**	**1 227.8**	**1 281.6**	**1 338.0**	**1 384.9**	**51**

Note: For details on definitions and sources, please refer to the metadata at the end of the tables.
StatLink http://dx.doi.org/10.1787/888932617550

STATISTICAL ANNEX

Table B.4. Stock of foreign-born population by country of birth
Thousands
SWITZERLAND

	2000	2001	2002	2003	2004	2005	2006	2007	2008	2009	2010	Of which: Women 2010 (%)
Italy	234.6	..	..	..	..	..	..	..	..	..	..	..
Germany	182.0	..	..	..	..	..	..	..	..	..	..	..
Serbia	158.1	..	..	..	..	..	..	..	..	..	..	..
Portugal	101.0	..	..	..	..	..	..	..	..	..	..	..
France	98.4	..	..	..	..	..	..	..	..	..	..	..
Spain	61.7	..	..	..	..	..	..	..	..	..	..	..
Turkey	58.5	..	..	..	..	..	..	..	..	..	..	..
Austria	54.6	..	..	..	..	..	..	..	..	..	..	..
Bosnia and Herzegovina	46.4	..	..	..	..	..	..	..	..	..	..	..
Former Yug. Rep. of Macedonia	41.5	..	..	..	..	..	..	..	..	..	..	..
United Kingdom	25.4	..	..	..	..	..	..	..	..	..	..	..
Croatia	24.1	..	..	..	..	..	..	..	..	..	..	..
Sri Lanka	22.4	..	..	..	..	..	..	..	..	..	..	..
United States	21.8	..	..	..	..	..	..	..	..	..	..	..
Netherlands	16.8	..	..	..	..	..	..	..	..	..	..	..
Other countries	423.5	..	..	..	..	..	..	..	..	..	..	..
Total	**1 570.8**	..	..	..	..	..	..	..	..	..	**2 075.2**	**52**

Note: For details on definitions and sources, please refer to the metadata at the end of the tables.
StatLink http://dx.doi.org/10.1787/888932617550

Table B.4. Stock of foreign-born population by country of birth
Thousands
TURKEY

	2000	2001	2002	2003	2004	2005	2006	2007	2008	2009	2010	Of which: Women 2010 (%)
Bulgaria	480.8	..	..	..	..	..	..	..	..	..	..	53
Germany	273.5	..	..	..	..	..	..	..	..	..	..	51
Greece	59.2	..	..	..	..	..	..	..	..	..	..	54
Netherlands	21.8	..	..	..	..	..	..	..	..	..	..	51
Russian Federation	19.9	..	..	..	..	..	..	..	..	..	..	61
United Kingdom	18.9	..	..	..	..	..	..	..	..	..	..	53
France	16.8	..	..	..	..	..	..	..	..	..	..	49
Austria	14.3	..	..	..	..	..	..	..	..	..	..	50
United States	13.6	..	..	..	..	..	..	..	..	..	..	45
Iran	13.0	..	..	..	..	..	..	..	..	..	..	38
Cyprus	10.4	..	..	..	..	..	..	..	..	..	..	54
Switzerland	10.4	..	..	..	..	..	..	..	..	..	..	52
Other countries	326.1	..	..	..	..	..	..	..	..	..	..	
Total	**1 278.7**	..	..	..	..	..	..	..	..	..	..	**52**

Notes: For details on definitions and sources, please refer to the metadata at the end of the tables. See notes on Cyprus in the introduction of this annex.
StatLink http://dx.doi.org/10.1787/888932617550

STATISTICAL ANNEX

Table B.4. Stock of foreign-born population by country of birth
Thousands
UNITED KINGDOM

	2000	2001	2002	2003	2004	2005	2006	2007	2008	2009	2010	Of which: Women 2010 (%)
India	..	468	..	..	..	..	570	553	601	661	687	48
Poland	..	61	..	..	..	..	229	423	495	540	534	50
Ireland	..	537	..	..	..	..	417	410	420	401	401	54
Pakistan	..	321	..	..	..	..	274	357	422	427	382	48
Germany	..	266	..	..	..	..	269	253	273	296	301	57
South Africa	..	141	..	..	..	..	198	194	204	220	227	54
Bangladesh	..	154	..	..	..	..	221	202	193	199	193	47
United States	..	158	..	..	..	..	169	162	173	160	193	54
Nigeria	..	88	..	..	..	..	117	147	137	166	167	50
Jamaica	..	146	..	..	..	..	135	173	142	130	134	54
Somalia	..	44	..	..	..	..	67	90	97	105	132	64
Italy	..	107	..	..	..	..	86	102	108	117	130	55
Australia	..	108	..	..	..	..	116	123	139	123	124	48
France	..	96	..	..	..	..	111	134	129	144	122	57
Sri Lanka	..	68	..	..	..	..	102	114	96	105	118	44
Other countries	..	2 101	..	..	..	..	2 676	2 755	3 004	3 105	3 211	
Total	..	**4 866**	..	..	..	..	**5 757**	**6 192**	**6 633**	**6 899**	**7 056**	**51**

Note: For details on definitions and sources, please refer to the metadata at the end of the tables.

StatLink http://dx.doi.org/10.1787/888932617550

Table B.4. Stock of foreign-born population by country of birth
Thousands
UNITED STATES

	2000	2001	2002	2003	2004	2005	2006	2007	2008	2009	2010	Of which: Women 2010 (%)
Mexico	8 881.8	9 287.7	9 889.0	10 078.7	10 256.9	10 993.9	11 535.0	11 739.6	11 451.3	11 478.2	11 746.5	46
India	1 072.5	1 205.2	1 238.0	1 297.9	1 372.3	1 410.7	1 505.4	1 514.0	1 626.9	1 665.1	1 796.5	48
Philippines	1 301.9	1 371.1	1 467.7	1 443.3	1 509.8	1 594.8	1 634.1	1 708.5	1 685.1	1 733.9	1 766.5	60
China	932.1	1 063.4	1 081.2	1 127.7	1 218.4	1 202.9	1 357.5	1 367.8	1 339.1	1 425.8	1 604.4	55
Viet Nam	1 054.7	946.1	1 024.1	1 066.0	1 052.0	1 072.9	1 116.2	1 102.2	1 154.7	1 149.4	1 243.8	52
El Salvador	789.2	787.2	856.2	872.6	931.9	988.0	1 042.2	1 108.3	1 078.3	1 157.2	1 207.1	49
Cuba	771.7	902.5	880.8	888.7	925.0	902.4	932.6	980.0	987.8	982.9	1 112.1	50
Korea	825.4	878.1	944.5	957.7	955.4	993.9	1 021.2	1 050.7	1 034.7	1 012.9	1 086.9	58
Dominican Republic	586.9	631.9	648.5	679.9	716.5	708.5	764.9	747.9	779.2	791.6	879.9	56
Guatemala	461.0	443.1	510.0	523.7	585.2	644.7	741.0	683.8	743.8	790.5	797.3	41
Canada	826.9	829.1	812.8	849.5	808.5	830.3	847.2	816.4	824.3	814.1	785.6	55
United Kingdom	672.1	670.4	662.6	677.8	658.0	676.6	677.1	678.1	692.4	688.3	676.6	53
Jamaica	560.5	536.3	580.4	600.8	590.1	579.2	643.1	587.6	631.7	645.0	650.8	56
Colombia	468.2	511.9	561.9	529.6	499.3	554.8	589.1	603.7	603.3	617.7	648.3	57
Germany	648.1	651.3	647.9	622.7	643.8	626.5	635.6	624.2	641.5	614.8	611.8	64
Other countries	10 420.3	10 832.8	11 290.3	11 451.0	11 534.7	11 989.5	12 427.4	12 735.8	12 741.9	12 885.5	13 302.8	
Total	**30 273.3**	**31 548.1**	**33 096.2**	**33 667.7**	**34 257.7**	**35 769.6**	**37 469.4**	**38 048.5**	**38 016.1**	**38 452.8**	**39 916.9**	**51**

Note: For details on definitions and sources, please refer to the metadata at the end of the tables.

StatLink http://dx.doi.org/10.1787/888932617550

STATISTICAL ANNEX

Metadata related to Tables A.4 and B.4. **Stocks of foreign-born population**

Legend: ® Observed figures.
ε Estimates (in italic) made by means of the component method (CM) or the parametric method (PM). For more details on the method of estimation, please refer to www.oecd.org/migration/foreignborn. No estimate is made by country of birth (Table B.4).

Data for foreign-born from Serbia include persons from Serbia, Montenegro and Serbia and Montenegro.

Country	Comments	Source
Australia	® Estimated resident population (ERP) based on Population Censuses. In between Censuses, the ERP is updated by data on births, deaths and net overseas migration. *Reference date:* 30 June.	Australian Bureau of Statistics (ABS).
Austria	® Stock of foreign-born residents recorded in the population register. Break in time series in 2002. Revised data for 2002-07 to be coherent with the results of register based test census of 2006. *Reference date:* 31 December (since 2002).	Population Register, Statistics Austria. Prior to 2002: Labour Force Survey, Statistics Austria.
Belgium	® Stock of foreign-born recorded in the population register. Excludes asylum seekers.	Population Register, Directorate General Statistics and Economic Information (DGSEI).
Canada	® 2001 and 2006: Total immigrants (excluding non-permanent residents). Immigrants are persons who are, or have ever been, landed immigrants in Canada. A landed immigrant is a person who has been granted the right to live in Canada permanently by immigration authorities. Some immigrants have resided in Canada for a number of years and have changed status, while others are recent arrivals. ε PM for other years.	Statistics Canada.
Chile	® 2002 Census. ® Register of permits of residence granted for other years.	Register of permits of residence granted, Chile Sistema B3000, Department of Foreigners and Migration, Ministry of the Interior.
Czech Republic	® 2001 Census. ε CM for other years.	Czech Statistical Office.
Denmark	® Immigrants are defined as persons born abroad to parents who are both foreign citizens or born abroad. When no information is available on the country of birth, the person is classified as an immigrant.	Statistics Denmark.
Estonia	® Population Register.	Ministry of the Interior.
Finland	® Population register. Includes foreign-born persons of Finnish origin.	Statistics Finland.
France	® 2006-08 annual Censuses. ® 2010 Census (B.4). ε PM for other years (A.4). Table B.4 includes persons who were born French abroad.	National Institute for Statistics and Economic Studies (INSEE).
Germany	® 2000 and 2005-10: Microcensus.	Federal Statistical Office.
Greece	® 2001 Census. Usual foreign-born resident population.	Hellenic Statistical Authority.
Hungary	® Includes foreigners and Hungarians. Includes refugees. From 2010 on, it includes third country nationals holding a residence permit. *Reference date:* 31 December.	Office of Immigration and Nationality, Central Population Register, Hungarian Central Statistical Office.
Iceland	® It is to be expected that a greater number of people is registered in the National Register of Persons than are actually residing in the country. *Reference date:* 31 December.	National Register of Persons, Statistics Iceland.
Ireland	® 2002 and 2006 Censuses. Persons usually resident and present in their usual residence on census night. ε PM for other years.	Central Statistics Office.
Israel	The data refer to permanent immigrants, that is, to persons who entered the country to take up permanent residence under the Law of Return or the Law of Entrance. Before 2006, the detail by country of origin (Table B.4) includes Jews and Others and excludes Arabs whereas from 2006 on, it includes Jews only. For the whole period, the total foreign-born population (A.4) includes Jews and Others and excludes Arabs. Data for Algeria include Tunisia. Data for former Czechoslovakia include Slovak Republic, Czech Republic, and Hungary. Data for Germany include Austria. The statistical data for Israel are supplied by and under the responsibility of the relevant Israeli authorities. The use of such data by the OECD is without prejudice to the status of the Golan Heights, East Jerusalem and Israeli settlements in the West Bank under the terms of international law.	Central Bureau of Statistics.

Metadata related to Tables A.4 and B.4. **Stocks of foreign-born population** (cont.)

Legend: ® Observed figures.
ε Estimates (in italic) made by means of the component method (CM) or the parametric method (PM). For more details on the method of estimation, please refer to *www.oecd.org/migration/foreignborn*. No estimate is made by country of birth (Table B.4).

Data for foreign-born from Serbia include persons from Serbia, Montenegro and Serbia and Montenegro.

Country	Comments	Source
Italy	® 2001 Census. ® ISTAT for other years.	National Institute of Statistics (ISTAT).
Luxembourg	® 2001 Census. ε CM for other years.	Central Office of Statistics and Economic Studies (Statec).
Mexico	® 2000 Census. ® From 2005 on, estimation of the total number of foreign-born from the National Survey of Occupation and Employment (ENOE).	National Migration Institute (INM) and National Institute of Statistics and Geography (INEGI).
Netherlands	® *Reference date:* 1 January of the following year.	Population register, Central Bureau of Statistics (CBS).
New Zealand	® 2001 and 2006 Censuses. ε PM for other years.	Statistics New Zealand.
Norway	® *Reference date:* 31 December.	Central Population Register, Statistics Norway.
Poland	® 2002 Census. Excluding foreign temporary residents who, at the time of the census, had been staying at a given address in Poland for less than 12 months. Country of birth in accordance with political (administrative) boundaries at the time of the census.	Central Statistical Office.
Portugal	® 2001 Census. ε CM for other years.	National Statistical Institute (INE)
Russian Federation	® 2002 Census.	Federal Migration Service, Ministry of the Interior.
Slovak Republic	® 2001 Census. Population who had permanent resident status at the date of the Census. ® 2004 Population Register.	Ministry of the Interior.
Slovenia	® Central Population Register.	Ministry of the Interior.
Spain	® Population register. *Reference date*: end of the year.	Municipal Registers, National Statistics Institute (INE).
Sweden	® *Reference date:* 31 December.	Population Register, Statistics Sweden.
Switzerland	® 2000 Census. ® 2010 Population Register of the Confederation. ε CM for other years.	Federal Statistical Office.
Turkey	® 2000 Census.	Turkish Statistical Institute.
United Kingdom	® 2001 Census. ® 2006-10 Labour Force Survey. Foreign-born residents. ε PM for other years. Figures are rounded.	Office for National Statistics.
United States	® American Community Survey.	Census Bureau.

Table A.5. Stocks of foreign population by nationality in OECD countries and the Russian Federation

Thousands and percentages

	2000	2001	2002	2003	2004	2005	2006	2007	2008	2009	2010
Austria	701.8	730.3	746.8	754.2	774.4	796.7	804.8	835.2	870.7	895.1	927.6
% of total population	8.7	9.1	9.2	9.3	9.5	9.7	9.7	10.1	10.4	10.7	11.1
Belgium	861.7	846.7	850.1	860.3	870.9	900.5	932.2	971.4	1 013.3	1 057.7	1 119.3
% of total population	8.4	8.2	8.2	8.3	8.4	8.6	8.8	9.1	9.5	9.8	10.2
Canada	..	1 568.6	..	..	..	..	1 758.9	..	..	..	..
% of total population	..	5.1	..	..	..	..	5.4	..	..	..	..
Czech Republic	201.0	210.8	231.6	240.4	254.3	278.3	321.5	392.3	437.6	432.5	424.3
% of total population	2.0	2.1	2.3	2.4	2.5	2.7	3.1	3.8	4.2	4.1	4.0
Denmark	258.6	266.7	265.4	271.2	267.6	270.1	278.1	298.5	320.2	329.9	346.0
% of total population	4.8	5.0	4.9	5.0	5.0	5.0	5.1	5.5	5.8	6.0	6.2
Estonia	287.1	273.8	269.5	266.5	262.6	255.1	243.8	232.2	223.6	219.2	..
% of total population	21.0	20.1	19.8	19.7	19.5	19.0	18.1	17.3	16.7	16.4	..
Finland	91.1	98.6	103.7	107.0	108.3	113.9	121.7	132.7	143.3	155.7	168.0
% of total population	1.8	1.9	2.0	2.1	2.1	2.2	2.3	2.5	2.7	2.9	3.1
France	..	..	..	..	..	..	3 541.8	3 696.9	3 731.2	..	3 769.0
% of total population	..	..	..	..	..	..	5.7	6.0	6.0	..	6.0
Germany	7 296.8	7 318.6	7 335.6	7 334.8	6 717.1	6 755.8	6 751.0	6 744.9	6 727.6	6 694.8	6 753.6
% of total population	8.9	8.9	8.9	8.9	8.1	8.2	8.2	8.2	8.2	8.2	8.3
Greece	304.6	355.8	436.8	472.8	533.4	553.1	570.6	643.1	733.6	839.7	810.0
% of total population	2.8	3.2	4.0	4.3	4.8	5.0	5.1	5.7	6.5	7.4	7.1
Hungary	110.0	116.4	115.9	130.1	142.2	154.4	166.0	174.7	184.4	197.8	209.2
% of total population	1.1	1.1	1.1	1.3	1.4	1.5	1.6	1.7	1.8	2.0	2.1
Iceland	8.8	9.9	10.2	10.2	10.6	13.8	18.6	23.4	24.4	21.7	21.1
% of total population	3.1	3.5	3.6	3.5	3.6	4.7	6.1	7.5	7.6	6.8	6.6
Ireland	..	..	219.3	..	..	..	413.2	..	..	..	..
% of total population	..	..	5.6	..	..	..	9.7	..	..	..	..
Italy	1 379.7	1 448.4	1 549.4	1 990.2	2 402.2	2 670.5	2 938.9	3 432.7	3 891.3	4 235.1	4 570.3
% of total population	2.4	2.5	2.7	3.5	4.2	4.6	5.0	5.8	6.6	7.1	7.6
Japan	1 686.4	1 778.5	1 851.8	1 915.0	1 973.7	2 011.6	2 083.2	2 151.4	2 215.9	2 184.7	2 132.9
% of total population	1.3	1.4	1.5	1.5	1.5	1.6	1.6	1.7	1.7	1.7	1.7
Korea	210.2	229.6	271.7	460.3	491.4	510.5	660.6	800.3	895.5	920.9	1 002.7
% of total population	0.4	0.5	0.6	1.0	1.0	1.1	1.4	1.7	1.8	1.9	2.0
Luxembourg	164.7	166.7	170.7	177.8	183.7	191.3	198.3	205.9	215.5	216.3	221.4
% of total population	37.7	37.8	38.3	39.5	40.4	41.5	42.3	43.2	44.5	43.8	44.1
Mexico	..	..	..	..	..	..	..	..	..	262.7	..
% of total population	..	..	..	..	..	..	..	..	..	0.2	..
Netherlands	667.8	690.4	700.0	702.2	699.4	691.4	681.9	688.4	719.5	735.2	760.4
% of total population	4.2	4.3	4.3	4.3	4.3	4.2	4.2	4.2	4.4	4.4	4.6
Norway	184.3	185.9	197.7	204.7	213.3	222.3	238.3	266.3	303.0	333.9	369.2
% of total population	4.1	4.1	4.4	4.5	4.6	4.8	5.1	5.7	6.4	6.9	7.6
Poland	..	..	49.2	..	..	..	54.9	57.5	60.4	49.6	..
% of total population	..	..	0.1	..	..	..	0.1	0.2	0.2	0.1	..
Portugal	207.6	360.8	423.8	444.6	469.1	432.0	437.1	446.3	443.1	457.3	448.1
% of total population	2.0	3.5	4.1	4.3	4.5	4.1	4.1	4.2	4.2	4.3	4.2
Russian Federation	..	..	1 025.4	..	..	..	..	..	..	..	..
% of total population	..	..	0.7	..	..	..	..	..	..	..	..
Slovak Republic	28.8	29.4	29.5	29.2	22.3	25.6	32.1	40.9	52.5	62.9	68.0
% of total population	0.5	0.5	0.5	0.5	0.4	0.5	0.6	0.8	1.0	1.2	1.3
Slovenia	42.3	45.3	44.7	45.3	44.3	49.0	53.6	68.6	70.7	82.3	82.7
% of total population	2.1	2.3	2.2	2.3	2.2	2.4	2.7	3.4	3.5	4.0	4.0

Table A.5. **Stocks of foreign population by nationality in OECD countries and the Russian Federation** (cont.)

Thousands and percentages

	2000	2001	2002	2003	2004	2005	2006	2007	2008	2009	2010
Spain	1 370.7	1 977.9	2 664.2	3 034.3	3 730.6	4 144.2	4 519.6	5 268.8	5 648.7	5 747.7	5 730.7
% of total population	3.4	4.9	6.4	7.2	8.7	9.5	10.3	11.7	12.4	12.5	12.4
Sweden	472.4	471.3	469.8	452.8	457.8	457.5	485.9	518.2	555.4	595.1	633.3
% of total population	5.3	5.3	5.3	5.1	5.1	5.1	5.4	5.7	6.0	6.4	6.8
Switzerland	1 384.4	1 419.1	1 447.3	1 471.0	1 495.0	1 511.9	1 523.6	1 571.0	1 638.9	1 680.2	1 720.4
% of total population	19.3	19.6	19.9	20.0	20.2	20.3	20.4	20.8	21.4	21.7	22.1
Turkey	271.3	..	..	..	..	..	..	..	..	..	..
% of total population	0.4	..	..	..	..	..	..	..	..	..	..
United Kingdom	2 342.0	2 587.0	2 584.0	2 742.0	2 857.0	3 035.0	3 392.0	3 824.0	4 186.0	4 348.0	4 524.0
% of total population	4.0	4.4	4.4	4.6	4.8	5.1	5.7	6.4	6.9	7.1	7.4
United States	17 757.7	18 533.7	20 490.6	20 634.1	21 115.7	21 707.1	21 775.4	22 741.1	22 213.9	21 274.3	21 581.3
% of total population	6.3	6.5	7.1	7.1	7.2	7.3	7.3	7.5	7.3	6.9	7.0

Note: For details on definitions and sources, refer to the metadata at the end of Tables B.5.

StatLink http://dx.doi.org/10.1787/888932617474

Table B.5. Stock of foreign population by nationality
Thousands
AUSTRIA

	2000	2001	2002	2003	2004	2005	2006	2007	2008	2009	2010	Of which: Women 2010 (%)
Germany	..	75.3	78.2	83.6	91.2	100.4	109.2	119.8	130.7	138.2	146.4	50
Serbia	..	140.9	141.8	137.6	136.8	137.9	135.8	132.6	134.9	134.2	135.7	48
Turkey	127.3	127.1	127.2	123.0	116.5	113.1	108.2	109.2	110.7	112.2	113.5	48
Bosnia and Herzegovina	..	95.5	96.1	94.2	90.9	88.3	86.2	85.0	84.6	84.3	84.2	45
Croatia	..	57.3	58.5	58.5	58.6	58.1	56.8	56.4	56.3	56.3	56.5	47
Romania	..	17.8	19.5	20.5	21.3	21.9	21.9	27.6	32.3	36.0	41.7	56
Poland	..	21.4	21.8	22.2	26.6	30.6	33.3	35.5	36.9	37.4	38.8	49
Hungary	..	13.1	13.7	14.2	15.1	16.3	17.4	19.3	21.5	23.5	26.0	52
Russian Federation	..	3.7	4.9	8.0	14.2	17.2	18.8	20.0	21.8	22.3	22.8	55
Slovak Republic	..	7.5	8.5	9.5	11.3	13.0	14.2	15.7	18.1	19.3	20.5	64
Former Yug. Rep. of Macedonia	..	13.2	14.4	15.3	16.0	16.3	16.3	16.5	17.0	17.3	18.0	46
Italy	..	10.7	10.9	11.3	11.7	12.2	12.7	13.4	14.3	15.1	16.0	41
Bulgaria	..	4.7	5.3	5.9	6.3	6.5	6.4	7.6	9.0	9.9	11.4	56
China	..	5.1	6.5	7.6	8.3	8.8	8.9	9.3	9.7	9.9	9.9	55
Czech Republic	..	6.2	6.6	6.9	7.4	7.7	8.0	8.3	9.1	9.2	9.4	63
Other countries	..	130.8	132.9	136.0	142.2	148.5	150.7	158.9	163.9	170.2	176.9	
Total	701.8	730.3	746.8	754.2	774.4	796.7	804.8	835.2	870.7	895.1	927.6	50

Note: For details on definitions and sources, please refer to the metadata at the end of the tables.

StatLink http://dx.doi.org/10.1787/888932617569

Table B.5. Stock of foreign population by nationality
Thousands
BELGIUM

	2000	2001	2002	2003	2004	2005	2006	2007	2008	2009	2010	Of which: Women 2007 (%)
Italy	195.6	190.8	187.0	183.0	179.0	175.5	171.9	169.0	167.0	165.1	162.8	46
France	109.3	111.1	113.0	114.9	117.3	120.6	125.1	130.6	136.6	140.2	145.3	52
Netherlands	88.8	92.6	96.6	100.7	105.0	110.5	117.0	123.5	130.2	133.5	137.8	46
Morocco	106.8	90.6	83.6	81.8	81.3	80.6	80.6	79.9	79.4	81.9	84.7	49
Poland	6.9	8.9	10.4	11.6	14.0	18.0	23.2	30.4	36.3	43.1	49.7	49
Spain	43.4	45.0	44.5	43.8	43.2	42.9	42.8	42.7	43.6	45.2	48.0	50
Turkey	56.2	45.9	42.6	41.3	39.9	39.7	39.4	39.5	39.6	39.6	39.8	50
Germany	34.6	34.7	35.1	35.5	36.3	37.0	37.6	38.4	39.1	39.4	39.8	50
Portugal	25.6	25.8	26.0	26.8	27.4	28.0	28.7	29.8	31.7	33.1	34.5	49
Romania	2.4	3.3	4.0	4.6	5.6	7.5	10.2	15.3	21.4	26.4	33.6	50
United Kingdom	26.6	26.4	26.2	26.2	26.0	25.7	25.1	25.1	25.5	25.0	25.0	45
Democratic Republic of the Congo	11.3	13.0	13.6	13.8	13.2	13.5	14.2	15.0	16.8	18.1	19.6	51
Bulgaria	1.0	1.5	1.9	2.2	2.7	3.3	3.9	6.7	10.4	13.2	17.3	51
Greece	18.0	17.6	17.3	17.1	16.6	16.3	15.7	15.2	14.9	14.8	14.8	49
Russian Federation	2.5	2.9	3.3	3.7	4.0	5.5	6.4	7.2	11.8	12.8	14.0	60
Other countries	132.6	136.8	144.9	153.2	159.5	175.9	190.3	203.3	208.9	226.3	252.6	
Total	861.7	846.7	850.1	860.3	870.9	900.5	932.2	971.4	1 013.3	1 057.7	1 119.3	49

Note: For details on definitions and sources, please refer to the metadata at the end of the tables.

StatLink http://dx.doi.org/10.1787/888932617569

Table B.5. Stock of foreign population by nationality
Thousands
CZECH REPUBLIC

	2000	2001	2002	2003	2004	2005	2006	2007	2008	2009	2010	Of which: Women 2010 (%)
Ukraine	50.2	51.8	59.1	62.3	78.3	87.8	102.6	126.7	131.9	131.9	124.3	43
Slovak Republic	44.3	53.2	61.1	64.9	47.4	49.4	58.4	67.9	76.0	73.4	71.8	46
Viet Nam	23.6	23.9	27.1	29.0	34.2	36.8	40.8	51.1	60.3	61.1	60.3	41
Russian Federation	13.0	12.4	12.8	12.6	14.7	16.3	18.6	23.3	27.1	30.3	31.8	54
Poland	17.1	16.5	16.0	15.8	16.3	17.8	18.9	20.6	21.7	19.3	18.2	53
Germany	5.0	4.9	5.2	5.2	5.8	7.2	10.1	15.7	17.5	13.8	13.9	21
Moldova	2.1	2.5	2.8	3.3	4.1	4.7	6.2	8.0	10.6	10.0	8.9	38
Bulgaria	4.0	4.1	4.2	4.0	4.4	4.6	4.6	5.0	5.9	6.4	6.9	37
United States	3.2	3.2	3.4	3.3	3.8	4.0	4.2	4.5	5.3	5.6	6.1	39
Mongolia	..	..	..	..	..	..	..	6.0	8.6	5.7	5.6	59
China	3.6	3.3	3.2	4.0	3.4	3.6	4.2	5.0	5.2	5.4	5.5	46
Romania	2.4	2.3	2.3	2.3	2.6	2.7	2.9	3.2	3.6	4.1	4.4	14
United Kingdom	1.5	1.6	1.8	1.7	1.8	2.2	3.5	3.8	4.5	4.4	4.4	23
Kazakhstan	..	..	..	..	..	..	..	3.0	3.4	3.9	4.2	54
Belarus	2.6	2.5	2.7	2.7	2.9	3.0	3.2	3.7	3.9	4.0	4.2	58
Other countries	28.5	28.4	29.9	29.4	34.7	38.3	43.3	44.9	52.1	53.1	53.9	
Total	**201.0**	**210.8**	**231.6**	**240.4**	**254.3**	**278.3**	**321.5**	**392.3**	**437.6**	**432.5**	**424.3**	**42**

Note: For details on definitions and sources, please refer to the metadata at the end of the tables.

StatLink http://dx.doi.org/10.1787/888932617569

Table B.5. Stock of foreign population by nationality
Thousands
DENMARK

	2000	2001	2002	2003	2004	2005	2006	2007	2008	2009	2010	Of which: Women 2010 (%)
Turkey	35.2	33.4	31.9	30.3	30.0	29.5	28.8	28.8	28.9	29.0	29.2	49
Poland	5.5	5.7	5.7	5.9	6.2	7.4	9.7	13.8	19.9	21.1	22.6	48
Germany	12.7	12.9	13.0	13.3	13.6	14.2	15.4	18.0	20.4	21.1	21.6	48
Iraq	13.8	16.5	18.0	19.4	19.2	18.7	18.1	18.3	17.6	16.7	16.7	47
Norway	13.0	13.2	13.4	13.8	13.9	13.9	14.2	14.4	14.8	15.0	15.1	60
United Kingdom	12.6	12.8	12.7	12.8	12.8	12.9	13.2	13.7	14.2	14.3	14.7	35
Sweden	10.8	10.8	10.7	10.8	10.9	11.2	11.6	12.1	12.7	12.8	12.9	59
Bosnia and Herzegovina	..	..	17.8	17.2	14.0	12.7	12.2	12.1	11.8	11.5	11.4	49
Afghanistan	4.2	7.1	8.2	9.1	9.3	9.4	9.4	9.5	9.4	9.1	9.5	47
Iceland	5.9	6.0	6.6	7.1	7.4	7.7	8.0	8.3	8.5	8.9	9.0	52
Former Yugoslavia	35.0	34.8	10.8	10.7	9.8	9.4	8.7	8.6	8.1	9.1	8.9	50
Thailand	4.4	4.9	5.2	5.4	5.6	5.9	6.2	6.7	7.3	7.7	8.3	84
Somalia	14.4	14.6	13.3	13.1	11.3	9.8	9.0	8.8	8.5	8.3	8.2	48
Pakistan	7.1	7.2	6.9	7.0	6.9	6.7	6.6	6.7	6.9	7.1	7.8	50
China	2.7	3.2	3.9	5.2	5.9	6.2	6.1	6.6	7.2	7.4	7.6	56
Other countries	81.2	83.7	87.2	90.2	90.9	94.6	100.8	112.1	124.1	130.8	142.7	
Total	**258.6**	**266.7**	**265.4**	**271.2**	**267.6**	**270.1**	**278.1**	**298.5**	**320.2**	**329.9**	**346.0**	**51**

Note: For details on definitions and sources, please refer to the metadata at the end of the tables.

StatLink http://dx.doi.org/10.1787/888932617569

STATISTICAL ANNEX

Table B.5. Stock of foreign population by nationality
Thousands
FINLAND

	2000	2001	2002	2003	2004	2005	2006	2007	2008	2009	2010	Of which: Women 2010 (%)
Estonia	10.8	11.7	12.4	13.4	14.0	15.5	17.6	20.0	22.6	25.5	29.1	52
Russian Federation	20.6	22.7	24.3	25.0	24.6	24.6	25.3	26.2	26.9	28.2	28.4	58
Sweden	7.9	8.0	8.0	8.1	8.2	8.2	8.3	8.3	8.4	8.5	8.5	42
Somalia	4.2	4.4	4.5	4.6	4.7	4.7	4.6	4.9	4.9	5.6	6.6	47
China	1.7	1.9	2.1	2.4	2.6	3.0	3.4	4.0	4.6	5.2	5.6	53
Iraq	3.1	3.2	3.4	3.5	3.4	3.3	3.0	3.0	3.2	4.0	5.0	36
Thailand	1.3	1.5	1.8	2.1	2.3	2.6	3.0	3.5	3.9	4.5	5.0	87
Turkey	1.8	2.0	2.1	2.3	2.4	2.6	2.9	3.2	3.4	3.8	4.0	29
Germany	2.2	2.3	2.5	2.6	2.6	2.8	3.0	3.3	3.5	3.6	3.7	40
India	0.8	0.9	1.0	1.2	1.3	1.6	2.0	2.3	2.7	3.2	3.5	37
United Kingdom	2.2	2.4	2.5	2.7	2.7	2.8	2.9	3.1	3.2	3.3	3.5	20
Serbia	1.2	1.9	2.2	2.8	3.3	3.3	3.4	3.5	3.5	3.6	3.8	45
Viet Nam	1.8	1.8	1.7	1.7	1.5	1.7	1.8	2.0	2.3	2.5	2.8	53
Iran	1.9	2.2	2.4	2.5	2.6	2.6	2.6	2.6	2.5	2.5	2.6	43
Afghanistan	0.4	0.7	1.1	1.3	1.6	1.8	2.0	2.2	2.2	2.3	2.5	44
Other countries	29.2	31.0	31.6	31.0	30.6	32.8	35.9	40.5	45.3	49.4	53.4	
Total	**91.1**	**98.6**	**103.7**	**107.0**	**108.3**	**113.9**	**121.7**	**132.7**	**143.3**	**155.7**	**168.0**	**47**

Note: For details on definitions and sources, please refer to the metadata at the end of the tables.

StatLink http://dx.doi.org/10.1787/888932617569

Table B.5. Stock of foreign population by nationality
Thousands
FRANCE

	2000	2001	2002	2003	2004	2005	2006	2007	2008	2009	2010	Of which: Women 2010 (%)
Portugal	..	..	..	..	..	..	490.6	491.0	492.5	..	..	..
Algeria	..	..	..	..	..	..	481.0	475.3	471.3	..	..	..
Morocco	..	..	..	..	..	..	460.4	452.0	444.8	..	..	..
Turkey	..	..	..	..	..	..	223.6	223.4	220.1	..	..	..
Italy	..	..	..	..	..	..	177.4	175.2	174.3	..	..	..
United Kingdom	..	..	..	..	..	..	136.5	146.6	151.8	..	..	..
Tunisia	..	..	..	..	..	..	145.9	144.2	143.9	..	..	..
Spain	..	..	..	..	..	..	133.8	131.0	130.1	..	..	..
Germany	..	..	..	..	..	..	92.4	93.4	93.9	..	..	..
Belgium	..	..	..	..	..	..	81.3	84.4	87.7	..	..	..
China	..	..	..	..	..	..	66.2	72.1	76.7	..	..	..
Haiti	..	..	..	..	..	..	40.4	62.0	62.2	..	..	..
Mali	..	..	..	..	..	..	56.7	59.5	59.7	..	..	..
Senegal	..	..	..	..	..	..	49.5	50.5	50.2	..	..	..
Congo	..	..	..	..	..	..	44.3	46.1	47.7	..	..	..
Other countries	..	..	..	..	..	..	861.7	990.2	1 024.3	..	..	
Total	..	..	..	..	..	..	**3 541.8**	**3 696.9**	**3 731.2**	..	**3 769.0**	..

Note: For details on definitions and sources, please refer to the metadata at the end of the tables.

StatLink http://dx.doi.org/10.1787/888932617569

STATISTICAL ANNEX

Table B.5. **Stock of foreign population by nationality**
Thousands
GERMANY

	2000	2001	2002	2003	2004	2005	2006	2007	2008	2009	2010	Of which: Women 2010 (%)
Turkey	1 998.5	1 947.9	1 912.2	1 877.7	1 764.3	1 764.0	1 738.8	1 713.6	1 688.4	1 658.1	1 629.5	48
Italy	619.1	616.3	609.8	601.3	548.2	540.8	534.7	528.3	523.2	517.5	517.5	41
Poland	301.4	310.4	317.6	326.9	292.1	326.6	361.7	384.8	393.8	398.5	419.4	51
Greece	365.4	362.7	359.4	354.6	316.0	309.8	303.8	294.9	287.2	278.1	276.7	46
Croatia	216.8	223.8	231.0	236.6	229.2	228.9	227.5	225.3	223.1	221.2	220.2	51
Russian Federation	115.9	136.1	155.6	173.5	178.6	185.9	187.5	187.8	188.3	189.3	191.3	62
Austria	187.7	189.0	189.3	189.5	174.0	174.8	175.7	175.9	175.4	174.5	175.2	47
Bosnia and Herzegovina	156.3	159.0	163.8	167.1	156.0	156.9	157.1	158.2	156.8	154.6	152.4	49
Netherlands	110.8	112.4	115.2	118.7	114.1	118.6	123.5	128.2	133.0	134.9	136.3	45
Romania	90.1	88.1	88.7	89.1	73.4	73.0	73.4	84.6	94.3	105.0	126.5	52
Serbia	..	..	..	..	125.8	297.0	316.8	330.6	319.9	298.0	232.4	49
Ukraine	89.3	103.5	116.0	126.0	128.1	130.7	129.0	127.0	126.2	125.6	124.3	62
Portugal	133.7	132.6	131.4	130.6	116.7	115.6	115.0	114.6	114.5	113.3	113.2	45
France	110.2	111.3	112.4	113.0	100.5	102.2	104.1	106.5	108.1	107.3	108.7	53
Spain	129.5	128.7	127.5	126.0	108.3	107.8	106.8	106.3	105.5	104.0	105.4	50
Other countries	2 672.2	2 696.7	2 705.8	2 704.3	2 291.9	2 123.1	2 095.8	2 078.4	2 090.0	2 115.0	2 224.5	
Total	**7 296.8**	**7 318.6**	**7 335.6**	**7 334.8**	**6 717.1**	**6 755.8**	**6 751.0**	**6 744.9**	**6 727.6**	**6 694.8**	**6 753.6**	**49**

Note: For details on definitions and sources, please refer to the metadata at the end of the tables.

StatLink ⟶ http://dx.doi.org/10.1787/888932617569

Table B.5. **Stock of foreign population by nationality**
Thousands
GREECE

	2000	2001	2002	2003	2004	2005	2006	2007	2008	2009	2010	Of which: Women 2010 (%)
Albania	185.7	209.5	262.1	294.7	325.6	341.0	347.4	384.6	413.9	501.7	485.0	47
Bulgaria	8.1	12.6	18.6	17.3	25.3	27.9	29.5	30.7	40.2	54.5	48.4	69
Romania	5.2	7.2	13.8	14.6	16.2	18.9	18.9	25.7	29.5	33.8	33.3	59
Georgia	4.4	10.2	12.0	9.5	14.1	16.9	15.1	23.8	33.6	33.9	32.8	68
Pakistan	3.7	2.9	4.8	6.2	4.2	5.5	6.7	13.9	18.0	23.0	21.2	11
Bangladesh	0.8	0.9	1.5	1.0	1.8	3.2	2.1	2.6	14.1	12.5	14.6	4
Russian Federation	15.6	19.9	22.0	17.8	16.8	17.6	18.9	21.6	16.7	19.5	14.1	83
Ukraine	2.5	6.4	11.3	10.2	13.1	12.2	12.2	14.1	11.9	13.7	12.2	73
Poland	11.2	13.5	14.1	15.9	17.0	16.1	16.6	21.4	18.9	11.2	10.2	60
Cyprus	6.8	5.2	7.7	8.1	12.2	11.0	10.6	11.2	14.2	11.8	9.9	49
Germany	4.8	3.5	2.3	4.3	3.8	5.6	6.7	7.1	8.1	7.3	9.6	74
Egypt	2.7	4.3	6.1	11.2	6.3	2.6	3.6	5.2	12.6	10.3	9.5	22
India	1.6	2.1	1.9	1.7	2.3	1.6	0.7	3.3	5.0	7.7	8.0	22
United Kingdom	4.0	5.3	3.6	6.2	7.1	7.7	7.6	8.0	7.5	7.5	7.3	54
Armenia	2.9	5.1	4.0	4.7	7.3	6.1	7.1	5.0	9.1	12.3	6.7	46
Other countries	44.5	47.3	50.8	49.5	60.1	58.9	66.8	64.8	80.2	79.0	87.2	
Total	**304.6**	**355.8**	**436.8**	**472.8**	**533.4**	**553.1**	**570.6**	**643.1**	**733.6**	**839.7**	**810.0**	**49**

Notes: For details on definitions and sources, please refer to the metadata at the end of the tables. See notes on Cyprus in the introduction of this annex.

StatLink ⟶ http://dx.doi.org/10.1787/888932617569

STATISTICAL ANNEX

Table B.5. Stock of foreign population by nationality
Thousands
HUNGARY

	2000	2001	2002	2003	2004	2005	2006	2007	2008	2009	2010	Of which: Women 2010 (%)
Romania	41.6	45.0	47.3	55.7	67.5	66.2	67.0	65.8	66.4	72.7	76.9	46
Germany	7.5	7.7	7.1	7.4	6.9	10.5	15.0	14.4	16.7	18.7	20.2	48
Ukraine	8.9	9.8	9.9	13.1	13.9	15.3	15.9	17.3	17.6	17.2	16.5	53
China	5.8	6.8	6.4	6.8	6.9	8.6	9.0	10.2	10.7	11.2	11.8	45
Serbia	8.6	8.4	7.9	8.3	13.6	8.4	8.5	13.7	13.7	11.5	10.7	48
Slovak Republic	1.6	2.2	1.5	2.5	1.2	3.6	4.3	4.9	6.1	6.4	7.3	60
Former Yugoslavia	..	..	..	4.1	..	3.7	4.2	3.5	3.3	5.7	5.8	45
Austria	0.7	0.8	0.8	0.8	0.5	1.5	2.2	2.6	3.0	3.7	3.9	37
Russian Federation	1.9	2.0	1.8	2.2	2.6	2.8	2.8	2.8	2.9	3.3	3.5	64
United States	..	..	..	..	..	..	1.9	2.3	2.4	3.1	3.3	44
Viet Nam	1.9	2.2	2.1	2.4	2.5	3.1	3.1	3.0	3.3	3.1	3.1	49
Former USSR	5.6	5.1	5.7	4.0	5.1	3.0	3.1	2.7	2.6	3.0	3.0	69
Poland	2.3	2.2	1.9	2.2	2.2	2.4	2.7	2.6	2.8	2.5	2.7	61
United Kingdom	0.6	0.7	0.9	1.0	0.4	1.5	1.9	2.1	2.4	2.4	2.5	33
France	0.5	0.6	0.7	0.8	0.3	1.3	1.5	1.5	2.2	1.9	2.1	41
Other countries	22.5	22.8	21.9	19.0	18.3	22.5	23.0	25.1	28.3	31.4	35.8	
Total	**110.0**	**116.4**	**115.9**	**130.1**	**142.2**	**154.4**	**166.0**	**174.7**	**184.4**	**197.8**	**209.2**	**47**

Note: For details on definitions and sources, please refer to the metadata at the end of the tables.

StatLink http://dx.doi.org/10.1787/888932617569

Table B.5. Stock of foreign population by nationality
Thousands
ICELAND

	2000	2001	2002	2003	2004	2005	2006	2007	2008	2009	2010	Of which: Women 2010 (%)
Poland	1.5	1.7	1.8	1.9	1.9	3.2	6.0	9.9	11.0	9.6	9.1	45
Lithuania	0.2	0.3	0.4	0.4	0.4	0.6	1.0	1.5	1.7	1.5	1.6	45
Germany	0.5	0.6	0.6	0.6	0.5	0.8	0.9	1.1	1.1	1.0	1.0	63
Denmark	1.0	0.9	0.9	0.9	0.9	0.9	0.9	1.0	1.0	0.9	0.9	55
Latvia	0.0	0.1	0.1	0.1	0.1	0.2	0.3	0.5	0.6	0.6	0.6	49
Philippines	0.5	0.5	0.6	0.6	0.6	0.8	0.8	0.7	0.7	0.6	0.6	57
United Kingdom	0.4	0.4	0.4	0.4	0.3	0.4	0.4	0.4	0.5	0.5	0.6	28
Thailand	0.4	0.5	0.5	0.5	0.5	0.5	0.5	0.5	0.6	0.5	0.5	69
Portugal	0.1	0.1	0.1	0.1	0.4	0.4	0.7	0.9	0.8	0.6	0.5	35
United States	0.6	0.6	0.6	0.5	0.5	0.6	0.6	0.6	0.5	0.5	0.5	44
France	0.2	0.2	0.2	0.1	0.1	0.1	0.2	0.2	0.3	0.3	0.3	49
Sweden	0.3	0.3	0.3	0.3	0.3	0.3	0.3	0.4	0.4	0.3	0.3	60
Norway	0.3	0.3	0.3	0.3	0.3	0.3	0.3	0.3	0.3	0.3	0.2	63
Spain	0.1	0.1	0.1	0.1	0.1	0.1	0.1	0.1	0.2	0.2	0.2	40
China	0.1	0.1	0.2	0.2	0.2	0.6	0.8	0.4	0.2	0.2	0.2	46
Other countries	2.6	3.0	3.2	3.3	3.4	3.9	4.5	4.8	4.6	4.0	3.8	
Total	**8.8**	**9.9**	**10.2**	**10.2**	**10.6**	**13.8**	**18.6**	**23.4**	**24.4**	**21.7**	**21.1**	**48**

Note: For details on definitions and sources, please refer to the metadata at the end of the tables.

StatLink http://dx.doi.org/10.1787/888932617569

Table B.5. Stock of foreign population by nationality
Thousands
IRELAND

	2000	2001	2002	2003	2004	2005	2006	2007	2008	2009	2010	Of which: Women 2010 (%)
United Kingdom	..	..	101.3	..	..	..	110.6	..	..	..	..	..
Poland	..	..	2.1	..	..	..	62.7	..	..	..	..	..
Lithuania	..	..	2.1	..	..	..	24.4	..	..	..	..	..
Nigeria	..	..	8.7	..	..	..	16.0	..	..	..	..	..
Latvia	..	..	1.8	..	..	..	13.2	..	..	..	..	..
United States	..	..	11.1	..	..	..	12.3	..	..	..	..	..
China	..	..	5.8	..	..	..	11.0	..	..	..	..	..
Germany	..	..	7.0	..	..	..	10.1	..	..	..	..	..
Philippines	..	..	3.7	..	..	..	9.3	..	..	..	..	..
France	..	..	6.2	..	..	..	8.9	..	..	..	..	..
India	..	..	2.5	..	..	..	8.3	..	..	..	..	..
Slovak Republic	..	..	..	..	..	..	8.0	..	..	..	..	..
Romania	..	..	4.9	..	..	..	7.6	..	..	..	..	..
Italy	..	..	3.7	..	..	..	6.1	..	..	..	..	..
Spain	..	..	4.3	..	..	..	6.0	..	..	..	..	..
Other countries	..	..	54.1	..	..	..	98.8	..	..	..	..	..
Total	..	..	**219.3**	..	..	..	**413.2**	..	..	..	..	..

Note: For details on definitions and sources, please refer to the metadata at the end of the tables.

StatLink http://dx.doi.org/10.1787/888932617569

Table B.5. Stock of foreign population by nationality
Thousands
ITALY

	2000	2001	2002	2003	2004	2005	2006	2007	2008	2009	2010	Of which: Women 2010 (%)
Romania	70.0	83.0	95.0	177.8	248.8	297.6	342.2	625.3	796.5	887.8	968.6	55
Albania	146.3	159.3	216.6	270.4	316.7	348.8	375.9	401.9	441.4	466.7	482.6	46
Morocco	162.3	167.9	215.4	253.4	294.9	319.5	343.2	365.9	403.6	431.5	452.4	44
China	60.1	62.1	69.6	86.7	111.7	127.8	144.9	156.5	170.3	188.4	209.9	48
Ukraine	9.1	12.6	12.7	58.0	93.4	107.1	120.1	132.7	154.0	174.1	200.7	80
Philippines	65.1	67.7	64.9	72.4	82.6	89.7	101.3	105.7	113.7	123.6	134.2	58
Moldova	3.3	5.7	7.0	24.6	38.0	47.6	55.8	68.6	89.4	105.6	130.9	67
India	30.0	32.5	35.5	44.8	54.3	61.8	69.5	77.4	91.9	105.9	121.0	39
Poland	30.4	32.9	30.0	40.3	50.8	60.8	72.5	90.2	99.4	105.6	109.0	71
Tunisia	46.0	53.4	59.5	68.6	78.2	83.6	88.9	93.6	100.1	103.7	106.3	37
Peru	30.1	31.7	34.2	43.0	53.4	59.3	66.5	70.8	77.6	87.7	98.6	60
Ecuador	11.2	12.3	15.3	33.5	53.2	62.0	68.9	73.2	80.1	85.9	91.6	59
Egypt	32.4	31.8	33.7	40.6	52.9	58.9	65.7	69.6	74.6	82.1	90.4	30
Bangladesh	20.8	22.0	20.6	27.4	35.8	41.6	49.6	55.2	65.5	74.0	82.5	33
Sri Lanka	33.8	38.8	34.2	39.2	45.6	50.5	56.7	61.1	68.7	75.3	81.1	45
Other countries	628.9	634.6	605.1	709.5	791.8	853.9	917.2	984.9	1 064.5	1 137.2	1 210.4	..
Total	**1 379.7**	**1 448.4**	**1 549.4**	**1 990.2**	**2 402.2**	**2 670.5**	**2 938.9**	**3 432.7**	**3 891.3**	**4 235.1**	**4 570.3**	**52**

Note: For details on definitions and sources, please refer to the metadata at the end of the tables.

StatLink http://dx.doi.org/10.1787/888932617569

STATISTICAL ANNEX

Table B.5. **Stock of foreign population by nationality**
Thousands
JAPAN

	2000	2001	2002	2003	2004	2005	2006	2007	2008	2009	2010	Of which: Women 2010 (%)
China	335.6	381.2	424.3	462.4	487.6	519.6	560.7	606.9	655.4	680.5	687.2	58
Korea	635.3	632.4	625.4	613.8	607.4	598.7	598.2	593.5	589.2	578.5	566.0	54
Brazil	254.4	266.0	268.3	274.7	286.6	302.1	313.0	317.0	312.6	267.5	230.6	46
Philippines	144.9	156.7	169.4	185.2	199.4	187.3	193.5	202.6	210.6	211.7	210.2	78
Peru	46.2	50.1	51.8	53.6	55.8	57.7	58.7	59.7	59.7	57.5	54.6	47
United States	44.9	46.2	48.0	47.8	48.8	49.4	51.3	51.9	52.7	52.1	50.7	34
Viet Nam	16.9	19.1	21.1	23.9	26.0	28.9	32.5	36.9	41.1	41.0	41.8	46
Thailand	29.3	31.7	33.7	34.8	36.3	37.7	39.6	41.4	42.6	42.7	41.3	75
Indonesia	19.3	20.8	21.7	22.9	23.9	25.1	24.9	25.6	27.3	25.5	24.9	35
India	10.1	11.7	13.3	14.2	15.5	17.0	18.9	20.6	22.3	22.9	22.5	30
Nepal	..	..	..	..	..	..	7.8	9.4	12.3	15.3	17.5	31
United Kingdom	16.5	17.5	18.5	18.2	18.1	17.5	17.8	17.3	17.0	16.6	16.0	27
Pakistan	7.5	7.9	8.2	8.4	8.6	8.8	9.1	9.3	9.9	10.3	10.3	20
Bangladesh	7.2	7.9	8.7	9.7	10.7	11.0	11.3	11.3	11.4	11.2	10.2	28
Canada	10.1	11.0	11.9	12.0	12.1	12.0	11.9	11.5	11.0	10.7	10.0	30
Other countries	108.4	118.2	127.5	133.3	137.0	138.8	133.9	136.7	140.8	140.9	139.2	
Total	**1 686.4**	**1 778.5**	**1 851.8**	**1 915.0**	**1 973.7**	**2 011.6**	**2 083.2**	**2 151.4**	**2 215.9**	**2 184.7**	**2 132.9**	**54**

Note: For details on definitions and sources, please refer to the metadata at the end of the tables.

StatLink ⟶ http://dx.doi.org/10.1787/888932617569

Table B.5. **Stock of foreign population by nationality**
Thousands
KOREA

	2000	2001	2002	2003	2004	2005	2006	2007	2008	2009	2010	Of which: Women 2010 (%)
China	59.0	73.6	84.5	185.5	208.8	217.0	311.8	421.5	487.1	489.1	505.4	..
Viet Nam	15.6	16.0	16.9	23.3	26.1	35.5	52.2	67.2	79.8	86.2	98.2	..
United States	22.8	22.0	37.6	40.0	39.0	41.8	46.0	51.1	56.2	63.1	57.6	..
Philippines	16.0	16.4	17.3	27.6	27.9	30.7	40.3	42.9	39.4	38.4	39.5	..
Thailand	3.2	3.6	4.8	20.0	21.9	21.4	30.2	31.7	30.1	28.7	27.6	..
Indonesia	16.7	15.6	17.1	28.3	26.1	22.6	23.7	23.7	27.4	25.9	27.4	..
Mongolia	..	..	1.4	9.2	11.0	13.7	19.2	20.5	21.2	21.0	21.8	..
Chinese Taipei	23.0	22.8	22.7	22.6	22.3	22.2	22.1	22.1	27.0	21.7	21.5	..
Uzbekistan	3.7	4.0	4.1	10.7	11.5	10.8	11.6	10.9	15.0	15.9	20.8	..
Japan	14.0	14.7	15.4	16.2	16.6	17.5	18.0	18.4	18.6	18.6	19.4	..
Sri Lanka	2.5	2.5	2.7	4.9	5.5	8.5	11.1	12.1	14.3	14.4	17.4	..
Canada	3.3	4.0	7.0	8.0	8.8	10.0	11.3	13.0	14.2	15.6	15.0	..
Cambodia	..	..	0.0	0.7	1.3	2.0	3.3	4.6	7.0	8.8	11.7	..
Bangladesh	7.9	9.1	9.0	13.6	13.1	9.1	8.6	7.8	7.7	7.3	9.3	..
Nepal	2.0	2.1	2.3	4.2	5.3	4.9	5.0	4.6	5.9	7.4	9.2	..
Other countries	20.5	23.3	28.8	45.6	46.3	43.0	46.3	48.1	44.7	58.8	100.9	
Total	**210.2**	**229.6**	**271.7**	**460.3**	**491.4**	**510.5**	**660.6**	**800.3**	**895.5**	**920.9**	**1 002.7**	**44**

Note: For details on definitions and sources, please refer to the metadata at the end of the tables.

StatLink ⟶ http://dx.doi.org/10.1787/888932617569

Table B.5. **Stock of foreign population by nationality**
Thousands
LUXEMBOURG

	2000	2001	2002	2003	2004	2005	2006	2007	2008	2009	2010	Of which: Women 2010 (%)
Portugal	58.5	59.8	61.4	64.9	67.8	70.8	73.7	76.6	80.0	79.8	81.3	..
France	20.1	20.9	21.6	22.2	23.1	24.1	25.2	26.6	28.5	29.7	31.1	..
Italy	20.3	19.1	19.0	19.0	19.0	19.1	19.1	19.1	19.4	18.2	17.7	..
Belgium	15.1	15.4	15.9	16.2	16.3	16.5	16.5	16.5	16.7	16.8	17.0	..
Germany	10.6	10.1	10.2	10.5	10.8	10.9	11.3	11.6	12.0	12.1	12.1	..
United Kingdom	4.9	4.5	4.7	4.7	4.7	4.8	4.9	5.0	5.3	5.5	5.6	..
Netherlands	3.9	3.6	3.6	3.6	3.7	3.7	3.8	3.8	3.9	3.9	3.8	..
Spain	3.0	2.8	2.9	2.9	3.0	3.1	3.2	3.2	3.3	3.3	3.4	..
Poland	..	..	0.7	0.8	1.0	1.3	1.6	1.8	2.2	2.5	2.7	..
Denmark	2.2	2.0	2.0	2.0	2.0	2.2	2.2	2.2	2.2	2.2	2.2	..
Sweden	1.2	1.2	1.2	1.2	1.3	1.4	1.5	1.7	1.8	1.8	1.8	..
Greece	1.4	1.2	1.2	1.2	1.2	1.3	1.4	1.4	1.5	1.5	1.6	..
Romania	..	..	0.4	0.4	0.4	0.5	0.6	0.9	1.1	1.3	1.5	..
Ireland	1.1	1.0	1.0	1.1	1.1	1.1	1.2	1.2	1.3	1.3	1.4	..
Finland	0.7	0.8	0.8	0.9	0.9	1.0	1.0	1.1	1.1	1.1	1.1	..
Other countries	21.9	24.1	24.1	26.2	27.6	29.4	31.1	33.3	35.2	35.6	37.1	
Total	**164.7**	**166.7**	**170.7**	**177.8**	**183.7**	**191.3**	**198.3**	**205.9**	**215.5**	**216.3**	**221.4**	..

Note: For details on definitions and sources, please refer to the metadata at the end of the tables.

StatLink http://dx.doi.org/10.1787/888932617569

Table B.5. **Stock of foreign population by nationality**
Thousands
MEXICO

	2000	2001	2002	2003	2004	2005	2006	2007	2008	2009	2010	Of which: Women 2010 (%)
United States	..	..	..	..	..	..	..	..	..	60.0	..	..
Spain	..	..	..	..	..	..	..	..	..	18.6	..	..
Argentina	..	..	..	..	..	..	..	..	..	15.2	..	..
Colombia	..	..	..	..	..	..	..	..	..	14.6	..	..
Canada	..	..	..	..	..	..	..	..	..	10.9	..	..
Cuba	..	..	..	..	..	..	..	..	..	10.3	..	..
China	..	..	..	..	..	..	..	..	..	10.2	..	..
Venezuela	..	..	..	..	..	..	..	..	..	10.1	..	..
France	..	..	..	..	..	..	..	..	..	9.4	..	..
Germany	..	..	..	..	..	..	..	..	..	8.9	..	..
Guatemala	..	..	..	..	..	..	..	..	..	8.4	..	..
Peru	..	..	..	..	..	..	..	..	..	6.6	..	..
Brazil	..	..	..	..	..	..	..	..	..	6.3	..	..
Korea	..	..	..	..	..	..	..	..	..	6.0	..	..
Italy	..	..	..	..	..	..	..	..	..	5.7	..	..
Other countries	..	..	..	..	..	..	..	..	..	61.6	..	..
Total	..	..	..	..	..	..	..	..	..	**262.7**	..	..

Note: For details on definitions and sources, please refer to the metadata at the end of the tables.

StatLink http://dx.doi.org/10.1787/888932617569

STATISTICAL ANNEX

Table B.5. **Stock of foreign population by nationality**
Thousands
NETHERLANDS

	2000	2001	2002	2003	2004	2005	2006	2007	2008	2009	2010	Of which: Women 2010 (%)
Turkey	100.8	100.3	100.3	101.8	100.6	98.9	96.8	93.7	92.7	90.8	88.0	50
Germany	54.8	55.6	56.1	56.5	57.1	58.5	60.2	62.4	65.9	68.4	71.4	55
Morocco	111.4	104.3	97.8	94.4	91.6	86.2	80.5	74.9	70.8	66.6	61.9	50
Poland	5.9	6.3	6.9	7.4	11.0	15.2	19.6	26.2	35.5	43.1	52.5	52
United Kingdom	41.4	43.6	44.1	43.7	42.5	41.5	40.3	40.2	41.1	41.4	41.4	40
Belgium	25.9	26.1	26.3	26.2	26.1	26.0	26.0	26.2	26.6	26.9	27.2	54
Italy	18.2	18.6	18.7	18.5	18.4	18.5	18.6	19.0	20.3	21.1	21.9	37
China	8.0	9.4	11.2	13.3	14.7	15.0	15.3	16.2	18.1	19.8	21.4	52
Spain	17.2	17.4	17.5	17.4	17.1	16.9	16.5	16.5	17.3	18.1	19.2	51
France	13.3	14.1	14.5	14.5	14.5	14.7	14.7	15.1	16.4	17.2	17.8	51
Portugal	9.8	10.6	11.3	11.8	12.0	12.1	12.2	12.9	14.2	15.4	15.7	45
United States	14.8	15.2	15.4	15.1	14.8	14.6	14.6	14.5	14.9	14.6	14.8	51
Bulgaria	0.9	1.1	1.4	1.7	1.9	2.1	2.2	6.4	10.2	12.3	14.1	51
Indonesia	9.3	10.1	10.8	11.2	11.4	11.5	11.4	11.4	11.6	11.6	11.7	68
India	3.4	3.4	3.4	3.6	3.7	4.3	5.4	6.4	8.0	8.7	9.6	39
Other countries	232.8	254.3	290.6	291.2	287.9	281.3	273.5	272.4	255.9	259.2	271.8	
Total	**667.8**	**690.4**	**700.0**	**702.2**	**699.4**	**691.4**	**681.9**	**688.4**	**719.5**	**735.2**	**760.4**	**50**

Note: For details on definitions and sources, please refer to the metadata at the end of the tables.

StatLink http://dx.doi.org/10.1787/888932617569

Table B.5. **Stock of foreign population by nationality**
Thousands
NORWAY

	2000	2001	2002	2003	2004	2005	2006	2007	2008	2009	2010	Of which: Women 2010 (%)
Poland	2.0	2.2	2.6	2.7	3.9	6.8	13.6	26.8	39.2	46.7	55.2	33
Sweden	25.2	25.1	25.2	25.4	25.8	26.6	27.9	29.9	32.8	35.8	39.2	48
Germany	7.1	7.5	8.2	8.8	9.6	10.6	12.2	15.3	18.9	20.8	22.4	45
Denmark	19.4	19.7	20.0	20.0	20.1	20.2	20.3	20.5	20.6	20.7	20.9	46
Lithuania	0.4	0.5	0.8	0.9	1.3	1.9	3.0	5.1	7.6	10.4	16.4	41
United Kingdom	11.1	11.0	11.2	11.0	11.2	11.2	11.6	12.0	12.6	13.3	14.0	36
Somalia	6.2	6.6	8.4	9.9	10.5	10.6	10.8	10.6	10.9	10.8	11.1	47
Russian Federation	3.3	3.9	4.8	6.2	7.4	8.2	8.8	9.7	10.4	10.6	10.8	63
Iraq	9.9	10.8	13.0	13.4	13.7	13.1	12.1	10.7	11.0	10.9	10.6	42
Thailand	2.7	3.0	3.6	4.2	5.0	5.7	6.4	6.9	7.9	8.6	9.3	85
United States	8.0	7.9	8.0	7.7	7.6	7.6	7.7	7.9	8.3	8.5	8.6	51
Philippines	2.0	2.1	2.4	2.6	2.9	3.3	3.9	4.8	6.1	6.8	7.8	82
Afghanistan	1.0	1.8	3.0	4.3	5.1	5.9	6.5	6.5	6.6	7.2	7.7	36
Netherlands	3.6	3.7	3.8	4.0	4.2	4.6	5.1	5.8	6.4	6.8	7.1	45
Iceland	3.9	4.0	4.2	4.1	3.9	3.8	3.8	3.8	4.0	5.3	6.4	47
Other countries	78.7	76.0	78.4	79.4	81.2	82.1	84.6	89.8	99.9	110.7	121.7	
Total	**184.3**	**185.9**	**197.7**	**204.7**	**213.3**	**222.3**	**238.3**	**266.3**	**303.0**	**333.9**	**369.2**	**47**

Note: For details on definitions and sources, please refer to the metadata at the end of the tables.

StatLink http://dx.doi.org/10.1787/888932617569

Table B.5. **Stock of foreign population by nationality**
Thousands
POLAND

	2000	2001	2002	2003	2004	2005	2006	2007	2008	2009	2010	Of which: Women 2010 (%)
Ukraine	..	..	9.9	..	..	..	5.2	6.1	7.2	10.2	..	..
Germany	..	..	3.7	..	..	..	11.4	11.8	12.2	4.4	..	..
Russian Federation	..	..	4.3	..	..	..	3.3	3.4	3.5	4.2	..	..
Belarus	..	..	2.9	..	..	..	1.5	1.8	2.2	3.2	..	..
Viet Nam	..	..	2.1	..	..	..	1.9	2.0	2.2	2.9	..	..
Armenia	..	..	1.6	..	..	..	0.8	0.8	0.9	1.4	..	..
Sweden	..	..	0.5	..	..	..	2.6	2.8	2.8	1.3	..	..
Bulgaria	..	..	1.1	..	..	..	1.0	1.0	1.1	1.1	..	..
United States	..	..	1.3	..	..	..	1.0	1.0	1.1	1.1	..	..
Former USSR	..	..	..	..	..	..	1.3	1.3	1.2	1.0	..	..
Austria	..	..	0.3	..	..	..	2.6	2.7	2.8	1.0	..	..
Greece	..	..	0.5	..	..	..	1.2	1.2	1.2	0.9	..	..
United Kingdom	..	..	1.0	..	..	..	0.6	0.6	0.6	0.8	..	..
France	..	..	1.0	..	..	..	0.6	0.6	0.6	0.7	..	..
Czech Republic	..	..	0.8	..	..	..	0.6	0.6	0.7	0.7	..	..
Other countries	..	..	18.2	..	..	..	19.4	19.6	20.1	14.8	..	..
Total	..	..	**49.2**	..	..	..	**54.9**	**57.5**	**60.4**	**49.6**	..	..

Note: For details on definitions and sources, please refer to the metadata at the end of the tables.

StatLink http://dx.doi.org/10.1787/888932617569

Table B.5. **Stock of foreign population by nationality**
Thousands
PORTUGAL

	2000	2001	2002	2003	2004	2005	2006	2007	2008	2009	2010	Of which: Women 2010 (%)
Brazil	22.2	48.7	61.6	66.3	78.6	70.4	74.0	69.8	107.3	116.6	119.6	56
Ukraine	..	45.7	63.0	66.4	67.0	44.9	42.8	40.1	52.6	52.4	49.5	45
Cape Verde	47.1	57.3	62.1	63.6	65.6	69.6	68.2	65.0	51.8	49.4	44.7	52
Romania	0.4	8.4	11.3	12.0	12.5	11.1	12.0	19.4	27.4	32.5	36.8	43
Angola	20.4	28.4	32.7	34.4	35.4	34.6	33.7	32.9	27.8	26.8	23.8	50
Guinea-Bissau	15.9	21.3	23.8	24.8	25.6	25.2	24.6	24.5	25.1	23.7	20.4	40
United Kingdom	14.1	15.0	15.9	16.9	18.0	19.0	19.8	23.6	15.4	16.4	17.2	48
China	3.3	7.3	8.5	9.1	9.7	9.4	10.6	10.8	13.4	14.4	15.8	48
Moldova	..	10.1	13.1	13.7	14.8	15.5	16.0	15.0	21.4	20.8	15.6	47
Sao Tome and Principe	5.4	8.3	9.6	10.1	10.9	11.9	11.4	11.0	12.0	11.8	10.9	53
Germany	10.4	11.1	11.9	12.5	13.1	13.6	13.9	15.5	8.2	8.6	9.0	52
Spain	12.2	13.6	14.6	15.3	15.9	16.4	16.6	18.0	7.2	8.1	8.9	47
Bulgaria	0.4	2.2	3.5	4.0	3.9	3.3	3.6	5.1	6.5	7.2	8.2	44
India	1.3	4.3	5.0	5.2	5.3	4.0	4.2	4.4	5.6	5.9	5.4	26
Russian Federation	0.5	6.5	8.0	7.8	8.2	5.4	5.7	5.4	6.3	6.3	5.3	59
Other countries	54.0	72.6	79.1	82.4	84.7	78.1	80.3	85.9	55.3	56.5	57.0	
Total	**207.6**	**360.8**	**423.8**	**444.6**	**469.1**	**432.0**	**437.1**	**446.3**	**443.1**	**457.3**	**448.1**	**49**

Note: For details on definitions and sources, please refer to the metadata at the end of the tables.

StatLink http://dx.doi.org/10.1787/888932617569

Table B.5. Stock of foreign population by nationality
Thousands
RUSSIAN FEDERATION

	2000	2001	2002	2003	2004	2005	2006	2007	2008	2009	2010	Of which: Women 2010 (%)
Ukraine	..	..	230.6	..	..	..	..	..	..	..	..	..
Azerbaijan	..	..	154.9	..	..	..	..	..	..	..	..	..
Armenia	..	..	136.8	..	..	..	..	..	..	..	..	..
Uzbekistan	..	..	70.9	..	..	..	..	..	..	..	..	..
Kazakhstan	..	..	69.5	..	..	..	..	..	..	..	..	..
Tajikistan	..	..	64.2	..	..	..	..	..	..	..	..	..
Georgia	..	..	52.9	..	..	..	..	..	..	..	..	..
Moldova	..	..	51.0	..	..	..	..	..	..	..	..	..
Belarus	..	..	40.3	..	..	..	..	..	..	..	..	..
China	..	..	30.6	..	..	..	..	..	..	..	..	..
Kyrgyzstan	..	..	28.8	..	..	..	..	..	..	..	..	..
Viet Nam	..	..	22.5	..	..	..	..	..	..	..	..	..
Afghanistan	..	..	8.2	..	..	..	..	..	..	..	..	..
Turkmenistan	..	..	6.4	..	..	..	..	..	..	..	..	..
India	..	..	5.4	..	..	..	..	..	..	..	..	..
Other countries	..	..	52.4	..	..	..	..	..	..	..	..	..
Total	..	..	**1 025.4**	..	..	..	..	..	..	..	..	..

Note: For details on definitions and sources, please refer to the metadata at the end of the tables.

StatLink http://dx.doi.org/10.1787/888932617569

Table B.5. Stock of foreign population by nationality
Thousands
SLOVAK REPUBLIC

	2000	2001	2002	2003	2004	2005	2006	2007	2008	2009	2010	Of which: Women 2010 (%)
Czech Republic	6.3	5.9	5.4	4.9	3.6	4.4	5.1	6.0	6.9	8.3	9.0	43
Ukraine	4.3	4.6	4.7	4.9	4.0	3.7	3.9	3.7	4.7	5.9	6.3	49
Romania	..	..	..	..	..	0.4	0.7	3.0	5.0	5.4	5.8	27
Poland	2.4	2.4	2.4	2.4	2.5	2.8	3.6	4.0	4.4	5.4	5.6	46
Hungary	..	..	..	..	..	1.8	2.1	2.7	3.6	4.6	5.3	29
Germany	..	..	..	..	..	1.6	2.3	2.9	3.8	4.0	4.1	22
Serbia	..	..	..	..	..	0.4	0.7	1.4	2.9	3.6	3.9	38
Viet Nam	..	..	..	..	..	0.8	1.1	1.4	2.5	2.3	2.3	39
Russian Federation	..	..	..	..	..	1.2	1.3	1.4	1.5	2.0	2.2	55
Austria	..	..	..	..	..	0.9	1.2	1.5	1.7	2.1	2.2	21
China	..	..	..	..	..	0.5	0.9	1.2	1.5	1.7	1.9	45
Korea	..	..	..	..	..	0.4	0.8	1.1	1.5	1.7	1.8	37
Italy	..	..	..	..	..	0.5	0.7	1.0	1.1	1.5	1.7	12
Bulgaria	..	..	..	..	..	0.6	0.5	1.0	1.4	1.5	1.7	26
France	..	..	..	..	..	0.6	0.9	1.1	1.3	1.6	1.7	30
Other countries	15.8	16.5	17.0	17.0	12.1	4.8	6.2	7.5	8.7	11.3	12.5	
Total	**28.8**	**29.4**	**29.5**	**29.2**	**22.3**	**25.6**	**32.1**	**40.9**	**52.5**	**62.9**	**68.0**	**36**

Note: For details on definitions and sources, please refer to the metadata at the end of the tables.

StatLink http://dx.doi.org/10.1787/888932617569

Table B.5. Stock of foreign population by nationality
Thousands
SLOVENIA

	2000	2001	2002	2003	2004	2005	2006	2007	2008	2009	2010	Of which: Women 2010 (%)
Bosnia and Herzegovina	21.4	22.8	22.0	21.8	21.3	21.9	24.4	32.5	33.1	39.0	38.8	21
Croatia	6.8	7.2	7.2	7.0	6.8	7.0	6.8	7.0	7.2	7.8	7.7	34
Serbia				7.6	7.9	9.3	10.3	14.0	11.4	9.3	8.2	30
Ukraine	0.6	0.7	0.7	0.9	0.9	0.9	0.9	1.1	1.0	1.1	1.2	74
Bulgaria	0.1	0.1	0.1	0.1	0.1	0.1	0.1	0.8	0.6	0.8	1.1	27
China	..	..	..	..	..	..	..	..	..	..	0.9	44
Italy	0.4	0.4	0.4	0.4	0.3	0.4	0.4	0.5	0.7	0.7	0.9	37
Germany	0.4	0.4	0.4	0.4	0.3	0.6	0.6	0.6	0.7	0.7	0.8	51
Montenegro	..	..	..	..	..	..	..	0.2	0.4	0.6	0.6	44
Russian Federation	0.3	0.4	0.4	0.4	0.3	0.4	0.4	0.4	0.4	0.5	0.6	71
United Kingdom	0.1	0.1	0.1	0.1	0.1	0.2	0.2	0.3	0.3	0.4	0.4	38
Austria	0.2	0.2	0.2	0.2	0.2	0.3	0.3	0.3	0.4	0.4	0.4	44
United States	..	..	..	..	..	..	..	..	..	..	0.2	44
Romania	0.1	0.1	0.1	0.1	0.1	0.1	0.2	0.2	0.2	0.2	0.2	63
Hungary	0.1	0.1	0.1	0.1	0.1	0.1	0.1	0.1	0.2	0.2	0.2	44
Other countries	12.0	12.8	13.0	6.2	5.9	7.7	8.8	10.6	14.2	20.6	20.5	
Total	**42.3**	**45.3**	**44.7**	**45.3**	**44.3**	**49.0**	**53.6**	**68.6**	**70.7**	**82.3**	**82.7**	**29**

Note: For details on definitions and sources, please refer to the metadata at the end of the tables.

StatLink http://dx.doi.org/10.1787/888932617569

Table B.5. Stock of foreign population by nationality
Thousands
SPAIN

	2000	2001	2002	2003	2004	2005	2006	2007	2008	2009	2010	Of which: Women 2010 (%)
Romania	31.6	67.3	137.3	208.0	317.4	407.2	527.0	731.8	798.9	831.2	864.3	48
Morocco	233.4	307.5	379.0	420.6	511.3	563.0	582.9	652.7	718.1	754.1	769.9	40
United Kingdom	107.3	128.1	161.5	174.8	227.2	274.7	315.0	353.0	375.7	387.7	390.9	49
Ecuador	139.0	259.5	390.3	475.7	497.8	461.3	427.1	427.7	421.4	399.6	359.1	50
Colombia	87.2	191.0	244.7	248.9	271.2	265.1	261.5	284.6	296.7	292.6	271.8	55
Bolivia	6.6	13.5	28.4	52.3	97.9	139.8	200.5	242.5	230.7	213.2	197.9	58
Germany	99.2	113.8	130.2	117.3	133.6	150.5	164.4	181.2	191.0	195.8	195.8	50
Italy	34.7	46.2	65.4	77.1	95.4	115.8	135.1	157.8	175.3	184.3	187.8	42
Bulgaria	12.0	29.7	52.8	69.9	93.0	101.6	122.1	154.0	164.7	169.6	172.6	47
China	27.6	37.7	51.2	62.5	87.7	104.7	106.7	125.9	147.5	158.2	166.2	47
Portugal	47.1	52.1	56.7	55.8	66.2	80.6	100.6	127.2	140.9	142.5	140.7	38
Peru	35.0	44.8	55.9	68.6	85.0	95.9	103.7	121.9	139.2	140.2	131.9	51
France	51.6	59.8	69.9	66.9	77.8	90.0	100.4	112.6	120.5	123.9	122.4	50
Argentina	32.4	56.7	109.4	130.9	153.0	150.3	141.2	147.4	142.3	132.2	120.0	51
Brazil	17.1	23.7	31.3	37.4	54.1	72.4	90.2	116.5	126.2	117.8	106.9	64
Other countries	408.8	546.6	700.0	767.8	961.9	1 071.2	1 141.3	1 332.0	1 459.7	1 504.8	1 532.4	
Total	**1 370.7**	**1 977.9**	**2 664.2**	**3 034.3**	**3 730.6**	**4 144.2**	**4 519.6**	**5 268.8**	**5 648.7**	**5 747.7**	**5 730.7**	**48**

Note: For details on definitions and sources, please refer to the metadata at the end of the tables.

StatLink http://dx.doi.org/10.1787/888932617569

Table B.5. Stock of foreign population by nationality
Thousands
SWEDEN

	2000	2001	2002	2003	2004	2005	2006	2007	2008	2009	2010	Of which: Women 2010 (%)
Finland	98.6	97.5	96.3	93.5	90.3	87.1	83.5	80.4	77.1	74.1	70.6	58
Iraq	33.1	36.2	40.1	41.5	39.8	31.9	30.3	40.0	48.6	55.1	56.6	46
Poland	16.7	15.5	13.9	13.4	14.7	17.2	22.4	28.9	34.7	38.6	40.9	50
Denmark	25.6	26.6	28.1	29.7	31.2	32.9	35.8	38.4	39.7	40.3	40.5	42
Norway	32.0	33.3	34.7	35.5	35.6	35.4	35.5	35.6	35.5	35.2	34.9	51
Somalia	11.5	9.6	8.7	8.8	9.0	9.6	11.6	14.7	18.3	24.7	30.8	50
Germany	16.4	17.3	18.1	19.1	19.9	21.0	22.5	24.7	26.6	27.5	27.6	48
Thailand	5.8	6.3	6.8	8.3	9.8	11.2	12.5	13.9	15.5	17.1	18.3	80
United Kingdom	13.1	13.8	14.2	14.4	14.6	14.7	15.1	15.7	16.5	17.3	17.4	30
China	4.4	4.9	5.2	5.7	6.2	6.7	6.9	7.7	9.4	11.8	14.1	53
Iran	14.3	13.5	12.9	12.5	12.4	11.5	10.5	10.2	10.6	11.8	13.5	47
Turkey	15.8	13.9	12.6	12.4	12.3	11.7	10.2	10.0	10.2	10.8	11.9	40
Afghanistan	3.8	4.6	5.3	6.1	6.8	6.9	7.7	7.9	8.2	8.6	9.8	41
United States	10.0	10.0	9.6	9.4	9.3	9.2	8.4	8.3	8.5	8.9	9.1	44
Romania	2.9	2.5	2.3	2.3	2.4	2.4	2.3	4.4	6.5	7.7	8.8	47
Other countries	168.4	165.9	160.9	140.3	143.7	148.2	170.8	177.4	189.4	205.6	228.6	
Total	**472.4**	**471.3**	**469.8**	**452.8**	**457.8**	**457.5**	**485.9**	**518.2**	**555.4**	**595.1**	**633.3**	**48**

Note: For details on definitions and sources, please refer to the metadata at the end of the tables.

StatLink http://dx.doi.org/10.1787/888932617569

Table B.5. Stock of foreign population by nationality
Thousands
SWITZERLAND

	2000	2001	2002	2003	2004	2005	2006	2007	2008	2009	2010	Of which: Women 2010 (%)
Italy	321.6	314.0	308.3	303.8	300.2	296.4	291.7	289.6	290.0	289.1	289.1	42
Germany	110.7	116.6	125.0	133.6	144.9	157.6	172.6	201.9	233.4	250.5	264.2	44
Portugal	140.2	135.5	141.1	149.8	159.7	167.3	173.5	182.3	196.2	205.3	213.2	45
Serbia	190.7	194.7	198.1	199.8	199.2	196.2	190.8	187.4	180.3	149.9	115.0	48
France	61.1	61.5	63.2	65.0	67.0	69.0	71.5	77.4	85.6	90.6	95.1	46
Turkey	79.5	79.5	78.8	77.7	76.6	75.4	73.9	72.6	71.7	71.0	70.6	46
Spain	83.8	81.0	78.9	76.8	74.3	71.4	68.2	65.1	64.4	64.1	64.2	45
Former Yug. Rep. of Macedonia	55.9	58.4	59.8	60.5	60.8	60.7	60.1	60.0	59.7	59.8	60.2	48
Austria	29.6	29.9	31.1	31.6	32.5	32.8	32.9	34.0	35.5	36.5	37.2	46
United Kingdom	20.8	22.2	22.8	23.4	24.1	24.9	26.0	28.7	31.9	34.1	36.4	42
Bosnia and Herzegovina	44.3	45.7	46.0	45.4	44.8	43.2	41.3	39.3	37.5	35.8	34.6	48
Croatia	43.6	43.9	43.4	42.7	41.8	40.6	39.1	37.8	36.1	34.9	33.8	50
Netherlands	14.4	14.6	15.0	15.2	15.4	15.8	16.1	17.0	18.1	18.5	19.1	45
Poland	4.0	4.3	4.5	4.7	4.9	5.3	6.0	7.3	8.9	10.2	11.5	57
Belgium	7.5	7.9	8.0	8.2	8.5	8.8	9.0	9.5	10.0	10.4	10.7	47
Other countries	176.6	209.3	223.4	232.8	240.4	246.6	250.8	261.1	279.7	319.5	365.7	
Total	**1 384.4**	**1 419.1**	**1 447.3**	**1 471.0**	**1 495.0**	**1 511.9**	**1 523.6**	**1 571.0**	**1 638.9**	**1 680.2**	**1 720.4**	**47**

Note: For details on definitions and sources, please refer to the metadata at the end of the tables.

StatLink http://dx.doi.org/10.1787/888932617569

Table B.5. Stock of foreign population by nationality
Thousands
TURKEY

	2000	2001	2002	2003	2004	2005	2006	2007	2008	2009	2010	Of which: Women 2010 (%)
Germany	86.4	..	..	..	..	..	..	..	..	..	..	..
Bulgaria	36.7	..	..	..	..	..	..	..	..	..	..	..
Russian Federation	13.8	..	..	..	..	..	..	..	..	..	..	..
United Kingdom	11.4	..	..	..	..	..	..	..	..	..	..	..
Azerbaijan	9.0	..	..	..	..	..	..	..	..	..	..	..
Netherlands	9.0	..	..	..	..	..	..	..	..	..	..	..
Iran	8.2	..	..	..	..	..	..	..	..	..	..	..
United States	7.6	..	..	..	..	..	..	..	..	..	..	..
Austria	6.1	..	..	..	..	..	..	..	..	..	..	..
Greece	6.0	..	..	..	..	..	..	..	..	..	..	..
Iraq	5.5	..	..	..	..	..	..	..	..	..	..	..
France	4.3	..	..	..	..	..	..	..	..	..	..	..
Sweden	3.8	..	..	..	..	..	..	..	..	..	..	..
Uzbekistan	3.7	..	..	..	..	..	..	..	..	..	..	..
Afghanistan	3.4	..	..	..	..	..	..	..	..	..	..	..
Other countries	56.3	..	..	..	..	..	..	..	..	..	..	..
Total	**271.3**	..	..	..	..	..	..	..	..	..	..	..

Note: For details on definitions and sources, please refer to the metadata at the end of the tables.
StatLink http://dx.doi.org/10.1787/888932617569

Table B.5. Stock of foreign population by nationality
Thousands
UNITED KINGDOM

	2000	2001	2002	2003	2004	2005	2006	2007	2008	2009	2010	Of which: Women 2010 (%)
Poland	..	34	24	34	48	110	209	406	498	549	550	50
India	153	132	145	154	171	190	258	258	294	293	354	46
Ireland	404	436	403	367	368	369	335	341	359	344	344	53
Pakistan	94	82	97	83	86	95	78	133	178	177	137	46
United States	114	148	100	120	133	106	132	109	117	112	133	55
Germany	64	59	68	70	96	100	91	88	91	121	129	60
Italy	95	102	98	91	121	88	76	95	96	107	117	52
France	85	82	92	102	95	100	110	122	123	148	116	51
China	22	24	..	..	..	..	73	89	109	76	107	49
Nigeria	..	45	42	33	43	62	61	89	81	106	106	45
Portugal	29	58	85	88	83	85	81	87	95	96	104	51
South Africa	..	68	64	95	92	100	105	90	94	113	102	52
Lithuania	..	..	..	..	..	..	47	54	73	67	99	54
Australia	75	67	75	73	80	79	88	100	101	84	92	48
Bangladesh	55	70	61	48	69	64	74	68	66	77	74	45
Other countries	..	1 180	1 230	1 384	1 372	1 487	1 574	1 695	1 811	1 878	1 960	
Total	**2 342**	**2 587**	**2 584**	**2 742**	**2 857**	**3 035**	**3 392**	**3 824**	**4 186**	**4 348**	**4 524**	**51**

Note: For details on definitions and sources, please refer to the metadata at the end of the tables.
StatLink http://dx.doi.org/10.1787/888932617569

Metadata related to Tables A.5 and B.5. **Stocks of foreign population**

Country	Comments	Source
Austria	Stock of foreign citizens recorded in the population register. *Reference date:* 31 December. Prior to 2002: annual average.	Population Register, Statistics Austria. Prior to 2002: Labour Force Survey, Statistics Austria.
Belgium	Stock of foreign citizens recorded in the population register. From 2008 on, asylum seekers are included. This results in some artificial increase for some nationalities between 2007 and 2008. *Reference date:* 31 December.	Population Register, Directorate for Statistics and Economic Information.
Canada	2001 and 2006 Censuses.	Statistics Canada.
Czech Republic	Holders of a permanent residence permit (mainly for family reasons), a long-term visa (over 90 days), a long-term residence permit (1-year permit, renewable) or a temporary residence permit (EU citizens). *Reference date:* 31 December.	Register of Foreigners, Ministry of the Interior.
Denmark	Stock of foreign citizens recorded in the population register. Excludes asylum seekers and all persons with temporary residence permits. *Reference date:* 31 December.	Central Population Register, Statistics Denmark.
Estonia		Police and Border Guard Board.
Finland	Stock of foreign citizens recorded in the population register. Includes foreign persons of Finnish origin. *Reference date:* 31 December.	Central Population Register, Statistics Finland.
France	Foreigners with permanent residence in France. Including trainees, students and illegal migrants who accept to be interviewed. Excluding seasonal and cross-border workers.	Censuses, National Institute for Statistics and Economic Studies (INSEE).
Germany	Stock of foreign citizens recorded in the population register. Includes asylum seekers living in private households. Excludes foreign-born persons of German origin *(Aussiedler)*. Decrease in 2004 is due to cross checking of residence register and central register of foreigners. *Reference date:* 31 December.	Central Population Register, Federal Office of Statistics.
Greece	Includes some undocumented foreigners. *Reference date:* 4th quarter.	Labour Force Survey, Hellenic Statistical Authority.
Hungary	Foreigners having a residence or a settlement document. From 2010 on, it includes refugees. *Reference date:* 31 December.	Office of Immigration and Nationality, Hungarian Central Statistical Office.
Iceland	Data are from the National Register of Persons. It is to be expected that figures are overestimates. *Reference date:* 31 December.	Statistics Iceland.
Ireland	2002 and 2006 Censuses.	Central Statistics Office (CSO).
Italy	Until 2003, data refer to holders of residence permits Children under 18 who are registered on their parents' permit are not counted. Data include foreigners who were regularised following the 1998 and 2002 programmes. In 2000, figures include 116 253 regularised persons. Since 2004, data refer to resident foreigners (those who are registered with municipal registry offices). *Reference date:* 31 December.	Ministry of the Interior and National Statistical Institute (ISTAT).
Japan	Foreigners staying in Japan more than 90 days and registered in the register of Foreigners. *Reference date:* 31 December.	Register of Foreigners, Ministry of Justice, Immigration Bureau.
Korea	Foreigners staying in Korea more than 90 days and registered in population registers. Data have been revised since 2002 in order to include foreign nationals with Korean ancestors (called overseas Koreans) who enter with F-4 visa and are also registered in population registers. The large increase in 2003 is mainly due to a regularisation programme introduced in that year.	Ministry of Justice.
Luxembourg	Stock of foreign citizens recorded in population register. Does not include visitors (less than three months) and cross-border workers. *Reference date:* 31 December.	Population Register, Central Office of Statistics and Economic Studies (Statec).
Mexico	Number of foreigners who hold a valid permit for permanent residence (immigrants, FM2) or temporary residence (non immigrants, FM3).	National Migration Institute (INM).

Metadata related to Tables A.5 and B.5. **Stocks of foreign population**

Country	Comments	Source
Netherlands	Stock of foreign citizens recorded in the population register. Figures include administrative corrections and asylum seekers (except those staying in reception centres). *Reference date:* 1 January of the following year.	Population Register, Central Bureau of Statistics (CBS).
Norway	Stock of foreign citizens recorded in the population register. It excludes visitors (less than six months) and cross-border workers. *Reference date:* 31 December.	Central Population Register, Statistics Norway.
Poland	Permanent residents. Excluding foreign permanent residents who had been staying abroad for more than 12 months and foreign temporary residents who had been staying in Poland for less than 12 months. From 2006 on, data are from the Central Population Register.	2002 Census, Central Statistical Office and Central Population Register.
Portugal	Holders of a valid residence permit. Data for 2001-04 include Stay Permits delivered following the 2001 regularisation programme as well as foreigners who received Long Term Permits (Temporary Stay, Study and Work) issued in each year. Data for 2005-06 include holders of valid Residence Permits, holders of valid Stay Permits (foreigners who renovated their Stay Permits in each year) and holders of Long Term Visas (both issued and renewed every year). Work Visas issued after 2004 include a certain number of foreigners that benefited from the regularisation scheme and also from the specific dispositions applying to Brazilian workers that resulted from a bilateral agreement signed between Portugal and Brazil. Data for women do not include the holders of long-term visas.	Ministry of the Interior, National Statistical Institute (INE) and Ministry of Foreign Affairs.
Russian Federation	2002 Census.	Federal Migration Service, Ministry of the Interior.
Slovak Republic	Holders of a permanent or long term residence permit.	Register of Foreigners, Ministry of the Interior.
Slovenia		Central Population Register, Ministry of the Interior.
Spain	Population register. Data include all registered foreign citizens independently of their administrative status. *Reference date:* end of the year.	Municipal Registers, National Statistics Institute (INE)
Sweden	Stock of foreign citizens recorded in the population register. *Reference date:* 31 December.	Population Register, Statistics Sweden.
Switzerland	Stock of all those with residence or settlement permits (permits B and C respectively). Holders of an L-permit (short duration) are also included if their stay in the country is longer than 12 months. Does not include seasonal or cross-border workers. *Reference date:* 31 December.	Register of Foreigners, Federal Office of Migration.
Turkey	2000 Census.	Population Census, Turkish Statistical Institute.
United Kingdom	Foreign residents. Those with unknown nationality from the New Commonwealth are not included (around 10 000 to 15 000 persons). There is a break in the series in 2004 as a result of a new weighting procedure. *Reference date:* 31 December.	Labour Force Survey, Home Office.
United States	Foreigners born abroad.	Current Population Survey, Census Bureau.

Data for Serbia include persons from Serbia, Montenegro and Serbia and Montenegro.

Acquisitions of nationality

Nationality law can have a significant impact on the measurement of the national and foreign populations. In France and Belgium, for example, where foreigners can fairly easily acquire the nationality of the country, increases in the foreign population through immigration and births can eventually contribute to a significant rise in the population of nationals. On the other hand, in countries where naturalisation is more difficult, increases in immigration and births among foreigners manifest themselves almost exclusively as growth in the foreign population. In addition, changes in rules regarding naturalisation can have significant impact. For example, during the 1980s, a number of OECD countries made naturalisation easier and this resulted in noticeable falls in the foreign population (and rises in the population of nationals).

However, host-country legislation is not the only factor affecting naturalisation. For example, where naturalisation involves forfeiting citizenship of the country of origin, there may be incentives to remain a foreign citizen. Where the difference between remaining a foreign citizen and becoming a national is marginal, naturalisation may largely be influenced by the time and effort required to make the application, and the symbolic and political value individuals attach to being citizens of one country or another.

Data on naturalisations are usually readily available from administrative sources. The statistics generally cover all means of acquiring the nationality of a country. These include standard naturalisation procedures subject to criteria such as age or residency, etc. as well as situations where nationality is acquired through a declaration or by option (following marriage, adoption or other situations related to residency or descent), recovery of former nationality and other special means of acquiring the nationality of the country.

Table A.6. **Acquisitions of nationality in OECD countries and the Russian Federation**
Numbers, and percentages of the stock of foreign population in the previous year

	2000	2001	2002	2003	2004	2005	2006	2007	2008	2009	2010
Australia	71 923	81 191	83 484	82 859	90 763	99 237	111 569	147 085	92 212	99 221	95 284
% of foreign population	..	..	..	..	..	..	..	..	..	..	..
Austria	24 320	31 731	36 011	44 694	41 645	34 876	25 746	14 010	10 258	7 978	6 135
% of foreign population	3.5	4.5	4.9	6.0	5.5	4.5	3.2	1.7	1.2	0.9	0.7
Belgium	62 082	62 982	46 417	33 709	34 754	31 512	31 860	36 063	37 710	32 767	..
% of foreign population	6.9	7.3	5.5	4.0	4.0	3.6	3.5	3.9	3.9	3.2	..
Canada	214 568	167 353	141 591	155 117	193 620	198 691	260 755	199 844	176 525	156 304	143 562
% of foreign population	..	9.0	..	..	..	..	11.4	..	..	..	..
Chile	..	..	..	..	..	..	..	..	..	812	629
% of foreign population	..	..	..	..	..	..	..	..	..	..	..
Czech Republic	8 335	6 321	4 532	3 410	5 020	2 626	2 346	1 877	1 837	1 621	1 495
% of foreign population	3.6	3.1	2.1	1.5	2.1	1.0	0.8	0.6	0.5	0.4	0.3
Denmark	18 811	11 902	17 300	6 583	14 976	10 197	7 961	3 648	5 772	6 537	3 006
% of foreign population	7.3	4.6	6.5	2.5	5.5	3.8	2.9	1.3	1.9	2.0	0.9
Estonia	3 425	3 090	4 091	3 706	6 523	7 072	4 753	4 228	2 124	1 670	1 184
% of foreign population	..	1.1	1.5	1.4	2.4	2.7	1.9	1.7	0.9	0.7	0.5
Finland	2 977	2 720	3 049	4 526	6 880	5 683	4 433	4 824	6 682	3 413	4 334
% of foreign population	3.4	3.0	3.1	4.4	6.4	5.2	3.9	4.0	5.0	2.4	2.8
France	150 026	127 548	128 092	144 640	168 826	154 827	147 868	131 738	137 452	135 842	143 275
% of foreign population	4.6	..	..	..	..	..	..	3.7	3.7	3.6	3.8
Germany	186 688	178 098	154 547	140 731	127 153	117 241	124 566	113 030	94 470	96 122	101 570
% of foreign population	2.5	2.4	2.1	1.9	1.7	1.7	1.8	1.7	1.4	1.4	1.5
Greece	..	..	..	..	..	..	..	10 806	16 922	17 019	..
% of foreign population	..	..	..	..	..	..	..	1.9	2.6	2.3	..
Hungary	7 538	8 590	3 369	5 261	5 432	9 870	6 172	8 442	8 104	5 802	6 086
% of foreign population	4.9	7.8	2.9	4.5	4.2	6.9	4.0	5.1	4.6	3.1	3.1
Iceland	286	352	356	463	671	726	844	647	914	728	450
% of foreign population	1.4	1.7	1.7	2.2	3.2	3.4	4.0	3.1	4.3	3.4	2.1
Ireland	1 143	2 443	2 817	3 993	3 784	4 079	5 763	6 656	4 350	4 594	6 387
% of foreign population	..	..	..	1.8	..	..	..	1.6	..	..	..
Italy	9 563	10 382	10 685	13 406	11 934	19 266	35 766	38 466	39 484	40 084	40 223
% of foreign population	0.7	0.8	0.7	0.9	0.6	0.8	1.3	1.3	1.2	1.0	0.9
Japan	15 812	15 291	14 339	17 633	16 336	15 251	14 108	14 680	13 218	14 785	13 072
% of foreign population	1.0	0.9	0.8	1.0	0.9	0.8	0.7	0.7	0.6	0.7	0.6
Korea	..	1 680	3 883	7 734	9 262	16 974	8 125	10 319	15 258	26 756	17 323
% of foreign population	..	0.8	1.7	2.8	2.0	3.5	1.6	1.6	1.9	3.0	1.9
Luxembourg	684	496	754	785	841	954	1 128	1 236	1 215	4 022	4 311
% of foreign population	0.4	0.3	0.5	0.5	0.5	0.5	0.6	0.6	0.6	1.9	2.0
Mexico	3 944	3 090	4 737	4 317	6 429	5 610	4 175	5 470	4 471	3 489	2 150
% of foreign population	..	..	..	..	..	..	..	..	..	..	..
Netherlands	49 968	46 667	45 321	28 799	26 173	28 488	29 089	30 653	28 229	29 754	26 275
% of foreign population	7.7	7.0	6.6	4.1	3.7	4.1	4.2	4.5	4.1	4.1	3.6
New Zealand	29 609	23 535	19 469	18 296	22 142	24 341	29 017	29 867	23 772	18 730	15 173
% of foreign population	..	..	..	..	..	..	..	..	..	..	..
Norway	9 517	10 838	9 041	7 867	8 154	12 655	11 955	14 877	10 312	11 442	11 903
% of foreign population	5.3	5.9	4.9	4.0	4.0	5.9	5.4	6.2	3.9	3.8	3.6
Poland	975	766	1 186	1 634	1 937	2 866	989	1 528	1 054	2 503	2 926
% of foreign population	..	..	..	3.3	..	..	..	2.8	1.8	4.1	5.9
Portugal	721	1 082	1 369	1 747	1 346	939	3 627	6 020	22 408	28 888	24 478
% of foreign population	0.4	0.5	0.4	0.4	0.3	0.2	0.8	1.4	5.0	6.5	5.4
Russian Federation	..	359 195	272 463	31 528	330 419	504 518	366 488	367 699	361 363	394 137	111 298
% of foreign population	..	..	..	3.1	..	..	..	..	..	..	..

STATISTICAL ANNEX

Table A.6. **Acquisitions of nationality in OECD countries and the Russian Federation** (cont.)
Numbers, and percentages of the stock of foreign population in the previous year

	2000	2001	2002	2003	2004	2005	2006	2007	2008	2009	2010
Slovak Republic	..	..	..	3 492	4 016	1 393	1 125	1 478	680	262	239
% of foreign population	..	..	..	11.8	13.8	6.3	4.4	4.6	1.7	0.5	0.4
Spain	11 999	16 743	21 810	26 556	38 335	42 829	62 339	71 810	84 170	79 597	123 721
% of foreign population	1.3	1.2	1.1	1.0	1.3	1.1	1.5	1.6	1.6	1.4	2.2
Sweden	42 495	35 458	36 978	32 351	26 130	35 531	46 995	32 473	29 330	28 562	32 457
% of foreign population	8.8	7.5	7.8	6.9	5.8	7.8	10.3	6.7	5.7	5.1	5.5
Switzerland	28 700	27 586	36 515	35 424	35 685	38 437	46 711	43 889	44 365	43 440	39 314
% of foreign population	2.1	2.0	2.6	2.4	2.4	2.6	3.1	2.9	2.8	2.7	2.3
Turkey	..	..	23 725	21 086	8 238	6 901	5 072	..	..	..	..
% of foreign population	..	..	..	..	..	..	..	..	..	..	..
United Kingdom	82 210	90 282	120 121	130 535	148 273	161 699	154 018	164 637	129 377	203 789	195 046
% of foreign population	3.7	3.9	4.6	5.1	5.4	5.7	5.1	4.9	3.4	4.9	4.5
United States	888 788	608 205	573 708	463 204	537 151	604 280	702 589	660 477	1 046 539	743 715	619 913
% of foreign population	4.1	2.8	2.7	2.1	2.5	2.8	3.3	3.1	4.8	3.4	2.9

Note: For details on definitions and sources, refer to the metadata at the end of Tables B.6.

StatLink http://dx.doi.org/10.1787/888932617493

Table B.6. **Acquisitions of nationality by country of former nationality**
AUSTRALIA

	2000	2001	2002	2003	2004	2005	2006	2007	2008	2009	2010	Of which: Women 2010 (%)
United Kingdom	14 314	14 073	16 473	14 971	19 980	21 750	23 274	30 452	20 209	19 216	19 101	48
India	2 475	2 356	2 781	3 391	4 068	6 408	9 363	12 864	7 756	12 789	12 948	39
China	5 437	4 936	5 105	5 996	6 164	6 846	8 425	11 357	6 696	8 369	8 898	58
South Africa	2 687	3 467	3 970	4 503	5 238	5 189	5 316	7 077	4 290	4 571	4 389	50
New Zealand	7 727	15 627	16 112	14 578	10 858	8 710	7 096	7 795	5 129	3 760	4 304	51
Philippines	2 256	2 688	2 855	3 009	3 470	3 677	4 142	5 179	3 264	3 974	4 051	59
Sri Lanka	1 791	1 506	1 316	1 436	1 743	1 750	2 536	3 812	2 324	2 598	2 520	47
Korea	700	985	743	826	1 088	1 291	1 876	2 946	1 560	1 562	2 321	54
Malaysia	1 163	1 303	1 573	1 672	1 971	2 008	2 158	3 350	2 033	1 799	2 207	54
Viet Nam	2 839	2 095	1 902	1 749	2 285	2 147	2 171	2 893	1 581	1 669	1 688	66
United States	984	1 160	1 298	1 307	1 578	1 675	1 951	2 347	1 575	1 524	1 680	51
Indonesia	698	725	759	882	984	1 206	1 703	2 431	1 276	1 098	1 349	59
Thailand	499	486	541	612	806	983	1 200	1 621	852	1 239	1 343	76
Ireland	666	816	825	744	1 084	1 183	1 213	1 667	928	1 105	1 302	44
Bangladesh	345	350	306	348	447	663	950	1 207	1 212	2 529	1 178	44
Other countries	27 342	28 618	26 925	26 835	28 999	33 751	38 195	50 087	31 527	31 419	26 005	
Total	**71 923**	**81 191**	**83 484**	**82 859**	**90 763**	**99 237**	**111 569**	**147 085**	**92 212**	**99 221**	**95 284**	**51**

Note: For details on definitions and sources, please refer to the metadata at the end of the tables.

StatLink http://dx.doi.org/10.1787/888932617588

Table B.6. Acquisitions of nationality by country of former nationality
AUSTRIA

	2000	2001	2002	2003	2004	2005	2006	2007	2008	2009	2010	Of which: Women 2010 (%)
Bosnia and Herzegovina	2 761	3 856	5 913	8 268	8 657	7 026	4 596	3 329	2 207	1 457	1 278	57
Serbia	2 810	4 296	4 806	9 836	7 245	6 681	4 825	4 254	2 595	2 003	1 268	51
Turkey	6 720	10 046	12 623	13 665	13 004	9 545	7 542	2 076	1 664	1 242	937	44
Croatia	1 642	1 986	2 537	2 588	2 212	2 276	2 494	1 349	824	440	456	62
Former Yug. Rep. of Macedonia	241	471	574	786	803	991	716	414	377	281	150	41
Russian Federation	168	166	161	83	194	235	228	128	127	135	137	58
Germany	102	106	85	106	135	135	122	113	67	174	132	55
Romania	2 682	2 813	1 774	2 096	1 373	1 128	981	455	382	246	114	59
Afghanistan	70	44	69	135	322	454	261	43	106	108	113	30
Iran	481	451	328	272	411	432	253	88	99	103	111	44
Poland	545	606	930	768	768	443	236	172	129	138	99	69
Egypt	657	807	599	615	616	506	382	100	121	124	94	43
India	486	638	656	525	562	421	159	137	122	90	84	58
Ukraine	49	71	104	146	230	182	145	81	70	80	75	80
Hungary	351	315	246	262	174	120	106	74	56	72	68	72
Other countries	4 555	5 059	4 606	4 543	4 939	4 301	2 700	1 197	1 312	1 285	1 019	
Total	**24 320**	**31 731**	**36 011**	**44 694**	**41 645**	**34 876**	**25 746**	**14 010**	**10 258**	**7 978**	**6 135**	**53**

Note: For details on definitions and sources, please refer to the metadata at the end of the tables.

StatLink http://dx.doi.org/10.1787/888932617588

Table B.6. Acquisitions of nationality by country of former nationality
BELGIUM

	2000	2001	2002	2003	2004	2005	2006	2007	2008	2009	2010	Of which: Women 2010 (%)
Morocco	21 917	24 018	15 832	10 565	8 704	7 977	7 753	8 722	8 427	6 919	..	..
Turkey	17 282	14 401	7 805	5 186	4 467	3 602	3 204	3 039	3 182	2 763	..	..
Italy	3 650	3 451	2 341	2 646	2 271	2 086	2 360	2 017	1 762	1 700	..	..
Russian Federation	..	265	301	153	244	297	487	1 533	2 599	1 647	..	..
Democratic Republic of the Congo	2 993	2 991	2 809	1 785	2 566	1 917	1 567	1 793	1 795	1 555	..	..
Former Yugoslavia	2 187	2 487	2 678	675	800	562	724	591	753	977	..	..
France	948	1 025	856	698	780	772	820	836	838	792	..	..
Algeria	1 071	1 281	926	826	826	739	658	687	744	739	..	..
Poland	551	677	630	460	465	470	550	586	619	640	..	..
Pakistan	75	474	404	270	298	306	348	666	559	628	..	..
Netherlands	492	601	646	522	665	672	692	668	683	608	..	..
India	345	558	463	296	271	294	329	365	423	458	..	..
Ghana	..	297	319	270	313	281	315	388	357	416	..	..
Rwanda	..	794	1 012	557	571	700	635	924	723	416	..	..
Cameroon	..	..	..	214	266	242	250	317	463	401	..	..
Other countries	10 571	9 662	9 395	8 586	11 247	10 595	11 168	12 931	13 783	12 108	..	..
Total	**62 082**	**62 982**	**46 417**	**33 709**	**34 754**	**31 512**	**31 860**	**36 063**	**37 710**	**32 767**	**..**	**..**

Note: For details on definitions and sources, please refer to the metadata at the end of the tables.

StatLink http://dx.doi.org/10.1787/888932617588

STATISTICAL ANNEX

Table B.6. Acquisitions of nationality by country of former nationality
CANADA

	2000	2001	2002	2003	2004	2005	2006	2007	2008	2009	2010	Of which: Women 2010 (%)
India	18 681	14 029	12 623	13 934	21 826	22 059	33 967	25 789	20 827	17 396	18 956	51
China	22 775	17 406	16 321	20 021	25 138	25 771	34 474	24 345	21 025	16 008	13 412	56
Philippines	14 024	9 485	7 622	8 225	9 022	11 035	15 566	12 196	11 666	11 068	11 608	58
Pakistan	8 073	8 610	7 292	6 494	10 676	12 429	17 121	11 623	9 430	7 838	8 062	50
United Kingdom	3 772	2 964	2 698	4 366	7 452	6 743	6 492	5 170	4 657	4 310	4 456	50
Colombia	451	554	724	953	1 510	2 084	3 136	3 782	4 671	4 286	3 811	51
United States	3 784	2 943	2 812	3 859	5 288	5 058	5 117	4 267	4 133	3 734	3 712	54
Iran	6 495	6 322	5 712	5 135	4 616	4 984	8 087	5 336	4 988	3 828	3 575	50
Korea	3 721	3 106	3 464	4 350	5 909	5 425	7 558	5 860	5 248	3 835	3 159	54
Romania	4 546	3 376	2 672	3 105	3 294	4 470	5 884	4 682	4 374	4 417	3 089	53
Sri Lanka	6 603	4 376	3 500	3 261	5 151	4 579	5 650	4 703	3 691	3 186	2 915	55
Algeria	1 834	1 756	1 557	1 687	1 500	2 146	3 329	2 552	2 150	3 159	2 451	47
Russian Federation	3 113	3 417	3 379	3 438	3 796	4 077	4 621	3 677	3 324	2 714	2 365	56
Bangladesh	2 631	2 282	1 553	1 527	2 053	2 859	3 415	2 023	1 873	2 140	2 282	47
Morocco	996	924	922	1 347	1 190	2 338	3 871	2 728	2 225	3 371	2 031	49
Other countries	113 069	85 803	68 740	73 415	85 199	82 634	102 467	81 111	72 243	65 014	57 678	
Total	**214 568**	**167 353**	**141 591**	**155 117**	**193 620**	**198 691**	**260 755**	**199 844**	**176 525**	**156 304**	**143 562**	**52**

Note: For details on definitions and sources, please refer to the metadata at the end of the tables.

StatLink http://dx.doi.org/10.1787/888932617588

Table B.6. Acquisitions of nationality by country of former nationality
CHILE

	2000	2001	2002	2003	2004	2005	2006	2007	2008	2009	2010	Of which: Women 2010 (%)
Peru	..	..	..	..	..	..	..	..	..	170	128	63
Cuba	..	..	..	..	..	..	..	..	..	107	98	41
Ecuador	..	..	..	..	..	..	..	..	..	72	81	57
Bolivia	..	..	..	..	..	..	..	..	..	114	78	58
Colombia	..	..	..	..	..	..	..	..	..	61	44	61
Chinese Taipei	..	..	..	..	..	..	..	..	..	60	38	55
China	..	..	..	..	..	..	..	..	..	46	25	60
Pakistan	..	..	..	..	..	..	..	..	..	17	15	0
Venezuela	..	..	..	..	..	..	..	..	..	14	14	36
Argentina	..	..	..	..	..	..	..	..	..	20	11	45
Other countries	..	..	..	..	..	..	..	..	..	131	97	
Total	..	..	..	..	..	..	..	..	..	**812**	**629**	**51**

Note: For details on definitions and sources, please refer to the metadata at the end of the tables.

StatLink http://dx.doi.org/10.1787/888932617588

Table B.6. Acquisitions of nationality by country of former nationality
CZECH REPUBLIC

	2000	2001	2002	2003	2004	2005	2006	2007	2008	2009	2010	Of which: Women 2010 (%)
Ukraine	373	173	251	419	446	239	425	424	398	520	391	..
Slovak Republic	5 377	3 593	2 109	989	1 741	1 259	786	625	521	431	377	..
Poland	8	163	304	170	298	167	86	50	53	58	63	..
Viet Nam	101	76	29	46	47	62	43	40	42	44	52	..
Russian Federation	71	87	65	7	86	134	107	102	84	58	50	..
Romania	58	140	109	116	101	143	131	36	83	35	36	..
Bulgaria	105	132	95	54	62	48	48	14	11	12	21	..
Kazakhstan	17	25	43	156	89	43	129	18	121	21	17	..
Moldova	..	2	4	4	1	11	9	33	21	23	15	..
Belarus	13	19	13	14	21	35	27	39	27	20	15	..
Kyrgyzstan	..	..	..	..	..	..	..	..	..	..	12	..
Armenia	8	11	8	18	23	32	61	28	19	16	11	..
Algeria	..	..	3	6	5	9	9	12	4	..	10	..
Bosnia and Herzegovina	11	13	20	47	62	63	37	19	11	9	9	..
Serbia	12	35	16	14	42	26	31	28	25	17	7	..
Other countries	2 181	1 852	1 463	1 350	1 996	355	417	409	417	357	409	
Total	**8 335**	**6 321**	**4 532**	**3 410**	**5 020**	**2 626**	**2 346**	**1 877**	**1 837**	**1 621**	**1 495**	..

Note: For details on definitions and sources, please refer to the metadata at the end of the tables.

StatLink ⟶ http://dx.doi.org/10.1787/888932617588

Table B.6. Acquisitions of nationality by country of former nationality
DENMARK

	2000	2001	2002	2003	2004	2005	2006	2007	2008	2009	2010	Of which: Women 2010 (%)
Iraq	2 210	871	1 161	153	1 015	961	1 113	515	1 166	1 201	368	42
Afghanistan	276	215	301	40	367	282	260	178	359	790	354	45
Turkey	2 787	3 130	2 418	2 158	732	878	1 125	527	581	511	239	48
Somalia	1 189	1 074	2 263	324	2 022	1 709	923	317	527	264	142	50
Bosnia and Herzegovina	..	..	..	..	..	..	519	224	270	265	131	54
China	228	195	289	203	339	382	281	162	181	199	103	47
Ethiopia	..	..	..	..	..	..	58	32	71	116	98	39
Viet Nam	647	318	508	280	318	232	213	129	78	144	86	55
Former Yugoslavia	917	355	784	239	835	324	594	165	196	228	83	48
Germany	240	129	174	82	178	144	99	42	44	84	81	58
Russian Federation	..	..	..	..	..	..	84	54	63	123	74	68
Thailand	214	124	172	62	180	114	95	61	79	96	64	45
Iran	1 105	437	519	120	505	317	203	89	207	155	63	51
Sweden	..	..	..	..	..	..	66	48	39	52	58	62
Norway	..	..	..	..	..	..	134	93	73	76	51	57
Other countries	8 998	5 054	8 711	2 922	8 485	4 854	2 194	1 012	1 838	2 233	1 011	
Total	**18 811**	**11 902**	**17 300**	**6 583**	**14 976**	**10 197**	**7 961**	**3 648**	**5 772**	**6 537**	**3 006**	**51**

Note: For details on definitions and sources, please refer to the metadata at the end of the tables.

StatLink ⟶ http://dx.doi.org/10.1787/888932617588

Table B.6. Acquisitions of nationality by country of former nationality
FINLAND

	2000	2001	2002	2003	2004	2005	2006	2007	2008	2009	2010	Of which: Women 2010 (%)
Russian Federation	666	533	418	1 682	2 313	2 094	1 399	1 665	2 211	1 026	1 925	68
Estonia	353	295	319	468	690	291	176	182	262	166	243	66
Iran	102	58	68	124	225	233	213	218	329	180	137	47
Turkey	85	82	112	141	171	128	110	102	195	94	132	39
Somalia	346	222	204	209	165	414	445	464	595	290	131	54
Serbia	4	14	41	32	338	346	248	240	371	173	122	52
Afghanistan	2	0	23	3	14	48	101	102	279	186	108	56
Sweden	44	57	61	94	149	198	178	163	274	126	104	43
Ukraine	32	8	28	66	130	65	46	45	62	53	92	60
China	92	106	136	126	95	60	57	68	84	53	85	66
Iraq	185	224	217	165	447	346	405	443	379	207	78	50
India	16	33	37	23	53	32	8	26	28	27	73	49
Morocco	39	37	41	31	70	32	35	46	49	22	65	42
Romania	50	35	16	38	32	17	11	17	34	25	58	55
Viet Nam	155	164	205	133	209	82	64	79	78	42	54	67
Other countries	806	852	1 123	1 191	1 779	1 297	937	964	1 452	743	927	
Total	**2 977**	**2 720**	**3 049**	**4 526**	**6 880**	**5 683**	**4 433**	**4 824**	**6 682**	**3 413**	**4 334**	**60**

Note: For details on definitions and sources, please refer to the metadata at the end of the tables.

StatLink http://dx.doi.org/10.1787/888932617588

Table B.6. Acquisitions of nationality by country of former nationality
FRANCE

	2000	2001	2002	2003	2004	2005	2006	2007	2008	2009	2010	Of which: Women 2010 (%)
Morocco	37 795	34 922	33 967	36 875	..	37 848	..	..	28 699	26 097	27 637	48
Algeria	17 627	15 498	15 711	20 245	..	25 435	..	..	20 256	20 659	20 941	49
Tunisia	12 763	10 251	9 956	11 412	..	12 012	..	..	9 471	9 268	8 520	44
Turkey	12 137	10 755	10 468	10 492	..	13 618	..	..	10 202	9 171	8 448	46
Portugal	11 201	9 182	8 844	9 576	..	8 888	..	..	7 778	6 415	4 903	49
Russian Federation	779	730	831	951	..	1 132	..	..	3 530	4 157	4 503	61
Senegal	1 595	1 463	1 858	2 185	..	2 345	..	..	3 038	3 364	3 508	50
Congo	1 083	1 100	1 475	1 769	..	2 390	..	..	2 933	3 269	3 327	53
Serbia	2 365	1 884	1 910	2 133	..	2 749	..	..	3 375	3 219	3 179	50
Côte d'Ivoire	1 409	1 194	1 495	1 869	..	1 987	..	..	2 197	2 565	3 003	58
Cameroon	1 556	1 381	1 770	2 196	..	2 081	..	..	2 014	2 411	2 824	62
Haiti	1 920	1 571	2 082	2 734	..	2 744	..	..	2 922	2 981	2 771	54
Mali	631	581	774	947	..	1 365	..	..	2 237	2 704	2 698	51
Democratic Republic of the Congo	1 765	1 401	1 572	2 012	..	2 631	..	..	2 402	2 294	2 293	53
Lebanon	1 695	1 113	1 210	1 363	..	1 359	..	..	1 190	1 358	1 726	42
Other countries	43 705	34 522	34 169	37 881	..	36 243	..	..	35 208	35 910	42 994	
Total	**150 026**	**127 548**	**128 092**	**144 640**	**168 826**	**154 827**	**147 868**	**131 738**	**137 452**	**135 842**	**143 275**	**51**

Note: For details on definitions and sources, please refer to the metadata at the end of the tables.

StatLink http://dx.doi.org/10.1787/888932617588

Table B.6. Acquisitions of nationality by country of former nationality
GERMANY

	2000	2001	2002	2003	2004	2005	2006	2007	2008	2009	2010	Of which: Women 2010 (%)
Turkey	82 861	76 573	64 631	56 244	44 465	32 661	33 388	28 861	24 449	24 647	26 192	44
Iraq	984	1 264	1 721	2 999	3 564	4 136	3 693	4 102	4 229	5 136	5 228	39
Poland	1 604	1 774	2 646	2 990	7 499	6 896	6 907	5 479	4 245	3 841	3 789	74
Afghanistan	4 773	5 111	4 750	4 948	4 077	3 133	3 063	2 831	2 512	3 549	3 520	49
Ukraine	2 978	3 295	3 656	3 889	3 844	3 363	4 536	4 454	1 953	2 345	3 118	62
Iran	14 410	12 020	13 026	9 440	6 362	4 482	3 662	3 121	2 734	3 184	3 046	50
Serbia	..	..	..	400	3 539	8 824	12 601	10 458	6 484	4 309	3 039	49
Morocco	5 008	4 425	3 800	4 118	3 820	3 684	3 546	3 489	3 130	3 042	2 806	37
Russian Federation	4 583	4 972	3 734	2 764	4 381	5 055	4 679	4 069	2 439	2 477	2 753	61
Romania	2 008	2 026	1 974	1 394	1 309	1 789	1 379	3 502	2 137	2 357	2 523	72
Bosnia and Herzegovina	4 002	3 791	2 357	1 770	2 103	1 907	1 862	1 797	1 878	1 733	1 945	56
Viet Nam	4 489	3 014	1 482	1 423	1 371	1 278	1 382	1 078	1 048	1 513	1 738	56
Lebanon	5 673	4 486	3 300	2 651	2 265	1 969	2 030	1 754	1 675	1 759	1 697	45
Israel	1 101	1 364	1 739	2 844	3 164	2 871	4 313	2 405	1 971	1 681	1 649	48
Kazakhstan	2 152	2 148	2 027	3 010	1 443	2 975	3 207	2 180	1 602	1 439	1 601	61
Other countries	50 062	51 835	43 704	39 847	33 947	32 218	34 318	33 450	31 984	33 110	36 926	
Total	**186 688**	**178 098**	**154 547**	**140 731**	**127 153**	**117 241**	**124 566**	**113 030**	**94 470**	**96 122**	**101 570**	**51**

Note: For details on definitions and sources, please refer to the metadata at the end of the tables.

StatLink http://dx.doi.org/10.1787/888932617588

Table B.6. Acquisitions of nationality by country of former nationality
GREECE

	2000	2001	2002	2003	2004	2005	2006	2007	2008	2009	2010	Of which: Women 2010 (%)
Albania	..	..	..	..	..	..	..	5 688	9 996	14 271	..	..
Georgia	..	..	..	..	..	..	..	489	1 285	550	..	..
Russian Federation	..	..	..	..	..	..	..	475	834	410	..	..
Turkey	..	..	..	..	..	..	..	223	212	175	..	..
Australia	..	..	..	..	..	..	..	105	164	138	..	..
Armenia	..	..	..	..	..	..	..	80	165	137	..	..
Ukraine	..	..	..	..	..	..	..	68	167	129	..	..
United States	..	..	..	..	..	..	..	105	175	127	..	..
Germany	..	..	..	..	..	..	..	39	85	105	..	..
Cyprus	..	..	..	..	..	..	..	109	68	87	..	..
Romania	..	..	..	..	..	..	..	83	79	63	..	..
Bulgaria	..	..	..	..	..	..	..	105	89	62	..	..
Canada	..	..	..	..	..	..	..	44	49	49	..	..
Egypt	..	..	..	..	..	..	..	62	50	45	..	..
Israel	..	..	..	..	..	..	..	82	81	40	..	..
Other countries	..	..	..	..	..	..	..	3 049	3 423	631	..	..
Total	..	..	..	..	..	..	..	**10 806**	**16 922**	**17 019**	..	..

Note: For details on definitions and sources, please refer to the metadata at the end of the tables. See notes on Cyprus in the introduction of this annex.

StatLink http://dx.doi.org/10.1787/888932617588

Table B.6. Acquisitions of nationality by country of former nationality
HUNGARY

	2000	2001	2002	2003	2004	2005	2006	2007	2008	2009	2010	Of which: Women 2010 (%)
Romania	4 231	5 644	2 238	3 415	3 605	6 890	4 303	6 052	5 535	3 805	3 939	57
Serbia	..	..	..	..	..	949	357	757	758	672	721	48
Ukraine	..	..	..	..	..	828	541	834	857	558	646	65
Belarus	..	..	..	..	..	194	99	136	167	127	123	71
Russian Federation	..	..	..	..	..	162	111	7	156	119	111	68
Slovak Republic	..	..	..	..	..	161	206	116	106	97	97	66
Czech Republic	..	..	..	..	..	142	14	60	75	60	76	72
Viet Nam	..	..	..	..	..	53	40	53	95	39	75	39
China	..	..	..	..	..	16	15	31	29	20	27	63
Croatia	..	..	..	..	..	50	148	26	34	25	26	69
Germany	..	..	..	..	..	25	22	28	33	35	25	52
Afghanistan	..	..	..	..	..	5	4	25	15	10	24	50
Bulgaria	..	..	..	..	..	14	11	5	4	8	23	52
Estonia	..	..	..	..	..	148	118	110	41	31	19	53
Mongolia	..	..	..	..	..	11	14	10	4	14	16	69
Other countries	3 307	2 946	1 131	1 846	1 827	222	169	192	195	182	138	
Total	**7 538**	**8 590**	**3 369**	**5 261**	**5 432**	**9 870**	**6 172**	**8 442**	**8 104**	**5 802**	**6 086**	**56**

Note: For details on definitions and sources, please refer to the metadata at the end of the tables.

StatLink ⟶ http://dx.doi.org/10.1787/888932617588

Table B.6. Acquisitions of nationality by country of former nationality
ICELAND

	2000	2001	2002	2003	2004	2005	2006	2007	2008	2009	2010	Of which: Women 2010 (%)
Philippines	35	64	45	64	59	45	105	69	126	106	67	60
Poland	35	39	48	67	133	184	222	162	164	153	50	56
Viet Nam	6	15	9	8	19	23	41	16	52	51	39	59
Thailand	49	40	50	51	48	50	54	45	62	40	28	82
Serbia	..	..	..	..	73	70	78	33	109	76	27	59
Russian Federation	13	4	5	11	33	23	24	17	38	17	21	76
United States	28	32	22	34	33	31	34	33	20	15	19	37
Ukraine	4	1	2	4	18	6	9	13	18	18	15	73
India	..	..	2	..	2	1	2	2	8	7	11	55
Lithuania	..	4	3	1	9	7	5	23	23	9	11	45
Bosnia and Herzegovina	4	4	3	1	1	17	7	24	14	16	9	56
Bulgaria	3	4	2	8	9	2	9	5	6	10	9	67
Morocco	1	7	5	3	7	7	4	9	22	3	8	25
China	4	7	6	7	13	13	17	19	24	15	7	43
Chile	1	1	1	1	5	2	1	15	6	3	6	50
Other countries	103	130	153	203	209	245	232	162	222	189	123	
Total	**286**	**352**	**356**	**463**	**671**	**726**	**844**	**647**	**914**	**728**	**450**	**59**

Note: For details on definitions and sources, please refer to the metadata at the end of the tables.

StatLink ⟶ http://dx.doi.org/10.1787/888932617588

Table B.6. Acquisitions of nationality by country of former nationality
IRELAND

	2000	2001	2002	2003	2004	2005	2006	2007	2008	2009	2010	Of which: Women 2010 (%)
Nigeria	..	..	..	..	..	155	189	142	319	454	1 012	51
Philippines	..	..	..	..	..	43	70	37	84	410	630	67
India	..	..	..	..	..	144	126	119	166	339	443	36
South Africa	..	..	..	..	..	257	363	219	205	318	343	48
Pakistan	..	..	..	..	..	213	239	189	196	201	306	38
China	..	..	..	..	..	57	85	45	102	131	258	52
Russian Federation	..	..	..	..	..	81	109	86	160	246	253	52
Bangladesh	..	..	..	..	..	8	20	25	41	146	238	27
Ukraine	..	..	..	..	..	31	25	34	97	153	202	49
Sudan	..	..	..	..	..	40	39	40	80	123	170	34
Zimbabwe	..	..	..	..	..	55	67	46	89	111	147	49
Romania	..	..	..	..	..	92	81	46	74	117	143	45
Moldova	..	..	..	..	..	21	22	11	67	72	115	44
United States	..	..	..	..	..	890	1 518	1 841	875	156	112	59
Belarus	..	..	..	..	..	11	14	7	38	72	106	57
Other countries	..	..	..	..	..	1 981	2 796	3 769	1 757	1 545	1 909	
Total	1 143	2 443	2 817	3 993	3 784	4 079	5 763	6 656	4 350	4 594	6 387	48

Note: For details on definitions and sources, please refer to the metadata at the end of the tables.

StatLink ⟶ http://dx.doi.org/10.1787/888932617588

Table B.6. Acquisitions of nationality by country of former nationality
ITALY

	2000	2001	2002	2003	2004	2005	2006	2007	2008	2009	2010	Of which: Women 2010 (%)
Morocco	573	579	624	1 132	1 046	..	3 295	3 850	..	5 917	6 952	..
Albania	521	687	703	830	882	..	2 330	2 605	..	6 101	5 628	..
Romania	665	855	968	977	847	..	2 775	3 509	..	2 032	2 929	..
Peru	228	263	305	383	253	..	..	883	..	1 147	1 377	..
Brazil	512	619	604	726	579	..	1 751	1 928	..	1 226	1 313	..
Tunisia	208	215	175	271	258	..	371	920	..	1 256	1 215	..
Ukraine	111	129	167	224	209	..	..	1 389	..	..	1 033	..
Poland	448	475	519	677	619	..	1 320	1 255	..	..	974	..
Egypt	266	235	195	264	283	..	217	704	..	926	912	..
Russian Federation	347	384	439	463	436	..	1 181	1 279	..	..	861	..
Cuba	377	512	542	646	539	..	1 535	1 355	..	..	840	..
Argentina	240	316	411	541	515	..	2 569	2 410	..	1 556	834	..
Dominican Republic	377	354	393	409	317	..	..	939	..	..	717	..
Moldova	..	..	..	..	..	..	..	754	..	..	703	..
Serbia	92	154	186	194	175	..	..	397	..	..	764	..
Other countries	4 598	4 605	4 454	5 669	4 976	..	18 422	14 289	..	19 923	13 171	
Total	9 563	10 382	10 685	13 406	11 934	19 266	35 766	38 466	39 484	40 084	40 223	..

Note: For details on definitions and sources, please refer to the metadata at the end of the tables.

StatLink ⟶ http://dx.doi.org/10.1787/888932617588

Table B.6. Acquisitions of nationality by country of former nationality
JAPAN

	2000	2001	2002	2003	2004	2005	2006	2007	2008	2009	2010	Of which: Women 2010 (%)
Korea	9 842	10 295	9 188	11 778	11 031	9 689	8 531	8 546	7 412	7 637	6 668	..
China	5 245	4 377	4 442	4 722	4 122	4 427	4 347	4 740	4 322	5 392	4 816	..
Other countries	725	619	709	1 133	1 183	1 135	1 230	1 394	1 484	1 756	1 588	
Total	**15 812**	**15 291**	**14 339**	**17 633**	**16 336**	**15 251**	**14 108**	**14 680**	**13 218**	**14 785**	**13 072**	..

Note: For details on definitions and sources, please refer to the metadata at the end of the tables.

StatLink http://dx.doi.org/10.1787/888932617588

Table B.6. Acquisitions of nationality by country of former nationality
KOREA

	2000	2001	2002	2003	2004	2005	2006	2007	2008	2009	2010	Of which: Women 2010 (%)
China	..	1 391	3 344	6 146	7 443	14 881	7 156	8 178	12 545	..	..	..
Viet Nam	..	8	30	81	147	362	243	461	1 147	..	..	..
Philippines	..	21	112	928	1 074	786	317	335	579	..	..	..
Mongolia	..	1	10	43	36	109	32	82	134	..	..	..
Uzbekistan	..	5	6	21	34	79	38	60	80	..	..	..
Thailand	..	7	12	41	53	69	39	57	73	..	..	..
Pakistan	..	9	13	63	58	66	18	34	27	..	..	..
Other countries	..	238	356	411	417	622	282	1 112	673	..	..	
Total	..	**1 680**	**3 883**	**7 734**	**9 262**	**16 974**	**8 125**	**10 319**	**15 258**	**26 756**	**17 323**	..

Note: For details on definitions and sources, please refer to the metadata at the end of the tables.

StatLink http://dx.doi.org/10.1787/888932617588

Table B.6. Acquisitions of nationality by country of former nationality
LUXEMBOURG

	2000	2001	2002	2003	2004	2005	2006	2007	2008	2009	2010	Of which: Women 2010 (%)
Portugal	150	106	147	158	188	252	338	352	293	1 242	1 351	51
Italy	157	105	119	120	111	97	161	138	109	362	665	50
France	52	33	65	57	44	51	74	75	76	277	342	58
Germany	50	45	47	50	62	79	74	95	76	322	333	56
Belgium	72	39	87	73	83	101	87	97	77	224	258	52
Bosnia and Herzegovina	1	5	6	8	22	29	46	72	76	270	202	43
Serbia	1	0	0	0	0	2	55	67	115	425	412	52
Former Yugoslavia	11	11	21	28	25	50	1	0	2	0	61	33
Spain	10	4	6	11	8	9	7	17	10	48	58	55
United Kingdom	1	0	1	2	3	1	8	5	0	62	53	57
Russian Federation	5	4	5	2	5	8	13	10	10	40	50	78
Netherlands	14	13	11	17	6	7	20	10	20	31	50	58
United States	1	0	0	0	2	2	0	2	3	47	44	45
Cape Verde	27	20	48	50	41	33	45	46	49	77	40	55
Former Yug. Rep. of Macedonia	3	4	6	10	12	10	7	17	10	51	37	54
Other countries	132	111	191	209	241	233	199	250	299	595	392	
Total	**684**	**496**	**754**	**785**	**841**	**954**	**1 128**	**1 236**	**1 215**	**4 022**	**4 311**	**52**

Note: For details on definitions and sources, please refer to the metadata at the end of the tables.

StatLink http://dx.doi.org/10.1787/888932617588

Table B.6. Acquisitions of nationality by country of former nationality
MEXICO

	2000	2001	2002	2003	2004	2005	2006	2007	2008	2009	2010	Of which: Women 2010 (%)
Colombia	..	..	434	..	901	813	689	892	690	390	..	..
Cuba	..	..	549	..	661	666	429	660	459	307	..	..
United States	..	..	94	..	215	286	334	287	246	266	..	..
Argentina	..	..	142	..	328	372	400	450	400	265	..	..
Spain	..	..	140	..	218	301	239	286	251	227	..	..
Guatemala	..	..	1 650	..	1 624	247	114	185	141	209	..	..
China	..	..	211	..	310	324	188	294	324	196	..	..
Peru	..	..	226	..	320	191	215	292	213	166	..	..
El Salvador	..	..	208	..	243	235	137	159	118	163	..	..
Venezuela	..	..	39	..	107	197	185	316	309	159	..	..
Honduras	..	..	77	..	118	156	59	123	98	131	..	..
France	..	..	62	..	105	93	105	71	77	82	..	..
Italy	..	..	57	..	93	99	89	94	108	76	..	..
Chile	..	..	29	..	77	86	58	90	69	72	..	..
Nicaragua	..	..	74	..	99	87	53	80	61	57	..	..
Other countries	..	..	745	..	1 010	1 457	881	1 191	907	723	..	..
Total	**3 944**	**3 090**	**4 737**	**4 317**	**6 429**	**5 610**	**4 175**	**5 470**	**4 471**	**3 489**	**2 150**	**..**

Note: For details on definitions and sources, please refer to the metadata at the end of the tables.

StatLink http://dx.doi.org/10.1787/888932617588

Table B.6. Acquisitions of nationality by country of former nationality
NETHERLANDS

	2000	2001	2002	2003	2004	2005	2006	2007	2008	2009	2010	Of which: Women 2010 (%)
Morocco	13 471	12 721	12 033	7 126	5 873	7 086	6 896	6 409	5 034	5 508	5 797	54
Turkey	4 708	5 513	5 391	3 726	4 026	3 493	3 407	4 073	3 147	4 167	4 984	55
Suriname	2 008	2 025	1 957	1 242	1 421	2 031	1 636	1 285	1 006	1 142	967	61
China	1 002	1 111	908	722	739	1 291	799	638	539	559	490	67
Germany	508	573	608	445	297	349	447	461	353	387	414	57
Thailand	277	355	289	171	161	160	171	195	220	383	413	84
Afghanistan	945	803	1 118	982	801	550	562	662	584	596	402	59
Ghana	348	360	357	157	74	199	296	314	283	411	367	57
Indonesia	456	416	380	291	203	293	248	302	262	306	298	76
Iraq	2 403	2 315	2 367	832	489	333	331	501	866	674	288	52
Russian Federation	422	335	347	207	242	521	466	413	436	400	275	84
Brazil	231	290	249	137	131	159	189	173	201	307	272	77
Nigeria	143	196	214	96	69	139	189	214	220	300	271	52
Philippines	300	348	263	159	129	198	209	226	209	308	263	83
Egypt	443	528	437	190	97	238	245	304	255	337	259	49
Other countries	22 303	18 778	18 403	12 316	11 421	11 448	12 998	14 483	14 614	13 969	10 515	
Total	**49 968**	**46 667**	**45 321**	**28 799**	**26 173**	**28 488**	**29 089**	**30 653**	**28 229**	**29 754**	**26 275**	**57**

Note: For details on definitions and sources, please refer to the metadata at the end of the tables.

StatLink http://dx.doi.org/10.1787/888932617588

Table B.6. Acquisitions of nationality by country of former nationality
NEW ZEALAND

	2000	2001	2002	2003	2004	2005	2006	2007	2008	2009	2010	Of which: Women 2010 (%)
United Kingdom	3 670	3 019	2 187	2 266	2 377	2 423	2 890	3 638	3 562	3 150	2 617	47
Samoa	1 702	1 590	1 307	1 189	1 065	1 153	1 363	1 445	1 433	1 605	1 908	47
India	1 847	1 376	1 350	1 255	2 127	2 905	4 330	5 177	3 429	2 303	1 567	51
South Africa	2 010	2 028	1 973	1 992	2 407	2 425	2 799	3 131	2 458	1 850	1 339	50
Fiji	1 253	1 273	1 139	1 047	1 452	1 543	1 689	1 722	1 931	1 581	1 307	52
Philippines	949	829	652	555	702	844	1 123	1 166	718	708	848	54
China	3 752	2 579	1 896	2 032	2 849	3 323	3 888	3 077	1 909	1 208	676	56
Korea	1 982	1 053	685	642	1 099	1 523	1 638	1 448	884	606	457	49
Malaysia	..	..	..	..	..	..	329	451	422	480	456	51
Tonga	365	408	271	207	198	167	191	259	278	324	378	49
United States	363	281	335	348	335	268	346	424	413	352	327	50
Zimbabwe	..	..	..	..	..	..	812	907	672	390	276	57
Sri Lanka	774	738	568	472	511	436	435	480	393	305	235	48
Chinese Taipei	1 970	1 619	1 069	546	355	414	428	373	330	256	203	53
Thailand	..	..	..	..	..	..	252	212	167	174	131	73
Other countries	8 972	6 742	6 037	5 745	6 665	6 917	6 504	5 957	4 773	3 438	2 448	
Total	**29 609**	**23 535**	**19 469**	**18 296**	**22 142**	**24 341**	**29 017**	**29 867**	**23 772**	**18 730**	**15 173**	**51**

Note: For details on definitions and sources, please refer to the metadata at the end of the tables.

StatLink http://dx.doi.org/10.1787/888932617588

Table B.6. Acquisitions of nationality by country of former nationality
NORWAY

	2000	2001	2002	2003	2004	2005	2006	2007	2008	2009	2010	Of which: Women 2010 (%)
Somalia	332	676	546	392	526	1 250	1 281	2 196	1 315	1 737	1 528	46
Iraq	524	331	497	403	619	2 141	2 142	2 577	1 072	1 267	1 338	56
Afghanistan	19	36	17	21	23	75	194	674	877	857	1 054	41
Russian Federation	222	192	308	280	365	548	458	436	515	622	673	51
Iran	481	361	324	228	508	832	535	740	495	785	554	49
Pakistan	1 077	409	829	497	568	694	590	544	773	469	430	53
Philippines	157	261	299	265	249	322	246	421	233	445	322	80
Thailand	142	302	257	193	234	299	263	427	247	483	267	78
Sweden	246	249	216	211	221	276	376	241	211	184	248	53
Eritrea	9	24	26	12	20	50	60	88	67	63	248	44
Ethiopia	59	79	63	55	83	116	140	313	341	216	225	52
Turkey	523	356	412	398	393	385	355	445	209	145	214	45
Sri Lanka	454	477	461	281	235	264	242	362	246	276	194	73
China	156	113	135	84	82	109	123	175	92	157	182	59
Viet Nam	738	594	292	210	222	216	216	178	248	161	177	74
Other countries	4 378	6 378	4 359	4 337	3 806	5 078	4 734	5 060	3 371	3 575	4 249	
Total	**9 517**	**10 838**	**9 041**	**7 867**	**8 154**	**12 655**	**11 955**	**14 877**	**10 312**	**11 442**	**11 903**	**52**

Note: For details on definitions and sources, please refer to the metadata at the end of the tables.

StatLink http://dx.doi.org/10.1787/888932617588

Table B.6. Acquisitions of nationality by country of former nationality
POLAND

	2000	2001	2002	2003	2004	2005	2006	2007	2008	2009	2010	Of which: Women 2010 (%)
Ukraine	46	62	214	431	538	759	417	662	369	877	992	69
Belarus	25	31	54	108	129	316	101	126	152	357	418	63
Russian Federation	23	14	22	52	145	257	129	114	64	162	215	74
Armenia	11	6	13	8	6	18	27	30	16	79	101	44
Viet Nam	7	13	17	11	11	36	29	47	12	64	97	38
Germany	101	47	49	60	62	156	1	39	37	47	92	48
Sweden	10	13	30	107	81	90	8	26	48	34	61	59
United States	26	11	9	32	41	59	8	23	27	47	50	34
Nigeria	21	4	12	8	11	16	7	17	2	35	45	0
Canada	44	23	22	46	36	73	7	17	24	35	40	63
Kazakhstan	54	43	53	68	38	62	10	10	18	41	38	55
Egypt	0	0	5	1	2	18	6	13	0	37	38	0
Tunisia	0	0	3	0	5	17	4	6	4	19	35	3
Turkey	4	15	1	5	11	19	36	11	1	35	33	0
Moldova	0	0	0	0	0	19	8	23	24	20	28	68
Other countries	603	484	682	697	821	951	191	364	256	614	643	
Total	975	766	1 186	1 634	1 937	2 866	989	1 528	1 054	2 503	2 926	53

Note: For details on definitions and sources, please refer to the metadata at the end of the tables.

StatLink http://dx.doi.org/10.1787/888932617588

Table B.6. Acquisitions of nationality by country of former nationality
PORTUGAL

	2000	2001	2002	2003	2004	2005	2006	2007	2008	2009	2010	Of which: Women 2010 (%)
Brazil	175	283	345	345	307	162	491	415	4 080	5 820	..	..
Cape Verde	69	228	271	370	274	132	1 047	2 189	6 013	5 021	..	..
Moldova	..	..	..	..	2	3	6	..	2 230	3 043	..	..
Angola	42	65	82	144	63	38	336	738	2 075	3 003	..	..
Guinea-Bissau	27	55	73	38	95	36	873	1 602	2 754	1 927	..	..
Ukraine	..	..	..	..	2	2	12	..	484	1 858	..	..
Sao Tome and Principe	7	20	34	58	22	7	134	448	1 391	1 468	..	..
India	10	6	9	11	3	6	25	32	417	790	..	..
Russian Federation	..	..	..	..	9	6	21	31	259	673	..	..
Pakistan	..	..	..	..	2	4	21	32	74	453	..	..
Romania	..	..	..	..	4	5	20	..	209	452	..	..
Bangladesh	..	..	..	..	..	..	..	31	316	413	..	..
Chinese Taipei	..	..	..	..	..	..	..	..	..	236	..	..
Georgia	..	..	..	..	..	..	..	..	..	123	..	..
China	7	2	6	5	1	2	15	36	93	120	..	..
Other countries	384	423	549	776	562	536	626	466	2 013	3 488	..	..
Total	721	1 082	1 369	1 747	1 346	939	3 627	6 020	22 408	28 888	24 478	..

Note: For details on definitions and sources, please refer to the metadata at the end of the tables.

StatLink http://dx.doi.org/10.1787/888932617588

Table B.6. Acquisitions of nationality by country of former nationality
RUSSIAN FEDERATION

	2000	2001	2002	2003	2004	2005	2006	2007	2008	2009	2010	Of which: Women 2010 (%)
Kyrgyzstan	..	21 217	17 324	1 717	27 449	38 422	33 166	61 239	51 210	48 720	37 348	..
Kazakhstan	..	133 341	101 756	8 678	106 613	123 286	68 087	64 831	58 736	50 628	27 130	..
Armenia	..	19 267	14 573	1 722	23 139	39 330	34 860	39 328	45 253	54 828	6 261	..
Ukraine	..	72 449	53 396	7 623	50 593	94 133	66 502	55 424	58 500	62 025	5 715	..
Azerbaijan	..	19 629	13 663	2 010	24 555	35 720	22 045	24 885	29 643	34 627	5 265	..
Uzbekistan	..	33 373	29 665	2 266	29 676	73 315	67 021	53 109	43 982	49 784	4 788	..
Tajikistan	..	8 748	7 944	869	10 749	16 148	12 198	16 444	21 891	39 214	4 393	..
Belarus	..	8 356	6 399	563	10 179	12 943	7 919	6 572	7 099	6 062	3 888	..
Georgia	..	20 748	12 297	1 459	20 695	25 225	14 008	12 156	11 110	9 876	2 513	..
Moldova	..	9 038	6 740	366	7 283	13 727	12 809	13 876	15 782	20 429	1 992	..
Turkmenistan	..	4 776	3 551	398	5 358	7 713	5 577	4 737	4 444	4 026	482	..
Afghanistan	..	575	214	0	53	136	101	109	153	124	188	..
Lithuania	..	1 032	609	56	488	722	496	460	539	430	149	..
Turkey	..	170	102	27	50	44	51	60	105	129	144	..
Latvia	..	1 869	1 184	196	954	1 062	756	516	466	469	135	..
Other countries	..	4 607	3 046	3 578	12 585	22 592	20 892	13 953	12 450	12 766	10 907	
Total	..	**359 195**	**272 463**	**31 528**	**330 419**	**504 518**	**366 488**	**367 699**	**361 363**	**394 137**	**111 298**	..

Note: For details on definitions and sources, please refer to the metadata at the end of the tables.

StatLink http://dx.doi.org/10.1787/888932617588

Table B.6. Acquisitions of nationality by country of former nationality
SLOVAK REPUBLIC

	2000	2001	2002	2003	2004	2005	2006	2007	2008	2009	2010	Of which: Women 2010 (%)
Serbia	..	..	..	443	506	185	42	112	53	46	57	54
Czech Republic	..	..	..	597	775	167	121	158	93	39	45	51
Ukraine	..	..	..	251	549	450	377	704	203	35	44	64
Viet Nam	..	..	..	405	619	40	40	62	37	7	15	53
Hungary	..	..	..	5	9	7	9	6	15	3	12	50
Romania	..	..	..	450	442	220	147	100	31	10	10	30
Russian Federation	..	..	..	65	96	37	35	42	31	4	8	50
United States	..	..	..	97	136	64	113	110	93	9	7	57
Poland	..	..	..	43	26	14	20	18	7	1	5	60
Israel	..	..	..	8	3	11	5	..	1	..	5	40
Germany	..	..	..	19	30	10	13	16	16	8	3	67
Bulgaria	..	..	..	66	42	24	35	19	7	1	3	67
Angola	..	..	..	8	7	2	1	7	1	2	2	50
Croatia	..	..	..	35	50	22	16	18	5	2	2	50
West Bank and Gaza Strip	..	..	..	20	8	3	1	..	..	1	2	..
Other countries	..	..	..	980	718	137	150	106	87	94	19	
Total	..	..	..	**3 492**	**4 016**	**1 393**	**1 125**	**1 478**	**680**	**262**	**239**	**51**

Note: For details on definitions and sources, please refer to the metadata at the end of the tables.

StatLink http://dx.doi.org/10.1787/888932617588

Table B.6. Acquisitions of nationality by country of former nationality
SPAIN

	2000	2001	2002	2003	2004	2005	2006	2007	2008	2009	2010	Of which: Women 2010 (%)
Ecuador	292	510	1 173	1 951	6 370	10 031	19 477	21 371	25 536	25 769	43 091	59
Colombia	302	848	1 267	1 801	4 194	7 334	12 720	13 852	15 409	16 527	23 995	61
Morocco	1 921	2 822	3 111	6 831	8 036	5 555	5 690	7 864	8 615	6 683	10 703	44
Peru	1 488	2 322	3 117	2 933	3 958	3 645	4 713	6 490	8 206	6 368	8 291	55
Argentina	661	791	997	1 009	1 746	2 293	3 536	4 810	5 188	4 629	6 395	51
Bolivia	66	89	104	129	218	289	648	709	1 103	1 813	4 778	61
Dominican Republic	1 755	2 126	2 876	2 648	2 834	2 322	2 805	2 800	3 496	2 766	3 801	66
Cuba	893	1 191	2 088	1 602	1 889	2 506	2 703	2 466	2 870	2 696	3 546	58
Venezuela	197	326	439	529	703	752	908	1 324	1 581	1 744	2 730	61
Uruguay	177	239	219	235	327	408	624	839	1 201	1 451	2 219	53
Brazil	273	411	477	500	683	695	782	779	1 049	943	1 738	69
Chile	594	359	353	350	484	620	844	838	1 141	1 090	1 688	51
Mexico	..	263	352	344	451	437	567	593	763	584	932	64
Portugal	452	568	627	536	634	478	430	381	566	485	800	54
Paraguay	..	42	46	23	42	60	87	78	179	298	766	69
Other countries	2 928	3 836	4 564	5 135	5 766	5 404	5 805	6 616	7 267	5 751	8 248	
Total	**11 999**	**16 743**	**21 810**	**26 556**	**38 335**	**42 829**	**62 339**	**71 810**	**84 170**	**79 597**	**123 721**	**57**

Note: For details on definitions and sources, please refer to the metadata at the end of the tables.

StatLink http://dx.doi.org/10.1787/888932617588

Table B.6. Acquisitions of nationality by country of former nationality
SWEDEN

	2000	2001	2002	2003	2004	2005	2006	2007	2008	2009	2010	Of which: Women 2010 (%)
Iraq	4 181	4 043	4 160	4 678	5 298	11 544	12 895	5 950	4 224	3 180	4 367	46
Finland	1 389	1 512	1 561	2 816	2 703	2 588	2 975	2 757	2 535	2 432	2 971	65
Poland	264	1 906	2 604	1 325	990	793	1 000	762	686	824	1 487	56
Thailand	525	454	606	443	500	585	876	1 007	1 261	1 314	1 429	83
Somalia	2 843	2 802	1 789	1 121	840	688	931	655	787	885	1 076	53
Turkey	1 398	2 796	2 127	1 375	1 269	1 702	2 921	1 456	1 125	1 200	1 049	45
Iran	2 798	2 031	1 737	1 350	1 296	1 889	2 796	1 459	1 113	1 110	967	56
Germany	154	198	243	209	244	294	457	386	606	700	923	51
Bosnia and Herzegovina	12 591	4 241	4 064	3 090	1 469	1 788	2 627	2 081	1 764	1 146	919	53
Afghanistan	395	329	285	278	361	623	1 062	777	812	1 180	848	45
Russian Federation	410	621	626	642	535	886	1 510	919	759	865	769	64
Chile	687	727	689	548	464	543	754	687	593	488	526	45
Denmark	310	271	316	310	335	329	431	388	404	409	485	43
Burundi	0	1	1	6	14	9	46	114	201	354	482	51
China	434	460	563	675	654	920	1 141	742	515	403	429	67
Other countries	14 116	13 066	15 607	13 485	9 158	10 350	14 573	12 333	11 945	12 072	13 730	
Total	**42 495**	**35 458**	**36 978**	**32 351**	**26 130**	**35 531**	**46 995**	**32 473**	**29 330**	**28 562**	**32 457**	**54**

Note: For details on definitions and sources, please refer to the metadata at the end of the tables.

StatLink http://dx.doi.org/10.1787/888932617588

Table B.6. Acquisitions of nationality by country of former nationality
SWITZERLAND

	2000	2001	2002	2003	2004	2005	2006	2007	2008	2009	2010	Of which: Women 2010 (%)
Serbia	3 285	3 686	5 803	6 332	7 854	9 503	11 721	10 441	10 252	8 453	6 859	..
Italy	6 652	5 386	6 633	5 085	4 196	4 032	4 502	4 629	4 921	4 804	4 111	..
Germany	646	586	817	670	639	773	1 144	1 361	3 022	4 035	3 617	..
Portugal	765	779	920	1 165	1 199	1 505	2 383	2 201	1 761	2 336	2 217	..
Turkey	3 127	3 116	4 128	4 216	3 565	3 467	3 457	3 044	2 866	2 593	2 091	..
Bosnia and Herzegovina	999	1 128	1 865	2 268	2 371	2 790	3 149	3 008	2 855	2 408	1 924	..
Former Yug. Rep. of Macedonia	857	1 022	1 639	1 802	1 981	2 171	2 596	2 210	2 287	1 831	1 586	..
Croatia	970	1 045	1 638	1 565	1 616	1 681	1 837	1 660	2 046	1 599	1 483	..
Spain	851	699	691	800	823	975	1 283	1 246	1 096	1 245	1 120	..
France	1 360	1 307	1 367	1 215	1 181	1 021	1 260	1 218	1 110	1 314	1 084	..
United Kingdom	339	310	350	306	289	287	323	353	319	365	298	..
Netherlands	74	90	90	155	254	178	210	234	189	229	227	..
Belgium	83	53	118	91	71	61	64	112	153	173	209	..
Austria	240	233	227	194	150	167	174	166	193	205	189	..
Romania	194	196	216	186	130	145	163	148	126	136	152	..
Other countries	8 258	7 950	10 013	9 465	9 437	9 742	12 509	11 970	11 169	11 714	12 147	
Total	**28 700**	**27 586**	**36 515**	**35 424**	**35 685**	**38 437**	**46 711**	**43 889**	**44 365**	**43 440**	**39 314**	**53**

Note: For details on definitions and sources, please refer to the metadata at the end of the tables.

StatLink http://dx.doi.org/10.1787/888932617588

Table B.6. Acquisitions of nationality by country of former nationality
TURKEY

	2000	2001	2002	2003	2004	2005	2006	2007	2008	2009	2010	Of which: Women 2010 (%)
Bulgaria	..	..	13 178	12 423	3 528	3 299	1 769	..	..	..	..	..
Azerbaijan	..	..	2 667	1 908	1 541	780	563	..	..	..	..	..
Russian Federation	..	..	1 264	1 033	700	346	287	..	..	..	..	..
Afghanistan	..	..	27	56	233	312	245	..	..	..	..	..
Kazakhstan	..	..	379	450	398	272	195	..	..	..	..	..
Syria	..	..	212	201	135	124	175	..	..	..	..	..
Iraq	..	..	136	103	153	146	143	..	..	..	..	..
Iran	..	..	121	112	178	156	137	..	..	..	..	..
Greece	..	..	48	37	119	104	107	..	..	..	..	..
United Kingdom	..	..	19	12	26	61	93	..	..	..	..	..
Kyrgyzstan	..	..	147	146	140	129	88	..	..	..	..	..
Uzbekistan	..	..	175	150	109	76	87	..	..	..	..	..
Ukraine	..	..	618	598	87	58	85	..	..	..	..	..
Former Yug. Rep. of Macedonia	..	..	85	84	72	82	80	..	..	..	..	..
Romania	..	..	886	455	52	84	76	..	..	..	..	..
Other countries	..	..	3 763	3 318	767	872	942	..	..	..	..	
Total	**..**	**..**	**23 725**	**21 086**	**8 238**	**6 901**	**5 072**	**..**	**..**	**..**	**..**	**..**

Note: For details on definitions and sources, please refer to the metadata at the end of the tables.

StatLink http://dx.doi.org/10.1787/888932617588

Table B.6. Acquisitions of nationality by country of former nationality
UNITED KINGDOM

	2000	2001	2002	2003	2004	2005	2006	2007	2008	2009	2010	Of which: Women 2010 (%)
India	8 135	8 177	10 003	10 799	13 598	14 137	15 134	14 507	11 835	26 541	29 405	..
Pakistan	8 631	10 144	10 946	12 769	14 094	12 605	10 260	8 143	9 442	20 945	22 054	..
Philippines	1 361	1 382	1 344	1 609	2 011	3 797	8 839	10 844	5 382	11 751	9 429	..
Bangladesh	5 380	5 385	5 737	6 133	5 786	3 637	3 724	2 257	3 633	12 041	7 966	..
Nigeria	5 594	6 277	6 486	6 302	6 242	6 622	5 874	6 031	4 531	6 953	7 873	..
China	1 962	1 580	2 362	1 863	1 918	2 425	2 601	3 117	2 677	6 041	7 581	..
South Africa	1 635	2 319	3 278	4 536	6 366	7 046	7 665	8 149	5 266	8 367	7 446	..
Zimbabwe	449	547	798	1 428	1 814	2 128	2 556	5 592	5 707	7 703	6 301	..
Somalia	2 586	5 495	7 498	8 544	11 164	8 297	9 029	7 450	7 163	8 139	5 817	..
Afghanistan	313	372	874	1 612	4 055	4 951	3 397	10 554	5 539	5 012	5 281	..
Sri Lanka	2 656	2 767	8 092	5 106	4 530	6 997	5 717	6 496	3 284	4 762	4 944	..
Turkey	4 875	4 037	8 040	4 916	4 860	6 767	5 583	4 709	4 641	7 207	4 630	..
Ghana	2 935	3 169	3 080	3 515	3 217	3 307	2 989	3 373	3 134	4 662	4 551	..
Iraq	2 340	1 831	3 449	2 257	2 335	3 259	4 120	5 479	8 894	5 497	4 385	..
Jamaica	1 882	2 062	2 026	2 799	3 161	3 520	2 526	3 165	2 715	3 148	2 958	..
Other countries	31 476	34 738	46 108	56 347	63 122	72 204	64 004	64 771	45 534	65 020	64 425	
Total	**82 210**	**90 282**	**120 121**	**130 535**	**148 273**	**161 699**	**154 018**	**164 637**	**129 377**	**203 789**	**195 046**	**53**

Note: For details on definitions and sources, please refer to the metadata at the end of the tables.

StatLink http://dx.doi.org/10.1787/888932617588

Table B.6. Acquisitions of nationality by country of former nationality
UNITED STATES

	2000	2001	2002	2003	2004	2005	2006	2007	2008	2009	2010	Of which: Women 2010 (%)
Mexico	189 705	103 234	76 531	56 093	63 840	77 089	83 979	122 258	231 815	111 630	67 062	..
India	42 198	34 311	33 774	29 790	37 975	35 962	47 542	46 871	65 971	52 889	61 142	..
Philippines	46 563	35 431	30 487	29 081	31 448	36 673	40 500	38 830	58 792	38 934	35 465	..
China	54 534	34 423	32 018	24 014	27 309	31 708	35 387	33 134	40 017	37 130	33 969	..
Viet Nam	55 934	41 596	36 835	25 995	27 480	32 926	29 917	27 921	39 584	31 168	19 313	..
Colombia	14 018	10 872	10 634	7 962	9 819	11 396	15 698	12 089	22 926	16 593	18 417	..
Dominican Republic	25 176	15 010	15 591	12 627	15 464	20 831	22 165	20 645	35 251	20 778	15 451	..
Cuba	15 661	11 393	10 889	7 727	11 236	11 227	21 481	15 394	39 871	24 891	14 050	..
Haiti	14 428	10 408	9 280	7 263	8 215	9 740	15 979	11 552	21 229	13 290	12 291	..
Jamaica	22 567	13 978	13 973	11 232	12 271	13 674	18 953	12 314	21 324	15 098	12 070	..
Pakistan	8 726	8 375	8 658	7 431	8 744	9 699	10 411	9 147	11 813	12 528	11 601	..
Korea	23 858	18 053	17 307	15 968	17 184	19 223	17 668	17 628	22 759	17 576	11 170	..
El Salvador	24 073	13 663	10 716	8 738	9 602	12 174	13 430	17 157	35 796	18 927	10 343	..
Iran	19 251	13 881	11 796	10 807	11 781	11 031	11 363	10 557	11 813	12 069	9 337	..
Nigeria	4 128	4 349	6 412	5 691	6 470	6 894	8 652	6 582	8 597	9 298	9 126	..
Other countries	327 968	239 228	248 807	202 785	238 313	264 033	309 464	258 398	378 981	310 916	279 106	
Total	**888 788**	**608 205**	**573 708**	**463 204**	**537 151**	**604 280**	**702 589**	**660 477**	**1 046 539**	**743 715**	**619 913**	**53**

Note: For details on definitions and sources, please refer to the metadata at the end of the tables.

StatLink http://dx.doi.org/10.1787/888932617588

Metadata related to Tables A.6 and B.6. Acquisitions of nationality

Country	Comments	Source
Australia		Department of Immigration and Citizenship.
Austria	Data refer to persons living in Austria at the time of acquisition.	Statistics Austria and BMI (Ministry of the Interior).
Belgium		Directorate for Statistics and Economic Information (DGSEI) and Ministry of Justice.
Canada	Data refer to country of birth, not to country of previous nationality. Persons who acquire Canadian citizenship may also hold other citizenships at the same time if allowed by the country of previous nationality.	Citizenship and Immigration Canada.
Chile	Residence permits (*Sistema B3000*).	Department of Foreigners and Migration, Ministry of the Interior.
Czech Republic	Acquisition of nationality by declaration or by naturalisation.	Ministry of the Interior.
Denmark		Statistics Denmark.
Estonia		Ministry of the Interior.
Finland	Includes naturalisations of persons of Finnish origin.	Statistics Finland.
France	Data by former nationality for naturalisations by "anticipated delaration" is unknown for the years 2004, 2006 and 2007.	Ministry of the Interior, Overseas Territories, Local Authorities and Immigration and Ministry of Justice.
Germany	Figures do not include ethnic Germans.	Federal Office of Statistics.
Greece	Data refer to all possible types of citizenship acquisition: naturalisation, declaration (for Greek descents), adoption by a Greek, etc.	Ministry of the Interior.
Hungary	Mainly Hungarian nationals from neighbouring countries who became Hungarian citizens, sometimes after their former Hungarian citizenship was abolished.	Central Office Administrative and Electronic Public Services (Central Population Register), Hungarian Central Statistical Office.
Iceland	Includes children who receive Icelandic citizenship with their parents.	Statistics Iceland.
Ireland	From 2005 on, figures include naturalisations and Post nuptial citizenship figures.	Department of Justice and Equality.
Italy		Ministry of the Interior.
Japan		Ministry of Justice, Civil Affairs Bureau.
Korea		Ministry of Justice.
Luxembourg	Excludes children acquiring nationality as a consequence of the naturalisation of their parents.	Ministry of Justice.
Mexico		Ministry of Foreign Affairs (SRE).
Netherlands		Central Bureau of Statistics (CBS).
New Zealand	The country of origin of persons granted New Zealand citizenship is the country of birth if birth documentation is available. If not, the country of origin is the country of citizenship as shown on the person's passport.	Department of Internal Affairs.
Norway		Statistics Norway.
Poland	From 2002 on, data include naturalisations by marriage and acknowledgment of persons of Polish descent, in addition to naturalisation by ordinary procedure.	Office for Repatriation and Aliens.
Portugal	From 2008 on, following the modification of the law on Portuguese citizenship in 2006 and 2007, the data include every foreigner who used to have a foreign citizenship and obtained Portuguese citizenship in the given year. Until 2007, data exclude acquisitions of nationality due to marriage or adoption.	National Statistical Office (INE) and Ministry of Justice (Central register).
Russian Federation	Excludes citizenship acquired through consulates. From 2009 on, applicants to Russian citizenship must have stayed in the country as temporary residents for at least a year, and as permanent residents for at least five years.	Ministry of Foreign Affairs and Federal Migration Service.
Slovak Republic	Data refer to persons living in Slovak Republic at the time of acquisition.	Ministry of the Interior.
Spain	Includes only naturalisations on grounds of residence in Spain. Excludes individuals recovering their former (Spanish) nationality.	Ministry of Labour and Immigration, based on naturalisations registered by the Ministry of Justice.
Sweden		Statistics Sweden.
Switzerland		Federal Office of Migration.
Turkey		Ministry of Interior, General Directorate of Population and Citizenship Affairs.
United Kingdom	The increase in 2009 is partly due to the processing of a backlog of applications filled prior to 2009.	Home Office.
United States	Data by country of birth refer to fiscal years (October to September of the year indicated).	US Department of Homeland Security.

Source: Data for Serbia include persons from Serbia, Montenegro and Serbia and Montenegro.

LIST OF CORRESPONDENTS OF THE CONTINUOUS REPORTING SYSTEM ON MIGRATION

AUSTRALIA	Mark CULLY
	Department of Immigration and Citizenship, Canberra
AUSTRIA	Gudrun BIFFL
	Danube University, Krems
BELGIUM	Frédéric POUPINEL de VALENCÉ
	Service public fédéral Emploi, Travail et Concertation sociale, Brussels
BULGARIA	Daniela BOBEVA
	Bulgarian National Bank, Sofia
CANADA	Martha JUSTUS
	Citizenship and Immigration Canada, Ottawa
CZECH REPUBLIC	Jarmila MAREŠOVÁ
	Czech Statistical Office, Prague
DENMARK	Maren SØRENSEN
	Danish Ministry for Social Affairs and Integration, Copenhagen
FINLAND	Arja SAARTO
	Ministry of Interior, Helsinki
FRANCE	Yves BREEM
	Ministry of the Interior, Overseas Territories, Local Authorities and Immigration, Paris
GERMANY	Farid EL KHOLY
	Ministry of Labour and Social Affairs, Berlin
GREECE	Anna TRIANDAFYLLIDOU
	Hellenic Foundation for European and Foreign Politic, Athens
HUNGARY	Orsolya KISGYÖRGY
	Ministry of National Economy, Budapest
IRELAND	Philip O'CONNELL
	The Economic and Social Research Institute, Dublin
ISRAEL	Gilad NATHAN
	Research and Information Center of the Israeli Parliament, Jerusalem
ITALY	Carla COLLICELLI and Maurizio MASTROLEMBO
	CENSIS, Rome
JAPAN	Hideharu MARUYAMA
	Ministry of Justice, Tokyo
	Mari YAMAMOTO
	Ministry of Health, Labour and Welfare, Tokyo

LIST OF CORRESPONDENTS OF THE CONTINUOUS REPORTING SYSTEM ON MIGRATION

KOREA	Young-bum PARK
	Hansung University, Seoul
LITHUANIA	Audra SIPAVIČIENÉ
	Vilnius
LUXEMBOURG	Christiane MARTIN
	Office luxembourgeois de l'Accueil et de l'Intégration
MEXICO	Gustavo MOHAR
	Ministry of the Interior, Mexico
NETHERLANDS	Godfried ENGENSEN and Eric SNEL
	Erasmus University, Rotterdam
NEW ZEALAND	Claire HARKESS
	Department of Labour, Wellington
NORWAY	Espen THORUD
	Ministry of Justice and the Police, Oslo
POLAND	Agnieszka FIHEL and Pawel KACZMARCZYK
	University of Warsaw
PORTUGAL	Jorge MALHEIROS
	University of Lisbon
ROMANIA	Mihaela MATEI
	Bucharest
RUSSIAN FEDERATION	Olga CHUDINOVSKIKH
	Centre for Population Studies, Moscow
SLOVAK REPUBLIC	Martina LUBYOVA
	Slovak Academy of Sciences, Bratislava
SPAIN	Ramon MAHIA
	Autonomous University of Madrid
SWEDEN	Michael HAGOS
	Ministry of Employment, Stockholm
SWITZERLAND	Claire de COULON
	Federal Office of Migration, Berne
TURKEY	Ahmet ICDUYGU
	Koç University, Istanbul
UNITED KINGDOM	John SALT University
	College London, Department of Geography, London
UNITED STATES	Lindsay LOWELL
	Institute for the Study of International Migration, Washington, DC

LIST OF OECD SECRETARIAT MEMBERS INVOLVED IN THE PREPARATION OF THIS PUBLICATION

International Migration Division

Jean-Christophe Dumont, Head of Division
Georges Lemaître, Principal Administrator
Theodora Xenogiani, Principal Administrator
Thomas Liebig, Administrator
Jonathan Chaloff, Administrator
Josep Mestres, Administrator
Cécile Thoreau, Administrator
Ana Damas de Matos, Administrator
Jason Gagnon, Administrator
Philippe Hervé, Statistician
Véronique Gindrey, Statistician
Sylviane Yvron, Assistant
Natalie Santiago, Assistant
Maria Vincenza Desiderio, Consultant
Sarah Widmaier, Consultant
Karoline Krause, Consultant
Julia Jauer, Consultant

ORGANISATION FOR ECONOMIC CO-OPERATION AND DEVELOPMENT

The OECD is a unique forum where governments work together to address the economic, social and environmental challenges of globalisation. The OECD is also at the forefront of efforts to understand and to help governments respond to new developments and concerns, such as corporate governance, the information economy and the challenges of an ageing population. The Organisation provides a setting where governments can compare policy experiences, seek answers to common problems, identify good practice and work to co-ordinate domestic and international policies.

The OECD member countries are: Australia, Austria, Belgium, Canada, Chile, the Czech Republic, Denmark, Estonia, Finland, France, Germany, Greece, Hungary, Iceland, Ireland, Israel, Italy, Japan, Korea, Luxembourg, Mexico, the Netherlands, New Zealand, Norway, Poland, Portugal, the Slovak Republic, Slovenia, Spain, Sweden, Switzerland, Turkey, the United Kingdom and the United States. The European Union takes part in the work of the OECD.

OECD Publishing disseminates widely the results of the Organisation's statistics gathering and research on economic, social and environmental issues, as well as the conventions, guidelines and standards agreed by its members.

OECD PUBLISHING, 2, rue André-Pascal, 75775 PARIS CEDEX 16
(81 2012 07 1 P) ISBN 978-92-64-17720-8 – No. 60067 2012